BIBLIOGRAPHY OF NORTH AMERICAN INDIAN MENTAL HEALTH

BIBLIOGRAPHY OF NORTH AMERICAN INDIAN MENTAL HEALTH

Compiled by DIANNE R. KELSO
and CAROLYN L. ATTNEAVE

Prepared under the auspices of the White Cloud Center

GREENWOOD PRESS
Westport, Connecticut • London, England

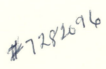

Library of Congress Cataloging in Publication Data

Kelso, Dianne R.
  Bibliography of North American Indian mental health.

  Includes indexes.
    1. Indians of North America—Mental health—Abstracts.
  2. Indians of North America—Mental health services—
  Abstracts. 3. Mental health services—North America—
  Abstracts. I. Attneave, Carolyn L. II. White Cloud
  Center. III. Title.
  RC451.5.I5K44   362.2'08997   81-800
  ISBN 0-313-22930-9 (lib. bdg.)   AACR2

Library of Congress Catalog Card Number: 81-800
ISBN: 0-313-22930-9

First published in 1981

Greenwood Press
A division of Congressional Information Service, Inc.
88 Post Road West, Westport, Connecticut 06881

Printed in the United States of America

10 9 8 7 6 5 4 3 2 1

Contents

Preface

This volume represents five years of collecting and indexing materials relevant to the mental health of Native American populations in the United States and Canada. Between 1975 and 1977, work on the bibliography was conducted at the University of Washington, and since the fall of 1977, it has been carried on at the White Cloud Center for American Indian/Alaska Native Mental Health Research and Development. White Cloud Center is located on the campus of the University of Oregon Health Sciences Center in Portland, Oregon.

During the first two years, the staff not only initiated the collection of documents but also designed the basic indexing and retrieval system and prepared a limited number of copies of an index of the first 500 accessions. This work was done under National Institute of Mental Health Grant No. 7-R01-28198 with Carolyn L. Attneave, Ph.D., and Dianne Kelso, M.L.S., as coprincipal investigators. Eleven American Indian graduate students and a technical staff assisted in various phases of the documentation, and a number of nationally known consultants contributed their expertise. About 800 documents were collected in this initial period.

In the fall of 1977, the project was transferred to the White Cloud Center, and Dianne Kelso joined that staff as an information analyst. Carolyn L. Attneave has continued as consultant and advisor, but the main day-to-day effort has been under Dianne Kelso's active supervision. The collection, accession, and indexing of documents has continued to the present base of 1,363.

A major activity of 1978 and 1979 has been entering the bibliographic data base into a computer for storage. This makes possible the retrieval of specialized and focused bibliographies to meet the needs of many people.

From the beginning the bibliography has been designed for two major groups of users: scholars of human behavior and personnel engaged in mental health service delivery. The bibliographic standards should meet the needs of those engaged in research, whether they be students or senior professionals. However, persons in the field, especially tribal and village leaders developing mental health programs and locating relevant material for in-service training, should also find the materials easy to use. Too often the lack of a centralized resource has people in one part of the country working without knowledge of similar efforts in another. We hope that this volume, together with continuing additions to the computerized data base, will make information available to all those who wish to use it in their day-to-day delivery of services as well as those who need it for research.

In today's world, knowledge is a key to power. The power to control one's own destiny as a people is a keenly felt need of the American Indian peoples whose mental health is the subject matter of this bibliography. The available publications have increased from a few articles written at the turn of the century describing psychiatric disorders to the more than 700 relevant documents published in the last decade. With a growing emphasis on strengths as well as problems, and on health adaptations as well as illnesses of American Indians, knowledge is accumulating at an accelerating pace. It is our hope that through this volume a major step is being taken to return this knowledge, and its latent power, to the people who can most benefit from its use.

Dianne R. Kelso
Carolyn L. Attneave

Acknowledgments

Any project that has continued for five years and that is as active as this bibliographic service has been, accrues debts to many people who have contributed expertise and support. Not all of these can be mentioned, but among them the most outstanding have been singled out to stand symbolically for others without whom this volume would never have come into being.

Norman Dinges, Ph.D., Culture Learning Center, East-West Center, University of Hawaii, deserves special acknowledgment for his contribution of articles and bibliographic data collected over many years of cross-cultural work.

Robert A. Ryan, Ed.D., Director of White Cloud Center, and James Shore, M.D., Chairman of the Department of Psychiatry, University of Oregon Health Sciences Center, have smoothed the administrative path and provided the logistic support essential to the success of this effort.

Paul Omen, M.S., a systems analyst for the Milne Computer Center, Oregon State University, adapted the Famulus program to online search capability, and he contributed many hours of time as well as expertise to make the retrieval system smooth and efficient.

Ann Goddard, Publications Coordinator of the White Cloud Center, has given time and energy to collecting and editing this material.

Richard Lopez, Ph.D., from the Center for Minority Group Mental Health Programs of the National Institute of Mental Health Center, has faithfully served as project officer, both under the original grant and for the activities which have been incorporated into the operations of the White Cloud Center. Under the direction of James Ralph, M.D., the Center for Minority Group Mental Health Programs of the National Institute of Mental Health was among the first institutions to recognize the need of minority populations for adequate bibliographic tools and to fund their development.

Many professional organizations have contributed their time, expertise, and materials. Particular mention should be made of the American Psychiatric Association's Council on Public Affairs under the leadership of James Bell, M.D., and of its Task Force, later the Standing Committee on American Indian Affairs, under Morton Beiser, M.D., and later Johanna Clevenger, M.D. The Canadian Psychiatric Association had a parallel history and its Task Force and Committee Chairman, Wolfgang Jilek, M.D., has been continually supportive.

Other organizations and institutions which have cooperated whenever an opportunity arose have been the Society of Indian Psychologists, the American Indian Physician's Association, the Canadian Office of Indian Education, the Indian Brotherhood of Canada, and the Indian Health Service.

Individuals who have offered consultation or assistance in the design and initiation of the bibliography include: Aiken Connor, Povl Toussieng, Loye Ryan, Gayla Twiss, Robert Bergman, Eleonora D'Arms, Terry Tafoya, Dennis Waggoner, Lita Sheldon, Michael Burgett, Sandra Lee, and Nancy Papador.

Finally, we acknowledge the many authors and research scholars without whose efforts to understand and to share their knowledge there would be no bibliography. We also extend appreciation to the many other American Indian people whose interest, requests for help, and increasingly successful research and service projects bear witness to the usefulness of these bibliographic tools. To those we know, both through correspondence and in person, and to those whose work will add new materials to the collection, we offer our heartfelt gratitude.

Introduction

Ever since fifteenth-century European explorers first aroused curiosity about New World peoples, scholars have been amassing data about American Indians.* Consequently, libraries, archives, and government depositories offer researchers a legacy of ethnographic bulletins, government reports, books, and scholarly articles devoted to their study. Scattered throughout these documents is a wealth of information pertinent to the study of mental health.

It is the purpose of this bibliography to provide an organized means of access to this storehouse of information. Reflecting the interdisciplinary nature and long history of American Indian research, the scope of the bibliography is very broad, and no limits have been set on the publication dates of references included. The bulk of Indian scholarly literature has traditionally been found in anthropological and historical publications. Since the 1960s, however, a growing multidisciplinary interst in minority groups has greatly increased the volume of literature found in medicine, psychiatry, social work, education, and the social and behavioral sciences. Anthropological and historical treatments from the early twentieth century and contemporary studies of reservation and urban life provide a context for understanding Indian mental health and mental illness. Therefore, these studies have been referenced in this volume along with medical, psychological, and psychiatric research that focuses more sharply on mental health issues. This collection should help to clarify and categorize the scattered mental health data pertaining to American Indians, while building a solid foundation for further research. By compiling a wide range of research published over the past eighty years, this comprehen-

---

*American Indian, Indian, Native American, or Native are used interchangeably to refer to all North American Indians, Eskimos, Aleuts, and Metis.

sive bibliography should also contribute insights into the long history of minority-majority relations on this continent and the resulting varied impacts on mental health.

It should be acknowledged that these documents reflect the changing attitudes and research biases of North American society during this century. Some authors present negative, exaggerated, or inaccurate images of American Indians (Trimble, 1975; Maynard, 1974; Medicine, 1971). Native people who have long depended on an oral tradition are rightly skeptical of published research which has been used to perpetuate stereotypes and justify discrimination. The recent identification of errors of earlier studies, especially misunderstandings of what was observed (and even accurately reported), is a strong argument in favor of American Indian people doing their own research. Some controversial or inaccurate studies have been included in this volume, as it is our policy to include everything within our scope without judgement as to merit or accuracy. The compilers and their sponsors disclaim any endorsement of the views presented in the research cited.

Some enlightened researchers of all races have questioned the cross-cultural applicability of psychological assumptions and research tools, and they have produced a small but growing body of culturally sensitive research that can be used to implement better mental health programs, train both Native and non-Native personnel, and develop school curricula. Much information found in this bibliography can give Indian people a powerful tool in establishing the need for culturally-sensitive services and in developing programs and service.

SCOPE AND SEARCH STRATEGY

The scope of the bibliography includes those studies which have American Indian subjects and which explore mental health issues or variables affecting mental health. No limit is set on the age of a document, but only articles written in English are included. No attempt has been made to evaluate the quality of research. Everything that is relevant is included, intuitive and expository writings as well as research articles. "Mental health" is loosely defined for our purposes as a continuum of states and behaviors ranging from the vigorous and healthy to the pathological. "American Indian" refers to all North American Native peoples including Indians, Aleuts, Eskimos, and Metis. For the purpose of brevity, the terms American Indian, Indian, Native American, or Native are used throughout this bibliography to denote all of these varied peoples.

The search strategy we used to sift through the multidisciplinary literature for relevant articles will also serve to illustrate the range of materials listed in the bibliography. A search strategy devised by Thomas Childers (1975) and adapted for our purposes uses three categories of possible index terms, key words, or subject headings that are perused in various reference lists, indexes, catalogues, and thesauri.

Category 1, "Native Americans," includes all terms naming Native American groups. These include all-inclusive terms as well as names of tribes, such as:

American Indian

Alaska Native

North American Indian

Sioux

Navajo

Crow

Category 2, "Mental Health/Illness," covers a wide range of psychological and psychiatric terms, such as:

Learning

Depression

Emotional adjustment

Cognition

Schizophrenia

Psychopathology

Also included in this category are coping behaviors and cultural characteristics of any part of the Native American population that have particular relevance for mental health, for example:

Traditional healers

Time perception

Ghost sickness

Ethnic identity

Category 3, "Related Subject Areas," is a loose category of terms describing the context in which mental issues are likely to be found. These include:

Education

Medicine

Urbanization

Foster care

Religion

Corrections

Once a document is retrieved, its content is analyzed and a decision is made as to its relevance. Any document that falls within all three categories or within both categories 1 and 2 is automatically accepted. Documents which fall in only a single category or within both categories 2 and 3 (but not 1) are rejected. Those within both categories 1 and 3 are carefully checked to determine their relevance to mental health. While an attempt is made to be systematic about decisions, many final choices of borderline documents are arbitrary (see figure 1).

FIGURE 1

Diagram of Search Strategy

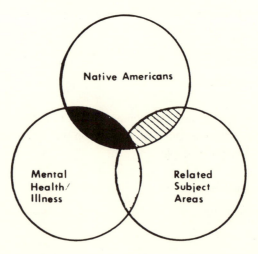

The following examples illustrate the type of coverage accorded to topics in the "Related Subject Areas" category:

Education: academic achievement, learning problems and disabilities, intelligence testing, school dropouts, learning styles, mental health programs in schools, bicultural and bilingual education, the effects of boarding schools on Indian students.

Medicine: psychosocial aspects of disease, psychophysiological disorders, psychological barriers to the delivery of medical services, use of traditional healers, use of Native paraprofessionals.

Urbanization: reasons for relocation, psychological adjustments to urban environment, delivery of mental health services, urban coping behaviors, family functioning, social networks.

SOURCES

Sources for both recent and retrospective literature have been searched for citations to be included in the bibliography. Both published and unpublished bibliographies compiled by researchers and scholars were used to establish a core of often cited references. Thorough searches of bibliographic data bases, such as Social Science Information Exchange (SSIE), Medical Library Information Network (Medline), Social Work Abstracts, Education Resources Information Center (ERIC), and Psychological Abstracting and Retrieval Service (PASAR), provided an overview of the literature published in the last five years. Bibliographies and reference lists attached to published documents have led to older literature as well as to articles that were never covered by abstracting or indexing services. Current works are identified by searches of data bases and indexes, by review of journals as they are published, and through information supplied by researchers and authors in contact with the White Cloud Center.

The majority of the citations are from refereed journals. The remaining references are to less accessible sources such as unpublished research reports, government documents, doctoral dissertations, and papers presented at professional meetings. Books have been excluded, although individually authored chapters are referenced. Not all sources are covered with equal thoroughness, nor are all topics given the same attention. Once an article or document is secured, bibliographies and reference lists should lead the reader to other sources, thereby expanding topics and source materials that are unevenly covered in this bibliography.

INDEX DEVELOPMENT

The Descriptor and Author Indexes provide a semantic map to help the user find the most suitable references in an unwieldy mass of citations. In addition to the indexes, a Glossary and a Culture Area and Tribe List are provided to increase the efficiency of the bibliographic search. The Glossary defines descriptors other than tribes and culture areas as they are used in this bibliography and provides cross-references. The Culture Area and Tribe List provides a complete list of tribes and culture areas found in the Descriptor Index, along with cross-references from alternative spellings. Explanations of the organization of the Descriptor Index, the Author Index, the Glossary, and the Culture Area and Tribe List are given in the User's Guide, as are instructions about their effective use. The following section outlines the philosophy that guided the development of the Descriptor Index.

The Descriptor Index has evolved slowly over five years of use, requiring frequent redefinition of some descriptors and the addition or removal of others. Semantic difficulties have arisen as a result of the attempt to reflect the terminology of several different disciplines, as well as the need to isolate culture-specific concepts of mental health and illness from Native points of view. Ideally, a group of Indian mental health experts would have generated a list of possible index terms or descriptors, but these individuals are scattered throughout the United States and Canada. It became necessary to compile a list of descriptors from careful reading and analysis of the literature itself and from the existing thesauri of relevant disciplines. This list has been evaluated and refined by Native mental health professionals as they became available for consultation. Many clarifications were the result of requests for bibliographies received from those in the front line of service delivery and program development, as well as from students and scholars engaged in research. The Descriptor Index presented here contains a mix of medical, psychological, sociological, anthropological, and culturally specific terms that should give access to the literature from many points of view. Descriptors other than names of culture areas and tribes are defined in the Glossary so that the reader will clearly understand their usage in the bibliography. Culture areas and tribes are listed separately.

It has been the intention of this project to devise an index which identifies both positive and negative behaviors, that is, both mental health and mental illness. This has been an unusually difficult task for a number of reasons. Most research efforts with Indian populations have focused on mental, social, and behavioral problems. The anthropological literature, for instance, has often described culturally defined behaviors that historically were considered deviant by American Indian groups. Such culture-specific syndromes vary from tribe to tribe and region to region. Examples range from Arctic hysteria in the far north and Windigo psychosis in the eastern sub-Arctic to witchcraft among the southwestern tribes. These culture-specific syndromes are listed and defined in the Glossary and Descriptor Index as well as other culture-specific syndromes such as Ghost sickness, Soul loss, and Taboo breaking. More familiar negative behaviors are shared with the dominant culture but have some specific Indian features. Suicide, alcoholism, academic failure, and poor psychological adjustment have also received attention from researchers, primarily because they cause the majority culture so much difficulty in administering educational, social, medical, and legal programs for Indians. This negative bias in research has been discussed by Dinges et al. in a review of the American Indian adolescent socialization literature (1979).

There are strong positive elements in Indian culture, however, many of which have implications for mental health. Wherever possible these have been identified and included in the index. There is a growing concern among researchers that authors from the dominant culture have misunderstood or mislabeled many healthy Indian responses to stress. For example, among many Native people an appropriate response to aggressive, coercive behavior is to remain silent or to withdraw from a potentially volatile situation. In a cultural context in which noncoercive behavior is the norm, passive resistance is seen as positive coping strategy. In another cultural context, such as a school classroom, withdrawal or passive resistance may be perceived by the teacher as negative behavior inhibiting the learning process. These particular coping behaviors are listed in the Glossary and Descriptor Index as Noninterference, Passive resistance, and Emotional restraint. Other positive American Indian norms and values that are listed include Cooperation, Generosity, and Universal harmony. As the growing trend throughout the mental health field is to look at holistic concepts and health as well as illness, these positively oriented entries will become increasingly important. It has already been demonstrated that they fill a vital role in defining American Indian identity and combatting racism and sterotypes.

TRENDS IN AMERICAN INDIAN MENTAL HEALTH LITERATURE

Many comprehensive reviews have been published on different topics in the field of Indian mental health (thirty-eight such reviews are listed in this bibliography), but a thorough review of the entire field has yet to be done. This bibliography, although far from complete, is the most comprehensive data base presently available. Hence, preliminary observations on the scope and trends of this field seem in order.

When references from this bibliography are sorted by topic and then listed chronologically, publishing trends emerge that reflect changing interests,

FIGURE 2

Research Trends

Research Topics	1930–1939 48 Citations		1940–1949 85 Citations	
	No.	% of Total	No.	% of Total
Acculturation	4	8%	13	15%
Traditional Child Rearing	14	29%	14	17%
Traditional Social Control	1	2%	9	11%
Religion	5	11%	14	17%
Traditional Healing	14	29%	14	17%
Culture-Specific Syndromes	13	27%	8	10%
Mental Disorders	9	19%	1	1%
Personality	4	8%	15	18%
Abilities	8	17%	11	13%
Drug Use	4	8%	6	7%
Suicide	0	0%	3	4%
Urbanization	0	0%	1	1%
Discrimination	1	2%	2	2%
Child Welfare	0	0%	0	0%
Mental Health Systems	0	0%	2	2%
Psychotherapy & Counseling	0	0%	3	4%
Alcohol Use	0	0%	4	5%
Self-Concept/Ethnic Identity	0	0%	0	0%
Crime & Corrections	0	0%	3	4%

The total number of citations listed in the bibliography for each decade is posted at the top of each column. Vertical columns do not add up to the total number of articles per decade or to

Figure 2—*Continued*

1950–1959 117 Citations		1960–1969 329 Citations		1970–1979 759 Citations	
No.	% of Total	No.	% of Total	No.	% of Total
24	20%	52	16%	72	9%
10	9%	24	7%	50	7%
9	8%	22	6%	19	3%
22	19%	28	9%	28	4%
11	9%	24	7%	55	7%
9	8%	22	6%	33	4%
9	8%	33	10%	56	7%
23	20%	30	9%	30	4%
3	3%	18	5%	36	5%
9	8%	13	4%	31	4%
2	2%	10	3%	31	4%
1	1%	12	4%	38	5%
4	4%	17	5%	58	8%
4	4%	11	3%	32	4%
1	1%	30	9%	88	12%
3	3%	7	2%	51	7%
7	6%	24	7%	110	15%
7	6%	20	6%	107	14%
2	2%	11	3%	39	5%

100%. This is because a single article may cover more than one of these topics, and some cover topics not listed here. This is only a sample of topics covered in this bibliography.

funding patterns, and the evolution of research emphases over the last five decades. Figure 2 displays the number and percentage of documents published in a few selected subject areas in Indian mental health. Some topics show a stronger interest early in the century, while others have only recently emerged in the literature. Percentages of the total number of documents published in a decade are a more stable measure of interest for a given topic than are the total numbers of articles written. However, it should be pointed out that 7 percent of the documents produced in the 1970s (fifty to fifty-five papers) is often more than the total number of reports on all topics from an earlier decade. Although a topic may represent a small percentage of a decade's publications, the number of articles published on that topic may well be a sufficient indication of continuing interest.

While recognizing that many complex factors contribute to changing research interests, some speculations about general influence can be inferred from the data in figure 2. Some topics relevant to Native mental health flourished during the early part of the century. At this time anthropology, as a discipline, was infused with enthusiasm for psychoanalytic theory and its potential for insights into and explanations of cultural behavior. Regardless of the inherent biases of this disciplinary marriage, it resulted in an early and continuing exchange between anthropology and the mental health-related fields. Some of these materials provide historical baselines for measuring cultural change, some provide classic descriptions of culture-specific syndromes, and others provide examples of misunderstanding and misinterpretations that stimulate correcting or clarifying research by Indian and non-Indian alike. The number of publications that reflect an anthropological approach to mental health remains quite high, although they represent a decreasing percentage of the total output of Indian mental health literature in the most recent years.

Research topics in psychology have also varied in popularity over time. Measurement of abilities, for example, is an area of concern that has become more controversial to explore in recent years, particularly with respect to cross-cultural comparisons. Early interest in the subject peaked in the 1930s and 1940s, whereas only 5 percent of the 1970s literature in this bibliography deals with abilities measurement. Related efforts to describe, categorize, and classify Indian people can be documented by the early prevalence of articles on mental disorders, culture-specific syndromes, and personality traits. Again, interest in these topics continues, but the percentage of the total literature per decade is declining as a function of the multiplicity of interests.

Though some topics show decreased proportional representation in the American Indian mental health literature, others have risen both in volume and importance since the 1950s. These topics illustrate a shift in emphasis away from Indian people as exotic objects of descriptive studies and towards a research focus on specific psychosocial problems and their resolutions. Family studies, for instance, are characterized by a recent increase in literature about child welfare and relatively fewer publications about traditional child rearing. Recent articles on crime, suicide, and alcoholism may reflect a current concern with disruptive behaviors. However, an expanding literature on urbanization, discrimination, and self-concept/ethnic identity may suggest a growing awareness of the relationship between these behavioral problems and the stress of rapid cultural change and minority status. A comparison of the waning interest in acculturation and the dramatic increase in self-concept/ethnic identity studies suggests a current philosophy of maintaining rather than eradicating Indian identity.

In recent decades there has also been a proliferation of articles on the development and evaluation of institutionalized solutions to behavioral and mental health problems, replacing the earlier interest in culture-specific methods such as traditional healing, traditional social control, and religion. The growth of literature on mental health services and the effectiveness of psychotherapy and counseling coincides with the formal introduction of mental health programs in the 1960s and 1970s, at which time mental health professionals joined other social scientists in American Indian research. It is interesting to note that a similar review of the Hispanic mental health literature shows many of the same trends (Padilla, Olmedo, Lopez, and Perez, 1978).

Figure 2 is only a rough indicator of research trends; it may be misleading in some cases as to the relative importance of research topics. For example, figure 2 indicates a shrinking percentage of publications about traditional healing. This tabular data does not adequately illustrate the growth of a small, but significant, new area of research. The fields of medical anthropology, holistic health, and cross-cultural psychiatry are currently exploring the integration of traditional healers and the mental health and health-delivery systems, as well as the use of therapies or counseling strategies that take Native belief systems into account. Similarly, figure 2 indicates fewer recent publications on drug use. The large body of drug use studies, which was primarily concerned with the traditional, religious ingestion of peyote, has, in fact, decreased over time. However, a recent concern about adolescent drug and inhalant abuse has sparked new drug research. Also emerging are new, innovative studies that explore the use of peyote in the treatment of alcoholism, particularly within the framework of the Native American Church. In both of these instances, fresh and creative approaches to research are evolving in areas previously dominated by ethnographic description. These new trends are not evidenced from data in figure 2. For more specific and detailed understanding of individual topics in Indian mental health, one must narrow the scope of literature examined. Topical reviews listed in the Descriptor Index of this bibliography under Review of literature serve this purpose.

WHITE CLOUD INFORMATION RETRIEVAL SYSTEM (WIRS)

This volume presents the results of five years of work in a printed form designed to provide those interested in this field with direct access to the information. Until now, the only access to the bibliography has been through a computerized data base at White Cloud Center, the White Cloud Information Retrieval System (WIRS). This bibliographic information service answers an average of twenty requests a month for bibliographies on Indian mental health topics.

Using computer storage and retrieval, WIRS offers other options for service not provided in a printed volume such as this. Because the computer allows timely updating of the data base, the number of citations increases as quickly as they can be entered at the terminal. The online computer search program is a powerful tool which is not limited by the designated descriptors. It can prepare individual bibliographies on any topic, geographic region, tribe, publication date, author, title, or source. Occasionally a reader will require an update of a topic covered in this volume, or need a more specialized bibliography than can be produced using the directions in the User's Guide. One such need might be a list of research articles on a specific psychological test used with American Indian populations. A telephone call or a letter to White Cloud Center will get a response.

WHITE CLOUD CENTER
Gaines Hall U.O.H.S.C.
840 S.W. Gaines Road
Portland, Oregon 97201
(503) 225-8939

REFERENCES

Childers, T. *The Information Poor in America*. Metuchen, N.J.: Scarecrow Press, 1975.

Dinges, N. G., Trimble, J. E., and Hollenbeck, A. R. "American Indian Adolescent Socialization: A Review of the Literature." *Journal of Adolescence* 2 (1979): 259-96.

Driver, H. *Indians of North America*. Chicago: University of Chicago Press, 1961.

Maynard, E. "The Growing Negative Image of the Anthropologist among American Indians." *Human Organization* 33 (1974): 402-4.

Medicine, B. "The Anthropologist as the Indian's Image-Maker." *Indian Historian* 4 (1971): 27-29.

Padilla, A. M., Olmedo, E. L., Lopez, S., and Perez, R. *Hispanic Mental Health Bibliography II*. Los Angeles: Spanish Speaking Mental Health Center, 1978.

Trimble, J. E. "The Intrusion of Western Psychological Thought on Native American Ethos: Divergence and Conflict among the Dakota." In J. W. Berry & W. J. Lomer, eds., *Proceedings of the Second International Conference of the International Association for Cross-Cultural Psychology*. Netherlands: Swets and Zeithinger, 1975.

User's Guide

This bibliography is a tool for locating materials relating to American Indian (as defined earlier) mental health. It is indexed by a wide variety of topics in this field, and by tribe, culture area, and author, so that specific, subject-related bibliographies can be quickly compiled. As the sheer volume of material makes serendipity an ineffective and frustrating method of locating relevant citations, it is advisable to first examine the Glossary, the Culture Area and Tribe List, and the Descriptor Index, and to develop a search strategy. The User's Guide explains what information is found in each section of the bibliography and how it can be used to compile bibliographies that are tailored to fit individual needs.

BIBLIOGRAPHY SECTION

References are listed in the Bibliography section in accession number order. Each entry consists of seven fields: accession number (NUMB), author (AUTH), title (TITL), source (SOUR), year (YEAR), descriptors (DESC), and identifiers (IDEN). Each field is clearly labeled for quick identification. These fields are defined below:

> NUMB: A unique number is assigned to each document as it is indexed. This accession number is used to identify the reference in the indexes, and it has no other meaning. The entries in the bibliography occur in accession number order.

> AUTH: Author(s) of the work are listed.

TITL: The title of the article, chapter, paper, report, dissertation, etc., is given.

SOUR: Complete bibliographic information about the source of the citation is provided in a standard format (adapted American Psychological Association style).

YEAR: The year of the document's publication is listed.

DESC: Assigned descriptors (index terms) are listed. Used as a substitute for an abstract, the list of descriptors provides information about the subject content of the article. Descriptors marked with plus signs indicate major topics. Descriptors appear in alphabetical order in the Descriptor Index.

IDEN: Names of the country, state, province, reservation, or reserve in which the research was done; names of psychological tests; and names of institutions or programs which figure importantly in the document are listed. Identifiers provide extra information about the contents of the document but are not considered "descriptors" and do not appear in any index.

GLOSSARY

The Glossary is the first section to consult when using this bibliography. Here, Indian mental health topics are listed alphabetically. Terms which are used as descriptors are written in upper case letters and defined. Terms which are not designated as descriptors are written in lower case letters and followed by cross-references to appropriate descriptors.

The Glossary is the section of the bibliography that allows the user to select the best descriptor or combination of descriptors to find the information needed. When one descriptor does not adequately cover a topic, a cross-reference may list several possible descriptors separated by commas. In a few cases, only those references listed simultaneously under two descriptors will have appropriate information. This overlap is indicated by an ampersand (&) between the two terms. For example, juvenile delinquency is not a descriptor but information about juvenile delinquency can be found in articles indexed under the combination Adolescents & Socially deviant behavior. A list of accession numbers appearing under both terms will produce a bibliography limited to juvenile delinquincy. Commonly requested topics that require this technique are included in the glossary, but researchers should feel free to make such combinations whenever their needs suggest it.

CULTURE AREA AND TRIBE LIST

This list is a continuation of the Glossary in format and usage. Culture areas are adapted from Harold Driver (1961), who defines a culture area as "a geographical area occupied by a number of peoples whose cultures show a significant degree of similarity with each other and at the same time a significant degree of dissimilarity with the cultures of peoples of other such areas." Examples of North American culture areas are Plains, Plateau, Eastern sub-Arctic, and Southeast woodland. Culture areas are listed alphabetically, and a map of their boundaries is provided.

The Culture Area and Tribe List includes all tribes whose populations are the subject of research or whose culture traits, mental health, etc., are discussed by documents listed in the bibliography. Since, for political and other reasons, tribal names vary from time to time, a standard name and spelling has been adopted. Large tribal groupings often contain identifiable subdivisions. These are grouped together for easier location of related material. Examples are Cheyenne-northern and Cheyenne-southern or Pueblo-Hopi, Pueblo-Taos, and Pueblo-Zuni.

DESCRIPTOR INDEX

All descriptors including tribes and culture areas are listed alphabetically in the Descriptor Index. Each descriptor is followed by a list of accession numbers that identify relevant documents. It is important to note that these numbers are not page numbers.

Descriptors can be combined and coordinated in ways that decrease the number of references that must be examined in order to find the specific information that is needed. For example, there are more than 100 references listed under Alcohol use. If the user is interested specifically in alcoholism on reservations, time and effort will be saved by looking at just those references listed under Alcohol use and Reservation.

Some precombinations have already been suggested in the Glossary by connecting two descriptors with an ampersand, but many others can be created to fit individual information needs. For example, descriptors particularly useful in narrowing a search for specific kind of study are: Experimental study, Clinical study, Epidemiological study, Demographic data, Review of literature, or Survey.

AUTHOR INDEX

Authors are listed alphabetically by last name or by the name of the agency responsible for the document. When a document has multiple authorship, each author is listed separately.

SEARCH STRATEGY

Most experienced researchers have techniques of their own for developing the bibliographies that they need. For the beginner these suggestions will be helpful:

1. Locate the topics in which you are interested in the Glossary, or if you wish to specify a culture area or tribe, locate these in the Culture Area and Tribe List.

2. Find the appropriate descriptors in the Descriptor Index, and copy the accession numbers on a sheet of paper.

3. Locate each reference in the Bibliography section. A look at the descriptor field (DESC) should give you an idea of the other subjects covered by this article, and identifiers (IDEN) give added information about the article, such as where the research was done. Together the descriptors and identifiers can be used as an abstract to help you decide if the article fits your needs. Descriptors that are followed by plus signs indicate that this subject is given considerable attention in the document. (Note: The plus sign does not imply quality of information.) Descriptors without plus signs indicate that this subject was accorded only a paragraph or two in this article.

4. On a convenient sized card, copy the bibliographic information for each reference you have selected. Enough information is provided to enable you to write an acceptable citation for most publications and scholarly reports. It gives sufficient information to locate the document in libraries throughout the United States and Canada.

5. Once you have a card for each document, you can arrange them in the order that best fits your needs—alphabetically by author, chronologically by date of publication, in the order in which you refer to them in your own work, or in the order you will collect them in the library.

Glossary

ABILITIES (see also: ACHIEVEMENT, COGNITIVE PROCESSES, LEARNING)
Capabilities of performing intellectual or creative tasks.

ACCIDENTS
Types of accidents, correlates of accidents, and accident rates of American Indian populations.

Acculturation (use: BICULTURALISM, CULTURAL ADAPTATION, URBANIZATION)

ACHIEVEMENT (see also: ABILITIES, LEARNING)
Studies which measure or discuss scholastic, career, or other accomplishments and the variables which influence achievement.

Adaptation (use: CULTURAL ADAPTATION, NATIVE AMERICAN COPING BEHAVIORS)

ADMINISTRATIVE ISSUES
Administrative policies and management problems concerning programs with a Native American focus.

ADOLESCENTS (see also: CHILDREN-INFANTS AND PRESCHOOL, CHILDREN-SCHOOL AGE)
Studies of subjects between the ages of 13 and 20.

ADOPTION AND FOSTER CARE (see also: CHILD ABUSE AND NEGLECT, FAMILY FUNCTIONING)
The placement of American Indian children with adoptive or foster families and the resulting effects.

ADULTS (see also: AGED)
Studies of subjects between the ages of 20 and 55.

AGE COMPARISONS
Comparisons of testing and research results in terms of two or more age groups.

AGED
Studies of subjects, ages 56 and older.

AGGRESSIVENESS
Forceful behavior, either self-assertive and self-protective or hostile to others or to oneself.

ALCOHOL USE (see also: ALCOHOLISM TREATMENT, DRUG USE, DRUG TREATMENT, TRADITIONAL USE OF DRUGS AND ALCOHOL)
1. Studies pertaining to alcoholism.
2. Studies of the frequency and duration of alcohol drinking as well as the history and social conditions surrounding alcohol use.

Alcoholism (use: ALCOHOL USE)

ALCOHOLISM TREATMENT
Descriptions of programs and services designed to treat alcoholism.

Alienation (use: ANOMIE)

American Indian Movement (use: NATIVE AMERICAN POLITICAL MOVEMENTS)

ANGLO AMERICANS
Studies which include Caucasian subjects, especially as comparison groups in research or psychological testing.

ANOMIE (see also: DEPRESSION, POWERLESSNESS)
A lack of values, purpose, and identity, often associated with social and cultural disorganization.

ANXIETY (see also: STRESS, HYSTERIA)
An intense state of apprehensiveness and uneasiness characterized by forms of hysteria.

Anthropologists (use: RESEARCHERS)

Aptitudes (use: ABILITIES)

ARCTIC HYSTERIA
A culture-specific syndrome of Arctic people characterized by forms of hysteria.

Arrest Rates (use: CORRECTIONAL INSTITUTIONS)

ASIAN AMERICANS
Studies which include Asian American subjects, especially as comparison groups in research or psychological testing.

Assessment (use: PSYCHOLOGICAL TESTING)

Assimilation (use: CULTURAL ADAPTATION, BICULTURALISM)

ATTITUDES (see also: NATIVE AMERICAN VALUES)
Mental positions or feelings, regarding ideas, situations, or objects.
B.I.A.
The role of the Bureau of Indian Affairs of the U.S. Department of the Interior in determining policy which affects mental health, its involvement in mental health programs, and its impact on the mental health of American Indians.

B.I.A. BOARDING SCHOOLS (see also: BOARDING HOMES, COLLEGES AND
UNIVERSITIES, ELEMENTARY SCHOOLS, SECONDARY SCHOOLS)
   Elementary and secondary schools, often located off-
reservation and administered by the Bureau of Indian Affairs.

BEHAVIOR MODIFICATION
   A theory of psychotherapy that is based on learning theory:
reinforcement, classical and instrumental conditioning,
primary and secondary sources of drive, and the nature of
frustrations and conflict.

Bereavement (use: DEATH AND DYING, GRIEF REACTION)

BICULTURALISM (see also: CULTURAL ADAPTATION)
   Two types of cultural behavior that can be learned by an
individual and employed under different circumstances where
appropriate.

BILINGUALISM (see also: LANGUAGE HANDICAPS)
   The learning of two languages or the use of two languages
with equal facility.

Birth (use: CHILDREN-INFANTS AND PRESCHOOL)

Birth Control (use: FAMILY PLANNING)

BLACK AMERICANS
   Studies which include Black American subjects, especially as
comparison groups in research or psychological testing.

BOARDING HOMES (see also: B.I.A. BOARDING SCHOOLS)
   Studies of mental health issues in boarding homes or
dormitories where students live in order to attend public
schools.

Boarding Schools (use: B.I.A. BOARDING SCHOOLS)

Brain Disorders (use: ORGANIC BRAIN DISORDERS)

Bureau of Indian Affairs (use: B.I.A.)

Cannibalism (use: WINDIGO PSYCHOSIS)

Canadian Indians (Tribes are indexed individually and the
   country, state, or province are listed in the IDEN field of
   each entry)

Catholics (use: RELIGIONS-NON-NATIVE)

Caucasians (use: ANGLO AMERICANS)

Census Data (use: DEMOGRAPHIC DATA, EPIDEMIOLOGICAL STUDY)

Ceremonies   (use: NATIVE AMERICAN RELIGIONS, POW-WOWS)

CHARACTER DISORDERS
A group of mental disorders characterized by habitual
maladaptive patterns of behavior, generally life-long in
duration.

CHEMOTHERAPY
The legal use of drugs by trained personnel for therapeutic
purposes.

Chicanos   (use: LATINOS)

CHILD ABUSE AND NEGLECT (See also: ADOPTION AND FOSTER CARE,
FAMILY FUNCTIONING)
The incidence of emotional and physical abuse or neglect of
children.

Child Rearing Practices   (use: TRADITIONAL CHILD REARING)

Child Welfare Issues (use: ADOPTION AND FOSTER CARE, CHILD
ABUSE AND NEGLECT)

Childbirth   (use: CHILDREN-INFANTS AND PRESCHOOL)

CHILDREN-INFANTS AND PRESCHOOL
Studies of subjects between the ages of 0 to 6 years.

CHILDREN-SCHOOL AGE   (see also: ADOLESCENTS)
Studies of subjects between the ages of 7 and 12 years.

Cigarette Smoking   (use: DRUG USE)

Cirrhosis of the Liver   (use: PHYSICAL HEALTH AND ILLNESS)

Cities   (use: URBAN AREAS)

Clergy   (use: RELIGIOUS-NON-NATIVE PERSONNEL)

CLINICAL STUDY
Descriptions of diagnostic observations and direct treatment
of patients.

Clinics   (use: MEDICAL INSTITUTIONS, MENTAL HEALTH
INSTITUTIONS)

COGNITIVE PROCESSES   (see also: ABILITIES, LEARNING, TIME
PERCEPTION)
Studies concerning perception, thought, memory, or judgment;
including studies of cognitive development, cognitive style,
field dependence, problem solving, and decision making.

COLLEGES AND UNIVERSITIES (see also: B.I.A. BOARDING SCHOOLS, ELEMENTARY SCHOOLS, SECONDARY SCHOOLS)

COMMUNITY INVOLVEMENT
Participation by community members in program development and maintenance.

Competition (use: NONCOMPETITIVENESS)

CONFESSION
A means by which some American Indian tribes cure illnesses associated with misconduct, particularly the breaking of a taboo.

CONSULTATION
The theory, methodology, and practice of consultation concerning American Indian programs.

Contraception (use: FAMILY PLANNING)

COOPERATION
A behavioral norm or value of some American Indian tribes which prescribes working or acting together for the social, emotional, economic, and spiritual well-being of the whole group rather than the benefit of the individual.

Coping Behaviors (use: NATIVE AMERICAN COPING BEHAVIORS)

CORRECTIONAL INSTITUTIONS (see also: CORRECTIONS PERSONNEL, LEGAL ISSUES, TRADITIONAL SOCIAL CONTROL)
References to prisons, jails, detention centers and other correctional facilities and to their impact on mental health.

CORRECTIONS PERSONNEL
The roles of policemen, prison guards, parole officers, etc., in dealing with the crime and socially deviant behavior.

Counseling (use: NATIVE AMERICAN COPING BEHAVIORS)

Counselors (use: MENTAL HEALTH PROFESSIONALS)

Cradleboard (use: TRADITIONAL CHILD REARING)

Creativity (use: ABILITIES)

CRIME (see also: CORRECTIONAL INSTITUTIONS, CORRECTIONS PERSONNEL, LEGAL ISSUES, SOCIALLY DEVIANT BEHAVIOR, TRADITIONAL SOCIAL CONTROL)
An act committed in violation of a law prohibiting it, or

omitted in violation of a law ordering it.

Cross-Cultural Comparisons (use: NATIVE-NON-NATIVE COMPARISONS)

Cross-Cultural Stress (use: STRESS)

CULTURAL   ADAPTATION   (see   also: BICULTURALISM,   CULTURAL
CONTINUITY, CULTURAL REVIVAL, URBANIZATION)
A change in the original cultural patterns of either of two
different cultures as they come into continuous contact.

CULTURAL CONTINUITY (see also: ETHNIC IDENTITY)
Maintenance   of   culturally   defined   goals,   values,
perceptions, and modes of expression.

CULTURAL   REVIVAL   (see   also: NATIVE   AMERICAN   POLITICAL
MOVEMENTS, NATIVE AMERICAN RELIGIONS, POW-WOWS)
The renewal of identity as a distinct cultural group by
revitalizing elements of a cultural heritage that have been
repressed, devalued, or left in disuse. The Ghost Dance
Religion is a well documented example.

CULTURE-BASED PSYCHOTHERAPY (see also: CONFESSION, CULTURE-
SPECIFIC SYNDROMES, NATIVE AMERICAN COPING BEHAVIORS, NATIVE
AMERICAN ETIOLOGY, PSYCHOTHERAPY AND COUNSELING, TRADITIONAL
HEALERS)
1. Healing   practices,   rituals,   and   ceremonies   of
    traditional Native healers which are used to maintain
    mental   health and to alleviate or correct mental
    disorders.
2. Therapy or counseling strategies used by mental   health
    professionals which take Native belief systems into
    consideration.

Culture Change (use: CULTURAL ADAPTATION)

CULTURE-FAIR TESTS (see also: PSYCHOLOGICAL TESTING)
Studies which discuss the usage of psychological tests in
cross-cultural settings.

CULTURE-SPECIFIC SYNDROMES (see   also: ARCTIC HYSTERIA,GHOST
SICKNESS, SOUL LOSS, SPIRIT INTRUSION, TABOO BREAKING,
WINDIGO PSYCHOSIS, WITCHCRAFT)
A number of symptoms occuring together characterizing a
certain illness or conditions. Both the symptoms and the
illness are defined in terms of the specific socio-cultural
environment.

DAYCARE
Preschools and day care centers which offer services for
preschool children.

DEATH AND DYING (see also: GRIEF REACTION, SUICIDE)
Studies pertaining to attitudes about death and dying and methods of coping with it.

Delinquent Behavior (use: SOCIALLY DEVIANT BEHAVIOR)

DELIVERY OF SERVICES
Studies pertaining to the delivery of human services to American Indian populations and to the physical, social, an cultural barriers to service delivery.

DEMOGRAPHIC DATA (see also: EPIDEMIOLOGICAL STUDY)
Studies which provide population descriptions including baseline data about the distribution, density, vital statistics, etc. of American Indian populations.

DEPRESSION (see also: ANOMIE, GRIEF REACTION, POWERLESSNESS)
An emotional condition, characterized by feelings of hopelessness, sadness, and inadequacy.

Developmental Age Groups (use: ADOLESCENTS, ADULTS, AGED, CHILDREN-INFANTS AND PRESCHOOL, CHILDREN-SCHOOL AGE)

Deviant Behavior (use: SOCIALLY DEVIANT BEHAVIOR))

Diabetes (use: PHYSICAL HEALTH AND ILLNESS)

Diet (use: NUTRITIONAL FACTORS)

DISCRIMINATION
A showing of partiality or prejudice in actions or policies.

Divorce (use: MARITAL RELATIONSHIPS)

Doctors (use: MEDICAL PROFESSIONALS)

DREAMS AND VISION QUESTS (see also: NATIVE AMERICAN RELIGIONS TRADITIONAL USE OF DRUGS AND ALCOHOL)
Studies of dreams, visions, and hallucinations, especially those which are regarded as contact with the supernatural.

Dropout Prevention (use: DROPOUTS & PREVENTIVE MENTAL HEALTH PROGRAMS)

DROPOUTS
Participants in education, training, or other programs who withdraw before completing the program.

Drug Abuse (use: DRUG USE)

Drug Therapy (use: CHEMOTHERAPY)

DRUG TREATMENT
Descriptions of programs and services designed to treat drug addiction.

DRUG USE (see also: ALCOHOL USE, ALCOHOLISM TREATMENT, DRUG TREATMENT, TRADITIONAL USE OF DRUGS AND ALCOHOL)
Studies of the nonmedical use of drugs and inhalants, not including alcohol.

Ecological factors (use: ENVIRONMENTAL FACTORS)

ECONOMIC ISSUES (see also: EMPLOYMENT)
References to economic concerns such as poverty or sudden wealth and how they affect mental well-being.

EDUCATION PARAPROFESSIONALS
Counselors, instructional aides, etc. who have received limited training for their specialty rather than a degree.

EDUCATION PROFESSIONALS
Professors, teachers, instructors, etc.

EDUCATION PROGRAMS AND SERVICES (see also: B.I.A. BOARDING SCHOOLS, COLLEGES AND UNIVERSITIES, ELEMENTARY SCHOOLS, READING PROGRAMS, SCIENCE PROGRAMS, SECONDARY SCHOOLS, TRAINING PROGRAMS)
Descriptions of education programs and services in terms of how they meet education, cultural, and mental health needs of American Indian students.

Elderly (use: AGED)

ELEMENTARY SCHOOLS (see also: B.I.A. BOARDING SCHOOLS, COLLEGES AND UNIVERSITIES, SECONDARY SCHOOLS)
References to elementary schools as environments for learning, psychological testing, and mental health issues.

Emotional adjustment (use: NATIVE AMERICAN COPING BEHAVIORS)

Emotional disorders (use: MENTAL DISORDERS)

EMOTIONAL RESTRAINT (see also: NONCOMPETITIVENESS, NONINTERFERENCE, PASSIVE RESISTANCE)
A behavioral norm or value of some American Indian tribes which promotes self-control and discourages the expression of strong or violent feelings.

EMPLOYMENT
Studies of employment rates, opportunities, etc., for American Indians as well as studies of employment and its accompanying problems.

EPIDEMIOLOGICAL STUDY
Descriptions of research which investigates patterns of mental health status and elements contributing to the ecology, etiology, and occurance of mental illness in American Indian populations.

ENVIRONMENTAL FACTORS
Studies which discuss the physical environment as it impacts mental health.

Ethnic Groups (use: ANGLO AMERICANS, ASIAN AMERICANS, BLACK AMERICANS, LATINOS)

ETHNIC IDENTITY (see also: CULTURAL CONTINUITY, SELF-CONCEPT)
Identification with members of an ethnic group and a sense of historical continuity with that group.

Ethnomedicine (use: CULTURE-BASED PSYCHOTHERAPY, TRADITIONAL HEALERS, TRADITIONAL USE OF DRUGS AAND ALCOHOL)

Etiology (use: NATIVE AMERICAN ETIOLOGY)

Evaluation (use: PROGRAM EVALUATION)

EXPERIMENTAL STUDY
Descriptions of research in which an hypothesis is tested by manipulation of one or more variables.

EXTENDED FAMILY (see also: FAMILY FUNCTIONING, MARITAL RELATIONSHIPS, TRADITIONAL CHILD REARING)
Descriptions of family networks beyond the nuclear family.

FAMILY FUNCTIONING (see also: ADOPTION AND FOSTER CARE, CHILD ABUSE AND NEGLECT, EXTENDED FAMILY, MARITAL RELATIONSHIPS, FAMILY PLANNING, TRADITIONAL CHILD REARING)
Studies concerning the functioning of the nuclear, extended, single parent, or other type of family.

FAMILY PLANNING
Attitudes, methods, etc., about controlling the size of one's family.

FEDERAL GOVERNMENT
The role of the federal government in determining policy which effects mental health.

Field Dependence (use: COGNITIVE PROCESSES)

FEMALES
Studies of female subjects.

Fertility (use: FAMILY PLANNING)

Foster Care (use: ADOPTION AND FOSTER CARE)

FULL BLOOD-MIXED BLOOD COMPARISONS
Comparisons of research results in terms of full blood and mixed blood American Indians.

GENEROSITY
A behavioral norm or value of some American Indian tribes which discourages the hoarding of material goods by an individual and encourages sharing within a group.

GENETIC FACTORS
Studies which take genetic variables into account.

GHOST SICKNESS
A culture-specific syndrome caused by returning ghosts, usually those of family members or close acquaintences.

Government (use: FEDERAL GOVERNMENT)

Graduate School (use: COLLEGES AND UNIVERSITIES)

GRIEF REACTION (see also: DEATH AND DYING, DEPRESSION)
Intense emotional suffering caused by important losses such as the death of a close relative.

Group Behaviors (use: GROUP NORMS AND SANCTIONS, SOCIAL GROUPS AND PEER GROUPS, SOCIAL NETWORKS)

GROUP NORMS AND SANCTIONS (see also: TRADITIONAL SOCIAL CONTROL)
Standards of behavior that are maintained through public opinion and group pressure rather than by authorities or legal force.

Group Therapy (use: PSYCHOTHERAPY AND COUNSELING & SOCIAL GROUPS AND PEER GROUP)

Hallucinations (use: DREAMS AND VISION QUESTS)

Handicaps (use: LANGUAGE HANDICAPS, LEARNING DISABILITES AND PROBLEMS, MENTAL RETARDATION)

Health (use: PHYSICAL HEALTH AND ILLNESS, UNIVERSAL HARMONY)

Heterosexuality (use: SEXUAL RELATIONS)

High Schools (use: SECONDARY SCHOOLS)

Hispanic (use: LATINOS)

Homicide (use: CRIME)

Homosexuality (use: SEXUAL RELATIONS)

Hospitalization (use: INSTITUTIONALIZATION & MEDICAL INSTITUTIONS, MENTAL HEALTH INSTITUTIONS)

Hospitals (use: MEDICAL INSTITUTIONS, MENTAL HEALTH INSTITUTIONS)

HYSTERIA (see also: ARCTIC HYSTERIA)
A feeling of unmanageable fear or emotional excess.

I.H.S.
The role of the U.S. Indian Health Service in determining policy which affects mental health, its involvement in mental health programs, and its impact on the mental health of American Indians.

Identity (use: ETHNIC IDENTITY, SELF-CONCEPT)

Illegitimacy (use: SEXUAL RELATIONS)

Incarceration (use: INSTITUTIONALIZATION & CORRECTIONAL INSTITUTIONS)

Indian Health Service (use: I.H.S.)

Indian Time (use: TIME PERCEPTION)

Infants (use: CHILDREN-INFANTS AND PRESCHOOL)

Inhalant Abuse (use: DRUG USE)

Inpatient Care (use: INSTITUTIONALIZATION & MEDICAL INSTITUTIONS, MENTAL HEALTH INSTITUTIONS)

Insanity (use: MENTAL DISORDERS)

INSTITUTIONALIZATION
Hospitalization, incarceration, etc.

INTERTRIBAL COMPARISONS
Comparisons of research results in terms of two or more tribal populations.

Job Training (use: TRAINING PROGRAMS)

Junior High Schools (use: SECONDARY SCHOOLS)

Juvenile Delinquency (use: ADOLESCENTS & SOCIALLY DEVIANT

BEHAVIOR)

LANGUAGE HANDICAPS (see also: BILINGUALISM, LEARNING
DISABILITIES AND PROBLEMS)
1. Communication and psychological barriers between tribes
or ethnic groups due to difference, in language.
2. Language and verbal problems encountered by Native
children in the classroom.
3. Psychophysiological language disorders such as
stuttering.

LATINOS
Studies which include Hispanic subjects, especially as
comparison groups in research or psychological testing.

LEADERSHIP (see also: SOCIAL STATUS, TRIBAL POLITICAL
ORGANIZATIONS) Studies which discuss or measure the capacity
to lead.

LEARNING (see also: ABILITIES, ACHIEVEMENT, COGNITIVE
PROCESSES)
The acquisition of knowledge or skills.

LEARNING DISABILITIES AND PROBLEMS (see also: LANGUAGE
HANDICAPS, MENTAL RETARDATION)
Syndromes which make learning more difficult (such as
dyslexia, dysgraphia, and dyscalculia), as well as more
general social and psychological barriers to learning in a
school setting.

LEGAL ISSUES (see also: CORRECTIONAL INSTITUTIONS, CORRECTIONS
PERSONNEL, CRIME)
Legal matters which may affect any of the other subject
categories, i.e., adoption, institutionlization, etc.

Literature Review (use: REVIEW OF LITERATURE)

MALES
Studies of male subjects

MARITAL RELATIONSHIPS (see also: FAMILY FUNCTIONING)
Studies pertaining to marriage and to the relationship
between marriage partners.

Math Programs (use: SCIENCE PROGRAMS)

Measurement (use: PSYCHOLOGICAL TESTING)

MEDICAL INSTITUTIONS (see also: MENTAL HEALTH INSTITUTIONS)
1. Studies of Native Americans in medical hospitals,
clinics, etc.
2. The effects of hospitalization on the individual, the

family, and the community.

MEDICAL PARAPROFESSIONALS
   Community health aides, community health medics, etc., who
   have received limited training for their specialty rather
   than a degree.

MEDICAL PROFESSIONALS (see also: TRADITIONAL HEALERS)
   Physicians, nurses, etc.

MEDICAL PROGRAMS AND SERVICES (see also: ALCOHOLISM
   TREATMENT, DRUG TREATMENT, PREVENTIVE MENTAL HEALTH
   PROGRAMS)
   Descriptions of programs and services which treat physical
   illness, with particular emphasis on psychological aspects
   such as attitudes toward treatment.

Medicine Men (use: TRADITIONAL HEALERS)

Men (use: MALES)

MENTAL DISORDERS (see also: CHARACTER DISORDERS, CULTURE-
   SPECIFIC SYNDROMES, DEPRESSION, HYSTERIA, NEUROSES,
   PARANOIA, PSYCHOSES, SCHIZOPHRENIA)
   Psychological and psychiatric disfunctions.

Mental Health Clinics (use: MENTAL HEALTH INSTITUTIONS)

MENTAL HEALTH INSTITUTIONS
   1. Studies of Native Americans in mental hospitals,
      clinics, etc.
   2. Studies of the effects of hospitalization on the
      individual, the family and the community.

MENTAL HEALTH PARAPROFESSIONALS
   Mental health technicians, mental health aides, psychiatric
   aides, etc., who have received limited training in their
   specialty rather than a degree.

MENTAL HEALTH PROFESSIONALS (see also: TRADITIONAL HEALERS)
   Psychiatrists, psychologists, social workers, psychiatric
   nurses and other professionals with degrees or licences
   working in a mental health setting.

MENTAL HEALTH PROGRAMS AND SERVICES (see also: ALCOHOLISM
   TREATMENT, DRUG TREATMENT, PREVENTIVE MENTAL HEALTH
   PROGRAMS)
   Descriptions of programs and services designed to improve
   mental health in any of a variety of settings--communities,
   hospitals, schools, prisons, etc.

Mental Hospitals (use: MENTAL HEALTH INSTITUTIONS)

Mental Illness   (use: MENTAL DISORDERS)

MENTAL RETARDATION (see also: LEARNING   DISABILITIES   AND
   PROBLEMS)
   Intellectual functioning which is significantly and
   consistently below average, often due to physical causes.

Migration   (use: RELOCATION)

MILITARY SERVICE
   1. Studies of American Indians in the military.
   2. Studies of how the military affects the mental health of
       individuals, their families, and their communities.

Ministers   (use: RELIGIOUS-NON-NATIVE PERSONNEL)

Missionaries   (use: RELIGIOUS-NON-NATIVE PERSONNEL)

Mormons   (use: RELIGIONS-NON-NATIVE)

Mourning   (use: DEATH AND DYING, GRIEF REACTION)

MOTIVATION
   Inner drive that emerges and directs behavior.

MOTOR PROCESSES
   Those processes involving muscular movement or coordination.

Narcotics (use: CHEMOTHERAPY, DRUG USE, TRADITIONAL USE OF
   DRUGS AND ALCOHOL)

NATIVE AMERICAN ADMINISTERED PROGRAMS (see also: COMMUNITY
   INVOLVEMENT)
   Descriptions of programs that are designed and administered
   by American Indians.

Native American Church   (use: NATIVE AMERICAN RELIGIONS)

NATIVE AMERICAN COPING BEHAVIORS (see also: CONFESSION,
   COOPERATION,   EMOTIONAL   RESTRAINT,   GENEROSITY,
   NONCOMPETITIVENESS, NONINTERFERENCE, PASSIVE RESISTANCE,
   TRADITIONAL USE OF DRUGS AND ALCOHOL)
   Culture-specific behaviors that are adaptive responses to
   anxiety and stress.

NATIVE   AMERICAN   ETIOLOGY   (see   also: CULTURE-BASED
   PSYCHOTHERAPY, CULTURE-SPECIFIC SYNDROMES, TRADITIONAL
   HEALERS)
   American Indian theories about the origins, causations, and
   mechanisms of illness.

NATIVE AMERICAN PERSONNEL
Studies of the roles of American Indians at all levels of employment.

NATIVE AMERICAN POLITICAL MOVEMENTS (see also: POLITICS-NONTRIBAL, TRIBAL POLITICAL ORGANIZATIONS)
Intertribal or pan - Indian political activities and organizations.

NATIVE AMERICAN RELIGIONS (sée also: CULTURAL REVIVAL, DREAMS AND VISION QUESTS, RELIGIONS-NON-NATIVE, TRADITIONAL HEALERS, TRADITIONAL USE OF DRUGS AND ALCOHOL)
American Indian systems of religious belief including the Northwest Shaker Church, Native American Church, Handsome Lake Religion, etc., as well as specific tribal beliefs.

NATIVE-NON-NATIVE COMPARISONS
Comparisons of research results between American Indians and other cultural or ethnic populations.

NATIVE AMERICAN VALUES (see also: COOPERATION, EMOTIONAL RESTRAINT, GENEROSITY, NONCOMPETITIVENESS, NONINTERFERENCE, UNIVERSAL HARMONY)
Studies that compare, measure, or discuss cultural principles, norms, and standards that are held by American Indian tribes.

Nativistic Movements (use: CULTURAL REVIVAL)

Negroes (use: BLACK AMERICANS)

Networks (use: SOCIAL NETWORKS)

NEUROSES (see also: ANXIETY, CULTURE-SPECIFIC SYNDROMES, DEPRESSION, HYSTERIA)
A group of emotional maladaptations arising from unresolved, unconscious conflict.

NONCOMPETITIVENESS (see also: EMOTIONAL RESTRAINT, NONINTERFERENCE, PASSIVE RESISTANCE)
A behavioral norm or value of some American Indian tribes which limits or represses intragroup rivalry.

NONINTERFERENCE (see also: EMOTIONAL RESTRAINT, NONCOMPETITIVENESS, PASSIVE RESISTANCE)
A behavioral norm or value of some American Indian tribes which discourages coercion of any kind, physical, verbal, or psychological.

Norms (use: GROUP NORMS AND SANCTIONS)

Nurses   (use: MEDICAL PROFESSIONALS)

NUTRITIONAL FACTORS
   Studies concerning diet and its effects.

Obesity   (use: PHYSICAL HEALTH AND ILLNESS)

Occupations   (use: EMPLOYMENT)

OFF-RESERVATION (see also: RESERVATION, URBAN AREAS)
   Studies   of   American   Indians   living   in   nonurban,
   nonreservation areas.

ORGANIC BRAIN SYNDROMES
   A group of symptoms characteristics of the acute and chronic
   brain disorders.

OUTPATIENT CARE
   Descriptions of psychiatric treatment which does not involve
   hospitalization.

Pan-Indian Movements (use: CULTURAL REVIVAL,   NATIVE AMERICAN
   RELIGIONS, NATIVE AMERICAN POLITICAL MOVEMENTS, POW-WOWS)

Paraprofessional personnel (use: EDUCATION PARAPROFESSIONALS,
   MEDICAL PARAPROFESSIONALS, MENTAL HEALTH PARAPROFESSIONALS,
   SOCIAL SERVICE PARAPROFESSIONALS)

Parole   (use: LEGAL ISSUES)

Parole Officers   (use: CORRECTIONS PERSONNEL)

PASSIVE   RESISTANCE   (see   also: EMOTIONAL   RESTRAINT,
   NONCOMPETITIVENESS, NONINTERFERENCE)
   A behavioral   norm   or value of some American Indian tribes
   which prescribes a passive response to aggressive, coercive
   behaviors and intimidating situations.

PARANOIA
   A tendency on the part of an individual or a group toward
   excessive or irrational suspiciousness or distrustfulness of
   others.

Peer Counseling (use: PSYCHOTHERAPY AND COUNSELING & SOCIAL
   GROUPS AND PEER GROUPS)

Peer Groups   (use: SOCIAL GROUPS AND PEER GROUPS)

Personality Disorders   (use: CHARACTER DISORDERS)

PERSONALITY TRAITS   (see also: NATIVE AMERICAN VALUES)
   Deeply engrained patterns of behavior that each person

evolves, both consciously and subconsciously, as his style of life or way of adapting to his environment.

Personnel (use: EDUCATION PARAPROFESSIONALS, EDUCATION PROFESSIONALS, MEDICAL PARAPROFESSIONALS, MEDICAL PROFESSIONALS, MENTAL HEALTH PARAPROFESSIONALS, MENTAL HEALTH PROFESSIONALS, NATIVE AMERICAN PERSONNEL, SOCIAL SERVICE PARAPROFESSIONALS, SOCIAL SERVICE PROFESSIONALS)

Peyote (use: TRADITIONAL USE OF DRUGS AND ALCOHOL)

PHYSICAL HEALTH AND ILLNESS (see also: PSYCHOPHYSIOLOGICAL DISORDERS)
The physical condition of American Indian populations, particularly as it relates to mental health variables.

Physicians (use: MEDICAL PROFESSIONALS)

Planning (use: PROGRAM DEVELOPMENT)

Police (use: CORRECTIONS PERSONNEL)

Politics (use: NATIVE AMERICAN POLITICAL MOVEMENTS, POLITICS-NONTRIBAL, TRIBAL POLITICAL ORGANIZATIONS)

POLITICS-NONTRIBAL (see also: NATIVE AMERICAN POLITICAL MOVEMENTS, TRIBAL POLITICAL ORGANIZATIONS)
The general political environment at local and federal levels and how it effects mental health issues and policy.

Population Statistics (use: DEMOGRAPHIC STUDY, EPIDEMIOLOGICAL STUDY)

Poverty (use: ECONOMIC ISSUES)

POWERLESSNESS (see also: ANOMIE)
A feeling of dependency on forces other than oneself for strength or resources.

POW-WOWS
American Indian ceremonies or social gatherings.

Prejudice (use: DISCRIMINATION)

PREVENTIVE MENTAL HEALTH PROGRAMS
Descriptions of programs designed to lower the incidence and prevalence of mental disorders and of social problems such as school dropouts, drug abuse, suicide, etc.

Preschool (use: DAY CARE)

Priests (use: RELIGIOUS-NON-NATIVE PERSONNEL)

Primary Schools   (use: ELEMENTARY SCHOOLS)

Prisons   (use: CORRECTIONAL INSTITUTIONS)

Prison Personnel   (use: CORRECTIONS PERSONNEL)

Problem Solving   (use: COGNITIVE PROCESSES)

Professional   Personnel   (use: CONSULTANTS,   EDUCATION
   PROFESSIONALS,   MEDICAL   PROFESSIONALS,   MENTAL   HEALTH
   PROFESSIONALS, RESEARCHERS, SOCIAL SERVICE PROFESSIONALS)

PROGRAM DEVELOPMENT
   Descriptions   of   the   theory,   method,   and   practice   of
   developing programs to   meet   the   mental   health   needs   of
   American Indians.

PROGRAM EVALUATION
   Descriptions   of   the criteria and methods of evaluating the
   effectiveness of programs designed to meet the mental health
   needs of American Indians.

Promiscuity   (use: SEXUAL RELATIONS)

Protestants   (use: RELIGIONS-NON-NATIVE)

Prostitution   (use: SEXUAL RELATIONS)

Psychiatric Aides   (use: MENTAL HEALTH PARAPROFESSIONALS)

Psychiatric Clinic   (use: MENTAL HEALTH INSTITUTIONS)

Psychiatric Disorders   (use: MENTAL DISORDERS)

Psychiatric Hospitals   (use: MENTAL HEALTH INSTITUTIONS)

Psychiatrists   (use: MENTAL HEALTH PROFESSIONALS)

PSYCHOANALYSIS
   Studies which use a Freudian theory of mental   disorders,   a
   Freudian   approach to personality development, or a Freudian
   approach to psychotherapy.

Psychological Stress   (use: STRESS)

PSYCHOLOGICAL TESTING   (see also: CULTURE-FAIR TESTS)
   Reports of the development and application   of   standardized
   psychological tests with American Indian subjects. The names
   of individual tests are listed in the Indentifiers (IDEN).

Psychologists   (use: MENTAL HEALTH PROFESSIONALS)

Psychopathology (use: MENTAL DISORDERS)

PSYCHOPHYSIOLOGICAL DISORDERS
A group of disorders characterized by physical symptoms that are related to emotional factors and that tend to involve a single organ system.

PSYCHOSES (see also: CULTURE-SPECIFIC SYNDROMES, DEPRESSION, ORGANIC BRAIN SYNDROMES, PARANOIA, SCHIZOPHRENIA)
A group of mental disorders of organic or emotional origin in which the individual's ability to interpret reality and behave appropriately is sufficiently impaired so as to interfere with his capacity to meet the ordinary demands of life.

PSYCHOTHERAPY AND COUNSELING (see also: BEHAVIOR MODIFICATION, CHEMOTHERAPY, CULTURE-BASED PSYCHOTHERAPY, PSYCHOANALYSIS)
Descriptions of treatment methods which attempt to modify behavior by psychological means.

Racism (use: DISCRIMINATION)

READING PROGRAMS
Education programs that help to break down psychological and cultural barriers to learning how to read.

RELIGIONS-NON-NATIVE (see also: NATIVE AMERICAN RELIGIONS)
References to non-Native religious doctrines and their impact on the mental health of American Indians and Alaska Natives.

RELIGIOUS-NON-NATIVE PERSONNEL
Priests, ministers, missionaries, etc.

RELOCATION (see also: URBANIZATION)
The migration of American Indians from one location to another, particularly the relocation from reservations to urban areas and vice versa.

RESEARCHERS
Studies which discuss research and researchers, particularly in reference to the impact they have on the people they study.

RESERVATION (see also: OFF-RESERVATION, URBAN AREAS)
Studies of American Indians living on reservations or reserves. Individual names of reservations are listed in the Identifiers, (IDEN).

Retardation (use: MENTAL RETARDATION)

REVIEW OF LITERATURE
Detailed review and often critical evaluations of prior research in any given subject area.

ROLE MODELS   (see also: SOCIAL ROLES)
Descriptions of exemplory American Indian individuals who serve as models for others.

Rural Areas   (use: OFF-RESERVATION, RESERVATION)

Sanctions   (use: GROUP NORMS AND SANCTIONS)

SCHIZOPHRENIA
A psychotic disorder characterized by severe disturbances of thought, mood, and behavior.

SCIENCE PROGRAMS
Education programs that help to break down psychological or cultural barriers to learning math and science.

SECONDARY SCHOOLS (see also: B.I.A. BOARDING SCHOOLS, COLLEGES AND UNIVERSITIES, ELEMENTARY SCHOOLS)
Junior and senior high schools as environments for learning, psychological testing and mental health issues.

School Dropouts   (use: DROPOUTS)

Schools   (use: B.I.A.   BOARDING   SCHOOLS,   COLLEGES   AND UNIVERSITIES, ELEMENTARY SCHOOLS, SECONDARY SCHOOLS)

Senior Citizens   (use: AGED)

SELF-CONCEPT   (see also: ETHNIC IDENTITY)
An individual's concept of him/herself and his/her abilites, particularly in relation to how he/she is perceived by others.

Senior High Schools   (use: SECONDARY SCHOOLS)

Service delivery   (use: DELIVERY OF SERVICES)

Servicemen   (use: MILITARY SERVICE)

SEX DIFFERENCES
Comparisons of research results in terms of male and female differences.

Sex Roles   (use: SOCIAL ROLES)

SEXUAL RELATIONS
Studies about sexual patterns and orientations.

Shamen (use: TRADITIONAL HEALERS)

Sharing (use: GENEROSITY)

Silence (use: EMOTIONAL RESTRAINT, LANGUAGE HANDICAPS, PASSIVE RESISTANCE)

Social Class (use: SOCIAL STATUS)

Social Control (use: TRADITIONAL SOCIAL CONTROL)

SOCIAL GROUPS AND PEER GROUPS
1. Groups of individuals in a social setting.
2. Groups of people with similar interests or of the same age, status, etc.

SOCIAL NETWORKS
Networks of people of all ages connected by ties of kinship, friendship, community, or work and usually not formalized. The Eskimo village, the band, and some clans are culture-specific examples, but other less distinctive networks often function as support systems.

SOCIAL ROLES (see also: ROLE MODELS)
The types of behavior expected from an individual because of his/her position on the social structure or his/her sex.

SOCIAL SERVICE PARAPROFESSIONALS
Social work aides, etc., who have received limited training for their speciality rather than a degree.

SOCIAL SERVICE PROFESSIONALS
Social workers, etc.

SOCIAL SERVICES
Descriptions of a wide range of informational, referral, guidance, and counseling services as well as adoption, child welfare, delinquency prevention, and various forms of public assistance.

SOCIAL STATUS (see also: LEADERSHIP)
Studies concerning an individual's rank in the social structure.

Social Workers (use: MENTAL HEALTH PROFESSIONALS, SOCIAL SERVICE PROFESSIONALS)

SOCIALLY DEVIANT BEHAVIOR (see also: ALCOHOL USE, CRIME DROPOUTS, DRUG USE, SUICIDE)
Behavior that deviates from what is considered normal and desirable by the society of which one is a member.

Sociologists (use: RESEARCHERS)

Soldiers (use: MILITARY SERVICE)

SOUL LOSS
A culture-specific syndrome caused by the separation of
the soul from the body through forcible abduction by
sorcerers and their supernatural agents or through the
accidental straying of the soul as in dreams.

Spatial Perception (use: COGNITIVE PROCESSES)

SPIRIT INTRUSION
A culture-specific syndrome caused by a spirit entering
and living in the body of an individual.

Status (use: SOCIAL STATUS)

STEREOTYPES
Oversimplified and often inaccurate ideas about the
appearance and behavior of a group of people.

STRESS (see also: ANXIETY)
Psychological or physiological tension associated with
cultural, social, institutional, or environmental
pressures and conflicts.

Students (use: B.I.A. BOARDING SCHOOLS, COLLEGES AND
UNIVERSITIES, ELEMENTARY SCHOOLS, SECONDARY SCHOOLS)

Stuttering (use: PSYCHOPHYSIOLOGICAL DISORDERS)

Substance Abuse (use: ALCOHOL USE, DRUG USE)

SUICIDE
Studies of the suicide rates and correlates of suicide in
American Native populations.

Suicide Prevention (use: SUICIDE & PREVENTIVE MENTAL HEALTH
PROGRAMS)

SURVEY
Research based on an empirical body of data which purports
to be representative of a larger population.

TABOO BREAKING
A culture-specific syndrome triggered by the transgression
of a prohibition against certain actions, food, or contact
with others.

Teachers (use: EDUCATION PROFESSIONALS)

Teenagers   (use: ADOLESCENTS)

Testing   (use: PSYCHOLOGICAL TESTING)

Therapists   (use: MENTAL   HEALTH   PROFESSIONALS, MENTAL HEALTH
PARAPROFESSIONALS)

Therapy   (use: ALCOHOLISM   TREATMENT,   BEHAVIOR   MODIFICATION,
CHEMOTHERAPY,   DRUG   TREATMENT,   PSYCHOANALYSIS, PSYCHOTHERAPY
AND COUNSELING)

TIME PERCEPTION   (see also: COGNITIVE PROCESSES)
Measurement of time in a socio-cultural context. "Indian
time," for example, measures time in terms of natural
phenomona like days, months, or seasons instead of a clock.

TRADITIONAL CHILD REARING (see also: CHILD ABUSE   AND   NEGLECT,
EXTENDED FAMILY, FAMILY FUNCTIONING)
Descriptions of American Indian child rearing practices,
emphasizing those practices that come from their own
tradition.

TRADITIONAL HEALERS   (see also: CULTURE-BASED PSYCHOTHERAPY)
Specialists often called medicine men or women, shamens,
etc., who have traditionally been called upon to heal the
physical, mental and spiritiual disorders.

TRADITIONAL SOCIAL CONTROL
Descriptions of traditional American Indians' means of
social control such as teasing, self-discipline,
witchcraft, and community ceremonies.

TRADITIONAL USE OF DRUGS AND ALCOHOL
Traditional use of alcoholic beverages made from agave,
dasylirion, cacti, and mesquite and of drugs such as
tobacco, peyote, and jimson weed.

TRAINING PROGRAMS   (see also: EDUCATION PROGRAMS AND SERVICES)
Descriptions of programs designed to provide or improve
skills.

Treatment   (use: ALCOHOLISM   TREATMENT, BEHAVIOR MODIFICATION,
CHEMOTHERAPY,   DRUG   TREATMENT,   INSTITUTIONALIZATION,
OUTPATIENT   CARE,   PSYCHOANALYSIS,   PSYCHOTHERAPY   AND
COUNSELING)

Treatment Dropouts   (use: DROPOUTS)

Treatment   Facilities   (use: MEDICAL   INSTITUTIONS,   MENTAL
HEALTH INSTITUTIONS)

Tribal Courts (use: LEGAL ISSUES)

TRIBAL POLITICAL ORGANIZATIONS (see also: LEADERSHIP, NATIVE
    AMERICAN POLITICAL MOVEMENTS, POLITICS-NONTRIBAL)
    Tribal governments and tribally based political groups on
    and off the reservation.

U.S. Government (use: FEDERAL GOVERNMENT)

Ulcers (use: PSYCHOPHYSIOLOGICAL DISORDERS)

Undergraduates (use: COLLEGES AND UNIVERSITIES)

Unemployment (use: EMPLOYMENT)

UNIVERSAL HARMONY
    A belief of some American Indian tribes that every element
    of the universe has a supernatural power which is related
    to every other element. If a proper balance between all
    things is maintained, health and well-being will follow.

Universities (use: COLLEGES AND UNIVERSITIES)

URBAN AREAS (see also: OFF-RESERVATION, RESERVATION)
    Studies of American Indians living in urban areas.

URBANIZATION
    Studies of adaptation to urban life, organization, problems,
    etc.

Utilization of Services (use: DELIVERY SERVICES)

Values (use: NATIVE AMERICAN VALUES)

Verbal Problems (use: LANGUAGE HANDICAPS)

Violence (use: AGGRESSIVENESS, CRIME)

Vison Quests (use: DREAMS AND VISION QUESTS)

Visual Perception (use: COGNITIVE PROCESSES)

Vocational Training (use: TRAINING PROGRAMS)

Vocations (use: EMPLOYMENT)

WINDIGO PSYCHOSIS
    A culture-specific syndrome of the Eastern Sub-Arctic
    Indians characterized by a craving for human flesh. An
    individual is believed to be transformed into or possessed
    by the spirit of a cannabalistic monster known as a
    windigo.

WITCHCRAFT
   A culture-specific syndrome characterized by illness
   and/or death and caused by the malevolent exercise of
   supernatural power by persons in league with evil spirits.

Women   (use: FEMALES)

Youth (use: ADOLESCENTS, CHILDREN-INFANTS AND PRESCHOOL,
   CHILDREN-SCHOOL AGE)

Culture Area
and Tribe List

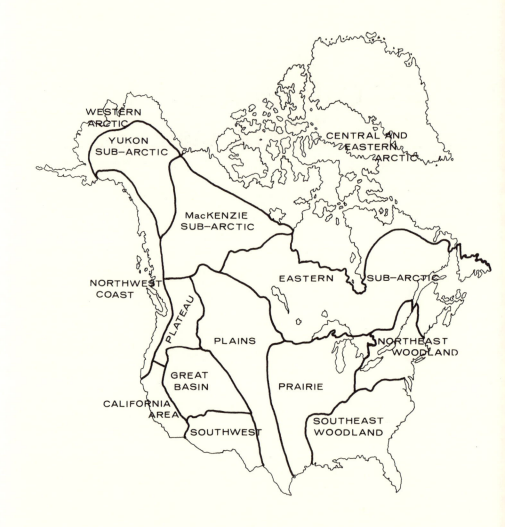

Culture Areas of North America

Culture Areas

CALIFORNIA AREA (see also: ASTUGEWI, CALIFORNIA INDIANS, CHUMASH, POMO, WINTU, YOKUTS, YUROK)

CENTRAL AND EASTERN ARCTIC (see also: ESKIMO)

EASTERN SUB-ARCTIC (see also: ALGONKIN, CHIPPEWA, CREE, MICMAC, NESKAPI)

GREAT BASIN (see also: CALIFORNIA INDIANS, GOSIUTE, PAIUTE, SHOSHONE, UTE, WASHO)

MACKENZIE SUB-ARCTIC (see also: ATHABASCAN, CHIPEWYAN, DOGRIB, SLAVE, YELLOWKNIFE)

NORTHEAST WOODLAND (see also: IROQUOIS, IROQUOIS-MOHAWK, IROQUOIS-ONEIDA, IROQUOIS-SENECA, IROQUOIS-TUSCARORA, MENOMINEE, MUNSEE, ONONODAGA, PASSAMAQUODDY)

NORTHWEST COAST (see also: ALASKA NATIVES, BELLA BELLA, COAST SALISH, HAIDA, HOOPA, KWAKIUTL, LUMMI, NOOKSACK, NOOTKA, QUINAULT, SKAGIT, SWINOMISH, TSIMSHIAN).

PLAINS (see also: ARAPAHO, ARAPAHO-NORTHERN, ASSINIBOINE-STONEY, BLACKFEET, BLACKFEET-BLOOD, BLACKFEET-PIEGAN, CHEYENNE, CHEYENNE-NORTHERN, CHEYENNE-SOUTHERN, COMANCHE, CROW, KIOWA, KIOWA APACHE, METIS, SHOSHONE, SIOUX, SIOUX-OGLALA).

PLATEAU (see also: BANNOCK, CARRIER, COLVILLE, FLATHEAD, KLAMATH, MODOC, NEZ PERCE, SHOSHONE, SPOKANE, TENINO, WARM SPRINGS, YAKIMA).

PRAIRIE (see also: ARIKARA, HIDATSA, IOWA, KICKAPOO, MANDAN, MESQUAKIE, OMAHA, OSAGE, OTO, PONCA, POTAWATOMI, STOCKBRIDGE, TONKAWA, WICHITA, WINNEBAGO).

SOUTHEAST WOODLAND (see also: CADDO, CHEROKEE, CHICKASAW, CHOCTAW, CREEK, DELAWARE, DELAWARE-CHEROKEE, HALIWA, LUMBEE, MICCOSUKEE, NANICOKE, SEMINOLE).

SOUTHWEST (see also: APACHE, APACHE-CHIRICAHUA, APACHE-JICARILLA, APACHE-LIPAN, APACHE-MESCALERO, APACHE-WHITE MOUNTAIN, CARRIZO, CHEMEHUEVI, COCOPAH, DIEGUENO, HAVASUPAI, HUALAPAI, MARICOPA, MOHAVE, MAYO NAVAJO, PAPAGO, PIMA, PUEBLO, PUEBLO-COCHITI, PUEBLO-HOPI, PUEBLO-SAN FELIPE, PUEBLO-SANTO DOMINGO, PUEBLO-TAOS, PUEBLO-TEWA, PUEBLO-ZIA, PUEBLO-ZUNI, TARAHUMAPA, YAQUI, YAVAPAI, YUMA).

WESTERN ARCTIC (see also: ESKIMO).

YUKON SUB-ARCTIC (see also: ALASKA NATIVES, ATHABASCAN, KASKA, KUTCHIN).

Tribes

ALASKA NATIVES

ALEUT

ALGONKIN

APACHE

APACHE-CHIRICAHUA

APACHE-JICARILLA

APACHE-LIPAN

APACHE-MESCALERO

APACHE-WHITE MOUNTAIN

ARAPAHO

ARAPAHO-NORTHERN

ARIKARA

ASSINIBOINE-STONEY

ATHABASCAN (see also: CARRIER, CHIPEWYAN, DOGRIB, HARE, KASKA, KUTCHIN, SLAVE, YELLOWKNIFE)

ATSUGEWI

BANNOCK

BELLA BELLA

BLACKFEET

BLACKFEET-BLOOD

BLACKFEET-PIEGAN

Blood (use: BLACKFEET-BLOOD)

CADDO

CALIFORNIA INDIANS

CARRIER

CARRIZO

CHEMEHUEVI

CHEROKEE

CHEYENNE

CHEYENNE-NORTHERN

CHEYENNE-SOUTHERN

CHICKASAW

CHIPEWYAN

CHIPPEWA

Chiricahua Apache (use: APACHE-CHIRICAHUA)

CHOCTAW

CHUMASH

COAST SALISH

Cochiti (use: PUEBLO-COCHITI)

COCOPAH

COLVILLE

COMANCHE

CREE

CREEK

CROW

Dakota (use: SIOUX)

DELAWARE

DELAWARE-CHEROKEE

DIEGUENO

DOGRIB

ESKIMO

FLATHEAD

Fox (use: MESQUAKIE)

GOSIUTE

HAIDA

HALIWA

HARE

HAVASUPAI

HIDATSA

HOOPA

Hopi (use: PUEBLO-HOPI)

HUALAPAI

IOWA

IROQUOIS

IROQUOIS-MOHAWK

IROQUOIS-ONEIDA

IROQUOIS-SENECA

IROQUOIS-TUSCARORA

Jicarilla Apache (use: APACHE-JICARILLA)

KASKA

KICKAPOO

KIOWA

KIOWA APACHE

KLAMATH

KUTCHIN

KWAKIUTL

Lakota (use: SIOUX)

Lipan Apache (use: APACHE-LIPAN)

LUMBEE

MANDAN

MARICOPA

MAYO

MENOMINEE

Mescalero Apache (use: APACHE-MESCALERO)

MESUAKIE

METIS

MICCOSUKEE

MICMAC

MODOC

MOHAVE

Mohawk (use: IROQUOIS-MOHAWK)

MUNSEE

NANICOKE

NAVAJO

NESKAPI

NEZ PERCE

NOOKSACK

NOOTKA

Northern Arapaho (use: ARAPAHO-NORTHERN)

Northern Cheyenne (use: CHEYENNE-NORTHERN)

Ojibway (use: CHIPPEWA)

OKLAHOMA INDIANS

OMAHA

Oneida (use: IROQUOIS-ONEIDA)

ONONONDAGA

OSAGE

OTO

PAIUTE

PAPAGO

PASSAMAQUODDY

Piegan (use: BLACKFEET-PIEGAN)

PIMA

POMO

PONCA

POTAWATOMI

PUEBLO

PUEBLO-COCHITI

PUEBLO-HOPI

PUEBLO-SAN FELIPE

PUEBLO-SANTO DOMINGO

PUEBLO-TAOS

PUEBLO-TEWA

PUEBLO-ZIA

PUEBLO-ZUNI

QUINAULT

Ree (use: ARIKARA)

Salish (use: COAST SALISH)

San Felipe (use: PUEBLO-SAN FELIPE)

Santo Domingo (use: PUEBLO-SANTO DOMINGO)

Saulteaux (use: CHIPPEWA)

Seneca (use: IROQUOIS-SENECA)

SHOSHONE

SIOUX

SIOUX-OGLALA

SKAGIT

SLAVE

Southern Cheyenne   (use: CHEYENNE-SOUTHERN)

SPOKANE

STOCKBRIDGE

SWINOMISH

Taos   (use: PUEBLO-TAOS)

TARAHUMARA

TENINO

Tewa   (use: PUEBLO-TEWA)

TONKAWA

TSIMSHIAN

Tuscarora   (use: IROQUOIS-TUSCARORA)

UTE

WARM SPRINGS

WASHO

White Mountain Apache   (use: APACHE-WHITE MOUNTAIN)

WICHITA

WINNEBAGO

WINTU

YAKIMA

YAQUI

YAVAPAI

YELLOWKNIFE

YOKUTS

YUMA

YUROK

Zia (use: PUEBLO-ZIA)

Zuni (use: PUEBLO-ZUNI)

Bibliography

1 AUTH ADAIR, JOHN
   TITL PHYSICIANS, MEDICINE MEN AND THEIR NAVAHO PATIENTS.
   SOUR IN IAGO GALDSTON (ED.), MAN'S IMAGE IN MEDICINE AND
         ANTHROPOLOGY, PP 237-257. NEW YORK: INTERNATIONAL
         UNIVERSITIES PRESS, 1963.
   YEAR 1963
   DESC NAVAJO, SOUTHWEST, CULTURAL ADAPTATION+, DELIVERY OF
         SERVICES+, TRADITIONAL HEALERS+, MEDICAL
         PROFESSIONALS+, BICULTURALISM, NATIVE AMERICAN
         PERSONNEL, RESERVATION
   IDEN ARIZONA, U.S., NAVAJO RESERVATION

2 AUTH ATTNEAVE, CAROLYN L.
   TITL MEDICINE MEN AND PSYCHIATRISTS IN THE INDIAN HEALTH
         SERVICE.
   SOUR PSYCHIATRIC ANNALS, NOV. 1974, V4(9), PP 49-55.
   YEAR 1974
   DESC TRADITIONAL HEALERS+, I.H.S.+, MENTAL HEALTH
         PROFESSIONALS+, NONINTERFERENCE+, STRESS, RESERVATION
   IDEN U.S.

3 AUTH BARTER, ELOISE RICHARDS; BARTER, JAMES T.
   TITL URBAN INDIANS AND MENTAL HEALTH PROBLEMS.
   SOUR PSYCHIATRIC ANNALS, NOV. 1974, V4(9), PP 37-43.
   YEAR 1974
   DESC URBANIZATION+, NATIVE AMERICAN POLITICAL MOVEMENTS,
         DELIVERY OF SERVICES+, NATIVE AMERICAN PERSONNEL,
         NATIVE AMERICAN ADMINISTERED PROGRAMS, URBAN AREAS,
         MENTAL HEALTH PROGRAMS AND SERVICES+
   IDEN U.S.

4 AUTH BEISER, MORTON; DEGROAT, ELLOISE
   TITL BODY AND SPIRIT MEDICINE: CONVERSATIONS WITH A NAVAHO
         SINGER.
   SOUR PSYCHIATRIC ANNALS, NOV. 1974, V4(9), PP 9-12.
   YEAR 1974
   DESC NAVAJO, RESERVATION, TRADITIONAL HEALERS+,
         WITCHCRAFT+, NATIVE AMERICAN ETIOLOGY, NATIVE AMERICAN
         RELIGIONS+, SOUTHWEST
   IDEN U.S., NAVAJO RESERVATION

5 AUTH BERGMAN, ROBERT L.
   TITL PARAPROFESSIONALS IN INDIAN MENTAL HEALTH PROGRAMS.
   SOUR PSYCHIATRIC ANNALS, NOV. 1974, V4(9), PP 76-84.
   YEAR 1974
   DESC NAVAJO, SOUTHWEST, RESERVATION, MENTAL HEALTH
         PARAPROFESSIONALS+, I.H.S., TRAINING PROGRAMS+,
         NATIVE AMERICAN PERSONNEL, LANGUAGE HANDICAPS,
         DELIVERY OF SERVICES, TABOO BREAKING
   IDEN U.S., ARIZONA, NEW MEXICO, NAVAJO RESERVATION

6 AUTH BLOOM, JOSEPH D.; RICHARDS, WILLIAM W.
   TITL ALASKA NATIVE REGIONAL CORPORATIONS AND COMMUNITY
         MENTAL HEALTH.
   SOUR PSYCHIATRIC ANNALS, NOV. 1974, V4(9), 67-75.

```
        YEAR  1974
        DESC  ALASKA NATIVES, NORTHWEST COAST, WESTERN ARCTIC, YUKON
              SUB-ARCTIC, NATIVE AMERICAN PERSONNEL, MENTAL HEALTH
              PARAPROFESSIONALS+, MENTAL HEALTH PROGRAMS AND
              SERVICES+, OFF-RESERVATION, CULTURAL REVIVAL
        IDEN  U.S., ALASKA, ALASKA NATIVE LAND CLAIMS SETTLEMENT
              ACT, ALASKA NATIVE HEALTH SERVICE

7    AUTH  BUXBAUM, ROBERT C.
     TITL  INDIAN HEALTH: THE ROLE OF THE MEDICAL SCHOOL.
     SOUR  HARVARD MEDICAL SCHOOL ALUMNI BULLETIN, JAN./FEB.
           1972, V46, PP 16-20.
     YEAR  1972
     DESC  MEDICAL PROFESSIONALS+, DISCRIMINATION+, COLLEGES AND
           UNIVERSITIES+, NATIVE AMERICAN PERSONNEL, B.I.A.
           BOARDING SCHOOLS, I.H.S., CHILDREN-SCHOOL AGE,
           ADOLESCENTS
     IDEN  U.S., HARVARD MEDICAL SCHOOL

8    AUTH  ATTNEAVE, CAROLYN L.
     TITL  THERAPY IN TRIBAL SETTINGS AND URBAN NETWORK
           INTERVENTION.
     SOUR  FAMILY PROCESS, SEP. 1969, V8(2), PP 192-210.
     YEAR  1969
     DESC  CLINICAL STUDY, URBAN AREAS,  SOCIAL NETWORKS+, MENTAL
           HEALTH PROFESSIONALS+, EXTENDED FAMILY, COOPERATION,
           PSYCHOTHERAPY AND COUNSELING+
     IDEN  U.S.

9    AUTH  GOLDSTEIN, GEORGE S.
     TITL  THE MODEL DORMITORY.
     SOUR  PSYCHIATRIC ANNALS, NOV. 1974, V4(9), PP 85-92.
     YEAR  1974
     DESC  NAVAJO, RESERVATION, SOUTHWEST, PSYCHOLOGICAL TESTING,
           CHILDREN-SCHOOL AGE+, SOCIALLY DEVIANT BEHAVIOR,
           B.I.A. BOARDING SCHOOLS+, EDUCATION
           PARAPROFESSIONALS+, PROGRAM EVALUATION, CULTURE-FAIR
           TESTS, EDUCATION PROGRAMS AND SERVICES
     IDEN  U.S., GOODENOUGH HARRIS DRAW A PERSON TEST, STANFORD
           ACHIEVEMENT TEST, BENDER GESTALT TEST, DEVELOPMENTAL
           FORM SEQUENCE

10   AUTH  GOOD TRACKS, JIMM G.
     TITL  NATIVE AMERICAN NON INTERFERENCE.
     SOUR  SOCIAL WORK, NOV. 1973, V18(6), PP 30-34.
     YEAR  1973
     DESC  SOCIAL SERVICE PROFESSIONALS+,  NONINTERFERENCE+,
           DELIVERY OF SERVICES+
     IDEN  U.S.

11   AUTH  HAVIGHURST, ROBERT J.
     TITL  EDUCATION AMONG AMERICAN INDIANS: INDIVIDUAL AND
           CULTURAL ASPECTS.
     SOUR  ANNALS OF THE AMERICAN ACADEMY OF POLITICAL AND SOCIAL
           SCIENCE, MAY 1957, V311, PP 105-115.
```

```
     YEAR  1957
     DESC  RESERVATION, PSYCHOLOGICAL TESTING,
           NONCOMPETITIVENESS, B.I.A. BOARDING SCHOOLS,
           ADOLESCENTS+, CHILDREN-SCHOOL AGE+, ACHIEVEMENT+,
           ABILITIES+, BICULTURALISM, PUEBLO-ZUNI, PUEBLO-ZIA,
           PUEBLO-HOPI, PAPAGO, NAVAJO, SOUTHWEST, SIOUX, PLAINS,
           MOTIVATION+, TRADITIONAL CHILD REARING
     IDEN  U.S., HOPI RESERVATION, ZUNI RESERVATION, ZIA
           RESERVATION, NAVAJO RESERVATION, PINE RIDGE
           RESERVATION, PAPAGO RESERVATION

12   AUTH  JILEK, WOLFGANG G.
     TITL  FROM CRAZY WITCHDOCTOR TO AUXILIARY PSYCHOTHERAPIST:
           THE CHANGING IMAGE OF THE MEDICINE MAN.
     SOUR  PSYCHIATRIA CLINICA, 1971, V4, PP 200-220.
     YEAR  1971
     DESC  ADULTS, MENTAL DISORDERS, TRADITIONAL HEALERS+,
           PSYCHOTHERAPY AND COUNSELING, CULTURE-SPECIFIC
           SYNDROMES, NEUROSES, PSYCHOSES, CHARACTER DISORDERS,
           STEREOTYPES, CULTURE-BASED PSYCHOTHERAPY, NATIVE
           AMERICAN ETIOLOGY+, REVIEW OF LITERATURE
     IDEN  U.S., CANADA

13   AUTH  JILEK, WOLFGANG G.
     TITL  INDIAN HEALING POWER: INDIGENOUS THERAPEUTIC PRACTICES
           IN THE PACIFIC NORTHWEST.
     SOUR  PSYCHIATRIC ANNALS, NOV. 1974, V4(9), PP 13-21.
     YEAR  1974
     DESC  RESERVATION, TRADITIONAL HEALERS+, SPIRIT INTRUSION+,
           DEPRESSION, ANOMIE, CULTURAL REVIVAL, COAST SALISH,
           NORTHWEST COAST, STRESS, CULTURE-BASED PSYCHOTHERAPY+
     IDEN  U.S., CANADA, WASHINGTON, BRITISH COLUMBIA

14   AUTH  JILEK, WOLFGANG G.; TODD, NORMAN
     TITL  WITCHDOCTORS SUCCEED WHERE DOCTORS FAIL: PSYCHOTHERAPY
           AMONG COAST SALISH INDIANS.
     SOUR  CANADIAN PSYCHIATRIC ASSOCIATION JOURNAL, AUG 1974,
           V19(4), PP 351-356.
     YEAR  1974
     DESC  COAST SALISH, NORTHWEST COAST, RESERVATION,
           TRADITIONAL HEALERS+, CULTURAL REVIVAL, PSYCHOTHERAPY
           AND COUNSELING, MENTAL HEALTH PROFESSIONALS, SPIRIT
           INTRUSION, CULTURE-BASED PSYCHOTHERAPY+
     IDEN  CANADA, BRITISH COLUMBIA

15   AUTH  JILEK-AALL, LOUISE
     TITL  PSYCHOSOCIAL ASPECTS OF DRINKING AMONG COAST SALISH
           INDIANS.
     SOUR  CANADIAN PSYCHIATRIC ASSOCIATION JOURNAL, AUG. 1974,
           V19(4), PP 357-361.
     YEAR  1974
     DESC  COAST SALISH, NORTHWEST COAST, RESERVATION, ALCOHOL
           USE+, STRESS+, NATIVE AMERICAN ADMINISTERED PROGRAMS,
           ALCOHOLISM TREATMENT
     IDEN  CANADA, BRITISH COLUMBIA, ALCOHOLICS ANONYMOUS
```

16   AUTH   KLUCKHOHN, CLYDE; ROSENZWEIG, JANINE C.
     TITL   TWO NAVAJO CHILDREN OVER A FIVE-YEAR PERIOD.
     SOUR   AMERICAN JOURNAL OF ORTHOPSYCHIATRY, APR. 1949,
            V19(2), PP 266-278.
     YEAR   1949
     DESC   NAVAJO, SOUTHWEST, RESERVATION, PERSONALITY TRAITS+,
            PSYCHOLOGICAL TESTING,CHILDREN-SCHOOL AGE+,
            CULTURE-FAIR TESTS
     IDEN   U.S., NAVAJO RESERVATION, RORSCHACH TEST, BANELAS
            MORAL AND IDEOLOG TEST, THEMATIC APPECEPTION TEST,
            STEWERT EMOTIONAL RESPONSE TEST

17   AUTH   LEIGHTON, ALEXANDER H.; LEIGHTON, DOROTHEA C.
     TITL   ELEMENTS OF PSYCHOTHERAPY IN NAVAJO RELIGION.
     SOUR   PSYCHIATRY: JOURNAL OF THE BIOLOGY AND PATHOLOGY OF
            INTERPERSONAL RELATIONS, NOV. 1941, V4(4), PP 515-523.
     YEAR   1941
     DESC   NAVAJO, RESERVATION, SOUTHWEST, CULTURAL ADAPTATION,
            PSYCHOTHERAPY AND COUNSELING, TRADITIONAL HEALERS,
            MEDICAL PROFESSIONALS, MENTAL HEALTH PROFESSIONALS,
            NATIVE AMERICAN RELIGIONS+, CULTURE-BASED
            PSYCHOTHERAPY+, NATIVE AMERICAN ETIOLOGY
     IDEN   U.S., NAVAJO RESERVATION

18   AUTH   LEON, ROBERT L.
     TITL   MALADAPTIVE INTERACTION BETWEEN BUREAU OF INDIAN
            AFFAIRS STAFF AND INDIAN CLIENTS.
     SOUR   AMERICAN JOURNAL OF ORTHOPSYCHIATRY, JUL. 1965,
            V35(4), PP 723-728.
     YEAR   1965
     DESC   B.I.A.+, ADMINISTRATIVE ISSUES+, PROGRAM EVALUATION+,
            FEDERAL GOVERNMENT, PASSIVE RESISTANCE
     IDEN   U.S.

19   AUTH   LEON, ROBERT L.
     TITL   SOME IMPLICATIONS FOR A PREVENTIVE PROGRAM FOR
            AMERICAN INDIANS.
     SOUR   AMERICAN JOURNAL OF PSYCHIATRY, AUG. 1968, V125(2), PP
            232-236.
     YEAR   1968
     DESC   B.I.A.+, STRESS, NATIVE AMERICAN ADMINISTERED
            PROGRAMS, ADMINISTRATIVE ISSUES+, NONCOMPETITIVENESS,
            TIME PERCEPTION, PROGRAM DEVELOPMENT+, PREVENTIVE
            MENTAL HEALTH PROGRAMS
     IDEN   U.S.

20   AUTH   LYSLO, ARNOLD.
     TITL   ADOPTIVE PLACEMENT OF AMERICAN INDIAN CHILDREN WITH
            NON-INDIAN FAMILIES: PART I.
     SOUR   CHILD WELFARE, MAY 1961, PP 4-6.
     YEAR   1961
     DESC   ADOPTION AND FOSTER CARE+, B.I.A., CHILDREN-INFANTS
            AND PRESCHOOL+, CHILDREN-SCHOOL AGE+, SOCIAL SERVICES,
            FAMILY FUNCTIONING+
     IDEN   U.S., INDIAN ADOPTION PROJECT

21 AUTH MCNICKLE, D'ARCY.
    TITL THE SOCIOCULTURAL SETTING OF INDIAN LIFE.
    SOUR AMERICAN JOURNAL OF PSYCHIATRY, AUG. 1968, V125(2), PP
          219-223.
    YEAR 1968
    DESC CULTURAL ADAPTATION+, NATIVE AMERICAN POLITICAL
          MOVEMENTS+, BICULTURALISM+, TRIBAL POLITICAL
          ORGANIZATIONS, CULTURAL CONTINUITY+, COLLEGES AND
          UNIVERSITIES, ADOLESCENTS+
    IDEN U.S.

22 AUTH MAY, PHILIP A.; DIZMANG, LARRY H.
    TITL SUICIDE AND THE AMERICAN INDIAN.
    SOUR PSYCHIATRIC ANNALS, NOV. 1974, V4(9), PP 22-28.
    YEAR 1974
    DESC SUICIDE+, STRESS+, ADULTS, ADOLESCENTS, SELF-CONCEPT,
          FAMILY FUNCTIONING, INTERTRIBAL COMPARISONS,
          STEREOTYPES, SOUTHWEST, GREAT BASIN, PLATEAU, PLAINS
    IDEN U.S.

23 AUTH MEYER, GEORGE G.
    TITL ON HELPING THE CASUALTIES OF RAPID CHANGE.
    SOUR PSYCHIATRIC ANNALS, NOV. 1974, V4(9), PP 44-48.
    YEAR 1974
    DESC RESERVATION, CULTURAL ADAPTATION, STRESS+, TRADITIONAL
          HEALERS, GHOST SICKNESS, MENTAL HEALTH PROFESSIONALS+,
          ETHNIC IDENTITY+
    IDEN U.S.

24 AUTH MILLER, SHELDON I.; SCHOENFELD, LAWRENCE S.
    TITL SUICIDE ATTEMPT PATTERNS AMONG THE NAVAJO INDIANS.
    SOUR INTERNATIONAL JOURNAL OF SOCIAL PSYCHIATRY, SUM. 1971,
          V17(3), PP 189-193.
    YEAR 1971
    DESC NAVAJO, RESERVATION, SOUTHWEST, ADOLESCENTS,
          DEPRESSION, DRUG USE, SEX DIFFERENCES, SUICIDE+,
          STEREOTYPES, ECONOMIC ISSUES, SOUTHWEST
    IDEN U.S., NAVAJO RESERVATION

25 AUTH PRAGER, KENNETH M.
    TITL ALCOHOLISM AND THE AMERICAN INDIAN.
    SOUR HARVARD MEDICAL ALUMNI BULLETIN, JAN./FEB. 1972, V46,
          PP 20-26.
    YEAR 1972
    DESC SIOUX, ADOLESCENTS, ALCOHOL USE+, PLAINS,
          SELF-CONCEPT,ADULTS, ETHNIC IDENTITY+, ACCIDENTS+,
          EPIDEMIOLOGICAL STUDY, RESERVATION
    IDEN U.S., SOUTH DAKOTA, CHEYENNE RIVER RESERVATION

26 AUTH SASLOW, HARRY L.; HARROVER, MAY J.
    TITL RESEARCH ON PSYCHOSOCIAL ADJUSTMENT OF INDIAN YOUTH.
    SOUR AMERICAN JOURNAL OF PSYCHIATRY, AUG. 1968, V125(2), PP
          224-231.
    YEAR 1968
    DESC PUEBLO-HOPI, PUEBLO-SAN FELIPE, PUEBLO-SANTO DOMINGO,

NAVAJO, APACHE-MESCALERO, SIOUX-OGLALA, ADOLESCENTS+,
PLAINS, SOUTHWEST, RESERVATION, CHILDREN-SCHOOL AGE+,
CHILDREN-INFANTS AND PRESCHOOL, ACHIEVEMENT+,
PSYCHOLOGICAL TESTING, , ANOMIE, EXTENDED FAMILY+,
TRADITIONAL CHILD REARING+, REVIEW OF LITERATURE
IDEN   U.S.

27 AUTH SHORE, JAMES H.
    TITL AMERICAN INDIAN SUICIDE: FACT AND FANTASY.
    SOUR PSYCHIATRY, FEB. 1975, V38, PP 86-91.
    YEAR 1975
    DESC RESERVATION, ADULTS, ADOLESCENTS, STEREOTYPES,
          INTERTRIBAL COMPARISONS, EPIDEMIOLOGICAL STUDY, SEX
          DIFFERENCES, SELF-CONCEPT, SUICIDE+, PREVENTIVE MENTAL
          HEALTH PROGRAMS, CORRECTIONAL INSTITUTIONS
    IDEN U.S.

28 AUTH SHORE, JAMES H.
    TITL PSYCHIATRIC EPIDEMIOLOGY AMONG AMERICAN INDIANS.
    SOUR PSYCHIATRIC ANNALS, NOV. 1974, V4(9), PP 56-66.
    YEAR 1974
    DESC MENTAL DISORDERS+, ALCOHOL USE, SUICIDE,
          EPIDEMIOLOGICAL STUDY, PSYCHOLOGICAL TESTING,
          SCHIZOPHRENIA, DEPRESSION, GRIEF REACTION,
          CULTURE-FAIR TESTS, INTERTRIBAL COMPARISONS, SURVEY
    IDEN U.S., CORNELL MEDICAL INDEX, HEALTH OPINION SURVEY

29 AUTH SINGER, KARL L.
    TITL HOW THE NAVAJO DEAL WITH ILLNESS.
    SOUR HARVARD MEDICAL ALUMNI BULLETIN, JAN./FEB. 1972, V46,
          PP 26-29.
    YEAR 1972
    DESC NAVAJO, SOUTHWEST, TRADITIONAL HEALERS+, DELIVERY OF
          SERVICES+, MEDICAL PROFESSIONALS+, NATIVE AMERICAN
          ETIOLOGY, I.H.S., NATIVE AMERICAN RELIGIONS,
          WITCHCRAFT, UNIVERSAL HARMONY
    IDEN U.S., NAVAJO RESERVATION

30 AUTH SPINDLER, GEORGE D.; SPINDLER, LOUISE S.
    TITL AMERICAN INDIAN PERSONALITY TYPES AND THEIR
          SOCIOCULTURAL ROOTS.
    SOUR ANNALS OF THE AMERICAN ACADEMY OF POLITICAL AND SOCIAL
          SCIENCE, MAY 1957, V311, PP 147-157.
    YEAR 1957
    DESC PSYCHOLOGICAL TESTING+, PERSONALITY TRAITS+, CULTURAL
          CONTINUITY+, CULTURAL ADAPTATION+, SEX DIFFERENCES,
          INTERTRIBAL COMPARISONS, NATIVE AMERICAN VALUES,
          GENEROSITY, MENOMINEE, CHIPPEWA, SIOUX, PUEBLO-ZUNI,
          IROQUOIS-TUSCARORA, PLAINS, NORTHEAST WOODLAND,
          SOUTHWEST, EASTERN SUB-ARCTIC
    IDEN U.S., RORSCHACH TEST, THEMATIC APPERCEPTION TEST

31 AUTH WALLACE, HELEN M.
    TITL THE HEALTH OF AMERICAN INDIAN CHILDREN.
    SOUR HEALTH SERVICE REPORTS, NOV. 1972, V87, PP 867-876.

```
      YEAR  1972
      DESC  CHILDREN-INFANTS AND PRESCHOOL+, CHILDREN-SCHOOL AGE+,
            EPIDEMIOLOGICAL STUDY, MEDICAL PROGRAMS AND SERVICES+,
            PHYSICAL HEALTH AND ILLNESS+, DEMOGRAPHIC DATA,
            NUTRITIONAL FACTORS
      IDEN  U.S.

32    AUTH  CARLSON, ERIC J.
      TITL  COUNSELLING IN NATIVE CONTEXT.
      SOUR  CANADA'S MENTAL HEALTH, 1975, V23, PP 7-9.
      YEAR  1975
      DESC  PSYCHOTHERAPY AND COUNSELING+, ETHNIC IDENTITY+,
            MENTAL HEALTH PROFESSIONALS+, ADOLESCENTS+
      IDEN  CANADA

33    AUTH  WESTERMEYER, JOSEPH
      TITL  THE DRUNKEN INDIAN: MYTHS AND REALITIES.
      SOUR  PSYCHIATRIC ANNALS, NOV. 1974, V4(9), PP 29-36.
      YEAR  1974
      DESC  STEREOTYPES+,  STRESS, ALCOHOL USE+, ALCOHOLISM
            TREATMENT, NATIVE AMERICAN ADMINISTERED PROGRAMS
      IDEN  U.S.

34    AUTH  LINTON, RALPH
      TITL  NATIVISTIC MOVEMENTS.
      SOUR  AMERICAN ANTHROPOLOGIST, 1943, V45, PP 230-240.
      YEAR  1943
      DESC  CULTURAL REVIVAL+, NATIVE AMERICAN RELIGIONS+,
            CULTURAL CONTINUITY+, STRESS+, NATIVE-NON-NATIVE
            COMPARISONS, LATINOS, ANGLO AMERICANS,
      IDEN  U.S.

35    AUTH  LEIGHTON, ALEXANDER H.; HUGHES, CHARLES C.
      TITL  NOTES ON ESKIMO PATTERNS OF SUICIDE.
      SOUR  SOUTHWESTERN JOURNAL OF ANTHROPOLOGY, 1955, V11, PP
            327-338.
      YEAR  1955
      DESC  ESKIMO, WESTERN ARCTIC, SUICIDE+, GROUP NORMS AND
            SANCTIONS+, ADULTS, AGED,EXTENDED FAMILY, DEATH AND
            DYING+, EPIDEMIOLOGICAL STUDY
      IDEN  U.S., ALASKA

36    AUTH  RITZENTHALER, ROBERT; SELLERS, MARY
      TITL  INDIANS IN AN URBAN SITUATION.
      SOUR  WISCONSIN ARCHEOLOGIST, 1955, V36(4), PP 147-161.
      YEAR  1955
      DESC  DEMOGRAPHIC DATA, URBAN AREAS, URBANIZATION+,
            IROQUOIS-ONEIDA, CHIPPEWA, EASTERN SUB-ARCTIC,
            EMPLOYMENT, RELOCATION+, NORTHEAST WOODLAND
      IDEN  U.S., WISCONSIN

37    AUTH  LAMPHERE, LOUISE
      TITL  CEREMONIAL CO-OPERATION AND NETWORKS: A REANALYSIS OF
            THE NAVAJO OUTFIT.
      SOUR  MAN, 1970, V5, PP 39-59.
```

         YEAR   1970
         DESC   NAVAJO, SOUTHWEST, SOCIAL NETWORKS+, RESERVATION,
                COOPERATION+, EXTENDED FAMILY+
         IDEN   U.S., NAVAJO RESERVATION

38   AUTH   MINZ, NORBETT L.
     TITL   DECULTURATION IN SCHIZOPHRENIC'S DRAWINGS.
     SOUR   IN IRENE JAKAB (ED.), TRANSCULTURAL ASPECTS OF
            PSYCHIATRIC ART, PP 137-155.PSYCHIATRY AND ART, V4.
            BASEL: S. KARGER, 1975.
     YEAR   1975
     DESC   NAVAJO, PUEBLO-HOPI, SOUTHWEST, RESERVATION, ADULTS,
            PSYCHOLOGICAL TESTING+, SCHIZOPHRENIA+
     IDEN   U.S., NAVAJO RESERVATION, GOODENOUGH HARRIS DRAW A
            PERSON TEST

39   AUTH   VOGT, EVON Z.
     TITL   THE AUTOMOBILE IN CONTEMPORARY NAVAJO CULTURE.
     SOUR   IN ANTHONY F. C. WALLACE (ED), MEN AND CULTURE:
            SELECTED PAPERS OF THE FIFTH INTERNATIONAL CONGRESS OF
            ANTHROPOLOGICAL AND ETHNOLOGICAL SCIENCES, PP 359-363.
            PHILADELPHIA: UNIVERSITY OF PENNSYLVANIA PRESS, 1960.
     YEAR   1960
     DESC   NAVAJO, RESERVATION, CULTURAL ADAPTATION+, CULTURAL
            CONTINUITY+, SOUTHWEST,EXTENDED FAMILY, COOPERATION,
            RELOCATION+

40   AUTH   DOZIER, EDWARD P.
     TITL   PROBLEM DRINKING AMONG AMERICAN INDIANS.
     SOUR   QUARTERLY JOURNAL OF STUDIES ON ALCOHOL, MAR. 1966,
            V27(1), PP 72-87.
     YEAR   1966
     DESC   ADULTS, ALCOHOL USE+, NATIVE AMERICAN RELIGIONS,
            GROUP NORMS AND SANCTIONS, NATIVE AMERICAN
            ADMINISTERED PROGRAMS, STRESS, RELIGIONS-NON-NATIVE,
            SOCIAL GROUPS AND PEER GROUPS+, PSYCHOTHERAPY AND
            COUNSELING, PUEBLO, SOUTHWEST, KLAMATH, NORTHWEST
            COAST, ALCOHOLISM TREATMENT+
     IDEN   U.S., ALCOHOLICS ANONYMOUS, HANDSOME LAKE RELIGION,
            GHOST DANCE, SHAKER RELIGION

41   AUTH   HAVIGHURST, ROBERT J.; GUNTHER, MINNA KOROL; PRATT,
            INEZ E.
     TITL   ENVIRONMENT AND THE DRAW-A-MAN TEST: THE PERFORMANCE
            OF INDIAN CHILDREN.
     SOUR   JOURNAL OF ABNORMAL AND SOCIAL PSYCHOLOGY, JAN. 1946,
            V41(1), PP 50-63.
     YEAR   1946
     DESC   RESERVATION, CHILDREN-SCHOOL AGE+, PUEBLO-HOPI,
            PUEBLO-ZUNI, PUEBLO-ZIA, PAPAGO, NAVAJO, SOUTHWEST,
            SIOUX, PLAINS, PSYCHOLOGICAL TESTING+, ABILITIES+, SEX
            DIFFERENCES, INTERTRIBAL COMPARISONS
     IDEN   U.S., GOODENOUGH HARRIS DRAW A PERSON TEST

42   AUTH   LITTMAN, GERARD

TITL ALCOHOLISM, ILLNESS, AND SOCIAL PATHOLOGY AMONG
      AMERICAN INDIANS IN TRANSITION.
SOUR AMERICAN JOURNAL OF PUBLIC HEALTH AND THE NATION'S
      HEALTH, SEP. 1970, V60(9), PP 1769-1785.
YEAR 1970
DESC URBAN AREAS, ECONOMIC ISSUES, ALCOHOL USE+, NATIVE
      AMERICAN COPING BEHAVIORS, ADULTS, NONINTERFERENCE,
      URBANIZATION+, NATIVE AMERICAN ETIOLOGY,   STRESS+,
      ALCOHOL USE+, ALCOHOLISM TREATMENT
IDEN U.S., ILLINOIS

43 AUTH THOMPSON, LAURA
    TITL ACTION RESEARCH AMONG AMERICAN INDIANS.
    SOUR SCIENTIFIC MONTHLY, JAN. 1950, V70(1), PP 34-40.
    YEAR 1950
    DESC PSYCHOLOGICAL TESTING+, PERSONALITY TRAITS+, EDUCATION
          PROFESSIONALS, CHILDREN-SCHOOL AGE, CULTURE-FAIR
          TESTS+, PUEBLO-HOPI, PUEBLO-ZUNI, NAVAJO, PAPAGO,
          SOUTHWEST, SIOUX, PLAINS, RESERVATION
    IDEN U.S., NEW MEXICO, HOPI RESERVATION

44 AUTH WESTERMEYER, JOSEPH
    TITL OPTIONS REGARDING ALCOHOL USE AMONG THE CHIPPEWA.
    SOUR AMERICAN JOURNAL OF ORTHOPSYCHIATRY, APR. 1972,
          V42(3), PP 398-403.
    YEAR 1972
    DESC CHIPPEWA, ADULTS, EASTERN SUB-ARCTIC, ALCOHOL USE+,
          GROUP NORMS AND SANCTIONS, NATIVE AMERICAN COPING
          BEHAVIORS
    IDEN U.S., MINNESOTA

45 AUTH KUNITZ, STEPHEN J.; LEVY, JERROLD E.
    TITL CHANGING IDEAS OF ALCOHOL USE AMONG NAVAJO INDIANS.
    SOUR QUARTERLY JOURNAL OF STUDIES ON ALCOHOL, MAR. 1974,
          V35, PP 243-259.
    YEAR 1974
    DESC NAVAJO, SOUTHWEST, RESERVATION, ADULTS, ALCOHOL USE+,
          MEDICAL PARAPROFESSIONALS, NATIVE AMERICAN PERSONNEL
    IDEN U.S., NAVAJO RESERVATION

46 AUTH GOLDSTINE, THEA; GUTMANN, DAVID
    TITL A TAT STUDY OF NAVAJO AGING.
    SOUR PSYCHIATRY, NOV. 1972, V35, PP 373-384.
    YEAR 1972
    DESC NAVAJO, SOUTHWEST, ADULTS, AGED+, PSYCHOLOGICAL
          TESTING+, PERSONALITY TRAITS+, RESERVATION, URBAN
          AREAS, AGGRESSIVENESS+, MALES+, PSYCHOANALYSIS
    IDEN U.S., THEMATIC APPERCEPTION TEST

47 AUTH CONRAD, REX D.; KAHN, MARVIN W.
    TITL AN EPIDEMIOLOGICAL STUDY OF SUICIDE AND ATTEMPTED
          SUICIDE AMONG PAPAGO INDIANS.
    SOUR AMERICAN JOURNAL OF PSYCHIATRY, JAN 1974, V131(1), PP
          69-72.
    YEAR 1974

```
       DESC   EPIDEMIOLOGICAL STUDY, SUICIDE+, ADULTS, MALES,
              SOUTHWEST, PAPAGO
       IDEN   U.S., ARIZONA

48  AUTH   HAMMERSCHLAG, CARL A.; ALDERFER, CLAYTON P.; BERG,
           DAVID.
    TITL   INDIAN EDUCATION: A HUMAN SYSTEMS ANALYSIS.
    SOUR   AMERICAN JOURNAL OF PSYCHIATRY, OCT. 1973, V130(10),
           PP 1098-1102.
    YEAR   1973
    DESC   CHILDREN-SCHOOL AGE, ADOLESCENTS, EDUCATION
           PROFESSIONALS, NATIVE AMERICAN PERSONNEL, B.I.A.
           BOARDING SCHOOLS+, ACHIEVEMENT, ETHNIC IDENTITY,
           DISCRIMINATION, POWERLESSNESS+, EDUCATION PROGRAMS AND
           SERVICES, PROGRAM EVALUATION+, SOCIALLY DEVIANT
           BEHAVIOR
    IDEN   U.S.

49  AUTH   FOULKS, EDWARD F.; KATZ, SOLOMON
    TITL   THE MENTAL HEALTH OF ALASKAN NATIVES.
    SOUR   ACTA PSYCHIATRICA SCANDINAVICA, 1973, V49, PP 91-96.
    YEAR   1973
    DESC   ALASKA NATIVES, OFF-RESERVATION, MENTAL DISORDERS+,
           EPIDEMIOLOGICAL STUDY,ALCOHOL USE, DEPRESSION,
           PARANOIA, URBANIZATION, NORTHWEST COAST, YUKON
           SUB-ARCTIC, WESTERN ARCTIC, URBAN AREAS, DEMOGRAPHIC
           DATA
    IDEN   U.S., ALASKA

50  AUTH   CUNDICK, BERT P.; GOTTFREDSON, DOUGLAS K.; WILLSON,
           LINDA
    TITL   CHANGES IN SCHOLASTIC ACHIEVEMENT AND INTELLIGENCE OF
           INDIAN CHILDREN ENROLLED IN A FOSTER PLACEMENT
           PROGRAM.
    SOUR   DEVELOPMENTAL PSYCHOLOGY, NOV. 1974, V10(6), PP
           815-820.
    YEAR   1974
    DESC   CHILDREN-SCHOOL AGE+, ADOPTION AND FOSTER CARE+,
           ABILITIES, ACHIEVEMENT+,RELIGIONS-NON-NATIVE
    IDEN   U.S., MORMON CHURCH

51  AUTH   COCKERHAM, WILLIAM C.
    TITL   DRINKING ATTITUDES AND PRACTICES AMONG WIND RIVER
           RESERVATION INDIAN YOUTH.
    SOUR   QUARTERLY JOURNAL OF STUDIES ON ALCOHOL, MAR. 1975,
           V36(3), PP 321-326.
    YEAR   1975
    DESC   SHOSHONE, ARAPAHO-NORTHERN, PLAINS, RESERVATION,
           ADOLESCENTS+, SOCIALLY DEVIANT BEHAVIOR+, SEX
           DIFFERENCES, ALCOHOL USE+, GROUP NORMS AND SANCTIONS,
           ATTITUDES+
    IDEN   WYOMING, U.S., WIND RIVER RESERVATION

52  AUTH   BREKKE, BEVERLY; WILLIAMS, JOHN D.
    TITL   CONSERVATION AND READING ACHIEVEMENT OF SECOND GRADE
```

BILINGUAL AMERICAN INDIAN CHILDREN.
SOUR JOURNAL OF PSYCHOLOGY, JAN.1974, V86, PP 65-69.
YEAR 1974
DESC PUEBLO-ZUNI, SOUTHWEST, RESERVATION, CHILDREN-SCHOOL
     AGE+, PSYCHOLOGICAL TESTING+, BILINGUALISM+,
     LEARNING+, CULTURE-FAIR TESTS
IDEN NEW MEXICO, U.S., GOODENOUGH HARRIS DRAW A PERSON
     TEST, CLASSROOM READING INVENTORY, PIAGETIAN TASKS

53 AUTH BAHR, HOWARD M.; CHADWICK, BRUCE A.
   TITL CONSERVATISM, RACIAL INTOLERANCE, AND ATTITUDES TOWARD
        RACIAL ASSIMILATION AMONG WHITES AND AMERICAN INDIANS.
   SOUR JOURNAL OF SOCIAL PSYCHOLOGY, OCT. 1974, V94, PP
        45-56.
   YEAR 1974
   DESC URBAN AREAS, DISCRIMINATION+, NATIVE-NON-NATIVE
        COMPARISONS+, CULTURAL ADAPTATION, PSYCHOLOGICAL
        TESTING, ADOPTION AND FOSTER CARE, DEMOGRAPHIC
        DATA,NATIVE AMERICAN VALUES, ANGLO AMERICANS ,
        ATTITUDES+
   IDEN U.S., WASHINGTON, WILSON PATTERSON CONSERVATISM SCALE

54 AUTH DLUGOKINSKI, ERIC; KRAMER, LYN
   TITL A SYSTEM OF NEGLECT: INDIAN BOARDING SCHOOLS.
   SOUR AMERICAN JOURNAL OF PSYCHIATRY, JUN. 1974, V131(6), PP
        670-673.
   YEAR 1974
   DESC CHILDREN-SCHOOL AGE, ADOLESCENTS+, B.I.A. BOARDING
        SCHOOLS+, GROUP NORMS AND SANCTIONS, SOCIAL GROUPS
        AND PEER GROUPS, ADMINISTRATIVE ISSUES+, PSYCHOTHERAPY
        AND COUNSELING+
   IDEN U.S.

55 AUTH ALBAUGH, BERNARD J.; ANDERSON, PHILIP O.
   TITL PEYOTE IN THE TREATMENT OF ALCOHOLISM AMONG AMERICAN
        INDIANS.
   SOUR AMERICAN JOURNAL OF PSYCHIATRY, NOV. 1974, V131(11),
        PP 1247-1250.
   YEAR 1974
   DESC CHEYENNE-SOUTHERN, ARAPAHO, PLAINS, OFF-RESERVATION,
        ADULTS, ANOMIE, NATIVE AMERICAN RELIGIONS, DRUG USE+,
        ALCOHOL USE+, ALCOHOLISM TREATMENT+, PROGRAM
        DEVELOPMENT+, TRADITIONAL USE OF DRUGS AND ALCOHOL+,
        CHEMOTHERAPY+
   IDEN U.S., OKLAHOMA, ALCOHOLICS ANONYMOUS, NATIVE AMERICAN
        CHURCH, CHEYENNE-ARAPAHOE LODGE

56 AUTH HOFFMANN, HELMUT; JACKSON, DOUGLAS N.
   TITL COMPARISON OF MEASURED PSYCHOPATHOLOGY IN INDIAN AND
        NON-INDIAN ALCOHOLICS.
   SOUR PSYCHOLOGICAL REPORTS, DEC. 1973, V33, PP 793-794.
   YEAR 1973
   DESC CHIPPEWA, EASTERN SUB-ARCTIC, PSYCHOLOGICAL TESTING+,
        ALCOHOL USE+, NATIVE-NON-NATIVE COMPARISONS,
        PERSONALITY TRAITS, ANGLO AMERICANS

```
        IDEN   U.S., DIFFERENTIAL PERSONALITY INVENTORY

57   AUTH   LEFLEY, HARRIET P.
     TITL   DIFFERENTIAL SELF-CONCEPT IN AMERICAN INDIAN CHILDREN
            AS A FUNCTION OF LANGUAGE AND EXAMINERS.
     SOUR   JOURNAL OF PERSONALITY AND SOCIAL PSYCHOLOGY, JAN.
            1975, V31(1), PP 36-41.
     YEAR   1975
     DESC   SEMINOLE, MICCOSUKEE, SOUTHEAST WOODLAND,
            SELF-CONCEPT+, BILINGUALISM+, CHILDREN-SCHOOL AGE+,
            RESERVATION, ETHNIC IDENTITY, CULTURE-FAIR TESTS,
            PSYCHOLOGICAL TESTING+, SEX DIFFERENCES, AGE
            COMPARISONS
     IDEN   FLORIDA, U.S., PIERS HARRIS CHILDRENS SELF-CONCEPT
            SCALE, SARASON AND GANZER WORD RATING SCALE,
            COOPERSMITH WORD RATING FORM, INDIAN STIMULUS SCALE,
            INDIAN SELF ESTEEM SCALE

58   AUTH   GOLDSTEIN, GEORGE S.
     TITL   BEHAVIOR MODIFICATION: SOME CULTURAL FACTORS.
     SOUR   PSYCHOLOGICAL RECORD, WIN. 1974, V24, PP 89-91.
     YEAR   1974
     DESC   NAVAJO, SOUTHWEST, RESERVATION, CHILDREN-SCHOOL AGE+,
            CULTURAL ADAPTATION, B.I.A. BOARDING SCHOOLS, SOCIALLY
            DEVIANT BEHAVIOR,  NONINTERFERENCE+, PSYCHOTHERAPY AND
            COUNSELING+, BEHAVIOR MODIFICATION+, CLINICAL STUDY
     IDEN   U.S., NAVAJO RESERVATION, MODEL DORMITORY

59   AUTH   CRESS, JOSEPH N.; O'DONNELL, JAMES P.
     TITL   INDIANNESS, SEX AND GRADE DIFFERENCES ON BEHAVIOR AND
            PERSONALITY MEASURES AMONG OGLALA SIOUX ADOLESCENTS.
     SOUR   PSYCHOLOGY IN THE SCHOOLS, 1974, V11, PP 306-309.
     YEAR   1974
     DESC   SIOUX-OGLALA, PLAINS, RESERVATION, ADOLESCENTS+,
            PSYCHOLOGICAL TESTING+, ETHNIC IDENTITY+, CULTURAL
            ADAPTATION, SELF-CONCEPT+, CULTURAL CONTINUITY, SEX
            DIFFERENCES, SOCIALLY DEVIANT BEHAVIOR, PERSONALITY
            TRAITS, ACHIEVEMENT
     IDEN   U.S., SOUTH DAKOTA, PINE RIDGE RESERVATION,
            COOPERSMITH BEHAVIOR RATING FORM, QUAY-PETERSON
            BEHAVIOR PROBLEM CHECKLIST, THINK ABOUT YOURSELF,
            SOCIOMETRIC TESTS

60   AUTH   BERGER, A.
     TITL   THE EDUCATION OF CANADIAN INDIANS: AN INDEPTH STUDY OF
            NINE FAMILIES.
     SOUR   ALBERTA JOURNAL OF EDUCATIONAL RESEARCH, DEC. 1973,
            V19(4), PP 334-342.
     YEAR   1973
     DESC   CREE, PLAINS, CHILDREN-SCHOOL AGE, RESERVATION,
            ELEMENTARY SCHOOLS, EDUCATION PROFESSIONALS,
            STEREOTYPES, CULTURAL CONTINUITY, DROPOUTS, EDUCATION
            PROGRAMS AND SERVICES+, FAMILY FUNCTIONING, COMMUNITY
            INVOLVEMENT
     IDEN   CANADA, HOBBEMA RESERVE, ALBERTA, WINTERBURN RESERVE
```

61 AUTH BRINKER, PAUL A.; TAYLOR, BENJAMIN J.
   TITL SOUTHERN PLAINS INDIAN RELOCATION RETURNEES.
   SOUR HUMAN ORGANIZATION, SUM. 1974, V33(2), PP 139-146.
   YEAR 1974
   DESC PLAINS, RESERVATION, OFF-RESERVATION, EMPLOYMENT,
        KIOWA, COMANCHE, NAVAJO, SOUTHWEST, URBANIZATION+,
        ALCOHOL USE, EXTENDED FAMILY, ADULTS, INTERTRIBAL
        COMPARISONS, ECONOMIC ISSUES, RELOCATION+
   IDEN OKLAHOMA, U.S.

62 AUTH BERGMAN, ROBERT L.
   TITL A SCHOOL FOR MEDICINE MEN.
   SOUR AMERICAN JOURNAL OF PSYCHIATRY, JUN. 1973, V130(6), PP
        663-666.
   YEAR 1973
   DESC NAVAJO, SOUTHWEST, TRADITIONAL HEALERS+, RESERVATION,
        CULTURE-BASED PSYCHOTHERAPY, UNIVERSAL HARMONY, NATIVE
        AMERICAN ETIOLOGY, TRAINING PROGRAMS+, PROGRAM
        DEVELOPMENT+
   IDEN ARIZONA, U.S., NAVAJO RESERVATION, ROUGH ROCK
        DEMONSTRATION SCHOOL

63 AUTH MILLER, ANTHONY G.
   TITL INTEGRATION AND ACCULTURATION OF COOPERATIVE BEHAVIOR
        AMONG BLACKFEET INDIAN AND NON-INDIAN CANADIAN
        CHILDREN.
   SOUR JOURNAL OF CROSS-CULTURAL PSYCHOLOGY, SEP. 1973,
        V4(3), PP 374-380.
   YEAR 1973
   DESC BLACKFEET, RESERVATION, PLAINS, CHILDREN-SCHOOL AGE+,
        COOPERATION+, NONCOMPETITIVENESS+, CULTURAL
        ADAPTATION+, PSYCHOLOGICAL TESTING+
   IDEN CANADA, ALBERTA, BLOOD RESERVE, MADSEN COOPERATION
        BOARD

64 AUTH GRANZBERG, GARY
   TITL A NOTE ON DELAY OF GRATIFICATION AMONG THE HOPI.
   SOUR JOURNAL OF SOCIAL PSYCHOLOGY, OCT. 1973, V91, PP
        151-152.
   YEAR 1973
   DESC PUEBLO-HOPI, CHILDREN-SCHOOL AGE+, ABILITIES+,
        ACHIEVEMENT+
   IDEN U.S.

65 AUTH DIZMANG, LARRY H.; WATSON, JANE; MAY, PHILIP A.; BOPP,
        JOHN F.
   TITL ADOLESCENT SUICIDE AT AN INDIAN RESERVATION.
   SOUR AMERICAN JOURNAL OF ORTHOPSYCHIATRY, JAN. 1974,
        V44(1), PP 43-49.
   YEAR 1974
   DESC SHOSHONE, BANNOCK, PLATEAU, TRADITIONAL CHILD
        REARING+, EXTENDED FAMILY, RESERVATION, SUICIDE+,
        PSYCHOLOGICAL TESTING, STRESS, PREVENTIVE MENTAL
        HEALTH PROGRAMS, NATIVE AMERICAN ADMINISTERED
        PROGRAMS, ADOLESCENTS+, FAMILY FUNCTIONING+

IDEN   U.S., IDAHO, FORT HALL RESERVATION

66 AUTH   LEFLEY, HARRIET P.
    TITL   EFFECTS OF A CULTURAL HERITAGE PROGRAM ON THE
            SELF-CONCEPT OF MICCOSUKEE INDIAN CHILDREN.
    SOUR   JOURNAL OF EDUCATIONAL RESEARCH, JUL.-AUG. 1974,
            V67(10), PP 462-466.
    YEAR   1974
    DESC   MICCOSUKEE, SEMINOLE, SOUTHEAST WOODLAND, RESERVATION,
            CHILDREN-SCHOOL AGE+, SELF-CONCEPT+, PSYCHOLOGICAL
            TESTING+, ETHNIC IDENTITY+, INTERTRIBAL COMPARISONS,
            CULTURAL CONTINUITY, EDUCATION PROGRAMS AND SERVICES+,
            PROGRAM EVALUATION+
    IDEN   U.S., FLORIDA, PIERS HARRIS SELF-CONCEPT SCALE,
            SARASON AND GANZER WORD RATING SCALE, INDIAN SELF
            ESTEEM SCALE, INDIAN STIMULUS SCALE, COOPERSMITH
            BEHAVIOR RATING FORM

67 AUTH   MAYNOR, WALTZ; KATZENMEYER, W.G.
    TITL   ACADEMIC PERFORMANCE AND SCHOOL INTEGRATION: A
            MULTI-ETHNIC ANALYSIS.
    SOUR   JOURNAL OF NEGRO EDUCATION, WIN. 1974, V43, PP 30-38.
    YEAR   1974
    DESC   CHILDREN-SCHOOL AGE, EDUCATION PROFESSIONALS,
            ACHIEVEMENT+, ADOLESCENTS, PSYCHOLOGICAL TESTING,
            NATIVE AMERICAN PERSONNEL, NATIVE-NON-NATIVE
            COMPARISONS, ELEMENTARY SCHOOLS, SECONDARY SCHOOLS+,
            BLACK AMERICANS, ANGLO AMERICANS
    IDEN   U.S., CALIFORNIA ACHIEVEMENT TEST, CALIFORNIA TEST OF
            MENTAL MATURITY

68 AUTH   HALLOWELL, A. IRVING
    TITL   THE SOCIAL FUNCTION OF ANXIETY IN A PRIMITIVE SOCIETY.
    SOUR   AMERICAN SOCIOLOGICAL REVIEW, 1941, V6, 869-881.
    YEAR   1941
    DESC   CHIPPEWA, EASTERN SUB-ARCTIC, ANXIETY+, NATIVE
            AMERICAN ETIOLOGY+, WITCHCRAFT, CULTURE-BASED
            PSYCHOTHERAPY, TRADITIONAL SOCIAL CONTROL, CONFESSION,
            NATIVE AMERICAN COPING BEHAVIORS+
    IDEN   CANADA, MANITOBA

69 AUTH   KAPLAN, BERT; JOHNSON, DALE L.
    TITL   THE SOCIAL MEANING OF NAVAJO PSYCHOPATHOLOGY AND
            PSYCHOTHERAPY.
    SOUR   IN A. KIEV (ED.), MAGIC, FAITH AND HEALING: STUDIES IN
            PRIMITIVE PSYCHIATRY TODAY, PP 203-229. NEW YORK: FREE
            PRESS, 1964.
    YEAR   1964
    DESC   NAVAJO, SOUTHWEST, NATIVE AMERICAN ETIOLOGY+, TABOO
            BREAKING, WITCHCRAFT, MENTAL DISORDERS+, GHOST
            SICKNESS, CULTURE-BASED PSYCHOTHERAPY+, RESERVATION,
            DREAMS AND VISION QUESTS, NATIVE AMERICAN COPING
            BEHAVIORS
    IDEN   U.S., NAVAJO RESERVATION

70 AUTH BOYER, L. BRYCE
   TITL FOLK PSYCHIATRY OF THE APACHES OF THE MESCALERO INDIAN
        RESERVATION.
   SOUR IN A. KIEV (ED.), MAGIC, FAITH, AND HEALING: STUDIES
        IN PRIMITIVE PSYCHIATRY TODAY, PP 384-419. NEW YORK:
        FREE PRESS, 1964.
   YEAR 1964
   DESC APACHE-CHIRICAHUA, APACHE-MESCALERO, SOUTHWEST,
        RESERVATION, TRADITIONAL SOCIAL CONTROL, SOCIALLY
        DEVIANT BEHAVIOR, TRADITIONAL CHILD REARING, SEXUAL
        RELATIONS, CHILD ABUSE AND NEGLECT, WITCHCRAFT+,
        TRADITIONAL HEALERS+, GHOST SICKNESS+, CULTURE-BASED
        PSYCHOTHERAPY+, EXTENDED FAMILY+, AGGRESSIVENESS,
        FAMILY FUNCTIONING, PSYCHOANALYSIS
   IDEN U.S., NEW MEXICO, MESCALERO RESERVATION

71 AUTH FOX, J. ROBIN.
   TITL WITCHCRAFT AND CLANSHIP IN COCHITI THERAPY.
   SOUR IN A. KIEV (ED.), MAGIC, FAITH AND HEALING: STUDIES IN
        PRIMITIVE PSYCHIATRY TODAY, PP 174-200. NEW YORK: FREE
        PRESS, 1964.
   YEAR 1964
   DESC PUEBLO-COCHITI, SOUTHWEST, RESERVATION, EXTENDED
        FAMILY+, NATIVE AMERICAN ETIOLOGY+, WITCHCRAFT+,
        TRADITIONAL HEALERS, CULTURE-BASED PSYCHOTHERAPY+,
        FEMALES, TRADITIONAL CHILD REARING
   IDEN U.S., NEW MEXICO

72 AUTH LABARRE, WESTON
   TITL CONFESSION AS CATHARTIC THERAPY IN AMERICAN INDIAN
        TRIBES.
   SOUR IN A. KIEV (ED.), MAGIC, FAITH AND HEALING: STUDIES IN
        PRIMITIVE PSYCHIATRY TODAY, PP 36-49. NEW YORK: FREE
        PRESS, 1964.
   YEAR 1964
   DESC CULTURE-BASED PSYCHOTHERAPY+, TABOO BREAKING+,
        TRADITIONAL USE OF DRUGS AND ALCOHOL, CONFESSION+,
        NATIVE AMERICAN COPING BEHAVIORS+
   IDEN U.S., CANADA

73 AUTH KESHENA, RITA
   TITL THE ROLE OF AMERICAN INDIANS IN MOTION PICTURES.
   SOUR AMERICAN INDIAN CULTURE AND RESEARCH JOURNAL, 1974,
        V1, PP 25-28.
   YEAR 1974
   DESC STEREOTYPES+, DISCRIMINATION+, ECONOMIC ISSUES, NATIVE
        AMERICAN PERSONNEL+
   IDEN U.S.

74 AUTH DINGES, NORMAN G.; YAZZIE, MYRA; TOLLEFSON, GWEN D.
   TITL DEVELOPMENTAL INTERVENTION FOR NAVAJO FAMILY MENTAL
        HEALTH.
   SOUR PERSONNEL AND GUIDANCE JOURNAL, FEB. 1974, V52(6), PP
        390-395.
   YEAR 1974

DESC   NAVAJO, SOUTHWEST, PROGRAM EVALUATION+,
        CHILDREN-INFANTS AND PRESCHOOL, ADULTS, EXTENDED
        FAMILY, BICULTURALISM, RESERVATION, CULTURAL
        CONTINUITY, PREVENTIVE MENTAL HEALTH PROGRAMS+, FAMILY
        FUNCTIONING+, NATIVE AMERICAN PERSONNEL, MENTAL HEALTH
        PARAPROFESSIONALS, PSYCHOTHERAPY AND COUNSELING,
        PROGRAM DEVELOPMENT
IDEN   U.S., ARIZONA, NEW MEXICO

75 AUTH   CONRAD, REX D.; DELK, JOHN L.; WILLIAMS, CECIL
    TITL   USE OF STIMULUS FADING PROCEDURES IN THE TREATMENT OF
            SITUATION SPECIFIC MUTISM: A CASE STUDY.
    SOUR   JOURNAL OF BEHAVIOR THERAPY AND EXPERIMENTAL
            PSYCHIATRY, JUL. 1974, V5, PP 99-100.
    YEAR   1974
    DESC   RESERVATION, SOUTHWEST, CHILDREN-SCHOOL AGE,
            PSYCHOTHERAPY AND COUNSELING+, CLINICAL STUDY, MENTAL
            HEALTH PARAPROFESSIONALS+, NATIVE AMERICAN PERSONNEL+,
            ELEMENTARY SCHOOLS, SOCIALLY DEVIANT BEHAVIOR+,
            PASSIVE RESISTANCE, BEHAVIOR MODIFICATION+
    IDEN   U.S.

76 AUTH   THORNBURG, HERSHEL D.
    TITL   AN INVESTIGATION OF A DROPOUT PROGRAM AMONG ARIZONA'S
            MINORITY YOUTH.
    SOUR   EDUCATION, FEB. 1974, V94(3), PP 249-265.
    YEAR   1974
    DESC   OFF-RESERVATION, ADOLESCENTS+, SECONDARY SCHOOLS+,
            SELF-CONCEPT, PSYCHOLOGICAL TESTING, NATIVE-NON-NATIVE
            COMPARISONS, EDUCATION PROGRAMS AND SERVICES+,
            SOUTHWEST, DROPOUTS+, PREVENTIVE MENTAL HEALTH
            PROGRAMS, BLACK AMERICANS, LATINOS, ANGLO AMERICANS,
            ATTITUDES
    IDEN   U.S., ARIZONA, TENNESSEE SELF CONCEPT SCALE,
            CALIFORNIA READING TEST, LORGE THORNDIKE INTELLIGENCE
            TEST, PUPIL OPINION QUESTIONNAIRE

77 AUTH   WILSON, LAWRENCE G.; SHORE, JAMES H.
    TITL   EVALUATION OF A REGIONAL INDIAN ALCOHOL PROGRAM.
    SOUR   AMERICAN JOURNAL OF PSYCHIATRY, MAR. 1975, V132(3), PP
            255-258.
    YEAR   1975
    DESC   COLVILLE, SPOKANE, YAKIMA, WARM SPRINGS, LUMMI,
            RESERVATION, NORTHWEST COAST, ADULTS, ALCOHOL USE+,
            ALCOHOLISM TREATMENT+, PROGRAM EVALUATION+, NATIVE
            AMERICAN ADMINISTERED PROGRAMS, PLATEAU
    IDEN   U.S., WASHINGTON, IDAHO, OREGON, LUMMI RESERVATION,
            COLVILLE RESERVATION, YAKIMA RESERVATION, WARM SPRINGS
            RESERVATION, SPOKANE RESERVATION

78 AUTH   SIEVERS, MAURICE L.; CYNAMON, MICHAEL H.; BITTKER,
            THOMAS E.
    TITL   INTENTIONAL ISONIAZID OVERDOSAGE AMONG SOUTHWESTERN
            AMERICAN INDIANS.
    SOUR   AMERICAN JOURNAL OF PSYCHIATRY, JUN. 1975, V132(6), PP

```
           662-665.
    YEAR   1975
    DESC   RESERVATION, APACHE, PIMA, PUEBLO-HOPI, MARICOPA,
           YAVAPAI, HUALAPAI, HAVASUPAI, CHEMEHUEVI, COCOPAH,
           MOHAVE, SUICIDE+, CHEMOTHERAPY, DRUG USE+, SEX
           DIFFERENCES, INTERTRIBAL COMPARISONS, ADULTS,
           SOUTHWEST
    IDEN   U.S., ARIZONA

79  AUTH   ALLAN, JAMES R.
    TITL   THE INDIAN ADOLESCENT: PSYCHOSOCIAL TASKS OF THE
           PLAINS INDIAN OF WESTERN OKLAHOMA.
    SOUR   AMERICAN JOURNAL OF ORTHOPSYCHIATRY, APR. 1973, V43,
           PP 368-375.
    YEAR   1973
    DESC   PLAINS, ADOLESCENTS+, OFF-RESERVATION, B.I.A. BOARDING
           SCHOOLS, STEREOTYPES, OKLAHOMA INDIANS, ETHNIC
           IDENTITY+, DISCRIMINATION, CULTURAL REVIVAL, CULTURAL
           ADAPTATION+, STRESS+
    IDEN   U.S., OKLAHOMA

80  AUTH   HENDRIE, HUGH C.; HANSON, DIANE
    TITL   A COMPARATIVE STUDY OF THE PSYCHIATRIC CARE OF INDIAN
           AND METIS.
    SOUR   AMERICAN JOURNAL OF ORTHOPSYCHIATRY, APR. 1972,
           V42(3), PP 480-489.
    YEAR   1972
    DESC   METIS, PLAINS, INSTITUTIONALIZATION+, EXPERIMENTAL
           STUDY, CLINICAL STUDY, MEDICAL INSTITUTIONS+, ECONOMIC
           ISSUES, DELIVERY OF SERVICES+, CHARACTER DISORDERS,
           URBAN AREAS, ADULTS
    IDEN   CANADA, MANITOBA

81  AUTH   SHUTT, DONALD L.; HANNON, THOMAS A.
    TITL   THE VALIDITY OF THE HNTLA FOR EVALUATION OF THE
           ABILITIES OF BILINGUAL CHILDREN.
    SOUR   EDUCATIONAL AND PSYCHOLOGICAL MEASUREMENT, SUM. 1974,
           V34, PP 429-432.
    YEAR   1974
    DESC   NAVAJO, SOUTHWEST, BILINGUALISM+, ELEMENTARY SCHOOLS,
           MENTAL HEALTH PROFESSIONALS, PSYCHOLOGICAL TESTING+,
           CULTURE-FAIR TESTS+, LEARNING, LANGUAGE HANDICAPS+,
           RESERVATION, CHILDREN-SCHOOL AGE, NATIVE-NON-NATIVE
           COMPARISONS, LATINOS
    IDEN   U.S., ARIZONA, HISKEY-NEBRASKA TEST OF LEARNING
           APTITUDE, WESCHLER INTELLIGENCE SCALE CHILDREN

82  AUTH   YOUNGMAN, GERALDINE; SADONGEI, MARGARET
    TITL   COUNSELING THE AMERICAN INDIAN CHILD.
    SOUR   ELEMENTARY SCHOOL GUIDANCE AND COUNSELING, MAY 1974,
           V8, PP 273-277.
    YEAR   1974
    DESC   CHILDREN-SCHOOL AGE+, GENEROSITY, NONCOMPETITIVENESS+,
           EDUCATION PROFESSIONALS, INTERTRIBAL COMPARISONS,
           PSYCHOTHERAPY AND COUNSELING+,
```

```
          IDEN  U.S.

83   AUTH  POLLARD, W. GROSVENOR
     TITL  IMPLICATIONS OF THE RANK CONCESSION SYNDROME FOR ADULT
           EDUCATION PROGRAMS: AN EXPLORATION IN SOCIAL ROLES AND
           PROGRAM EFFECTIVENESS.
     SOUR  ADULT EDUCATION, 1974, V24(4), PP 225-269.
     YEAR  1974
     DESC  ETHNIC IDENTITY+, SOCIAL NETWORKS, PROGRAM
           DEVELOPMENT+, STOCKBRIDGE, MUNSEE, NORTHEAST WOODLAND,
           RESERVATION, ECONOMIC ISSUES, BICULTURALISM+, ADULTS,
           EDUCATION PROGRAMS AND SERVICES, SOCIAL STATUS+,
           COOPERATION+
     IDEN  U.S., WISCONSIN

84   AUTH  MURPHY, ELIZABETH A.
     TITL  THE CLASSROOM: MEETING THE NEEDS OF THE CULTURALLY
           DIFFERENT CHILD--THE NAVAJO NATION.
     SOUR  EXCEPTIONAL CHILDREN, MAY 1974, V40, PP 601-608.
     YEAR  1974
     DESC  CHILDREN-SCHOOL AGE+, NAVAJO, SOUTHWEST, RESERVATION,
           ELEMENTARY SCHOOLS, EDUCATION PROGRAMS AND SERVICES+,
           LEARNING DISABILITIES AND PROBLEMS+, PROGRAM
           DEVELOPMENT, NATIVE AMERICAN PERSONNEL, NATIVE
           AMERICAN ADMINISTERED PROGRAMS+
     IDEN  U.S., NAVAJO RESERVATION

85   AUTH  BOWD, ALAN D.
     TITL  A CROSS-CULTURAL STUDY OF THE FACTORIAL COMPOSITION OF
           MECHANICAL APTITUDE.
     SOUR  CANADIAN JOURNAL OF BEHAVIOURAL SCIENCES, JAN. 1973,
           V5(1), PP 13-23.
     YEAR  1973
     DESC  ADOLESCENTS, RESERVATION, PSYCHOLOGICAL TESTING+,
           ABILITIES+, MALES, CULTURE-FAIR TESTS, BELLA BELLA,
           BLACKFEET, ASSINIBOINE-STONEY, METIS, NORTHWEST COAST,
           PLAINS, OFF-RESERVATION, INTERTRIBAL COMPARISONS,
           NATIVE-NON-NATIVE COMPARISONS, ANGLO AMERICANS
     IDEN  CANADA, ALBERTA, BRITISH COLUMBIA, BLACKFEET RESERVE,
           STONEY RESERVE, MINNESOTA PAPER FORMBOARD, MACQUARRIE
           TEST FOR MECHANICAL APTITUDE, TEST OF MECHANICAL
           COMPREHENSION, PROGRESSIVE MATRICES, MILL HILL
           VOCABULARY SCALE

86   AUTH  KEMNITZER, LUIS S.
     TITL  ADJUSTMENT AND VALUE CONFLICT IN URBANIZING DAKOTA
           INDIANS MEASURED BY Q-SORT TECHNIQUES.
     SOUR  AMERICAN ANTHROPOLOGIST, JUN. 1973, V75, PP 687-707.
     YEAR  1973
     DESC  PSYCHOLOGICAL TESTING+, URBAN AREAS, ADULTS,
           URBANIZATION+, ETHNIC IDENTITY, SIOUX, PLAINS,
           SELF-CONCEPT+, CULTURAL CONTINUITY, STRESS+,
           RELOCATION+, NATIVE AMERICAN VALUES+
     IDEN  U.S., CALIFORNIA, Q SORT TESTING TECHNIQUE
```

87 AUTH SHORE, JAMES H.; STONE, DENNIS L.
   TITL DUODENAL ULCER AMONG NORTHWEST COASTAL INDIAN WOMEN.
   SOUR AMERICAN JOURNAL OF PSYCHIATRY, JUL. 1973, V130(7), PP
        774-777.
   YEAR 1973
   DESC NORTHWEST COAST, OFF-RESERVATION, ADULTS,
        PSYCHOPHYSIOLOGICAL DISORDERS+, FEMALES+,
        EPIDEMIOLOGICAL STUDY, SOCIAL ROLES+, SEX DIFFERENCES,
        PSYCHOLOGICAL TESTING, SOUTHWEST, INTERTRIBAL
        COMPARISONS, PHYSICAL HEALTH AND ILLNESS,STRESS
   IDEN CORNELL MEDICAL INDEX, U.S.

88 AUTH SHORE, JAMES H.; NICHOLLS, WILLIAM M.
   TITL INDIAN CHILDREN AND TRIBAL GROUP HOMES: NEW
        INTERPRETATION OF THE WHIPPER MAN.
   SOUR AMERICAN JOURNAL OF PSYCHIATRY, APR. 1975, V132(4), PP
        454-456.
   YEAR 1975
   DESC PLATEAU, ADOLESCENTS+, CHILDREN-SCHOOL AGE+,
        TRADITIONAL SOCIAL CONTROL, TRADITIONAL CHILD REARING,
        CHILDREN-INFANTS AND PRESCHOOL+, NATIVE AMERICAN
        ADMINISTERED PROGRAMS+, FAMILY FUNCTIONING+, ADOPTION
        AND FOSTER CARE+, CHILD ABUSE AND NEGLECT,
        RESERVATION, SOCIALLY DEVIANT BEHAVIOR, SOCIAL
        SERVICES, CLINICAL STUDY
   IDEN U.S., OREGON, WHIPPER MAN PROGRAM

89 AUTH ROBBINS, RICHARD H.
   TITL ALCOHOL AND THE IDENTITY STRUGGLE: SOME EFFECTS OF
        ECONOMIC CHANGE ON INTERPERSONAL RELATIONS.
   SOUR AMERICAN ANTHROPOLOGIST, FEB. 1973, V75, PP 99-122.
   YEAR 1973
   DESC NESKAPI, EASTERN SUB-ARCTIC, GENEROSITY+,
        NONINTERFERENCE, ALCOHOL USE+, ECONOMIC ISSUES, ETHNIC
        IDENTITY+, SOCIAL GROUPS AND PEER GROUPS, EXTENDED
        FAMILY, AGGRESSIVENESS, SOCIAL STATUS+
   IDEN CANADA, QUEBEC

90 AUTH HAYES, EDWARD J.
   TITL ENVIRONMENTAL PRESS AND PSYCHOLOGICAL NEED AS RELATED
        TO ACADEMIC SUCCESS OF MINORITY GROUP STUDENTS.
   SOUR JOURNAL OF COUNSELING PSYCHOLOGY, JUL. 1974, V21(4),
        PP 299-304.
   YEAR 1974
   DESC COLLEGES AND UNIVERSITIES+, ACHIEVEMENT+, ADOLESCENTS,
        NATIVE-NON-NATIVE COMPARISONS, PSYCHOLOGICAL TESTING,
        BLACK AMERICANS, ANGLO AMERICANS
   IDEN U.S., COLLEGE CHARACTERISTICS INDEX, SCHOLASTIC
        APTITUDE TEST,, STERN ACTIVITIES INDEX, MANIFEST
        ANXIETY SCALE, ROTTERS INTERNAL-EXTERNAL SCALE

91 AUTH HIPPLER, ARTHUR E.
   TITL THE ATHABASKANS OF INTERIOR ALASKA: A CULTURE AND
        PERSONALITY PERSPECTIVE.
   SOUR AMERICAN ANTHROPOLOGIST, OCT. 1973, V75, PP 1529-1541.

```
         YEAR   1973
         DESC   ATHABASCAN, YUKON SUB-ARCTIC, TRADITIONAL CHILD
                REARING+, EXTENDED FAMILY+, PERSONALITY TRAITS+,
                STRESS+, TRADITIONAL SOCIAL CONTROL, OFF-RESERVATION,
                AGGRESSIVENESS, NATIVE AMERICAN COPING BEHAVIORS
         IDEN   U.S., ALASKA

   92    AUTH   WOOD, ROSEMARY
         TITL   HEALTH PROBLEMS FACING NATIVE AMERICAN WOMEN.
         SOUR   PAPER PRESENTED AT THE INVITATIONAL CONFERENCE OF
                AMERICAN WOMEN, SPONSORED BY THE NATIONAL INSTITUTE OF
                EDUCATION, WOMEN'S DIVISION, ALBUQUERQUE, NEW MEXICO,
                OCT. 12, 1976. (48P)
         YEAR   1976
         DESC   FEMALES+, PHYSICAL HEALTH AND ILLNESS+, TRADITIONAL
                HEALERS, MEDICAL PROGRAMS AND SERVICES, DELIVERY OF
                SERVICES+, DISCRIMINATION+, STEREOTYPES, I.H.S.,
                NATIVE AMERICAN PERSONNEL+, MEDICAL PROFESSIONALS+,
                SOCIAL ROLES, ADULTS
         IDEN   U.S.

   93    AUTH   GRAVES, THEODORE D.
         TITL   URBAN INDIAN PERSONALITY AND THE 'CULTURE OF POVERTY'.
         SOUR   AMERICAN ETHNOLOGIST, FEB. 1974, V1, PP 65-86.
         YEAR   1974
         DESC   ADULTS, URBAN AREAS, NAVAJO, MALES, PERSONALITY
                TRAITS+, STEREOTYPES, EMPLOYMENT, ACHIEVEMENT,
                PSYCHOLOGICAL TESTING, CORRECTIONAL INSTITUTIONS,
                ECONOMIC ISSUES+, NONCOMPETITIVENESS, RELOCATION, TIME
                PERCEPTION, URBANIZATION+
         IDEN   U.S., COLORADO, LIFE SPACE SAMPLE, LOCUS OF CONTROL
                SCALE, THEMATIC APPERCEPTION TEST

   94    AUTH   FRIESON, J.W.
         TITL   EDUCATION AND VALUES IN AN INDIAN COMMUNITY.
         SOUR   ALBERTA JOURNAL OF EDUCATIONAL RESEARCH, JUN. 1974,
                V20(2), PP 146-156.
         YEAR   1974
         DESC   BLACKFEET, PLAINS, PSYCHOLOGICAL TESTING,
                NATIVE-NON-NATIVE COMPARISONS, ACHIEVEMENT+, CULTURAL
                ADAPTATION, ELEMENTARY SCHOOLS, CULTURAL CONTINUITY+,
                CHILDREN-SCHOOL AGE+, RESERVATION, SELF-CONCEPT,
                EDUCATION PROGRAMS AND SERVICES, NATIVE AMERICAN
                VALUES+, ANGLO AMERICANS,
         IDEN   CANADA, BLACKFOOT RESERVE

   95    AUTH   JILEK, WOLFGANG G.
         TITL   CANADIAN M.D.'S HAVE THINK SESSION WITH INDIANS.
         SOUR   PSYCHIATRIC NEWS, JAN. 1976, V11 (1), PP 40, 44.
         YEAR   1976
         DESC   TRADITIONAL HEALERS+, MENTAL HEALTH PROFESSIONALS+,
                CULTURAL ADAPTATION+
         IDEN   CANADA

   96    AUTH   MICKELSON, NORMA I.; GALLOWAY, CHARLES G.
```

```
     TITL  VERBAL CONCEPTS OF INDIAN AND NON-INDIAN SCHOOL
           BEGINNERS.
     SOUR  JOURNAL OF EDUCATIONAL RESEARCH, OCT 1973, V67(2), PP
           55-56.
     YEAR  1973
     DESC  CHILDREN-SCHOOL AGE+, ACHIEVEMENT+, PSYCHOLOGICAL
           TESTING+, ELEMENTARY SCHOOLS, NATIVE-NON-NATIVE
           COMPARISONS, ANGLO AMERICANS
     IDEN  U.S., BOEHM TEST OF BASIC CONCEPTS

97   AUTH  LEVY, JERROLD E.
     TITL  NAVAJO SUICIDE.
     SOUR  HUMAN ORGANIZATION, WIN. 1965, V24, PP 308-318.
     YEAR  1965
     DESC  NAVAJO, SOUTHWEST, SUICIDE+, STRESS, SEX DIFFERENCES,
           AGE COMPARISONS, RESERVATION, ADULTS, EXTENDED FAMILY,
           FAMILY FUNCTIONING, NATIVE-NON-NATIVE COMPARISONS,
           EPIDEMIOLOGICAL STUDY, PERSONALITY TRAITS+,
           AGGRESSIVENESS+, MARITAL RELATIONSHIPS, ASIAN
           AMERICANS, BLACK AMERICANS, ANGLO AMERICANS, LATINOS
     IDEN  U.S., NAVAJO RESERVATION

98   AUTH  STEWART, OMER C.
     TITL  QUESTIONS REGARDING AMERICAN INDIAN CRIMINALITY.
     SOUR  HUMAN ORGANIZATION, SPR. 1964, V23, PP 61-66.
     YEAR  1964
     DESC  CRIME+, ALCOHOL USE, URBAN AREAS, OFF-RESERVATION,
           NATIVE-NON-NATIVE COMPARISONS, DISCRIMINATION,
           ADOLESCENTS, ADULTS, EPIDEMIOLOGICAL STUDY, BLACK
           AMERICANS, ANGLO AMERICANS, LATINOS
     IDEN  U.S.

99   AUTH  FERGUSON, FRANCES N.
     TITL  NAVAJO DRINKING: SOME TENTATIVE HYPOTHESES.
     SOUR  HUMAN ORGANIZATION, SUM. 1968, V27, PP 159-167.
     YEAR  1968
     DESC  NAVAJO, SOUTHWEST, RESERVATION,  STRESS, ANXIETY,
           ALCOHOL USE, ALCOHOLISM TREATMENT+, GROUP NORMS AND
           SANCTIONS, SOCIAL GROUPS AND PEER GROUPS, PROGRAM
           EVALUATION+, CLINICAL STUDY, PSYCHOLOGICAL TESTING,
           EXPERIMENTAL STUDY, ADULTS
     IDEN  U.S., NAVAJO RESERVATION

100  AUTH  LEVY, JERROLD E.; KUNITZ, STEPHEN J.
     TITL  INDIAN RESERVATIONS, ANOMIE, AND SOCIAL PATHOLOGIES.
     SOUR  SOUTHWESTERN JOURNAL OF ANTHROPOLOGY, SUM. 1971,
           V27(2), PP 97-128.
     YEAR  1971
     DESC  SOCIALLY DEVIANT BEHAVIOR+, ANOMIE+, RESERVATION,
           NAVAJO, SOUTHWEST, CRIME, SUICIDE, ADULTS, ALCOHOL
           USE, ALCOHOL USE, STRESS+, ECONOMIC ISSUES,
           PUEBLO-HOPI
     IDEN  U.S., HOPI RESERVATION, NAVAJO RESERVATION

101  AUTH  BERGMAN, ROBERT L.
```

```
       TITL  NAVAJO PEYOTE USE; ITS APPARENT SAFETY.
       SOUR  AMERICAN JOURNAL OF PSYCHIATRY, DEC. 1971, V128(6), PP
             695-699.
       YEAR  1971
       DESC  NAVAJO, SOUTHWEST, RESERVATION, NATIVE AMERICAN
             RELIGIONS+, DRUG USE+, SOCIAL GROUPS AND PEER GROUPS,
             TRADITIONAL USE OF DRUGS AND ALCOHOL+
       IDEN  U.S., NAVAJO RESERVATION, NATIVE AMERICAN CHURCH

102    AUTH  KUTTNER, ROBERT E.; LORINCZ, ALBERT B.
       TITL  ALCOHOLISM AND ADDICTION IN URBANIZED SIOUX INDIANS.
       SOUR  MENTAL HYGIENE, OCT. 1967, V51, PP 530-542.
       YEAR  1967
       DESC  SIOUX, PLAINS,  ALCOHOL USE+, URBAN AREAS, ADULTS,
             DRUG USE+, INTERTRIBAL COMPARISONS, EPIDEMIOLOGICAL
             STUDY, ADOLESCENTS, NATIVE-NON-NATIVE COMPARISONS,
             SOCIAL GROUPS AND PEER GROUPS+, FAMILY FUNCTIONING,
             BLACK AMERICANS
       IDEN  U.S., NEBRASKA

103    AUTH  CURLEY, R.
       TITL  DRINKING PATTERNS OF THE MESCALERO APACHE.
       SOUR  QUARTERLY JOURNAL OF STUDIES ON ALCOHOL, MAR. 1967,
             V28, PP 116-131.
       YEAR  1967
       DESC  APACHE-MESCALERO, SOUTHWEST, RESERVATION, ALCOHOL
             USE+, SOCIAL GROUPS AND PEER GROUPS, ADULTS,
             TRADITIONAL USE OF DRUGS AND ALCOHOL, GROUP NORMS AND
             SANCTIONS+, SELF-CONCEPT, ADOLESCENTS, SEX DIFFERENCES
       IDEN  U.S., MESCALERO RESERVATION, NEW MEXICO

104    AUTH  LEMERT, EDWIN M.
       TITL  THE USE OF ALCOHOL IN THREE SALISH INDIAN TRIBES.
       SOUR  QUARTERLY JOURNAL OF STUDIES ON ALCOHOL, MAR. 1958,
             V19, PP 90-107.
       YEAR  1958
       DESC  COAST SALISH, ALCOHOL USE+, SOCIAL GROUPS AND PEER
             GROUPS, AGGRESSIVENESS, SEXUAL RELATIONS,
             STEREOTYPES+, NORTHWEST COAST, GROUP NORMS AND
             SANCTIONS
       IDEN  CANADA, BRITISH COLUMBIA

105    AUTH  DEVEREUX, GEORGE
       TITL  THE FUNCTION OF ALCOHOL IN MOHAVE SOCIETY.
       SOUR  QUARTERLY JOURNAL OF STUDIES ON ALCOHOL, SEP. 1948,
             V9, PP 207-251.
       YEAR  1948
       DESC  MOHAVE, SOUTHWEST, SEXUAL RELATIONS+, ALCOHOL USE+,
             GENEROSITY, FEMALES, AGGRESSIVENESS+, GROUP NORMS AND
             SANCTIONS, ADULTS, RESERVATION, WITCHCRAFT
       IDEN  U.S., ARIZONA, CALIFORNIA

106    AUTH  WHITTAKER, JAMES O.
       TITL  ALCOHOL AND THE STANDING ROCK SIOUX TRIBE, PART II:
             PSYCHODYNAMIC AND CULTURAL FACTORS IN DRINKING.
```

SOUR QUARTERLY JOURNAL OF STUDIES ON ALCOHOL, MAR. 1963,
      V24, PP 80-90.
YEAR 1963
DESC SIOUX, PLAINS, RESERVATION, ALCOHOL USE+,
      NATIVE-NON-NATIVE COMPARISONS, SEX DIFFERENCES,
      ADULTS, AGGRESSIVENESS, EMPLOYMENT, SOCIAL GROUPS AND
      PEER GROUPS+, GROUP NORMS AND SANCTIONS+, ANGLO
      AMERICANS
IDEN U.S., NORTH DAKOTA, SOUTH DAKOTA

107 AUTH HONIGMANN, JOHN J.; HONIGMANN, IRMA
     TITL DRINKING IN AN INDIAN-WHITE COMMUNITY.
     SOUR QUARTERLY JOURNAL OF STUDIES ON ALCOHOL, MAR. 1945,
         V5, PP 575-619.
     YEAR 1945
     DESC ATHABASCAN, YUKON SUB-ARCTIC, GROUP NORMS AND
         SANCTIONS, ALCOHOL USE+, SEXUAL RELATIONS, SOCIAL
         GROUPS AND PEER GROUPS, AGGRESSIVENESS,
         NATIVE-NON-NATIVE COMPARISONS, ANXIETY,
         OFF-RESERVATION, ANGLO AMERICANS
     IDEN CANADA

108 AUTH BERREMAN, GERALD D.
     TITL DRINKING PATTERNS OF THE ALEUTS.
     SOUR QUARTERLY JOURNAL OF STUDIES ON ALCOHOL, SEP. 1956,
         V17, PP 503-514.
     YEAR 1956
     DESC ALEUT, WESTERN ARCTIC, ALCOHOL USE+, STRESS, ANXIETY,
         CHILDREN-SCHOOL AGE
     IDEN U.S., ALASKA

109 AUTH KLINE, JAMES A.; ROBERTS, ARTHUR C.
     TITL A RESIDENTIAL ALCOHOLISM TREATMENT PROGRAM FOR
         AMERICAN INDIANS.
     SOUR QUARTERLY JOURNAL OF STUDIES ON ALCOHOL, SEP. 1973,
         V34, PP 860-868.
     YEAR 1973
     DESC ALCOHOL USE+, URBAN AREAS, ALCOHOLISM TREATMENT+,
         ADULTS, MALES, TIME PERCEPTION, PROGRAM DEVELOPMENT+,
         CLINICAL STUDY, NATIVE AMERICAN PERSONNEL,
         PSYCHOTHERAPY AND COUNSELING, SOCIAL GROUPS AND PEER
         GROUPS
     IDEN U.S., CALIFORNIA

110 AUTH BLOOM, JOSEPH D.
     TITL MIGRATION AND PSYCHOPATHOLOGY OF ESKIMO WOMEN.
     SOUR AMERICAN JOURNAL OF PSYCHIATRY, APR. 1973, V130(4), PP
         446-449.
     YEAR 1973
     DESC FEMALES+, ESKIMO, WESTERN ARCTIC, URBANIZATION, URBAN
         AREAS, SEX DIFFERENCES, MENTAL DISORDERS+, ARCTIC
         HYSTERIA, EPIDEMIOLOGICAL STUDY, ADULTS, STRESS,
         RELOCATION+, SOCIAL ROLES
     IDEN U.S., ALASKA

111 AUTH SUE, STANLEY
    TITL TRAINING OF THIRD WORLD STUDENTS TO FUNCTION AS
          COUNSELORS.
    SOUR JOURNAL OF COUNSELING PSYCHOLOGY, JAN. 1973, V20(1),
          PP 73-78.
    YEAR 1973
    DESC ADULTS, URBAN AREAS, COLLEGES AND UNIVERSITIES,
          TRAINING PROGRAMS+, MENTAL HEALTH PARAPROFESSIONALS+,
          NATIVE AMERICAN PERSONNEL, NATIVE-NON-NATIVE
          COMPARISONS, PSYCHOTHERAPY AND COUNSELING+, BLACK
          AMERICANS, ANGLO AMERICANS, LATINOS
    IDEN U.S.

112 AUTH QUERY, WILLIAM T.; QUERY, JOY M.
    TITL AGGRESSIVE RESPONSES TO THE HOLTZMAN INKBLOT TECHNIQUE
          BY INDIAN AND WHITE ALCOHOLICS.
    SOUR JOURNAL OF CROSS-CULTURAL PSYCHOLOGY, DEC. 1972,
          V3(4), PP 413-416.
    YEAR 1972
    DESC SIOUX, CHIPPEWA, ALCOHOL USE+, ADULTS,
          NATIVE-NON-NATIVE COMPARISONS, PSYCHOLOGICAL TESTING,
          PERSONALITY TRAITS+, PLAINS, EASTERN SUB-ARCTIC,
          AGGRESSIVENESS+, ANGLO AMERICANS
    IDEN U.S., HOLTZMAN INKBLOT TECHNIQUE

113 AUTH WADDELL, JACK O.
    TITL FOR INDIVIDUAL POWER AND SOCIAL CREDIT: THE USE OF
          ALCOHOL AMONG TUCSON PAPAGOS.
    SOUR HUMAN ORGANIZATION, SPR. 1975, V34(1), PP 9-15.
    YEAR 1975
    DESC PAPAGO, OFF-RESERVATION, ADULTS, EXTENDED FAMILY,
          ECONOMIC ISSUES, URBAN AREAS, GENEROSITY,
          NONCOMPETITIVENESS,ALCOHOL USE+, COOPERATION,
          SOUTHWEST
    IDEN U.S., ARIZONA

114 AUTH WILLIAMS, JOHN D.; TEUBNER, JOHANNA; HARLOW, STEVEN D.
    TITL CREATIVITY IN RURAL, URBAN, AND INDIAN CHILDREN.
    SOUR JOURNAL OF PSYCHOLOGY, JAN. 1973, V83, PP 111-116.
    YEAR 1973
    DESC PLAINS, URBAN AREAS, OFF-RESERVATION, ECONOMIC ISSUES,
          CHILDREN-SCHOOL AGE+, PSYCHOLOGICAL TESTING+,
          ABILITIES+, SELF-CONCEPT
    IDEN U.S., NORTH DAKOTA, TORRENCE TESTS OF CREATIVE
          THINKING

115 AUTH WITHYCOMBE, JERALDINE S.
    TITL RELATIONSHIPS OF SELF-CONCEPT, SOCIAL STATUS, AND
          SELF-PERCEIVED SOCIAL STATUS AND RACIAL DIFFERENCES OF
          PAIUTE INDIAN AND WHITE ELEMENTARY SCHOOL CHILDREN.
    SOUR JOURNAL OF SOCIAL PSYCHOLOGY, DEC. 1973, V91, PP
          337-338.
    YEAR 1973
    DESC PAIUTE, GREAT BASIN, RESERVATION, OFF-RESERVATION,
          CHILDREN-SCHOOL AGE+, PSYCHOLOGICAL TESTING+,

```
         SELF-CONCEPT+, SOCIAL GROUPS AND PEER GROUPS,
         NATIVE-NON-NATIVE COMPARISONS, ELEMENTARY SCHOOLS+,
         SOCIAL STATUS+, ANGLO AMERICANS
    IDEN U.S., NEVADA, CLASSROOM SOCIAL DISTANCE SCALE, THIS IS
         ME SCALE, BILL"S INDEX OF ADJUSTMENT AND VALUES

116 AUTH GRANZBERG, GARY
    TITL THE PSYCHOLOGICAL INTEGRATION OF CULTURE: A
         CROSS-CULTURAL STUDY OF HOPI TYPE INITIATION RITES.
    SOUR JOURNAL OF SOCIAL PSYCHOLOGY, JUN. 1973, V90, PP 3-7.
    YEAR 1973
    DESC PUEBLO-HOPI, SOUTHWEST, RESERVATION, CHILDREN-INFANTS
         AND PRESCHOOL+, CHILDREN-SCHOOL AGE+, TRADITIONAL
         CHILD REARING+, PERSONALITY TRAITS, AGGRESSIVENESS
    IDEN U.S.

117 AUTH PARKIN, MICHAEL
    TITL SUICIDE AND CULTURE IN FAIRBANKS: A COMPARISON OF
         THREE CULTURAL GROUPS IN A SMALL CITY OF INTERIOR
         ALASKA.
    SOUR PSYCHIATRY, FEB. 1974, V37, PP 60-67.
    YEAR 1974
    DESC ATHABASCAN, YUKON SUB-ARCTIC, WESTERN ARCTIC,
         SUICIDE+, SEX DIFFERENCES, NATIVE-NON-NATIVE
         COMPARISONS,URBAN AREAS, STRESS, ESKIMO, DEPRESSION,
         EPIDEMIOLOGICAL STUDY, ANGLO AMERICANS
    IDEN U.S., ALASKA

118 AUTH TYLER, JOHN D.; HOLSINGER, DAVID N.
    TITL LOCUS OF CONTROL DIFFERENCES BETWEEN RURAL AMERICAN
         INDIAN AND WHITE CHILDREN.
    SOUR JOURNAL OF SOCIAL PSYCHOLOGY, APR. 1975, V95, PP
         149-155.
    YEAR 1975
    DESC PERSONALITY TRAITS+, ADOLESCENTS, NATIVE-NON-NATIVE
         COMPARISONS, SEX DIFFERENCES, CHIPPEWA, EASTERN
         SUB-ARCTIC, RESERVATION, PSYCHOLOGICAL TESTING+, AGE
         COMPARISONS, BLACK AMERICANS, ANGLO AMERICANS
    IDEN U.S., NOWICKI-STRICKLAND LOCUS OF CONTROL SCALE FOR
         CHILDREN

119 AUTH MARTIN, DAVID S.
    TITL ETHNOCENTRISM TOWARD FOREIGN CULTURE IN ELEMENTARY
         SOCIAL STUDIES.
    SOUR ELEMENTARY SCHOOL JOURNAL, MAR. 1975, V75, PP 381-388.
    YEAR 1975
    DESC ELEMENTARY SCHOOLS, CHILDREN-SCHOOL AGE+, ESKIMO,
         WESTERN ARCTIC, STEREOTYPES, EDUCATION PROGRAMS AND
         SERVICES+, PROGRAM DEVELOPMENT+, DISCRIMINATION+,
         EXPERIMENTAL STUDY, PSYCHOLOGICAL TESTING+, ATTITUDES+
    IDEN U.S., KUHLMANN-ANDERSON INTELLIGENCE TEST, (FIGERT)
         DOGMATISM SCALE, LIKERT SCALE, SEMANTIC DIFFERENTIAL

120 AUTH SHORE, JAMES H.; KINZIE, J. DAVID; HAMPSON, JOHN L.;
         PATTISON, E. MANSELL
```

```
        TITL  PSYCHIATRIC EPIDEMIOLOGY OF AN INDIAN VILLAGE.
        SOUR  PSYCHIATRY, FEB. 1973, V36, PP 70-81.
        YEAR  1973
        DESC  NORTHWEST COAST, EPIDEMIOLOGICAL STUDY, RESERVATION,
              AGE COMPARISONS, SEX DIFFERENCES, ADULTS, ALCOHOL USE,
              PSYCHOSES, NEUROSES, CHARACTER DISORDERS,
              PSYCHOPHYSIOLOGICAL DISORDERS, SOCIAL STATUS+,
              STRESS+, MENTAL DISORDERS+
        IDEN  U.S.

121  AUTH  ROSENTHAL, BERNARD G.
     TITL  DEVELOPMENT OF SELF-IDENTIFICATION IN RELATION TO
           ATTITUDES TOWARDS THE SELF IN THE CHIPPEWA INDIANS.
     SOUR  GENETIC PSYCHOLOGY MONOGRAPHS, AUG. 1974, V90, PP
           43-141.
     YEAR  1974
     DESC  SELF-CONCEPT+, CHILDREN-SCHOOL AGE+, CHILDREN-INFANTS
           AND PRESCHOOL+, CHIPPEWA, EASTERN SUB-ARCTIC, ECONOMIC
           ISSUES, ETHNIC IDENTITY+, STRESS, RESERVATION,
           PSYCHOLOGICAL TESTING, AGE COMPARISONS, DEMOGRAPHIC
           DATA, ATTITUDES+
     IDEN  U.S., WISCONSIN, LAC DU FLAMBEAU RESERVATION

122  AUTH  KLOPFER, BRUNO; BOYER, L. BRYCE
     TITL  NOTES ON THE PERSONALITY STRUCTURE OF A NORTH AMERICAN
           INDIAN SHAMAN: RORSCHACH INTERPRETATION.
     SOUR  JOURNAL OF PROJECTIVE TECHNIQUES, 1961, V25, PP
           169-178.
     YEAR  1961
     DESC  TRADITIONAL HEALERS+, PSYCHOLOGICAL TESTING+,
           APACHE-MESCALERO, SOUTHWEST, PERSONALITY TRAITS+,
           HYSTERIA, PSYCHOANALYSIS
     IDEN  U.S., MESCALERO RESERVATION, RORSCHACH TEST

123  AUTH  LYON, JUANA P.
     TITL  THE INDIAN ELDER, A FORGOTTEN AMERICAN: FINAL REPORT
           ON THE FIRST FIRST NATIONAL INDIAN CONFERENCE ON
           AGING, PHOENIX, ARIZONA, JUNE 15-17, 1976.
     SOUR  ALBUQUERQUE: NATIONAL INDIAN COUNCIL ON AGING, 1978.
     YEAR  1978
     DESC  ENVIRONMENTAL FACTORS, NUTRITIONAL FACTORS, LEGAL
           ISSUES, ECONOMIC ISSUES, AGED+, INSTITUTIONALIZATION,
           DELIVERY OF SERVICES, DEMOGRAPHIC DATA, PHYSICAL
           HEALTH AND ILLNESS, MENTAL DISORDERS, MEDICAL PROGRAMS
           AND SERVICES, MENTAL HEALTH PROGRAMS AND SERVICES,
           SOCIAL SERVICES, URBAN AREAS, RESERVATION
     IDEN  U.S.

124  AUTH  LUBART, JOSEPH M.
     TITL  FIELD STUDY OF THE PROBLEMS OF ADAPTATION OF MACKENZIE
           DELTA ESKIMOS TO SOCIAL AND ECONOMIC CHANGE.
     SOUR  PSYCHIATRY, 1969, V32, PP 447-458.
     YEAR  1969
     DESC  ESKIMO, CENTRAL AND EASTERN ARCTIC, ANOMIE+, STRESS+,
           OFF-RESERVATION, PERSONALITY TRAITS+, MALES, FEMALES,
```

```
                DISCRIMINATION, COOPERATION+, GROUP NORMS AND
                SANCTIONS, SOCIAL ROLES, SOCIAL STATUS
        IDEN    CANADA

125     AUTH    KUNCE, JOSEPH; RANKIN, L.S.; CLEMENT, ELAINE
        TITL    MAZE PERFORMANCE AND PERSONAL, SOCIAL, AND ECONOMIC
                ADJUSTMENT OF ALASKAN NATIVES.
        SOUR    JOURNAL OF SOCIAL PSYCHOLOGY, 1967, V73, PP 37-45.
        YEAR    1967
        DESC    ESKIMO, WESTERN ARCTIC, PSYCHOLOGICAL TESTING+,
                ADULTS, OFF-RESERVATION, SEX DIFFERENCES, ABILITIES+
        IDEN    U.S., ALASKA, CORNELL MEDICAL INDEX, CIRCULAR PENCIL
                MAZE TEST

126     AUTH    KUNITZ, STEPHEN J.; LEVY, JERROLD E.; ODOROFF, CHARLES
                L.; BOLLINGER, J.
        TITL    THE EPIDEMIOLOGY OF ALCOHOLIC CIRRHOSIS IN TWO
                SOUTHWESTERN INDIAN TRIBES.
        SOUR    QUARTERLY JOURNAL OF STUDIES ON ALCOHOL, 1971, V32, PP
                706-720.
        YEAR    1971
        DESC    PUEBLO-HOPI, SOUTHWEST, NAVAJO, RESERVATION,
                EPIDEMIOLOGICAL STUDY,  PHYSICAL HEALTH AND ILLNESS+,
                INTERTRIBAL COMPARISONS, OFF-RESERVATION, STRESS+, SEX
                DIFFERENCES, ALCOHOL USE+, DEMOGRAPHIC DATA, MARITAL
                RELATIONSHIPS
        IDEN    U.S., ARIZONA, NAVAJO RESERVATION, HOPI RESERVATION

127     AUTH    GRAVES, THEODORE D.
        TITL    ACCULTURATION, ACCESS AND ALCOHOL IN A TRI-ETHNIC
                COMMUNITY.
        SOUR    AMERICAN ANTHROPOLOGIST, 1967, V69, PP 306-321.
        YEAR    1967
        DESC    ALCOHOL USE+, NATIVE-NON-NATIVE COMPARISONS, ADULTS,
                CULTURAL ADAPTATION+, ECONOMIC ISSUES+, SOCIALLY
                DEVIANT BEHAVIOR+, ANOMIE, TRADITIONAL SOCIAL CONTROL,
                NONINTERFERENCE, PSYCHOLOGICAL TESTING,
                EPIDEMIOLOGICAL STUDY, OFF-RESERVATION, SOUTHWEST,
                LATINOS, ANGLO AMERICANS
        IDEN    U.S.

128     AUTH    MASON, EVELYN P.
        TITL    CROSS-VALIDATION STUDY OF PERSONALITY CHARACTERISTICS
                OF JUNIOR HIGH STUDENTS FROM AMERICAN INDIAN, MEXICAN
                AND CAUCASIAN ETHNIC BACKGROUNDS.
        SOUR    JOURNAL OF SOCIAL PSYCHOLOGY, 1969, V77, PP 15-24.
        YEAR    1969
        DESC    PERSONALITY TRAITS+, ADOLESCENTS, SECONDARY SCHOOLS,
                ACHIEVEMENT+, NATIVE-NON-NATIVE COMPARISONS, SEX
                DIFFERENCES, SELF-CONCEPT+, DISCRIMINATION,
                MOTIVATION, PSYCHOLOGICAL TESTING+, EDUCATION PROGRAMS
                AND SERVICES+, NORTHWEST COAST, LATINOS, ANGLO
                AMERICANS
        IDEN    PROJECT CATCH-UP, U.S., WASHINGTON
```

129 AUTH MASON, EVELYN P.
     TITL PROGRESS REPORT: PROJECT CATCH-UP: AN EDUCATIONAL
           PROGRAM FOR JUNIOR HIGH STUDENTS OF AMERICAN INDIAN,
           MEXICAN, AND CAUCASIAN ETHNIC BACKGROUNDS.
     SOUR PSYCHOLOGY IN THE SCHOOLS, 1968, V5, PP 272-276.
     YEAR 1968
     DESC LUMMI, NOOKSACK, SWINOMISH, NORTHWEST COAST, EDUCATION
           PROGRAMS AND SERVICES+, SECONDARY SCHOOLS+, PROGRAM
           EVALUATION+, ACHIEVEMENT+, LEARNING DISABILITIES AND
           PROBLEMS, MOTIVATION, DROPOUTS, PREVENTIVE MENTAL
           HEALTH PROGRAMS, NATIVE-NON-NATIVE COMPARISONS,
           ADOLESCENTS, ANGLO AMERICANS, LATINOS
     IDEN U.S., WASHINGTON, PROJECT CATCH-UP

130 AUTH MASON, EVELYN P.
     TITL PROJECT CATCH -UP: AN EDUCATIONAL PROGRAM OF SOCIALLY
           DISADVANTAGED THIRTEEN AND FOURTEEN YEAR OLDS.
     SOUR PSYCHOLOGY IN THE SCHOOLS, 1969, V6, PP 253-257.
     YEAR 1969
     DESC ADOLESCENTS, SECONDARY SCHOOLS+, ACHIEVEMENT, PROGRAM
           EVALUATION+, EDUCATION PROGRAMS AND SERVICES+,
           DROPOUTS, PREVENTIVE MENTAL HEALTH PROGRAMS,
           NATIVE-NON-NATIVE COMPARISONS, LATINOS, ANGLO
           AMERICANS, NORTHWEST COAST
     IDEN U.S., WASHINGTON, PROJECT CATCH-UP

131 AUTH JENKINS, ALMA
     TITL SOME EVALUATIVE FACTORS IN THE SELECTION OF ADOPTIVE
           HOMES FOR INDIAN CHILDREN.
     SOUR CHILD WELFARE, JUN. 1961, V40, PP 16-20.
     YEAR 1961
     DESC ADOPTION AND FOSTER CARE+, CHILDREN-SCHOOL AGE+,
           CHILDREN-INFANTS AND PRESCHOOL+, SOCIAL SERVICES+,
           B.I.A.
     IDEN U.S., INDIAN ADOPTION PROJECT

132 AUTH WESTERMEYER, JOSEPH; HAUSMAN, WILLIAM
     TITL MENTAL HEALTH CONSULTATION WITH GOVERNMENT AGENCIES: A
           COMPARISON OF TWO CASES.
     SOUR SOCIAL PSYCHIATRY, 1974, V9(4), PP 137-141.
     YEAR 1974
     DESC MENTAL HEALTH PROFESSIONALS+, DELIVERY OF SERVICES+,
           MENTAL HEALTH PROGRAMS AND SERVICES, PROGRAM
           EVALUATION+, CONSULTATION+, FEDERAL GOVERNMENT
     IDEN U.S.

133 AUTH RESNIK, H.L.P.; DIZMANG, LARRY H.
     TITL OBSERVATIONS ON SUICIDAL BEHAVIOR AMONG AMERICAN
           INDIANS.
     SOUR AMERICAN JOURNAL OF PSYCHIATRY, JAN. 1971, V127(7), PP
           882-887.
     YEAR 1971
     DESC SUICIDE+, INTERTRIBAL COMPARISONS, ETHNIC IDENTITY+,
           STRESS+, RESERVATION, CHEYENNE-NORTHERN, PLAINS,
           SHOSHONE, BANNOCK, PLATEAU, FAMILY FUNCTIONING,

ADOLESCENTS
IDEN U.S.

134 AUTH NELSON, LEONARD B.
    TITL ALCOHOLISM IN ZUNI, NEW MEXICO: A COMMUNITY DIAGNOSIS.
    SOUR HARVARD MEDICAL ALUMNI BULLETIN, JAN.-FEB. 1976, V50,
         PP 18-23.
    YEAR 1976
    DESC PUEBLO-ZUNI, SOUTHWEST, ALCOHOL USE+, FAMILY
         FUNCTIONING, WITCHCRAFT, ALCOHOLISM TREATMENT+,
         TRADITIONAL HEALERS, CORRECTIONS PERSONNEL, PROGRAM
         DEVELOPMENT+, ADULTS
    IDEN U.S., NEW MEXICO

135 AUTH ERIKSON, ERIK H.
    TITL OBSERVATIONS ON SIOUX EDUCATION.
    SOUR JOURNAL OF PSYCHOLOGY, 1939, V7, PP 101-156.
    YEAR 1939
    DESC SIOUX, PLAINS, CHILDREN-SCHOOL AGE+, ADOLESCENTS+,
         MALES, CHILDREN-INFANTS AND PRESCHOOL+, TRADITIONAL
         CHILD REARING+, SEX DIFFERENCES, FEMALES, GENEROSITY,
         NONCOMPETITIVENESS, B.I.A. BOARDING SCHOOLS, STRESS,
         SEXUAL RELATIONS, RESERVATION, GROUP NORMS AND
         SANCTIONS+, DREAMS AND VISION QUESTS
    IDEN U.S., SOUTH DAKOTA, PINE RIDGE RESERVATION

136 AUTH WILSON, LOLITA
    TITL CANADIAN INDIAN CHILDREN WHO HAD NEVER ATTENDED
         SCHOOL.
    SOUR ALBERTA JOURNAL OF EDUCATIONAL RESEARCH, DEC. 1973,
         V19, PP 309-313.
    YEAR 1973
    DESC CHILDREN-SCHOOL AGE+, PSYCHOLOGICAL TESTING+,
         ABILITIES+
    IDEN CANADA, ALBERTA, WECHSLER INTELLIGENCE SCALE CHILDREN,
         RAVEN PROGRESSIVE MATRICES

137 AUTH HAVIGHURST, ROBERT J.; HILKEVITCH, RHEA R.
    TITL THE INTELLIGENCE OF INDIAN CHILDREN AS MEASURED BY A
         PERFORMANCE SCALE.
    SOUR JOURNAL OF ABNORMAL AND SOCIAL PSYCHOLOGY, OCT. 1944,
         V39, PP 419-433.
    YEAR 1944
    DESC CHILDREN-SCHOOL AGE+, PLAINS, SOUTHWEST, SIOUX,
         PUEBLO-HOPI, PUEBLO-ZUNI,PUEBLO-ZIA, PAPAGO, NAVAJO,
         PSYCHOLOGICAL TESTING+, ABILITIES+, CULTURE-FAIR
         TESTS, ADOLESCENTS+, INTERTRIBAL COMPARISONS,
         RESERVATION, NATIVE-NON-NATIVE COMPARISONS, ANGLO
         AMERICANS
    IDEN U.S., GRACE ARTHUR POINT PERFORMANCE SCALE

138 AUTH HURT, WESLEY R.; BROWN, RICHARD M.
    TITL SOCIAL DRINKING PATTERNS OF THE YANKTON SIOUX
    SOUR HUMAN ORGANIZATION, 1965, V24, PP 222-230.
    YEAR 1965

```
      DESC  ALCOHOL USE+, CULTURAL CONTINUITY+, SIOUX, PLAINS,
            OFF-RESERVATION, SEX DIFFERENCES, AGE COMPARISONS,
            MALES, FEMALES, AGED, ADULTS, SEXUAL RELATIONS, SOCIAL
            ROLES
      IDEN  U.S., SOUTH DAKOTA

139   AUTH  SHEPARDSON, MARY ; HAMMOND, BLODWEN
      TITL  CHANGE AND PERSISTANCE IN AN ISOLATED NAVAJO
            COMMUNITY.
      SOUR  AMERICAN ANTHROPOLOGIST, 1964, V66, PP 1029-1050.
      YEAR  1964
      DESC  NAVAJO, SOUTHWEST, CULTURAL CONTINUITY+, DEMOGRAPHIC
            DATA, CULTURAL ADAPTATION+, BICULTURALISM+
      IDEN  U.S., NAVAJO RESERVATION

140   AUTH  HACKENBERG, ROBERT A.; GALLAGHER, MARY M.
      TITL  THE COSTS OF CULTURAL CHANGE: ACCIDENTAL INJURY AND
            MODERNIZATION AMONG THE PAPAGO INDIANS.
      SOUR  HUMAN ORGANIZATION, SUM. 1972, V31(2), PP 211-226.
      YEAR  1972
      DESC  EPIDEMIOLOGICAL STUDY, PAPAGO, SOUTHWEST, STRESS+,
            ADULTS, RESERVATION, SEX DIFFERENCES, CULTURAL
            ADAPTATION+, ACCIDENTS, DEMOGRAPHIC DATA
      IDEN  U.S., ARIZONA, PAPAGO RESERVATION

141   AUTH  GOLD, DELORES
      TITL  PSYCHOLOGICAL CHANGES ASSOCIATED WITH ACCULTURATION OF
            SASKATCHEWAN INDIANS.
      SOUR  JOURNAL OF SOCIAL PSYCHOLOGY, 1967, V71, PP 177-184.
      YEAR  1967
      DESC  CHIPEWYAN, CREE, PLAINS, URBANIZATION+, RESERVATION,
            URBAN AREAS, FEMALES, PSYCHOLOGICAL TESTING, ADULTS,
            PERSONALITY TRAITS+, MACKENZIE SUB-ARCTIC,
            NATIVE-NON-NATIVE COMPARISONS, ANGLO AMERICANS
      IDEN  CANADA, SASKATCHEWAN, CAMPISI SCALE, CULTURAL
            INFORMATION TEST

142   AUTH  HAVIGHURST, ROBERT J.
      TITL  THE EXTENT AND SIGNIFICANCE OF SUICIDE AMONG AMERICAN
            INDIANS TODAY.
      SOUR  MENTAL HYGIENE, APR. 1971, V55(2), PP 174-177.
      YEAR  1971
      DESC  QUINAULT, NORTHWEST COAST, NATIVE-NON-NATIVE
            COMPARISONS, EPIDEMIOLOGICAL STUDY, SUICIDE+,
            ADOLESCENTS+, SEX DIFFERENCES, AGE COMPARISONS,
            ECONOMIC ISSUES
      IDEN  U.S.

143   AUTH  GRANZBERG, GARY
      TITL  HOPI INITIATION RITES: A CASE STUDY OF THE VALIDITY OF
            THE FREUDIAN THEORY OF CULTURE.
      SOUR  JOURNAL OF SOCIAL PSYCHOLOGY, AUG. 1972, V87, PP
            189-195.
      YEAR  1972
      DESC  CHILDREN-SCHOOL AGE+, PUEBLO-HOPI, SOUTHWEST,
```

RESERVATION, PSYCHOLOGICAL TESTING, MALES, TRADITIONAL
CHILD REARING+, PERSONALITY TRAITS+, AGGRESSIVENESS,
PSYCHOANALYSIS
IDEN   U.S., ARIZONA, HOPI RESERVATION

144 AUTH GALLOWAY, CHARLES G.; MICKELSON, NORMA I.
      TITL MODIFICATION OF BEHAVIOR PATTERNS OF INDIAN CHILDREN.
      SOUR ELEMENTARY SCHOOL JOURNAL, DEC. 1971, V72, PP 150-155.
      YEAR 1971
      DESC CHILDREN-SCHOOL AGE+, EDUCATION PROGRAMS AND
           SERVICES+, PSYCHOTHERAPY AND COUNSELING+, RESERVATION,
           CHILDREN-INFANTS AND PRESCHOOL+, SOCIALLY DEVIANT
           BEHAVIOR+, CLINICAL STUDY, PASSIVE RESISTANCE,
           ELEMENTARY SCHOOLS, BEHAVIOR MODIFICATION+
      IDEN CANADA, BRITISH COLUMBIA

145 AUTH WOODWARD, RICHARD G.
      TITL TITLE VIII AND THE OGLALA SIOUX.
      SOUR PHI DELTA KAPPAN, DEC. 1973, V55, PP 249-251.
      YEAR 1973
      DESC SIOUX-OGLALA, PLAINS, RESERVATION, DROPOUTS+,
           PREVENTIVE MENTAL HEALTH PROGRAMS+, ADOLESCENTS+,
           NATIVE AMERICAN POLITICAL MOVEMENTS, EDUCATION
           PROGRAMS AND SERVICES+, ADULTS, SECONDARY SCHOOLS+,
      IDEN U.S., SOUTH DAKOTA, PINE RIDGE RESERVATION, TITLE VIII
           DROPOUT PREVENTION PROGRAM

146 AUTH FREDERICK, CALVIN
      TITL SUICIDE, HOMICIDE AND ALCOHOLISM AMONG AMERICAN
           INDIANS: GUIDELINES FOR HELP.
      SOUR (U.S. NIMH CENTER FOR THE STUDIES OF CRIME AND
           DELINQUENCY). WASHINGTON, D.C.: GOVERNMENT PRINTING
           OFFICE, 1973.
      YEAR 1973
      DESC SUICIDE+, CRIME+, ALCOHOL USE+, PREVENTIVE MENTAL
           HEALTH PROGRAMS+, CORRECTIONAL INSTITUTIONS,
           ALCOHOLISM TREATMENT
      IDEN U.S.

147 AUTH AMERICAN INDIAN NURSES ASSOCIATION
      TITL ALTERNATIVES FOR PLANNING A CONTINUUM OF CARE FOR
           ELDERLY AMERICAN INDIANS.
      SOUR (IHS CONTRACT NO. 246-76-C-3241). WASHINGTON, D.C.:
           GOVERNMENT PRINTING OFFICE, 1978.
      YEAR 1978
      DESC AGED+, DELIVERY OF SERVICES+, INSTITUTIONALIZATION+,
           OUTPATIENT CARE+, PROGRAM DEVELOPMENT, MEDICAL
           PROGRAMS AND SERVICES, SOCIAL SERVICES, RESERVATION,
           URBAN AREAS, MENTAL HEALTH PROGRAMS AND SERVICES,
           TRAINING PROGRAMS, PROGRAM EVALUATION
      IDEN U.S.

148 AUTH ALEXANDER, THERON; ANDERSON, ROBERT
      TITL CHILDREN IN A SOCIETY UNDER STRESS.
      SOUR BEHAVIORAL SCIENCE, 1957, V2, PP 46-55.

```
     YEAR  1957
     DESC  CHEYENNE-NORTHERN, PLAINS, CHILDREN-SCHOOL AGE+,
           RESERVATION, GENEROSITY, STRESS+, PSYCHOLOGICAL
           TESTING+, EXTENDED FAMILY, FAMILY FUNCTIONING+,
           CULTURE-FAIR TESTS
     IDEN  U.S., MONTANA, TONGUE RIVER RESERVATION, THEMATIC
           APPERCEPTION TEST

149  AUTH  BARGER, KENNETH; EARL, DAPHNE
     TITL  DIFFERENTIAL ADAPTATION TO NORTHERN TOWN LIFE BY THE
           ESKIMOS AND INDIANS OF GREAT WHALE RIVER.
     SOUR  HUMAN ORGANIZATION, SPR. 1971, V30(1), PP 25-30.
     YEAR  1971
     DESC  OFF-RESERVATION, ESKIMO, CREE, CENTRAL AND EASTERN
           ARCTIC, CULTURAL ADAPTATION+, EMPLOYMENT+, ECONOMIC
           ISSUES, CULTURAL CONTINUITY+, ADULTS, EASTERN
           SUB-ARCTIC, URBAN AREAS, INTERTRIBAL COMPARISONS
     IDEN  CANADA, QUEBEC

150  AUTH  ABLON, JOAN
     TITL  RETENTION OF CULTURAL VALUES AND DIFFERENTIAL URBAN
           ADAPTION: SAMOANS AND AMERICAN INDIANS IN A WEST COAST
           CITY
     SOUR  SOCIAL FORCES, MAR. 1971, V49, PP 385-393.
     YEAR  1971
     DESC  URBAN AREAS, NATIVE-NON-NATIVE COMPARISONS,
           URBANIZATION+, RELOCATION+, STRESS+, CULTURAL
           CONTINUITY+, EXTENDED FAMILY, NATIVE AMERICAN
           VALUES+, ASIAN AMERICANS
     IDEN  U.S., CALIFORNIA

151  AUTH  CONN, STEPHEN
     TITL  AT RAMAH, NEW MEXICO: BILINGUAL LEGAL EDUCATION.
     SOUR  JOURNAL OF AMERICAN INDIAN EDUCATION, JAN. 1973, V12,
           PP 3-10.
     YEAR  1973
     DESC  NAVAJO, SOUTHWEST, EDUCATION PROGRAMS AND SERVICES+,
           SECONDARY SCHOOLS+, ADOLESCENTS, LEGAL ISSUES+,
           BILINGUALISM, BICULTURALISM
     IDEN  U.S., NEW MEXICO, NAVAJO RESERVATION

152  AUTH  DLUGOKINSKI, ERIC
     TITL  REVIEW OF AN OLD STEREOTYPE: THE SILENT INDIAN.
     SOUR  JOURNAL OF AMERICAN INDIAN EDUCATION, MAY 1972, V11,
           PP 23-25.
     YEAR  1972
     DESC  B.I.A. BOARDING SCHOOLS+, ADOLESCENTS+, PSYCHOTHERAPY
           AND COUNSELING+, SOCIAL GROUPS AND PEER GROUPS+,
           PASSIVE RESISTANCE+, STEREOTYPES+
     IDEN  U.S., OKLAHOMA

153  AUTH  BERRY, JOHN W.
     TITL  PSYCHOLOGICAL RESEARCH IN THE NORTH.
     SOUR  ANTHROPOLOGICA, 1971, V13, PP 141-157.
     YEAR  1971
```

DESC ESKIMO, CENTRAL AND EASTERN ARCTIC, COGNITIVE
PROCESSES+, PERSONALITY TRAITS+, CULTURAL ADAPTATION+,
REVIEW OF LITERATURE
IDEN CANADA

154 AUTH BITTKER, THOMAS E.
TITL DILEMMAS OF MENTAL HEALTH SERVICE DELIVERY TO
OFF-RESERVATION INDIANS.
SOUR ANTHROPOLOGICAL QUARTERLY, JUL. 1973, V46, PP 172-182.
YEAR 1973
DESC OFF-RESERVATION, DELIVERY OF SERVICES+, GREAT BASIN,
SOUTHWEST, CALIFORNIA AREA,ALCOHOL USE, MENTAL
DISORDERS, MENTAL HEALTH PROGRAMS AND SERVICES+,
PROGRAM DEVELOPMENT+
IDEN U.S., ARIZONA, NEVADA, UTAH, CALIFORNIA

155 AUTH WESTERMEYER, JOSEPH
TITL CHIPPEWA AND MAJORITY ALCOHOLISM IN THE TWIN CITIES: A
COMPARISON.
SOUR JOURNAL OF NERVOUS AND MENTAL DISEASE, NOV. 1972,
V155(5), PP 322-327.
YEAR 1972
DESC CHIPPEWA, EASTERN SUB-ARCTIC, URBAN AREAS, ALCOHOL
USE+, MEDICAL INSTITUTIONS, ALCOHOLISM TREATMENT,
NATIVE-NON-NATIVE COMPARISONS, ADULTS, SEX
DIFFERENCES, EPIDEMIOLOGICAL STUDY, ANGLO AMERICANS
IDEN U.S., MINNESOTA

156 AUTH FURST, PETER T.
TITL THE ROOTS AND CONTINUITIES OF SHAMANISM.
SOUR ARTSCANADA, DEC. 1974, PP 33-60.
YEAR 1974
DESC TRADITIONAL HEALERS+, NATIVE AMERICAN RELIGIONS+,
NATIVE AMERICAN ETIOLOGY,TRADITIONAL USE OF DRUGS AND
ALCOHOL+, WITCHCRAFT, SOUL LOSS
IDEN MEXICO, U.S., CANADA, ASIA, SOUTH AMERICA

157 AUTH TORREY, E. FULLER
TITL MENTAL HEALTH SERVICES FOR AMERICAN INDIANS AND
ESKIMOS
SOUR COMMUNITY MENTAL HEALTH JOURNAL, DEC. 1970, V6(6), PP
455-463.
YEAR 1970
DESC MENTAL HEALTH PROGRAMS AND SERVICES+, PROGRAM
DEVELOPMENT+, NATIVE AMERICAN PERSONNEL, TRADITIONAL
HEALERS+, MENTAL HEALTH PARAPROFESSIONALS+,
CULTURE-BASED PSYCHOTHERAPY, CULTURE-SPECIFIC
SYNDROMES, ESKIMO, WESTERN ARCTIC, OFF-RESERVATION,
ALASKA NATIVES
IDEN U.S., ALASKA

158 AUTH MATCHETT, WILLIAM F.
TITL REPEATED HALLUCINATORY EXPERIENCES AS A PART OF THE
MOURNING PROCESS AMONG HOPI INDIAN WOMEN.
SOUR PSYCHIATRY, MAY 1972, V35, PP 185-194.

```
        YEAR  1972
        DESC  PUEBLO-HOPI, SOUTHWEST, ADULTS, FEMALES, RESERVATION,
              DEPRESSION+, GRIEF REACTION+, CLINICAL STUDY, GHOST
              SICKNESS+, DREAMS AND VISION QUESTS, EMOTIONAL
              RESTRAINT, DEATH AND DYING+
        IDEN  U.S., ARIZONA, HOPE RESERVATION

159  AUTH  HOYT, ELIZABETH A.
     TITL  YOUNG INDIANS: SOME PROBLEMS AND ISSUES OF MENTAL
           HYGIENE.
     SOUR  MENTAL HYGIENE, JAN. 1962, V46, PP 41-47.
     YEAR  1962
     DESC  PREVENTIVE MENTAL HEALTH PROGRAMS+, ADOLESCENTS+,
           SOUTHWEST, SELF-CONCEPT, EMPLOYMENT, STRESS+, PROGRAM
           DEVELOPMENT+, NATIVE AMERICAN VALUES
     IDEN  U.S.

160  AUTH  KINZIE, J. DAVID; SHORE, JAMES H.; PATTISON, E.
           MANSELL
     TITL  ANATOMY OF PSYCHIATRIC CONSULTATION TO RURAL INDIANS.
     SOUR  COMMUNITY MENTAL HEALTH JOURNAL, AUG. 1972, V8(3), PP
           196-207.
     YEAR  1972
     DESC  CONSULTATION+, MENTAL HEALTH PROGRAMS AND SERVICES+,
           RESERVATION, NORTHWEST COAST, MENTAL HEALTH
           PARAPROFESSIONALS, PROGRAM DEVELOPMENT+, NATIVE
           AMERICAN PERSONNEL, EPIDEMIOLOGICAL STUDY, MENTAL
           DISORDERS, DELIVERY OF SERVICES+
     IDEN  U.S.

161  AUTH  KUNITZ, STEPHEN J.; LEVY, JERROLD E.; EVERETT, MICHAEL
     TITL  ALCOHOLIC CIRRHOSIS AMONG THE NAVAHO.
     SOUR  QUARTERLY JOURNAL OF STUDIES ON ALCOHOL, 1969, V30, PP
           672-685.
     YEAR  1969
     DESC  ALCOHOL USE+, NAVAJO, SOUTHWEST, PHYSICAL HEALTH AND
           ILLNESS+, EPIDEMIOLOGICAL STUDY, RESERVATION, I.H.S.,
           SEX DIFFERENCES, NATIVE-NON-NATIVE COMPARISONS,
           ADULTS, DEMOGRAPHIC DATA, ANGLO AMERICANS
     IDEN  U.S., NAVAJO RESERVATION

162  AUTH  LANDES, RUTH
     TITL  THE ABNORMAL AMONG THE OJIBWA INDIANS.
     SOUR  JOURNAL OF ABNORMAL AND SOCIAL PSYCHOLOGY, 1938, V33,
           PP 14-33.
     YEAR  1938
     DESC  CHIPPEWA, EASTERN SUB-ARCTIC, TRADITIONAL HEALERS,
           WINDIGO PSYCHOSIS+, ANXIETY+, DEPRESSION+, PSYCHOSES,
           NEUROSES
     IDEN  CANADA, ONTARIO

163  AUTH  HERREID, CLYDE F.; HERREID, JANET, R.
     TITL  DIFFERENCES IN MMPI SCORES IN NATIVE AND NON-NATIVE
           ALASKANS.
     SOUR  JOURNAL OF SOCIAL PSYCHOLOGY, 1966, V70, PP 191-198.
```

```
       YEAR  1966
       DESC  ALASKA NATIVES, WESTERN ARCTIC, PSYCHOLOGICAL
             TESTING+, NATIVE-NON-NATIVE COMPARISONS, PERSONALITY
             TRAITS+, ANGLO AMERICANS
       IDEN  U.S., ALASKA, M.M.P.I.

 164   AUTH  HONIGMANN, JOHN J.; HONIGMANN, IRMA
       TITL  HOW BAFFIN ISLAND ESKIMO HAVE LEARNED TO USE ALCOHOL.
       SOUR  SOCIAL FORCES, 1965, V44, PP 73-83.
       YEAR  1965
       DESC  ESKIMO, CENTRAL AND EASTERN ARCTIC, ALCOHOL USE+,
             LEGAL ISSUES, CULTURAL ADAPTATION+, ADULTS,
             OFF-RESERVATION
       IDEN  CANADA

 165   AUTH  MASON, EVELYN P.
       TITL  STABILITY OF DIFFERENCES IN PERSONALITY
             CHARACTERISTICS OF JUNIOR HIGH STUDENTS FROM AMERICAN
             INDIAN, MEXICAN, AND ANGLO ETHNIC BACKGROUNDS.
       SOUR  PSYCHOLOGY IN THE SCHOOLS, JAN. 1971, V8, PP 86-89.
       YEAR  1971
       DESC  SECONDARY SCHOOLS, PERSONALITY TRAITS+,
             NATIVE-NON-NATIVE COMPARISONS+, SEX DIFFERENCES,
             SELF-CONCEPT, ACHIEVEMENT, MOTIVATION, PSYCHOLOGICAL
             TESTING+,ADOLESCENTS+, LATINOS, ANGLO AMERICANS
       IDEN  U.S., PROJECT CATCH-UP, CALIFORNIA PSYCHOLOGICAL
             INVENTORY, WASHINGTON

 166   AUTH  STRIMBU, JERRY L.; SCHOENFELDT, LYLE F.; SIMS, O.
             SUTHERN
       TITL  DRUG USAGE IN COLLEGE STUDENTS AS A FUNCTION OF RACIAL
             CLASSIFICATION AND MINORITY GROUP STATUS.
       SOUR  RESEARCH IN HIGHER EDUCATION, 1973, V1, PP 263-272.
       YEAR  1973
       DESC  DRUG USE+, NATIVE-NON-NATIVE COMPARISONS, COLLEGES AND
             UNIVERSITIES+, ADOLESCENTS, EPIDEMIOLOGICAL STUDY,
             BLACK AMERICANS, ANGLO AMERICANS, ASIAN AMERICANS
       IDEN  U.S.

 167   AUTH  WANGLER, DAVID G.
       TITL  SCIENCE, MAGIC, AND CULTURE.
       SOUR  AMERICAN INDIAN CULTURE AND RESEARCH JOURNAL, 1974,
             VI, PP 14-16.
       YEAR  1974
       DESC  NATIVE AMERICAN RELIGIONS+, STRESS, NAVAJO, SOUTHWEST,
             EDUCATION PROGRAMS AND SERVICES, RESEARCHERS+
       IDEN  U.S.

 168   AUTH  JILEK-AALL, LOUISE
       TITL  THE WESTERN PSYCHIATRIST AND HIS NON-WESTERN
             CLIENTELE.
       SOUR  CANADIAN PSYCHIATRIC ASSOCIATION JOURNAL, OCT. 1976,
             V21(6), PP 353-359.
       YEAR  1976
       DESC  MENTAL HEALTH PROFESSIONALS+, PSYCHOTHERAPY AND
```

```
                COUNSELING+, COAST SALISH, NORTHWEST COAST,
                CULTURE-BASED PSYCHOTHERAPY+, STRESS, CULTURE-SPECIFIC
                SYNDROMES+
        IDEN    CANADA, BRITISH COLUMBIA

169  AUTH   SONTAG, ED
     TITL   WASHINGTON REPORT.
     SOUR   EDUCATION AND TRAINING OF THE MENTALLY RETARDED, OCT.
            1972, V7, PP 157-159.
     YEAR   1972
     DESC   MENTAL RETARDATION+, I.H.S., B.I.A., PROGRAM
            DEVELOPMENT+, EDUCATION PROGRAMS AND SERVICES+
     IDEN   U.S.

170  AUTH   SCHUBERT, JOSEF; CROPLEY, A.J.
     TITL   VERBAL REGULATION OF BEHAVIOR AND I.Q. IN CANADIAN
            INDIAN AND WHITE CHILDREN.
     SOUR   DEVELOPMENTAL PSYCHOLOGY, NOV. 1972, V7(3), PP 295-301.
     YEAR   1972
     DESC   CHILDREN-SCHOOL AGE+, ABILITIES+, PSYCHOLOGICAL
            TESTING+, NATIVE-NON-NATIVE COMPARISONS, CULTURE-FAIR
            TESTS+, CREE, PLAINS, ANGLO AMERICANS
     IDEN   CANADA, WECHSLER INTELLIGENCE SCALE CHILDREN,
            SASKATCHEWAN

171  AUTH   JEWELL, DONALD P.
     TITL   A CASE OF A "PSYCHOTIC" NAVAHO INDIAN MALE.
     SOUR   HUMAN ORGANIZATION, SPR. 1952, V11, PP 32-36.
     YEAR   1952
     DESC   NAVAJO, SOUTHWEST, SCHIZOPHRENIA+, PSYCHOTHERAPY AND
            COUNSELING+, LANGUAGE HANDICAPS, CULTURAL CONTINUITY,
            INSTITUTIONALIZATION+, MENTAL HEALTH INSTITUTIONS,
            PSYCHOLOGICAL TESTING, PASSIVE RESISTANCE, CLINICAL
            STUDY
     IDEN   U.S., NEW MEXICO, GOODENOUGH HARRIS DRAW A PERSON TEST

172  AUTH   KLEINFELD, JUDITH S.
     TITL   CHARACTERISTICS OF SUCCESSFUL BOARDING HOME PARENTS OF
            ESKIMO AND ATHABASCAN INDIAN STUDENTS.
     SOUR   HUMAN ORGANIZATION, SUM. 1973, V32(2), PP 191-199.
     YEAR   1973
     DESC   ESKIMO, WESTERN ARCTIC, ATHABASCAN, YUKON SUB-ARCTIC,
            ADOLESCENTS+, FAMILY FUNCTIONING+, ADOPTION AND FOSTER
            CARE+, NONINTERFERENCE+, EMOTIONAL RESTRAINT, BOARDING
            HOMES
     IDEN   ALASKA, U.S.

173  AUTH   MASON, EVELYN P.; LOCASSO, RICHARD M.
     TITL   EVALUATION OF POTENTIAL FOR CHANGE IN JUNIOR-HIGH-AGE
            YOUTH FROM AMERICAN INDIAN, MEXICAN, AND ANGLO ETHNIC
            BACKGROUNDS.
     SOUR   PSYCHOLOGY IN THE SCHOOLS, OCT. 1972, V9, PP 423-427.
     YEAR   1972
     DESC   SECONDARY SCHOOLS+, CHILDREN-SCHOOL AGE+,
            PSYCHOLOGICAL TESTING+, NATIVE-NON-NATIVE COMPARISONS,
```

```
          SEX DIFFERENCES, ACHIEVEMENT+, DROPOUTS+,
          SELF-CONCEPT, ANGLO AMERICANS, LATINOS
     IDEN U.S., CALIFORNIA TEST OF MENTAL MATURITY, CALIFORNIA
          ACHIEVEMENT TEST, CALIFORNIA PSYCHOLOGICAL INVENTORY,
          WASHINGTON, PROJECT CATCH-UP

174 AUTH SHORE, JAMES H.; VON FUMMETTI, BILLEE
    TITL THREE ALCOHOL PROGRAMS FOR AMERICAN INDIANS.
    SOUR AMERICAN JOURNAL OF PSYCHIATRY, MAY 1972, V128(11), PP
         134-138.
    YEAR 1972
    DESC ALCOHOLISM TREATMENT+, NATIVE AMERICAN ADMINISTERED
         PROGRAMS+, ADULTS, PROGRAM EVALUATION+, UTE,
         APACHE-JICARILLA, SOUTHWEST, RESERVATION
    IDEN U.S., UINTAH AND OURAY RESERVATION, UTAH, NEW MEXICO,
         NEVADA

175 AUTH WALLACE, ANTHONY F.C.
    TITL DREAMS AND WISHES OF THE SOUL: A TYPE OF
         PSYCHO-ANALYTIC THEORY AMONG SEVENTEENTH-CENTURY
         IROQUOIS.
    SOUR AMERICAN ANTHROPOLOGIST, APR. 1958, V60, PP 234-248.
    YEAR 1958
    DESC IROQUOIS, NATIVE AMERICAN RELIGIONS+, NORTHEAST
         WOODLAND, NATIVE AMERICAN ETIOLOGY, CULTURE-BASED
         PSYCHOTHERAPY+, MALES, REVIEW OF LITERATURE, DREAMS
         AND VISION QUESTS+
    IDEN U.S.

176 AUTH MILLER, ANTHONY G.; THOMAS, RON
    TITL COOPERATION AND COMPETITION AMONG BLACKFOOT INDIAN AND
         URBAN CANADIAN CHILDREN.
    SOUR CHILD DEVELOPMENT, SEP. 1972, V43, PP 1104-1110.
    YEAR 1972
    DESC BLACKFEET, PLAINS, URBAN AREAS, CHILDREN-SCHOOL AGE+,
         NATIVE-NON-NATIVE COMPARISONS, COOPERATION+,
         NONCOMPETITIVENESS, ELEMENTARY SCHOOLS, PSYCHOLOGICAL
         TESTING+, ANGLO AMERICANS
    IDEN CANADA, ALBERTA, MADSEN COOPERATION BOARD

177 AUTH REBOUSSIN, ROLAND; GOLDSTEIN, JOEL W.
    TITL ACHIEVEMENT MOTIVATION IN NAVAJO AND WHITE STUDENTS.
    SOUR AMERICAN ANTHROPOLOGIST, 1966, V68, PP 740-745.
    YEAR 1966
    DESC MOTIVATION+, COLLEGES AND UNIVERSITIES, SOUTHWEST,
         ACHIEVEMENT, PSYCHOLOGICAL TESTING+, CULTURAL
         ADAPTATION, NATIVE-NON-NATIVE COMPARISONS, ANGLO
         AMERICANS
    IDEN U.S., HASKELL INSTITUTE, FRENCH TEST OF INSIGHT,
         KANSAS

178 AUTH SIMON, RITA J.
    TITL AN ASSESSMENT OF THE RACIAL AWARENESS, PREFERENCE AND
         SELF IDENTITY AMONG WHITE AND ADOPTED NON-WHITE
         CHILDREN.
```

```
       SOUR  SOCIAL PROBLEMS, OCT. 1974, V22(1), PP 43-57.
       YEAR  1974
       DESC  ETHNIC IDENTITY+, ADOPTION AND FOSTER CARE+,
             CHILDREN-INFANTS AND PRESCHOOL+, CHILDREN-SCHOOL AGE+,
             PSYCHOLOGICAL TESTING+, SELF-CONCEPT+,
             NATIVE-NON-NATIVE COMPARISONS, EXPERIMENTAL STUDY,
             BLACK AMERICANS, ANGLO AMERICANS
       IDEN  U.S.

179    AUTH  HAMAMSY, LAILA S.
       TITL  THE ROLE OF WOMEN IN A CHANGING NAVAJO SOCIETY.
       SOUR  AMERICAN ANTHROPOLOGIST, 1957, V59, PP 101-111.
       YEAR  1957
       DESC  FEMALES+, ADULTS, NAVAJO, SOUTHWEST, RESERVATION,
             ECONOMIC ISSUES, EXTENDED FAMILY+, FAMILY
             FUNCTIONING+, STRESS+, SOCIAL ROLES+
       IDEN  U.S., NAVAJO RESERVATION

180    AUTH  NELSON, MARY
       TITL  PROBLEMS INDIAN STUDENTS FACE.
       SOUR  INDIAN HISTORIAN, SUM. 1972, V5, PP 22-24
       YEAR  1972
       DESC  GENEROSITY, SELF-CONCEPT+, COLLEGES AND UNIVERSITIES+,
             NONCOMPETITIVENESS, LANGUAGE HANDICAPS, STRESS+
       IDEN  U.S.

181    AUTH  BOYER, L. BRYCE; BOYER, RUTH M.; HIPPLER, ARTHUR E.
       TITL  ECOLOGY, SOCIALIZATION, AND PERSONALITY DEVELOPMENT
             AMONG ATHABASCANS.
       SOUR  JOURNAL OF COMPARATIVE FAMILY STUDIES, SPR. 1974,
             V5(1), PP 61-73.
       YEAR  1974
       DESC  ATHABASCAN, YUKON SUB-ARCTIC, PERSONALITY TRAITS+,
             TRADITIONAL CHILD REARING+, ENVIRONMENTAL FACTORS,
             EMOTIONAL RESTRAINT, PSYCHOANALYSIS
       IDEN  U.S., ALASKA

182    AUTH  STULL, DONALD D.
       TITL  VICTIMS OF MODERNIZATION: ACCIDENT RATES AND PAPAGO
             INDIAN ADJUSTMENT.
       SOUR  HUMAN ORGANIZATION, SUM. 1972, V31(2), PP 227-240.
       YEAR  1972
       DESC  PAPAGO, SOUTHWEST, CULTURAL ADAPTATION+,
             EPIDEMIOLOGICAL STUDY, RESERVATION, STRESS+,
             ACCIDENTS+, ADULTS, DEMOGRAPHIC DATA
       IDEN  U.S., ARIZONA

183    AUTH  MARTIN, HARRY W.; SUTKER, SARA SMITH; LEON, ROBERT L.;
             JALES, WILLIAM M.
       TITL  MENTAL HEALTH OF EASTERN OKLAHOMA INDIANS: AN
             EXPLORATION.
       SOUR  HUMAN ORGANIZATION, WIN. 1968, V27(4), PP 308-315.
       YEAR  1968
       DESC  EPIDEMIOLOGICAL STUDY, PLAINS, SOUTHEAST WOODLAND,
             PSYCHOLOGICAL TESTING+, MENTAL DISORDERS+,
```

NATIVE-NON-NATIVE COMPARISONS, SEX DIFFERENCES,
DEMOGRAPHIC DATA, BLACK AMERICANS
IDEN   U.S., OKLAHOMA, CORNELL MEDICAL INDEX, LANGER SCALE

184 AUTH   BARTER, JAMES T.; WEIST, KATHERINE M.
     TITL   HISTORICAL AND CONTEMPORARY PATTERNS OF NORTHERN
             CHEYENNE SUICIDE.
     SOUR   PAPER PRESENTED AT THE MEETING OF THE AMERICAN
             PSYCHIATRIC ASSOCIATION, SAN FRANCISCO, 1970. (25
             PAGES)
     YEAR   1970
     DESC   EPIDEMIOLOGICAL STUDY, SUICIDE+, RESERVATION,
             CHEYENNE-NORTHERN, CULTURAL CONTINUITY+, FAMILY
             FUNCTIONING+, SEX DIFFERENCES, PLAINS, DEMOGRAPHIC
             DATA
     IDEN   U.S., MONTANA

185 AUTH   REH, EMMA; MCNICKLE, D'ARCY
     TITL   PEYOTE AND THE INDIAN.
     SOUR   SCIENTIFIC MONTHLY, SEP. 1943, V57, PP 220-229.
     YEAR   1943
     DESC   DRUG USE+, NATIVE AMERICAN RELIGIONS+, TRADITIONAL USE
             OF DRUGS AND ALCOHOL+, ADULTS
     IDEN   NATIVE AMERICAN CHURCH, U.S., CANADA

186 AUTH   WESTERMEYER, JOSEPH
     TITL   INDIAN POWERLESSNESS IN MINNESOTA.
     SOUR   SOCIETY, MAR.-APR. 1973, PP 45-51.
     YEAR   1973
     DESC   DISCRIMINATION+, NATIVE AMERICAN ADMINISTERED
             PROGRAMS, INSTITUTIONALIZATION, PASSIVE RESISTANCE,
             DELIVERY OF SERVICES, POWERLESSNESS
     IDEN   U.S., MINNESOTA

187 AUTH   DAVIS, MARY J.
     TITL   ADOPTIVE PLACEMENT OF AMERICAN INDIAN CHILDREN WITH
             NON-INDIAN FAMILIES--PART II.
     SOUR   CHILD WELFARE, JUN. 1961, PP 12-15.
     YEAR   1961
     DESC   ADOPTION AND FOSTER CARE+, CHILDREN-INFANTS AND
             PRESCHOOL+, CHILDREN-SCHOOL AGE+, SOCIAL SERVICES+,
             B.I.A.
     IDEN   U.S., INDIAN ADOPTION PROJECT

188 AUTH   HOSTBJOR, STELLA
     TITL   SOCIAL SERVICES TO THE INDIAN UNMARRIED MOTHER.
     SOUR   CHILD WELFARE, MAY 1961, PP 7-9.
     YEAR   1961
     DESC   SEXUAL RELATIONS, FAMILY FUNCTIONING, SIOUX, PLAINS,
             GROUP NORMS AND SANCTIONS, ADOPTION AND FOSTER CARE+,
             EXTENDED FAMILY+, FEMALES, SOCIAL SERVICES+
     IDEN   U.S., INDIAN ADOPTION PROJECT

189 AUTH   HIPPLER, ARTHUR E.
     TITL   THAWING OUT SOME MAGIC.

```
        SOUR  MENTAL HYGIENE, SPR. 1975, V59, PP 20-24.
        YEAR  1975
        DESC  DELIVERY OF SERVICES+, MENTAL HEALTH PROGRAMS AND
              SERVICES+, ALASKA NATIVES, NATIVE AMERICAN ETIOLOGY+,
              TRADITIONAL HEALERS+, OFF-RESERVATION
        IDEN  U.S., ALASKA

190  AUTH  MILLER, SHELDON I.; SCHOENFELD, LAWRENCE S.
     TITL  GRIEF IN THE NAVAJO: PSYCHODYNAMICS AND CULTURE.
     SOUR  INTERNATIONAL JOURNAL OF SOCIAL PSYCHIATRY, AUT. 1973,
           V19, PP 187-191.
     YEAR  1973
     DESC  CLINICAL STUDY, GRIEF REACTION+, NAVAJO, SOUTHWEST,
           NATIVE AMERICAN RELIGIONS, ADULTS,CULTURE-BASED
           PSYCHOTHERAPY, PSYCHOTHERAPY AND COUNSELING+,
           CHEMOTHERAPY, GHOST SICKNESS, AGGRESSIVENESS,
           EMOTIONAL RESTRAINT, DEATH AND DYING
     IDEN  U.S., NAVAJO RESERVATION

191  AUTH  MILLER, FRANK C.; CAULKINS, D. DOUGLAS
     TITL  CHIPPEWA ADOLESCENTS: A CHANGING GENERATION.
     SOUR  HUMAN ORGANIZATION, SUM. 1964, V23, PP 150-159.
     YEAR  1964
     DESC  CHIPPEWA, EASTERN SUB-ARCTIC, ADOLESCENTS+,
           RESERVATION, SECONDARY SCHOOLS,CULTURAL ADAPTATION+,
           SOCIAL GROUPS AND PEER GROUPS, ANOMIE+, STRESS+
     IDEN  U.S., MINNESOTA, DEER LAKE RESERVATION

192  AUTH  MINDELL, CARL; GURWITT, ALAN
     TITL  THE PLACEMENT OF AMERICAN INDIAN CHILDREN: THE NEED
           FOR CHANGE.
     SOUR  IN THE DESTRUCTION OF AMERICAN INDIAN FAMILIES,
           STEPHEN UNGER (ED.), PP 61-66.  NEW YORK: ASSOCIATION
           ON AMERICAN INDIAN AFFAIRS, 1977.
     YEAR  1977
     DESC  ADOPTION AND FOSTER CARE+, CHILDREN-INFANTS AND
           PRESCHOOL+, CHILDREN-SCHOOL AGE+, NATIVE AMERICAN
           ADMINISTERED PROGRAMS+, SOCIAL SERVICES, CULTURAL
           CONTINUITY
     IDEN  U.S.

193  AUTH  ASSOCIATION OF AMERICAN INDIAN PHYSICIANS
     TITL  AGING: ITS IMPACT ON THE HEALTH OF AMERICAN INDIANS.
     SOUR  (IHS CONTRACT NO. 246-78-C-6001). WASHINGTON, D.C.:
           GOVERNMENT PRINTING OFFICE, 1978.
     YEAR  1978
     DESC  AGED+, DELIVERY OF SERVICES+, PHYSICAL HEALTH AND
           ILLNESS+, MENTAL DISORDERS+, DEMOGRAPHIC DATA, MEDICAL
           PROGRAMS AND SERVICES, MENTAL HEALTH PROGRAMS AND
           SERVICES,EPIDEMIOLOGICAL STUDY, URBAN AREAS,
           RESERVATION, INSTITUTIONALIZATION
     IDEN  U.S.

194  AUTH  AMERICAN INDIAN NURSES ASSOCIATION
     TITL  THE ENVIRONMENT OF ELDERLY NATIVE AMERICANS.
```

SOUR   (IHS CONTRACT NO. 246-76-C-3241). WASHINGTON, D.C.:
GOVERNMENT PRINTING OFFICE, 1978.
YEAR   1978
DESC   AGED+, ENVIRONMENTAL FACTORS+, ECONOMIC ISSUES,
DEMOGRAPHIC DATA, SOCIAL SERVICES, NUTRITIONAL FACTORS
IDEN   U.S.

195   AUTH   HAY, THOMAS H.
TITL   A TECHNIQUE OF FORMALIZING AND TESTING MODELS OF
BEHAVIOR: TWO MODELS OF OJIBWA RESTRAINT.
SOUR   AMERICAN ANTHROPOLOGIST, JUN. 1973, V75, PP 708-730.
YEAR   1973
DESC   CHIPPEWA, EASTERN SUB-ARCTIC, PERSONALITY TRAITS+,
AGGRESSIVENESS+, TRADITIONAL SOCIAL CONTROL+, ADULTS,
WITCHCRAFT, NONINTERFERENCE+, RESERVATION, EMOTIONAL
RESTRAINT
IDEN   U.S., WISCONSIN

196   AUTH   DOWLING, JOHN H.
TITL   A "RURAL" INDIAN COMMUNITY IN AN URBAN SETTING.
SOUR   HUMAN ORGANIZATION, AUG. 1968, V27(3), PP 236-240.
YEAR   1968
DESC   OFF-RESERVATION, EMPLOYMENT+, RELOCATION+,
DISCRIMINATION+, IROQUOIS-ONEIDA, NORTHEAST WOODLAND,
DEMOGRAPHIC DATA
IDEN   U.S., WISCONSIN, WISCONSIN ONEIDA RESERVATION

197   AUTH   PRICE, JOHN A.
TITL   THE MIGRATION AND ADAPTATION OF AMERICAN INDIANS TO
LOS ANGELES.
SOUR   HUMAN ORGANIZATION, SUM. 1968, V27(2), PP 168-175.
YEAR   1968
DESC   URBAN AREAS, RELOCATION+, SOCIAL NETWORKS+,
URBANIZATION, INTERTRIBAL COMPARISONS, DEMOGRAPHIC
DATA, NATIVE AMERICAN POLITICAL MOVEMENTS, NAVAJO,
SIOUX, OKLAHOMA INDIANS
IDEN   U.S., CALIFORNIA

198   AUTH   JAMIESON, ELMER; SANDIFORD, PETER
TITL   THE MENTAL CAPACITY OF SOUTHERN ONTARIO INDIANS.
SOUR   JOURNAL OF EDUCATIONAL PSYCHOLOGY. 1928, V19, PP
536-551.
YEAR   1928
DESC   ABILITIES+, IROQUOIS, NORTHEAST WOODLAND, ELEMENTARY
SCHOOLS, PSYCHOLOGICAL TESTING+, SEX DIFFERENCES,
CHILDREN-SCHOOL AGE+, ACHIEVEMENT, LANGUAGE
HANDICAPS+, SOCIAL STATUS, ADOLESCENTS+, SECONDARY
SCHOOLS
IDEN   CANADA, ONTARIO, PINTER-CUNNINGHAM PRIMARY MENTAL
TEST, AYRES BURGESS SILENT READING TEST, AYRES
SPELLING SCALE, AYRES GETTYSBURG SCALE, CANADIAN
NATIONAL INTELLIGENCE TEST

199   AUTH   SPEISS, JEFFREY M.; SPEISS, MADELEINE L.
TITL   REINFORCED READINESS: A CULTURALLY RELEVANT BEHAVIOR

MODIFICATION PROGRAM FOR MEXICAN-AMERICAN, INDIAN, AND
BLACK CHILDREN.
SOUR PROCEEDINGS OF THE 81ST ANNUAL CONVENTION OF THE
AMERICAN PSYCHOLOGICAL ASSOCIATION, 1973, V8, PP
639-640.
YEAR 1973
DESC PSYCHOTHERAPY AND COUNSELING+, EXPERIMENTAL STUDY,
READING PROGRAMS+, EDUCATION PROGRAMS AND SERVICES+,
NATIVE-NON-NATIVE COMPARISONS, LEARNING+,
CHILDREN-SCHOOL AGE+, BEHAVIOR MODIFICATION, LATINOS,
BLACK AMERICANS
IDEN U.S., NEW MEXICO

200 AUTH CONRAD, REX D.; KAHN, MARVIN W.
TITL AN EPIDEMIOLOGICAL STUDY OF SUICIDE AND SUICIDE
ATTEMPTS AMONG THE PAPAGO INDIANS.
SOUR PROCEEDINGS OF THE 81ST ANNUAL CONVENTION OF THE
AMERICAN PSYCHOLOGICAL ASSOCIATION, 1973, V8, PP
449-450.
YEAR 1973
DESC EPIDEMIOLOGICAL STUDY, SUICIDE+, PAPAGO, SOUTHWEST,
MALES, ADOLESCENTS, ADULTS, SOCIAL ROLES
IDEN U.S., ARIZONA

201 AUTH DOZIER, EDWARD P.; SIMPSON, GEORGE E.; YINGER, J.
MILTON
TITL THE INTEGRATION OF AMERICANS OF INDIAN DESCENT.
SOUR ANNALS OF THE AMERICAN ACADEMY OF POLITICAL AND SOCIAL
SCIENCES, MAY 1957, V311, PP 158-165.
YEAR 1957
DESC CULTURAL CONTINUITY+, CULTURAL ADAPTATION+
IDEN U.S.

202 AUTH MARTIN, HARRY W.
TITL CORRELATES OF ADJUSTMENT AMONG AMERICAN INDIANS IN AN
URBAN ENVIRONMENT.
SOUR HUMAN ORGANIZATION, WIN. 1964, V23, PP 290-295.
YEAR 1964
DESC NAVAJO, SIOUX, CHOCTAW, SOUTHWEST, PLAINS, SOUTHEAST
WOODLAND, AGE COMPARISONS, ADULTS, SEX DIFFERENCES,
CULTURAL ADAPTATION+, INTERTRIBAL COMPARISONS,
INSTITUTIONALIZATION, CORRECTIONAL INSTITUTIONS,
RELOCATION+, URBANIZATION+, URBAN AREAS
IDEN U.S.

203 AUTH DUTOIT, BRIAN M.
TITL SUBSTITUTION, A PROCESS IN CULTURE CHANGE.
SOUR HUMAN ORGANIZATION, SPR. 1964, V23, PP 16-23.
YEAR 1964
DESC RESERVATION, ALCOHOL USE+, SOCIAL GROUPS AND PEER
GROUPS+, CULTURAL ADAPTATION+, ADULTS, STRESS+
IDEN U.S.

204 AUTH SCHOENFELD, LAWRENCE S.; LYERLY, R. JEANNINE; MILLER,
SHELDON I.

```
     TITL  WE LIKE US.
     SOUR  MENTAL HYGIENE, APR. 1971, V55(2), PP 171-173.
     YEAR  1971
     DESC  MENTAL HEALTH PROGRAMS AND SERVICES+, NAVAJO,
           SOUTHWEST, MENTAL HEALTH PROFESSIONALS+, PROGRAM
           EVALUATION+, B.I.A., I.H.S.
     IDEN  U.S., NAVAJO RESERVATION

205  AUTH  SCHOENFELD, LAWRENCE S.; MILLER, SHELDON I.
     TITL  THE NAVAJO INDIAN: A DESCRIPTIVE STUDY OF THE
           PSYCHIATRIC POPULATION.
     SOUR  INTERNATIONAL JOURNAL OF SOCIAL PSYCHIATRY, 1973, V19,
           PP 31-37.
     YEAR  1973
     DESC  EPIDEMIOLOGICAL STUDY, NAVAJO, SOUTHWEST, RESERVATION,
           I.H.S., MENTAL DISORDERS+, NEUROSES, PSYCHOSES,
           CHARACTER DISORDERS, MENTAL HEALTH PROGRAMS AND
           SERVICES+, DEMOGRAPHIC DATA
     IDEN  U.S., NAVAJO RESERVATION

206  AUTH  WESTERMEYER, JOSEPH
     TITL  THE RAVAGE OF INDIAN FAMILIES IN CRISIS.
     SOUR  IN THE DESTRUCTION OF AMERICAN INDIAN FAMILIES,
           STEPHEN UNGER (ED.), PP 47-56.  NEW YORK: ASSOCIATION
           ON AMERICAN INDIAN AFFAIRS, 1977.
     YEAR  1977
     DESC  EPIDEMIOLOGICAL STUDY, FAMILY FUNCTIONING+, ADOPTION
           AND FOSTER CARE+, SOCIAL SERVICES+, PROGRAM
           EVALUATION+, DEMOGRAPHIC DATA
     IDEN  U.S., MINNESOTA

207  AUTH  WEPPNER, ROBERT S.
     TITL  SOCIOECONOMIC BARRIERS TO ASSIMILATION OF NAVAJO
           MIGRANTS.
     SOUR  HUMAN ORGANIZATION, AUT. 1972, V31(3), PP 303-314.
     YEAR  1972
     DESC  RELOCATION, URBAN AREAS, EMPLOYMENT+, DISCRIMINATION+,
           CULTURAL ADAPTATION+, URBANIZATION+, NAVAJO,
           SOUTHWEST, DEMOGRAPHIC DATA, ADULTS
     IDEN  U.S., COLORADO

208  AUTH  WADDELL, JACK O.
     TITL  RESURGENT PATRONAGE AND LAGGING BUREAUCRACY IN A
           PAPAGO OFF-RESERVATION COMMUNITY.
     SOUR  HUMAN ORGANIZATION, SPR. 1970, V29(1), PP 37-42.
     YEAR  1970
     DESC  EMPLOYMENT+, PAPAGO, SOUTHWEST, DISCRIMINATION+,
           ADULTS, OFF-RESERVATION, PASSIVE RESISTANCE, CULTURAL
           CONTINUITY
     IDEN  U.S., ARIZONA

209  AUTH  VOGET, FRED W.
     TITL  THE AMERICAN INDIAN IN TRANSITION: REFORMATION AND
           ACCOMODATION.
     SOUR  AMERICAN ANTHROPOLOGIST, 1956, V58(2), PP 249-263.
```

```
        YEAR  1956
        DESC  CULTURAL REVIVAL+, CULTURAL ADAPTATION+, CULTURAL
              CONTINUITY+, NATIVE AMERICAN RELIGIONS, SOCIAL STATUS,
              BICULTURALISM+
        IDEN  U.S., HANDSOME LAKE RELIGION, NATIVE AMERICAN CHURCH,
              GHOST DANCE, SHAKER RELIGION

210  AUTH  BIGART, ROBERT J.
     TITL  PATTERNS OF CULTURAL CHANGE IN A SALISH FLATHEAD
           COMMUNITY.
     SOUR  HUMAN ORGANIZATION, AUT. 1971, V30(3), PP 229-237.
     YEAR  1971
     DESC  FLATHEAD, PLATEAU, CULTURAL ADAPTATION+, CULTURAL
           CONTINUITY+, SECONDARY SCHOOLS, PSYCHOLOGICAL
           TESTING+, RESERVATION, ADOLESCENTS+, ACHIEVEMENT,
           ECONOMIC ISSUES, NATIVE-NON-NATIVE COMPARISONS,
           BICULTURALISM+, ANGLO AMERICANS
     IDEN  U.S., MONTANA, FLATHEAD RESERVATION, THEMATIC
           APPERCEPTION TEST, KLUCKHOHN VALUES ORIENTATION TEST,
           BROWNFAIN SELF-RATING SCALE, SEMANTIC DIFFERENTIAL

211  AUTH  BLANCHARD, JOSEPH D.; BLANCHARD, EVELYN; ROLL, SAMUEL
     TITL  A PSYCHOLOGICAL AUTOPSY OF AN INDIAN ADOLESCENT
           SUICIDE WITH IMPLICATIONS FOR COMMUNITY SERVICES.
     SOUR  SUICIDE AND LIFE THREATENING BEHAVIOR, SPR. 1976, V6,
           PP 3-10.
     YEAR  1976
     DESC  SUICIDE+, ADOLESCENTS+, FAMILY FUNCTIONING,
           PSYCHOLOGICAL TESTING, PUEBLO, SOUTHWEST,
           AGGRESSIVENESS, EXTENDED FAMILY, ANOMIE, PREVENTIVE
           MENTAL HEALTH PROGRAMS+, MENTAL HEALTH PROGRAMS AND
           SERVICES+
     IDEN  U.S., MEMORY FOR DESIGNS TEST, BENDER GESTALT TEST,
           RORSCHACH TEST, NEW MEXICO, INTERNAL EXTERNAL SCALE

212  AUTH  CLINTON, LAWRENCE; CHADWICK, BRUCE A.; BAHR, HOWARD M.
     TITL  VOCATIONAL TRAINING FOR INDIAN MIGRANTS: CORRELATES OF
           "SUCCESS" IN A FEDERAL PROGRAM.
     SOUR  HUMAN ORGANIZATION, SPR. 1973, V32(1), PP 17-27.
     YEAR  1973
     DESC  EMPLOYMENT, TRAINING PROGRAMS+, URBAN AREAS,
           RELOCATION+, DROPOUTS+, PROGRAM EVALUATION+,
           EXPERIMENTAL STUDY, ADULTS, B.I.A., SEX DIFFERENCES,
           MARITAL RELATIONSHIPS
     IDEN  U.S., OREGON,ADULT VOCATIONAL TRAINING PROGRAM

213  AUTH  EDWARDS, DAN; EDWARDS, MARGE
     TITL  SOCIAL GROUP WORK IN YOUNG AMERICAN INDIANS.
     SOUR  MONOGRAPH NO. 9, BOULDER, CO.: WESTERN INTERSTATE
           COMMISSION FOR HIGHER EDUCATION, 1974. (22P)
     YEAR  1974
     DESC  SOCIAL GROUPS AND PEER GROUPS+, TIME PERCEPTION,
           PROGRAM DEVELOPMENT+, CHILDREN-SCHOOL AGE+,
           ADOLESCENTS, SOCIAL SERVICE PROFESSIONALS, SOCIAL
           SERVICES, PASSIVE RESISTANCE
```

```
         IDEN   U.S.

214  AUTH   GRAVES, THEODORE D.; LAVE, CHARLES A.
     TITL   DETERMINANTS OF URBAN MIGRANT INDIAN WAGES.
     SOUR   HUMAN ORGANIZATION, SPR. 1972, V31(1), PP 47-61.
     YEAR   1972
     DESC   URBAN AREAS, NAVAJO, SOUTHWEST, RELOCATION+,
            URBANIZATION+, EMPLOYMENT+, ECONOMIC ISSUES+,
            ACHIEVEMENT, MOTIVATION,  B.I.A., DISCRIMINATION,
            MARITAL RELATIONSHIPS
     IDEN   U.S., COLORADO

215  AUTH   PERETTI, PETER O.
     TITL   ENFORCED ACCULTURATION AND INDIAN-WHITE RELATIONS.
     SOUR   INDIAN HISTORIAN, 1973, V6, PP 38-52.
     YEAR   1973
     DESC   CULTURAL CONTINUITY+, CULTURAL ADAPTATION+, FEDERAL
            GOVERNMENT+, ADMINISTRATIVE ISSUES,  COOPERATION,
            EXTENDED FAMILY, PASSIVE RESISTANCE
     IDEN   U.S.

216  AUTH   TOWNSLEY, H.C.; GOLDSTEIN, GEORGE S.
     TITL   ONE VIEW OF THE ETIOLOGY OF DEPRESSION IN THE AMERICAN
            INDIAN.
     SOUR   PUBLIC HEALTH REPORTS, SEP.-OCT. 1977, V92, PP 458-461.
     YEAR   1977
     DESC   DEPRESSION+, SELF-CONCEPT+,  B.I.A. BOARDING SCHOOLS,
            ADOLESCENTS, ADULTS, ADMINISTRATIVE ISSUES, PASSIVE
            RESISTANCE, NATIVE AMERICAN COPING BEHAVIORS
     IDEN   U.S., M.M.P.I.

217  AUTH   REED, T. EDWARD; KALANT, HAROLD; GIBBINS, ROBERT J.;
            KAPUR, BUSHAN M.; RANKIN, JAMES G.
     TITL   ALCOHOL AND ACETALDEHYDE METABOLISM IN CAUCASIANS,
            CHINESE AND AMERINDS.
     SOUR   CANADIAN MEDICAL ASSOCIATION JOURNAL, NOV. 1976, V115,
            PP 851-855.
     YEAR   1976
     DESC   CHIPPEWA, EASTERN SUB-ARCTIC, NATIVE-NON-NATIVE
            COMPARISONS, ANGLO AMERICANS, ASIAN AMERICANS, ALCOHOL
            USE+, INTERTRIBAL COMPARISONS, PIMA, SOUTHWEST,GENETIC
            FACTORS+
     IDEN   CANADA, ONTARIO

218  AUTH   SLOTKIN, J.S.
     TITL   SOCIAL PSYCHIATRY OF A MENOMINI COMMUNITY.
     SOUR   JOURNAL OF ABNORMAL AND SOCIAL PSYCHOLOGY, 1953,
            V48(1), PP 10-16.
     YEAR   1953
     DESC   MENOMINEE, NORTHEAST WOODLAND, AGGRESSIVENESS+,
            NONCOMPETITIVENESS+, COOPERATION, TRADITIONAL SOCIAL
            CONTROL+, ADULTS, RESERVATION, WITCHCRAFT, PSYCHOSES,
            NEUROSES, ALCOHOL USE, NATIVE AMERICAN COPING
            BEHAVIORS
     IDEN   U.S.
```

219 AUTH SHORE, JAMES H.; BOPP, JOHN F.; WALLER, THELMA R.;
           DAWES, JAMES W.
     TITL A SUICIDE PREVENTION CENTER ON AN INDIAN RESERVATION.
     SOUR AMERICAN JOURNAL OF PSYCHIATRY, MAR. 1972, V128(9), PP
           76-81.
     YEAR 1972
     DESC PREVENTIVE MENTAL HEALTH PROGRAMS+, RESERVATION,
           PLATEAU, ADOLESCENTS, SUICIDE+, MENTAL HEALTH PROGRAMS
           AND SERVICES+, CORRECTIONAL INSTITUTIONS, NATIVE
           AMERICAN PERSONNEL, PROGRAM DEVELOPMENT+
     IDEN U.S.

220 AUTH MILLER, D.D.; JOHNSON, GAIL
     TITL WHAT WE"VE LEARNED ABOUT TEACHING READING TO NAVAJO
           INDIANS.
     SOUR READING TEACHER, MAR. 1974, V27, PP 550-554.
     YEAR 1974
     DESC LEARNING+, LANGUAGE HANDICAPS+, CULTURAL CONTINUITY+,
           ETHNIC IDENTITY, CHILDREN-SCHOOL AGE+, NAVAJO,
           SOUTHWEST, REVIEW OF LITERATURE, READING PROGRAMS+
     IDEN U.S.

221 AUTH NELSON, L.G.; TADLOCK, L.D.; DAWES, JAMES W.; HIPPLE,
           J.L.; JETMALANI, N.B.
     TITL SCREENING FOR EMOTIONALLY DISTURBED STUDENTS IN AN
           INDIAN BOARDING SCHOOL: EXPERIENCE WITH THE CORNELL
           MEDICAL INDEX HEALTH QUESTIONNAIRE.
     SOUR AMERICAN JOURNAL OF PSYCHIATRY, JUN. 1964, V120, PP
           1155-1159.
     YEAR 1964
     DESC ADOLESCENTS+, B.I.A. BOARDING SCHOOLS, NAVAJO,
           SOUTHWEST, ESKIMO, WESTERN ARCTIC, MENTAL DISORDERS+,
           PREVENTIVE MENTAL HEALTH PROGRAMS, NATIVE AMERICAN
           VALUES
     IDEN U.S., CORNELL MEDICAL INDEX, CHEMAWA INDIAN SCHOOL,
           OREGON

222 AUTH HELPER, MALCOLM M.; GARFIELD, SOL L.
     TITL USE OF THE SEMANTIC DIFFERENTIAL TO STUDY
           ACCULTURATION IN AMERICAN INDIAN ADOLESCENTS.
     SOUR JOURNAL OF PERSONALITY AND SOCIAL PSYCHOLOGY, 1965,
           V2(6), PP 817-822.
     YEAR 1965
     DESC ADOLESCENTS+, PSYCHOLOGICAL TESTING, NATIVE-NON-NATIVE
           COMPARISONS, CULTURAL ADAPTATION+, PLAINS, B.I.A.
           BOARDING SCHOOLS, ACHIEVEMENT+, SEX DIFFERENCES,
           NATIVE AMERICAN VALUES+, ANGLO AMERICANS
     IDEN U.S., SEMANTIC DIFFERENTIAL, SOUTH DAKOTA, FLANDREAU
           INDIAN VOCATIONAL HIGHSCHOOL

223 AUTH KUTTNER, ROBERT E.; LORINCZ, ALBERT B.
     TITL PROMISCUITY AND PROSTITUTION IN URBANIZED INDIAN
           COMMUNITIES.
     SOUR MENTAL HYGIENE, JAN. 1970, V54(1), PP 79-91.
     YEAR 1970

```
     DESC   SEXUAL RELATIONS+, FEMALES, URBAN AREAS, SIOUX,
            WINNEBAGO, OMAHA, PLAINS, PRAIRIE, URBANIZATION,
            ECONOMIC ISSUES, ALCOHOL USE, SOCIAL GROUPS AND PEER
            GROUPS, ADULTS, EPIDEMIOLOGICAL STUDY, GROUP NORMS AND
            SANCTIONS
     IDEN   U.S., NEBRASKA

224  AUTH   BEE, ROBERT L.
     TITL   POTAWATOMI PEYOTISM: THE INFLUENCE OF TRADITIONAL
            PATTERNS.
     SOUR   SOUTHWESTERN JOURNAL OF ANTHROPOLOGY, 1966, V22, PP
            194-205.
     YEAR   1966
     DESC   POTAWATOMI, PRAIRIE, DRUG USE+, TRADITIONAL USE OF
            DRUGS AND ALCOHOL+, RESERVATION, NATIVE AMERICAN
            RELIGIONS, TRIBAL POLITICAL ORGANIZATIONS+
     IDEN   U.S., KANSAS, NATIVE AMERICAN CHURCH

225  AUTH   GOLDSCHMIDT, WALTER; EDGERTON, ROBERT B.
     TITL   A PICTURE TECHNIQUE FOR THE STUDY OF VALUES.
     SOUR   AMERICAN ANTHROPOLOGIST, 1961, V63, PP 26-47.
     YEAR   1961
     DESC   MENOMINEE, NORTHEAST WOODLAND, PSYCHOLOGICAL TESTING+,
            NONINTERFERENCE, NATIVE AMERICAN RELIGIONS,
            GENEROSITY, ADULTS, RESERVATION, CULTURE-FAIR TESTS+,
            CULTURAL ADAPTATION+, CULTURAL CONTINUITY+, NATIVE
            AMERICAN VALUES+
     IDEN   U.S., WISCONSIN

226  AUTH   HALLOWELL, A. IRVING
     TITL   PSYCHIC STRESSES AND CULTURE PATTERNS.
     SOUR   AMERICAN JOURNAL OF PSYCHIATRY, MAY 1936, V92, PP
            1291-1310.
     YEAR   1936
     DESC   MENTAL DISORDERS+, NEUROSES, PSYCHOSIS, NATIVE
            AMERICAN ETIOLOGY, GROUP NORMS AND SANCTIONS+,
            CHIPPEWA, EASTERN SUB-ARCTIC, CULTURE-BASED
            PSYCHOTHERAPY+, TRADITIONAL HEALERS, SOUL LOSS, TABOO
            BREAKING, SOCIALLY DEVIANT BEHAVIOR+, WINDIGO
            PSYCHOSIS, RESERVATION, DREAMS AND VISION QUESTS+,
            NATIVE AMERICAN COPING BEHAVIORS, CONFESSION+, STRESS
     IDEN   CANADA, MANITOBA

227  AUTH   HALLOWELL, A. IRVING
     TITL   AGGRESSION IN SAULTEAUX SOCIETY.
     SOUR   PSYCHIATRY, 1940, V3, PP 395-407.
     YEAR   1940
     DESC   CHIPPEWA, EASTERN SUB-ARCTIC, AGGRESSIVENESS+,
            COOPERATION, TRADITIONAL SOCIAL CONTROL+, WITCHCRAFT,
            NATIVE AMERICAN ETIOLOGY, RESERVATION, DREAMS AND
            VISION QUESTS
     IDEN   CANADA

228  AUTH   KROHN, ALAN; GUTMANN, DAVID
     TITL   CHANGES IN MASTERY STYLES WITH AGE: A STUDY OF NAVAJO
```

```
          DREAMS.
     SOUR PSYCHIATRY, AUG. 1971, V34, PP 289-300.
     YEAR 1971
     DESC AGED+, ADULTS+, NAVAJO, SOUTHWEST, RESERVATION,
          MALES+, AGE COMPARISONS, PERSONALITY TRAITS+,
          AGGRESSIVENESS+, SELF-CONCEPT+, PSYCHOLOGICAL TESTING,
          DREAMS AND VISION QUESTS+, PSYCHOANALYSIS
     IDEN U.S., NAVAJO RESERVATION, THEMATIC APPERCEPTION TEST,
          SYNTONIC ORALITY SCORE

229  AUTH CULVER, CHARLES M.; DUNHAM, FRANCES
     TITL HUMAN RELATIONS TRAINING WITH COMPLEMENTARY SOCIAL
          GROUPS: AN EXPERIMENT IN FACE-TO-FACE INTERACTION.
     SOUR PSYCHIATRY, 1970, V33, PP 344-351.
     YEAR 1970
     DESC TRAINING PROGRAMS+, SOCIAL GROUPS AND PEER GROUPS,
          PSYCHOTHERAPY AND COUNSELING+, SOCIAL SERVICE
          PROFESSIONALS+, CORRECTIONS PERSONNEL+,
          DISCRIMINATION, PASSIVE RESISTANCE
     IDEN U.S., T GROUP

230  AUTH POLGAR, STEVEN
     TITL BICULTURATION OF MESQUAKIE TEENAGE BOYS.
     SOUR AMERICAN ANTHROPOLOGIST, 1960, V62, PP 217-235.
     YEAR 1960
     DESC ADOLESCENTS+, MESQUAKIE, PRAIRIE, BICULTURALISM+,
          TRADITIONAL CHILD REARING, TRADITIONAL SOCIAL CONTROL,
          PASSIVE RESISTANCE, SOCIALLY DEVIANT BEHAVIOR, SOCIAL
          GROUPS AND PEER GROUPS+, OFF-RESERVATION, NATIVE
          AMERICAN RELIGIONS,CULTURAL ADAPTATION+
     IDEN U.S., IOWA

231  AUTH DEVEREUX, GEORGE
     TITL THREE TECHNICAL PROBLEMS IN THE PSYCHOTHERAPY OF
          PLAINS INDIAN PATIENTS.
     SOUR AMERICAN JOURNAL OF PSYCHOTHERAPY, 1951, V5, PP
          411-423.
     YEAR 1951
     DESC PLAINS, CLINICAL STUDY, PSYCHOTHERAPY AND COUNSELING+,
          EXTENDED FAMILY, PERSONALITY TRAITS+, CULTURAL
          CONTINUITY, FEMALES, MALES, DREAMS AND VISION QUESTS+,
          PSYCHOANALYSIS
     IDEN U.S.

232  AUTH HACKENBERG, ROBERT A.
     TITL AN ANTHROPOLOGICAL STUDY OF DEMOGRAPHIC TRANSITION:
          THE PAPAGO INFORMATION SYSTEM.
     SOUR MILBANK MEMORIAL FUND QUARTERLY, 1966, V44, PP 470-493.
     YEAR 1966
     DESC DEMOGRAPHIC DATA, PAPAGO, SOUTHWEST, RESERVATION,
          PROGRAM DEVELOPMENT+, PROGRAM EVALUATION+, I.H.S.,
          MEDICAL PROGRAMS AND SERVICES+, ADMINISTRATIVE ISSUES+
     IDEN U.S., ARIZONA

233  AUTH BROWNLEE, ALETA
```

TITL THE AMERICAN INDIAN CHILD.
SOUR CHILDREN, MAR.-APR. 1958, V5(2), PP 55-60.
YEAR 1958
DESC CHILDREN-SCHOOL AGE+, CHILDREN-INFANTS AND PRESCHOOL+,
     RESERVATION, TIME PERCEPTION, MOTIVATION, FEDERAL
     GOVERNMENT, CHILD ABUSE AND NEGLECT+, SOCIAL SERVICES+
IDEN U.S.

234 AUTH KRUSH, THADDEUS P.; BJORK, JOHN W.; SINDELL, PETER S.;
     NELLE, JOANNA
   TITL SOME THOUGHTS ON THE FORMATION OF PERSONALITY
     DISORDER: STUDY OF AN INDIAN BOARDING SCHOOL
     POPULATION.
   SOUR AMERICAN JOURNAL OF PSYCHIATRY, FEB. 1966, V122, PP
     868-876.
   YEAR 1966
   DESC B.I.A. BOARDING SCHOOLS+, PSYCHOLOGICAL TESTING+,
     ETHNIC IDENTITY, SIOUX, PLAINS, SECONDARY SCHOOLS,
     ADOLESCENTS, EDUCATION PROFESSIONALS, PERSONALITY
     TRAITS+, RELOCATION, NATIVE AMERICAN VALUES
   IDEN SOUTH DAKOTA, U.S., FLANDREAU INDIAN VOCATIONAL HIGH
     SCHOOL, KLUCKHOHN VALUE ORIENTATION SCALE, M.M.P.I.,
     CALIFORNIA PSYCHOLOGICAL INVENTORY, QUAY-PETERSON
     DELINQUENCY SCALE, TIME FACTOR EVALUATION, STUDENT
     SENTENCE COMPLETION TEST, SEMANTIC DIFFERENTIAL,
     BAUER-LAMBERT SCREENING SCALE

235 AUTH KLEINFELD, JUDITH S.
   TITL INTELLECTUAL STRENGTHS IN CULTURALLY DIFFERENT GROUPS:
     AN ESKIMO ILLUSTRATION.
   SOUR REVIEW OF EDUCATIONAL RESEARCH, SUM. 1973, V43(3), PP
     341-359.
   YEAR 1973
   DESC ESKIMO, WESTERN ARCTIC, ABILITIES+, PSYCHOLOGICAL
     TESTING+, CULTURE-FAIR TESTS+, CHILDREN-SCHOOL AGE,
     OFF-RESERVATION, COGNITIVE PROCESSES+, LANGUAGE
     HANDICAPS, ELEMENTARY SCHOOLS, GENETIC FACTORS
   IDEN U.S., ALASKA, GUILFORD MODEL OF INTELLIGENCE

236 AUTH BOYER, L. BRYCE; KLOPFER, BRUNO; BRAWER, FLORENCE B.;
     KAWAI, HAYAO
   TITL COMPARISONS OF THE SHAMANS AND PSEUDOSHAMANS OF THE
     APACHES OF THE MESCALERO INDIAN RESERVATION: A
     RORSCHACH STUDY.
   SOUR JOURNAL OF PROJECTIVE TECHNIQUES AND PERSONALITY,
     1964, V28, PP 173-180.
   YEAR 1964
   DESC APACHE, SOUTHWEST, TRADITIONAL HEALERS+, WITCHCRAFT,
     PSYCHOLOGICAL TESTING+, HYSTERIA+, AGED,
     PSYCHOANALYSIS
   IDEN U.S., MESCALERO RESERVATION, RORSCHACH TEST, SCHAFER
     HYSTERIC SIGNS

237 AUTH GRAVES, THEODORE D.; ARSDALE, MINOR V.
   TITL VALUES, EXPECTATIONS AND RELOCATION: THE NAVAJO

MIGRANT TO DENVER.
SOUR HUMAN ORGANIZATION, WIN. 1966, V25(4), PP 300-307.
YEAR 1966
DESC NAVAJO, SOUTHWEST, URBAN AREAS, RELOCATION+,
URBANIZATION, PSYCHOLOGICAL TESTING+, ECONOMIC
ISSUES+, CULTURAL CONTINUITY+, EMPLOYMENT, NATIVE
AMERICAN VALUES
IDEN U.S., COLORADO

238 AUTH CHADWICK, BRUCE A.; WHITE, LYNN C.
TITL CORRELATES OF LENGTH OF URBAN RESIDENCE AMONG THE
SPOKANE INDIANS.
SOUR HUMAN ORGANIZATION, SPR. 1973, V32(1), PP 9-16.
YEAR 1973
DESC SPOKANE, PLATEAU, URBANIZATION+, ETHNIC IDENTITY+,
CULTURAL ADAPTATION+, ECONOMIC ISSUES, ADULTS,
RELOCATION+, PSYCHOLOGICAL TESTING, EXPERIMENTAL
STUDY, URBAN AREAS
IDEN U.S., WASHINGTON

239 AUTH DUNNING, R.W.
TITL ETHNIC RELATIONS AND THE MARGINAL MAN IN CANADA.
SOUR HUMAN ORGANIZATION, AUT. 1959, V18, PP 117-122.
YEAR 1959
DESC DISCRIMINATION+, EDUCATION PROFESSIONALS, MEDICAL
PROFESSIONALS, CORRECTIONS PERSONNEL,
RELIGIOUS-NON-NATIVE PERSONNEL, STRESS+, SOCIAL STATUS
IDEN CANADA

240 AUTH HURT, WESLEY R.
TITL THE URBANIZATION OF THE YANKTON SIOUX.
SOUR HUMAN ORGANIZATION, WIN. 1961-62, V20, PP 226-231.
YEAR 1961-62
DESC URBAN AREAS, URBANIZATION+, SIOUX, PLAINS, EMPLOYMENT,
DEMOGRAPHIC DATA, RELOCATION+, PERSONALITY TRAITS+,
DISCRIMINATION, ADULTS, SOCIAL NETWORKS
IDEN U.S., SOUTH DAKOTA

241 AUTH HILL, W.W.
TITL THE STATUS OF THE HERMAPHRODITE AND TRANSVESTITE IN
NAVAJO CULTURE.
SOUR AMERICAN ANTHROPOLOGIST, 1935, V37, PP 273-279.
YEAR 1935
DESC SEXUAL RELATIONS+, NAVAJO, SOUTHWEST, GROUP NORMS AND
SANCTIONS+, ADULTS, SOCIAL STATUS, SOCIAL ROLES+,
MALES+, FEMALES+
IDEN U.S., NAVAJO RESERVATION

242 AUTH PARKER, SEYMOUR
TITL ESKIMO PSYCHOPATHOLOGY IN THE CONTEXT OF ESKIMO
PERSONALITY AND CULTURE.
SOUR AMERICAN ANTHROPOLOGIST, 1962, V64, PP 76-96 ·
YEAR 1962
DESC CHIPPEWA, EASTERN SUB-ARCTIC, ESKIMO, CENTRAL AND
EASTERN ARCTIC, INTERTRIBAL COMPARISONS, MENTAL

DISORDERS+, PERSONALITY TRAITS+, ARCTIC HYSTERIA+,
TRADITIONAL CHILD REARING+, FEMALES, COOPERATION,
NATIVE AMERICAN RELIGIONS, AGGRESSIVENESS, SOCIAL
ROLES
   IDEN   CANADA, GREENLAND

243 AUTH SAVISHINSKY, JOEL S.
   TITL MOBILITY AS AN ASPECT OF STRESS IN AN ARCTIC
COMMUNITY.
   SOUR AMERICAN ANTHROPOLOGIST, 1971, V73, PP 604-618.
   YEAR 1971
   DESC HARE, MACKENZIE SUB-ARCTIC, AGGRESSIVENESS+,
COOPERATION+, OFF-RESERVATION,SOCIAL GROUPS AND PEER
GROUPS+, RELOCATION+, EMOTIONAL RESTRAINT+, NATIVE
AMERICAN COPING BEHAVIORS, ENVIRONMENTAL
FACTORS+,STRESS
   IDEN CANADA, NORTHWEST TERRITORIES

244 AUTH MAYNARD, EILEEN
   TITL THE GROWING NEGATIVE IMAGE OF THE ANTHROPOLOGIST AMONG
AMERICAN INDIANS.
   SOUR HUMAN ORGANIZATION, WIN. 1974, V33(4), PP 402-404.
   YEAR 1974
   DESC SIOUX, PLAINS, RESERVATION, RESEARCHERS+
   IDEN U.S., SOUTH DAKOTA, PINE RIDGE RESERVATION

245 AUTH BRILL, A.A.
   TITL PIBLOKTO OR HYSTERIA AMONG PEARY"S ESKIMOS.
   SOUR JOURNAL OF NERVOUS AND MENTAL DISORDERS, 1913, V40, PP
514-520.
   YEAR 1913
   DESC ESKIMO, CENTRAL AND EASTERN ARCTIC, ARCTIC HYSTERIA+,
ADULTS, FEMALES+, SEXUAL RELATIONS+, HYSTERIA,
PSYCHOANALYSIS
   IDEN GREENLAND

246 AUTH WALLACE, WILLIAM J.
   TITL THE DREAM IN MOHAVE LIFE.
   SOUR JOURNAL OF AMERICAN FOLKLORE, 1947, V60, PP 252-258.
   YEAR 1947
   DESC DREAMS AND VISION QUESTS+, MOHAVE, SOUTHWEST
   IDEN U.S.

247 AUTH TEFFT, STANTON K.
   TITL ANOMY, VALUES, AND CULTURE CHANGE AMONG TEEN-AGE
INDIANS: AN EXPLORATORY STUDY.
   SOUR SOCIOLOGY OF EDUCATION, SPR. 1967, PP 145-157.
   YEAR 1967
   DESC ANOMIE+, ADOLESCENTS+, RESERVATION, STRESS+, SHOSHONE,
ARAPAHO-NORTHERN, PLAINS, INTERTRIBAL COMPARISONS,
NATIVE-NON-NATIVE COMPARISONS, COOPERATION, UNIVERSAL
HARMONY, GENEROSITY, SOCIAL STATUS+, DISCRIMINATION+,
NATIVE AMERICAN VALUES+,SECONDARY SCHOOLS
   IDEN U.S., WIND RIVER RESERVATION, HARVARD VALUE STUDY
QUESTIONNAIRE, WYOMING

248 AUTH ROBERTS, BERYL J.; MICO, PAUL R. ; CLARK, ELIZABETH W.
    TITL AN EXPERIMENTAL STUDY OF TWO APPROACHES TO
         COMMUNICATION.
    SOUR AMERICAN JOURNAL OF PUBLIC HEALTH, SEP. 1963, V53(9),
         PP 1361-1381.
    YEAR 1963
    DESC EXPERIMENTAL STUDY, NAVAJO, SOUTHWEST, FEMALES+,
         ADULTS+, MEDICAL INSTITUTIONS+, I.H.S., FAMILY
         FUNCTIONING, CHILDREN-INFANTS AND PRESCHOOL+, DELIVERY
         OF SERVICES+, EDUCATION PROGRAMS AND SERVICES+,
         MOTIVATION, CLINICAL STUDY, RESERVATION
    IDEN U.S., NAVAJO RESERVATION

249 TITL SENATE PROBES CHILD WELFARE.
    SOUR INDIAN FAMILY DEFENSE, SUM. 1974, (6P).
    YEAR 1974
    DESC ADOPTION AND FOSTER CARE+, CHILDREN-INFANTS AND
         PRESCHOOL+, CHILDREN-SCHOOL AGE+, SOCIAL SERVICES,
         FEMALES+, FAMILY FUNCTIONING+, ETHNIC IDENTITY+
    IDEN U.S.

250 AUTH REICHARD, GLADYS A.
    TITL HUMAN NATURE AS CONCEIVED BY THE NAVAJO INDIANS.
    SOUR REVIEW OF RELIGION, 1943, V7, PP 353-360.
    YEAR 1943
    DESC NAVAJO, SOUTHWEST, UNIVERSAL HARMONY+, NATIVE AMERICAN
         RELIGIONS+, NATIVE AMERICAN ETIOLOGY+
    IDEN U.S.

251 AUTH WALLACE, ANTHONY F.C.; ACKERMAN, ROBERT E.
    TITL AN INTERDISCIPLINARY APPROACH TO MENTAL DISORDER AMONG
         THE POLAR ESKIMO OF NORTHWEST GREENLAND.
    SOUR ANTHROPOLOGICA, 1960, V2, PP 249-260.
    YEAR 1960
    DESC ESKIMO, CENTRAL AND EASTERN ARCTIC, ARCTIC HYSTERIA+,
         ADULTS, PHYSICAL HEALTH AND ILLNESS+, REVIEW OF
         LITERATURE, NUTRITIONAL FACTORS
    IDEN GREENLAND

252 AUTH LEIGHTON, ALEXANDER H.; LEIGHTON, DOROTHEA C.
    TITL SOME TYPES OF UNEASINESS AND FEAR IN A NAVAJO
         COMMUNITY.
    SOUR AMERICAN ANTHROPOLOGIST, 1942, V44, PP 194-209.
    YEAR 1942
    DESC NAVAJO, SOUTHWEST, OFF-RESERVATION, ANXIETY+, PHYSICAL
         HEALTH AND ILLNESS+,NATIVE AMERICAN ETIOLOGY,
         ENVIRONMENTAL FACTORS
    IDEN U.S., NAVAJO RESERVATION

253 AUTH WYMAN, LELAND C.; THORNE, BETTY
    TITL NOTES ON NAVAJO SUICIDE.
    SOUR AMERICAN ANTHROPOLOGIST, 1945, V47, PP 278-287.
    YEAR 1945
    DESC NAVAJO, SOUTHWEST, SUICIDE+, ADULTS, SEX DIFFERENCES,
         RESERVATION

```
      IDEN   U.S., NAVAJO RESERVATION

254   AUTH   PETERSON, JOHN H.
      TITL   ASSIMILATION, SEPARATION, AND OUT-MIGRATION IN AN
             AMERICAN INDIAN GROUP.
      SOUR   AMERICAN ANTHROPOLOGIST, 1972, V74, PP 1286-1295.
      YEAR   1972
      DESC   CHOCTAW, SOUTHEAST WOODLAND, OFF-RESERVATION, CULTURAL
             ADAPTATION, NATIVE-NON-NATIVE COMPARISONS,
             DISCRIMINATION+, RELOCATION+, EMPLOYMENT, ANGLO
             AMERICANS, BLACK AMERICANS
      IDEN   MISSISSIPPI, U.S.

255   AUTH   ABLON, JOAN
      TITL   RELOCATED AMERICAN INDIANS IN THE SAN FRANCISCO BAY
             AREA: SOCIAL INTERACTION AND INDIAN IDENTITY.
      SOUR   HUMAN ORGANIZATION, WIN. 1964, V23, PP 296-304.
      YEAR   1964
      DESC   RELOCATION+, URBAN AREAS, URBANIZATION+, EMPLOYMENT,
             FAMILY FUNCTIONING+, SIOUX, NAVAJO, CHIPPEWA, PLAINS,
             SOUTHWEST, EASTERN SUB-ARCTIC, SOCIAL NETWORKS,
             INTERTRIBAL COMPARISONS, CULTURAL CONTINUITY+, ANGLO
             AMERICANS
      IDEN   CALIFORNIA, U.S.

256   AUTH   DANE, J.K.; GRIESSMAN, B. EUGENE
      TITL   THE COLLECTIVE IDENTITY OF MARGINAL PEOPLES: THE NORTH
             CAROLINA EXPERIENCE.
      SOUR   AMERICAN ANTHROPOLOGIST, 1972, V74, PP 694-703.
      YEAR   1972
      DESC   ETHNIC IDENTITY+, DEMOGRAPHIC DATA, CULTURAL REVIVAL+,
             HALIWA, LUMBEE, SOUTHEAST WOODLAND
      IDEN   U.S., NORTH CAROLINA

257   AUTH   ACKERMAN, LILLIAN A.
      TITL   MARITAL INSTABILITY AND JUVENILE DELINQUENCY AMONG THE
             NEZ PERCES.
      SOUR   AMERICAN ANTHROPOLOGIST, 1971, V73, PP 595-603.
      YEAR   1971
      DESC   ADOLESCENTS+, SOCIALLY DEVIANT BEHAVIOR+, NEZ PERCE,
             PLATEAU, NONINTERFERENCE, EXTENDED FAMILY+, FAMILY
             FUNCTIONING+, TRADITIONAL SOCIAL CONTROL+, TRADITIONAL
             CHILD REARING+, SEXUAL RELATIONS+, MARITAL
             RELATIONSHIPS
      IDEN   U.S., IDAHO

258   AUTH   DIMOCK, EDMUND; RIEGEL, BARBARA
      TITL   VOLUNTEERING TO HELP INDIANS HELP THEMSELVES.
      SOUR   CHILDREN, JAN.-FEB. 1971, V18(1), PP 23-27.
      YEAR   1971
      DESC   CALIFORNIA AREA, RESERVATION, ECONOMIC ISSUES, SOCIAL
             SERVICES+, STEREOTYPES+, ELEMENTARY SCHOOLS+,
             DROPOUTS+, PREVENTIVE MENTAL HEALTH PROGRAMS,
             CHILDREN-SCHOOL AGE+, DISCRIMINATION+
      IDEN   U.S., CALIFORNIA, VIEJAS RESERVATION
```

259 AUTH BIGART, ROBERT J.
    TITL INDIAN CULTURE AND INDUSTRIALIZATION.
    SOUR AMERICAN ANTHROPOLOGIST, 1972, V74, PP 1180-1188.
    YEAR 1972
    DESC CULTURAL ADAPTATION+, TRADITIONAL SOCIAL CONTROL,
         NONCOMPETITIVENESS, UNIVERSAL HARMONY, GENEROSITY,
         TIME PERCEPTION, EMPLOYMENT+, PERSONALITY TRAITS,
         RESERVATION, TRIBAL POLITICAL ORGANIZATIONS+, CULTURAL
         CONTINUITY+
    IDEN U.S.

260 AUTH MOHATT, GERALD
    TITL THE SACRED WATER: THE QUEST FOR PERSONAL POWER THROUGH
         DRINKING AMONG THE TETON SIOUX.
    SOUR IN DAVID C. MCCLELLAN, W.S. DAVIS, R. KALIN, AND E.
         WANNER (EDS.), THE DRINKING MAN: ALCOHOL AND HUMAN
         MOTIVATION, PP 261-275, NEW YORK: FREE PRESS, 1972.
    YEAR 1972
    DESC SIOUX, PLAINS, SOCIAL STATUS+, STRESS+, DREAMS AND
         VISION QUESTS, AGGRESSIVENESS, RESERVATION, ALCOHOL
         USE+, ADOLESCENTS
    IDEN U.S., SOUTH DAKOTA

261 AUTH BOWMAN, BEULAH; CARLIN, WALTER; GARCIA, ANTHONY;
         MAYBEE, CHRIS; MILLER, DOROTHY; SIERRAS, PEGGY
    TITL AMERICAN INDIAN SOCIALIZATION TO URBAN LIFE: FINAL
         REPORT.
    SOUR SAN FRANCISCO: SCIENTIFIC ANALYSIS CORPORATION, N.D.
         (110P), (NIMH GRANT NO.MH 22719)
    DESC URBAN AREAS, URBANIZATION+, SIOUX, PLAINS, NAVAJO,
         SOUTHWEST, CALIFORNIA AREA, CALIFORNIA INDIANS,
         CULTURAL CONTINUITY+, DEMOGRAPHIC DATA, EXTENDED
         FAMILY+, SOCIAL NETWORKS, FAMILY FUNCTIONING+, ADULTS,
         CHILDREN-SCHOOL AGE,TRADITIONAL CHILD REARING+, ETHNIC
         IDENTITY+, CHILDREN-INFANTS AND PRESCHOOL,
         ADOLESCENTS, NATIVE AMERICAN VALUES+
    IDEN U.S., CALIFORNIA

262 AUTH WESTERMEYER, JOSEPH
    TITL COMPARATIVE STUDIES AND THEIR PROBLEMS.
    SOUR OFFICIAL NEWSLETTER OF THE ASSOCIATION OF AMERICAN
         INDIAN PHYSICIANS, JUN. 1976, V4(3), PP 4-6.
    YEAR 1976
    DESC EPIDEMIOLOGICAL STUDY, ALCOHOL USE+, PHYSICAL HEALTH
         AND ILLNESS
    IDEN U.S., MINNESOTA

263 AUTH KAHN, MARVIN W.; LEWIS, JESSE; GALVEZ, EUGENE
    TITL AN EVALUATION STUDY OF A GROUP THERAPY PROCEDURE WITH
         RESERVATION ADOLESCENT INDIANS.
    SOUR PSYCHOTHERAPY: THEORY, RESEARCH AND PRACTICE, AUT.
         1974, V11(3), PP 239-242.
    YEAR 1974
    DESC PSYCHOTHERAPY AND COUNSELING+, SOCIAL GROUPS AND PEER
         GROUPS+, ADOLESCENTS+, PAPAGO, SOUTHWEST, RESERVATION,

```
              MALES, SOCIALLY DEVIANT BEHAVIOR+, PREVENTIVE MENTAL
              HEALTH PROGRAMS
       IDEN   U.S., ARIZONA

264    AUTH   REED, T. EDWARD; KALANT, HAROLD
       TITL   METABOLISM OF ETHANOL IN DIFFERENT RACIAL GROUPS.
       SOUR   CANADIAN MEDICAL ASSOCIATION JOURNAL, MAR. 1977, V116,
              P 476.
       YEAR   1977
       DESC   ALCOHOL USE+, NATIVE-NON-NATIVE COMPARISONS, ANGLO
              AMERICANS, ASIAN AMERICANS, INTERTRIBAL COMPARISONS,
              SOUTHWEST, EASTERN SUB-ARCTIC,GENETIC FACTORS+
       IDEN   CANADA

265    AUTH   SLOCUMB, JOHN C.; ODOROFF, CHARLES L.; KUNITZ, STEPHEN
              J.
       TITL   THE USE-EFFECTIVENESS OF TWO CONTRACEPTIVE METHODS IN
              A NAVAJO POPULATION: THE PROBLEM OF PROGRAM DROPOUTS.
       SOUR   AMERICAN JOURNAL OF OBSTETRICS AND GYNECOLOGY, JUL.
              1975, V122 (6), PP 717-726
       YEAR   1975
       DESC   NAVAJO, SOUTHWEST, FEMALES+, ADULTS+, FAMILY
              PLANNING+, DROPOUTS+, RESERVATION, DEMOGRAPHIC DATA,
              I.H.S., PROGRAM EVALUATION+
       IDEN   U.S. , NAVAJO RESERVATION

266    AUTH   BERLIN, IRVING N.
       TITL   ANGLO ADOPTIONS OF NATIVE AMERICANS: REPERCUSSIONS IN
              ADOLESCENCE.
       SOUR   JOURNAL OF THE AMERICAN ACADEMY OF CHILD PSYCHIATRY,
              1978, V17 (2), PP 387-388.
       YEAR   1978
       DESC   ANGLO AMERICANS, ADOPTION AND FOSTER CARE+,
              ADOLESCENTS+
       IDEN   U.S.

267    AUTH   BROWN, JOSEPH EPES
       TITL   THE PERSISTENCE OF ESSENTIAL VALUES AMONG NORTH
              AMERICAN PLAINS INDIANS.
       SOUR   STUDIES IN COMPARATIVE RELIGION, AUT. 1969, V3, PP
              216-225
       YEAR   1969
       DESC   PLAINS, CULTURAL CONTINUITY+, NATIVE AMERICAN
              RELIGIONS+, CULTURAL REVIVAL
       IDEN   U.S.

268    AUTH   MCCLENDON, WILLIAM H.
       TITL   THE BLACK SCHOLAR INTERVIEW: DENNIS BANKS.
       SOUR   THE BLACK SCHOLAR, JUN. 1976, V7, PP 29-36.
       YEAR   1976
       DESC   NATIVE AMERICAN POLITICAL MOVEMENTS+, DISCRIMINATION+,
              URBAN AREAS, URBANIZATION+, CULTURAL REVIVAL+
       IDEN   U.S., AMERICAN INDIAN MOVEMENT

269    AUTH   DEMONTIGNY, LIONEL H.
```

```
          TITL  THE BUREAUCRATIC GAME AND A PROPOSED INDIAN PLOY.
          SOUR  INDIAN HISTORIAN, AUT. 1975, V8(2), PP 25-30.
          YEAR  1975
          DESC  FEDERAL GOVERNMENT,  POLITICS-NONTRIBAL+, NATIVE
                AMERICAN PERSONNEL+, B.I.A., I.H.S.
          IDEN  U.S.

270  AUTH  HOOD, WILLIAM R.
          TITL  DIRTY WORDS: GENETIC DIFFERENCES IN RESPONSE TO
                ALCOHOL.
          SOUR  PAPER PRESENTED AT THE MEETING OF THE AMERICAN
                PSYCHOLOGICAL ASSOCIATION, HONOLULU, SEP. 1972.
          YEAR  1972
          DESC  ALCOHOL USE+, SOUTHWEST, PHYSICAL HEALTH AND ILLNESS,
                NATIVE-NON-NATIVE COMPARISONS, TARAHUMARA, REVIEW OF
                LITERATURE, NUTRITIONAL FACTORS, ANGLO
                AMERICANS,GENETIC FACTORS+
          IDEN  U.S., MEXICO

271  AUTH  CARDELL, GEORGE W.; CROSS, WILLIAM C.; LUTZ, W. JAMES
          TITL  EXTENDING COUNSELOR INFLUENCE INTO THE CLASSROOM.
          SOUR  JOURNAL OF AMERICAN INDIAN EDUCATION, JAN. 1978, V17
                (2), PP 7-12.
          YEAR  1978
          DESC  PSYCHOTHERAPY AND COUNSELING+, SOCIAL GROUPS AND PEER
                GROUPS+, APACHE-MESCALERO, SOUTHWEST, CHILDREN-SCHOOL
                AGE+, ELEMENTARY SCHOOLS, EXPERIMENTAL STUDY,
                LEARNING+
          IDEN  U.S.

272  AUTH  DENNIS, WAYNE
          TITL  THE PERFORMANCE OF HOPI CHILDREN ON THE THE GOODENOUGH
                DRAW-A-MAN TEST
          SOUR  JOURNAL OF COMPARATIVE PSYCHOLOGY, DEC. 1942, V34 (3),
                PP 341-348.
          YEAR  1942
          DESC  PUEBLO-HOPI, SOUTHWEST, RESERVATION, CHILDREN-SCHOOL
                AGE+, PSYCHOLOGICAL TESTING+, CULTURE-FAIR TESTS+,
                ABILITIES+, NATIVE-NON-NATIVE COMPARISONS, ANGLO
                AMERICANS
          IDEN  U.S., ARIZONA, GOODENOUGH HARRIS DRAW A PERSON TEST

273  AUTH  DENNIS, WAYNE; DENNIS, MARSENA G.
          TITL  THE EFFECT OF CRADLING PRACTICES UPON THE ONSET OF
                WALKING IN HOPI CHILDREN.
          SOUR  JOURNAL OF GENETIC PSYCHOLOGY, MAR. 1940, V56, PP
                77-86.
          YEAR  1940
          DESC  CHILDREN-INFANTS AND PRESCHOOL+, TRADITIONAL CHILD
                REARING+, PUEBLO-HOPI, SOUTHWEST, MOTOR
                PROCESSES+,RESERVATION, NATIVE-NON-NATIVE COMPARISONS,
                ANGLO AMERICANS
          IDEN  U.S., ARIZONA, HOPI RESERVATION

274  AUTH  LEMERT, EDWIN M.
```

```
      TITL   LETTERS TO THE EDITOR: ON ALCOHOLISM AMONG THE
             NORTHWEST COAST INDIANS.
      SOUR   AMERICAN ANTHROPOLOGIST, 1956, V58, PP 561-562.
      YEAR   1956
      DESC   NORTHWEST COAST, ALCOHOL USE+
      IDEN   U.S., CANADA

275   AUTH   INDIAN HEALTH SERVICE
      TITL   MENTAL HEALTH ACTIVITIES IN THE INDIAN HEALTH PROGRAM.
      SOUR   INDIAN HEALTH SERVICE, WASHINGTON, D.C.: AUTHOR, 1968.
      YEAR   1968
      DESC   MENTAL HEALTH PROGRAMS AND SERVICES+, DELIVERY OF
             SERVICES+, RESERVATION, MENTAL HEALTH INSTITUTIONS,
             CONSULTATION, MENTAL HEALTH PROFESSIONALS, PROGRAM
             DEVELOPMENT+, I.H.S.
      IDEN   U.S.

276   AUTH   BASS, WILLARD P.
      TITL   AN EVALUATION OF THE BORDERTOWN DORMITORY PROGRAM.
      SOUR   (B.I.A. CONTRACT NO. NOOC 1420 3411). ALBUQUERQUE, NEW
             MEXICO: SOUTHWESTERN COOPERATIVE EDUCATIONAL
             LABORATORY, 1971. (63P)
      YEAR   1971
      DESC   NAVAJO, SECONDARY SCHOOLS+, ACHIEVEMENT, PROGRAM
             EVALUATION+, BOARDING HOMES+, EDUCATION PROGRAMS AND
             SERVICES+, SOUTHWEST
      IDEN   U.S.

277   AUTH   DEVEREUX, GEORGE
      TITL   STATUS, SOCIALIZATION, AND INTERPERSONAL RELATIONS OF
             MOHAVE CHILDREN.
      SOUR   PSYCHIATRY, NOV. 1950, V13 (4), PP 489-502
      YEAR   1950
      DESC   TRADITIONAL CHILD REARING+, MOHAVE, SOUTHWEST, SOCIAL
             STATUS+, CHILDREN-SCHOOL AGE, AGE COMPARISONS,
             CHILDREN-INFANTS AND PRESCHOOL, SOCIAL ROLES+,
             GENEROSITY, EXTENDED FAMILY+
      IDEN   U.S.

278   AUTH   DEVEREUX, GEORGE
      TITL   MOHAVE INDIAN OBSTETRICS: A PSYCHOANALYTIC STUDY.
      SOUR   AMERICAN IMAGO, JULY 1948, V5(2), PP 95-139.
      YEAR   1948
      DESC   MOHAVE, SOUTHWEST, FEMALES+, CHILDREN-INFANTS AND
             PRESCHOOL+, TRADITIONAL HEALERS+, SEXUAL RELATIONS+,
             PSYCHOANALYSIS
      IDEN   U.S.

279   AUTH   ALASKA NATIVE HEALTH BOARD
      TITL   EVALUATION OF ALCOHOLISM TREATMENT SERVICES IN THE
             STATE OF ALASKA: A DESCRIPTION OF SERVICE AGENCY
             OPERATIONS.
      SOUR   (HSMA CONTRACT NO. HSM 76-72-328). ANCHORAGE: AUTHOR,
             1973. (36P)
      YEAR   1973
```

```
          DESC  ALCOHOL USE+, ALASKA NATIVES, ALCOHOLISM TREATMENT+,
                PROGRAM EVALUATION+, DELIVERY OF SERVICES+, MEDICAL
                INSTITUTIONS, OFF-RESERVATION
          IDEN  U.S., ALASKA

    280   AUTH  AMES, DAVID W.; BURTON, R. FISHER
          TITL  THE MENOMINEE TERMINATION CRISIS: BARRIERS IN THE WAY
                OF A RAPID CULTURAL TRANSITION.
          SOUR  HUMAN ORGANIZATION, AUT. 1959, V18, PP 101-111.
          YEAR  1959
          DESC  MENOMINEE, NORTHEAST WOODLAND, RESERVATION, FEDERAL
                GOVERNMENT+, ANXIETY+, CULTURAL ADAPTATION+, ECONOMIC
                ISSUES, EMPLOYMENT, NATIVE AMERICAN PERSONNEL, ETHNIC
                IDENTITY, TRIBAL POLITICAL ORGANIZATIONS
          IDEN  U.S., WISCONSIN, MENOMINEE RESERVATION, U.S. PUBLIC
                LAW 399

    281   AUTH  DENNIS, WAYNE; RUSSELL, R.W.
          TITL  PIAGET'S QUESTIONS APPLIED TO ZUNI CHILDREN.
          SOUR  CHILD DEVELOPMENT, SEP. 1940, V11 (3), PP 181-187.
          YEAR  1940
          DESC  PUEBLO-ZUNI, SOUTHWEST, CHILDREN-SCHOOL AGE,
                ADOLESCENTS, PSYCHOLOGICAL TESTING+,
                RESERVATION,ABILITIES+, NATIVE-NON-NATIVE COMPARISONS,
                ANGLO AMERICANS, COGNITIVE PROCESSES+, ENVIRONMENTAL
                FACTORS
          IDEN  U.S., PIAGETIAN TASKS

    282   AUTH  DINGES, NORMAN G.; HOLLENBECK, ALBERT R.
          TITL  FIELD DEPENDENCE-INDEPENDENCE IN NAVAJO CHILDREN.
          SOUR  INTERNATIONAL JOURNAL OF PSYCHOLOGY, 1978, V13 (3), PP
                215-220.
          YEAR  1978
          DESC  NAVAJO, SOUTHWEST, CHILDREN-SCHOOL AGE, PSYCHOLOGICAL
                TESTING+, NATIVE-NON-NATIVE COMPARISONS, ANGLO
                AMERICANS, EXTENDED FAMILY, SEX DIFFERENCES, FAMILY
                FUNCTIONING, COGNITIVE PROCESSES+, RESERVATION
          IDEN  U.S., NAVAJO RESERVATION, EMBEDDED FIGURES TEST

    283   AUTH  STREIB, GORDON F.
          TITL  THE USE OF SURVEY METHODS AMONG THE NAVAJO.
          SOUR  AMERICAN ANTHROPOLOGIST, JAN.-MAR. 1952, V54, PP 30-40.
          YEAR  1952
          DESC  NAVAJO, SOUTHWEST, SURVEY, RESEARCHERS+, RESERVATION
          IDEN  U.S., NAVAJORESERVATION

    284   AUTH  FELDSTEIN, AARON
          TITL  THE METABOLISM OF ALCOHOL: ON THE VALIDITY OF THE
                WIDMARK EQUATIONS, IN OBESITY, AND IN RACIAL AND
                ETHNIC GROUPS.
          SOUR  JOURNAL OF STUDIES ON ALCOHOL, 1978, V39 (5), PP
                926-932.
          YEAR  1978
          DESC  ALCOHOL USE+, NATIVE-NON-NATIVE COMPARISONS, ANGLO
                AMERICANS, PHYSICAL HEALTH AND ILLNESS+, CHIPPEWA,
```

```
           EASTERN SUB-ARCTIC, NUTRITIONAL FACTORS+, GENETIC
           FACTORS+
      IDEN U.S.

285   AUTH KALANT, HAROLD; REED, T. EDWARD
      TITL LIMITATIONS OF THE WIDMARK CALCULATION: A REPLY TO
           FELDSTEIN'S CRITIQUE.
      SOUR JOURNAL OF STUDIES ON ALCOHOL, 1978, V39 (5), PP
           933-935.
      YEAR 1978
      DESC ALCOHOL USE+, CHIPPEWA, EASTERN SUB-ARCTIC,
           NATIVE-NON-NATIVE COMPARISONS, ANGLO AMERICANS,
           PHYSICAL HEALTH AND ILLNESS
      IDEN CANADA

286   AUTH ROZYNKO, VITALI V.; FERGUSON, LARA C.
      TITL ADMISSION CHARACTERISTICS OF INDIAN AND WHITE
           ALCOHOLIC PATIENTS IN A RURAL MENTAL HOSPITAL.
      SOUR INTERNATIONAL JOURNAL OF THE ADDICTIONS, 1978, V13
           (4), PP 591-604.
      YEAR 1978
      DESC MENTAL HEALTH INSTITUTIONS, ALCOHOL USE+,
           NATIVE-NON-NATIVE COMPARISONS, ANGLO AMERICANS,
           ALCOHOLISM TREATMENT+, RESEARCHERS+, PROGRAM
           DEVELOPMENT, COMMUNITY INVOLVEMENT
      IDEN U.S., CALIFORNIA

287   AUTH VOGEL, VIRGIL J.
      TITL AMERICAN INDIAN INFLUENCE ON THE AMERICAN
           PHARMACOPEIA.
      SOUR AMERICAN INDIAN CULTURE AND RESEARCH, 1977, V2 (1), PP
           3-7.
      YEAR 1977
      DESC TRADITIONAL USE OF DRUGS AND ALCOHOL+, DRUG USE+
      IDEN U.S., CANADA

288   AUTH TRIMBLE, JOSEPH E.
      TITL AN INDEX OF THE SOCIAL INDICATORS OF THE AMERICAN
           INDIAN IN OKLAHOMA.
      SOUR REPORT PREPARED FOR OFFICE OF COMMUNITY AFFAIRS AND
           PLANNING, STATE OF OKLAHOMA.  OKLAHOMA CITY, 1972.
           (564P)
      YEAR 1972
      DESC OKLAHOMA INDIANS, DEMOGRAPHIC DATA, OFF-RESERVATION,
           MENTAL HEALTH INSTITUTIONS, INSTITUTIONALIZATION,
           OUTPATIENT CARE, CRIME, ADOLESCENTS, SOCIALLY DEVIANT
           BEHAVIOR, EMPLOYMENT, EDUCATION PROGRAMS AND
           SERVICES+, MEDICAL PROGRAMS AND SERVICES+, SOCIAL
           SERVICES+, MENTAL HEALTH PROGRAMS AND SERVICES+
      IDEN U.S., OKLAHOMA

289   AUTH WESTERMEYER, JOSEPH
      TITL SUGGESTIONS FOR NON-INDIAN MENTAL HEALTH WORKER
           WORKING WITH AMERICAN INDIAN ALCOHOLICS.
      SOUR PAPER PRESENTED AT THE MEETING OF THE AMERICAN
```

```
               PSYCHOLOGICAL ASSOCIATION, 1972.   (10P)
      YEAR  1972
      DESC  ALCOHOL USE+, MENTAL HEALTH PARAPROFESSIONALS+,
            ALCOHOLISM TREATMENT+, PROGRAM DEVELOPMENT+,
            STEREOTYPES
      IDEN  U.S.

290   AUTH  MCNICKLE, D'ARCY
      TITL  THE INDIAN IN AMERICAN SOCIETY.
      SOUR  SOCIAL WELFARE FORUM, 1955, PP 68-77.
      YEAR  1955
      DESC  CULTURAL CONTINUITY+, ADMINISTRATIVE ISSUES+, FEDERAL
            GOVERNMENT, CULTURAL ADAPTATION
      IDEN  U.S.

291   AUTH  BONNEY, RACHEL A.
      TITL  THE ROLE OF AIM LEADERS IN INDIAN NATIONALISM.
      SOUR  AMERICAN INDIAN QUARTERLY, AUT. 1977, V3 (3), PP
            209-224.
      YEAR  1977
      DESC  ETHNIC IDENTITY+, NATIVE AMERICAN POLITICAL
            MOVEMENTS+, URBAN AREAS, DISCRIMINATION+
      IDEN  U.S., AMERICAN INDIAN MOVEMENT

292   AUTH  MEDICINE, BEATRICE
      TITL  THE ANTHROPOLOGIST AS THE INDIAN"S IMAGE-MAKER.
      SOUR  INDIAN HISTORIAN, FALL 1971, V4, PP 27-29.
      YEAR  1971
      DESC  RESEARCHERS+, STEREOTYPES+, SELF-CONCEPT

293   AUTH  LESSER, ALEXANDER
      TITL  EDUCATION AND THE FUTURE OF TRIBALISM IN THE UNITED
            STATES: THE CASE OF THEAMERICAN INDIAN.
      SOUR  SOCIAL SERVICE REVIEW, JUN. 1961, V35(2), PP 135-143.
      YEAR  1961
      DESC  CULTURAL CONTINUITY+, CULTURAL ADAPTATION+, EDUCATION
            PROGRAMS AND SERVICES+
      IDEN  U.S.

294   AUTH  HOFFMANN, HELMUT
      TITL  HOSPITALIZED ALCOHOLIC OJIBWAY INDIANS: METHODOLOGICAL
            PROBLEMS OF A CROSS-CULTURAL COMPARISON.
      SOUR  PAPER PRESENTED AT THE ANTHROPOLOGY AND MENTAL HEALTH
            SESSIONS OF THE 9TH INTERNATIONAL CONGRESS OF
            ANTHROPOLOGICAL AND ETHNOLOGICAL SCIENCES, CHICAGO,
            AUG./SEP. 1973.   (23P)
      YEAR  1973
      DESC  CHIPPEWA, EASTERN SUB-ARCTIC,  INSTITUTIONALIZATION+,
            DEMOGRAPHIC DATA, EPIDEMIOLOGICAL STUDY, PSYCHOLOGICAL
            TESTING, ALCOHOL USE+, EXPERIMENTAL STUDY, CLINICAL
            STUDY, NATIVE-NON-NATIVE COMPARISONS, MENTAL HEALTH
            INSTITUTIONS
      IDEN  U.S., M.M.P.I. PERSONALITY RESEARCH FORM, DIFFERENTIAL
            PERSONALITY INVENTORY
```

295 AUTH HOWARD, JAMES H.
     TITL THE NATIVE AMERICAN IMAGE IN WESTERN EUROPE.
     SOUR AMERICAN INDIAN QUARTERLY, FEB. 1978, V4 (1), PP 33-56.
     YEAR 1978
     DESC STEREOTYPES+, CULTURAL ADAPTATION, NATIVE-NON-NATIVE
           COMPARISONS
     IDEN NORTH AMERICA, EUROPE

296 AUTH MARRIOTT, ALICE; RACHLIN, CAROL
     TITL INDIANS 1966: FOUR CASE HISTORIES.
     SOUR SOUTHWEST REVIEW, SPR. 1966, PP 149-160.
     YEAR 1966
     DESC URBAN AREAS, URBANIZATION+, FAMILY FUNCTIONING+,
           SEXUAL RELATIONS+, ADOLESCENTS, ADULTS, SOCIAL
           NETWORKS
     IDEN U.S.

297 AUTH BLANCHARD, EVELYN
     TITL THE QUESTION OF BEST INTEREST.
     SOUR IN THE DESTRUCTION OF AMERICAN INDIAN FAMILIES,
           STEPHEN UNGER (ED.), PP 57-60. NEW YORK: ASSOCIATION
           ON AMERICAN INDIAN AFFAIRS, 1977.
     YEAR 1977
     DESC CHILDREN-SCHOOL AGE+, SOCIAL SERVICES+, ADOPTION AND'
           FOSTER CARE+
     IDEN U.S.

298 AUTH LOPEZ, BARRY
     TITL THE AMERICAN INDIAN MIND.
     SOUR QUEST, SEP.-OCT. 1978, V2 (5), PP 109-124.
     YEAR 1978
     DESC NATIVE AMERICAN VALUES+, NATIVE AMERICAN RELIGIONS+,
           TIME PERCEPTION, TRADITIONAL USE OF DRUGS AND ALCOHOL,
           COGNITIVE PROCESSES
     IDEN U.S.

299 AUTH WAX, ROSALIE H.; THOMAS, ROBERT K.
     TITL AMERICAN INDIANS AND WHITE PEOPLE.
     SOUR PHYLON, WIN. 1961, V22(4), PP 305-317.
     YEAR 1961
     DESC STRESS+, NONINTERFERENCE+, TRADITIONAL CHILD REARING+,
           PASSIVE RESISTANCE+
     IDEN U.S.

300 AUTH FRENCH, LAURENCE A.; HORNBUCKLE, JIM
     TITL AN ANALYSIS OF INDIAN VIOLENCE: THE CHEROKEE EXAMPLE.
     SOUR AMERICAN INDIAN QUARTERLY, WIN. 1977-78, V3 (4), PP
           335-356.
     YEAR 1977-78
     DESC CHEROKEE, SOUTHEAST WOODLAND, AGGRESSIVENESS+,
           TRADITIONAL SOCIAL CONTROL+, RESERVATION, STRESS+,
           CRIME+
     IDEN U.S., QUALLA BOUNDARY

301 AUTH TEICHER, MORTON I.

```
         TITL  THREE CASES OF PSYCHOSIS AMONG THE ESKIMOS.
         SOUR  JOURNAL OF MENTAL SCIENCE, 1954, V100, PP 527-535.
         YEAR  1954
         DESC  PSYCHOSES+, ESKIMO, CENTRAL AND EASTERN ARCTIC, NATIVE
               AMERICAN ETIOLOGY+, SCHIZOPHRENIA+, CLINICAL STUDY
         IDEN  CANADA, NORTHWEST TERRITORIES

302      AUTH  BROWN, JOSEPH EPES
         TITL  MODES OF CONTEMPLATION THROUGH ACTION: NORTH AMERICAN
               INDIANS.
         SOUR  PAPER PRESENTED AT THE COLLOQUIUM ON TRADITIONAL MODES
               OF CONTEMPLATION ANDACTION, HOUSTON, JULY 1973, (15P).
         YEAR  1973
         DESC  NATIVE AMERICAN RELIGIONS+, SIOUX, PLAINS, UNIVERSAL
               HARMONY+, DREAMS AND VISION QUESTS+

303      AUTH  GREEN, RAYNA D.
         TITL  TRAITS OF INDIAN CHARACTER: THE "INDIAN" ANECDOTE IN
               AMERICAN VERNACULAR TRADITION.
         SOUR  SOUTHERN FOLKLORE QUARTERLY, SEP. 1975, V39(3), PP
               233-262.
         YEAR  1975
         DESC  STEREOTYPES+, STRESS

304      AUTH  SUTTLES, WAYNE
         TITL  THE PLATEAU PROPHET DANCE AMONG THE COAST SALISH.
         SOUR  SOUTHWESTERN JOURNAL OF ANTHROPOLOGY, 1957, V13, PP
               352-396.
         YEAR  1957
         DESC  CULTURAL REVIVAL+, COAST SALISH, NORTHWEST COAST,
               NATIVE AMERICAN RELIGIONS+, PLATEAU,
               RELIGIONS-NON-NATIVE
         IDEN  U.S., WASHINGTON, PROPHET DANCE

305      AUTH  GREEN, RAYNA D.
         TITL  THE POCAHONTAS PERPLEX: THE IMAGE OF INDIAN WOMEN IN
               AMERICAN CULTURE.
         SOUR  MASSACHUSETTS REVIEW, 1975, V14, PP 698-714.
         YEAR  1975
         DESC  FEMALES+, STEREOTYPES+, SEXUAL RELATIONS+,
               DISCRIMINATION+, SOCIAL ROLES+, ROLE MODELS+
         IDEN  U.S., POCAHONTAS

306      AUTH  OGDEN, MICHAEL; SPECTOR, MOZART I,; HILL, CHARLES A.
         TITL  SUICIDE AND HOMICIDES AMONG INDIANS.
         SOUR  PUBLIC HEALTH REPORTS, JAN. 1970, V85(1), PP 75-80.
         YEAR  1970
         DESC  SUICIDE+, CRIME+, EPIDEMIOLOGICAL STUDY, AGE
               COMPARISONS, SEX DIFFERENCES, PREVENTIVE MENTAL HEALTH
               PROGRAMS+, ADOLESCENTS, I.H.S.
         IDEN  U.S.

307      AUTH  ALASKA NATIVE HEALTH BOARD
         TITL  ADULT ALCOHOLISM SEVERITY AND CLIENT CHARACTERISTICS
               IN ALASKA.
```

```
    SOUR  (NIAAA GRANT NO. 2R18-AA-01922-01). ANCHORAGE: AUTHOR,
          1976.
    YEAR  1976
    DESC  ALCOHOLISM TREATMENT, ALCOHOL USE+, ALASKA NATIVES,
          ADULTS, EPIDEMIOLOGICAL STUDY
    IDEN  U.S., ALASKA

308 AUTH  ALLINSMITH, WESLEY; GOETHALS, GEORGE W.
    TITL  CULTURAL FACTORS IN MENTAL HEALTH: AN ANTHROPOLOGICAL
          PERSPECTIVE.
    SOUR  REVIEW OF EDUCATIONAL RESEARCH, DEC. 1956, V26, PP
          429-450.
    YEAR  1956
    DESC  STRESS+, CULTURAL ADAPTATION+, NATIVE-NON-NATIVE
          COMPARISONS, TRADITIONAL CHILD REARING, EDUCATION
          PROGRAMS AND SERVICES+, LATINOS, ASIAN AMERICANS

309 AUTH  JENNESS, DIAMOND
    TITL  AN INDIAN METHOD OF TREATING HYSTERIA.
    SOUR  PRIMITIVE MAN, 1933, V6, PP 13-20.
    YEAR  1933
    DESC  CARRIER, PLATEAU, CULTURE-BASED PSYCHOTHERAPY, NATIVE
          AMERICAN ETIOLOGY, CULTURE-SPECIFIC SYNDROMES,
          HYSTERIA+, DREAMS AND VISION QUESTS
    IDEN  CANADA, BRITISH COLUMBIA

310 AUTH  ALASKA NATIVE HEALTH BOARD
    TITL  ADOLESCENT ALCOHOLISM: A RELATIONSHIP TO OTHER MENTAL
          PROBLEMS.
    SOUR  (NIAAA GRANT NO. 1R18-AA-01922-01). ANCHORAGE: AUTHOR,
          1976.
    YEAR  1976
    DESC  ALCOHOL USE+, ADOLESCENTS+, B.I.A. BOARDING SCHOOLS,
          EPIDEMIOLOGICAL STUDY
    IDEN  U.S., ALASKA

311 AUTH  JOHNSON, LUSITA G.; PROSKAUER, STEPHEN
    TITL  HYSTERICAL PSYCHOSIS IN A PREPUBESCENT NAVAJO GIRL.
    SOUR  JOURNAL OF THE AMERICAN ACADEMY OF CHILD PSYCHIATRY,
          WIN. 1974, V13, PP 1-19.
    YEAR  1974
    DESC  HYSTERIA+, NAVAJO, SOUTHWEST, STRESS+, GHOST SICKNESS,
          EXTENDED FAMILY, PSYCHOTHERAPY AND COUNSELING+,
          CULTURE-BASED PSYCHOTHERAPY+, FEMALES, CHILDREN-SCHOOL
          AGE, RESERVATION, B.I.A. BOARDING SCHOOLS, CLINICAL
          STUDY
    IDEN  U.S., NAVAJO RESERVATION

312 AUTH  HALLOWELL, A. IRVING
    TITL  VALUES, ACCULTURATION AND MENTAL HEALTH.
    SOUR  AMERICAN JOURNAL OF ORTHOPSYCHIATRY, OCT. 1950, V20,
          PP 732-743.
    YEAR  1950
    DESC  PERSONALITY TRAITS+, CHIPPEWA, CULTURAL CONTINUITY+,
          DREAMS AND VISION QUESTS, MALES, UNIVERSAL HARMONY,
```

EMOTIONAL RESTRAINT, EASTERN SUB-ARCTIC, PSYCHOLOGICAL
TESTING+, SEX DIFFERENCES
IDEN   CANADA, U.S., RORSCHACH TEST

313 AUTH   HALLOWELL, A. IRVING
     TITL   SIN, SEX, AND SICKNESS IN SAULTAUX BELIEF.
     SOUR   BRITISH JOURNAL OF MEDICAL PSYCHOLOGY, 1939, V18, PP
            191-197.
     YEAR   1939
     DESC   CHIPPEWA, EASTERN SUB-ARCTIC, NATIVE AMERICAN
            ETIOLOGY+, SEXUAL RELATIONS+,TABOO BREAKING+,
            CULTURE-BASED PSYCHOTHERAPY+, NATIVE AMERICAN COPING
            BEHAVIORS, CONFESSION+
     IDEN   CANADA, ONTARIO

314 AUTH   DUCK VALLEY INDIAN RESERVATION. TRIBAL MENTAL HEALTH
            COMMITTEE
     TITL   SUICIDE AMONG THE SHOSHONE-PAIUTE ON THE DUCK VALLEY
            INDIAN RESERVATION.
     SOUR   DUCK VALLEY INDIAN RESERVATION. TRIBAL MENTAL HEALTH
            COMMITTEE. (CONTRACT NO. HSM 73-70-235), JUN. 1970.
            (18P)
     YEAR   1970
     DESC   SUICIDE+, SHOSHONE, PAIUTE, GREAT BASIN, RESERVATION,
            DEMOGRAPHIC DATA, EPIDEMIOLOGICAL STUDY, SEX
            DIFFERENCES, AGE COMPARISONS, PREVENTIVE MENTAL HEALTH
            PROGRAMS+
     IDEN   U.S., NEVADA, DUCK VALLEY RESERVATION

315 AUTH   BEALE, CALVIN L.
     TITL   AN OVERVIEW OF THE PHENOMENON OF MIXED RACIAL ISOLATES
            IN THE UNITED STATES.
     SOUR   AMERICAN ANTHROPOLOGIST, 1972, V74, PP 704-709.
     YEAR   1972
     DESC   ETHNIC IDENTITY+, DISCRIMINATION, LUMBEE, HALIWA,
            SOUTHEAST WOODLAND, CHEROKEE, BLACK AMERICANS, ANGLO
            AMERICANS
     IDEN   U.S., NORTH CAROLINA

316 AUTH   SHAUGHNESSY, TIM
     TITL   WHITE STEREOTYPES OF INDIANS.
     SOUR   JOURNAL OF AMERICAN INDIAN EDUCATION, JAN. 1978, V17
            (2), PP 20-24.
     YEAR   1978
     DESC   STEREOTYPES+
     IDEN   U.S.

317 AUTH   WINTROB, RONALD M.; DIAMEN, SHARON
     TITL   COMMITMENT AND ALIENATION: THE IMPACT OF CULTURE
            CHANGE ON MISTASSINI CREE YOUTH.
     SOUR   PAPER PRESENTED AT THE ANNUAL MEETING OF THE CANADIAN
            PSYCHIATRIC ASSOCIATION, VANCOUVER, JUN. 1973. (33P)
     YEAR   1973
     DESC   CREE, EASTERN SUB-ARCTIC, RESERVATION, ADOLESCENTS+,
            STRESS+, FAMILY FUNCTIONING+, CULTURAL ADAPTATION+,

```
           SELF-CONCEPT, NATIVE AMERICAN POLITICAL MOVEMENTS
      IDEN CANADA, QUEBEC

318   AUTH FREEMAN, DANIEL M.A.
      TITL ADOLESCENT CRISES OF THE KIOWA-APACHE INDIAN MALE.
      SOUR IN EUGENE BRODY (ED.), MINORITY GROUP ADOLESCENTS IN
           THE UNITED STATES, PP 157-204.  BALTIMORE: WILLIAMS
           AND WILKINS, 1968.
      YEAR 1968
      DESC ADOLESCENTS+, KIOWA APACHE, PLAINS, MALES+,
           PERSONALITY TRAITS+, TRADITIONAL CHILD REARING+,
           TRADITIONAL SOCIAL CONTROL+, EXTENDED FAMILY+, SOCIAL
           STATUS+
      IDEN U.S., OKLAHOMA

319   AUTH BOURKE, JOHN G.
      TITL DISTILLATION BY EARLY AMERICAN INDIANS.
      SOUR AMERICAN ANTHROPOLOGIST, 1894, V7, PP 297-299.
      YEAR 1894
      DESC TRADITIONAL USE OF DRUGS AND ALCOHOL+
      IDEN U.S., MEXICO

320   AUTH HILL, THOMAS W.
      TITL DRUNKEN COMPORTMENT OF URBAN INDIANS: TIME-OUT
           BEHAVIOR?
      SOUR JOURNAL OF ANTHROPOLOGICAL RESEARCH, FALL 1978,
           V34(3), PP 442-467.
      YEAR 1978
      DESC ALCOHOL USE+, GROUP NORMS AND SANCTIONS+, URBAN AREAS,
           AGGRESSIVENESS+, SOCIALLY DEVIANT BEHAVIOR+
      IDEN U.S., IOWA

321   AUTH HAY, THOMAS H.
      TITL THE WINDIGO PSYCHOSIS: PSYCHODYNAMIC, CULTURAL, AND
           SOCIAL FACTORS IN ABERRANT BEHAVIOR.
      SOUR AMERICAN ANTHROPOLOGIST, 1971, V73, PP 1-19.
      YEAR 1971
      DESC WINDIGO PSYCHOSIS+, EASTERN SUB-ARCTIC, CHIPPEWA,
           DEPRESSION, DREAMS AND VISION QUESTS

322   AUTH HALLOWELL, A. IRVING
      TITL SOME PSYCHOLOGICAL CHARACTERISTICS OF THE NORTHEASTERN
           INDIANS.
      SOUR IN F. JOHNSON (ED.), MAN IN NORTHEASTERN NORTH
           AMERICA, PP 195-225.  CAMBRIDGE: PAPERS OF THE R.S.
           PEABODY FOUNDATION OF ARCHEOLOGY, ILL., 1946.
      YEAR 1946
      DESC PERSONALITY TRAITS+, NORTHEAST WOODLAND, EASTERN
           SUB-ARCTIC, ABILITIES+, AGGRESSIVENESS, PSYCHOLOGICAL
           TESTING, EMOTIONAL RESTRAINT+,
           NONINTERFERENCE,TRADITIONAL CHILD REARING, ANXIETY+
      IDEN U.S., CANADA, RORSCHACH TEST

323   AUTH GREEN, RAYNA D.; BROWN, JANET W.; LONG, ROGER
      TITL REPORT AND RECOMMENDATIONS: CONFERENCE ON MATHEMATICS
```

```
            IN AMERICAN INDIAN EDUCATION.
      SOUR  WASHINGTON, D.C.: AAAS PROJECT ON NATIVE AMERICANS IN
            SCIENCE, 1978.
      YEAR  1978
      DESC  EDUCATION PROGRAMS AND SERVICES+, SCIENCE PROGRAMS+,
            EDUCATION PROFESSIONALS+, ROLE MODELS
      IDEN  U.S.

324   AUTH  ROGERS, DONALD D.
      TITL  INCIDENCE OF PSYCHOPATHOLOGY AND INSTABILITY OF
            ECO-SYSTEMS IN TWO NORTHERN COMMUNITIES.
      SOUR  CANADIAN PSYCHIATRIC ASSOCIATION JOURNAL, AUG. 1974,
            V19(4), PP 369-373.
      YEAR  1974
      DESC  MENTAL DISORDERS+, ESKIMO, CENTRAL AND EASTERN ARCTIC,
            EPIDEMIOLOGICAL STUDY, ADMINISTRATIVE ISSUES,
            ENVIRONMENTAL FACTORS
      IDEN  CANADA

325   AUTH  SAMPATH, H.M.
      TITL  PREVALENCE OF PSYCHIATRIC DISORDERS IN A SOUTHERN
            BAFFIN ISLAND ESKIMO SETTLEMENT.
      SOUR  CANADIAN PSYCHIATRIC ASSOCIATION JOURNAL, AUG. 1974,
            V19, PP 363-367.
      YEAR  1974
      DESC  ESKIMO, CENTRAL AND EASTERN ARCTIC, EPIDEMIOLOGICAL
            STUDY, MENTAL DISORDERS+, ADULTS, SEX DIFFERENCES,
            OFF-RESERVATION,  DEPRESSION, HYSTERIA+
      IDEN  CANADA

326   AUTH  BERNARD, JESSIE
      TITL  POLITICAL LEADERSHIP AMONG NORTH AMERICAN INDIANS.
      SOUR  AMERICAN JOURNAL OF SOCIOLOGY, 1928, V34, PP 296-315.
      YEAR  1928
      DESC  TRIBAL POLITICAL ORGANIZATIONS+, PERSONALITY TRAITS+,
            LEADERSHIP+
      IDEN  U.S.

327   AUTH  SMITH, FREDERICK D.
      TITL  AN ANTHROPOLOGICAL PERSPECTIVE OF NATIVE AMERICAN
            CULTURAL STUDIES.
      SOUR  JOURNAL OF AMERICAN INDIAN EDUCATION, MAY 1978, V17.
            (3), PP 8-12
      YEAR  1978
      DESC  CULTURAL REVIVAL+, EDUCATION PROGRAMS AND SERVICES+,
            NATIVE AMERICAN POLITICAL MOVEMENTS+
      IDEN  U.S.

328   AUTH  MERIAM, LEWIS
      TITL  THE EFFECT OF BOARDING SCHOOLS ON INDIAN FAMILY LIFE:
            1928.
      SOUR  IN STEPHEN UNGER (ED.), THE DESTRUCTION OF AMERICAN
            INDIAN FAMILIES, PP 14-17.  NEW YORK: ASSOCIATION ON
            AMERICAN INDIAN AFFAIRS, 1977.
      YEAR  1977
```

```
        DESC  FAMILY FUNCTIONING+, BOARDING HOMES, CHILDREN-SCHOOL
              AGE+
        IDEN  U.S.

329  AUTH  STRAUS, ANNE S.
     TITL  THE MEANING OF DEATH IN NORTHERN CHEYENNE CULTURE.
     SOUR  PLAINS ANTHROPOLOGIST, FEB. 1978, V23 (79),  PP 1-6.
     YEAR  1978
     DESC  CHEYENNE-NORTHERN, PLAINS, DEATH AND DYING+, GRIEF
           REACTION

330  AUTH  ALBAUGH, BERNARD J.
     TITL  ETHNIC THERAPY WITH AMERICAN INDIAN ALCOHOLICS AS AN
           ANTIDOTE TO ANOMIE.
     SOUR  PAPER PRESENTED AT THE MEETING OF THE PROFESSIONAL
           ASSOCIATION OF THE U.S. PUBLIC HEALTH SERVICE,
           PHOENIX, MAY 1973.(4P)
     YEAR  1973
     DESC  ALCOHOL USE+, ANOMIE+, ALCOHOLISM TREATMENT+,
           BICULTURALISM+, CHEYENNE-SOUTHERN, ARAPAHO, PLAINS,
           NATIVE AMERICAN RELIGIONS
     IDEN  U.S., OKLAHOMA, NATIVE AMERICAN CHURCH, CHEYENNE AND
           ARAPAHO LODGE

331  AUTH  BARNOUW, VICTOR
     TITL  ACCULTURATION AND PERSONALITY AMONG THE WISCONSIN
           CHIPPEWA.
     SOUR  AMERICAN ANTHROPOLOGICAL ASSOCIATION. MEMOIRS, OCT.
           1950, V52(4, SERIES NO.72).   (152P)
     YEAR  1950
     DESC  CHIPPEWA, EASTERN SUB-ARCTIC, PERSONALITY TRAITS+,
           CULTURAL ADAPTATION+, PSYCHOLOGICAL TESTING,
           RESERVATION, SOCIAL NETWORKS, PLAINS, WITCHCRAFT,
           SIOUX, INTERTRIBAL COMPARISONS, TRADITIONAL CHILD
           REARING, EXTENDED FAMILY, PSYCHOANALYSIS
     IDEN  U.S., WISCONSIN, THEMATIC APPERCEPTION TEST, RORSCHACH
           TEST

332  AUTH  ANDRE, JAMES M.; GHUCHU, STANLEY
     TITL  SUICIDAL OCCURENCES IN AN AMERICAN INDIAN COMMUNITY.
     SOUR  PAPER PRESENTED AT THE MEETING OF THE PROFESSIONAL
           ASSOCIATION OF THE U.S. PUBLIC HEALTH SERVICE, LAS
           VEGAS, JUN. 1975. (17P)
     YEAR  1975
     DESC  SUICIDE+, PUEBLO-ZUNI, SOUTHWEST, SEX DIFFERENCES
     IDEN  U.S.

333  AUTH  BENNION, LYNN; LI, TING-KAI
     TITL  ALCOHOL METABOLISM IN AMERICAN INDIANS AND WHITES.
     SOUR  NEW ENGLAND JOURNAL OF MEDICINE, JAN. 1976, V294, PP
           9-13.
     YEAR  1976
     DESC  NATIVE-NON-NATIVE COMPARISONS, ALCOHOL USE+, ANGLO
           AMERICANS,GENETIC FACTORS+
```

334 AUTH   BOAG, THOMAS A.
     TITL   MENTAL HEALTH OF NATIVE PEOPLES OF THE ARCTIC.
     SOUR   CANADIAN PSYCHIATRIC ASSOCIATION JOURNAL, APR. 1970,
            V15(2), PP 115-120.
     YEAR   1970
     DESC   ARCTIC HYSTERIA+, ESKIMO, GROUP NORMS AND SANCTIONS,
            MENTAL DISORDERS+, CENTRAL AND EASTERN ARCTIC,
            CHIPPEWA, EASTERN SUB-ARCTIC, WINDIGO PSYCHOSIS,
            STRESS+, REVIEW OF LITERATURE, CREE
     IDEN   CANADA

335 AUTH   BAKER, JAMES L.
     TITL   INDIANS, ALCOHOL, AND HOMICIDE.
     SOUR   JOURNAL OF SOCIAL THERAPY, 1959, V5, PP 270-275.
     YEAR   1959
     DESC   CRIME+, ALCOHOL USE+, AGGRESSIVENESS+, ADULTS,
            CORRECTIONAL INSTITUTIONS+, PASSIVE RESISTANCE, NATIVE
            AMERICAN COPING BEHAVIORS
     IDEN   U.S.

336 AUTH   BOYER, L. BRYCE
     TITL   PSYCHOANALYTIC INSIGHT IN WORKING WITH ETHNIC
            MINORITIES.
     SOUR   SOCIAL CASEWORK, NOV. 1964, V45, PP 519-526.
     YEAR   1964
     DESC   APACHE-MESCALERO, RESERVATION, SOUTHWEST,
            STEREOTYPES+, PERSONALITY TRAITS+, TRADITIONAL CHILD
            REARING, SOCIAL SERVICE PROFESSIONALS+,
            PSYCHOANALYSIS
     IDEN   U.S., NEW MEXICO, MESCALERO RESERVATION

337 AUTH   BROD, THOMAS M.
     TITL   ALCOHOLISM AS A MENTAL HEALTH PROBLEM OF NATIVE
            AMERICANS: A REVIEW OF THE LITERATURE.
     SOUR   ARCHIVES OF GENERAL PSYCHIATRY, NOV. 1975, V32, PP
            1385-1391.
     YEAR   1975
     DESC   ALCOHOL USE+, REVIEW OF LITERATURE, TRADITIONAL USE OF
            DRUGS AND ALCOHOL

338 AUTH   BYNUM, JACK
     TITL   SUICIDE AND THE AMERICAN INDIAN: AN ANALYSIS OF RECENT
            TRENDS.
     SOUR   IN H.M. BAHR, B.A. CHADWICK, AND R.C. DAY (EDS.),
            NATIVE AMERICANS TODAY: SOCIOLOGICAL PERSPECTIVES, PP.
            367-377. NEW YORK: HARPER AND ROW, 1972.
     YEAR   1972
     DESC   SUICIDE+, REVIEW OF LITERATURE

339 AUTH   TOPPER, MARTIN D.
     TITL   MORMON PLACEMENT: THE EFFECTS OF MISSIONARY FOSTER
            FAMILIES ON NAVAJO ADOLESCENTS.
     SOUR   ETHOS, 1979, V7(2), PP 142-160.
     YEAR   1979
     DESC   NAVAJO, SOUTHWEST, ADOLESCENTS+, RESERVATION,

```
          RELIGIONS-NON-NATIVE+, RELIGIOUS-NON-NATIVE
          PERSONNEL+, ADOPTION AND FOSTER CARE+, STRESS+, FAMILY
          FUNCTIONING+, EXTENDED FAMILY, ETHNIC IDENTITY+,
          ALCOHOL USE, HYSTERIA, SEX DIFFERENCES,
          OFF-RESERVATION
     IDEN U.S., NAVAJO RESERVATION

340  AUTH BERGMAN, ROBERT L.
     TITL THE HUMAN COST OF REMOVING INDIAN CHILDREN FROM THEIR
          FAMILIES.
     SOUR IN STEPHEN UNGER (ED.), THE DESTRUCTION OF AMERICAN
          INDIAN FAMILIES, PP 34-36.  NEW YORK: ASSOCIATION ON
          AMERICAN INDIAN AFFAIRS, 1977.
     YEAR 1977
     DESC CHILDREN-SCHOOL AGE+, ADOPTION AND FOSTER CARE+,
          B.I.A. BOARDING SCHOOLS+
     IDEN U.S.

341  AUTH BIENVENUE, RITA M.; LATIF, A.H.
     TITL ARRESTS, DISPOSITION, AND RECIDIVISM: A COMPARISON OF
          INDIANS AND WHITES.
     SOUR CANADIAN JOURNAL OF CORRECTIONS, 1974, V16, PP 105-116.
     YEAR 1974
     DESC CORRECTIONAL INSTITUTIONS+, INSTITUTIONALIZATION+,
          CRIME+, SOCIAL STATUS+, DISCRIMINATION+, SEX
          DIFFERENCES, EPIDEMIOLOGICAL STUDY, NATIVE-NON-NATIVE
          COMPARISONS
     IDEN CANADA

342  AUTH FIELDS, SUZANNE
     TITL FOLK HEALING FOR THE WOUNDED SPIRIT: II. MEDICINE MEN:
          PURVEYORS OF AN ANCIENT ART.
     SOUR INNOVATIONS, WIN. 1976, V3, PP 12-18.
     YEAR 1976
     DESC TRADITIONAL HEALERS+, NAVAJO, SOUTHWEST, UNIVERSAL
          HARMONY, CULTURE-BASED PSYCHOTHERAPY+, SOCIAL
          NETWORKS, TRAINING PROGRAMS, RESERVATION
     IDEN U.S., NEW MEXICO, NAVAJO RESERVATION, ROUGH ROCK
          DEMONSTRATION SCHOOL

343  AUTH JIMSON, LEONARD B.
     TITL PARENT AND CHILD RELATIONSHIPS IN LAW AND IN NAVAJO
          CUSTOM.
     SOUR IN STEPHEN UNGER (ED.), THE DESTRUCTION OF AMERICAN
          INDIAN FAMILIES, PP 67-78.  NEW YORK: ASSOCIATION ON
          AMERICAN INDIAN AFFAIRS, 1977.
     YEAR 1977
     DESC NAVAJO, SOUTHWEST, LEGAL ISSUES+, SOCIAL SERVICES+,
          CHILD ABUSE AND NEGLECT+, EXTENDED FAMILY+, ADOPTION
          AND FOSTER CARE+, RESERVATION
     IDEN U.S., NAVAJO RESERVATION

344  AUTH BRODY, HUGH
     TITL THE ROLE OF ALCOHOL AND COMMUNITY IN THE ADAPTIVE
          PROCESS OF INDIAN URBAN MIGRANTS.
```

```
         SOUR   CANADA. DEPARTMENT OF INDIAN AFFAIRS AND NORTHERN
                DEVELOPMENT.  NORTHERN RESEARCH GROUP.  OTTAWA:
                INFORMATION CANADA, 1971.  (92P)
         YEAR   1971
         DESC   URBAN AREAS, SOCIAL GROUPS AND PEER GROUPS, SEXUAL
                RELATIONS, CRIME, ALCOHOL USE+, ECONOMIC ISSUES+,
                RELOCATION, AGGRESSIVENESS, DISCRIMINATION+,
                STEREOTYPES+, CORRECTIONAL INSTITUTIONS
         IDEN   CANADA

345      AUTH   ATTNEAVE, CAROLYN L.
         TITL   MENTAL HEALTH OF AMERICAN INDIAN: PROBLEMS, PROSPECTS,
                AND CHALLENGE FOR THE DECADE AHEAD.
         SOUR   PAPER PRESENTED AT THE MEETING OF THE AMERICAN
                PSYCHOLOGICAL ASSOCIATION, HONOLULU, SEP. 1972.  (23P)
         YEAR   1972
         DESC   MENTAL DISORDERS, MENTAL HEALTH PROGRAMS AND
                SERVICES+, PROGRAM DEVELOPMENT+, STRESS+, UNIVERSAL
                HARMONY, GENEROSITY, TIME PERCEPTION

346      AUTH   OPLER, MORRIS E.
         TITL   FURTHER COMPARATIVE ANTHROPOLOGICAL DATA BEARING THE
                SOLUTION OF A PSYCHOLOGICAL PROBLEM.
         SOUR   JOURNAL OF SOCIAL PSYCHOLOGY, NOV. 1938, V9, PP
                477-483.
         YEAR   1938
         DESC   APACHE-MESCALERO, APACHE-CHIRICAHUA, SOUTHWEST, GRIEF
                REACTION+, APACHE-JICARILLA, APACHE-LIPAN, GHOST
                SICKNESS+, AGED+, DEATH AND DYING+

347      AUTH   TEICHER, MORTON I.
         TITL   WINDIGO PSYCHOSIS: A STUDY OF A RELATIONSHIP BETWEEN
                BELIEF AND BEHAVIOR AMONG THE INDIANS OF NORTHEASTERN
                CANADA.
         SOUR   IN VERNE F. RAY (ED.), PROCEEDINGS OF THE 1960 ANNUAL
                SPRING MEETING OF THE AMERICAN ETHNOLOGICAL SOCIETY.
                SEATTLE: UNIVERSITY OF WASHINGTON PRESS, 1960.  (129P)
         YEAR   1960
         DESC   WINDIGO PSYCHOSIS+, EASTERN SUB-ARCTIC, EMOTIONAL
                RESTRAINT, ANXIETY

348      AUTH   PARKER, SEYMOUR
         TITL   THE KWAKIUTL INDIANS: "AMIABLE" AND "ATROCIOUS."
         SOUR   ANTHROPOLOGICA, 1964, V6(2), PP 131-158
         YEAR   1964
         DESC   KWAKIUTL, NORTHWEST COAST, PERSONALITY TRAITS+,
                COOPERATION+, SOCIAL STATUS+, AGGRESSIVENESS+,
                EMOTIONAL RESTRAINT, TRADITIONAL CHILD REARING,
                TRADITIONAL SOCIAL CONTROL
         IDEN   CANADA, BRITISH COLUMBIA

349      AUTH   BELMONT, FRANCOIS VACHON DE
         TITL   PECULIAR QUALITY OF INSOBRIETY AMONG SAVAGES.
         SOUR   MID-AMERICA, N.S., 1951-1952, V34, PP
                44-63.(TRANSLATED FROM HISTOIRE DE L' EAU-DE-VIE EN
```

CANADA BY F.V. BELMONT. ORIGINALLY PUBLISHED BY THE
SOCIETE LITTERAIRE DE QUEBEC IN THE 1840 VOLUME OF ITS
COLLECTION DE RELATIONS SUR L'HISTOIRE ANCIENNE DU
CANADA.)
YEAR 1951-1952
DESC ALCOHOL USE+, AGGRESSIVENESS+, IROQUOIS, NORTHEAST
WOODLAND, RELIGIOUS-NON-NATIVE PERSONNEL
IDEN CANADA

350 AUTH DOWNS, JAMES F.
TITL THE COWBOY AND THE LADY: MODELS AS A DETERMINANT OF
THE RATE OF ACCULTURATION AMONG THE PINON NAVAJO.
SOUR IN HOWARD M. BAHR, BRUCE A. CHADWICK, AND ROBERT C.
DAY (EDS.), NATIVE AMERICANS TODAY: SOCIOLOGICAL
PERSPECTIVES, PP 275-290. NEW YORK: HARPER AND ROW,
1972.
YEAR 1972
DESC FEMALES+, ADULTS, NAVAJO, SOUTHWEST, CULTURAL
ADAPTATION+, SEX DIFFERENCES,RESERVATION, CULTURAL
CONTINUITY+, EXTENDED FAMILY, MALES+, ETHNIC
IDENTITY+, ROLE MODELS+, SOCIAL ROLES+
IDEN U.S.

351 AUTH FENTON, WILLIAM N.
TITL IROQUOIS SUICIDE: A STUDY IN THE STABILITY OF A
CULTURE PATTERN.
SOUR ANTHROPOLOGICAL PAPERS, NO. 14 (SMITHSONIAN
INSTITUTION, BUREAU OF AMERICAN ETHNOLOGY BULLETIN NO.
128), 1941, PP 79-139.
YEAR 1941
DESC IROQUOIS-SENECA, NORTHEAST WOODLAND, SUICIDE+,
RESERVATION, TRADITIONAL USE OF DRUGS AND ALCOHOL+,
SEX DIFFERENCES, CRIME, AGE COMPARISONS, MARITAL
RELATIONSHIPS
IDEN U.S., NEW YORK

352 AUTH BOYER, L. BRYCE
TITL PSYCHOLOGICAL PROBLEMS OF A GROUP OF APACHES:
ALCOHOLIC HALLUCINOSIS AND LATENT HOMOSEXUALITY AMONG
TYPICAL MEN.
SOUR PSYCHOANALYTIC STUDY OF SOCIETY, 1964, V3, PP 203-277.
YEAR 1964
DESC APACHE-MESCALERO, SOUTHWEST, APACHE-CHIRICAHUA, SEXUAL
RELATIONS+, RESERVATION, GROUP NORMS AND SANCTIONS,
TRADITIONAL CHILD REARING+, CHILD ABUSE AND NEGLECT+,
GHOST SICKNESS, PSYCHOTHERAPY AND COUNSELING+,
CLINICAL STUDY, PSYCHOANALYSIS, MALES+, SOCIAL ROLES
IDEN U.S., NEW MEXICO, MESCALERO RESERVATION

353 AUTH JILEK, WOLFGANG G.; JILEK-AALL, LOUISE
TITL A TRANSCULTURAL APPROACH TO PSYCHOTHERAPY WITH
CANADIAN INDIANS. EXPERIENCES FROM THE FRASER VALLEY
OF BRITISH COLUMBIA.
SOUR IN PSYCHIATRY (PART II.) PROCEEDINGS OF THE 5TH WORLD
CONGRESS OF PSYCHIATRY, PP 1181-1186. EXCERPTA MEDICA

```
                    INTERNATIONAL CONGRESS SERIES, NO. 274. MEXICO, D.F.,
                    1971.
          YEAR      1971
          DESC      PSYCHOTHERAPY AND COUNSELING+, COAST SALISH, NORTHWEST
                    COAST, ALCOHOLISM TREATMENT, SPIRIT INTRUSION,
                    CULTURE-BASED PSYCHOTHERAPY+, TRADITIONAL HEALERS,
                    MENTAL HEALTH PROFESSIONALS, MENTAL DISORDERS+,
                    STRESS+
          IDEN      CANADA, BRITISH COLUMBIA, ALCOHOLICS ANONYMOUS

   354    AUTH      ATCHESON, J.D.
          TITL      PROBLEMS OF MENTAL HEALTH IN THE CANADIAN ARCTIC.
          SOUR      CANADA"S MENTAL HEALTH, JAN.-FEB. 1972, V20(1), PP
                    10-17.
          YEAR      1972
          DESC      STRESS+, MENTAL DISORDERS+, ESKIMO, CENTRAL AND
                    EASTERN ARCTIC, NATIVE-NON-NATIVE COMPARISONS, ARCTIC
                    HYSTERIA, ADOLESCENTS, ADULTS, DELIVERY OF SERVICES,
                    MENTAL HEALTH PROGRAMS AND SERVICES+
          IDEN      CANADA, YUKON

   355    AUTH      FENNA, D.; MIX, L.; SCHAEFER, OTTO ; GILBERT, J.A.L.
          TITL      ETHANOL METABOLISM IN VARIOUS RACIAL GROUPS.
          SOUR      CANADIAN MEDICAL ASSOCIATION JOURNAL, 1971, V105, PP
                    472-475.
          YEAR      1971
          DESC      NATIVE-NON-NATIVE COMPARISONS, ALCOHOL USE+, CLINICAL
                    STUDY, PREVENTIVE MENTAL HEALTH PROGRAMS,GENETIC
                    FACTORS+
          IDEN      CANADA

   356    AUTH      CURLEE, W.V.
          TITL      SUICIDE AND SELF-DESTRUCTIVE BEHAVIOR ON THE CHEYENNE
                    RIVER RESERVATION.
          SOUR      IN SUICIDE AMONG THE AMERICAN INDIANS, PP 34-36.
                    (USPHS PUBLICATION NO. 1903) WASHINGTON, D.C.:
                    GOVERNMENT PRINTING OFFICE, 1969.
          YEAR      1969
          DESC      SUICIDE+, ADOLESCENTS, ETHNIC IDENTITY+, SIOUX,
                    PLAINS, STRESS, ADULTS
          IDEN      U.S., SOUTH DAKOTA, CHEYENNE RIVER RESERVATION

   357    AUTH      CLIFTON, JAMES A.
          TITL      CULTURE CHANGE, STRUCTURAL STABILITY AND FACTIONALISM
                    IN THE PRAIRIE POTAWATOMIE RESERVATION.
          SOUR      MIDCONTINENT AMERICAN STUDIES JOURNAL, 1965, V6, PP
                    101-123.
          YEAR      1965
          DESC      POTAWATOMI, PRAIRIE, TRIBAL POLITICAL ORGANIZATIONS+,
                    RESERVATION, CULTURAL ADAPTATION+
          IDEN      U.S.

   358    AUTH      CHANCE, NORMAN A.
          TITL      ACCULTURATION, SELF-IDENTIFICATION, AND PERSONALITY
                    ADJUSTMENT.
```

```
       SOUR   AMERICAN ANTHROPOLOGIST, 1965, V67, PP 372-393.
       YEAR   1965
       DESC   SELF-CONCEPT+, ESKIMO, WESTERN ARCTIC, CULTURAL
              ADAPTATION+, PERSONALITY TRAITS+, PSYCHOLOGICAL
              TESTING+, ADULTS+, SEX DIFFERENCES, STRESS,
              OFF-RESERVATION
       IDEN   U.S., CORNELL MEDICAL INDEX, ALASKA

359    AUTH   GILLIN, JOHN
       TITL   ACQUIRED DRIVES IN CULTURE CONTACT.
       SOUR   AMERICAN ANTHROPOLOGIST, OCT.-DEC. 1942, V44(4), PP
              545-554.
       YEAR   1942
       DESC   ANXIETY+, CHIPPEWA, EASTERN SUB-ARCTIC, CULTURAL
              ADAPTATION+, STRESS+, SOCIAL STATUS, DISCRIMINATION,
              RESERVATION
       IDEN   U.S.

360    AUTH   RIFFENBURGH, ARTHUR S.
       TITL   CULTURAL INFLUENCES AND CRIME AMONG INDIAN-AMERICANS
              OF THE SOUTHWEST.
       SOUR   FEDERAL PROBATION, SEP. 1964, V28, PP 38-46.
       YEAR   1964
       DESC   CRIME+, SOUTHWEST, GROUP NORMS AND SANCTIONS+,
              STRESS+, LEGAL ISSUES, RESERVATION, URBAN AREAS,
              ALCOHOL USE, DISCRIMINATION, ETHNIC IDENTITY+,
              CORRECTIONAL INSTITUTIONS
       IDEN   U.S.

361    AUTH   FAIRBANKS, ROBERT A.
       TITL   THE CHEYENNE-ARAPAHO AND ALCOHOLISM: DOES THE TRIBE
              HAVE A LEGAL RIGHT TO A MEDICAL REMEDY.
       SOUR   AMERICAN INDIAN LAW REVIEW, WIN. 1973, V1(1), PP 55-77.
       YEAR   1973
       DESC   ALCOHOL USE+, CHEYENNE, ARAPAHO, PLAINS, I.H.S.+,
              ALCOHOLISM TREATMENT+,RESERVATION, B.I.A., NATIVE
              AMERICAN ADMINISTERED PROGRAMS
       IDEN   U.S., OKLAHOMA

362    AUTH   DRILLING, VERN
       TITL   PROBLEMS WITH ALCOHOL AMONG URBAN INDIANS IN
              MINNEAPOLIS.
       SOUR   SECTION OF THE FINAL REPORT OF THE NATIONAL STUDY OF
              AMERICAN INDIAN EDUCATION (USOE GRANT NO.
              OEC-0-8-080147-2805), AUG. 1970. (52P)
       YEAR   1970
       DESC   URBAN AREAS, ALCOHOL USE+, ALCOHOLISM TREATMENT,
              NATIVE-NON-NATIVE COMPARISONS, CORRECTIONAL
              INSTITUTIONS+, MALES, ADULTS, PSYCHOLOGICAL TESTING+,
              REVIEW OF LITERATURE, CLINICAL STUDY, ANGLO AMERICANS,
              BLACK AMERICANS
       IDEN   U.S., MINNESOTA, M.M.P.I.

363    AUTH   VON HENTIG, HANS
       TITL   THE DELINQUENCY OF THE AMERICAN INDIAN.
```

```
       SOUR   JOURNAL OF CRIMINAL LAW AND CRIMINOLOGY, 1945-46, V36
              (2), PP 75-86.
       YEAR   1945-46
       DESC   ADOLESCENTS+, SOCIALLY DEVIANT BEHAVIOR+, CORRECTIONAL
              INSTITUTIONS+, NATIVE-NON-NATIVE COMPARISONS, ANGLO
              AMERICANS,CRIME+, LEGAL ISSUES+
       IDEN   U.S.

364    AUTH   GARBARENO, MERWYN S.
       TITL   LIFE IN THE CITY: CHICAGO.
       SOUR   IN JACK O. WADDELL AND MICHAEL O. WATSON (EDS.), THE
              AMERICAN INDIAN IN URBAN SOCIETY, PP. 168-205.
              BOSTON: LITTLE, BROWN, AND CO., 1971.
       YEAR   1971
       DESC   URBAN AREAS, URBANIZATION+, ETHNIC IDENTITY+,
              RELOCATION, CULTURAL ADAPTATION+, FAMILY FUNCTIONING+,
              ALCOHOL USE, NATIVE AMERICAN POLITICAL MOVEMENTS,
              MARITAL RELATIONSHIPS
       IDEN   U.S., ILLINOIS

365    AUTH   HODGE, WILLIAM H.
       TITL   NAVAJO URBAN MIGRATION: AN ANALYSIS FROM THE
              PERSPECTIVE OF THE FAMILY.
       SOUR   IN JACK O. WADDELL AND MICHAEL O. WATSON (EDS.), THE
              AMERICAN INDIAN IN URBAN SOCIETY, PP. 347-391.
              BOSTON: LITTLE, BROWN, AND CO., 1971.
       YEAR   1971
       DESC   RESERVATION, URBAN AREAS, NAVAJO, SOUTHWEST,
              RELOCATION+, CULTURAL ADAPTATION+, BICULTURALISM+,
              URBANIZATION+
       IDEN   U.S.

366    AUTH   GRAVES, THEODORE D.
       TITL   DRINKING AND DRUNKENESS AMONG URBAN INDIANS.
       SOUR   IN JACK O. WADDELL AND MICHAEL O. WATSON (EDS.), THE
              AMERICAN INDIAN IN URBAN SOCIETY, PP. 274-311.
              BOSTON: LITTLE, BROWN, AND CO., 1971.
       YEAR   1971
       DESC   ALCOHOL USE+, URBAN AREAS, NAVAJO, SOUTHWEST,
              RELOCATION+, EMPLOYMENT+, ECONOMIC ISSUES+,
              PSYCHOLOGICAL TESTING, CORRECTIONAL INSTITUTIONS,
              INSTITUTIONALIZATION, NATIVE AMERICAN COPING BEHAVIORS
       IDEN   U.S., COLORADO

367    AUTH   LEVY, JERROLD E.; KUNITZ, STEPHEN J.
       TITL   NOTES ON SOME WHITE MOUNTAIN APACHE SOCIAL
              PATHOLOGIES.
       SOUR   PLATEAU, 1969, V42, PP 11-19.
       YEAR   1962
       DESC   SUICIDE+, ACCIDENTS+, CRIME+, APACHE-WHITE MOUNTAIN,
              SOUTHWEST, EPIDEMIOLOGICAL STUDY, DEMOGRAPHIC DATA,
              RESERVATION, ALCOHOL USE, PHYSICAL HEALTH AND ILLNESS
       IDEN   U.S.

368    AUTH   DAILY, R.C.
```

TITL THE ROLE OF ALCOHOL AMONG NORTH AMERICAN INDIAN TRIBES
      AS REPORTED IN THE JESUIT RELATIONS.
SOUR ANTHROPOLOGICA, 1968-69, V10-11, PP 45-57,
YEAR 1968-69
DESC RELIGIONS-NON-NATIVE+, ALCOHOL USE+, AGGRESSIVENESS,
      STRESS
IDEN CANADA, CATHOLIC CHURCH

369 AUTH FERGUSON, FRANCES N.
     TITL A TREATMENT PROGRAM FOR NAVAJO ALCOHOLICS.
     SOUR QUARTERLY JOURNAL OF STUDIES ON ALCOHOL, 1970, V31, PP
           898-919.
     YEAR 1970
     DESC NAVAJO, SOUTHWEST, ALCOHOLISM TREATMENT+, URBAN AREAS,
           ALCOHOL USE+, CHEMOTHERAPY+, PROGRAM EVALUATION+,
           CORRECTIONAL INSTITUTIONS+, PSYCHOLOGICAL TESTING,
           CLINICAL STUDY, INSTITUTIONALIZATION+
     IDEN U.S., NEW MEXICO

370 AUTH HIPPLER, ARTHUR E.
     TITL PATTERNS OF SEXUAL BEHAVIOR: THE ATHABASCANS OF
           INTERIOR ALASKA.
     SOUR ETHOS, SPR. 1974, V2, PP 47-68.
     YEAR 1974
     DESC ATHABASCAN, YUKON SUB-ARCTIC, SEXUAL RELATIONS+,
           TRADITIONAL CHILD REARING, ANXIETY, EXTENDED FAMILY,
           AGGRESSIVENESS, FAMILY FUNCTIONING+, OFF-RESERVATION,
           ADOLESCENTS, ADULTS
     IDEN U.S., ALASKA

371 AUTH TELFORD, C.W.
     TITL TEST PERFORMANCE OF FULL AND MIXED-BLOOD NORTH DAKOTA
           INDIANS.
     SOUR JOURNAL OF COMPARATIVE PSYCHOLOGY, 1932, V14,
           PP123-145.
     YEAR 1932
     DESC SIOUX, PLAINS, PSYCHOLOGICAL TESTING+, CHILDREN-SCHOOL
           AGE+, B.I.A. BOARDING SCHOOLS, CHIPPEWA, EASTERN
           SUB-ARCTIC, NATIVE-NON-NATIVE COMPARISONS, ABILITIES,
           INTERTRIBAL COMPARISONS, ANGLO AMERICANS, BLACK
           AMERICANS
     IDEN U.S., NORTH DAKOTA, GOODENOUGH HARRIS DRAW A PERSON
           TEST, PETERSON RATIONAL LEARNING TEST, MARE AND FOAL
           TEST, HEALY PUZZLE "A" TEST

372 AUTH ZENTNER, HENRY
     TITL FACTORS IN THE SOCIAL PATHOLOGY OF NORTH AMERICAN
           INDIAN SOCIETY.
     SOUR ANTHROPOLOGICA, 1963, V5, PP 119-130.
     YEAR 1963
     DESC SOCIALLY DEVIANT BEHAVIOR+, SOCIAL STATUS+, STRESS,
           CULTURAL CONTINUITY
     IDEN U.S.

373 AUTH BERGMAN, ROBERT L.

```
        TITL  NAVAJO MEDICINE AND PSYCHOANALYSIS.
        SOUR  HUMAN BEHAVIOR, JUL. 1973, V2, PP 8-15,
        YEAR  1973
        DESC  NAVAJO, SOUTHWEST, MENTAL HEALTH PROFESSIONALS+,
              TRADITIONAL HEALERS+, CULTURE-BASED PSYCHOTHERAPY+,
              NATIVE AMERICAN RELIGIONS, PSYCHOTHERAPY AND
              COUNSELING+, PSYCHOANALYSIS+
        IDEN  U.S.

   374  AUTH  HALLOWELL, A. IRVING
        TITL  AMERICAN INDIANS, WHITE AND BLACK: THE PHENOMENON OF
              TRANSCULTURATION.
        SOUR  CURRENT ANTHROPOLOGY, 1963, V4, PP 519-531.
        YEAR  1963
        DESC  CULTURAL ADAPTATION+, ADOPTION AND FOSTER CARE,
              EXTENDED FAMILY+, NATIVE-NON-NATIVE COMPARISONS,
              REVIEW OF LITERATURE, ANGLO AMERICANS, BLACK AMERICANS

   375  AUTH  BERREMAN, GERALD D.
        TITL  ALEUT REFERENCE GROUP ALIENATION, MOBILITY, AND
              ACCULTURATION.
        SOUR  AMERICAN ANTHROPOLOGIST, APR. 1964, V66, PP 231-250.
        YEAR  1964
        DESC  ALEUT, WESTERN ARCTIC, CULTURAL ADAPTATION+, SOCIAL
              GROUPS AND PEER GROUPS+, SOCIAL STATUS+,
              BICULTURALISM, GROUP NORMS AND SANCTIONS+,
              OFF-RESERVATION
        IDEN  U.S., ALASKA

   376  AUTH  GARDNER, RICHARD E.
        TITL  THE ROLE OF THE PAN-INDIAN CHURCH IN URBAN INDIAN
              LIFE.
        SOUR  ANTHROPOLOGY UCLA, 1969, V1, PP 14-26.
        YEAR  1969
        DESC  URBAN AREAS, NATIVE AMERICAN RELIGIONS+, SOCIAL
              NETWORKS+, RELIGIONS-NON-NATIVE+, ADULTS,
              URBANIZATION+
        IDEN  U.S., CALIFORNIA

   377  AUTH  ROY, CHUNILAL
        TITL  PREVALENCE OF MENTAL DISORDERS AMONG SASKATCHEWAN
              INDIANS.
        SOUR  JOURNAL OF CROSS-CULTURAL PSYCHOLOGY, DEC. 1970,
              V1(4), PP 383-392.
        YEAR  1970
        DESC  CREE, PLAINS, CHIPPEWA, EPIDEMIOLOGICAL STUDY,
              DEMOGRAPHIC DATA, MENTAL DISORDERS+, RESERVATION
        IDEN  CANADA, SASKATCHEWAN

   378  AUTH  BLANCHARD, JOSEPH D.; WARREN, RICHARD L.
        TITL  ROLE STRESS OF DORMITORY AIDES AT AN OFF-RESERVATION
              BOARDING SCHOOL.
        SOUR  HUMAN ORGANIZATION, SPR. 1975, V34(1), PP 41-49.
        YEAR  1975
        DESC  B.I.A. BOARDING SCHOOLS+, URBAN AREAS, , NATIVE
```

```
          AMERICAN PERSONNEL+, EDUCATION PARAPROFESSIONALS+,
          ADMINISTRATIVE ISSUES+, INSTITUTIONALIZATION+,
          CHILDREN-SCHOOL AGE, ADOLESCENTS, SOCIAL ROLES, STRESS
     IDEN U.S.

379  AUTH BLANCHARD, KENDALL
     TITL CHANGING SEX ROLES AND PROTESTANTISM AMONG THE NAVAJO
          WOMEN IN RAMAH.
     SOUR JOURNAL FOR THE SCIENTIFIC STUDY OF RELIGION, MAR.
          1975, V14, PP 43-50.
     YEAR 1975
     DESC FEMALES+, NAVAJO, SOUTHWEST, ADULTS,
          RELIGIONS-NON-NATIVE+, RESERVATION, SOCIAL STATUS+,
          CULTURAL ADAPTATION+, SOCIAL ROLES+, STRESS
     IDEN U.S., NAVAJO RESERVATION

380  AUTH ABLON, JOAN
     TITL AMERICAN INDIAN RELOCATION: PROBLEMS OF DEPENDENCY AND
          MANAGEMENT IN THE CITY.
     SOUR PHYLON, 1965, V26, PP 362-371.
     YEAR 1965
     DESC RELOCATION+, URBAN AREAS, URBANIZATION+, PERSONALITY
          TRAITS+, GENEROSITY, NONCOMPETITIVENESS, B.I.A.,
          CULTURAL CONTINUITY+
     IDEN U.S.

381  AUTH LEVY, JERROLD E.; KUNITZ, STEPHEN J.; EVERETT, MICHAEL
     TITL NAVAJO CRIMINAL HOMICIDE.
     SOUR SOUTHWESTERN JOURNAL OF ANTHROPOLOGY, 1969, V25, PP
          124-152.
     YEAR 1969
     DESC CRIME+, NAVAJO, SOUTHWEST, EPIDEMIOLOGICAL STUDY, SEX
          DIFFERENCES, AGE COMPARISONS, ADULTS, MALES,
          NATIVE-NON-NATIVE COMPARISONS, RESERVATION, SUICIDE+,
          FAMILY FUNCTIONING, ANGLO AMERICANS, BLACK AMERICANS
     IDEN U.S., NAVAJO RESERVATION

382  AUTH CHADWICK, BRUCE A.; STAUSS, JOSEPH H.
     TITL THE ASSIMILATION OF AMERICAN INDIANS INTO URBAN
          SOCIETY: THE SEATTLE CASE.
     SOUR HUMAN ORGANIZATION, WIN. 1975, V34(4), PP 359-369.
     YEAR 1975
     DESC CULTURAL CONTINUITY+, URBAN AREAS, CULTURAL
          ADAPTATION+, DISCRIMINATION, PSYCHOLOGICAL TESTING,
          DEMOGRAPHIC DATA, URBANIZATION+
     IDEN U.S., WASHINGTON

383  AUTH ADAIR, JOHN; VOGT, EVON Z.
     TITL NAVAJO AND ZUNI VETERANS: A STUDY IN CONTRASTING MODES
          OF CULTURE CHANGE.
     SOUR AMERICAN ANTHROPOLOGIST, OCT.-DEC. 1949, V51(4), PP
          547-561.
     YEAR 1949
     DESC NAVAJO, PUEBLO-ZUNI, SOUTHWEST, MALES, CULTURAL
          ADAPTATION+, CULTURAL CONTINUITY, NATIVE AMERICAN
```

RELIGIONS+, GROUP NORMS AND SANCTIONS, MILITARY
SERVICE
IDEN   U.S., NEW MEXICO

384   AUTH   ROY, PRODIPTO
      TITL   THE MEASUREMENT OF ASSIMILATION: THE SPOKANE INDIANS.
      SOUR   AMERICAN JOURNAL OF SOCIOLOGY, 1962, V67, PP 541-551.
      YEAR   1962
      DESC   SPOKANE, PLATEAU, CULTURAL ADAPTATION+, RESERVATION,
             EXPERIMENTAL STUDY
      IDEN   U.S., WASHINGTON

385   AUTH   LURIE, NANCY O.
      TITL   THE WORLD"S OLDEST ON-GOING PROTEST DEMONSTRATION:
             NORTH AMERICAN INDIAN DRINKING PATTERNS.
      SOUR   PACIFIC HISTORICAL REVIEW, 1971, V40, PP 311-332.
      YEAR   1971
      DESC   ALCOHOL USE+, ETHNIC IDENTITY+, STEREOTYPES+, CULTURAL
             CONTINUITY+, NATIVE AMERICAN COPING BEHAVIORS

386   AUTH   SILVERMAN, JULIAN
      TITL   SHAMANS AND ACUTE SCHIZOPHRENIA.
      SOUR   AMERICAN ANTHROPOLOGIST, 1967, V69, PP 21-31.
      YEAR   1967
      DESC   TRADITIONAL HEALERS+, SCHIZOPHRENIA+, REVIEW OF
             LITERATURE

387   AUTH   FRIEDL, ERNESTINE
      TITL   PERSISTENCE IN CHIPPEWA CULTURE AND PERSONALITY.
      SOUR   AMERICAN ANTHROPOLOGIST, 1956, V58, PP 814-825.
      YEAR   1956
      DESC   CHIPPEWA, EASTERN SUB-ARCTIC, PERSONALITY TRAITS+,
             CULTURAL CONTINUITY+
      IDEN   U.S.

388   AUTH   GRAVES, THEODORE D.
      TITL   THE NAVAJO URBAN MIGRANT AND HIS PSYCHOLOGICAL
             SITUATION.
      SOUR   ETHOS, AUT. 1973, V1, PP 321-324.
      YEAR   1973
      DESC   NAVAJO, SOUTHWEST, URBAN AREAS, RELOCATION+,
             PERSONALITY TRAITS+, ECONOMIC ISSUES+, PSYCHOLOGICAL
             TESTING, TIME PERCEPTION, EMPLOYMENT+, ADULTS
      IDEN   U.S., COLORADO

389   AUTH   BOCK, PHILIP K.
      TITL   PATTERNS OF ILLEGITIMACY ON A CANADA INDIAN RESERVE,
             1860-1960.
      SOUR   JOURNAL OF MARRIAGE AND THE FAMILY, MAY 1964, V26, PP
             142-148.
      YEAR   1964
      DESC   RESERVATION, SEXUAL RELATIONS+, FEMALES+, ADULTS,
             ADOLESCENTS, EPIDEMIOLOGICAL STUDY, STRESS, GROUP
             NORMS AND SANCTIONS+
      IDEN   CANADA, QUEBEC

390 AUTH BRUNER, EDWARD M.
     TITL THE MISSING TINS OF CHICKEN: A SYMBOLIC INTERACTIONIST
           APPROACH TO CULTURE CHANGE.
     SOUR ETHOS, SUM. 1973, V1, PP 219-238.
     YEAR 1973
     DESC BICULTURALISM+, CULTURAL ADAPTATION+, ETHNIC
           IDENTITY+, NATIVE-NON-NATIVE COMPARISONS
     IDEN U.S., INDONESIA

391 AUTH YOUNG, PHILIP
     TITL THE MOTHER OF US ALL.
     SOUR KENYON REVIEW, SUM. 1962, V24, PP 391-415.
     YEAR 1962
     DESC FEMALES+, STEREOTYPES+, REVIEW OF LITERATURE, ADULTS,
           ROLE MODELS+
     IDEN U.S., POCAHONTAS

392 AUTH ANASTASI, ANNE; FOLEY, JOHN P.
     TITL A STUDY OF ANIMAL DRAWINGS BY INDIAN CHILDREN OF THE
           NORTH PACIFIC COAST.
     SOUR JOURNAL OF SOCIAL PSYCHOLOGY, AUG. 1938, V9, PP
           363-374.
     YEAR 1938
     DESC NORTHWEST COAST, KWAKIUTL, CHILDREN-SCHOOL AGE+,
           ELEMENTARY SCHOOLS, PSYCHOLOGICAL TESTING+, SEX
           DIFFERENCES, AGE COMPARISONS, CULTURAL CONTINUITY+
     IDEN CANADA, BRITISH COLUMBIA

393 AUTH OPLER, MORRIS E.
     TITL AN INTERPRETATION OF AMBIVALENCE OF TWO AMERICAN
           INDIAN TRIBES.
     SOUR JOURNAL OF SOCIAL PSYCHOLOGY, 1936, V7, PP 82-116.
     YEAR 1936
     DESC APACHE-CHIRICAHUA, APACHE-MESCALERO, SOUTHWEST,
           WITCHCRAFT, GHOST SICKNESS+, GRIEF REACTION+, EXTENDED
           FAMILY+, DEATH AND DYING+
     IDEN U.S., MESCALERO RESERVATION

394 AUTH GRIMMET, SADIE A.
     TITL THE INFLUENCE OF ETHNICITY AND AGE ON SOLVING TWENTY
           QUESTIONS.
     SOUR JOURNAL OF SOCIAL PSYCHOLOGY, 1971, V83, PP 143-144.
     YEAR 1971
     DESC PSYCHOLOGICAL TESTING+, MALES, NATIVE-NON-NATIVE
           COMPARISONS, ABILITIES+, CHILDREN-SCHOOL AGE, LATINOS,
           ANGLO AMERICANS, BLACK AMERICANS, AGE COMPARISONS
     IDEN U.S., TWENTY QUESTIONS

395 AUTH VALLEE, FRANK G.
     TITL ESKIMO THEORIES OF MENTAL ILLNESS IN THE HUDSON BAY
           REGION.
     SOUR ANTHROPOLOGICA, 1966, V8, PP 53-83.
     YEAR 1966
     DESC ESKIMO, CENTRAL AND EASTERN ARCTIC, NATIVE AMERICAN
           ETIOLOGY+, ARCTIC HYSTERIA+, MENTAL DISORDERS+,

```
            HYSTERIA, SCHIZOPHRENIA,   EPIDEMIOLOGICAL STUDY,
            ADULTS,DEPRESSION
     IDEN   CANADA

396  AUTH   ZUNICH, M.
     TITL   PERCEPTIONS OF INDIAN, MEXICAN, NEGRO, AND WHITE
            CHILDREN CONCERNING THE DEVELOPMENT OF RESPONSIBILITY.
     SOUR   PERCEPTUAL AND MOTOR SKILLS, 1971, V32, PP 796-798.
     YEAR   1971
     DESC   PSYCHOLOGICAL TESTING+, CHILDREN-SCHOOL AGE+, ECONOMIC
            ISSUES+, COGNITIVE PROCESSES, NATIVE-NON-NATIVE
            COMPARISONS, LATINOS, BLACK AMERICANS, ANGLO AMERICANS
     IDEN   U.S., CHILDREN"S RESPONSIBILITY INVENTORY

397  AUTH   LURIE, NANCY O.
     TITL   MENOMINEE TERMINATION FROM RESERVATION TO COLONY.
     SOUR   HUMAN ORGANIZATION, AUT. 1972, V31(3), PP 257-270.
     YEAR   1972
     DESC   MENOMINEE, NORTHEAST WOODLAND, FEDERAL GOVERNMENT+,
            B.I.A.,   RESERVATION, LEGAL ISSUES+, ECONOMIC ISSUES+,
            TRIBAL POLITICAL ORGANIZATIONS+
     IDEN   U.S., WISCONSIN

398  AUTH   ABLON, JOAN
     TITL   CULTURAL CONFLICT IN URBAN INDIANS.
     SOUR   MENTAL HYGIENE, APR. 1971, V55(2), PP 199-205.
     YEAR   1971
     DESC   URBAN AREAS, STRESS+, NONCOMPETITIVENESS+,
            GENEROSITY+, EXTENDED FAMILY, SIOUX, PLAINS,
            RELOCATION+, URBANIZATION+, NATIVE AMERICAN VALUES
     IDEN   U.S., CALIFORNIA

399  AUTH   KRUSH, THADDEUS P.; BJORK, JOHN W.
     TITL   MENTAL HEALTH FACTORS IN AN INDIAN BOARDING SCHOOL.
     SOUR   MENTAL HYGIENE, 1965, V49, PP 94-103.
     YEAR   1965
     DESC   B.I.A. BOARDING SCHOOLS+, SECONDARY SCHOOLS+,
            ADOLESCENTS+, PLAINS, MENTAL HEALTH PROGRAMS AND
            SERVICES+, MENTAL DISORDERS+
     IDEN   U.S., SOUTH DAKOTA, FLANDREAU INDIAN VOCATIONAL HIGH
            SCHOOL

400  AUTH   JONES, DOROTHY
     TITL   CHILD WELFARE PROBLEMS IN AN ALASKAN NATIVE VILLAGE.
     SOUR   SOCIAL SERVICE REVIEW, 1969, V43, PP 297-309.
     YEAR   1969
     DESC   ALASKA NATIVES, OFF-RESERVATION, CHILD ABUSE AND
            NEGLECT+, SOCIAL SERVICES+, ADOPTION AND FOSTER CARE+,
            SOCIAL SERVICE PROFESSIONALS, FAMILY FUNCTIONING+,
            STRESS, PROGRAM EVALUATION, NATIVE AMERICAN
            PERSONNEL,ADMINISTRATIVE ISSUES+, CHILDREN-SCHOOL AGE,
            CHILDREN-INFANTS AND PRESCHOOL
     IDEN   U.S., ALASKA

401  AUTH   JOHNSON, GUY V.
```

```
      TITL  PERSONALITY IN A WHITE-INDIAN-NEGRO COMMUNITY.
      SOUR  AMERICAN SOCIOLOGICAL REVIEW, 1939, V4, PP 516-523.
      YEAR  1939
      DESC  SOUTHEAST WOODLAND, SOCIAL STATUS+, DISCRIMINATION+,
            NATIVE-NON-NATIVE COMPARISONS, PERSONALITY TRAITS+,
            OFF-RESERVATION, ANGLO AMERICANS, BLACK AMERICANS
      IDEN  U.S., NORTH CAROLINA

402   AUTH  OPLER, MORRIS E.
      TITL  SOME POINTS OF COMPARISON AND CONTRAST BETWEEN THE
            TREATMENT OF FUNCTIONAL DISORDERS BY APACHE SHAMANS
            AND MODERN PSYCHIATRIC PRACTICE.
      SOUR  AMERICAN JOURNAL OF PSYCHIATRY, MAY 1936, V92, PP
            1371-1387.
      YEAR  1936
      DESC  TRADITIONAL HEALERS+, SOUTHWEST, APACHE-MESCALERO,
            APACHE-CHIRICAHUA, RESERVATION, CULTURE-BASED
            PSYCHOTHERAPY, ANXIETY, WITCHCRAFT
      IDEN  U.S., NEW MEXICO, MESCALERO RESERVATION

403   AUTH  KAPLAN, BERT; RICKERS-OVSIANKINA, MARIA A.; JOSEPH,
            ALICE
      TITL  AN ATTEMPT TO SORT RORSCHACH RECORDS FROM FOUR
            CULTURES.
      SOUR  JOURNAL OF PROJECTIVE TECHNIQUES, 1956, V20, PP
            172-180.
      YEAR  1956
      DESC  PSYCHOLOGICAL TESTING+, NAVAJO, PUEBLO-ZUNI,
            SOUTHWEST, NATIVE-NON-NATIVE COMPARISONS, PERSONALITY
            TRAITS+, ANGLO AMERICANS, LATINOS
      IDEN  U.S., NEW MEXICO, RORSCHACH TEST

404   AUTH  KAPLAN, BERT
      TITL  REFLECTIONS OF THE ACCULTURATION PROCESS IN THE
            RORSCHACH TEST.
      SOUR  JOURNAL OF PROJECTIVE TECHNIQUES, 1955, V19, PP 30-35.
      YEAR  1955
      DESC  PSYCHOLOGICAL TESTING+, PERSONALITY TRAITS+, NAVAJO,
            PUEBLO-ZUNI, SOUTHWEST, CULTURAL ADAPTATION+, ANGLO
            AMERICANS, LATINOS
      IDEN  U.S., RORSCHACH TEST, NEW MEXICO

405   AUTH  WOLMAN, CAROL
      TITL  GROUP THERAPY IN TWO LANGUAGES, ENGLISH AND NAVAJO.
      SOUR  AMERICAN JOURNAL OF PSYCHOTHERAPY, 1970, V24, PP
            677-685.
      YEAR  1970
      DESC  PSYCHOTHERAPY AND COUNSELING+, SOCIAL GROUPS AND PEER
            GROUPS+, NAVAJO, SOUTHWEST, ALCOHOLISM TREATMENT+,
            TRADITIONAL SOCIAL CONTROL, GROUP NORMS AND SANCTIONS,
            BILINGUALISM+, LANGUAGE HANDICAPS+, CLINICAL STUDY
      IDEN  U.S., NEW MEXICO

406   AUTH  DEVEREUX, GEORGE
      TITL  MOHAVE INDIAN VERBAL AND MOTOR PROFANITY.
```

```
         SOUR  PSYCHOANALYSIS AND THE SOCIAL SCIENCES, 1951, V3, PP
               99-127.
         YEAR  1951
         DESC  MOHAVE, SOUTHWEST, SEXUAL RELATIONS+, AGGRESSIVENESS,
               MALES, FEMALES, ADULTS, GROUP NORMS AND SANCTIONS,
               PSYCHOANALYSIS
         IDEN  U.S.

407      AUTH  GOLDFRANK, ESTHER S.
         TITL  OBSERVATIONS ON SEXUALITY AMONG THE BLOOD INDIANS OF
               ALBERTA, CANADA.
         SOUR  PSYCHOANALYSIS AND THE SOCIAL SCIENCES, 1951, V3, PP
               71-98.
         YEAR  1951
         DESC  BLACKFEET-BLOOD, PLAINS, SEXUAL RELATIONS+,
               RESERVATION, TRADITIONAL CHILD REARING, FEMALES,
               ADULTS, GROUP NORMS AND SANCTIONS, PSYCHOANALYSIS
         IDEN  CANADA, ALBERTA

408      AUTH  DEVEREUX, GEORGE
         TITL  HETEROSEXUAL BEHAVIOR OF THE MOHAVE INDIANS.
         SOUR  PSYCHOANALYSIS AND THE SOCIAL SCIENCES, 1950, V2, PP
               85-128.
         YEAR  1950
         DESC  MOHAVE, SOUTHWEST, SEXUAL RELATIONS+, GROUP NORMS AND
               SANCTIONS+, PSYCHOANALYSIS

409      AUTH  ABEL, THEODORA M.; METRAUX, RHODA
         TITL  UNIVERSALS AND CULTURAL REGULARITIES: ASPECTS OF
               PERFORMANCE IN THE LOWENFELD MOSAIC TEST.
         SOUR  PAPER PRESENTED AT THE 73RD ANNUAL MEETING OF THE
               AMERICAN ANTHROPOLOGICAL ASSOCIATION, MEXICO, D.F.,
               NOV. 1974.(15P)
         YEAR  1974
         DESC  PSYCHOLOGICAL TESTING+, NATIVE-NON-NATIVE COMPARISONS,
               PERSONALITY TRAITS+,ADOLESCENTS, PUEBLO, NAVAJO,
               SOUTHWEST
         IDEN  NORTH AMERICA, ASIA, LOWENFELD MOSAIC TEST

410      AUTH  WESTERMEYER, JOSEPH
         TITL  VIOLENT DEATH AND ALCOHOL USE AMONG THE CHIPPEWA IN
               MINNESOTA.
         SOUR  MINNESOTA MEDICINE, 1972, V55, PP 749-752.
         YEAR  1972
         DESC  ALCOHOL USE+, ACCIDENTS+, CHIPPEWA, EASTERN
               SUB-ARCTIC, DEMOGRAPHIC DATA, NATIVE-NON-NATIVE
               COMPARISONS, CRIME, AGE COMPARISONS, ADULTS
         IDEN  U.S., MINNESOTA

411      AUTH  WADDELL, JACK O.
         TITL  "DRINK, FRIEND " SOCIAL CONTEXTS OF CONVIVIAL
               DRINKING AND DRUNKENESS AMONG PAPAGO INDIANS IN AN
               URBAN SETTING.
         SOUR  PAPER PRESENTED AT THE CONFERENCE ON ALCOHOL ABUSE AND
               ALCOHOLISM, WASHINGTON, D.C., 1971. (24P)
```

```
        YEAR  1971
        DESC  TRADITIONAL USE OF DRUGS AND ALCOHOL, PAPAGO,
              SOUTHWEST, RESERVATION,  ADULTS, MALES, SOCIAL GROUPS
              AND PEER GROUPS+, URBAN AREAS, ALCOHOL USE+
        IDEN  U.S., ARIZONA

412  AUTH  PARKER, ARTHUR C.
     TITL  THE SOCIAL ELEMENTS OF THE INDIAN PROBLEM.
     SOUR  AMERICAN JOURNAL OF SOCIOLOGY, 1916, V22(2), PP
           252-267.
     YEAR  1916
     DESC  FEDERAL GOVERNMENT+, RESERVATION, DISCRIMINATION+,
           LEGAL ISSUES, RELIGIONS-NON-NATIVE+
     IDEN  U.S.

413  AUTH  PATTISON, E. MANSELL
     TITL  EXORCISM AS PSYCHOTHERAPY: A CASE COLLABORATION.
     SOUR  IN R.H.COX (ED.), RELIGIOUS SYSTEMS AND PSYCHOTHERAPY.
           SPRINGFIELD, ILL.: CHARLES C. THOMAS, 1974.
     YEAR  1974
     DESC  TRADITIONAL HEALERS, PSYCHOTHERAPY AND COUNSELING+,
           MENTAL HEALTH PROFESSIONALS, NATIVE AMERICAN ETIOLOGY,
           YAKIMA, PLATEAU, STRESS, SCHIZOPHRENIA+, RESERVATION,
           ADOLESCENTS, GHOST SICKNESS+, CLINICAL STUDY,
           CULTURE-BASED PSYCHOTHERAPY+, PSYCHOANALYSIS
     IDEN  U.S., WASHINGTON

414  AUTH  STRATTON, JOHN
     TITL  COPS AND DRUNKS: POLICE ATTITUDES AND ACTIONS IN
           DEALING WITH INDIAN DRUNKS.
     SOUR  INTERNATIONAL JOURNAL OF ADDICTION, 1973, V8(4), PP
           613-621.
     YEAR  1973
     DESC  CORRECTIONS PERSONNEL+, ALCOHOL USE+, NAVAJO,
           SOUTHWEST, URBAN AREAS, DISCRIMINATION, CORRECTIONAL
           INSTITUTIONS+, INSTITUTIONALIZATION+, ALCOHOLISM
           TREATMENT, ATTITUDES+
     IDEN  U.S.

415  AUTH  SIEVERS, MAURICE L.
     TITL  CIGARETTE AND ALCOHOL USAGE BY SOUTHWESTERN AMERICAN
           INDIANS.
     SOUR  AMERICAN JOURNAL OF PUBLIC HEALTH, JAN. 1968, V58(1),
           PP 71-78.
     YEAR  1968
     DESC  ALCOHOL USE+, DRUG USE+, SOUTHWEST, SEX DIFFERENCES,
           NATIVE-NON-NATIVE COMPARISONS, INTERTRIBAL
           COMPARISONS, EPIDEMIOLOGICAL STUDY, ANGLO AMERICANS
     IDEN  U.S., ARIZONA

416  AUTH  REASONS, CHARLES
     TITL  CRIME AND THE AMERICAN INDIAN.
     SOUR  IN HOWARD M. BAHR, BRUCE A. CHADWICK, AND ROBERT C.
           DAY (EDS.), NATIVE AMERICANS TODAY: SOCIOLOGICAL
           PERSPECTIVES, PP. 319-326.  NEW YORK: HARPER AND ROW,
```

```
                1972.
       YEAR     1972
       DESC     CRIME+, CORRECTIONAL INSTITUTIONS+,
                INSTITUTIONALIZATION+, NATIVE-NON-NATIVE COMPARISONS,
                ANOMIE, STRESS, ALCOHOL USE, REVIEW OF LITERATURE,
                ASIAN AMERICANS, BLACK AMERICANS, ANGLO AMERICANS
       IDEN     U.S.

417    AUTH     SLEMENDA, CHARLES W.
       TITL     SOCIOCULTURAL FACTORS AFFECTING ACCEPTANCE OF FAMILY
                PLANNING SERVICES BY NAVAJO WOMEN.
       SOUR     HUMAN ORGANIZATION, SUM. 1978, V37 (2), PP 190-194.
       YEAR     1978
       DESC     RESERVATION, FAMILY PLANNING+, ADULTS+, FEMALES+,
                NAVAJO, SOUTHWEST, ECONOMIC ISSUES, NATIVE AMERICAN
                ETIOLOGY, FAMILY FUNCTIONING
       IDEN     U.S., NAVAJO RESERVATION

418    AUTH     ERICKSON, GERALD
       TITL     MENTAL HEALTH NEEDS AND RESOURCES IN A NORTHERN
                COMMUNITY.
       SOUR     (NATIONAL HEALTH AND WELFARE GRANT NO. 556-22-4).
                WINNIPEG: UNIVERSITY OF MANITOBA, 1971.  (33P)
       YEAR     1971
       DESC     DELIVERY OF SERVICES+, MENTAL DISORDERS, MENTAL HEALTH
                PROGRAMS AND SERVICES+, INSTITUTIONALIZATION, MENTAL
                HEALTH INSTITUTIONS, OFF-RESERVATION, PROGRAM
                DEVELOPMENT+
       IDEN     CANADA, MANITOBA

419    AUTH     PRICE, JOHN A.
       TITL     AN APPLIED ANALYSIS OF NORTH AMERICAN INDIAN DRINKING
                PATTERNS.
       SOUR     HUMAN ORGANIZATION, SPR. 1975, V34(1), PP 17-26.
       YEAR     1975
       DESC     ALCOHOL USE+, GROUP NORMS AND SANCTIONS, TRADITIONAL
                USE OF DRUGS AND ALCOHOL+, REVIEW OF LITERATURE,
                INSTITUTIONALIZATION, CORRECTIONAL INSTITUTIONS,
                TRADITIONAL SOCIAL CONTROL
       IDEN     U.S., CANADA

420    AUTH     MINNIS, MHYRA S.
       TITL     THE RELATIONSHIP OF THE SOCIAL STRUCTURE OF AN INDIAN
                COMMUNITY TO ADULT AND JUVENILE DELINQUENCY.
       SOUR     SOCIAL FORCES, MAY 1963, V41(4), PP 395-403.
       YEAR     1963
       DESC     ADOLESCENTS+, SOCIALLY DEVIANT BEHAVIOR+, SHOSHONE,
                BANNOCK, PLATEAU, RESERVATION, ECONOMIC ISSUES+,
                DEMOGRAPHIC DATA, EXTENDED FAMILY, CRIME
       IDEN     U.S., IDAHO, FORT HALL RESERVATION

421    AUTH     SWENSON, DAVID D.
       TITL     SUICIDE IN THE UNITED STATES.
       SOUR     IN SUICIDE AMONG THE AMERICAN INDIANS, PP 1-6 (USPHS
                PUBLICATION NO. 1903) WASHINGTON, D.C.: GOVERNMENT
```

```
         PRINTING OFFICE, 1969.
    YEAR 1969
    DESC SUICIDE+, EPIDEMIOLOGICAL STUDY, DEMOGRAPHIC DATA,
         PREVENTIVE MENTAL HEALTH PROGRAMS+, PROGRAM
         DEVELOPMENT+
    IDEN U.S.

422 AUTH INDIAN HEALTH SERVICE
    TITL ALCOHOLISM: A HIGH PRIORITY HEALTH PROBLEM.
    SOUR INDIAN HEALTH SERVICE (DHEW PUBLICATION NO. (HSM)
         73-12002) WASHINGTON, D.C.: GOVERNMENT PRINTING
         OFFICE, 1972.(27P)
    YEAR 1972
    DESC ALCOHOL USE, I.H.S.+, ALCOHOLISM TREATMENT+, PROGRAM
         DEVELOPMENT+
    IDEN U.S.

423 AUTH TAYLOR, HENRY D.; THWEATT, ROGER C.
    TITL CROSS-CULTURAL DEVELOPMENTAL PERFORMANCE OF NAVAJO
         CHILDREN ON THE BENDER-GESTALT TEST.
    SOUR PERCEPTUAL AND MOTOR SKILLS, AUG. 1972, V35, PP
         307-309.
    YEAR 1972
    DESC PSYCHOLOGICAL TESTING+, CHILDREN-SCHOOL AGE+,
         NATIVE-NON-NATIVE COMPARISONS, RESERVATION, ELEMENTARY
         SCHOOLS, OFF-RESERVATION, COGNITIVE PROCESSES+,MOTOR
         PROCESSES+, NAVAJO, SOUTHWEST, ANGLO AMERICANS
    IDEN U.S., BENDER GESTALT TEST, ARIZONA

424 AUTH ACKERKNECHT, ERWIN H.
    TITL PSYCHOPATHOLOGY, PRIMITIVE MEDICINE AND PRIMITIVE
         CULTURE.
    SOUR BULLETIN OF THE HISTORY OF MEDICINE, 1943, V14, PP
         30-67.
    YEAR 1943
    DESC TRADITIONAL HEALERS+, MENTAL DISORDERS+, CULTURE-BASED
         PSYCHOTHERAPY+, GROUP NORMS AND SANCTIONS,
         CULTURE-SPECIFIC SYNDROMES+
    IDEN ASIA, AFRICA, NORTH AMERICA

425 AUTH DEVEREUX, GEORGE
    TITL PRIMITIVE PSYCHIATRY.
    SOUR BULLETIN OF THE HISTORY OF MEDICINE, 1940, V8, PP
         1194-1213.
    YEAR 1940
    DESC NATIVE AMERICAN ETIOLOGY, MOHAVE, SOUTHWEST,
         CULTURE-SPECIFIC SYNDROMES+, SEXUAL RELATIONS+, FAMILY
         FUNCTIONING+
    IDEN U.S.

426 AUTH SCHMITT, N.; HOLE, L.W.; BARCLAY, W.S.
    TITL ACCIDENTAL DEATHS AMONG BRITISH COLUMBIA INDIANS.
    SOUR CANADIAN MEDICAL ASSOCIATION JOURNAL, JAN. 1966, V94,
         PP 228-234.
    YEAR 1966
```

    DESC NORTHWEST COAST, ACCIDENTS+, EPIDEMIOLOGICAL STUDY,
          DEMOGRAPHIC DATA, AGE COMPARISONS, SEX DIFFERENCES,
          ECONOMIC ISSUES
    IDEN CANADA, BRITISH COLUMBIA

427 AUTH FUCHS, ESTELLE
    TITL INNOVATION AT ROUGH ROCK.
    SOUR SATURDAY REVIEW, SEP. 1967, V50, PP 82-84.
    YEAR 1967
    DESC NAVAJO, SOUTHWEST, EDUCATION PROGRAMS AND SERVICES+,
          CHILDREN-INFANTS AND PRESCHOOL, CHILDREN-SCHOOL AGE,
          NATIVE AMERICAN ADMINISTERED PROGRAMS+, CULTURAL
          CONTINUITY+, ELEMENTARY SCHOOLS+
    IDEN U.S., NAVAJO RESERVATION, ROUGH ROCK DEMONSTRATION
          SCHOOL

428 AUTH SIEVERS, MAURICE L.; MARQUIS, JAMES R.
    TITL DUODENAL ULCER AMONG SOUTHWESTERN AMERICAN INDIANS.
    SOUR GASTROENTEROLOGY, 1962, V42, PP 566-569.
    YEAR 1962
    DESC PSYCHOPHYSIOLOGICAL DISORDERS+, SOUTHWEST,
          RESERVATION, EPIDEMIOLOGICAL STUDY, CLINICAL STUDY,
          ADULTS, PHYSICAL HEALTH AND ILLNESS
    IDEN U.S.

429 AUTH JAMES, BERNARD J.
    TITL SOME CRITICAL OBSERVATIONS CONCERNING ANALYSIS OF
          CHIPPEWA "ATOMISM" AND CHIPPEWA PERSONALITY.
    SOUR AMERICAN ANTHROPOLOGIST, 1954, V56, PP 283-286.
    YEAR 1954
    DESC EASTERN SUB-ARCTIC, PERSONALITY TRAITS+, REVIEW OF
          LITERATURE, ANOMIE+
    IDEN U.S.

430 AUTH BENEDICT, ROBERT
    TITL A PROFILE OF INDIAN AGED.
    SOUR OCCASIONAL PAPERS IN GERONTOLOGY, 1972, V10, PP 51-58
    YEAR 1972
    DESC AGED+, DEMOGRAPHIC DATA, ECONOMIC ISSUES+,
          EMPLOYMENT+, RESERVATION, PHYSICAL HEALTH AND ILLNESS
    IDEN U.S.

431 AUTH KAHN, MARVIN W.; DELK, JOHN L.
    TITL DEVELOPING A COMMUNITY MENTAL HEALTH CLINIC ON THE
          PAPAGO RESERVATION.
    SOUR INTERNATIONAL JOURNAL OF SOCIAL PSYCHIATRY, AUT. 1973,
          V19, PP 299-306.
    YEAR 1973
    DESC MENTAL HEALTH INSTITUTIONS+, RESERVATION, PAPAGO,
          SOUTHWEST, PROGRAM DEVELOPMENT+, MENTAL DISORDERS,
          DEMOGRAPHIC DATA, NATIVE AMERICAN PERSONNEL
    IDEN U.S., ARIZONA

432 AUTH SLATER, ARTHUR D.; ALBRECHT, STAN L.
    TITL THE EXTENT AND COST OF EXCESSIVE DRINKING AMONG THE

```
           UINTAH-OURAY INDIANS.
      SOUR IN HOWARD M. BAHR, BRUCE CHADWICK, AND ROBERT C. DAY
           (EDS.), NATIVE AMERICAN TODAY: SOCIOLOGICAL
           PERSPECTIVES, PP 358-367. NEW YORK: HARPER AND ROW,
           1972.
      YEAR 1972
      DESC ALCOHOL USE+, UTE, GREAT BASIN, INSTITUTIONALIZATION+,
           CORRECTIONAL INSTITUTIONS+, ECONOMIC ISSUES+
      IDEN U.S., UTAH, UINTAH-OURAY RESERVATION

433   AUTH BROMBERG, WALTER; HUTCHISON, SARAH H.
      TITL SELF IMAGE OF THE AMERICAN INDIAN: A PRELIMINARY
           STUDY.
      SOUR INTERNATIONAL JOURNAL OF SOCIAL PSYCHIATRY, SPR.-SUM.
           1974, V20, PP 39-44.
      YEAR 1974
      DESC SELF-CONCEPT+, COGNITIVE PROCESSES+, PSYCHOLOGICAL
           TESTING+
      IDEN U.S., GOODENOUGH HARRIS DRAW A PERSON TEST

434   AUTH RICHEK, HERBERT G.; CHUCULATE, OWEN; KLINERT, DOROTHY
      TITL AGING AND ETHNICITY IN HEALTHY ELDERLY WOMEN.
      SOUR GERIATRICS, MAY 1971, V26(5), PP 146-152.
      YEAR 1971
      DESC AGED+, FEMALES+, NATIVE-NON-NATIVE COMPARISONS,
           SELF-CONCEPT+, PSYCHOLOGICAL TESTING+, ANGLO AMERICANS
      IDEN U.S., BROWN SELF-REPORT INVENTORY

435   AUTH HAMMERSCHLAG, CARL A.
      TITL USING T-GROUPS TO TRAIN AMERICAN INDIANS AS PHYSICIAN
           ASSISTANTS.
      SOUR HOSPITAL AND COMMUNITY PSYCHIATRY, 1974, V25, PP 210,
           213.
      YEAR 1974
      DESC TRAINING PROGRAMS+, MEDICAL PARAPROFESSIONALS+, NATIVE
           AMERICAN PERSONNEL+,PSYCHOTHERAPY AND COUNSELING+,
           SOCIAL GROUPS AND PEER GROUPS
      IDEN U.S.

436   AUTH LEWIS, THOMAS H.
      TITL AN INDIAN HEALER"S PREVENTIVE MEDICINE PROCEDURE.
      SOUR HOSPITAL AND COMMUNITY PSYCHIATRY, FEB. 1974, V25, PP
           94-95.
      YEAR 1974
      DESC SIOUX, PLAINS, TRADITIONAL HEALERS+, RESERVATION,
           NATIVE AMERICAN RELIGIONS+
      IDEN U.S., SOUTH DAKOTA, PINE RIDGE RESERVATION

437   AUTH BRETT, BRIAN
      TITL MENTAL HEALTH CARE FOR CHILDREN OF THE WESTERN ARCTIC.
      SOUR CANADIAN JOURNAL OF PUBLIC HEALTH, SEP.-OCT. 1971,
           V62, PP 386-394.
      YEAR 1971
      DESC ESKIMO, CENTRAL AND EASTERN ARCTIC, CHILDREN-SCHOOL
           AGE+, ADOLESCENTS+, PREVENTIVE MENTAL HEALTH
```

```
           PROGRAMS+, DELIVERY OF SERVICES+, PROGRAM DEVELOPMENT
      IDEN CANADA, NORTHWEST TERRITORIES

438  AUTH SCHMITT, N.; BARCLAY, W.S.
     TITL ACCIDENTAL DEATHS AMONG WEST COAST INDIANS.
     SOUR CANADIAN JOURNAL OF PUBLIC HEALTH, OCT. 1962, V53, PP
          409-412.
     YEAR 1962
     DESC NORTHWEST COAST, ACCIDENTS+, EPIDEMIOLOGICAL STUDY,
          NATIVE-NON-NATIVE COMPARISONS, SEX DIFFERENCES, AGE
          COMPARISONS, ANGLO AMERICANS
     IDEN CANADA, BRITISH COLUMBIA

439  AUTH DRYFOOS, ROBERT J., JR.
     TITL TWO TACTICS FOR ETHNIC SURVIVAL--ESKIMO AND INDIAN.
     SOUR TRANS-ACTION, JAN. 1970, V7, PP 51-54.
     YEAR 1970
     DESC ESKIMO, CENTRAL AND EASTERN ARCTIC, CULTURAL
          CONTINUITY+, CULTURAL ADAPTATION+, INTERTRIBAL
          COMPARISONS, CREE
     IDEN CANADA, QUEBEC

440  AUTH NORRIS, PHIL; OVERBECK, DANIEL B.
     TITL THE INSTITUTIONALIZED MENTALLY RETARDED NAVAJO: A
          SERVICE PROGRAM.
     SOUR MENTAL RETARDATION, JUN. 1974, V12, PP 18-20.
     YEAR 1974
     DESC NAVAJO, SOUTHWEST, MENTAL RETARDATION+, B.I.A.,
          LANGUAGE HANDICAPS+, PSYCHOLOGICAL TESTING,
          INSTITUTIONALIZATION+, MENTAL HEALTH PROGRAMS AND
          SERVICES
     IDEN U.S.

441  AUTH KAUFMAN, ARTHUR; BRICKNER, PHILIP W.; VARNER, RICHARD;
          MASHBURN, WILLIAM
     TITL TRANQUILIZER CONTROL.
     SOUR JAMA: JOURNAL OF THE AMERICAN MEDICAL ASSOCIATION,
          SEP. 1972, V221(13), PP 1504-1506.
     YEAR 1972
     DESC DRUG USE+, CHEMOTHERAPY+, ANXIETY, MENTAL HEALTH
          PROGRAMS AND SERVICES+
     IDEN U.S., SOUTH DAKOTA

442  AUTH FISKE, SHIRLEY
     TITL RULES OF ADDRESS: NAVAJO WOMEN IN LOS ANGELES.
     SOUR JOURNAL OF ANTHROPOLOGICAL RESEARCH, SPR. 1978,
          V34(1), PP 72-91.
     YEAR 1978
     DESC NAVAJO, SOUTHWEST, COGNITIVE PROCESSES+, FEMALES+,
          ADULTS, URBAN AREAS, SOCIAL ROLES+, LANGUAGE
          HANDICAPS+, SOCIAL STATUS+, RELOCATION, URBANIZATION+,
          AGED
     IDEN U.S., CALIFORNIA

443  AUTH WILLIAMSON, ROBERT
```

TITL THE CANADIAN ARCTIC: SOCIOCULTURAL CHANGE.
SOUR ARCHIVES OF ENVIRONMENTAL HEALTH, OCT. 1968, V17, PP
484-491.
YEAR 1968
DESC ESKIMO, CENTRAL AND EASTERN ARCTIC, CULTURAL
ADAPTATION+, PHYSICAL HEALTH AND ILLNESS, FEDERAL
GOVERNMENT
IDEN CANADA, NORTHWEST TERRITORIES

444 AUTH BOYD, DAVID L.; MAYNARD, JAMES E.; HAMMES, LAUREL M.
TITL ACCIDENT MORTALITY IN ALASKA, 1958-1962.
SOUR ARCHIVES OF ENVIRONMENTAL HEALTH, JUL. 1968, V17, PP
101-106.
YEAR 1968
DESC ACCIDENTS+, NATIVE-NON-NATIVE COMPARISONS,
EPIDEMIOLOGICAL STUDY, YUKON SUB-ARCTIC, WESTERN
ARCTIC, ALASKA NATIVES, OFF-RESERVATION, ANGLO
AMERICANS
IDEN U.S., ALASKA

445 AUTH WALLACE, ANTHONY F.C.
TITL CULTURAL DETERMINANTS OF RESPONSE TO HALLUCINATORY
EXPERIENCE.
SOUR ARCHIVES OF GENERAL PSYCHIATRY, JUL. 1959, V1, PP
58-69.
YEAR 1959
DESC DREAMS AND VISION QUESTS+, DRUG USE+, TRADITIONAL USE
OF DRUGS AND ALCOHOL,NATIVE-NON-NATIVE COMPARISONS,
TRADITIONAL HEALERS, MENTAL DISORDERS
IDEN U.S., AUSTRALIA

446 AUTH MACARTHUR, RUSSELL
TITL SOME DIFFERENTIAL ABILITIES OF NORTHERN CANADIAN
NATIVE YOUTH.
SOUR INTERNATIONAL JOURNAL OF PSYCHOLOGY, 1968, V3(1), PP
43-51.
YEAR 1968
DESC ADOLESCENTS+, PSYCHOLOGICAL TESTING+, ABILITIES+,
ESKIMO, CENTRAL AND EASTERN ARCTIC, NATIVE-NON-NATIVE
COMPARISONS, CULTURE-FAIR TESTS+, CHILDREN-SCHOOL
AGE+, COGNITIVE PROCESSES, ANGLO AMERICANS
IDEN CANADA, PIAGETIAN TASKS

447 AUTH WAX, ROSALIE H.
TITL THE WARRIOR DROPOUTS
SOUR TRANS-ACTION, MAY 1967, V4, PP 40-46.
YEAR 1967
DESC SIOUX, PLAINS, RESERVATION, ADOLESCENTS+, DROPOUTS+,
MALES+, SOCIAL GROUPS AND PEER GROUPS+, SECONDARY
SCHOOLS+, B.I.A. BOARDING SCHOOLS
IDEN U.S., SOUTH DAKOTA, PINE RIDGE RESERVATION

448 AUTH SCHAEFER, OTTO
TITL ALCOHOL WITHDRAWAL SYNDROME IN A NEWBORN INFANT OF A
YUKON INDIAN MOTHER.

```
         SOUR   CANADIAN MEDICAL ASSOCIATION JOURNAL, DEC. 1962, V87,
                PP 1333-1334.
         YEAR   1962
         DESC   CHILDREN-INFANTS AND PRESCHOOL+, ALCOHOL USE+, YUKON
                SUB-ARCTIC, PHYSICAL HEALTH AND ILLNESS+
         IDEN   CANADA

449   AUTH   SHORE, JAMES H.
      TITL   SUICIDE AND SUICIDE ATTEMPTS AMONG AMERICAN INDIANS OF
             THE PACIFIC NORTHWEST.
      SOUR   INTERNATIONAL JOURNAL OF SOCIAL PSYCHIATRY, SUM. 1972,
             V18, PP 91-96.
      YEAR   1972
      DESC   SUICIDE+, NORTHWEST COAST, EPIDEMIOLOGICAL STUDY,
             I.H.S., REVIEW OF LITERATURE, B.I.A. BOARDING SCHOOLS,
             PLATEAU
      IDEN   U.S., WASHINGTON, OREGON, IDAHO

450   AUTH   WESTERMEYER, JOSEPH; HAUSMAN, WILLIAM
      TITL   CROSS CULTURAL CONSULTATION FOR MENTAL HEALTH
             PLANNING.
      SOUR   INTERNATIONAL JOURNAL OF SOCIAL PSYCHIATRY, SPR.-SUM.
             1974, V20(1-2), PP 34-38.
      YEAR   1974
      DESC   MENTAL HEALTH PROGRAMS AND SERVICES+, CONSULTATION+,
             PROGRAM DEVELOPMENT+, MENTAL HEALTH PROFESSIONALS+
      IDEN   U.S.

451   AUTH   SPANG, ALONZO T.
      TITL   COUNSELING THE INDIAN.
      SOUR   JOURNAL OF AMERICAN INDIAN EDUCATION, OCT. 1965, V5,
             PP 10-15.
      YEAR   1965
      DESC   PSYCHOTHERAPY AND COUNSELING+, TIME PERCEPTION,
             GENEROSITY, COOPERATION, UNIVERSAL HARMONY,
             NONCOMPETITIVENESS, CULTURE-FAIR TESTS

452   AUTH   WILTSHIRE, E. BEVAN; GRAY, JOHN E.
      TITL   DRAW-A-MAN AND RAVAN"S PROGRESSIVE MATRICES (1938)
             INTELLIGENCE TEST PERFORMANCE OF RESERVE INDIAN
             CHILDREN.
      SOUR   CANADIAN JOURNAL OF BEHAVIORAL SCIENCE, 1969, V1(2),
             PP 119-122.
      YEAR   1969
      DESC   PSYCHOLOGICAL TESTING+, ADOLESCENTS+, ABILITIES+,
             RESERVATION, CHILDREN-SCHOOL AGE+, AGE COMPARISONS,
             SEX DIFFERENCES, CREE, EASTERN SUB-ARCTIC
      IDEN   CANADA, RAVEN PROGRESSIVE MATRICES, GOODENOUGH HARRIS
             DRAW A PERSON TEST

453   AUTH   HENDERSON, NORMAN B.
      TITL   CROSS-CULTURAL ACTION RESEARCH: SOME LIMITATIONS,
             ADVANTAGES, AND PROBLEMS.
      SOUR   JOURNAL OF SOCIAL PSYCHOLOGY, OCT. 1967, V73, PP 61-70
      YEAR   1967
```

```
     DESC   NAVAJO, PUEBLO-ZUNI, SOUTHWEST, ALCOHOLISM TREATMENT+,
            STEREOTYPES, PROGRAM EVALUATION+
     IDEN   U.S.

454  AUTH   LEWIS, OSCAR
     TITL   MANLY HEARTED WOMEN AMONG THE NORTH PIEGAN.
     SOUR   AMERICAN ANTHROPOLOGIST, 1941, V43, PP 173-187.
     YEAR   1941
     DESC   BLACKFEET-PIEGAN, PLAINS, FEMALES+, GROUP NORMS AND
            SANCTIONS+, AGED, ADULTS, EXTENDED FAMILY, SEXUAL
            RELATIONS+, AGGRESSIVENESS+, SOCIAL ROLES
     IDEN   CANADA, ALBERTA

455  AUTH   DOZIER, EDWARD P.
     TITL   RESISTANCE TO ACCULTURATION AND ASSIMILATION IN AN
            INDIAN PUEBLO.
     SOUR   AMERICAN ANTHROPOLOGIST, 1951, V53, PP 56-66.
     YEAR   1951
     DESC   SOUTHWEST, PUEBLO-TEWA, PUEBLO-HOPI, CULTURAL
            CONTINUITY+, INTERTRIBAL COMPARISONS, RESERVATION,
            CULTURAL ADAPTATION+, EXTENDED FAMILY, BILINGUALISM+
     IDEN   U.S., ARIZONA

456  AUTH   VOGET, FRED W.
     TITL   ACCULTURATION AT CAUGHNAWAGA: A NOTE ON THE
            NATIVE-MODIFIED GROUP.
     SOUR   AMERICAN ANTHROPOLOGIST, 1951, V53, PP 220-231.
     YEAR   1951
     DESC   IROQUOIS, NORTHEAST WOODLAND, RESERVATION, CULTURAL
            ADAPTATION+, RELIGIONS-NON-NATIVE, NATIVE AMERICAN
            RELIGIONS+, TRIBAL POLITICAL ORGANIZATIONS, CULTURAL
            REVIVAL+
     IDEN   CANADA, QUEBEC, CAUGHNAWAGA IROQUOIS RESERVE, HANDSOME
            LAKE RELIGION

457  AUTH   CARPENTER, EDMUND S.
     TITL   ALCOHOL IN THE IROQUOIS DREAM QUEST.
     SOUR   AMERICAN JOURNAL OF PSYCHIATRY, AUG. 1959, V116, PP
            148-151.
     YEAR   1959
     DESC   IROQUOIS, NORTHEAST WOODLAND, TRADITIONAL USE OF DRUGS
            AND ALCOHOL+, NATIVE AMERICAN RELIGIONS+,
            RELIGIONS-NON-NATIVE+, DREAMS AND VISION QUESTS
     IDEN   CANADA, ONTARIO

458  AUTH   CHANCE, NORMAN A.
     TITL   CULTURE CHANGE AND INTEGRATION: AN ESKIMO EXAMPLE.
     SOUR   AMERICAN ANTHROPOLOGIST, 1960, V62, PP 1028, 1044.
     YEAR   1960
     DESC   ESKIMO, WESTERN ARCTIC, STRESS+, CULTURAL ADAPTATION+,
            BICULTURALISM, TRADITIONAL SOCIAL CONTROL, GROUP NORMS
            AND SANCTIONS, OFF-RESERVATION, NATIVE AMERICAN
            VALUES, LEADERSHIP
     IDEN   U.S., ALASKA
```

459 AUTH   EISENMAN, RUSSELL
     TITL   SCAPEGOATING AND SOCIAL CONTROL.
     SOUR   JOURNAL OF PSYCHOLOGY, NOV. 1965, V61, PP 203-209.
     YEAR   1965
     DESC   TRADITIONAL SOCIAL CONTROL+, NAVAJO, SOUTHWEST,
            ESKIMO, TABOO BREAKING, GROUP NORMS AND SANCTIONS+,
            NATIVE AMERICAN COPING BEHAVIORS
     IDEN   U.S.

460 AUTH   CASTELLANO, MARLENE
     TITL   VOCATION OR IDENTITY: THE DILEMMA OF INDIAN YOUTH.
     SOUR   IN WAUBAGESHIG (ED.), THE ONLY GOOD INDIAN: ESSAYS BY
            CANADIAN INDIANS, PP 52-60. TORONTO: NEW PRESS, 1970
     YEAR   1970
     DESC   ETHNIC IDENTITY+, EMPLOYMENT+, ADOLESCENTS+, STRESS,
            BICULTURALISM+, CULTURAL REVIVAL+, EDUCATION PROGRAMS
            AND SERVICES, TRAINING PROGRAMS
     IDEN   CANADA

461 AUTH   BLACK HORSE, FRANCIS D.
     TITL   PRISON AND NATIVE PEOPLE.
     SOUR   INDIAN HISTORIAN, SPR. 1975, V8, PP 54-56.
     YEAR   1975
     DESC   CORRECTIONAL INSTITUTIONS+, CULTURAL CONTINUITY+,
            STRESS, NATIVE AMERICAN RELIGIONS+, UNIVERSAL HARMONY,
            INSTITUTIONALIZATION+

462 AUTH   WESTERMEYER, JOSEPH
     TITL   EROSION OF INDIAN MENTAL HEALTH IN CITIES.
     SOUR   MINNESOTA MEDICINE, JUN. 1976, V59, PP 431-433.
     YEAR   1976
     DESC   URBAN AREAS, CHIPPEWA, SIOUX, PLAINS, EASTERN
            SUB-ARCTIC, NATIVE AMERICAN COPING BEHAVIORS+,
            URBANIZATION+, STRESS, PREVENTIVE MENTAL HEALTH
            PROGRAMS
     IDEN   U.S., MINNESOTA

463 AUTH   JAMES, BERNARD J.
     TITL   SOCIAL-PSYCHOLOGICAL DIMENSIONS OF OJIBWA
            ACCULTURATION.
     SOUR   AMERICAN ANTHROPOLOGIST, 1961, V63, PP 721-746.
     YEAR   1961
     DESC   CHIPPEWA, EASTERN SUB-ARCTIC, PERSONALITY TRAITS+,
            RESERVATION, CULTURAL ADAPTATION+, STRESS, ECONOMIC
            ISSUES, SOCIAL STATUS, STEREOTYPES+, ANXIETY+,
            SELF-CONCEPT+, DISCRIMINATION+, NONINTERFERENCE,
            PASSIVE RESISTANCE
     IDEN   U.S., WISCONSIN

464 AUTH   BOLMAN, WILLIAM M.; KATZ, ALAN S.
     TITL   HAMBURGER HOARDING: A CASE OF SYMBOLIC CANNIBALISM
            RESEMBLING WHITICO PSYCHOSIS.
     SOUR   JOURNAL OF NERVOUS AND MENTAL DISORDERS, MAY 1966,
            V142(5), PP 424-428.
     YEAR   1966

DESC WINDIGO PSYCHOSIS+, EASTERN SUB-ARCTIC, PSYCHOTHERAPY
AND COUNSELING+, ANXIETY+, SCHIZOPHRENIA+, CLINICAL
STUDY

465 AUTH TYLER, INEZ M.; THOMPSON, SOPHIE D.
TITL CULTURAL FACTORS IN CASEWORK TREATMENT OF A NAVAJO
MENTAL PATIENT.
SOUR SOCIAL CASEWORK, APR. 1965, V46, PP 215-220.
YEAR 1965
DESC NAVAJO, SOUTHWEST, I.H.S., RESERVATION, SOCIAL SERVICE
PROFESSIONALS+, INSTITUTIONALIZATION+, MENTAL HEALTH
INSTITUTIONS, EXTENDED FAMILY+, WITCHCRAFT,
CULTURE-BASED PSYCHOTHERAPY, ADULTS, LANGUAGE
HANDICAPS, NATIVE AMERICAN PERSONNEL+, OUTPATIENT
CARE+
IDEN U.S., NAVAJO RESERVATION

466 AUTH HACKENBERG, ROBERT A.; WILSON, C. RODERICK
TITL RELUCTANT EMIGRANTS: THE ROLE OF MIGRATION IN PAPAGO
INDIAN ADAPTATION.
SOUR HUMAN ORGANIZATION, SUM. 1972, V31(2), PP 171-186.
YEAR 1972
DESC PAPAGO, SOUTHWEST, RELOCATION+, DEMOGRAPHIC DATA, SEX
DIFFERENCES, AGE COMPARISONS, ECONOMIC ISSUES,
RESERVATION, OFF-RESERVATION, ADULTS
IDEN U.S., ARIZONA, PAPAGO RESERVATION

467 AUTH LOCKLEAR, HERBERT H.
TITL AMERICAN INDIAN MYTHS.
SOUR SOCIAL WORK, MAY 1972, V17, PP 72-80.
YEAR 1972
DESC STEREOTYPES+, CULTURAL CONTINUITY+, UNIVERSAL HARMONY,
EXTENDED FAMILY, URBANIZATION+, TIME PERCEPTION,
NONCOMPETITIVENESS, URBAN AREAS, GENEROSITY
IDEN U.S.

468 AUTH WINKLER, ALLAN M.
TITL DRINKING ON THE AMERICAN FRONTIER.
SOUR QUARTERLY JOURNAL OF STUDIES ON ALCOHOL, JUN. 1968,
V29, PP 413-445.
YEAR 1968
DESC ALCOHOL USE+, OFF-RESERVATION, NATIVE-NON-NATIVE
COMPARISONS,ANGLO AMERICANS
IDEN U.S.

469 AUTH GALLOWAY, CHARLES G.; MICKELSON, NORMA I.
TITL CHANGES IN PERSONAL-SOCIAL DISTANCE OF TEACHERS OF
INDIAN CHILDREN.
SOUR AMERICAN JOURNAL OF ORTHOPSYCHIATRY, JUL.1970, V40(4),
PP 681-683.
YEAR 1970
DESC EDUCATION PROFESSIONALS+, EDUCATION PROGRAMS AND
SERVICES+, CHILDREN-SCHOOL AGE, PSYCHOLOGICAL TESTING,
DISCRIMINATION+
IDEN CANADA, BRITISH COLUMBIA

470 AUTH SAVARD, ROBERT J.
    TITL EFFECTS OF DISULFIRAM THERAPY ON RELATIONSHIPS WITHIN
         THE NAVAJO DRINKING GROUP.
    SOUR QUARTERLY JOURNAL OF STUDIES ON ALCOHOL, DEC. 1968,
         V29, PP 909-916.
    YEAR 1968
    DESC CHEMOTHERAPY+, ALCOHOLISM TREATMENT+, NAVAJO,
         SOUTHWEST, MALES, ADULTS, SOCIAL GROUPS AND PEER
         GROUPS+, GROUP NORMS AND SANCTIONS+
    IDEN U.S., ARIZONA

471 AUTH HAMER, JOHN H.
    TITL ACCULTURATION STRESS AND THE FUNCTIONS OF ALCOHOL
         AMONG THE FOREST COUNTY POTAWATOMI.
    SOUR QUARTERLY JOURNAL OF STUDIES ON ALCOHOL, 1965, V26, PP
         285-302.
    YEAR 1965
    DESC POTAWATOMI, PRAIRIE, STRESS+, EMOTIONAL RESTRAINT+,
         SOCIAL GROUPS AND PEER GROUPS, ALCOHOL USE+, GROUP
         NORMS AND SANCTIONS+, PERSONALITY TRAITS+,
         AGGRESSIVENESS, SOCIAL STATUS+, STEREOTYPES
    IDEN U.S., MICHIGAN

472 AUTH DOBYNS, HENRY F.
    TITL THE THERAPEUTIC EXPERIENCE OF RESPONSIBLE DEMOCRACY.
    SOUR IN S. LEVINE AND N. LURIE (EDS.), THE AMERICAN INDIAN
         TODAY, PP 268-291. DELAND, FLORIDA: EVERETT/EDWARDS,
         1968.
    YEAR 1968
    DESC FEDERAL GOVERNMENT+, ADMINISTRATIVE ISSUES, B.I.A.,
         TRIBAL POLITICAL ORGANIZATIONS+, RESERVATION,
         POLITICS-NONTRIBAL, LEGAL ISSUES+,
    IDEN U.S.

473 AUTH KEREKHOFF, ALAN C.
    TITL ANOMIE AND ACHIEVEMENT MOTIVATION: A STUDY OF
         PERSONALITY DEVELOPMENT WITHIN CULTURAL
         DISORGANIZATION.
    SOUR SOCIAL FORCES, 1959, V37, PP 196-202.
    YEAR 1959
    DESC ANOMIE+, ACHIEVEMENT+, MOTIVATION+, PSYCHOLOGICAL
         TESTING+, CHIPPEWA, EASTERN SUB-ARCTIC, RESERVATION,
         CHILDREN-SCHOOL AGE+, PERSONALITY TRAITS+, TRADITIONAL
         CHILD REARING, ELEMENTARY SCHOOLS
    IDEN U.S., WISCONSIN, THEMATIC APPERCEPTION TEST

474 AUTH ROHRL, VIVIAN J.
    TITL A NUTRITIONAL FACTOR IN WINDIGO PSYCHOSIS.
    SOUR AMERICAN ANTHROPOLOGIST, FEB. 1970, V72, PP 97-101.
    YEAR 1970
    DESC WINDIGO PSYCHOSIS+, PHYSICAL HEALTH AND ILLNESS,
         EASTERN SUB-ARCTIC, CHIPPEWA, CREE, REVIEW OF
         LITERATURE, NUTRITIONAL FACTORS+
    IDEN U.S.

475 AUTH FRENCH, JEAN; SCHWARTZ, DORIS R.
     TITL TERMINAL CARE AT HOME IN TWO CULTURES.
     SOUR AMERICAN JOURNAL OF NURSING, MAR. 1973, V73, PP
           502-505.
     YEAR 1973
     DESC TRADITIONAL HEALERS, NAVAJO, SOUTHWEST, NATIVE
           AMERICAN ETIOLOGY+, DELIVERY OF SERVICES, MEDICAL
           PROFESSIONALS+, RESERVATION, AGED+, DEATH AND DYING+
     IDEN U.S., ARIZONA, NAVAJO RESERVATION

476 AUTH MOREY, SYLVESTER M.; GILLIAM, OLIVIA L.
     TITL RESPECT FOR LIFE: REPORT OF A CONFERENCE AT HARPER"S
           FERRY, WEST VIRGINIA ON THE TRADITIONAL UPBRINGING OF
           AMERICAN INDIAN CHILDREN.
     SOUR GARDEN CITY, N.Y.: WALDORF PRESS, 1974. (202P)
     YEAR 1974
     DESC TRADITIONAL CHILD REARING+, NATIVE AMERICAN VALUES+,
           CHILDREN-INFANTS AND PRESCHOOL+, CHILDREN-SCHOOL AGE+,
           ADOLESCENTS+, TRADITIONAL SOCIAL CONTROL+
     IDEN U.S.

477 AUTH O"DONNELL, JAMES P.; CRESS, JOSEPH N.
     TITL DIMENSIONS OF BEHAVIOR PROBLEMS AMONG OGLALA SIOUX
           ADOLESCENTS.
     SOUR JOURNAL OF ABNORMAL CHILD PSYCHOLOGY, 1975, V3(3), PP
           163-169.
     YEAR 1975
     DESC SIOUX-OGLALA, PLAINS, ADOLESCENTS+, PSYCHOLOGICAL
           TESTING+, SECONDARY SCHOOLS, RESERVATION, SEX
           DIFFERENCES, PERSONALITY TRAITS, SOCIALLY DEVIANT
           BEHAVIOR, PASSIVE RESISTANCE, NATIVE-NON-NATIVE
           COMPARISONS
     IDEN U.S., QUAY-PETERSON BEHAVIOR PROBLEM CHECKLIST

478 AUTH SWANSON, DAVID M.; BRATRUDE, AMON P.; BROWN, EDWARD M.
     TITL ALCOHOL ABUSE IN A POPULATION OF INDIAN CHILDREN.
     SOUR DISEASES OF THE NERVOUS SYSTEM, DEC. 1971, V32, PP
           835-842.
     YEAR 1971
     DESC ALCOHOL USE+, CHILDREN-SCHOOL AGE+, CHILDREN-INFANTS
           AND PRESCHOOL, FAMILY FUNCTIONING+, ADOLESCENTS+,
           SOCIALLY DEVIANT BEHAVIOR, NONINTERFERENCE,
           TRADITIONAL CHILD REARING+, CHILD ABUSE AND NEGLECT,
           COLVILLE, PLATEAU

479 AUTH KAUFMAN, ARTHUR
     TITL GASOLINE SNIFFING AMONG CHILDREN IN A PUEBLO INDIAN
           VILLAGE.
     SOUR PEDIATRICS, JUN. 1973, V51, PP 1060-1064.
     YEAR 1973
     DESC DRUG USE+, CHILDREN-SCHOOL AGE+, PUEBLO, SOUTHWEST,
           ADOLESCENTS, FAMILY FUNCTIONING+, RESERVATION
     IDEN U.S.

480 AUTH HELLON, C.P.

TITL   MENTAL ILLNESS AND ACCULTURATION IN THE CANADIAN
         ABORIGINAL.
SOUR   CANADIAN PSYCHIATRIC ASSOCIATION JOURNAL, APR. 1970,
         V15(2), PP 135-139.
YEAR   1970
DESC   MENTAL DISORDERS+, CLINICAL STUDY, CHARACTER
         DISORDERS+, MENTAL HEALTH INSTITUTIONS, SOCIALLY
         DEVIANT BEHAVIOR+, STRESS+, EPIDEMIOLOGICAL STUDY
IDEN   CANADA

481   AUTH   LEWIS, THOMAS H.
       TITL   OGLALA (SIOUX) CONCEPTS OF HOMOSEXUALITY AND THE
            DETERMINANTS OF SEXUAL IDENTIFICATION.
       SOUR   JAMA, JOURNAL OF THE AMERICAN MEDICAL ASSOCIATION,JUL.
            1973, V225(3), PP 312-313.
       YEAR   1973
       DESC   SEXUAL RELATIONS+, SIOUX-OGLALA, PLAINS, GROUP NORMS
            AND SANCTIONS+, RESERVATION, SOCIAL ROLES+, MALES
       IDEN   U.S., SOUTH DAKOTA, PINE RIDGE RESERVATION

482   AUTH   JILEK-AALL, LOUISE
       TITL   WHAT IS A SASQUATCH--OR, THE PROBLEMATICS OF REALITY
            TESTING.
       SOUR   CANADIAN PSYCHIATRIC ASSOCIATION JOURNAL, JUN. 1972,
            V17, PP 243-247.
       YEAR   1972
       DESC   NORTHWEST COAST, CULTURAL ADAPTATION,
            NATIVE-NON-NATIVE COMPARISONS, CULTURE-SPECIFIC
            SYNDROMES+, ANGLO AMERICANS
       IDEN   CANADA, BRITISH COLUMBIA

483   AUTH   MILES, JAMES E.
       TITL   THE PSYCHIATRIC ASPECTS OF THE TRADITIONAL MEDICINE OF
            THE BRITISH COLUMBIACOAST INDIANS.
       SOUR   CANADIAN PSYCHIATRIC ASSOCIATION JOURNAL, AUG. 1967,
            V12, PP 429-431.
       YEAR   1967
       DESC   NATIVE AMERICAN ETIOLOGY, NORTHWEST COAST, TRADITIONAL
            HEALERS+, CULTURE-BASED PSYCHOTHERAPY
       IDEN   CANADA, BRITISH COLUMBIA

484   AUTH   PELNER, LOUIS
       TITL   PEYOTE CULT, MESCALINE HALLUCINATIONS, AND MODEL
            PSYCHOSIS.
       SOUR   NEW YORK STATE JOURNAL OF MEDICINE, NOV. 1967, PP
            2838-2843.
       YEAR   1967
       DESC   NATIVE AMERICAN RELIGIONS, TRADITIONAL USE OF DRUGS
            AND ALCOHOL+, DRUG USE+, DREAMS AND VISION QUESTS+,
            SCHIZOPHRENIA+
       IDEN   U.S., NATIVE AMERICAN CHURCH

485   AUTH   LANTIS, MARGARET
       TITL   ENVIRONMENTAL STRESSES ON HUMAN BEHAVIOR: SUMMARY AND
            SUGGESTIONS.

SOUR ARCHIVES OF ENVIRONMENTAL HEALTH, OCT. 1968, V17, PP
      578-585.
YEAR 1968
DESC STRESS+, ECONOMIC ISSUES, CULTURAL ADAPTATION, WESTERN
      ARCTIC, CENTRAL AND EASTERN ARCTIC, ENVIRONMENTAL
      FACTORS

486 AUTH CHANCE, NORMAN A.
     TITL IMPLICATIONS OF ENVIRONMENTAL STRESS: STRATEGIES OF
           DEVELOPMENTAL CHANGE IN THE NORTH.
     SOUR ARCHIVES OF ENVIRONMENTAL HEALTH, OCT. 1968, V17, PP
           571-577.
     YEAR 1968
     DESC CREE, EASTERN SUB-ARCTIC, COGNITIVE PROCESSES,
           STRESS+, EMOTIONAL RESTRAINT, RESERVATION, URBAN
           AREAS, NONINTERFERENCE, NONCOMPETITIVENESS, NATIVE
           AMERICAN COPING BEHAVIORS+, NATIVE AMERICAN VALUES+,
           ENVIRONMENTAL FACTORS+
     IDEN CANADA, QUEBEC

487 AUTH VALLEE, FRANK G.
     TITL STRESSES OF CHANGE AND MENTAL HEALTH AMONG THE
           CANADIAN ESKIMOS.
     SOUR ARCHIVES OF ENVIRONMENTAL HEALTH, OCT. 1968, V17, PP
           565-570.
     YEAR 1968
     DESC ESKIMO, CENTRAL AND EASTERN ARCTIC, STRESS, MENTAL
           DISORDERS+, CULTURAL ADAPTATION, NATIVE AMERICAN
           ETIOLOGY+, MENTAL HEALTH PROGRAMS AND SERVICES+,
           OFF-RESERVATION, ENVIRONMENTAL FACTORS+
     IDEN CANADA, NORTHWEST TERRITORIES

488 AUTH ANDROES, SHARON T.
     TITL FLATHEAD VALLEY COMMUNITY COLLEGE ASSOCIATE DEGREE
           MENTAL HEALTH/HUMAN SERVICES PROGRAM.
     SOUR (NIMH GRANT NO. T41MH-12961). KALISPELL, MT.:
           FLATHEAD VALLEY COMMUNITY COLLEGE, 1976.
     YEAR 1976
     DESC MENTAL HEALTH PARAPROFESSIONALS+, SOCIAL SERVICE
           PARAPROFESSIONALS+, EDUCATION PROGRAMS AND SERVICES,
           COLLEGES AND UNIVERSITIES, TRAINING PROGRAMS+, PROGRAM
           DEVELOPMENT+, PLATEAU
     IDEN U.S., MONTANA

489 AUTH BERREMAN, GERALD D.
     TITL INQUIRY INTO COMMUNITY INTEGRATION IN AN ALEUTIAN
           VILLAGE.
     SOUR AMERICAN ANTHROPOLOGIST, 1955, V57, PP 49-59,
     YEAR 1955
     DESC ALEUT, WESTERN ARCTIC, STRESS+, OFF-RESERVATION,
           CULTURAL ADAPTATION
     IDEN U.S., ALASKA

490 AUTH LEON, ROBERT L.; MARTIN, HARRY W.; GLADFELTER, JOHN H.
     TITL AN EMOTIONAL AND EDUCATIONAL EXPERIENCE FOR URBAN

```
              MIGRANTS.
       SOUR   AMERICAN JOURNAL OF PSYCHIATRY, SEP. 1967, V124(3), PP
              381-384.
       YEAR   1967
       DESC   URBAN AREAS, RELOCATION+, ALASKA NATIVES, WESTERN
              ARCTIC, YUKON SUB-ARCTIC,NORTHWEST COAST,
              URBANIZATION+, B.I.A., CONSULTATION+, PREVENTIVE
              MENTAL HEALTH PROGRAMS
       IDEN   U.S., ALASKA, WASHINGTON

491    AUTH   LABARRE, WESTON
       TITL   A CULTIST DRUG ADDICTION IN AN INDIAN ALCOHOLIC.
       SOUR   BULLETIN OF THE MENNINGER CLINIC, 1941, V5, PP 40-46.
       YEAR   1941
       DESC   DRUG USE+, TRADITIONAL USE OF DRUGS AND ALCOHOL+,
              DREAMS AND VISION QUESTS+, OSAGE, PRAIRIE, ALCOHOL
              USE, PSYCHOTHERAPY AND COUNSELING+, CLINICAL STUDY,
              PSYCHOANALYSIS
       IDEN   U.S., OKLAHOMA

492    AUTH   BOYER, L. BRYCE; KLOPFER, BRUNO; BOYER, RUTH M.;
              BRAWER, FLORENCE B.; KAWAI, HAYAO
       TITL   EFFECTS OF ACCULTURATION ON THE PERSONALITY TRAITS OF
              THE OLD PEOPLE OF THE MESCALERO AND CHIRICAHUA
              APACHES.
       SOUR   INTERNATIONAL JOURNAL OF SOCIAL PSYCHIATRY, AUT. 1965,
              V11, PP 264-271.
       YEAR   1965
       DESC   APACHE-MESCALERO, APACHE-CHIRICAHUA, SOUTHWEST,
              PERSONALITY TRAITS+, RESERVATION, PSYCHOLOGICAL
              TESTING+, MALES+, AGED+, CULTURAL ADAPTATION, GRIEF
              REACTION, DEPRESSION, ETHNIC IDENTITY
       IDEN   U.S., NEW MEXICO, MESCALERO RESERVATION, RORSCHACH
              TEST

493    AUTH   LISMER, MARJORIE
       TITL   ADOPTION PRACTICES OF THE BLOOD INDIANS OF ALBERTA,
              CANADA.
       SOUR   PLAINS ANTHROPOLOGIST, FEB. 1974, V19, PP 25-33.
       YEAR   1974
       DESC   BLACKFEET-BLOOD, PLAINS, ADOPTION AND FOSTER CARE+,
              RESERVATION, EXTENDED FAMILY+, CHILDREN-INFANTS AND
              PRESCHOOL+, CHILDREN-SCHOOL AGE+
       IDEN   CANADA, ALBERTA, BLOOD RESERVE

494    AUTH   KLUCKHOHN, CLYDE
       TITL   PERSONALITY FORMATION AMONG THE NAVAJO INDIANS.
       SOUR   SOCIOMETRY, 1946, V9,  PP 128-132.
       YEAR   1946
       DESC   NAVAJO, SOUTHWEST, CHILDREN-SCHOOL AGE+, PERSONALITY
              TRAITS+, RESERVATION
       IDEN   U.S., NAVAJO RESERVATION

495    AUTH   CAVENAUGH, MARY ANN
       TITL   NATIVE AMERICAN BILINGUAL BICULTURAL DAY CARE.
```

SOUR REPORT BY THE NATIVE AMERICAN COMPONENT OF THE IRA DAY
      CARE GRANT NO. H-3939A/H/O, 1972. (49P)
YEAR 1972
DESC BILINGUALISM+, BICULTURALISM+, CHILDREN-INFANTS AND
      PRESCHOOL+, EDUCATION PROGRAMS AND SERVICES+, CULTURAL
      CONTINUITY+, NATIVE AMERICAN VALUES, NATIVE AMERICAN
      ADMINISTERED PROGRAMS+, MESQUAKIE, SIOUX, ALASKA
      NATIVES, UTE, DAY CARE+
IDEN U.S., UTAH, ALASKA, SOUTH DAKOTA, NORTH DAKOTA, IOWA,
      PINE RIDGE RESERVATION, UTE RESERVATION, FORT TOTTEN
      RESERVATION

496 AUTH FATHAUER, GEORGE H.
    TITL THE MOHAVE "GHOST DOCTOR".
    SOUR AMERICAN ANTHROPOLOGIST, 1951, V53, PP 605-607.
    YEAR 1951
    DESC MOHAVE, SOUTHWEST, TRADITIONAL HEALERS+, GHOST
          SICKNESS, DREAMS AND VISION QUESTS
    IDEN U.S.

497 AUTH GURIAN, JAY
    TITL THE IMPORTANCE OF DEPENDENCY IN NATIVE AMERICAN-WHITE
          CONTACT.
    SOUR AMERICAN INDIAN QUARTERLY, SPR. 1977, V3 (1), PP 16-36.
    YEAR 1977
    DESC POWERLESSNESS+, COOPERATION+, NATIVE AMERICAN VALUES+,
          NATIVE AMERICAN COPING BEHAVIORS+, SOCIAL NETWORKS
    IDEN U.S.

498 AUTH KLEINFELD, JUDITH S.
    TITL EFFECTS OF NONVERBALLY COMMUNICATED PERSONAL WARMTH ON
          THE INTELLIGENCE TEST PERFORMANCE OF INDIAN AND ESKIMO
          ADOLESCENTS.
    SOUR JOURNAL OF SOCIAL PSYCHOLOGY, OCT. 1973, V91, PP
          149-150.
    YEAR 1973
    DESC ADOLESCENTS+, PSYCHOLOGICAL TESTING+, ABILITIES+,
          WESTERN ARCTIC, YUKON SUB-ARCTIC, ESKIMO, ATHABASCAN,
          SECONDARY SCHOOLS, NONCOMPETITIVENESS,
          NONINTERFERENCE, COOPERATION, URBAN AREAS
    IDEN U.S., ALASKA, WECHSLER ADULT INTELLIGENCE SCALE, DIGIT
          SYMBOL SUBTEST, MANNWHITNEY U TEST

499 AUTH HAMMERSCHLAG, CARL A.
    TITL IDENTITY GROUPS WITH AMERICAN INDIAN ADOLESCENTS.
    SOUR PAPER PRESENTED AT THE ANNUAL MEETING OF THE AMERICAN
          GROUP PSYCHOTHERAPY ASSOCIATION, NEW YORK, FEB. 1974.
          (16 P)
    YEAR 1974
    DESC ADOLESCENTS+, SELF-CONCEPT+, ETHNIC IDENTITY+,
          STRESS+, SOCIAL GROUPS AND PEER GROUPS+, PSYCHOTHERAPY
          AND COUNSELING+, RESERVATION, URBAN AREAS

500 AUTH PORTER, FRANK W.
    TITL ANTHROPOLOGISTS AT WORK: A CASE STUDY OF THE NANTICOKE

```
        INDIAN COMMUNITY.
   SOUR AMERICAN INDIAN QUARTERLY, FEB. 1978, V4 (1), PP 1-18.
   YEAR 1978
   DESC NANTICOKE, SOUTHEAST WOODLAND, ETHNIC IDENTITY+,
        OFF-RESERVATION, CULTURAL ADAPTATION+, CULTURAL
        CONTINUITY+, RESEARCHERS+, BLACK AMERICANS, ANGLO
        AMERICANS, DISCRIMINATION
   IDEN U.S., DELAWARE

501 AUTH UHLMANN, JULIE M.
   TITL BOUNDARY MAINTENANCE IN THE URBAN ENVIRONMENT: THE
        PAPAGO CASE.
   SOUR PAPER PRESENTED AT THE MEETING OF THE AMERICAN
        ANTHROPOLOGICAL ASSOCIATION, MEXICO CITY, NOV.
        1974.(13P)
   YEAR 1974
   DESC PAPAGO, SOUTHWEST, CULTURAL ADAPTATION+, SOCIAL
        STATUS+, URBAN AREAS, NATIVE-NON-NATIVE COMPARISONS,
        CULTURAL CONTINUITY+, LATINOS, BLACK AMERICANS, ANGLO
        AMERICANS
   IDEN U.S., ARIZONA

502 AUTH SPENCER, BARBARA G.; WINDHAM, GERALD O.
   TITL OCCUPATIONAL PRESTIGE AMONG THE CHOCTAW INDIANS.
   SOUR PAPER PRESENTED AT THE ANNUAL MEETING OF THE SOUTHERN
        SOCIOLOGICAL SOCIETY, ATLANTA, APR. 1974. (24P)
   YEAR 1974
   DESC SOCIAL STATUS+, EMPLOYMENT+, CHOCTAW, SOUTHEAST
        WOODLAND, NATIVE-NON-NATIVE COMPARISONS, RESERVATION,
        CULTURAL ADAPTATION, ANGLO AMERICANS
   IDEN U.S., MISSISSIPPI

503 AUTH PRICE, JOHN A.
   TITL U.S. AND CANADIAN NATIVE VOLUNTARY ASSOCIATIONS:
        CONTINUITIES WITHIN THE EVOLUTION OF CULTURE.
   SOUR PAPER PREPARED FOR A SYMPOSIUM ON NATIVE CANADIAN
        VOLUNTARY ASSOCIATIONS, CANADIAN SOCIOLOGY AND
        ANTHROPOLOGY ASSOCIATION, EDMONTON, ALBERTA, MAY 1975.
        (30P)
   YEAR 1975
   DESC SOCIAL GROUPS AND PEER GROUPS+, SOCIAL NETWORKS+,
        URBAN AREAS, RESERVATION,CULTURAL CONTINUITY+, GROUP
        NORMS AND SANCTIONS, CULTURAL REVIVAL+, NATIVE
        AMERICAN POLITICAL MOVEMENTS+, SOCIAL ROLES
   IDEN U.S., CANADA

504 AUTH FRENCH, LAURENCE A.
   TITL SOCIAL PROBLEMS AMONG CHEROKEE FEMALES: A STUDY OF
        CULTURAL AMBIVALENCE AND ROLE IDENTITY.
   SOUR PAPER PRESENTED AT JOINT MEETING OF THE AMERICAN
        SOCIOLOGICAL ASSOCIATION AND THE RURAL SOCIOLOGICAL
        SOCIETY, MONTREAL, QUEBEC, AUG. 1974. (21P)
   YEAR 1974
   DESC CHEROKEE, SOUTHEAST WOODLAND, FEMALES+, RESERVATION,
        ETHNIC IDENTITY+, SEX DIFFERENCES, ANOMIE+, NATIVE
```

AMERICAN VALUES+, STRESS+, UNIVERSAL HARMONY,
NONINTERFERENCE, TRADITIONAL SOCIAL CONTROL,
AGGRESSIVENESS,ADULTS, POWERLESSNESS
IDEN U.S., NORTH CAROLINA, QUALLA BOUNDARY

505 AUTH NAGATA, SHUICHI
      TITL THE RESERVATION COMMUNITY AND THE URBAN COMMUNITY:
            HOPI INDIANS OF MOENKOPI.
      SOUR IN JACK O. WADDELL AND O. MICHAEL WATSON (EDS.), THE
            AMERICAN INDIAN IN URBAN SOCIETY, PP. 115-159.
            BOSTON: LITTLE, BROWN AND CO., 1971.
      YEAR 1971
      DESC RESERVATION, URBAN AREAS, PUEBLO-HOPI, NAVAJO,
            URBANIZATION+, SOCIAL NETWORKS+, ECONOMIC ISSUES+,
            DISCRIMINATION, COOPERATION, RELOCATION+,
            OFF-RESERVATION, SOUTHWEST
      IDEN U.S., ARIZONA, NAVAJO RESERVATION, HOPI RESERVATION

506 AUTH JORGENSON, JOSEPH G.
      TITL INDIANS AND THE METROPOLIS.
      SOUR IN JACK O. WADDELL AND O. MICHAEL WATSON (EDS.), THE
            AMERICAN INDIAN IN URBAN SOCIETY, PP. 67-113. BOSTON:
            LITTLE, BROWN AND CO., 1971.
      YEAR 1971
      DESC ECONOMIC ISSUES+, FEDERAL GOVERNMENT+, CALIFORNIA
            INDIANS, CALIFORNIA AREA,RESERVATION, URBAN AREAS,
            OFF-RESERVATION, COOPERATION, EMPLOYMENT,
            DISCRIMINATION, POLITICS-NONTRIBAL+, UTE, GREAT BASIN,
            CULTURAL REVIVAL, NATIVE AMERICAN COPING BEHAVIORS
      IDEN U.S., CALIFORNIA, UTAH

507 AUTH OLSON, JOHN W.
      TITL THE URBAN INDIAN AS VIEWED BY AN INDIAN CASEWORKER.
      SOUR IN JACK O. WADDELL AND O. MICHAEL WATSON (EDS.), THE
            AMERICAN INDIAN IN URBAN SOCIETY, PP. 398-408.
            BOSTON: LITTLE, BROWN AND CO., 1971.
      YEAR 1971
      DESC SOCIAL SERVICES+, EDUCATION PROGRAMS AND SERVICES,
            NONCOMPETITIVENESS, URBAN AREAS, URBANIZATION+,
            RELOCATION+, ETHNIC IDENTITY+, PSYCHOTHERAPY AND
            COUNSELING+
      IDEN U.S., ILLINOIS

508 AUTH SAMPSON,PAUL
      TITL INDIAN HEALTH SERVICE MODERNIZES MEDICAL CARE ON
            RESERVATIONS.
      SOUR JOURNAL OF THE AMERICAN MEDICAL ASSOCIATION, OCT.
            1971, V218 (4), PP 511-124.
      YEAR 1971
      DESC RESERVATION, I.H.S.+, DELIVERY OF SERVICES+, NAVAJO,
            SOUTHWEST, NATIVE AMERICAN ETIOLOGY, TRADITIONAL
            HEALERS+, MEDICAL PROFESSIONALS+, MENTAL HEALTH
            PROFESSIONALS
      IDEN U.S., NAVAJO RESERVATION

509   AUTH   METCALF, ANN
      TITL   FROM SCHOOLGIRL TO MOTHER: THE EFFECTS OF EDUCATION ON
             NAVAJO WOMEN.
      SOUR   SOCIAL PROBLEMS, 1976, V23, PP 535-544.
      YEAR   1976
      DESC   NAVAJO, SOUTHWEST, FEMALES+, CHILDREN-SCHOOL AGE+,
             B.I.A. BOARDING SCHOOLS+, FAMILY FUNCTIONING+, ETHNIC
             IDENTITY, SELF-CONCEPT, PSYCHOLOGICAL TESTING,
             TRADITIONAL CHILD REARING+, URBAN AREAS
      IDEN   U.S.

510   AUTH   FREDERIKSEN, SVEND
      TITL   SOME PRELIMINARIES ON THE SOUL COMPLEX IN ESKIMO
             SHAMANISTIC BELIEF.
      SOUR   JOURNAL OF THE WASHINGTON ACADEMY OF SCIENCE, APR.
             1964, V54, PP 109-112.
      YEAR   1964
      DESC   ESKIMO, CENTRAL AND EASTERN ARCTIC, WESTERN ARCTIC,
             SOUL LOSS+, TRADITIONAL HEALERS+, NATIVE AMERICAN
             RELIGIONS+
      IDEN   U.S., CANADA

511   AUTH   PRICE, JOHN A.
      TITL   U.S. AND CANADIAN INDIAN URBAN ETHNIC INSTITUTIONS.
      SOUR   URBAN ANTHROPOLOGY, APR. 1975, V4(1), PP 035-052
      YEAR   1975
      DESC   SOCIAL NETWORKS+, NATIVE AMERICAN ADMINISTERED
             PROGRAMS+, URBAN AREAS, URBANIZATION+, CULTURAL
             CONTINUITY, SOCIAL SERVICES, LEADERSHIP
      IDEN   U.S., CANADA

512   AUTH   HAMER, JOHN H.
      TITL   GUARDIAN SPIRITS, ALCOHOL, AND CULTURAL DEFENSE
             MECHANISMS.
      SOUR   ANTHROPOLOGICA, 1969, V11, PP 215-241.
      YEAR   1969
      DESC   POTAWATOMI, EMOTIONAL RESTRAINT, AGGRESSIVENESS,
             TRADITIONAL CHILD REARING+, DREAMS AND VISION QUESTS+,
             CHIPPEWA, EASTERN SUB-ARCTIC, RESERVATION, ALCOHOL
             USE+, POWERLESSNESS
      IDEN   U.S., MICHIGAN

513   AUTH   LABARRE, WESTON
      TITL   TWENTY YEARS OF PEYOTE STUDIES.
      SOUR   CURRENT ANTHROPOLOGY, JAN. 1960, V1(1), PP 45-60.
      YEAR   1960
      DESC   DRUG USE+, TRADITIONAL USE OF DRUGS AND ALCOHOL+,
             REVIEW OF LITERATURE, NATIVE AMERICAN RELIGIONS
      IDEN   U.S., NATIVE AMERICAN CHURCH

514   AUTH   PENISTON, EUGENE; BURMAN, WILLIAM
      TITL   RELAXATION AND ASSERTIVE TRAINING AS TREATMENT FOR A
             PSYCHOSOMATIC AMERICAN INDIAN PATIENT.
      SOUR   WHITE CLOUD JOURNAL, SPR. 1978, V1 (1), PP 7-10.
      YEAR   1978

```
      DESC  ANXIETY+, PSYCHOTHERAPY AND COUNSELING+, BEHAVIOR
            MODIFICATION+, CLINICAL STUDY, PSYCHOPHYSIOLOGICAL
            DISORDERS+, ADULTS, FEMALES
      IDEN  U.S.

515   AUTH  SHIMKIN, D.B.
      TITL  DYNAMICS OF RECENT WIND RIVER SHOSHONE HISTORY.
      SOUR  AMERICAN ANTHROPOLOGIST, 1942, V44, PP 451-462.
      YEAR  1942
      DESC  SHOSHONE, PLAINS, CULTURAL ADAPTATION+, NATIVE
            AMERICAN RELIGIONS+, CULTURAL REVIVAL,
            RELIGIONS-NON-NATIVE+, RESERVATION, LEADERSHIP
      IDEN  U.S., WIND RIVER RESERVATION, WYOMING

516   AUTH  KUTTNER, ROBERT E.
      TITL  COMPARATIVE PERFORMANCE OF DISADVANTAGED ETHNIC AND
            RACIAL GROUPS.
      SOUR  PSYCHOLOGICAL REPORTS, OCT. 1970, V27, P 372.
      YEAR  1970
      DESC  PSYCHOLOGICAL TESTING+, NATIVE-NON-NATIVE
            COMPARISONS+, ABILITIES+, CHILDREN-SCHOOL AGE, GENETIC
            FACTORS, BLACK AMERICANS
      IDEN  U.S.

517   AUTH  CRESS, JOSEPH N.; O"DONNELL, JAMES P.
      TITL  THE SELF-ESTEEM INVENTORY AND THE OGLALA SIOUX: A
            VALIDATION STUDY.
      SOUR  JOURNAL OF SOCIAL PSYCHOLOGY, OCT. 1975, V97, PP
            135-136.
      YEAR  1975
      DESC  SELF-CONCEPT+, PSYCHOLOGICAL TESTING+, SIOUX-OGLALA,
            PLAINS, ACHIEVEMENT+, ADOLESCENTS+, NATIVE AMERICAN
            VALUES, NATIVE-NON-NATIVE COMPARISONS, SECONDARY
            SCHOOLS, RESERVATION, ANGLO AMERICANS
      IDEN  U.S., SOUTH DAKOTA, PINE RIDGE RESERVATION,
            COOPERSMITH SELF-ESTEEM INVENTORY, BEHAVIOR RATING
            FORM, THINKING ABOUT YOURSELF

518   AUTH  KEMNITZER, LUIS S.
      TITL  THE STRUCTURE OF COUNTRY DRINKING PARTIES ON THE PINE
            RIDGE RESERVATION, SOUTH DAKOTA.
      SOUR  PLAINS ANTHROPOLOGIST, 1972, V17, PP 134-142.
      YEAR  1972
      DESC  ALCOHOL USE+, SIOUX-OGLALA, PLAINS, RESERVATION,
            SOCIAL NETWORKS, ECONOMIC ISSUES, GENEROSITY+, NATIVE
            AMERICAN VALUES, STRESS, NATIVE AMERICAN COPING
            BEHAVIORS, ADULTS, FULL BLOOD-MIXED BLOOD COMPARISONS
      IDEN  U.S., SOUTH DAKOTA, PINE RIDGE RESERVATION

519   AUTH  HOFFMANN, HELMUT; NOEM, AVIS A.
      TITL  ADJUSTMENT OF CHIPPEWA INDIAN ALCOHOLICS TO A
            PREDOMINANTLY WHITE TREATMENT PROGRAM.
      SOUR  PSYCHOLOGICAL REPORTS, DEC. 1975, V37, PP 1284-1286.
      YEAR  1975
      DESC  CHIPPEWA, EASTERN SUB-ARCTIC, ALCOHOLISM TREATMENT+,
```

```
                NATIVE-NON-NATIVE COMPARISONS+, MALES, MEDICAL
                INSTITUTIONS+, ADULTS, ANGLO AMERICANS
          IDEN  U.S.

520  AUTH  BOYER, L. BRYCE; BOYER, RUTH M.; KLOPFER, BRUNO;
           SCHEINER, SUZANNE B.
     TITL  APACHE "LEARNERS" AND "NONLEARNERS." II.   QUANTITATIVE
           RORSCHACH SIGNS OF INFLUENTIAL ADULTS.
     SOUR  JOURNAL OF PROJECTIVE TECHNIQUES AND PERSONALITY
           ASSESSMENT, APR. 1968, V32, PP 146-159.
     YEAR  1968
     DESC  APACHE-MESCALERO, APACHE-CHIRICAHUA, SOUTHWEST,
           RESERVATION, CHILDREN-SCHOOL AGE+, CULTURAL
           ADAPTATION+, INTERTRIBAL COMPARISONS, PSYCHOLOGICAL
           TESTING+, COGNITIVE PROCESSES+, LEARNING+, TRADITIONAL
           CHILD REARING
     IDEN  U.S., MESCALERO RESERVATION, NEW MEXICO, RORSCHACH
           TEST

521  AUTH  MCCASKILL, J.C.
     TITL  SOCIAL HYGIENE IN RACIAL PROBLEMS: THE INDIAN.
     SOUR  JOURNAL OF SOCIAL HYGIENE, 1932, V18, PP 438-446.
     YEAR  1932
     DESC  B.I.A. BOARDING SCHOOLS+, SEXUAL RELATIONS+, EDUCATION
           PROGRAMS AND SERVICES, CHILDREN-SCHOOL AGE,
           ADOLESCENTS
     IDEN  U.S.

522  AUTH  SUE, STANLEY
     TITL  COMMUNITY MENTAL HEALTH SERVICES TO MINORITY GROUPS:
           SOME OPTIMISM, SOME PESSIMISM.
     SOUR  AMERICAN PSYCHOLOGIST, AUG. 1977, V32, PP 616-624.
     YEAR  1977
     DESC  MENTAL HEALTH PROGRAMS AND SERVICES+,
           NATIVE-NON-NATIVE COMPARISONS, DISCRIMINATION+,
           DELIVERY OF SERVICES+, MENTAL HEALTH INSTITUTIONS,
           URBAN AREAS, ASIAN AMERICANS, LATINOS, ANGLO
           AMERICANS, BLACK AMERICANS
     IDEN  U.S., WASHINGTON

523  AUTH  HEATH, DWIGHT B.
     TITL  PROHIBITION AND POST-REPEAL DRINKING PATTERNS AMONG
           THE NAVAJO.
     SOUR  QUARTERLY JOURNAL OF STUDIES ON ALCOHOL, 1964, V25, PP
           119-135.
     YEAR  1964
     DESC  NAVAJO, SOUTHWEST, RESERVATION, ALCOHOL USE+, AGE
           COMPARISONS, SEX DIFFERENCES, SOCIAL GROUPS AND PEER
           GROUPS, GROUP NORMS AND SANCTIONS
     IDEN  U.S., NAVAJO RESERVATION

524  AUTH  FERNBERGER, SAMUEL W.
     TITL  FURTHER OBSERVATIONS ON PEYOTE INTOXICATION.
     SOUR  JOURNAL OF ABNORMAL AND SOCIAL PSYCHOLOGY, 1932, V26,
           PP 367-378.
```

YEAR 1932
DESC DRUG USE+, TRADITIONAL USE OF DRUGS AND ALCOHOL+
IDEN U.S.

525 AUTH LEVINE, SAUL V.; EASTWOOD, M.R.; RAE-GRANT, QUENTIN
    TITL PSYCHIATRIC SERVICE TO NORTHERN INDIANS.
    SOUR CANADIAN PSYCHIATRIC ASSOCIATION JOURNAL, AUG. 1974,
         V19(4), PP 343-349.
    YEAR 1974
    DESC DELIVERY OF SERVICES+, MENTAL HEALTH PROGRAMS AND
         SERVICES+, CREE, CHIPPEWA, EASTERN SUB-ARCTIC, PROGRAM
         DEVELOPMENT+, CONSULTATION+, MEDICAL INSTITUTIONS,
         NATIVE AMERICAN COPING BEHAVIORS, OFF-RESERVATION
    IDEN CANADA, ONTARIO, SIOUX LOOKOUT PROJECT

526 AUTH MILLER, W.H.; SANDOVAL, N.; MUSHOLT, E.
    TITL VOCATIONAL AND PERSONAL EFFECTIVENESS TRAINING OF A
         DEVELOPMENTALLY DELAYED NAVAJO GIRL.
    SOUR WHITE CLOUD JOURNAL, SPR. 1978, V1 (1), PP 11-14.
    YEAR 1978
    DESC EMPLOYMENT+, NAVAJO, SOUTHWEST, TRAINING PROGRAMS+,
         MENTAL RETARDATION+, RESERVATION, ELEMENTARY SCHOOLS,
         FEMALES, ADOLESCENTS
    IDEN U.S., ARIZONA, CHINLE VALLEY SCHOOL

527 AUTH RYAN, ROBERT A.; SPENCE, JOHN D.
    TITL EDITORIAL: AMERICAN INDIAN MENTAL HEALTH RESEARCH.
    SOUR WHITE CLOUD JOURNAL, SPR. 1978, V1 (1), PP 15-18.
    YEAR 1978
    DESC RESEARCHERS+, NATIVE AMERICAN PERSONNEL+, NATIVE
         AMERICAN ADMINISTERED PROGRAMS+
    IDEN U.S.

528 AUTH KLINE, JAMES A.; ROZYNKO, VITALI V.; FLINT, GARRY;
         ROBERTS, ARTHUR C.
    TITL PERSONALITY CHARACTERISTICS OF MALE NATIVE AMERICAN
         ALCOHOLIC PATIENTS.
    SOUR INTERNATIONAL JOURNAL OF ADDICTIONS, 1973, V8(4), PP
         729-732.
    YEAR 1973
    DESC MALES+, ALCOHOL USE, ADULTS+, PERSONALITY TRAITS+,
         CLINICAL STUDY, PSYCHOLOGICAL TESTING+, ALCOHOLISM
         TREATMENT+
    IDEN U.S., CALIFORNIA, M.M.P.I.

529 AUTH WOLFF, PETER H.
    TITL VASOMOTOR SENSITIVITY TO ALCOHOL IN DIVERSE MONGOLOID
         POPULATIONS.
    SOUR AMERICAN JOURNAL OF HUMAN GENETICS, 1973, V25, PP
         193-199.
    YEAR 1973
    DESC ALCOHOL USE+, ADULTS, CREE, EASTERN SUB-ARCTIC,
         NATIVE-NON-NATIVE COMPARISONS, GENETIC FACTORS, ANGLO
         AMERICANS, ASIAN AMERICANS
    IDEN U.S.

530 AUTH BROWDER, J. ALBERT
     TITL LETTER: FACTORS IN CHILD NEGLECT--WORKING INDIAN
           MOTHERS.
     SOUR PEDIATRICS, DEC. 1973, V52(6), PP 888-889.
     YEAR 1973
     DESC CHILD ABUSE AND NEGLECT+, NAVAJO, SOUTHWEST
     IDEN U.S.

531 AUTH KANE, ROBERT L.; MCCONATHA, P. DOUGLAS
     TITL THE MEN IN THE MIDDLE: A DILEMMA OF MINORITY HEALTH
           WORKERS.
     SOUR MEDICAL CARE, SEP. 1975, V13(9), PP 736-743.
     YEAR 1975
     DESC MEDICAL PARAPROFESSIONALS+, I.H.S.+, NAVAJO,
           SOUTHWEST, DELIVERY OF SERVICES+, NATIVE AMERICAN
           PERSONNEL+, STRESS+, BICULTURALISM+, MEDICAL
           PROFESSIONALS, PHYSICAL HEALTH AND ILLNESS,
           RESERVATION, SOCIAL ROLES
     IDEN U.S., NAVAJO RESERVATION

532 AUTH FUCHS, MICHAEL; BASHSHUR, RASHID
     TITL USE OF TRADITIONAL INDIAN MEDICINE AMONG URBAN NATIVE
           AMERICANS.
     SOUR MEDICAL CARE, NOV. 1975, V13(11), PP 915-927.
     YEAR 1975
     DESC URBAN AREAS, TRADITIONAL HEALERS+, NATIVE AMERICAN
           ETIOLOGY+, CULTURAL CONTINUITY+, PHYSICAL HEALTH AND
           ILLNESS, MEDICAL PROGRAMS AND SERVICES, RELOCATION+
     IDEN U.S., CALIFORNIA

533 AUTH RICHEK, HERBERT G.
     TITL A NOTE ON PREJUDICE IN PROSPECTIVE PROFESSIONAL
           HELPERS.
     SOUR NURSING RESEARCH, MAR.-APR. 1970, V19(2), PP 172-175.
     YEAR 1970
     DESC DISCRIMINATION+, SOCIAL SERVICE PROFESSIONALS+,
           MEDICAL PROFESSIONALS+, FEMALES+, PSYCHOLOGICAL
           TESTING
     IDEN U.S., MINORITY GROUPS ATTITUDE SCALE, OKLAHOMA

534 AUTH ROBERTSON, G.G.; BAIZERMAN, MICHAEL
     TITL PSYCHIATRIC CONSULTATION ON TWO INDIAN RESERVATIONS.
     SOUR HOSPITAL AND COMMUNITY PSYCHIATRY, JAN. 1969, V20,
           P186.
     YEAR 1969
     DESC CROW, CHEYENNE-NORTHERN, PLAINS, MENTAL HEALTH
           PROGRAMS AND SERVICES+, DELIVERY OF SERVICES+, I.H.S.,
           RESERVATION, PROGRAM DEVELOPMENT+, CONSULTATION+
     IDEN U.S., MONTANA, NORTHERN CHEYENNE RESERVATION, CROW
           RESERVATION

535 AUTH SCHNUR, LEO
     TITL NAVAJOS TRAIN WARD AIDES TO COUNTERACT "MEDICINE MEN."
     SOUR MODERN HOSPITAL, NOV. 1942, V59, P80.
     YEAR 1942

```
     DESC   NAVAJO, SOUTHWEST, RESERVATION, TRADITIONAL HEALERS,
            NATIVE AMERICAN PERSONNEL+, TRAINING PROGRAMS+,
            MEDICAL PROGRAMS AND SERVICES, MEDICAL
            PARAPROFESSIONALS+
     IDEN   U.S., NAVAJO RESERVATION

536  AUTH   OAKLAND, LYNN; KANE, ROBERT L.
     TITL   THE WORKING MOTHER AND CHILD NEGLECT ON THE NAVAJO
            RESERVATION.
     SOUR   PEDIATRICS, MAY 1973, V51, PP 849-853.
     YEAR   1973
     DESC   FAMILY FUNCTIONING+, CHILD ABUSE AND NEGLECT+, NAVAJO,
            SOUTHWEST, FEMALES+,ADULTS+, CHILDREN-INFANTS AND
            PRESCHOOL, EMPLOYMENT+, RESERVATION, EXTENDED FAMILY+,
            MEDICAL INSTITUTIONS
     IDEN   U.S., NAVAJO RESERVATION

537  AUTH   DEVEREUX, GEORGE
     TITL   INSTITUTIONALIZED HOMOSEXUALITY OF THE MOHAVE INDIANS.
     SOUR   HUMAN BIOLOGY, 1937, V9, PP 498-527.
     YEAR   1937
     DESC   MOHAVE, SOUTHWEST, SEXUAL RELATIONS+, MALES+,
            FEMALES+, ADULTS, ADOLESCENTS
     IDEN   U.S.

538  AUTH   NIEUWENHUIS, A.W.
     TITL   PRINCIPLES OF INDIAN MEDICINE IN AMERICAN ETHNOLOGY
            AND THEIR PSYCHOLOGICAL SIGNIFICANCE.
     SOUR   JANUS, 1924, V28, PP 305-356.
     YEAR   1924
     DESC   NATIVE AMERICAN ETIOLOGY+, NORTHWEST COAST, HAIDA,
            TSIMSHIAN, KWAKIUTL, PHYSICAL HEALTH AND ILLNESS,
            TRADITIONAL HEALERS+, SOUL LOSS+, WITCHCRAFT+,
            INTERTRIBAL COMPARISONS, CULTURE-BASED PSYCHOTHERAPY+
     IDEN   CANADA, SOUTH AMERICA

539  AUTH   BUTLER, G.C.
     TITL   INCIDENCE OF SUICIDE AMONG THE ETHNIC GROUPS OF THE
            NORTHWEST TERRITORIES AND YUKON TERRITORY.
     SOUR   MEDICAL SERVICES JOURNAL, CANADA, APR. 1965, V21, PP
            252-256.
     YEAR   1965
     DESC   SUICIDE+, ESKIMO, WESTERN ARCTIC, CENTRAL AND EASTERN
            ARCTIC, YUKON SUB-ARCTIC, MACKENZIE SUB-ARCTIC,
            EPIDEMIOLOGICAL STUDY
     IDEN   CANADA

540  AUTH   BROMBERG, WALTER; TRANTER, CHARLES L.
     TITL   PEYOTE INTOXICATION: SOME PSYCHOLOGICAL ASPECTS OF THE
            PEYOTE RITE.
     SOUR   JOURNAL OF NERVOUS AND MENTAL DISEASE, 1943, V97, PP
            518-527.
     YEAR   1943
     DESC   DRUG USE+, TRADITIONAL USE OF DRUGS AND ALCOHOL+,
            NATIVE AMERICAN RELIGIONS, UNIVERSAL HARMONY+,
```

                    ANXIETY, STRESS
          IDEN   U.S., CANADA

541 AUTH   TRIMBLE, JOSEPH E.
     TITL   SAY GOODBYE TO THE HOLLYWOOD INDIAN: RESULTS OF A
               NATIONWIDE SURVEY OF THE SELF-IMAGE OF THE AMERICAN
               INDIAN.
     SOUR   PAPER PRESENTED AT THE AMERICAN PSYCHOLOGICAL
               ASSOCIATION, NEW ORLEANS, AUG.-SEP. 1974.(14P)
     YEAR   1974
     DESC   STEREOTYPES+, SELF-CONCEPT+, RESEARCHERS+, CULTURAL
               REVIVAL+
     IDEN   U.S.

542 AUTH   DEVEREUX, GEORGE
     TITL   PRIMITIVE PSYCHIATRY II: FUNERAL SUICIDE AND THE
               MOHAVE SOCIAL STRUCTURE.
     SOUR   BULLETIN OF THE HISTORY OF MEDICINE, 1942, V11, PP
               522-542.
     YEAR   1942
     DESC   SUICIDE+, MOHAVE, SOUTHWEST, GRIEF REACTION+, DEATH
               AND DYING+
     IDEN   U.S.

543 AUTH   FAHY, AGNES; MUSCHENHEIM, CARL
     TITL   THIRD NATIONAL CONFERENCE ON AMERICAN INDIAN HEALTH.
     SOUR   JOURNAL OF AMERICAN MEDICAL ASSOCIATION. DEC. 1965,
               V194(10), PP 1093-1096.
     YEAR   1965
     DESC   MENTAL DISORDERS, STRESS, PREVENTIVE MENTAL HEALTH
               PROGRAMS+, DELIVERY OF SERVICES+, MENTAL HEALTH
               PROGRAMS AND SERVICES+, PHYSICAL HEALTH AND ILLNESS+,
               ECONOMIC ISSUES, PROGRAM DEVELOPMENT+
     IDEN   U.S.

544 AUTH   QUINAN, CLARENCE
     TITL   THE AMERICAN MEDICINE MAN AND THE ASIATIC SHAMAN: A
               COMPARISON.
     SOUR   ANNALS OF MEDICAL HISTORY, 1938, V10, PP 508-533.
     YEAR   1938
     DESC   TRADITIONAL HEALERS+, INTERTRIBAL COMPARISONS,
               NATIVE-NON-NATIVE COMPARISONS, CULTURE-BASED
               PSYCHOTHERAPY+
     IDEN   NORTH AMERICA, SOUTH AMERICA, ASIA

545 AUTH   STAGE, THOMAS B.; KEAST, THOMAS J.
     TITL   A PSYCHIATRIC SERVICE FOR PLAINS INDIANS.
     SOUR   HOSPITAL AND COMMUNITY PSYCHIATRY, 1966, V17, PP 74-76.
     YEAR   1966
     DESC   PLAINS, CHEYENNE-NORTHERN, CROW, RESERVATION,
               CONSULTATION, I.H.S., OUTPATIENT CARE+, DELIVERY OF
               SERVICES+, MENTAL HEALTH PROGRAMS AND SERVICES+,
               PSYCHOPHYSIOLOGICAL DISORDERS, EXTENDED FAMILY, STRESS
     IDEN   U.S., MONTANA, CROW RESERVATION, NORTHERN CHEYENNE
               RESERVATION

546 AUTH TRILLIN, CALVIN
     TITL U.S. JOURNAL: GALLUP, NEW MEXICO: DRUNKEN INDIANS.
     SOUR THE NEW YORKER, SEP. 1971, V47, PP 108-114.
     YEAR 1971
     DESC ALCOHOL USE+, NAVAJO, SOUTHWEST, CORRECTIONAL
           INSTITUTIONS, GROUP NORMS AND SANCTIONS, SOCIAL GROUPS
           AND PEER GROUPS, RESERVATION, ADULTS
     IDEN U.S., NEW MEXICO, NAVAJO RESERVATION

547 AUTH BALIKCI, ASEN
     TITL SHAMANISTIC BEHAVIOR AMONG THE NETSILIK ESKIMOS.
     SOUR SOUTHWESTERN JOURNAL OF ANTHROPOLOGY, 1963, V19, PP
           380-396.
     YEAR 1963
     DESC ESKIMO, CENTRAL AND EASTERN ARCTIC, TRADITIONAL
           HEALERS+, NATIVE AMERICAN ETIOLOGY+, TABOO BREAKING+,
           WITCHCRAFT+, AGGRESSIVENESS, NATIVE AMERICAN
           RELIGIONS, CULTURE-BASED PSYCHOTHERAPY, SPIRIT
           INTRUSION+
     IDEN CANADA

548 AUTH MURDOCK, GEORGE P.
     TITL TENINO SHAMANISM.
     SOUR ETHNOLOGY, 1965, V4, PP 165-171.
     YEAR 1965
     DESC TENINO, PLATEAU, RESERVATION, NATIVE AMERICAN
           RELIGIONS+, DREAMS AND VISION QUESTS, NATIVE AMERICAN
           ETIOLOGY+, SOUL LOSS+, WITCHCRAFT+, TRADITIONAL
           HEALERS+, TRADITIONAL SOCIAL CONTROL+, CULTURE-BASED
           PSYCHOTHERAPY+, SPIRIT INTRUSION+
     IDEN U.S., OREGON, WARM SPRINGS RESERVATION

549 AUTH WALKER, DEWARD E.
     TITL NEZ PERCE SORCERY.
     SOUR ETHNOLOGY, 1967, V6, PP 66-96.
     YEAR 1967
     DESC NEZ PERCE, PLATEAU, WITCHCRAFT+, TRADITIONAL SOCIAL
           CONTROL+, RELIGIONS-NON-NATIVE
     IDEN U.S.

550 AUTH HALLOWELL, A. IRVING
     TITL CULTURE AND MENTAL DISORDER.
     SOUR JOURNAL OF ABNORMAL AND SOCIAL PSYCHOLOGY, APR.-JUN.
           1934, V29(1), PP 1-9.
     YEAR 1934
     DESC CHIPPEWA, EASTERN SUB-ARCTIC, MENTAL DISORDERS+,
           NATIVE AMERICAN ETIOLOGY+,TABOO BREAKING+, WINDIGO
           PSYCHOSIS+, RESERVATION, ADULTS
     IDEN CANADA, MANITOBA, ONTARIO

551 AUTH DEVEREUX, GEORGE
     TITL THE SOCIAL AND CULTURAL IMPLICATIONS OF INCEST AMONG
           THE MOHAVE INDIANS.
     SOUR PSYCHOANALYTIC QUARTERLY, 1939, V8, PP 510-533.
     YEAR 1939

DESC   MOHAVE, SOUTHWEST, TABOO BREAKING+, SEXUAL RELATIONS+,
       WITCHCRAFT
IDEN   U.S.

552   AUTH   ARTHUR, GRACE
      TITL   AN EXPERIENCE IN EXAMINING AN INDIAN TWELFTH-GRADE
             GROUP WITH THE MULTIPHASIC PERSONALITY INVENTORY.
      SOUR   MENTAL HYGIENE, 1944, V28, PP 243-250.
      YEAR   1944
      DESC   ADOLESCENTS, PSYCHOLOGICAL TESTING+, SECONDARY
             SCHOOLS, EMOTIONAL RESTRAINT, NATIVE-NON-NATIVE
             COMPARISONS, PERSONALITY TRAITS+, NATIVE AMERICAN
             COPING BEHAVIORS+, ANGLO AMERICANS
      IDEN   U.S., M.M.P.I.

553   AUTH   LEMERT, EDWIN M.
      TITL   SOME INDIANS WHO STUTTER.
      SOUR   JOURNAL OF SPEECH AND HEARING DISORDERS, JUN. 1953,
             V18, PP 168-174.
      YEAR   1953
      DESC   NORTHWEST COAST, PSYCHOPHYSIOLOGICAL DISORDERS+,
             LANGUAGE HANDICAPS+, ANXIETY, TSIMSHIAN, NOOTKA, COAST
             SALISH, ATTITUDES, ATTITUDES
      IDEN   CANADA, BRITISH COLUMBIA

554   AUTH   WALLIS, RUTH S.; WALLIS, WILSON D.
      TITL   THE SINS OF THE FATHERS: CONCEPT OF DISEASE AMONG THE
             CANADIAN DAKOTA.
      SOUR   SOUTHWESTERN JOURNAL OF ANTHROPOLOGY, WIN. 1953, V9
             (4), PP 431-435.
      YEAR   1953
      DESC   SIOUX, PLAINS, RESERVATION, NATIVE AMERICAN ETIOLOGY+,
             TABOO BREAKING+
      IDEN   CANADA, MANITOBA

555   AUTH   LEIGHTON, ALEXANDER H.
      TITL   THE THERAPEUTIC PROCESS IN CROSS-CULTURAL PERSPECTIVE:
             A SYMPOSIUM: FRAGMENTS FROM A NAVAJO CEREMONIAL.
      SOUR   AMERICAN JOURNAL OF PSYCHIATRY, MAR. 1968, V124(9), PP
             1176-1178.
      YEAR   1968
      DESC   NAVAJO, SOUTHWEST, TRADITIONAL HEALERS+, CULTURE-BASED
             PSYCHOTHERAPY, RESERVATION
      IDEN   U.S., NEW MEXICO, NAVAJO RESERVATION

556   AUTH   BALIKCI, ASEN
      TITL   PERSPECTIVES ON THE ATOMISTIC TYPE OF SOCIETY: BAD
             FRIENDS.
      SOUR   HUMAN ORGANIZATION, AUT. 1968, V27(3), PP 191-199.
      YEAR   1968
      DESC   KUTCHIN, YUKON SUB-ARCTIC, AGGRESSIVENESS+, FAMILY
             FUNCTIONING+, SEXUAL RELATIONS, ADULTS,
             OFF-RESERVATION, EMOTIONAL RESTRAINT+, STRESS,
             ANOMIE+, MARITAL RELATIONSHIPS
      IDEN   CANADA, YUKON TERRITORY

557 AUTH MOYER, DAVID S.
    TITL THE SOCIAL CONTEXT OF ECONOMIC CHANGE: A STUDY OF
         ESKIMO BOAT MANAGEMENT.
    SOUR HUMAN ORGANIZATION, SPR. 1971, V30(1), PP 11-24.
    YEAR 1971
    DESC ESKIMO, CENTRAL AND EASTERN ARCTIC, EMPLOYMENT+,
         ECONOMIC ISSUES+, COOPERATION, EXTENDED FAMILY+,
         OFF-RESERVATION, SOCIAL NETWORKS
    IDEN CANADA, NORTHWEST TERRITORIES

558 AUTH SIMPSON, JAMES R.
    TITL USES OF CULTURAL ANTHROPOLOGY IN ECONOMIC ANALYSIS: A
         PAPAGO INDIAN CASE.
    SOUR HUMAN ORGANIZATION, AUT. 1970, V29(3), PP 162-168.
    YEAR 1970
    DESC RESEARCHERS, PAPAGO, SOUTHWEST, TRIBAL POLITICAL
         ORGANIZATIONS+, ECONOMIC ISSUES+, RESERVATION,
         COOPERATION, NATIVE AMERICAN VALUES+, B.I.A.,
    IDEN U.S., ARIZONA, PAPAGO RESERVATION

559 AUTH OLSON, DEAN F.
    TITL COOPERATIVE OWNERSHIP EXPERIENCE OF ALASKA ESKIMO
         REINDEER HERDERS.
    SOUR HUMAN ORGANIZATION, SPR. 1970, V29(1), PP 57-62.
    YEAR 1970
    DESC COOPERATION+, ESKIMO, WESTERN ARCTIC, OFF-RESERVATION,
         EXTENDED FAMILY+, TRIBAL POLITICAL ORGANIZATIONS+
    IDEN U.S., ALASKA

560 AUTH LEWIS, THOMAS H.
    TITL A SYNDROME OF DEPRESSION AND MUTISM IN THE OGLALA
         SIOUX.
    SOUR AMERICAN JOURNAL OF PSYCHIATRY, JUL. 1975, V132, PP
         753-755.
    YEAR 1975
    DESC SIOUX-OGLALA, PLAINS, RESERVATION, MEDICAL
         INSTITUTIONS, DEPRESSION+, CULTURE-SPECIFIC SYNDROMES
    IDEN U.S., SOUTH DAKOTA, PINE RIDGE RESERVATION

561 AUTH TRIMBLE, JOSEPH E.
    TITL VALUE DIFFERENCES AMONG THE AMERICAN INDIANS: CONCERNS
         FOR THE CONCERNED COUNSELOR.
    SOUR IN P. PEDERSEN , W. LONNER, AND J. DRAGUNS (EDS.),
         COUNSELING ACROSS CULTURES. HONOLULU: UNIVERSITY PRESS
         OF HAWAII, 1976.
    YEAR 1976
    DESC PSYCHOTHERAPY AND COUNSELING+, STRESS+, PSYCHOLOGICAL
         TESTING+, NATIVE AMERICAN VALUES+, ETHNIC IDENTITY+,
         GENEROSITY, TIME PERCEPTION, COOPERATION, UNIVERSAL
         HARMONY, PASSIVE RESISTANCE, CULTURAL CONTINUITY+
    IDEN U.S., CANADA

562 AUTH BEISER, MORTON
    TITL EDITORIAL: A HAZARD TO MENTAL HEALTH: INDIAN BOARDING
         SCHOOLS.

```
        SOUR   AMERICAN JOURNAL OF PSYCHIATRY, MAR. 1974, V131, PP
               305-306.
        YEAR   1974
        DESC   B.I.A. BOARDING SCHOOLS+, EDUCATION PROGRAMS AND
               SERVICES+, NATIVE AMERICAN ADMINISTERED PROGRAMS+
        IDEN   U.S., MODEL DORMITORY

  563   AUTH   SHERWIN, DUANE; MEAD, BEVERLEY
        TITL   DELIRIUM TREMENS IN A NINE-YEAR-OLD CHILD.
        SOUR   AMERICAN JOURNAL OF PSYCHIATRY, NOV. 1975, V132(11),
               PP 1210-1212.
        YEAR   1975
        DESC   CHILDREN-SCHOOL AGE+, ALCOHOL USE+, TRADITIONAL CHILD
               REARING, CHILDREN-INFANTS AND PRESCHOOL+
        IDEN   U.S.

  564   AUTH   BEIGEL, ALLEN A.; HUNTER, E. JAMES; TAMERIN, JOHN S.;
               CHAPIN, EDWIN H.; LOWERY, MARY J.
        TITL   PLANNING FOR THE DEVELOPMENT OF COMPREHENSIVE
               COMMUNITY ALCOHOLISM SERVICES: I. THE PREVALENCE
               SURVEY.
        SOUR   AMERICAN JOURNAL OF PSYCHIATRY, OCT. 1974, V131(10),
               PP 1112-1116.
        YEAR   1974
        DESC   ALCOHOLISM TREATMENT+, PROGRAM DEVELOPMENT+,
               EPIDEMIOLOGICAL STUDY, ADULTS,MALES, SOUTHWEST,
               NATIVE-NON-NATIVE COMPARISONS, CORRECTIONAL
               INSTITUTIONS+, ALCOHOL USE+, BLACK AMERICANS, ANGLO
               AMERICANS, LATINOS
        IDEN   U.S., ARIZONA

  565   AUTH   TRIMBLE, JOSEPH E.
        TITL   THE INTRUSION OF WESTERN PSYCHOLOGICAL THOUGHT ON
               NATIVE AMERICAN ETHOS: DIVERGENCE AND CONFLICT AMONG
               THE LAKOTA.
        SOUR   IN J.W. BERRY AND W.J. LONNER (EDS.), APPLIED
               CROSS-CULTURAL PSYCHOLOGY, PP 303-308. AMSTERDAM:
               SWETS AND ZEITINGER B.V., 1975.
        YEAR   1975
        DESC   RESEARCHERS+, SIOUX, PLAINS, RESERVATION, EXTENDED
               FAMILY+, FAMILY FUNCTIONING+, PERSONALITY TRAITS+,
               CULTURAL ADAPTATION
        IDEN   U.S.

  566   AUTH   MORGAN, WILLIAM
        TITL   NAVAJO TREATMENT OF SICKNESS: DIAGNOSTICIANS.
        SOUR   AMERICAN ANTHROPOLOGIST, 1931, V33, PP 390-402.
        YEAR   1931
        DESC   NAVAJO, SOUTHWEST, TRADITIONAL HEALERS+, DREAMS AND
               VISION QUESTS+, CULTURE-BASED PSYCHOTHERAPY+
        IDEN   U.S.

  567   AUTH   WYMAN, LELAND C.
        TITL   NAVAJO DIAGNOSTICIANS.
        SOUR   AMERICAN ANTHROPOLOGIST, 1936, V38, PP 236-246.
```

```
        YEAR  1936
        DESC  NAVAJO, SOUTHWEST, TRADITIONAL HEALERS+, CULTURE-BASED
              PSYCHOTHERAPY
        IDEN  U.S.

568  AUTH  ANDERSON, FORREST N.
     TITL  A MENTAL-HYGIENE SURVEY OF PROBLEM INDIAN CHILDREN IN
           OKLAHOMA.
     SOUR  MENTAL HYGIENE, 1936, V20, PP 472-476.
     YEAR  1936
     DESC  OKLAHOMA INDIANS, CHILDREN-SCHOOL AGE+, ELEMENTARY
           SCHOOLS+, PSYCHOLOGICAL TESTING+, MENTAL RETARDATION,
           SURVEY
     IDEN  U.S., OKLAHOMA

569  AUTH  BEIGEL, ALLEN A.; MCCABE, THOMAS R.; TAMERIN, JOHN S.;
           LOWERY, MARY J.; CHAPIN, EDWIN H.; HUNTER, E. JAMES
     TITL  PLANNING FOR THE DEVELOPMENT OF COMPREHENSIVE
           COMMUNITY ALCOHOLISM SERVICES: II. ASSESSING COMMUNITY
           AWARENESS AND ATTITUDES.
     SOUR  AMERICAN JOURNAL OF PSYCHIATRY, OCT. 1974, V131(10),
           PP 1116-1121.
     YEAR  1974
     DESC  ALCOHOLISM TREATMENT+, PROGRAM DEVELOPMENT+,
           SOUTHWEST, NATIVE-NON-NATIVE COMPARISONS, ALCOHOL
           USE+, ADULTS, EPIDEMIOLOGICAL STUDY,  BLACK AMERICANS,
           ANGLO AMERICANS, LATINOS,ATTITUDES+
     IDEN  U.S., ARIZONA, ALCOHOLICS ANONYMOUS

570  AUTH  CODERE, HELEN
     TITL  REVIEW OF "ALCOHOL AND THE NORTHWEST COAST INDIANS."
     SOUR  AMERICAN ANTHROPOLOGIST, 1955, V57, PP 1303-1305.
     YEAR  1955
     DESC  ALCOHOL USE+, NORTHWEST COAST
     IDEN  CANADA, BRITISH COLUMBIA

571  AUTH  LABARRE, WESTON
     TITL  PRIMITIVE PSYCHOTHERAPY IN NATIVE AMERICAN CULTURES:
           PEYOTISM AND CONFESSION.
     SOUR  JOURNAL OF ABNORMAL AND SOCIAL PSYCHOLOGY, 1947, V42,
           PP 294-309.
     YEAR  1947
     DESC  CULTURE-BASED PSYCHOTHERAPY+, TRADITIONAL USE OF DRUGS
           AND ALCOHOL+, DRUG USE+, DREAMS AND VISION QUESTS+,
           ANXIETY, TABOO BREAKING+, NATIVE AMERICAN COPING
           BEHAVIORS, CONFESSION+
     IDEN  U.S.

572  AUTH  DEVEREUX, GEORGE
     TITL  THE MENTAL HYGIENE OF THE AMERICAN INDIAN.
     SOUR  MENTAL HYGIENE, 1942, V26, PP 71-84.
     YEAR  1942
     DESC  STRESS+, ANXIETY+, PSYCHOTHERAPY AND COUNSELING+,
           MENTAL HEALTH INSTITUTIONS+, INSTITUTIONALIZATION+,
           MENTAL DISORDERS, SOCIAL SERVICE PROFESSIONALS, NATIVE
```

```
              AMERICAN PERSONNEL, POWERLESSNESS
       IDEN   U.S.

573   AUTH   CARPENTER, EDMUND S.
      TITL   WITCH-FEAR AMONG THE AIVILIK ESKIMOS.
      SOUR   AMERICAN JOURNAL OF PSYCHIATRY, 1953, V110, PP 194-199.
      YEAR   1953
      DESC   ESKIMO, CENTRAL AND EASTERN ARCTIC, WITCHCRAFT+,
             NATIVE AMERICAN ETIOLOGY+,SCHIZOPHRENIA,
             OFF-RESERVATION
      IDEN   CANADA

574   AUTH   OPLER, MORRIS E.
      TITL   THE USE OF PEYOTE BY THE CARRIZO AND LIPAN APACHE
             TRIBES.
      SOUR   AMERICAN ANTHROPOLOGIST, 1938, V40, PP 271-285.
      YEAR   1938
      DESC   APACHE-LIPAN, RESERVATION, TRADITIONAL USE OF DRUGS
             AND ALCOHOL+, DRUG USE+, SOUTHWEST, CARRIZO
      IDEN   U.S., MESCALERO RESERVATION, NEW MEXICO

575   AUTH   SCHULTES, RICHARD E.
      TITL   THE APPEAL OF PEYOTE (LOPHOPHORA WILLIAMSII) AS A
             MEDICINE.
      SOUR   AMERICAN ANTHROPOLOGIST, 1938, V40, PP 698-715.
      YEAR   1938
      DESC   TRADITIONAL USE OF DRUGS AND ALCOHOL+, DRUG USE+,
             NATIVE AMERICAN RELIGIONS, DREAMS AND VISION QUESTS
      IDEN   U.S., MEXICO

576   AUTH   JOSEPH, ALICE
      TITL   PHYSICIAN AND PATIENT: SOME ASPECTS OF INTER-PERSONAL
             RELATIONS BETWEEN PHYSICIANS AND PATIENTS, WITH
             SPECIAL REGARD TO THE RELATIONSHIP OF WHITE PHYSICIANS
             AND INDIAN PATIENTS.
      SOUR   APPLIED ANTHROPOLOGY, JUL.-AUG.-SEP. 1942, V1, PP 1-6.
      YEAR   1942
      DESC   MEDICAL PROFESSIONALS+, PASSIVE RESISTANCE+,
             RESERVATION, DELIVERY OF SERVICES

577   AUTH   BOYER, RUTH M.
      TITL   THE MATRIFOCAL FAMILY AMONG THE MESCALERO: ADDITIONAL
             DATA, PART I.
      SOUR   AMERICAN ANTHROPOLOGIST, 1964, V66, PP 593-602
      YEAR   1964
      DESC   EXTENDED FAMILY+, FEMALES+, MALES+, ADULTS+,
             APACHE-MESCALERO, SOUTHWEST, EMPLOYMENT, RESERVATION,
             SOCIAL ROLES
      IDEN   U.S., MESCALERO RESERVATION, NEW MEXICO

578   AUTH   DEVEREUX, GEORGE
      TITL   MOHAVE ORALITY: AN ANALYSIS OF NURSING AND WEANING
             CUSTOMS.
      SOUR   PSYCHOANALYTIC QUARTERLY, 1947, V16, PP 519-546
      YEAR   1947
```

```
      DESC  MOHAVE, SOUTHWEST, CHILDREN-INFANTS AND PRESCHOOL+,
            TRADITIONAL CHILD REARING+, SEXUAL RELATIONS+,
            FEMALES+, ADULTS
      IDEN  U.S.

579   AUTH  SLOBODIN, RICHARD
      TITL  SOME SOCIAL FUNCTIONS OF KUTCHIN ANXIETY.
      SOUR  AMERICAN ANTHROPOLOGIST, 1960, V62, PP 122-133.
      YEAR  1960
      DESC  ANXIETY+, KUTCHIN, YUKON SUB-ARCTIC, SOCIAL STATUS,
            MACKENZIE SUB-ARCTIC
      IDEN  CANADA

580   AUTH  PARKER, SEYMOUR
      TITL  THE WITTIKO PSYCHOSIS IN THE CONTEXT OF OJIBWA
            PERSONALITY AND CULTURE.
      SOUR  AMERICAN ANTHROPOLOGIST, 1960, V62, PP 603-623.
      YEAR  1960
      DESC  CHIPPEWA, CREE, WINDIGO PSYCHOSIS+, EASTERN
            SUB-ARCTIC, PERSONALITY TRAITS+, ANXIETY+, TRADITIONAL
            CHILD REARING, DREAMS AND VISION QUESTS,
            AGGRESSIVENESS
      IDEN  CANADA

581   AUTH  MICKELSON, NORMA I.; GALLOWAY, CHARLES G.
      TITL  CUMULATIVE LANGUAGE DEFICIT AMONG INDIAN CHILDREN.
      SOUR  EXCEPTIONAL CHILDREN, NOV. 1969, V36, PP 187-190.
      YEAR  1969
      DESC  LANGUAGE HANDICAPS+, EDUCATION PROGRAMS AND SERVICES+,
            LEARNING+, CHILDREN-INFANTS AND PRESCHOOL+,
            RESERVATION
      IDEN  CANADA

582   AUTH  GADDES, W.H.; MCKENZIE, AUDREY; BARNSLEY, ROGER.
      TITL  PSYCHOMETRIC INTELLIGENCE AND SPATIAL IMAGERY IN TWO
            NORTHWEST INDIAN AND TWO WHITE GROUPS OF CHILDREN.
      SOUR  JOURNAL OF SOCIAL PSYCHOLOGY, JUN. 1968, V75, PP 35-42.
      YEAR  1968
      DESC  ELEMENTARY SCHOOLS, CHILDREN-SCHOOL AGE+, ABILITIES+,
            PSYCHOLOGICAL TESTING+, COAST SALISH, KWAKIUTL,
            NORTHWEST COAST, NATIVE-NON-NATIVE COMPARISONS,
            CULTURE-FAIR TESTS+, ANGLO AMERICANS
      IDEN  CANADA, GOODENOUGH HARRIS DRAW A PERSON TEST, WECHSLER
            INTELLIGENCE SCALE CHILDREN, KOHS BLOCK DESIGN TEST,
            CULTURE FAIR INTELLIGENCE TEST, PORTEUS MAZE TEST

583   AUTH  JILEK-AALL, LOUISE
      TITL  IDENTIFICATION OF SPECIFIC PSYCHOSOCIAL STRESSES IN
            BRITISH COLUMBIA INDIAN PATIENTS.
      SOUR  PAPER PRESENTED AT THE SECOND TRANSCULTURAL WORKSHOP
            ON NATIVE PEOPLES MENTAL HEALTH, UNDER THE AUSPICES OF
            THE CANADIAN PSYCHIATRIC ASSOCIATION, QUEBEC, CANADA,
            SEP. 1976.
      YEAR  1976
      DESC  NORTHWEST COAST, COAST SALISH, RESERVATION, MENTAL
```

```
            HEALTH PROFESSIONALS+, STRESS
      IDEN  CANADA, BRITISH COLUMBIA

584   AUTH  MARGETTS, EDWARD L.
      TITL  INDIAN AND ESKIMO MEDICINE, WITH NOTES ON THE EARLY
            HISTORY OF PSYCHIATRY AMONG FRENCH AND BRITISH
            COLONISTS.
      SOUR  IN JOHN G. HOWELLS (ED.), WORLD HISTORY OF PSYCHIATRY,
            PP 400-431.  NEW YORK: BRUNNER/MAZEL, 1975.
      YEAR  1975
      DESC  MENTAL DISORDERS+, TRADITIONAL HEALERS+, MENTAL HEALTH
            INSTITUTIONS+
      IDEN  CANADA

585   AUTH  HURT, WESLEY R.
      TITL  FACTORS IN THE PERSISTENCE OF PEYOTE IN THE NORTHERN
            PLAINS.
      SOUR  PLAINS ANTHROPOLOGIST, MAY, 1960, V5(9), PP 16-27.
      YEAR  1960
      DESC  PLAINS, TRADITIONAL USE OF DRUGS AND ALCOHOL+, DRUG
            USE+, NATIVE AMERICAN RELIGIONS+, WINNEBAGO, SIOUX,
            RESERVATION, RELIGIONS-NON-NATIVE, TRIBAL POLITICAL
            ORGANIZATIONS+
      IDEN  U.S., NATIVE AMERICAN CHURCH, NEBRASKA, NORTH DAKOTA,
            SOUTH DAKOTA, WINNEBAGO RESERVATION, PINE RIDGE
            RESERVATION, ROSEBUD RESERVATION, FORT BERTHOLD
            RESERVATION, FORT TOTTEN RESERVATION, CHEYENNE RIVER
            RESERVATION, TURTLE MOUNTAIN RESERVATION

586   AUTH  INDIAN HEALTH SERVICE
      TITL  BASELINE DATA STUDY--PRELIMINARY FINDINGS: GENERAL
            CHARACTERISTICS OF THE INDIAN POPULATION.
      SOUR  IN PINE RIDGE RESEARCH BULLETIN, NO 1, PP 2-13.
            WASHINGTON, D.C.: GOVERNMENT PRINTING OFFICE, 1968.
      YEAR  1968
      DESC  SIOUX-OGLALA, PLAINS, RESERVATION, DEMOGRAPHIC DATA,
            AGE COMPARISONS, SEX DIFFERENCES, NATIVE-NON-NATIVE
            COMPARISONS, ACHIEVEMENT+, EMPLOYMENT+, EXTENDED
            FAMILY+, FULL BLOOD-MIXED BLOOD COMPARISONS
      IDEN  U.S., SOUTH DAKOTA, PINE RIDGE RESERVATION

587   AUTH  MINDELL, CARL; STUART, PAUL
      TITL  SUICIDE AND SELF-DESTRUCTIVE BEHAVIOR IN THE OGLALA
            SIOUX: SOME CLINICAL ASPECTS AND COMMUNITY APPROACHES.
      SOUR  IN PINE RIDGE RESEARCH BULLETIN, NO 1, PP 14-23.
            (INDIAN HEALTH SERVICE) WASHINGTON, D.C.: GOVERNMENT
            PRINTING OFFICE, 1968.
      YEAR  1968
      DESC  SIOUX-OGLALA, SUICIDE+, PREVENTIVE MENTAL HEALTH
            PROGRAMS+, PLAINS, RESERVATION, MENTAL HEALTH PROGRAMS
            AND SERVICES+, MENTAL HEALTH PARAPROFESSIONALS,
            EPIDEMIOLOGICAL STUDY, ACCIDENTS+
      IDEN  U.S., SOUTH DAKOTA, PINE RIDGE RESERVATION

588   AUTH  WILLS, J.E.
```

```
     TITL   ACCIDENT INVESTIGATION THROUGH REVIEW OF LITERATURE, A
            REVIEW OF HOSPITAL RECORDS, AND A CASE STUDY.
     SOUR   IN PINE RIDGE RESEARCH BULLETIN, NO 1, PP 24-25.
            (INDIAN HEALTH SERVICE) WASHINGTON, D.C.: GOVERNMENT
            PRINTING OFFICE, 1968.
     YEAR   1968
     DESC   ACCIDENTS+, SIOUX-OGLALA, PLAINS, RESERVATION,
            PERSONALITY TRAITS
     IDEN   U.S., SOUTH DAKOTA, PINE RIDGE RESERVATION

589  AUTH   MINDELL, CARL; MAYNARD, EILEEN
     TITL   AMBIVALENCE TOWARD EDUCATION AMONG INDIAN HIGH SCHOOL
            STUDENTS.
     SOUR   IN PINE RIDGE RESEARCH BULLETIN, NO 1, PP 26-31.
            (INDIAN HEALTH SERVICE) WASHINGTON, D.C.: GOVERNMENT
            PRINTING OFFICE, 1968.
     YEAR   1968
     DESC   SIOUX-OGLALA, PLAINS, RESERVATION, SECONDARY SCHOOLS+,
            ADOLESCENTS+, DROPOUTS+, ACHIEVEMENT+, MOTIVATION+,
            B.I.A. BOARDING SCHOOLS, PREVENTIVE MENTAL HEALTH
            PROGRAMS+
     IDEN   U.S., SOUTH DAKOTA, PINE RIDGE RESERVATION

590  AUTH   INDIAN HEALTH SERVICE
     TITL   CHARACTERISTICS OF THE INDIAN POPULATION BY
            EDUCATIONAL LEVEL: GENERAL SOCIAL CHARACTERISTICS.
     SOUR   IN PINE RIDGE RESEARCH BULLETIN, NO 2, PP 1-24.
            WASHINGTON, D.C.: GOVERNMENT PRINTING OFFICE, 1968.
     YEAR   1968
     DESC   SIOUX-OGLALA, PLAINS, RESERVATION, AGE COMPARISONS,
            SEX DIFFERENCES, ACHIEVEMENT+, ECONOMIC ISSUES,
            EMPLOYMENT+, DEMOGRAPHIC DATA, FULL BLOOD-MIXED BLOOD
            COMPARISONS, ELEMENTARY SCHOOLS+, SECONDARY SCHOOLS+
     IDEN   U.S., SOUTH DAKOTA, PINE RIDGE RESERVATION

591  AUTH   MESTETH, LEVI
     TITL   COMMUNITY PORTRAIT NO 1: KYLE COMMUNITY.
     SOUR   IN PINE RIDGE RESEARCH BULLETIN, NO 2, PP 25-40.
            (INDIAN HEALTH SERVICE) WASHINGTON, D.C.: GOVERNMENT
            PRINTING OFFICE, 1968.
     YEAR   1968
     DESC   SIOUX-OGLALA, PLAINS, RESERVATION, DEMOGRAPHIC DATA,
            PHYSICAL HEALTH AND ILLNESS+, EMPLOYMENT+, ECONOMIC
            ISSUES, TRIBAL POLITICAL ORGANIZATIONS,
            RELIGIONS-NON-NATIVE, ELEMENTARY SCHOOLS, SECONDARY
            SCHOOLS
     IDEN   U.S., SOUTH DAKOTA, PINE RIDGE RESERVATION

592  AUTH   INDIAN HEALTH SERVICE
     TITL   EMPLOYMENT AND INCOME AMONG INDIAN RESIDENTS OF THE
            PINE RIDGE RESERVATION.
     SOUR   IN PINE RIDGE RESEARCH BULLETIN, NO 3, PP 1-12.
            WASHINGTON, D.C.: GOVERNMENT PRINTING OFFICE, 1968.
     YEAR   1968
     DESC   SIOUX-OGLALA, PLAINS, RESERVATION, DEMOGRAPHIC DATA,
```

```
              EMPLOYMENT+, ECONOMIC ISSUES+
       IDEN   U.S., SOUTH DAKOTA, PINE RIDGE RESERVATION

593    AUTH   MINDELL, CARL
       TITL   INDIANS AND POVERTY.
       SOUR   IN PINE RIDGE RESEARCH BULLETIN, NO 3, PP 13-16.
              (INDIAN HEALTH SERVICE) WASHINGTON, D.C.: GOVERNMENT
              PRINTING OFFICE, 1968.
       YEAR   1968
       DESC   SIOUX-OGLALA, PLAINS, RESERVATION, ECONOMIC ISSUES+,
              NATIVE AMERICAN VALUES+, EMPLOYMENT+, GENEROSITY,
              NONCOMPETITIVENESS, NATIVE AMERICAN COPING BEHAVIORS+,
              LEADERSHIP
       IDEN   U.S., SOUTH DAKOTA, PINE RIDGE RESERVATION

594    AUTH   RIGGS, R.L.
       TITL   SOME PROBLEMS IN THE EDUCATION OF INDIAN YOUTH.
       SOUR   IN PINE RIDGE RESEARCH BULLETIN, NO 3, PP 17-20.
              (INDIAN HEALTH SERVICE) WASHINGTON, D.C.: GOVERNMENT
              PRINTING OFFICE, 1968.
       YEAR   1968
       DESC   SIOUX-OGLALA, PLAINS, RESERVATION, CHILDREN-SCHOOL
              AGE, LEARNING DISABILITIES AND PROBLEMS+, LANGUAGE
              HANDICAPS, BILINGUALISM, EDUCATION PROGRAMS AND
              SERVICES+
       IDEN   U.S., SOUTH DAKOTA, PINE RIDGE RESERVATION

595    AUTH   MAYNARD, EILEEN
       TITL   VICISSITUDES IN COUNTING THE OGLALA SIOUX.
       SOUR   IN PINE RIDGE RESEARCH BULLETIN, NO 3, PP 21-30.
              (INDIAN HEALTH SERVICE) WASHINGTON, D.C.: GOVERNMENT
              PRINTING OFFICE, 1968.
       YEAR   1968
       DESC   SIOUX-OGLALA, PLAINS, RESERVATION, DEMOGRAPHIC DATA,
              I.H.S.
       IDEN   U.S., SOUTH DAKOTA, PINE RIDGE RESERVATION

596    AUTH   INDIAN HEALTH SERVICE
       TITL   CHARACTERISTICS OF THE INDIAN STUDENT POPULATION.
       SOUR   IN PINE RIDGE RESEARCH BULLETIN, NO 4, PP 1-8.
              WASHINGTON, D.C.: GOVERNMENT PRINTING OFFICE, 1968.
       YEAR   1968
       DESC   SIOUX-OGLALA, PLAINS, RESERVATION, ADOLESCENTS+,
              SECONDARY SCHOOLS, DEMOGRAPHIC DATA, CHILDREN-SCHOOL
              AGE, ELEMENTARY SCHOOLS, FULL BLOOD-MIXED BLOOD
              COMPARISONS
       IDEN   U.S., SOUTH DAKOTA, PINE RIDGE RESERVATION

597    AUTH   INDIAN HEALTH SERVICE
       TITL   JUVENILE OFFENSES AND OFFENDERS ON THE PINE RIDGE
              RESERVATION.
       SOUR   IN PINE RIDGE RESEARCH BULLETIN, NO 4, PP 9-24.
              WASHINGTON, D.C.: GOVERNMENT PRINTING OFFICE, 1968.
       YEAR   1968
       DESC   ADOLESCENTS+, SOCIALLY DEVIANT BEHAVIOR+,
```

```
            SIOUX-OGLALA, PLAINS, RESERVATION, CRIME+,
            EPIDEMIOLOGICAL STUDY, SEX DIFFERENCES, DEMOGRAPHIC
            DATA, CHILDREN-SCHOOL AGE, FULL BLOOD-MIXED BLOOD
            COMPARISONS
     IDEN   U.S., SOUTH DAKOTA, PINE RIDGE RESERVATION

598  AUTH   WILLS, J.E.
     TITL   CHILDREN IN THE HOSPITAL: A REVIEW OF THE LITERATURE
            AND ITS APPLICATION TO THE OGLALA SIOUX.
     SOUR   IN PINE RIDGE RESEARCH BULLETIN, NO 4, PP 23-34.
            (INDIAN HEALTH SERVICE) WASHINGTON, D.C.: GOVERNMENT
            PRINTING OFFICE, 1968.
     YEAR   1968
     DESC   SIOUX-OGLALA, PLAINS, RESERVATION, MEDICAL
            INSTITUTIONS+, INSTITUTIONALIZATION+, CHILDREN-SCHOOL
            AGE+, CHILDREN-INFANTS AND PRESCHOOL+, ANXIETY+,
            TRADITIONAL CHILD REARING+
     IDEN   U.S., SOUTH DAKOTA, PINE RIDGE RESERVATION

599  AUTH   MESTETH, LEVI
     TITL   GAS AND GLUE SNIFFING AMONG THE SCHOOL AGE POPULATION.
     SOUR   IN PINE RIDGE RESEARCH BULLETIN, NO 4, PP 36-40.
            (INDIAN HEALTH SERVICE) WASHINGTON, D.C.: GOVERNMENT
            PRINTING OFFICE, 1968.
     YEAR   1968
     DESC   SIOUX-OGLALA, PLAINS, RESERVATION, DRUG USE+,
            ADOLESCENTS+, CHILDREN-SCHOOL AGE+, EPIDEMIOLOGICAL
            STUDY, SOCIAL GROUPS AND PEER GROUPS+, DREAMS AND
            VISION QUESTS, MALES+, FULL BLOOD-MIXED BLOOD
            COMPARISONS
     IDEN   U.S., SOUTH DAKOTA, PINE RIDGE RESERVATION

600  AUTH   MINDELL, CARL
     TITL   GASOLINE INHALATION: A PARTIAL REVIEW OF THE
            LITERATURE.
     SOUR   IN PINE RIDGE RESEARCH BULLETIN, NO 4, PP 41-42.
            (INDIAN HEALTH SERVICE) WASHINGTON, D.C.: GOVERNMENT
            PRINTING OFFICE, 1968.
     YEAR   1968
     DESC   SIOUX-OGLALA, PLAINS, RESERVATION, DRUG USE+,
            CHILDREN-SCHOOL AGE, ADOLESCENTS
     IDEN   U.S., SOUTH DAKOTA, PINE RIDGE RESERVATION

601  AUTH   MINDELL, CARL
     TITL   SOME PSYCHOLOGICAL ASPECTS OF NORMAL INDIAN
            ADOLESCENTS AND TWO GROUPS OF NON-INDIAN ADOLESCENTS.
     SOUR   IN PINE RIDGE RESEARCH BULLETIN, NO 4, PP 43-47.
            (INDIAN HEALTH SERVICE) WASHINGTON, D.C.: GOVERNMENT
            PRINTING OFFICE, 1968.
     YEAR   1968
     DESC   ADOLESCENTS+, SECONDARY SCHOOLS, PSYCHOLOGICAL
            TESTING+, RESERVATION, NATIVE-NON-NATIVE COMPARISONS,
            ANGLO AMERICANS, PERSONALITY TRAITS+, AGGRESSIVENESS,
            ANXIETY, SIOUX-OGLALA, PLAINS
     IDEN   U.S., SOUTH DAKOTA, PINE RIDGE RESERVATION
```

602 AUTH INDIAN HEALTH SERVICE
     TITL OGLALA SIOUX AND FAMILY ORGANIZATION, A STATISTICAL
           ANALYSIS.
     SOUR IN PINE RIDGE RESEARCH BULLETIN, NO 5, PP 1-23.
           WASHINGTON, D.C.: GOVERNMENT PRINTING OFFICE, 1968.
     YEAR 1968
     DESC SIOUX-OGLALA, PLAINS, RESERVATION, EXTENDED FAMILY+,
           DEMOGRAPHIC DATA, NATIVE-NON-NATIVE COMPARISONS,
           ADOPTION AND FOSTER CARE, ANGLO AMERICANS, FULL
           BLOOD-MIXED BLOOD COMPARISONS, MARITAL RELATIONSHIPS+
     IDEN U.S., SOUTH DAKOTA, PINE RIDGE RESERVATION

603 AUTH MILLER, MAURICE
     TITL COMMUNITY PORTRAIT NO. 2: WANBLEE COMMUNITY.
     SOUR IN PINE RIDGE RESEARCH BULLETIN, NO 5, PP 24-51.
           (INDIAN HEALTH SERVICE) WASHINGTON, D.C.: GOVERNMENT
           PRINTING OFFICE, 1968.
     YEAR 1968
     DESC SIOUX-OGLALA, PLAINS, RESERVATION, DEMOGRAPHIC DATA,
           EMPLOYMENT, PHYSICAL HEALTH AND ILLNESS, URBAN AREAS,
           EXTENDED FAMILY, TRIBAL POLITICAL ORGANIZATIONS,
           RELIGIONS-NON-NATIVE, ELEMENTARY SCHOOLS, SECONDARY
           SCHOOLS, FULL BLOOD-MIXED BLOOD COMPARISONS
     IDEN U.S., SOUTH DAKOTA, PINE RIDGE RESERVATION

604 AUTH LEWIS, THOMAS H.; MESTETH, LEVI
     TITL SUNDANCE, 1968.
     SOUR IN PINE RIDGE RESEARCH BULLETIN, NO 5, PP 52-64.
           (INDIAN HEALTH SERVICE) WASHINGTON, D.C.: GOVERNMENT
           PRINTING OFFICE, 1968.
     YEAR 1968
     DESC SIOUX-OGLALA, PLAINS, RESERVATION, NATIVE AMERICAN
           RELIGIONS+, CULTURAL CONTINUITY+, CULTURAL REVIVAL+
     IDEN U.S., SOUTH DAKOTA, PINE RIDGE RESERVATION, SUN DANCE

605 AUTH INDIAN HEALTH SERVICE
     TITL PINE RIDGE RESERVATION POPULATION BY DISTRICTS,
           COMMUNITIES AND VILLAGE-RURAL DISTRIBUTION.
     SOUR IN PINE RIDGE RESEARCH BULLETIN, NO 6, PP 1-10.
           WASHINGTON, D.C.: GOVERNMENT PRINTING OFFICE, 1968.
     YEAR 1968
     DESC SIOUX-OGLALA, PLAINS, RESERVATION, DEMOGRAPHIC DATA,
           URBAN AREAS
     IDEN U.S., SOUTH DAKOTA, PINE RIDGE RESERVATION

606 AUTH PRIMACK, W.
     TITL FAMILY PLANNING AT PINE RIDGE.
     SOUR IN PINE RIDGE RESEARCH BULLETIN, NO 6, PP 11-17.
           (INDIAN HEALTH SERVICE) WASHINGTON, D.C.: GOVERNMENT
           PRINTING OFFICE, 1968.
     YEAR 1968
     DESC SIOUX-OGLALA, PLAINS, RESERVATION, SEXUAL RELATIONS+,
           FEMALES+, ADULTS, DROPOUTS, EDUCATION PROGRAMS AND
           SERVICES+, FAMILY PLANNING+
     IDEN U.S., SOUTH DAKOTA, PINE RIDGE RESERVATION

607 AUTH MAYNARD, EILEEN
    TITL NEGATIVE ETHNIC IMAGE AMONG OGLALA SIOUX HIGH SCHOOL
         STUDENTS.
    SOUR IN PINE RIDGE RESEARCH BULLETIN, NO 6, PP 18-25.
         (INDIAN HEALTH SERVICE) WASHINGTON, D.C.: GOVERNMENT
         PRINTING OFFICE, 1968.
    YEAR 1968
    DESC ETHNIC IDENTITY+, SIOUX-OGLALA, RESERVATION, PLAINS,
         ADOLESCENTS+, SECONDARY SCHOOLS, NATIVE-NON-NATIVE
         COMPARISONS, STEREOTYPES+, DISCRIMINATION+, ANGLO
         AMERICANS, POWERLESSNESS, FULL BLOOD-MIXED BLOOD
         COMPARISONS
    IDEN U.S., SOUTH DAKOTA, PINE RIDGE RESERVATION

608 AUTH MINDELL, CARL
    TITL POVERTY, MENTAL HEALTH AND THE SIOUX.
    SOUR IN PINE RIDGE RESEARCH BULLETIN, NO 6, PP 26-34.
         (INDIAN HEALTH SERVICE) WASHINGTON, D.C.: GOVERNMENT
         PRINTING OFFICE, 1968.
    YEAR 1968
    DESC SIOUX-OGLALA, PLAINS, RESERVATION, ECONOMIC ISSUES+,
         DEMOGRAPHIC DATA, PASSIVE RESISTANCE+, FAMILY
         FUNCTIONING+, EPIDEMIOLOGICAL STUDY, SOCIALLY DEVIANT
         BEHAVIOR, POWERLESSNESS+
    IDEN U.S., SOUTH DAKOTA, PINE RIDGE RESERVATION

609 AUTH ZIMMERLY, W.
    TITL WHEN THE PEOPLE GATHER.
    SOUR IN PINE RIDGE RESEARCH BULLETIN, NO 6, PP 35-40.
         (INDIAN HEALTH SERVICE) WASHINGTON, D.C.: GOVERNMENT
         PRINTING OFFICE, 1968.
    YEAR 1968
    DESC NATIVE AMERICAN RELIGIONS+, NATIVE AMERICAN VALUES+,
         CULTURAL REVIVAL, SIOUX-OGLALA, PLAINS, RESERVATION,
         CULTURAL CONTINUITY+
    IDEN U.S., SOUTH DAKOTA, PINE RIDGE RESERVATION, SUN DANCE

610 AUTH INDIAN HEALTH SERVICE
    TITL FELT NEEDS, DEPENDENCY AND COMMUNITY DEVELOPMENT.
    SOUR IN PINE RIDGE RESEARCH BULLETIN, NO 7, PP 1-10.
         WASHINGTON, D.C.: GOVERNMENT PRINTING OFFICE, 1969.
    YEAR 1969
    DESC SIOUX-OGLALA, PLAINS, RESERVATION, FEDERAL
         GOVERNMENT+, DELIVERY OF SERVICES+, ECONOMIC ISSUES,
         NATIVE AMERICAN ADMINISTERED PROGRAMS+,
         NATIVE-NON-NATIVE COMPARISONS, POWERLESSNESS+, ANGLO
         AMERICANS, FULL BLOOD-MIXED BLOOD COMPARISONS
    IDEN U.S., SOUTH DAKOTA, PINE RIDGE RESERVATION

611 AUTH INDIAN HEALTH SERVICE
    TITL FAMILY PROBLEMS AND DEPENDENCY.
    SOUR IN PINE RIDGE RESEARCH BULLETIN, NO 7, PP 11-17.
         WASHINGTON, D.C.: GOVERNMENT PRINTING OFFICE, 1969.
    YEAR 1969
    DESC SIOUX-OGLALA, PLAINS, RESERVATION, FAMILY

```
                 FUNCTIONING+, FEDERAL GOVERNMENT+, DELIVERY OF
                 SERVICES, NATIVE-NON-NATIVE COMPARISONS, ANGLO
                 AMERICANS, POWERLESSNESS+
            IDEN U.S., SOUTH DAKOTA, PINE RIDGE RESERVATION

612  AUTH  TWISS, GAYLA
     TITL  COMMUNITY PORTRAIT NO. 3: PINE RIDGE VILLAGE.
     SOUR  IN PINE RIDGE RESEARCH BULLETIN, NO 7, PP 18-66.
           (INDIAN HEALTH SERVICE) WASHINGTON, D.C.: GOVERNMENT
           PRINTING OFFICE, 1969.
     YEAR  1969
     DESC  SIOUX-OGLALA, PLAINS, RESERVATION, DEMOGRAPHIC DATA,
           URBAN AREAS, I.H.S., DELIVERY OF SERVICES+,
           EMPLOYMENT, CORRECTIONAL INSTITUTIONS,
           RELIGIONS-NON-NATIVE, TRIBAL POLITICAL ORGANIZATIONS,
           SECONDARY SCHOOLS, ELEMENTARY SCHOOLS, FULL
           BLOOD-MIXED BLOOD COMPARISONS
     IDEN  U.S., SOUTH DAKOTA, PINE RIDGE RESERVATION

613  AUTH  STUART, PAUL
     TITL  THE RESERVATION COMMUNITY.
     SOUR  IN PINE RIDGE RESEARCH BULLETIN, NO 7, PP 67-82.
           (INDIAN HEALTH SERVICE) WASHINGTON, D.C.: GOVERNMENT
           PRINTING OFFICE, 1969.
     YEAR  1969
     DESC  SIOUX-OGLALA, PLAINS, RESERVATION, NATIVE AMERICAN
           VALUES+, FEDERAL GOVERNMENT+, TRIBAL POLITICAL
           ORGANIZATIONS, NATIVE AMERICAN ADMINISTERED PROGRAMS,
           POWERLESSNESS+
     IDEN  U.S., SOUTH DAKOTA, PINE RIDGE RESERVATION

614  AUTH  INDIAN HEALTH SERVICE
     TITL  HEALTH AND ATTITUDES TOWARDS THE PUBLIC HEALTH SERVICE
           AMONG THE OGLALA SIOUX.
     SOUR  IN PINE RIDGE RESEARCH BULLETIN, NO 8, PP 1-11.
           WASHINGTON, D.C.: GOVERNMENT PRINTING OFFICE, 1969.
     YEAR  1969
     DESC  SIOUX-OGLALA, PLAINS, RESERVATION, PHYSICAL HEALTH AND
           ILLNESS+, I.H.S.+, NATIVE-NON-NATIVE COMPARISONS, SEX
           DIFFERENCES, MEDICAL INSTITUTIONS+, DELIVERY OF
           SERVICES+, PROGRAM EVALUATION+, ANGLO AMERICANS, FULL
           BLOOD-MIXED BLOOD COMPARISONS, ATTITUDES+
     IDEN  U.S., SOUTH DAKOTA, PINE RIDGE RESERVATION

615  AUTH  KEMNITZER, LUIS S.
     TITL  WHITE MAN"S MEDICINE, INDIAN MEDICINE, AND INDIAN
           IDENTITY ON PINE RIDGE RESERVATION.
     SOUR  IN PINE RIDGE RESEARCH BULLETIN, NO 8, PP 12-23.
           (INDIAN HEALTH SERVICE) WASHINGTON, D.C.: GOVERNMENT
           PRINTING OFFICE, 1969.
     YEAR  1969
     DESC  SIOUX-OGLALA, PLAINS, RESERVATION, NATIVE AMERICAN
           VALUES, TRADITIONAL HEALERS+, I.H.S., MEDICAL
           INSTITUTIONS+, MEDICAL PROFESSIONALS+, DELIVERY OF
           SERVICES+, CULTURAL CONTINUITY+, NONINTERFERENCE
```

```
      IDEN   U.S., SOUTH DAKOTA, PINE RIDGE RESERVATION

616   AUTH   MCCRACKEN, C.H.
      TITL   THE BABY IS NOT SICK.
      SOUR   IN PINE RIDGE RESEARCH BULLETIN, NO 8, PP 24-27.
             (INDIAN HEALTH SERVICE) WASHINGTON, D.C.: GOVERNMENT
             PRINTING OFFICE, 1969.
      YEAR   1969
      DESC   SIOUX-OGLALA, PLAINS, RESERVATION, CHILDREN-INFANTS
             AND PRESCHOOL+, MEDICAL INSTITUTIONS+, DELIVERY OF
             SERVICES+, NATIVE AMERICAN ETIOLOGY+
      IDEN   U.S., SOUTH DAKOTA, PINE RIDGE RESERVATION

617   AUTH   DEMONTIGNY, LIONEL H.
      TITL   DOCTOR-INDIAN PATIENT RELATIONSHIPS.
      SOUR   IN PINE RIDGE RESEARCH BULLETIN, NO 8, PP 28-39.
             (INDIAN HEALTH SERVICE) WASHINGTON, D.C.: GOVERNMENT
             PRINTING OFFICE, 1969,
      YEAR   1969
      DESC   SIOUX-OGLALA, PLAINS, RESERVATION, MEDICAL
             PROFESSIONALS+, I.H.S., DELIVERY OF SERVICES+,
             EXTENDED FAMILY+, NATIVE AMERICAN VALUES+
      IDEN   U.S., SOUTH DAKOTA, PINE RIDGE RESERVATION

618   AUTH   TWISS, GAYLA
      TITL   THE COMMUNITY HEALTH AIDE PROGRAM: AN EVALUATION OF
             THE INDIGENOUS AIDES IN THE PROVISION OF HEALTH
             SERVICE.
      SOUR   IN PINE RIDGE RESEARCH BULLETIN, NO 8, PP 40-48.
             (INDIAN HEALTH SERVICE) WASHINGTON, D.C.: GOVERNMENT
             PRINTING OFFICE, 1969,
      YEAR   1969
      DESC   SIOUX-OGLALA, PLAINS, RESERVATION, MEDICAL
             PARAPROFESSIONALS+, MEDICAL PROGRAMS AND SERVICES+,
             PROGRAM EVALUATION+, DELIVERY OF SERVICES+, I.H.S.,
             NATIVE AMERICAN PERSONNEL+
      IDEN   U.S., SOUTH DAKOTA, PINE RIDGE RESERVATION

619   AUTH   WILLS, J.E.
      TITL   PSYCHOLOGICAL PROBLEMS OF SIOUX INDIANS RESULTING IN
             THE ACCIDENT PHENOMENA.
      SOUR   IN PINE RIDGE RESEARCH BULLETIN, NO 8, PP 49-63.
             (INDIAN HEALTH SERVICE) WASHINGTON, D.C.: GOVERNMENT
             PRINTING OFFICE, 1969.
      YEAR   1969
      DESC   ACCIDENTS+, SIOUX-OGLALA, PLAINS, RESERVATION,
             EPIDEMIOLOGICAL STUDY, SEX
             DIFFERENCES,NATIVE-NON-NATIVE COMPARISONS, ANXIETY+,
             ADULTS, NATIVE AMERICAN COPING BEHAVIORS+, PREVENTIVE
             MENTAL HEALTH PROGRAMS, ANGLO AMERICANS,
             POWERLESSNESS, FULL BLOOD-MIXED BLOOD COMPARISONS
      IDEN   U.S., SOUTH DAKOTA, PINE RIDGE RESERVATION

620   AUTH   MEDICINE, BEATRICE
      TITL   THE CHANGING DAKOTA FAMILY AND THE STRESSES THEREIN.
```

```
        SOUR   IN PINE RIDGE RESEARCH BULLETIN, NO 9, PP 1-20.
               (INDIAN HEALTH SERVICE) WASHINGTON, D.C.: GOVERNMENT
               PRINTING OFFICE, 1969.
        YEAR   1969
        DESC   SIOUX-OGLALA, PLAINS, RESERVATION, FAMILY
               FUNCTIONING+, EXTENDED FAMILY+, TRADITIONAL CHILD
               REARING+, GENEROSITY, TRADITIONAL SOCIAL CONTROL,
               CHILD ABUSE AND NEGLECT, NATIVE AMERICAN VALUES,
               SEXUAL RELATIONS+, MALES+, FEMALES+,STRESS+,
               ADOLESCENTS+, ADULTS, AGED, SOCIAL ROLES
        IDEN   U.S., PINE RIDGE RESERVATION, SOUTH DAKOTA

621     AUTH   THREE STAR, L.
        TITL   THE CHANGING STATUS OF THE SIOUX MALE.
        SOUR   IN PINE RIDGE RESEARCH BULLETIN, NO 9, PP 21-20.
               (INDIAN HEALTH SERVICE) WASHINGTON, D.C.: GOVERNMENT
               PRINTING OFFICE, 1969.
        YEAR   1969
        DESC   SIOUX-OGLALA, PLAINS, RESERVATION, MALES+, ETHNIC
               IDENTITY+, SOCIAL STATUS+
        IDEN   U.S., SOUTH DAKOTA, PINE RIDGE RESERVATION

622     AUTH   DEMONTIGNY, LIONEL H.
        TITL   ATTITUDES OF LOW EXPECTANCY.
        SOUR   IN PINE RIDGE RESEARCH BULLETIN, NO 9, PP 31-34.
               (INDIAN HEALTH SERVICE) WASHINGTON, D.C.: GOVERNMENT
               PRINTING OFFICE, 1969.
        YEAR   1969
        DESC   SIOUX-OGLALA, PLAINS, RESERVATION, ACHIEVEMENT+,
               MOTIVATION+, DISCRIMINATION+, ELEMENTARY SCHOOLS,
               SECONDARY SCHOOLS, ATTITUDES+
        IDEN   U.S., SOUTH DAKOTA, PINE RIDGE RESERVATION

623     AUTH   MAYNARD, EILEEN
        TITL   DRINKING AS A PART OF AN ADJUSTMENT SYNDROME AMONG THE
               OGLALA SIOUX.
        SOUR   IN PINE RIDGE RESEARCH BULLETIN, NO 9, PP 35-51.
               (INDIAN HEALTH SERVICE) WASHINGTON, D.C.: GOVERNMENT
               PRINTING OFFICE, 1969.
        YEAR   1969
        DESC   SIOUX-OGLALA, PLAINS, RESERVATION, ALCOHOL USE+, GROUP
               NORMS AND SANCTIONS+, SOCIAL GROUPS AND PEER GROUPS,
               SEX DIFFERENCES, EPIDEMIOLOGICAL STUDY, NATIVE
               AMERICAN COPING BEHAVIORS+, FULL BLOOD-MIXED BLOOD
               COMPARISONS
        IDEN   U.S., SOUTH DAKOTA, PINE RIDGE RESERVATION

624     AUTH   TWISS, GAYLA
        TITL   THE SECOND BATTLE OF WOUNDED KNEE: THE CONTROVERSY
               OVER THE PROPOSED WOUNDED KNEE MONUMENT.
        SOUR   IN PINE RIDGE RESEARCH BULLETIN, NO 9, PP 52-65.
               (INDIAN HEALTH SERVICE) WASHINGTON, D.C.: GOVERNMENT
               PRINTING OFFICE, 1969.
        YEAR   1969
        DESC   SIOUX-OGLALA, PLAINS, RESERVATION, ECONOMIC ISSUES,
```

```
          TRIBAL POLITICAL ORGANIZATIONS+, POLITICS-NONTRIBAL+
     IDEN U.S., SOUTH DAKOTA, PINE RIDGE RESERVATION

625  AUTH INDIAN HEALTH SERVICE
     TITL SOME NOTES ON DENOMINATIONAL PREFERENCES AMONG THE
          OGLALAS.
     SOUR IN PINE RIDGE RESEARCH BULLETIN, NO 10, PP 1-6.
          WASHINGTON, D.C.: GOVERNMENT PRINTING OFFICE, 1969.
     YEAR 1969
     DESC SIOUX-OGLALA, PLAINS, RESERVATION,
          RELIGIONS-NON-NATIVE+
     IDEN U.S., SOUTH DAKOTA, PINE RIDGE RESERVATION, CATHOLIC
          CHURCH, EPISCOPAL CHURCH

626  AUTH TWISS, GAYLA
     TITL THE ROLE OF THE PIPE IN DAKOTA RELIGION.
     SOUR IN PINE RIDGE RESEARCH BULLETIN, NO 10, PP 7-19.
          (INDIAN HEALTH SERVICE) WASHINGTON, D.C.: GOVERNMENT
          PRINTING OFFICE, 1969
     YEAR 1969
     DESC SIOUX-OGLALA, PLAINS, RESERVATION, NATIVE AMERICAN
          RELIGIONS+
     IDEN U.S., SOUTH DAKOTA, PINE RIDGE RESERVATION, SACRED
          PIPE

627  AUTH STEINMETZ, PAUL
     TITL EXPLANATION OF THE SACRED PIPE AS A PRAYER INSTRUMENT.
     SOUR IN PINE RIDGE RESEARCH BULLETIN, NO 10, PP 20-25.
          (INDIAN HEALTH SERVICE) WASHINGTON, D.C.: GOVERNMENT
          PRINTING OFFICE, 1969.
     YEAR 1969
     DESC SIOUX-OGLALA, PLAINS, RESERVATION, NATIVE AMERICAN
          RELIGIONS+, RELIGIONS-NON-NATIVE+, CULTURAL
          CONTINUITY+
     IDEN U.S., SOUTH DAKOTA, PINE RIDGE RESERVATION, SACRED
          PIPE, CATHOLIC CHURCH

628  AUTH KEMNITZER, LUIS S.
     TITL YUWIPI.
     SOUR IN PINE RIDGE RESEARCH BULLETIN, NO 10, PP 26-33.
          (INDIAN HEALTH SERVICE) WASHINGTON, D.C.: GOVERNMENT
          PRINTING OFFICE, 1969.
     YEAR 1969
     DESC SIOUX-OGLALA, PLAINS, RESERVATION, TRADITIONAL
          HEALERS+, NATIVE AMERICAN RELIGIONS+, CULTURE-BASED
          PSYCHOTHERAPY+
     IDEN U.S., SOUTH DAKOTA, PINE RIDGE RESERVATION, SACRED
          PIPE

629  AUTH FERACA, S.E.
     TITL PEYOTISM.
     SOUR IN PINE RIDGE RESEARCH BULLETIN, NO 10, PP 34-45.
          (INDIAN HEALTH SERVICE) WASHINGTON, D.C.: GOVERNMENT
          PRINTING OFFICE, 1969.
     YEAR 1969
```

```
        DESC  SIOUX-OGLALA, PLAINS, RESERVATION, TRADITIONAL USE OF
              DRUGS AND ALCOHOL+, DRUG USE+, NATIVE AMERICAN
              RELIGIONS+
        IDEN  U.S., SOUTH DAKOTA, PINE RIDGE RESERVATION, NATIVE
              AMERICAN CHURCH

  630   AUTH  ZIMMERLY, D.
        TITL  ON BEING AN ASCETIC: PERSONAL DOCUMENT OF A SIOUX
              MEDICINE MAN.
        SOUR  IN PINE RIDGE RESEARCH BULLETIN, NO 10, PP 46-69.
              (INDIAN HEALTH SERVICE) WASHINGTON, D.C.: GOVERNMENT
              PRINTING OFFICE, 1969.
        YEAR  1969
        DESC  SIOUX-OGLALA, PLAINS, RESERVATION, NATIVE AMERICAN
              RELIGIONS+, RELIGIONS-NON-NATIVE, TRADITIONAL
              HEALERS+, DREAMS AND VISION QUESTS
        IDEN  U.S., SOUTH DAKOTA, PINE RIDGE RESERVATION, SUN DANCE,
              SACRED PIPE

  631   AUTH  INDIAN HEALTH SERVICE
        TITL  SOME NOTES ON SCHOOL DROPOUTS.
        SOUR  IN PINE RIDGE RESEARCH BULLETIN, NO 11, PP 1-6.
              WASHINGTON, D.C.: GOVERNMENT PRINTING OFFICE, 1970
        YEAR  1970
        DESC  SIOUX-OGLALA, PLAINS, RESERVATION, SECONDARY SCHOOLS+,
              DROPOUTS+, ADOLESCENTS+, SEX DIFFERENCES, FULL
              BLOOD-MIXED BLOOD COMPARISONS, EPIDEMIOLOGICAL STUDY,
              NATIVE-NON-NATIVE COMPARISONS, ANGLO AMERICANS, BLACK
              AMERICANS
        IDEN  U.S., SOUTH DAKOTA, PINE RIDGE RESERVATION

  632   AUTH  LEWIS, THOMAS H.
        TITL  NOTES ON THE HEYOKA: THE TETON DAKOTA "CONTRARY" CULT.
        SOUR  IN PINE RIDGE RESEARCH BULLETIN, NO 11, PP 7-19.
              (INDIAN HEALTH SERVICE) WASHINGTON, D.C.: GOVERNMENT
              PRINTING OFFICE, 1970.
        YEAR  1970
        DESC  SIOUX-OGLALA, PLAINS, RESERVATION, NATIVE AMERICAN
              RELIGIONS+, MENTAL DISORDERS, SOCIALLY DEVIANT
              BEHAVIOR+, GROUP NORMS AND SANCTIONS+
        IDEN  U.S., SOUTH DAKOTA, PINE RIDGE RESERVATION, HEYOKA
              CULT

  633   AUTH  RUBY, R.H.
        TITL  YUWIPI, ANCIENT RITE OF THE SIOUX.
        SOUR  IN PINE RIDGE RESEARCH BULLETIN, NO 11, PP 20-30.
              (INDIAN HEALTH SERVICE) WASHINGTON, D.C.: GOVERNMENT
              PRINTING OFFICE, 1970.
        YEAR  1970
        DESC  SIOUX-OGLALA, PLAINS, RESERVATION, NATIVE AMERICAN
              RELIGIONS+, TRADITIONAL HEALERS+
        IDEN  U.S., PINE RIDGE RESERVATION, SOUTH DAKOTA, YUWIPI
              CEREMONY

  634   AUTH  MAYNARD, EILEEN
```

```
      TITL   COMMUNITY PORTRAIT NO. 4: MANDERSON COMMUNITY.
      SOUR   IN PINE RIDGE RESEARCH BULLETIN, NO 11, PP 31-49.
             (INDIAN HEALTH SERVICE) WASHINGTON, D.C.: GOVERNMENT
             PRINTING OFFICE, 1970.
      YEAR   1970
      DESC   SIOUX-OGLALA, PLAINS, RESERVATION, URBAN AREAS,
             DEMOGRAPHIC DATA, DELIVERY OF SERVICES+
      IDEN   U.S., SOUTH DAKOTA, PINE RIDGE RESERVATION

635   AUTH   VOYAT, GILBERT; SILK, S.
      TITL   CROSS-CULTURAL STUDY OF COGNITIVE DEVELOPMENT ON THE
             PINE RIDGE RESERVATION.
      SOUR   IN PINE RIDGE RESEARCH BULLETIN, NO 11, PP 50-73.
             WASHINGTON, \D.C.: GOVERNMENT PRINTING OFFICE, 1970.
      YEAR   1970
      DESC   SIOUX-OGLALA, PLAINS, COGNITIVE PROCESSES+,
             CHILDREN-SCHOOL AGE+, CULTURE-FAIR TESTS+, ABILITIES+,
             PSYCHOLOGICAL TESTING+, RESERVATION, LEARNING
      IDEN   U.S., SOUTH DAKOTA, PINE RIDGE RESERVATION, PIAGETIAN
             TASKS

636   AUTH   TRELEASE, MURRAY L.
      TITL   DYING AMONG ALASKAN INDIANS: A MATTER OF CHOICE.
      SOUR   IN ELISABETH KUBLER-ROSS (ED.), DEATH: THE FINAL STAGE
             OF GROWTH, PP 33-37.LONDON: PRENTICE-HALL, 1975.
      YEAR   1975
      DESC   DEATH AND DYING+, RELIGIOUS-NON-NATIVE PERSONNEL+,
             AGED+, ESKIMO, WESTERN ARCTIC
      IDEN   U.S., ALASKA

637   AUTH   BOYCE, GEORGE A.
      TITL   ALCOHOL AND AMERICAN INDIAN STUDENTS.
      SOUR   WASHINGTON, D.C.: BUREAU OF INDIAN AFFAIRS, 1965.
      YEAR   1965
      DESC   ADOLESCENTS+, ALCOHOL USE+, SOCIAL STATUS+, SOCIAL
             GROUPS AND PEER GROUPS, NATIVE-NON-NATIVE COMPARISONS,
             ALEUT, WESTERN ARCTIC, ANGLO AMERICANS, PLAINS, SIOUX,
             PUEBLO-HOPI, SOUTHWEST, NAVAJO, SECONDARY SCHOOLS+,
             PREVENTIVE MENTAL HEALTH PROGRAMS+
      IDEN   U.S.

638   AUTH   TOPPER, MARTIN D.
      TITL   DRINKING PATTERNS, CULTURE CHANGE, SOCIABILITY, AND
             NAVAJO "ADOLESCENTS."
      SOUR   ADDICTIVE DISEASES, 1974, V1(10), PP 97-116.
      YEAR   1974
      DESC   ALCOHOL USE+, NAVAJO, SOUTHWEST, RESERVATION, CULTURAL
             ADAPTATION+, ADOLESCENTS+, SOCIAL GROUPS AND PEER
             GROUPS, MALES+, FEMALES, STRESS+
      IDEN   U.S., NAVAJO RESERVATION

639   AUTH   HANSON, WYNNE
      TITL   GRIEF COUNSELING WITH NATIVE AMERICANS.
      SOUR   WHITE CLOUD JOURNAL, SUM. 1978, V1 (2), PP 19-21.
      YEAR   1978
```

DESC GRIEF REACTION+, PSYCHOTHERAPY AND COUNSELING+, URBAN
        AREAS, STEREOTYPES
IDEN U.S.

640 AUTH BEISER, MORTON; ATTNEAVE, CAROLYN L.
      TITL MENTAL HEALTH SERVICES FOR AMERICAN INDIANS: NEITHER
            FEAST NOR FAMINE.
      SOUR WHITE CLOUD JOURNAL, SUM. 1978, V1 (2), PP 3-10.
      YEAR 1978
      DESC I.H.S.+, DELIVERY OF SERVICES+, MENTAL HEALTH PROGRAMS
            AND SERVICES+, PROGRAM EVALUATION+, TRADITIONAL
            HEALERS, DISCRIMINATION, MENTAL HEALTH
            PARAPROFESSIONALS
      IDEN U.S.

641 AUTH PENISTON, EUGENE
      TITL THE EGO STRENGTH SCALE AS A PREDICTOR OF UTE INDIAN
            SUICIDE RISK.
      SOUR WHITE CLOUD JOURNAL, SUM. 1978, V1 (2), PP 15-18.
      YEAR 1978
      DESC SUICIDE+, PSYCHOLOGICAL TESTING+, UTE, GREAT BASIN,
            RESERVATION, PERSONALITY TRAITS, DEPRESSION, SEX
            DIFFERENCES, ADULTS, EXPERIMENTAL STUDY
      IDEN U.S., UINTAH AND OURAY RESERVATION, M.M.P.I.

642 AUTH SHORE, JAMES H.
      TITL DESTRUCTION OF INDIAN FAMILIES: BEYOND THE BEST
            INTERESTS OF INDIAN CHILDREN.
      SOUR WHITE CLOUD JOURNAL, SUM. 1978, V1 (2), PP 13-16.
      YEAR 1978
      DESC EXTENDED FAMILY, ADOPTION AND FOSTER CARE+, ETHNIC
            IDENTITY+, CHILDREN-INFANTS AND PRESCHOOL,
            CHILDREN-SCHOOL AGE, ADOLESCENTS
      IDEN U.S.

643 AUTH GOODLUCK, CHARLOTTE T.; ECKSTEIN, FLORENCE
      TITL AMERICAN INDIAN ADOPTION PROGRAM: AN ETHNIC APPROACH
            TO CHILD WELFARE.
      SOUR WHITE CLOUD JOURNAL, SPR. 1978, V1 (1), PP 3-7.
      YEAR 1978
      DESC ADOPTION AND FOSTER CARE+, EXTENDED FAMILY, SOCIAL
            SERVICES+
      IDEN U.S., INDIAN ADOPTION PROGRAM

644 AUTH OETTING, E.R.; GOLDSTEIN, GEORGE S.
      TITL NATIVE AMERICAN DRUG USE.
      SOUR (NIDA GRANT NO. 2 R01 DA01054-02). FT. COLLINS,
            COLORADO STATE UNIVERSITY,1978.
      YEAR 1978
      DESC DRUG USE+, ADOLESCENTS+, CHILDREN-SCHOOL AGE+, SURVEY,
            INTERTRIBAL COMPARISONS, NATIVE-NON-NATIVE
            COMPARISONS, ANGLO AMERICANS, AGE COMPARISONS, SEX
            DIFFERENCES
      IDEN U.S.

645 AUTH BUSHNELL, JOHN H.
    TITL LIVES IN PROFILE: A LONGITUDINAL STUDY OF CONTEMPORARY
          HUPA MEN FROM YOUNG ADULTHOOD TO THE MIDDLE YEARS.
    SOUR TRANSACTIONS OF THE NEW YORK ACADEMY OF SCIENCES,
          1971, V32(7), PP 787-801.
    YEAR 1971
    DESC HOOPA, CALIFORNIA AREA, MALES+, ADULTS+, PSYCHOLOGICAL
          TESTING+, PERSONALITY TRAITS+, RESERVATION, PASSIVE
          RESISTANCE, EMOTIONAL RESTRAINT, CULTURAL CONTINUITY+,
          MILITARY SERVICE
    IDEN U.S., CALIFORNIA, HOOPA VALLEY RESERVATION, SOCIAL
          MATURITY SCALE, IMPULSE EXPRESSION TEST, THEMATIC
          APPERCEPTION TEST

646 AUTH RYAN, ROBERT A.
    TITL SELF-IDENTITY IN AN URBAN INDIAN SOCIAL STRUGGLE.
    SOUR PAPER PRESENTED AT THE AMERICAN PSYCHOLOGICAL
          ASSOCIATION ANNUAL CONVENTION, CHICAGO, 30 AUG.- 3
          SEP., 1975. (15P)
    YEAR 1975
    DESC SELF-CONCEPT+, URBAN AREAS, URBANIZATION+,
          PSYCHOLOGICAL TESTING+, OMAHA, WINNEBAGO, SIOUX,
          PLAINS, PRAIRIE, ETHNIC IDENTITY+
    IDEN U.S., IOWA, TENNESSEE SELF-CONCEPT SCALE

647 AUTH CHANCE, NORMAN A.; FOSTER, DOROTHY A.
    TITL SYMPTOM FORMATION AND PATTERNS OF PSYCHOPATHOLOGY IN A
          RAPIDLY CHANGING ALASKAN ESKIMO SOCIETY.
    SOUR ANTHROPOLOGICAL PAPERS OF THE UNIVERSITY OF ALASKA,
          DEC. 1962, V11(1), PP 32-42.
    YEAR 1962
    DESC ESKIMO, STRESS+, MENTAL DISORDERS+, WESTERN ARCTIC,
          PSYCHOLOGICAL TESTING+, SEX DIFFERENCES, ADULTS,
          EPIDEMIOLOGICAL STUDY, MALES, FEMALES, AGE
          COMPARISONS, PHYSICAL HEALTH AND ILLNESS+, SURVEY
    IDEN U.S., ALASKA, CORNELL MEDICAL INDEX

648 AUTH ROSS, DONALD D.
    TITL A REACTION TO STRUGGLE OF IDENTITY AND SURVIVAL AMIDST
          SOCIAL CHANGE.
    SOUR PAPER PRESENTED AT THE AMERICAN PSYCHOLOGICAL
          ASSOCIATION ANNUAL CONVENTION, CHICAGO, 30 AUG.- 3
          SEP., 1975. (6P)
    YEAR 1975
    DESC ETHNIC IDENTITY+, NATIVE AMERICAN VALUES, CULTURAL
          CONTINUITY+, CULTURAL ADAPTATION+
    IDEN U.S., CANADA

649 AUTH TRIMBLE, JOSEPH E.
    TITL SELF AND CULTURAL IDENTITY OF THE "BREED": A
          SOCIOPSYCHOLOGICAL PERSPECTIVE.
    SOUR PAPER PRESENTED AT THE AMERICAN PSYCHOLOGICAL
          ASSOCIATION ANNUAL CONVENTION, CHICAGO, 30 AUG.-3
          SEP., 1975. (12P)
    YEAR 1975

        DESC ETHNIC IDENTITY+, SELF-CONCEPT+, DISCRIMINATION,
              CULTURAL REVIVAL+, FULL BLOOD-MIXED BLOOD COMPARISONS,
              NATIVE AMERICAN POLITICAL MOVEMENTS
        IDEN U.S.

650   AUTH KNIEP-HARDY, MARY; BURKHARDT, MARGARET A.
        TITL NURSING THE NAVAJO.
        SOUR AMERICAN JOURNAL OF NURSING, JAN. 1977, V77 (1), PP
              95-96.
        YEAR 1977
        DESC MEDICAL PROFESSIONALS+, NAVAJO, SOUTHWEST,
              INSTITUTIONALIZATION+, DELIVERY OF SERVICES+, MEDICAL
              INSTITUTIONS
        IDEN U.S.

651   AUTH CAMERON, ANN; STORM, THOMAS
        TITL ACHIEVEMENT MOTIVATION IN CANADIAN INDIAN, MIDDLE-AND
              WORKING-CLASS CHILDREN.
        SOUR PSYCHOLOGICAL REPORTS, APR. 1965, V16, PP 459-463.
        YEAR 1965
        DESC ACHIEVEMENT+, MOTIVATION+, PSYCHOLOGICAL TESTING+,
              SOCIAL STATUS+, ELEMENTARY SCHOOLS, CHILDREN-SCHOOL
              AGE+, NATIVE-NON-NATIVE COMPARISONS
        IDEN CANADA, BRITISH COLUMBIA, THEMATIC APPERCEPTION TEST

652   AUTH ERSKINE, J.S.
        TITL INDIAN DILEMMA.
        SOUR DALHOUSIE REVIEW, SPR. 1970, V50, PP 34-39.
        YEAR 1970
        DESC MICMAC, EASTERN SUB-ARCTIC, DISCRIMINATION+, CULTURAL
              CONTINUITY+, CULTURAL ADAPTATION, RESERVATION
        IDEN CANADA, NOVA SCOTIA

653   AUTH HANDELMAN, DON
        TITL SHAMANIZING ON AN EMPTY STOMACH.
        SOUR AMERICAN ANTHROPOLOGIST, 1968, V70, PP 353-356.
        YEAR 1968
        DESC TRADITIONAL HEALERS+, PERSONALITY TRAITS+,
              RESEARCHERS, MENTAL DISORDERS, SOCIAL ROLES, CULTURAL
              ADAPTATION+
        IDEN U.S.

654   TITL BRIEF REPORT: SUICIDE AMONG THE BLACKFEET INDIANS.
        SOUR BULLETIN OF SUICIDOLOGY, AUT. 1970, V7, PP 42-43.
        YEAR 1970
        DESC BLACKFEET, PLAINS, SUICIDE+, MEDICAL PROFESSIONALS,
              PREVENTIVE MENTAL HEALTH PROGRAMS, ADOLESCENTS
        IDEN U.S.

655   AUTH EDWARDS, EUGENE D.
        TITL A DESCRIPTION AND EVALUATION OF AMERICAN INDIAN SOCIAL
              WORK TRAINING PROGRAMS.
        SOUR ABSTRACTS FOR SOCIAL WORKERS, AUG. 1976, V12(3), P 13.
        YEAR 1976
        DESC SOCIAL SERVICE PROFESSIONALS+, TRAINING PROGRAMS+,

NATIVE AMERICAN PERSONNEL+, COLLEGES AND
UNIVERSITIES+, PROGRAM EVALUATION+
IDEN   U.S.

656 AUTH   OPLER, MORRIS E.
     TITL   THE CREATIVE ROLE OF SHAMANISM IN MESCALERO APACHE
            MYTHOLOGY.
     SOUR   JOURNAL OF AMERICAN FOLKLORE, 1946, V59, PP 268-281.
     YEAR   1946
     DESC   APACHE-MESCALERO, SOUTHWEST, TRADITIONAL HEALERS+
     IDEN   U.S.

657 AUTH   HONIGMANN, JOHN J.
     TITL   SOCIAL DISINTEGRATION IN FIVE NORTHERN COMMUNITIES.
     SOUR   CANADIAN REVIEW OF SOCIOLOGY AND ANTHROPOLOGY, 1965,
            V2, PP 199-214.
     YEAR   1965
     DESC   ESKIMO, CENTRAL AND EASTERN ARCTIC, OFF-RESERVATION,
            ANOMIE+, SOCIALLY DEVIANT BEHAVIOR+, KASKA, YUKON
            SUB-ARCTIC, KUTCHIN, SEXUAL RELATIONS, MARITAL
            RELATIONSHIPS, FAMILY FUNCTIONING, CREE, ANXIETY+,
            LEADERSHIP, ADULTS, ADOLESCENTS, ATHABASCAN
     IDEN   CANADA

658 AUTH   CHANCE, NORMAN A.
     TITL   CONCEPTUAL AND METHODOLOGICAL PROBLEMS IN
            CROSS-CULTURAL HEALTH RESEARCH.
     SOUR   AMERICAN JOURNAL OF PUBLIC HEALTH AND THE NATION"S
            HEALTH, 1962, V52(3), PP 410-417.
     YEAR   1962
     DESC   EPIDEMIOLOGICAL STUDY, MENTAL DISORDERS, NATIVE
            AMERICAN ETIOLOGY+, CULTURAL ADAPTATION+, ESKIMO,
            WESTERN ARCTIC, SEX DIFFERENCES, PHYSICAL HEALTH AND
            ILLNESS+, ANXIETY+, CULTURE-FAIR TESTS+
     IDEN   U.S., ALASKA

659 AUTH   DUNNING, R.W.
     TITL   SOME PROBLEMS OF RESERVE INDIAN COMMUNITIES: A CASE
            STUDY.
     SOUR   ANTHROPOLOGICA, 1964, V6, PP 3-18.
     YEAR   1964
     DESC   RESERVATION, CHIPPEWA, DEMOGRAPHIC DATA, ECONOMIC
            ISSUES, POWERLESSNESS, ETHNIC IDENTITY+, SOCIAL
            STATUS+, FEDERAL GOVERNMENT
     IDEN   CANADA

660 AUTH   DEVEREUX, GEORGE
     TITL   DREAM LEARNING AND INDIVIDUAL RITUAL DIFFERENCES IN
            MOJAVE SHAMANISM.
     SOUR   AMERICAN ANTHROPOLOGIST, 1957, V59, PP 1036-1045.
     YEAR   1957
     DESC   MOHAVE, SOUTHWEST, TRADITIONAL HEALERS+, DREAMS AND
            VISION QUESTS+, PSYCHOANALYSIS, CULTURE-BASED
            PSYCHOTHERAPY, NEUROSES, PSYCHOTHERAPY AND COUNSELING
     IDEN   U.S.

661   AUTH   DEVEREUX, GEORGE
      TITL   SHAMANS AS NEUROTICS.
      SOUR   AMERICAN ANTHROPOLOGIST, 1961, V63, PP 1088-1090.
      YEAR   1961
      DESC   TRADITIONAL HEALERS+, NEUROSES+, MENTAL DISORDERS+
      IDEN   U.S.

662   AUTH   OPLER, MARVIN K.
      TITL   ON DEVEREUX"S DISCUSSION OF UTE SHAMANISM.
      SOUR   AMERICAN ANTHROPOLOGIST, 1961, V63, PP 1088-1090
      YEAR   1961
      DESC   TRADITIONAL HEALERS+, NEUROSES+

663   AUTH   HANDELMAN, DON
      TITL   THE DEVELOPMENT OF A WASHO SHAMAN.
      SOUR   ETHNOLOGY, 1967, V6(4), PP 444-464.
      YEAR   1967
      DESC   WASHO, GREAT BASIN, TRADITIONAL HEALERS+, ROLE MODELS,
             DREAMS AND VISION QUESTS+, CULTURE-BASED
             PSYCHOTHERAPY+
      IDEN   U.S.

664   AUTH   LIEBOW, ELLIOT; TRUDEAU, JOHN
      TITL   A PRELIMINARY STUDY OF ACCULTURATION AMONG THE CREE
             INDIANS OF WINISK, ONTARIO.
      SOUR   ARCTIC, SEP. 1962, V14-15, PP 190-204.
      YEAR   1962
      DESC   CREE, EASTERN SUB-ARCTIC, CULTURAL ADAPTATION+,
             EMPLOYMENT+, SOCIALLY DEVIANT BEHAVIOR, URBAN AREAS,
             URBANIZATION+
      IDEN   CANADA, ONTARIO

665   AUTH   WELLMANN, KLAUS F.
      TITL   NORTH AMERICAN INDIAN ROCK ART AND HALLUCINOGENIC
             DRUGS.
      SOUR   JOURNAL OF THE AMERICAN MEDICAL ASSOCIATION, APR.
             1978, V239(15), PP 1524-1527.
      YEAR   1978
      DESC   TRADITIONAL USE OF DRUGS AND ALCOHOL+, DRUG USE+,
             TRADITIONAL HEALERS+, CHUMASH, YOKUTS, CALIFORNIA
             AREA, SOUTHWEST
      IDEN   U.S., CALIFORNIA, TEXAS

666   AUTH   DIZMANG, LARRY H.
      TITL   SUICIDE AMONG THE CHEYENNE INDIANS.
      SOUR   BULLETIN OF SUICIDOLOGY, JUL. 1967, V1, PP 8-11.
      YEAR   1967
      DESC   SUICIDE+, CHEYENNE-NORTHERN, PLAINS, AGGRESSIVENESS,
             RESERVATION, PREVENTIVE MENTAL HEALTH PROGRAMS+,
             MENTAL HEALTH PARAPROFESSIONALS+
      IDEN   U.S.

667   AUTH   MASON-BROWNE, N.L.
      TITL   THE INDIAN--BETWEEN TWO FIRES.
      SOUR   PAPER PRESENTED AT THE CANADIAN PSYCHIATRIC

ASSOCIATION WORKSHOP TO EXAMINE THE PROBLEMS OF THE
NORTHERN CANADIAN INDIANS, QUEBEC, CANADA, SEP. 1976.
(26P)
YEAR 1976
DESC TIME PERCEPTION, GENEROSITY, NATIVE AMERICAN VALUES+,
NONINTERFERENCE, STRESS+
IDEN CANADA

668 AUTH TOFFELMIER, GERTRUDE; LUOMALA, KATHARINE
TITL DREAMS AND DREAM INTERPRETATION OF THE DIEGUENO
INDIANS OF SOUTHERN CALIFORNIA.
SOUR PSYCHOANALYTIC QUARTERLY, 1936, V5, PP 195-225.
YEAR 1936
DESC DIEGUENO, SOUTHWEST, DREAMS AND VISION QUESTS+,
CULTURE-BASED PSYCHOTHERAPY, TRADITIONAL HEALERS+,
SEXUAL RELATIONS, CULTURE-SPECIFIC SYNDROMES
IDEN U.S., CALIFORNIA

669 AUTH PINTO, LEONARD J.
TITL ALCOHOL AND DRUG ABUSE AMONG NATIVE AMERICAN YOUTH ON
RESERVATIONS: A GROWING CRISIS.
SOUR IN DRUG USE IN AMERICA: PROBLEM IN PERSPECTIVE: VOL.
I, PATTERNS AND CONSEQUENCES OF DRUG USE, PP
1157-1178. (NATIONAL COMMISSION ON MARIJUANA AND DRUG
USE). WASHINGTON, D.C.: GOVERNMENT PRINTING OFFICE,
1973.
YEAR 1973
DESC ALCOHOL USE+, DRUG USE+, ADOLESCENTS+, ADULTS, CRIME,
SECONDARY SCHOOLS, ETHNIC IDENTITY, STEREOTYPES,
TRADITIONAL USE OF DRUGS AND ALCOHOL, REVIEW OF
LITERATURE
IDEN U.S.

670 AUTH COX, BRUCE
TITL MODERNIZATION AMONG THE MESTASSINI-WASWANIPI CREE: A
COMMENT.
SOUR CANADIAN REVIEW OF SOCIOLOGY AND ANTHROPOLOGY, APR.
1970, V7(3), PP 212-217.
YEAR 1970
DESC CREE, CULTURAL ADAPTATION+, EMPLOYMENT+, CULTURAL
CONTINUITY+, EASTERN SUB-ARCTIC
IDEN CANADA, QUEBEC

671 AUTH CROMPTON, DON W.
TITL THE BIOGRAPHICAL INVENTORY AS A PREDICTIVE INSTRUMENT
IN THE SELECTION OF INDIANS FOR TRAINING AS
PARAPROFESSIONAL ALCOHOLISM COUNSELORS.
SOUR ABSTRACTS FOR SOCIAL WORKERS, AUT. 1967, V12(3), P11.
YEAR 1967
DESC ALCOHOLISM TREATMENT+, TRAINING PROGRAMS+, NATIVE
AMERICAN PERSONNEL+, SOCIAL SERVICE
PARAPROFESSIONALS+, PSYCHOLOGICAL TESTING, PERSONALITY
TRAITS+
IDEN U.S., BIOGRAPHICAL INVENTORIES

672 AUTH DEVEREUX, GEORGE; LOEB, EDWIN M.
    TITL SOME NOTES ON APACHE CRIMINALITY.
    SOUR JOURNAL OF CRIMINAL PSYCHOPATHOLOGY, APR. 1943, V4, PP
          424-430.
    YEAR 1943
    DESC APACHE-CHIRICAHUA, SOUTHWEST, CRIME+, RESERVATION,
          SOCIALLY DEVIANT BEHAVIOR+, TRADITIONAL SOCIAL
          CONTROL+, LEGAL ISSUES
    IDEN U.S., NEW MEXICO, MESCALERO RESERVATION

673 AUTH KAPLAN, BERT
    TITL PSYCHOLOGICAL THEMES IN ZUNI MYTHOLOGY AND ZUNI
          T.A.T."S.
    SOUR IN GEZA ROHEIM (ED.), PSYCHOANALYTIC STUDY OF SOCIETY,
          VOL. 2, PP 255-262. NEW YORK: INTERNATIONAL
          UNIVERSITIES PRESS, 1962.
    YEAR 1962
    DESC PUEBLO-ZUNI, SOUTHWEST, PSYCHOLOGICAL TESTING,
          PERSONALITY TRAITS+, ADULTS, MALES
    IDEN U.S., THEMATIC APPERCEPTION TEST

674 AUTH LEIGHTON, ALEXANDER H.
    TITL THE MENTAL HEALTH OF THE AMERICAN INDIAN.
    SOUR AMERICAN JOURNAL OF PSYCHIATRY, AUG. 1968, V125(2), PP
          217-218.
    YEAR 1968
    DESC MENTAL DISORDERS, STRESS, MENTAL HEALTH PROGRAMS AND
          SERVICES+
    IDEN U.S.

675 AUTH SLOBODIN, RICHARD
    TITL THE SUBARCTIC METIS AS PRODUCTS AND AGENTS OF CULTURE
          CONTACT.
    SOUR ARCTIC ANTHROPOLOGY, 1964, V2(2), PP 50-55.
    YEAR 1964
    DESC YUKON SUB-ARCTIC, MACKENZIE SUB-ARCTIC, SOCIAL
          NETWORKS, METIS, OFF-RESERVATION, CULTURAL ADAPTATION+
    IDEN CANADA, U.S., ALASKA, NORTHWEST TERRITORIES

676 AUTH SUTTLES, WAYNE
    TITL THE PERSISTENCE OF INTERVILLAGE TIES AMONG THE COAST
          SALISH.
    SOUR ETHNOLOGY, 1963, V2, PP 512-525.
    YEAR 1963
    DESC COAST SALISH, NORTHWEST COAST, SOCIAL NETWORKS,
          COOPERATION, RESERVATION, NATIVE AMERICAN RELIGIONS+,
          CULTURAL CONTINUITY+
    IDEN CANADA, BRITISH COLUMBIA, U.S., WASHINGTON

677 AUTH WHITTAKER, JAMES O.
    TITL ALCOHOL AND THE STANDING ROCK SIOUX TRIBE: PART I, THE
          PATTERNS OF DRINKING.
    SOUR QUARTERLY JOURNAL OF STUDIES ON ALCOHOL, SEP. 1962,
          V23, PP 468-479.
    YEAR 1962

DESC   SIOUX, PLAINS, ALCOHOL USE, EPIDEMIOLOGICAL STUDY, SEX
          DIFFERENCES, AGE COMPARISONS, NATIVE-NON-NATIVE
          COMPARISONS, ANGLO AMERICANS, ADULTS, RESERVATION
IDEN   U.S., NORTH DAKOTA, SOUTH DAKOTA, STANDING ROCK
          RESERVATION

678 AUTH   VANSTONE, JAMES W.
    TITL   SOME ASPECTS OF RELIGIOUS CHANGE AMONG NATIVE
          INHABITANTS IN WEST ALASKA AND THE NORTHWEST
          TERRITORIES.
    SOUR   ARCTIC ANTHROPOLOGY, 1964, V2(2), PP 21-24.
    YEAR   1964
    DESC   RELIGIONS-NON-NATIVE+, ESKIMO, WESTERN ARCTIC,
          RELIGIOUS-NON-NATIVE PERSONNEL, YUKON SUB-ARCTIC,
          MACKENZIE SUB-ARCTIC
    IDEN   U.S., ALASKA

679 AUTH   ATTNEAVE, CAROLYN L.
    TITL   OUTPATIENT SERVICE TO AMERICAN INDIAN PATIENTS.
    SOUR   POCA, 1969, V6, PP 8-9, 11-12.
    YEAR   1969
    DESC   MENTAL HEALTH PROGRAMS AND SERVICES+, OUTPATIENT
          CARE+, CLINICAL STUDY, LANGUAGE HANDICAPS, DELIVERY OF
          SERVICES+, OKLAHOMA INDIANS, PSYCHOTHERAPY AND
          COUNSELING+, MENTAL RETARDATION
    IDEN   U.S., OKLAHOMA

680 AUTH   HERMAN, FREDERICK
    TITL   THE PROXIMITY OF PERSONALITY AND COGNITIVE FACTORS IN
          INDIAN STUDENTS.
    SOUR   DISSERTATION ABSTRACTS INTERNATIONAL, MAR. 1973, V33,
          P 4938-A.
    YEAR   1973
    DESC   PSYCHOLOGICAL TESTING+, PERSONALITY TRAITS+, COGNITIVE
          PROCESSES+, NATIVE-NON-NATIVE COMPARISONS, ANGLO
          AMERICANS, CHIPPEWA, CREE, EASTERN
          SUB-ARCTIC,CHILDREN-SCHOOL AGE+, ADOLESCENTS+,
          ELEMENTARY SCHOOLS+, SECONDARY SCHOOLS+
    IDEN   CANADA, ONTARIO

681 AUTH   BONGERS, LAEL
    TITL   A DEVELOPMENTAL STUDY OF TIME PERCEPTION AND TIME
          PERSPECTIVE IN THREE CULTURAL GROUPS: ANGLO AMERICAN,
          INDIAN AMERICAN, AND MEXICAN AMERICAN.
    SOUR   DISSERTATION ABSTRACTS INTERNATIONAL, 1972, V32(7), PP
          3774A-3775A.
    YEAR   1972
    DESC   TIME PERCEPTION+, NATIVE-NON-NATIVE COMPARISONS, ANGLO
          AMERICANS, LATINOS, AGE COMPARISONS, PSYCHOLOGICAL
          TESTING+, CHILDREN-SCHOOL AGE, ADOLESCENTS, ADULTS
    IDEN   U.S.

682 AUTH   CORRIGAN, FRANCIS VINCENT
    TITL   A COMPARISON OF SELF CONCEPTS OF AMERICAN INDIAN
          STUDENTS FROM PUBLIC OR FEDERAL SCHOOL BACKGROUNDS.

SOUR DISSERTATION ABSTRACTS INTERNATIONAL, DEC. 1970,
V31(6), PP 2679A-2680A.
YEAR 1970
DESC SELF-CONCEPT+, B.I.A. BOARDING SCHOOLS+, PSYCHOLOGICAL
TESTING+, SEX DIFFERENCES, AGE COMPARISONS,
INTERTRIBAL COMPARISONS, CHILDREN-SCHOOL AGE,
ADOLESCENTS, ELEMENTARY SCHOOLS+, SECONDARY SCHOOLS+
IDEN U.S., CALIFORNIA, TENNESSEE SELF CONCEPT SCALE,
CALIFORNIA TEST OF MENTAL MATURITY

683 AUTH LAMMERS, DONALD
TITL SELF CONCEPTS OF AMERICAN INDIAN ADOLESCENTS HAVING
SEGREGATED AND DESEGREGATED ELEMENTARY BACKGROUNDS.
SOUR DISSERTATION ABSTRACTS INTERNATIONAL, SEP. 1970,
V31(3), PP 930A.
YEAR 1970
DESC ADOLESCENTS, ELEMENTARY SCHOOLS+, ACHIEVEMENT+,
SELF-CONCEPT+, ONONONDAGA, NORTHEAST WOODLAND,
SECONDARY SCHOOLS+, PSYCHOLOGICAL TESTING+,
NATIVE-NON-NATIVE COMPARISONS, ANXIETY, ANGLO
AMERICANS, ATTITUDES
IDEN U.S., NEW YORK, SELF-SOCIAL SYMBOLS TASKS,
SELF-CONCEPT OF ABILITY SCALE, QUESTIONNAIRE ON
ATTITUDES TOWARD DIFFERENT TESTING SITUATIONS

684 AUTH SCHAD, CHARLES MERTON
TITL A COMPARISON OF ENTERING FIRST GRADE INDIAN AND
NON-INDIAN CHILDREN"S RECOGNITION AND VERBAL
IDENTIFICATION OF THE NINETY-FIVE MOST COMMON NOUNS AS
FOUND IN THE DOLCH PICTURE-WORD LIST.
SOUR DISSERTATION ABSTRACTS INTERNATIONAL, 1967, V28(5), PP
1631A-1632A.
YEAR 1967
DESC SIOUX-OGLALA, CHILDREN-SCHOOL AGE, ELEMENTARY SCHOOLS,
BILINGUALISM+, PLAINS, RESERVATION, LANGUAGE
HANDICAPS+, PSYCHOLOGICAL TESTING+, SEX DIFFERENCES
IDEN U.S., PINE RIDGE RESERVATION, DOLCH PICTURE-WORD LIST

685 AUTH GLASS, THOMAS EUGENE
TITL A DESCRIPTIVE AND COMPARATIVE STUDY OF AMERICAN INDIAN
CHILDREN IN THE DETROIT PUBLIC SCHOOLS.
SOUR DISSERTATION ABSTRACTS INTERNATIONAL, NOV. 1972,
V33(5), PP 2167A-2168A.
YEAR 1972
DESC ELEMENTARY SCHOOLS+, ACHIEVEMENT+, ABILITIES+, URBAN
AREAS, PSYCHOLOGICAL TESTING+, CHILDREN-SCHOOL AGE,
ECONOMIC ISSUES+, SELF-CONCEPT+, NATIVE-NON-NATIVE
COMPARISONS, LATINOS, BLACK AMERICANS
IDEN U.S., MICHIGAN

686 AUTH TRIMBLE, JOSEPH E.
TITL PSYCHOSOCIAL CHARACTERISTICS OF EMPLOYED AND
UNEMPLOYED WESTERN OKLAHOMA MALE AMERICAN INDIANS.
SOUR DISSERTATION ABSTRACTS INTERNATIONAL, 1969, V30(5), PP
2156A.

```
      YEAR  1969
      DESC  OKLAHOMA INDIANS, MALES+, ADULTS, EMPLOYMENT+, NATIVE
            AMERICAN VALUES, OFF-RESERVATION, CULTURAL
            ADAPTATION+, PSYCHOLOGICAL TESTING+, PERSONALITY
            TRAITS+
      IDEN  U.S., OKLAHOMA, CALIFORNIA PSYCHOLOGICAL INVENTORY,
            LABOR FORCE SURVEY

687   AUTH  PECK, RAYMOND LESTER
      TITL  A COMPARATIVE ANALYSIS OF THE PERFORMANCE OF INDIAN
            AND WHITE CHILDREN FROM NORTH CENTRAL MONTANA ON THE
            WECHSLER INTELLIGENCE SCALE FOR CHILDREN.
      SOUR  DISSERTATION ABSTRACTS INTERNATIONAL, FEB. 1973, V33,
            PP 4097A.
      YEAR  1973
      DESC  ABILITIES+, PSYCHOLOGICAL TESTING+, CHILDREN-SCHOOL
            AGE+, NATIVE-NON-NATIVE COMPARISONS, ANGLO AMERICANS,
            ELEMENTARY SCHOOLS, SEX DIFFERENCES
      IDEN  U.S., MONTANA, WECHSLER INTELLIGENCE SCALE CHILDREN

688   AUTH  GARDNER, RUTH
      TITL  THE RELATIONSHIP OF SELF ESTEEM AND VARIABLES
            ASSOCIATED WITH READING FOR FOURTH GRADE PIMA INDIAN
            CHILDREN.
      SOUR  DISSERTATION ABSTRACTS INTERNATIONAL, OCT. 1972,
            V33(4), P 1512A.
      YEAR  1972
      DESC  SELF-CONCEPT+, PIMA, SOUTHWEST, CHILDREN-SCHOOL AGE+,
            LEARNING+, RESERVATION, ELEMENTARY SCHOOLS, READING
            PROGRAMS+, ATTITUDES
      IDEN  U.S., ARIZONA, SELF ESTEEM INVENTORY, CALIFORNIA TEST
            OF MENTAL MATURITY, METROPOLITAN ACHIEVEMENT TEST,
            INVENTORY OF READING ATTITUDES

689   AUTH  WILLIAMS, LILLIE
      TITL  THE RELATIONSHIPS BETWEEN DOGMATISM, ACADEMIC
            ADJUSTMENT, AND GRADE POINT AVERAGES FOR AMERICAN
            INDIAN COLLEGE STUDENTS.
      SOUR  DISSERTATION ABSTRACTS INTERNATIONAL, NOV. 1970,
            V31(5), P 2028A.
      YEAR  1970
      DESC  COLLEGES AND UNIVERSITIES+, ADOLESCENTS, ACHIEVEMENT+
      IDEN  U.S., ARIZONA, ROKEACH DOGMATISM SCALE, COLLEGE
            INVENTORY OF ACADEMIC ADJUSTMENT

690   AUTH  NORRIS, ROBERT
      TITL  THE EFFECTS OF SELECTED CULTURAL VARIABLES INFLUENCING
            THE COLLEGE PERFORMANCES OF NATIVE AMERICAN INDIANS.
      SOUR  DISSERTATION ABSTRACTS INTERNATIONAL, JUN. 1972,
            V32(12), P 6783A.
      YEAR  1972
      DESC  COLLEGES AND UNIVERSITIES+, ACHIEVEMENT+, ADOLESCENTS,
            BICULTURALISM, EDUCATION PROGRAMS AND SERVICES+,
            DROPOUTS, PREVENTIVE MENTAL HEALTH PROGRAMS
      IDEN  U.S., NEW MEXICO
```

691 AUTH DEMMERT, WILLIAM G.
    TITL INDIAN EDUCATION: WHERE AND WHITHER?
    SOUR AMERICAN EDUCATION, AUG.-SEP. 1976, V12, PP 6-9.
    YEAR 1976
    DESC EDUCATION PROGRAMS AND SERVICES+, CHILDREN-SCHOOL AGE,
         BICULTURALISM+, ETHNIC IDENTITY+, NATIVE AMERICAN
         ADMINISTERED PROGRAMS+, NATIVE AMERICAN PERSONNEL,
         ELEMENTARY SCHOOLS, BILINGUALISM, FEDERAL GOVERNMENT,
         CULTURAL CONTINUITY
    IDEN U.S., INDIAN EDUCATION ACT (PL 92-318, TITLE IV)

692 AUTH MOOREFIELD, STORY
    TITL ALASKAN JOURNAL.
    SOUR AMERICAN EDUCATION, AUG.-SEP. 1976, V12, PP 15-22.
    YEAR 1976
    DESC EDUCATION PROGRAMS AND SERVICES+, BILINGUALISM+,
         ALASKA NATIVES, BICULTURALISM+, NATIVE AMERICAN
         PERSONNEL+,CULTURAL CONTINUITY, NATIVE AMERICAN
         ADMINISTERED PROGRAMS+, ADMINISTRATIVE ISSUES,
         ELEMENTARY SCHOOLS, SECONDARY SCHOOLS
    IDEN U.S., ALASKA, INDIAN EDUCATION ACT (PL 92-318, TITLE
         IV)

693 AUTH ROTH, EDITH BRILL
    TITL LATO; LATS-HUNTING IN THE INDIAN LANGUAGES.
    SOUR AMERICAN EDUCATION, AUG.-SEP. 1976, V12, PP 10-14.
    YEAR 1976
    DESC CHIPPEWA, EASTERN SUB-ARCTIC, BILINGUALISM+, EDUCATION
         PROGRAMS AND SERVICES, PREVENTIVE MENTAL HEALTH
         PROGRAMS, CULTURAL CONTINUITY, NATIVE AMERICAN
         ADMINISTERED PROGRAMS+, NATIVE AMERICAN PERSONNEL+,
         ADMINISTRATIVE ISSUES+, EDUCATION PROFESSIONALS+,
         ELEMENTARY SCHOOLS, SECONDARY SCHOOLS,DROPOUTS+
    IDEN U.S., WISCONSIN, INDIAN EDUCATION ACT (P.L. 92-318,
         TITLE IV)

694 AUTH ANNIS, ROBERT C.; FROST, BARRIE
    TITL HUMAN VISUAL ECOLOGY AND ORIENTATION ANISOTROPIES IN
         ACUITY.
    SOUR SCIENCE, NOV. 1973, V182, PP 729-731.
    YEAR 1973
    DESC CREE, EASTERN SUB-ARCTIC, ENVIRONMENTAL FACTORS+,
         COGNITIVE PROCESSES+, NATIVE-NON-NATIVE COMPARISONS,
         ANGLO AMERICANS
    IDEN CANADA, QUEBEC

695 AUTH JOHNSON, DALE L.; JOHNSON, CARMEN A.
    TITL TOTALLY DISCOURAGED: A DEPRESSIVE SYNDROME OF THE
         DAKOTA SIOUX.
    SOUR TRANSCULTURAL PSYCHIATRIC RESEARCH, APR. 1965, V2, PP
         141-143.
    YEAR 1965
    DESC SIOUX, RESERVATION, PLAINS, EPIDEMIOLOGICAL STUDY,
         MENTAL DISORDERS,CULTURE-SPECIFIC SYNDROMES+,
         DEPRESSION+, GRIEF REACTION+

```
     IDEN   U.S., NORTH DAKOTA, SOUTH DAKOTA, STANDING ROCK
            RESERVATION

696  AUTH   LANE, ROBERT B.
     TITL   CANADIAN INDIANS.
     SOUR   THE CANADIAN PSYCHOLOGIST, OCT. 1972, V13(4), PP
            350-359.
     YEAR   1972
     DESC   CHILDREN-SCHOOL AGE+, ELEMENTARY SCHOOLS+,
            ACHIEVEMENT+, NATIVE AMERICAN COPING BEHAVIORS+,
            PASSIVE RESISTANCE, NATIVE AMERICAN VALUES+,
            NONCOMPETITIVENESS
     IDEN   CANADA

697  AUTH   DEMPSEY, ARTHUR D.
     TITL   TIME CONSERVATION ACROSS CULTURES.
     SOUR   INTERNATIONAL JOURNAL OF PSYCHOLOGY, 1971, V6(2), PP
            115-120.
     YEAR   1971
     DESC   TIME PERCEPTION+, PSYCHOLOGICAL TESTING+,
            NATIVE-NON-NATIVE COMPARISONS, ANGLO AMERICANS,
            LATINOS, PUEBLO-HOPI, PAPAGO, NAVAJO, PIMA, SOUTHWEST,
            APACHE, AGE COMPARISONS, COGNITIVE PROCESSES+
     IDEN   U.S., ARIZONA, PIAGETIAN TASKS

698  AUTH   MACARTHUR, RUSSELL
     TITL   SOME ABILITY PATTERNS: CENTRAL ESKIMOS AND NSENGA
            AFRICANS.
     SOUR   INTERNATIONAL JOURNAL OF PSYCHOLOGY, 1973, V8(4), PP
            239-247.
     YEAR   1973
     DESC   ABILITIES+, PSYCHOLOGICAL TESTING+, NATIVE-NON-NATIVE
            COMPARISONS, ESKIMO, CENTRAL AND EASTERN ARCTIC,
            ADOLESCENTS, ANGLO AMERICANS, COGNITIVE PROCESSES+
     IDEN   CANADA

699  AUTH   SMALL, G.W.
     TITL   THE USEFULNESS OF CANADIAN ARMY SELECTION TESTS IN A
            CULTURALLY RESTRICTED POPULATION.
     SOUR   CANADIAN PSYCHOLOGIST, FEB. 1969, V10(1), PP 9-19
     YEAR   1969
     DESC   YUKON SUB-ARCTIC, MACKENZIE SUB-ARCTIC, ABILITIES+,
            PSYCHOLOGICAL TESTING+,CULTURE-FAIR TESTS+, MILITARY
            SERVICE+, MALES, ADULTS, DISCRIMINATION+
     IDEN   CANADA

700  AUTH   EISENMAN, RUSSELL
     TITL   SCAPEGOATING THE DEVIANT IN TWO CULTURES.
     SOUR   INTERNATIONAL JOURNAL OF PSYCHOLOGY, 1967, V2(2), PP
            133-138.
     YEAR   1967
     DESC   SOCIALLY DEVIANT BEHAVIOR+, WESTERN ARCTIC, ESKIMO,
            TABOO BREAKING+, TRADITIONAL SOCIAL CONTROL+,
            WITCHCRAFT+, NAVAJO, SOUTHWEST, NATIVE AMERICAN COPING
            BEHAVIORS+, CONFESSION
```

```
     IDEN  U.S.

701  AUTH  MACARTHUR, RUSSELL
     TITL  SEX DIFFERENCES IN FIELD DEPENDENCE FOR THE ESKIMO:
           REPLICATION OF BERRY"S FINDINGS.
     SOUR  INTERNATIONAL JOURNAL OF PSYCHOLOGY, 1967, V2(2), PP
           139-140.
     YEAR  1967
     DESC  ESKIMO, WESTERN ARCTIC, COGNITIVE PROCESSES+, SEX
           DIFFERENCES, CHILDREN-SCHOOL AGE, OFF-RESERVATION
     IDEN  CANADA

702  AUTH  GUILMET, GEORGE M.
     TITL  COGNITIVE RESEARCH AMONG THE ESKIMO: A SURVEY.
     SOUR  ANTHROPOLOGICA, 1975, V17, PP 61-84.
     YEAR  1975
     DESC  ESKIMO, CENTRAL AND EASTERN ARCTIC, COGNITIVE
           PROCESSES+, ABILITIES+, PSYCHOLOGICAL TESTING+, SEX
           DIFFERENCES, REVIEW OF LITERATURE, WESTERN ARCTIC,
           CULTURE-FAIR TESTS, OFF-RESERVATION
     IDEN  CANADA, U.S.,GOODENOUGH HARRIS DRAW A PERSON TEST,
           PIAGETIAN TASKS, WITKINS EMBEDDED FIGURES TEST,
           WECHSLER ADULT INTELLIGENCE SCALE, PETER"S CIRCULAR
           MAZE, PORTEUS MAZE TEST

703  AUTH  DENIS, MARGARET
     TITL  RELIGIOUS EDUCATION AMONG NORTH AMERICAN INDIAN
           PEOPLES.
     SOUR  RELIGIOUS EDUCATION, MAY-JUN. 1974, V69(3), PP 343-354.
     YEAR  1974
     DESC  RELIGIONS-NON-NATIVE+, NATIVE AMERICAN VALUES+,
           GENEROSITY, TIME PERCEPTION, NONINTERFERENCE
     IDEN  CANADA, CATHOLIC CHURCH

704  AUTH  BOYER, L. BRYCE
     TITL  REMARKS ON THE PERSONALITY OF SHAMANS, WITH SPECIAL
           REFERENCE TO THE APACHE OF THE MESCALERO INDIAN
           RESERVATION.
     SOUR  IN GEZA ROHEIM (ED.), PSYCHOANALYTIC STUDY OF SOCIETY,
           V2, PP 233-254.  NEW YORK: INTERNATIONAL UNIVERSITIES
           PRESS, 1962.
     YEAR  1962
     DESC  PERSONALITY TRAITS+, CHARACTER DISORDERS+, TRADITIONAL
           HEALERS+, APACHE-MESCALERO, SOUTHWEST, RESERVATION,
           HYSTERIA+, SOCIAL ROLES, PSYCHOANALYSIS, PSYCHOLOGICAL
           TESTING, GROUP NORMS AND SANCTIONS, APACHE-CHIRICAHUA
     IDEN  U.S., NEW MEXICO, MESCALERO RESERVATION, RORSCHACH
           TEST

705  AUTH  MACARTHUR, RUSSELL
     TITL  SOME COGNITIVE ABILITIES OF ESKIMO, WHITE, AND
           INDIAN-METIS PUPILS AGED 9 TO 12 YEARS.
     SOUR  CANADIAN JOURNAL OF BEHAVIOURAL SCIENCE, 1969, V1(1),
           PP 50-59.
     YEAR  1969
```

DESC COGNITIVE PROCESSES+, ESKIMO, METIS, ANGLO AMERICANS, NATIVE-NON-NATIVE COMPARISONS, ABILITIES+, CHILDREN-SCHOOL AGE+, ELEMENTARY SCHOOLS, PSYCHOLOGICAL TESTING+, CULTURE-FAIR TESTS+, CENTRAL AND EASTERN ARCTIC, OFF-RESERVATION
IDEN CANADA

706 AUTH SIGNORI, EDRO I.; BUTT, DORCAS S.
TITL RATINGS OF THE SOCIAL IMAGES OF DISADVANTAGED GROUPS BY MALES AND FEMALES.
SOUR PSYCHOLOGICAL REPORTS, APR. 1972, V30, PP 575-580.
YEAR 1972
DESC MALES, FEMALES, ADULTS, SEX DIFFERENCES, PSYCHOLOGICAL TESTING+, DISCRIMINATION+, STEREOTYPES+
IDEN CANADA

707 AUTH ZURCHER, LOUIS A.
TITL THE LEADER AND THE LOST: A CASE STUDY OF INDIGENOUS LEADERSHIP IN A POVERTY PROGRAM COMMUNITY ACTION COMMITTEE.
SOUR GENETIC PSYCHOLOGY MONOGRAPHS, 1967, V76, PP 23-93.
YEAR 1967
DESC LEADERSHIP+, ECONOMIC ISSUES, POTAWATOMI, PRAIRIE, URBAN AREAS, SOCIAL SERVICES+, PASSIVE RESISTANCE+, NATIVE AMERICAN ADMINISTERED PROGRAMS+, NONCOMPETITIVENESS, SOCIAL ROLES+, ADMINISTRATIVE ISSUES+
IDEN U.S., KANSAS

708 AUTH MASON, EVELYN P.
TITL COMPARISON OF PERSONALITY CHARACTERISTICS OF JUNIOR HIGH STUDENTS FROM AMERICAN INDIAN, MEXICAN, AND CAUCASIAN ETHNIC BACKGROUNDS.
SOUR JOURNAL OF SOCIAL PSYCHOLOGY, 1967, V73, PP 145-155.
YEAR 1967
DESC SECONDARY SCHOOLS, NORTHWEST COAST, NATIVE-NON-NATIVE COMPARISONS, ANGLO AMERICANS, LATINOS, PSYCHOLOGICAL TESTING+, PERSONALITY TRAITS+, EDUCATION PROGRAMS AND SERVICES+, ADOLESCENTS, SEX DIFFERENCES
IDEN U.S., WASHINGTON, PROJECT CATCH-UP, CALIFORNIA PSYCHOLOGICAL INVENTORY

709 AUTH DENTON, TREVOR
TITL CANADIAN INDIAN MIGRANTS AND IMPRESSION MANAGEMENT OF ETHNIC STIGMA.
SOUR CANADIAN REVIEW OF SOCIOLOGY AND ANTHROPOLOGY, 1975, V12(1), PP 65-71.
YEAR 1975
DESC ETHNIC IDENTITY+, STEREOTYPES+, URBAN AREAS, DISCRIMINATION+, NATIVE AMERICAN COPING BEHAVIORS+, URBANIZATION, RELOCATION
IDEN CANADA

710 AUTH BERRY, JOHN W.
TITL TEMNE AND ESKIMO PERCEPTUAL SKILLS.

SOUR INTERNATIONAL JOURNAL OF PSYCHOLOGY, 1966, V1(3), PP
207-229.
YEAR 1966
DESC ESKIMO, COGNITIVE PROCESSES+, CENTRAL AND EASTERN
ARCTIC, NATIVE-NON-NATIVE COMPARISONS, PSYCHOLOGICAL
TESTING+, PERSONALITY TRAITS+, TRADITIONAL CHILD
REARING+, TRADITIONAL SOCIAL CONTROL+, SEX
DIFFERENCES, AGE COMPARISONS, ENVIRONMENTAL FACTORS,
GENETIC FACTORS
IDEN CANADA, AFRICA, EUROPE

711 AUTH CHARLES, C.M.
TITL A SCIENCE-MYTHOLOGY RELATIONSHIP AMONG INDIAN
CHILDREN.
SOUR JOURNAL OF EDUCATIONAL RESEARCH, JAN. 1964, V57(5), PP
261-264.
YEAR 1964
DESC LEARNING DISABILITIES AND PROBLEMS+, ACHIEVEMENT+,
ELEMENTARY SCHOOLS, CHILDREN-SCHOOL AGE+, CULTURAL
CONTINUITY+, PSYCHOLOGICAL TESTING+, NATIVE AMERICAN
VALUES, NATIVE-NON-NATIVE COMPARISONS, ANGLO
AMERICANS, SCIENCE PROGRAMS+, NAVAJO, APACHE, PUEBLO
IDEN U.S., NATIONAL ACHIEVEMENT TESTS, ELEMENTARY SCIENCE
TEST, CULTURALLY-BIASED SCIENCE TEST

712 AUTH CAVAN, RUTH S.; CAVAN, JORDAN T.
TITL THE ESKIMOS: DELINQUENCY AND CRIME IN A PRIMITIVE
SOCIETY.
SOUR CHAPTER IN DELINQUENCY AND CRIME: CROSS-CULTURAL
PERSPECTIVES, PP 13-41. NEW YORK: LIPPINCOTT, 1968.
YEAR 1968
DESC ESKIMO, CENTRAL AND EASTERN ARCTIC, SOCIALLY DEVIANT
BEHAVIOR+, ADOLESCENTS+, OFF-RESERVATION, EXTENDED
FAMILY, COOPERATION, LEADERSHIP, NATIVE AMERICAN
COPING BEHAVIORS+, TRADITIONAL CHILD REARING, CRIME+,
ADULTS+, TABOO BREAKING, GROUP NORMS AND SANCTIONS,
TRADITIONAL SOCIAL CONTROL
IDEN CANADA

713 AUTH ARMSTRONG, HARVEY; PATTERSON, PAUL
TITL SEIZURES IN CANADIAN INDIAN CHILDREN: INDIVIDUAL,
FAMILY AND COMMUNITY APPROACHES.
SOUR CANADIAN PSYCHIATRIC ASSOCIATION JOURNAL, JUN. 1975,
V20(4), PP 247-255.
YEAR 1975
DESC HYSTERIA+, EASTERN SUB-ARCTIC, CHIPPEWA, CREE,
ADOLESCENTS+, STRESS+, FAMILY FUNCTIONING+,
PSYCHOTHERAPY AND COUNSELING+, MENTAL HEALTH
PROFESSIONALS+, CLINICAL STUDY
IDEN CANADA, ONTARIO

714 AUTH HOLDEN, DAVID E.W.
TITL MODERNIZATION AMONG TOWN AND BUSH CREE IN QUEBEC.
SOUR CANADIAN REVIEW OF SOCIOLOGY AND ANTHROPOLOGY, 1969,
V6(4), PP 237-248.

```
        YEAR  1969
        DESC  CREE, EASTERN SUB-ARCTIC, URBANIZATION+, RELOCATION+,
              SOCIAL ROLES, EMPLOYMENT+, URBAN AREAS, ADULTS, MALES
        IDEN  CANADA, QUEBEC

715     AUTH  MCBRIDE, DUANE C.; PAGE, J. BRYAN
        TITL  ADOLESCENT INDIAN SUBSTANCE ABUSE: ECOLOGICAL AND
              SOCIOCULTURAL FACTORS.
        SOUR  YOUTH AND SOCIETY, JUN. 1980, V11(4), PP 475-492.
        YEAR  1980
        DESC  GROUP NORMS AND SANCTIONS+, DRUG USE+, TRADITIONAL USE
              OF DRUGS AND ALCOHOL+, EPIDEMIOLOGICAL STUDY,
              ADOLESCENTS+, SURVEY, REVIEW OF LITERATURE, ALCOHOL
              USE+, ANOMIE, URBANIZATION, RESERVATION, URBAN AREAS,
              DRUG TREATMENT
        IDEN  U.S.

716     AUTH  KIRK, SAMUEL A.
        TITL  ETHNIC DIFFERENCES IN PSYCHOLINGUISTIC ABILITIES.
        SOUR  EXCEPTIONAL CHILDREN, OCT. 1972, V39, PP 112-118.
        YEAR  1972
        DESC  PSYCHOLOGICAL TESTING+, NATIVE-NON-NATIVE COMPARISONS,
              LATINOS, BLACK AMERICANS, TRADITIONAL CHILD REARING+,
              ANGLO AMERICANS, ABILITIES+, BILINGUALISM,
              CHILDREN-SCHOOL AGE
        IDEN  U.S., ILLINOIS TEST OF PSYCHOLINGUISTIC ABILITIES

717     AUTH  OLSEN, G.
        TITL  SEXUAL NORMS UNDER THE INFLUENCE OF ALTERED CULTURAL
              PATTERNS IN GREENLAND.
        SOUR  ACTA PSYCHIATRICA SCANDINAVICA, 1973, V49, PP 148-158.
        YEAR  1973
        DESC  GROUP NORMS AND SANCTIONS+, SEXUAL RELATIONS+, ESKIMO,
              CENTRAL AND EASTERN ARCTIC, ADOLESCENTS+,
              NATIVE-NON-NATIVE COMPARISONS, CULTURAL ADAPTATION+,
              OFF-RESERVATION
        IDEN  GREENLAND, DENMARK

718     AUTH  GOLDFRANK, ESTHER S.
        TITL  SOCIALIZATION, PERSONALITY, AND THE STRUCTURE OF
              PUEBLO SOCIETY (WITH PARTICULAR REFERENCE TO HOPI AND
              ZUNI).
        SOUR  AMERICAN ANTHROPOLOGIST, 1945, V47, PP 516-539.
        YEAR  1945
        DESC  PUEBLO-HOPI, PUEBLO-ZUNI, SOUTHWEST, PERSONALITY
              TRAITS+, TRADITIONAL CHILD REARING+, CHILDREN-INFANTS
              AND PRESCHOOL+, COOPERATION+, CHILDREN-SCHOOL AGE,
              ADOLESCENTS, TRADITIONAL SOCIAL CONTROL+, EMOTIONAL
              RESTRAINT+, WITCHCRAFT, FAMILY FUNCTIONING
        IDEN  U.S.

719     AUTH  DICK, JOHN
        TITL  NAVAJO MENTAL HEALTH.
        SOUR  IN RALPH SIMON, SAM SILVERSTEIN, AND BEATRICE M.
              SHRIVER, (EDS.), EXPLORATION IN MENTAL HEALTH
```

TRAINING, PP 134-135. (DHEW PUBLICATION NO. (ADM) 74-109). ROCKVILLE, MD: NATIONAL INSTITUTE OF MENTAL HEALTH, 1975.
YEAR 1975
DESC TRAINING PROGRAMS+, NAVAJO, SOUTHWEST, TRADITIONAL HEALERS+, MENTAL HEALTH PROGRAMS AND SERVICES+, I.H.S.
IDEN U.S.

720 AUTH THOMPSON, HILDEGARD
    TITL TEACHING ENGLISH TO INDIAN CHILDREN.
    SOUR ELEMENTARY ENGLISH, 1966, V43, PP 333-340.
    YEAR 1966
    DESC BILINGUALISM+, LEARNING+, LANGUAGE HANDICAPS+, B.I.A. BOARDING SCHOOLS+, EDUCATION PROGRAMS AND SERVICES+, ELEMENTARY SCHOOLS+, EDUCATION PROFESSIONALS, CHILDREN-SCHOOL AGE+, PROGRAM DEVELOPMENT+
    IDEN U.S.

721 AUTH WERNER, RUTH E.
    TITL AN ORAL ENGLISH EXPERIMENT WITH NAVAJO CHILDREN.
    SOUR ELEMENTARY ENGLISH, 1966, V43, PP 777-784.
    YEAR 1966
    DESC B.I.A. BOARDING SCHOOLS+, LANGUAGE HANDICAPS+, LEARNING+, BILINGUALISM, EDUCATION PROGRAMS AND SERVICES+, NAVAJO, SOUTHWEST, CHILDREN-SCHOOL AGE+, ELEMENTARY SCHOOLS+, RESERVATION, EDUCATION PROFESSIONALS, PROGRAM DEVELOPMENT+
    IDEN U.S., SHIPROCK BOARDING SCHOOL, NAVAJO RESERVATION

722 AUTH THOMPSON, LAURA
    TITL ATTITUDES AND ACCULTURATION.
    SOUR AMERICAN ANTHROPOLOGIST, 1948, V50(2), PP 200-215.
    YEAR 1948
    DESC SIOUX-OGLALA, PLAINS, CULTURAL ADAPTATION+, PSYCHOLOGICAL TESTING+, RESERVATION, CULTURAL CONTINUITY+, CHIPPEWA, EASTERN SUB-ARCTIC, NAVAJO, SOUTHWEST, NATIVE AMERICAN RELIGIONS, CHILDREN-SCHOOL AGE, PAPAGO, NATIVE AMERICAN COPING BEHAVIORS+, PUEBLO-HOPI, UNIVERSAL HARMONY, DREAMS AND VISION QUESTS, POWERLESSNESS, ATTITUDES+
    IDEN U.S., SOUTH DAKOTA, EMOTIONAL RESPONSE TEST, MORAL IDEOLOGY TEST, THEMATIC APPERCEPTION TEST, RORSCHACH TEST

723 AUTH SAINDON, J.E.
    TITL MENTAL DISORDERS AMONG THE JAMES BAY CREE.
    SOUR PRIMITIVE MAN, JAN. 1933, V6(1), PP 1-12.
    YEAR 1933
    DESC MENTAL DISORDERS+, CREE, EASTERN SUB-ARCTIC, HYSTERIA+, RELIGIOUS-NON-NATIVE PERSONNEL+, WINDIGO PSYCHOSIS, PSYCHOTHERAPY AND COUNSELING+
    IDEN CANADA, ONTARIO

724 AUTH PRIMEAUX, MARTHA H.
    TITL CARING FOR THE AMERICAN INDIAN PATIENT.

```
      SOUR  AMRICAN JOURNAL OF NURSING, JAN. 1977, V77 (1), PP
            91-94.
      YEAR  1977
      DESC  DELIVERY OF SERVICES+, MEDICAL INSTITUTIONS, MEDICAL
            PROFESSIONALS+, TRADITIONAL HEALERS+, EXTENDED FAMILY,
            TIME PERCEPTION, DEATH AND DYING,
            INSTITUTIONALIZATION+, TRADITIONAL CHILD REARING
      IDEN  U.S.

725   AUTH  MURDOCK, GEORGE P.
      TITL  TENINO SHAMANISM.
      SOUR  TRANSCULTURAL PSYCHIATRIC RESEARCH, APR. 1965, V2, PP
            144-146.
      YEAR  1965
      DESC  TENINO, PLATEAU, TRADITIONAL HEALERS+, CULTURE-BASED
            PSYCHOTHERAPY, SPIRIT INTRUSION
      IDEN  U.S., OREGON

726   AUTH  NEWCOMB, WILLIAM W.
      TITL  A NOTE ON CHEROKEE-DELAWARE PAN-INDIANISM.
      SOUR  AMERICAN ANTHROPOLOGIST, 1955, V57, PP 1041-1045.
      YEAR  1955
      DESC  DELAWARE-CHEROKEE, SOUTHEAST WOODLAND,
            OFF-RESERVATION, SOCIAL NETWORKS+, POW-WOWS, CULTURAL
            CONTINUITY+, ETHNIC IDENTITY+, TRADITIONAL USE OF
            DRUGS AND ALCOHOL, DRUG USE, CULTURAL REVIVAL+,
            CULTURAL ADAPTATION
      IDEN  U.S., OKLAHOMA

727   AUTH  MALOUF, CARLING
      TITL  GOSIUTE PEYOTISM.
      SOUR  AMERICAN ANTHROPOLOGIST, 1942, V44, PP 93-103.
      YEAR  1942
      DESC  TRADITIONAL USE OF DRUGS AND ALCOHOL+, DRUG USE+,
            GOSIUTE, GREAT BASIN, NATIVE AMERICAN RELIGIONS+
      IDEN  U.S., UTAH, NATIVE AMERICAN CHURCH

728   AUTH  YOUNG, BILOINE W.
      TITL  THE AMERICAN INDIAN: CITIZEN IN CAPTIVITY.
      SOUR  SATURDAY REVIEW, DEC. 1965, V48, PP 25-26.
      YEAR  1965
      DESC  POWERLESSNESS+, B.I.A.+,  NATIVE AMERICAN ADMINISTERED
            PROGRAMS, NAVAJO, SOUTHWEST, RESERVATION
      IDEN  U.S., NAVAJO RESERVATION

729   AUTH  FARB, PETER
      TITL  THE AMERICAN INDIAN: A PORTRAIT IN LIMBO.
      SOUR  SATURDAY REVIEW, OCT. 1968, V51, PP 26-29.
      YEAR  1968
      DESC  ECONOMIC ISSUES, DISCRIMINATION+, NATIVE AMERICAN
            ADMINISTERED PROGRAMS+, STEREOTYPES, FEDERAL
            GOVERNMENT+
      IDEN  U.S.

730   AUTH  POLACCA, KATHRYN
```

TITL WAYS OF WORKING WITH THE NAVAJOS WHO HAVE NOT LEARNED
THE WHITE MAN"S WAY.
SOUR JOURNAL OF AMERICAN INDIAN EDUCATION, 1962, V2, PP
6-16.
YEAR 1962
DESC NAVAJO, SOUTHWEST, RESERVATION, DELIVERY OF SERVICES+,
LANGUAGE HANDICAPS, NONINTERFERENCE, NATIVE AMERICAN
VALUES+, TIME PERCEPTION, TRADITIONAL SOCIAL CONTROL,
GENEROSITY, GROUP NORMS AND SANCTIONS+
IDEN U.S., NAVAJO RESERVATION

731 AUTH DEVEREUX, GEORGE
TITL MOHAVE SOUL CONCEPTS.
SOUR AMERICAN ANTHROPOLOGIST, 1937, V39, PP 417-422.
YEAR 1937
DESC MOHAVE, SOUTHWEST, DREAMS AND VISION QUESTS+, SOUL
LOSS+, WITCHCRAFT+, DEATH AND DYING, RESERVATION
IDEN U.S.

732 AUTH THOMPSON, LAURA; JOSEPH, ALICE
TITL WHITE PRESSURES ON INDIAN PERSONALITY AND CULTURE.
SOUR AMERICAN JOURNAL OF SOCIOLOGY, 1951, V53, PP 17-22.
YEAR 1951
DESC PUEBLO-HOPI, SOUTHWEST, PERSONALITY TRAITS+,
PSYCHOLOGICAL TESTING+, CHILDREN-SCHOOL AGE,
ADOLESCENTS, RESERVATION, SEX DIFFERENCES, EXTENDED
FAMILY, NATIVE AMERICAN RELIGIONS+,
RELIGIONS-NON-NATIVE+, STRESS+
IDEN U.S., HOPI RESERVATION, EMOTIONAL RESPONSE TEST, MORAL
IDEOLOGY TEST

733 AUTH VOGET, FRED W.
TITL THE AMERICAN INDIAN IN TRANSITION: REFORMATION AND
STATUS INNOVATIONS.
SOUR AMERICAN JOURNAL OF SOCIOLOGY, 1957, V62, PP 369-378.
YEAR 1957
DESC RESERVATION, CULTURAL REVIVAL+, SOCIAL STATUS+, NATIVE
AMERICAN RELIGIONS+
IDEN U.S., HANDSOME LAKE RELIGION, SHAKER RELIGION, NATIVE
AMERICAN CHURCH

734 AUTH LANDES, RUTH
TITL THE PERSONALITY OF THE OJIBWA.
SOUR CHARACTER AND PERSONALITY, 1937, V6, PP 51-60.
YEAR 1937
DESC CHIPPEWA, EASTERN SUB-ARCTIC, PERSONALITY TRAITS+,
EMOTIONAL RESTRAINT+, DREAMS AND VISION QUESTS,
ANXIETY+, WINDIGO PSYCHOSIS, TRADITIONAL SOCIAL
CONTROL+, TRADITIONAL CHILD REARING
IDEN CANADA, ONTARIO

735 AUTH DEVEREUX, GEORGE
TITL MOHAVE CULTURE AND PERSONALITY.
SOUR CHARACTER AND PERSONALITY, 1939, V8, PP 91-109.
YEAR 1939

    DESC MOHAVE, SOUTHWEST, PERSONALITY TRAITS+,
           CHILDREN-INFANTS AND PRESCHOOL, TRADITIONAL CHILD
           REARING+, EXTENDED FAMILY, TRADITIONAL HEALERS,
           PSYCHOANALYSIS
    IDEN U.S.

736 AUTH ALEXANDER, ROSEMARY
    TITL READERS FOR NAVAJO CHILDREN.
    SOUR INSTRUCTOR, NOV. 1969, V69, P 97.
    YEAR 1969
    DESC EDUCATION PROGRAMS AND SERVICES+, LEARNING+,
           ELEMENTARY SCHOOLS, CHILDREN-SCHOOL AGE+, NAVAJO,
           SOUTHWEST, RESERVATION, ETHNIC IDENTITY+, READING
           PROGRAMS+
    IDEN U.S., NAVAJO RESERVATION

737 AUTH BALES, ROBERT
    TITL CULTURAL DIFFERENCES IN RATES OF ALCOHOLISM.
    SOUR QUARTERLY JOURNAL OF STUDIES ON ALCOHOL, 1946, V6, PP
           480-499.
    YEAR 1946
    DESC ALCOHOL USE+, NATIVE-NON-NATIVE
           COMPARISONS,INTERTRIBAL COMPARISONS, NORTHEAST
           WOODLAND, SOUTHWEST, ANXIETY+, NATIVE AMERICAN COPING
           BEHAVIORS+
    IDEN U.S.

738 AUTH DEVEREUX, GEORGE
    TITL MOHAVE INDIAN INFANTICIDE.
    SOUR PSYCHOANALYTIC REVIEW, 1948, V35, PP 126-139.
    YEAR 1948
    DESC MOHAVE, SOUTHWEST, CHILDREN-INFANTS AND PRESCHOOL+,
           FAMILY PLANNING+
    IDEN U.S.

739 AUTH BOYER, L. BRYCE; BOYER, RUTH M.
    TITL SOME EFFECTS OF ACCULTURATION ON THE VICISSITUDES OF
           THE AGGRESSIVE DRIVE.
    SOUR TRANSCULTURAL PSYCHIATRIC RESEARCH, APR. 1965, V2, PP
           143-144.
    YEAR 1965
    DESC APACHE-MESCALERO, APACHE-CHIRICAHUA, SOUTHWEST,
           AGGRESSIVENESS+, RESERVATION, EMOTIONAL RESTRAINT+,
           NATIVE AMERICAN COPING BEHAVIORS+, SOCIAL ROLES+
    IDEN U.S., MESCALERO RESERVATION

740 AUTH HOFFMAN, VIRGINIA
    TITL LANGUAGE LEARNING AT ROUGH ROCK.
    SOUR CHILDHOOD EDUCATION, DEC. 1969, V46, PP 139-145.
    YEAR 1969
    DESC NAVAJO, SOUTHWEST, BILINGUALISM+, RESERVATION,
           LEARNING+, EDUCATION PROGRAMS AND SERVICES+, NATIVE
           AMERICAN PERSONNEL+, CHILDREN-SCHOOL AGE+,
           BICULTURALISM+, ELEMENTARY SCHOOLS+, NATIVE AMERICAN
           ADMINISTERED PROGRAMS+, CULTURAL CONTINUITY, EDUCATION

```
              PROFESSIONALS
         IDEN U.S., ROUGH ROCK DEMONSTRATION SCHOOL

741 AUTH DITTMANN, ALLEN T.; MORRE, HARVEY C.
    TITL DISTURBANCE IN DREAMS AS RELATED TO PEYOTISM AMONG THE
         NAVAJO.
    SOUR AMERICAN ANTHROPOLOGIST, 1957, V59, PP 642-649.
    YEAR 1957
    DESC NAVAJO, SOUTHWEST, DREAMS AND VISION QUESTS+, DRUG
         USE+, TRADITIONAL USE OF DRUGS AND ALCOHOL+,
         RESEARCHERS
    IDEN U.S.

742 AUTH EGGAN, DOROTHY
    TITL THE GENERAL PROBLEM OF HOPI ADJUSTMENT.
    SOUR AMERICAN ANTHROPOLOGIST, 1943, V45, PP 357-373.
    YEAR 1943
    DESC PUEBLO-HOPI, SOUTHWEST, PERSONALITY TRAITS+,
         AGGRESSIVENESS+, RESERVATION, EMOTIONAL RESTRAINT+,
         EXTENDED FAMILY+, TRADITIONAL CHILD REARING+, SEXUAL
         RELATIONS, ANXIETY+
    IDEN U.S., ARIZONA, HOPI RESERVATION

743 AUTH VOGET, FRED W.
    TITL CURRENT TRENDS IN THE WIND RIVER SHOSHONE SUN DANCE.
    SOUR ANTHROPOLOGICAL PAPERS NO. 42 (SMITHSONIAN
         INSTITUTION, BUREAU OF AMERICAN ETHNOLOGY BULLETIN NO.
         151), 1953, PP 485-499.
    YEAR 1953
    DESC SHOSHONE, PLAINS, CULTURAL ADAPTATION+, LEADERSHIP,
         NATIVE AMERICAN RELIGIONS+, RELIGIONS-NON-NATIVE,
         RESERVATION
    IDEN U.S., WYOMING, SUN DANCE

744 AUTH KLUCKHOHN, CLYDE
    TITL NAVAJO WITCHCRAFT.
    SOUR PAPERS OF THE PEABODY MUSEUM OF AMERICAN ARCHAEOLOGY
         AND ETHNOLOGY, HARVARD UNIVERSITY, 1944, V22(2), PP
         1-149.
    YEAR 1944
    DESC WITCHCRAFT+, NAVAJO, SOUTHWEST, TRADITIONAL HEALERS,
         NATIVE AMERICAN RELIGIONS, NATIVE AMERICAN COPING
         BEHAVIORS, TRADITIONAL SOCIAL CONTROL, RESERVATION
    IDEN U.S., NAVAJO RESERVATION

745 AUTH WHITING, BEATRICE B.
    TITL PAIUTE SORCERY.
    SOUR VIKING FUND PUBLICATIONS IN ANTHROPOLOGY, NO. 15.  NEW
         YORK: VIKING FUND, 1950.  (110P)
    YEAR 1950
    DESC PAIUTE, GREAT BASIN, WITCHCRAFT+, TRADITIONAL SOCIAL
         CONTROL+, GROUP NORMS AND SANCTIONS, NATIVE AMERICAN
         ETIOLOGY+, GHOST SICKNESS, CULTURE-BASED
         PSYCHOTHERAPY+, TRADITIONAL HEALERS, DREAMS AND VISION
         QUESTS, AGGRESSIVENESS+, SOCIALLY DEVIANT BEHAVIOR+
```

IDEN   U.S., OREGON

746 AUTH   PHILION, WILLIAM E.; GALLOWAY, CHARLES G.
    TITL   INDIAN CHILDREN AND THE READING PROGRAM.
    SOUR   JOURNAL OF READING, APR. 1969, PP 553-560, 598-602.
    YEAR   1969
    DESC   CHILDREN-SCHOOL AGE, ELEMENTARY SCHOOLS, LANGUAGE
            HANDICAPS+, TRADITIONAL CHILD REARING, LEARNING
            DISABILITIES AND PROBLEMS+, READING PROGRAMS+,
            ENVIRONMENTAL FACTORS
    IDEN   CANADA, BRITISH COLUMBIA

747 AUTH   MCFEE, MALCOLM
    TITL   THE 150% MAN, A PRODUCT OF BLACKFEET ACCULTURATION.
    SOUR   AMERICAN ANTHROPOLOGIST, 1968, V70, PP 1096-1107.
    YEAR   1968
    DESC   BLACKFEET, PLAINS, CULTURAL ADAPTATION+, RESERVATION,
            BICULTURALISM+, NATIVE AMERICAN VALUES, GENEROSITY,
            SOCIAL GROUPS AND PEER GROUPS, SOCIAL STATUS+,
            LEADERSHIP+, SOCIAL ROLES+
    IDEN   U.S., MONTANA, BLACKFEET RESERVATION

748 AUTH   DAVIS, J.C.; CROPLEY, A.J.
    TITL   PSYCHOLOGICAL FACTORS IN JUVENILE DELINQUENCY.
    SOUR   CANADIAN JOURNAL OF BEHAVIORAL SCIENCE, JAN. 1976,
            V8(1), PP 68-77.
    YEAR   1976
    DESC   ADOLESCENTS+, SOCIALLY DEVIANT BEHAVIOR+,
            PSYCHOLOGICAL TESTING+, MALES
    IDEN   CANADA, WECHSLER INTELLIGENCE SCALE CHILDREN

749 AUTH   FLANNERY, REGINA
    TITL   THE POSITION OF WOMAN AMONG THE MESCALERO APACHE.
    SOUR   PRIMITIVE MAN, 1932, V5, PP 26-32.
    YEAR   1932
    DESC   APACHE-MESCALERO, SOUTHWEST, FEMALES+, ADULTS, SOCIAL
            ROLES, ADOLESCENTS, SOCIAL STATUS+
    IDEN   U.S., NEW MEXICO

750 AUTH   GUNTHER, ERNA
    TITL   THE SHAKER RELIGION OF THE NORTHWEST.
    SOUR   IN MARION WESLEY SMITH (ED.), INDIANS OF THE URBAN
            NORTHWEST, PP 37-76. NEW YORK: COLUMBIA UNIVERSITY
            PRESS, 1949. (76P)
    YEAR   1949
    DESC   NATIVE AMERICAN RELIGIONS+, NORTHWEST COAST, CULTURAL
            ADAPTATION+, TRADITIONAL HEALERS, CULTURE-BASED
            PSYCHOTHERAPY+, PLATEAU, RELIGIONS-NON-NATIVE
    IDEN   U.S., WASHINGTON, OREGON, CALIFORNIA, SHAKER RELIGION,
            CANADA, BRITISH COLUMBIA

751 AUTH   HIRABAYASHI, JAMES; KEMNITZER, LUIS S.
    TITL   REVIEW OF INDIANS IN THE CITY: A CASE STUDY OF THE
            URBANIZATION OF INDIANS IN TORONTO, BY THE CANADIAN
            RESEARCH CENTRE FOR ANTHROPOLOGY, OTTAWA.

```
        SOUR   AMERICAN ANTHROPOLOGIST, 1972, V74, PP 1419-1422.
        YEAR   1972
        DESC   URBAN AREAS, URBANIZATION+, CULTURAL ADAPTATION+,
               NATIVE AMERICAN VALUES, SOCIAL NETWORKS, RESEARCHERS+,
               BICULTURALISM+
        IDEN   CANADA, ONTARIO

752     AUTH   ELKIN, HENRY
        TITL   THE NORTHERN ARAPAHO OF WYOMING.
        SOUR   IN RALPH LINTON (ED.), ACCULTURATION IN SEVEN AMERICAN
               INDIAN TRIBES, PP 207-255.  NEW YORK:
               APPLETON-CENTURY, 1940.
        YEAR   1940
        DESC   ARAPAHO-NORTHERN, PLAINS, CULTURAL ADAPTATION+,
               RESERVATION, CULTURAL CONTINUITY+, PERSONALITY TRAITS,
               EMOTIONAL RESTRAINT, POWERLESSNESS, NATIVE AMERICAN
               COPING BEHAVIORS+, STRESS+, PASSIVE RESISTANCE+
        IDEN   U.S., WYOMING, WIND RIVER RESERVATION

753     AUTH   HEIDENREICH, C. ADRIAN
        TITL   ALCOHOL AND DRUG USE AND ABUSE AMONG INDIAN-AMERICANS:
               A REVIEW OF ISSUES AND SOURCES.
        SOUR   JOURNAL OF DRUG ISSUES, SUM. 1976, V6(3), PP 256-272.
        YEAR   1976
        DESC   ALCOHOL USE+, DRUG USE+, REVIEW OF LITERATURE, ALCOHOL
               USE+
        IDEN   U.S.

754     AUTH   RAMSTAD, VIVIAN V.; POTTER, ROBERT E.
        TITL   DIFFERENCES IN VOCABULARY AND SYNTAX USAGE BETWEEN NEZ
               PERCE INDIANS AND WHITE KINDERGARTEN CHILDREN.
        SOUR   JOURNAL OF LEARNING DISABILITIES, OCT. 1974, V7(8), PP
               491-497.
        YEAR   1974
        DESC   BILINGUALISM, NEZ PERCE, PLATEAU, CHILDREN-INFANTS AND
               PRESCHOOL+, PSYCHOLOGICAL TESTING, LANGUAGE
               HANDICAPS+, LEARNING DISABILITIES AND PROBLEMS+,
               NATIVE-NON-NATIVE COMPARISONS, ANGLO AMERICANS,
               RESERVATION
        IDEN   U.S., IDAHO, LAPWAI RESERVATION, PEABODY PICTURE
               VOCABULARY TEST, NORTHWEST SYNTAX SCREENING TEST

755     AUTH   MEKEEL, SCUDDER
        TITL   A DISCUSSION OF CULTURE CHANGE AS ILLUSTRATED BY
               MATERIAL FROM A TETON-DAKOTA COMMUNITY.
        SOUR   AMERICAN ANTHROPOLOGIST, APR. 1932, V34, PP 273-285.
        YEAR   1932
        DESC   SIOUX-OGLALA, PLAINS, RESERVATION, TRIBAL POLITICAL
               ORGANIZATIONS+, LEADERSHIP+, CULTURAL ADAPTATION+,
               POW-WOWS, RELOCATION+
        IDEN   U.S., SOUTH DAKOTA, PINE RIDGE RESERVATION

756     AUTH   COLLINS, JUNE M.
        TITL   AN INTERPRETATION OF SKAGIT INTRAGROUP CONFLICT DURING
               ACCULTURATION.
```

SOUR AMERICAN ANTHROPOLOGIST, JUL. 1952, V54, PP 347-355.
YEAR 1952
DESC SKAGIT, NORTHWEST COAST, AGGRESSIVENESS+, TRADITIONAL
SOCIAL CONTROL+, EXTENDED FAMILY+, FAMILY
FUNCTIONING+, MARITAL RELATIONSHIPS+, CHILD ABUSE AND
NEGLECT+
IDEN U.S., WASHINGTON

757 AUTH CAUDILL, WILLIAM
TITL PSYCHOLOGICAL CHARACTERISTICS OF ACCULTURATED
WISCONSIN OJIBWA CHILDREN.
SOUR AMERICAN ANTHROPOLOGIST, 1949, V51, PP 409-427.
YEAR 1949
DESC CHIPPEWA, EASTERN SUB-ARCTIC, RESERVATION, PERSONALITY
TRAITS+, PSYCHOLOGICAL TESTING+, CHILDREN-SCHOOL AGE+,
ELEMENTARY SCHOOLS, EMOTIONAL RESTRAINT+,
AGGRESSIVENESS+, ANXIETY+
IDEN U.S., WISCONSIN, RORSCHACH TEST, THEMATIC APPERCEPTION
TEST, LAC DU FLAMBEAU RESERVATION

758 AUTH COOPER, JOHN M.
TITL THE CREE WITIKO PSYCHOSIS.
SOUR PRIMITIVE MAN, 1933, V6, PP 20-24.
YEAR 1933
DESC CREE, EASTERN SUB-ARCTIC, WINDIGO PSYCHOSIS+,
ENVIRONMENTAL FACTORS+
IDEN CANADA

759 AUTH ASTROV, MARGOT
TITL THE CONCEPT OF MOTION AS THE PSYCHOLOGICAL LEITMOTIF
OF NAVAJO LIFE AND LITERATURE.
SOUR JOURNAL OF AMERICAN FOLKLORE, 1950, V63, PP 45-56.
YEAR 1950
DESC NAVAJO, SOUTHWEST, PERSONALITY TRAITS+, CULTURE-BASED
PSYCHOTHERAPY, COGNITIVE PROCESSES+, RELOCATION+,
RESERVATION
IDEN U.S., NAVAJO RESERVATION

760 AUTH BITTLE, WILLIAM E.
TITL THE MANATIDIE: A FOCUS FOR KIOWA APACHE TRIBAL
IDENTITY.
SOUR PLAINS ANTHROPOLOGIST, AUG. 1962, V7(17), PP 152-163.
YEAR 1962
DESC ETHNIC IDENTITY+, KIOWA APACHE, PLAINS, CULTURAL
REVIVAL+, POW-WOWS, MILITARY SERVICE
IDEN U.S., OKLAHOMA

761 AUTH SYDIAHA, D.; REMPEL, J.
TITL MOTIVATIONAL AND ATTITUDINAL CHARACTERISTICS OF INDIAN
SCHOOL CHILDREN AS MEASURED BY THE THEMATIC
APPERCEPTION TEST.
SOUR CANADIAN PSYCHOLOGIST, JUL. 1964, V5(3), PP 139-148.
YEAR 1964
DESC METIS, PLAINS, PSYCHOLOGICAL TESTING+, ADOLESCENTS,
SECONDARY SCHOOLS, NATIVE-NON-NATIVE COMPARISONS,

```
              ECONOMIC ISSUES+, ACHIEVEMENT+, ANGLO
              AMERICANS,OFF-RESERVATION, URBAN AREAS, SOCIAL STATUS,
              MOTIVATION+
     IDEN     CANADA, SASKATCHEWAN, THEMATIC APPERCEPTION TEST

762  AUTH     LURIE, NANCY O.
     TITL     INDIAN DRINKING PATTERNS.
     SOUR     LETTER TO THE EDITOR: AMERICAN JOURNAL OF
              ORTHOPSYCHIATRY, 1972, V42, P 554.
     YEAR     1972
     DESC     ALCOHOL USE+, ETHNIC IDENTITY+, NATIVE AMERICAN COPING
              BEHAVIORS+
     IDEN     U.S.

763  AUTH     GLADWIN, THOMAS
     TITL     PERSONALITY STRUCTURE IN THE PLAINS.
     SOUR     ANTHROPOLOGICAL QUARTERLY, 1957, V30, PP 111-124.
     YEAR     1957
     DESC     PLAINS, PERSONALITY TRAITS+, COMANCHE, CHEYENNE,
              AGGRESSIVENESS+, EMOTIONAL RESTRAINT+, SEXUAL
              RELATIONS+, INTERTRIBAL COMPARISONS, TRADITIONAL CHILD
              REARING+, ANXIETY+
     IDEN     U.S.

764  AUTH     KLEINFELD, JUDITH S.
     TITL     VISUAL MEMORY IN VILLAGE ESKIMO AND URBAN CAUCASIAN
              CHILDREN.
     SOUR     ARCTIC, 1971, V24, PP 132-138.
     YEAR     1971
     DESC     COGNITIVE PROCESSES+, ESKIMO, PSYCHOLOGICAL TESTING+,
              ADOLESCENTS, OFF-RESERVATION, SECONDARY SCHOOLS,
              WESTERN ARCTIC, NATIVE-NON-NATIVE COMPARISONS, ANGLO
              AMERICANS
     IDEN     U.S., ALASKA, SULLIVAN SQUIGGLE TEST

765  AUTH     DELK, JOHN L.; URBANCIK, GERALD; WILLIAMS, CECIL;
              BERG, GREG; KAHN, MARVIN W.
     TITL     DROP-OUTS FROM AN AMERICAN INDIAN RESERVATION SCHOOL:
              A POSSIBLE PREVENTION PROGRAM.
     SOUR     JOURNAL OF COMMUNITY PSYCHOLOGY, JAN. 1974, V2(1), PP
              15-17.
     YEAR     1974
     DESC     DROPOUTS+, RESERVATION, PAPAGO, SOUTHWEST, MENTAL
              HEALTH INSTITUTIONS, COMMUNITY INVOLVEMENT, SECONDARY
              SCHOOLS, NATIVE AMERICAN PERSONNEL, MENTAL
              RETARDATION, PREVENTIVE MENTAL HEALTH PROGRAMS+,
              ADOLESCENTS
     IDEN     U.S., ARIZONA

766  AUTH     OPLER, MORRIS E.
     TITL     NOTES ON CHIRICAHUA APACHE CULTURE. I. SUPERNATURAL
              POWER AND THE SHAMAN.
     SOUR     PRIMITIVE MAN, 1947, V20(1-2), PP 1-14.
     YEAR     1947
     DESC     APACHE-CHIRICAHUA, TRADITIONAL HEALERS+, NATIVE
```

```
         AMERICAN RELIGIONS+, SOUTHWEST
    IDEN U.S.

767 AUTH SAVISHINSKY, JOEL S.
    TITL THE CHILD IS FATHER TO THE DOG: CANINES AND
         PERSONALITY PROCESSES IN THE ARCTIC COMMUNITY.
    SOUR HUMAN DEVELOPMENT, 1974, V17(6), PP 460-466.
    YEAR 1974
    DESC FAMILY FUNCTIONING+, HARE, MACKENZIE SUB-ARCTIC,
         TRADITIONAL CHILD REARING+, CHILDREN-INFANTS AND
         PRESCHOOL+, CHILDREN-SCHOOL AGE+
    IDEN CANADA, NORTHWEST TERRITORIES

768 AUTH BRANT, CHARLES S.
    TITL PEYOTISM AMONG THE KIOWA-APACHE AND NEIGHBORING
         TRIBES.
    SOUR SOUTHWESTERN JOURNAL OF ANTHROPOLOGY, 1950, V6, PP
         212-222.
    YEAR 1950
    DESC KIOWA APACHE, PLAINS, DRUG USE+, TRADITIONAL USE OF
         DRUGS AND ALCOHOL+, NATIVE AMERICAN RELIGIONS+,
         TRADITIONAL HEALERS
    IDEN U.S., NATIVE AMERICAN CHURCH, OKLAHOMA

769 AUTH HAUGHTON, ANSON B.
    TITL PLANNING FOR SUICIDE PREVENTION.
    SOUR IN SUICIDE AMONG THE AMERICAN INDIANS, PP 16-20.
         (USPHS PUBLICATION NO. 1903) WASHINGTON, D.C.:
         GOVERNMENT PRINTING OFFICE, 1969.
    YEAR 1969
    DESC PREVENTIVE MENTAL HEALTH PROGRAMS+, DELIVERY OF
         SERVICES+, RESERVATION, , PROGRAM
         DEVELOPMENT+,SUICIDE+
    IDEN U.S.

770 AUTH LANDES, RUTH
    TITL THE OJIBWA OF CANADA.
    SOUR IN M. MEAD (ED.), COOPERATION AND COMPETITION AMONG
         PRIMITIVE PEOPLES, PP 87-126.  BOSTON: BEACON PRESS,
         1961.
    YEAR 1961
    DESC CHIPPEWA, RESERVATION, EASTERN SUB-ARCTIC,
         COOPERATION+, NONCOMPETITIVENESS+, TRADITIONAL
         HEALERS, DREAMS AND VISION QUESTS, TRADITIONAL CHILD
         REARING, SOCIAL ROLES+, MALES+, FEMALES+, ECONOMIC
         ISSUES
    IDEN CANADA, ONTARIO, MANITOU RESERVE

771 AUTH GOLDMAN, IRVING
    TITL THE KWAKIUTL INDIANS ON VANCOUVER ISLAND.
    SOUR IN M. MEAD (ED.), COOPERATION AND COMPETITITON AMONG
         PRIMITIVE PEOPLES, PP 180-209.  BOSTON: BEACON PRESS,
         1961.
    YEAR 1961
    DESC KWAKIUTL, NORTHWEST COAST, ECONOMIC ISSUES+,
```

```
                COOPERATION, NONCOMPETITIVENESS, SOCIAL STATUS+,
                AGGRESSIVENESS+
        IDEN    CANADA, BRITISH COLUMBIA

772     AUTH    GAGNE, RAYMOND C.
        TITL    SPATIAL CONCEPTS IN THE ESKIMO LANGUAGE.
        SOUR    IN V.F. VALENTINE AND F.C. VALLEE (EDS.), ESKIMO OF
                THE CANADIAN ARCTIC, PP30-38.  TORONTO: MCCLELLAND AND
                STEWART, 1968.
        YEAR    1968
        DESC    ESKIMO, COGNITIVE PROCESSES+, WESTERN ARCTIC, CENTRAL
                AND EASTERN ARCTIC, OFF-RESERVATION
        IDEN    U.S., CANADA

773     AUTH    LURIE, NANCY O.
        TITL    THE WILL-O"-THE-WISP OF INDIAN UNITY.
        SOUR    INDIAN HISTORIAN, SUM. 1976, V9(3), PP 19-24.
        YEAR    1976
        DESC    TRIBAL POLITICAL ORGANIZATIONS+, ADMINISTRATIVE
                ISSUES+, LEADERSHIP+,  PASSIVE RESISTANCE
        IDEN    U.S., INDIAN REORGANIZATION ACT

774     AUTH    WITT, SHIRLEY
        TITL    NATIVE WOMEN TODAY: SEXISM AND THE INDIAN WOMAN.
        SOUR    CIVIL RIGHTS DIGEST, SPR. 1974, V6(3), PP 29-35.
        YEAR    1974
        DESC    FEMALES+, ADULTS+, STEREOTYPES+, NEUROSES, EMPLOYMENT,
                POWERLESSNESS, FAMILY PLANNING

775     AUTH    MEDICINE, BEATRICE
        TITL    THE ROLE OF WOMEN IN NATIVE AMERICAN SOCIETIES: A
                BIBLIOGRAPHY.
        SOUR    INDIAN HISTORIAN, SUM. 1975, V8(3), PP 50-54.
        YEAR    1975
        DESC    FEMALES+, REVIEW OF LITERATURE, SOCIAL ROLES+

776     AUTH    BARTER, JAMES T.
        TITL    SELF-DESTRUCTIVE BEHAVIOR IN ADOLESCENTS AND ADULTS:
                SIMILARITIES AND DIFFERENCES.
        SOUR    IN SUICIDE AMONG THE AMERICAN INDIANS, PP 7-10.
                (USPHS PUBLICATION NO. 1903) WASHINGTON, D.C.:
                GOVERNMENT PRINTING OFFICE, 1969.
        YEAR    1969
        DESC    SUICIDE+, ADULTS+, ADOLESCENTS+, AGE COMPARISONS,
                DEPRESSION, PREVENTIVE MENTAL HEALTH PROGRAMS,
                SELF-CONCEPT
        IDEN    U.S.

777     AUTH    TABACHNICK, NORMAN
        TITL    TWO TYPES OF SUICIDAL BEHAVIOR.
        SOUR    IN SUICIDE AMONG THE AMERICAN INDIANS, PP 11-15.
                (USPHS PUBLICATION NO. 1903)  WASHINGTON, D.C.:
                GOVERNMENT PRINTING OFFICE, 1969.
        YEAR    1969
        DESC    SUICIDE+, PREVENTIVE MENTAL HEALTH PROGRAMS+, CLINICAL
```

```
        STUDY, PSYCHOTHERAPY AND COUNSELING+
   IDEN U.S.

778 AUTH MINDELL, CARL; STUART, PAUL
    TITL SUICIDE AND SELF-DESTRUCTIVE BEHAVIOR IN THE OGLALA
         SIOUX: SOME CLINICAL ASPECTS AND COMMUNITY APPROACHES.
    SOUR IN SUICIDE AMONG THE AMERICAN INDIANS, PP 25-33.
         (USPHS PUBLICATION NO. 1903)  WASHINGTON, D.C.:
         GOVERNMENT PRINTING OFFICE, 1969.
    YEAR 1969
    DESC SUICIDE+, RESERVATION, ADOLESCENTS+, SEX DIFFERENCES,
         PREVENTIVE MENTAL HEALTH PROGRAMS+, DEATH AND DYING,
         ACCIDENTS+, MENTAL HEALTH PARAPROFESSIONALS
    IDEN U.S., SOUTH DAKOTA, PINE RIDGE RESERVATION

779 AUTH WALLACE, ANTHONY F.C.
    TITL THE MODAL PERSONALITY STRUCTURE OF THE TUSCARORA
         INDIANS AS REVEALED BY THE RORSCHACH TEST.
    SOUR (SMITHSONIAN INSTITUTION, BUREAU OF AMERICAN
         ETHNOGRAPHY BULLETIN NO. 150) WASHINGTON, D.C.:
         GOVERNMENT PRINTING OFFICE, 1952.  (120P)
    YEAR 1952
    DESC PSYCHOLOGICAL TESTING+, PERSONALITY TRAITS+,
         IROQUOIS-TUSCARORA, NORTHEAST WOODLAND, RESERVATION,
         SEX DIFFERENCES
    IDEN U.S., NEW YORK, TUSCARORA RESERVATION, RORSCHACH TEST

780 AUTH COLLINS, JUNE M.
    TITL THE INDIAN SHAKER CHURCH: A STUDY OF CONTINUITY AND
         CHANGE IN RELIGION.
    SOUR SOUTHWESTERN JOURNAL OF ANTHROPOLOGY, 1950, V6, PP
         399-411.
    YEAR 1950
    DESC COAST SALISH, NORTHWEST COAST, NATIVE AMERICAN
         RELIGIONS+, DREAMS AND VISION QUESTS+, CULTURAL
         CONTINUITY+, TRADITIONAL HEALERS, SPIRIT INTRUSION+
    IDEN U.S., WASHINGTON, SHAKER RELIGION

781 AUTH KLEINFELD, JUDITH S.
    TITL CLASSROOM CLIMATE AND THE VERBAL PARTICIPATION OF
         INDIAN AND ESKIMO STUDENTS IN INTEGRATED CLASSROOMS.
    SOUR JOURNAL OF EDUCATIONAL RESEARCH, OCT. 1973, V67(2), PP
         51-52.
    YEAR 1973
    DESC SECONDARY SCHOOLS, ADOLESCENTS+, ALASKA NATIVES,
         PSYCHOLOGICAL TESTING, NATIVE AMERICAN COPING
         BEHAVIORS+, ENVIRONMENTAL FACTORS, PASSIVE RESISTANCE+
    IDEN U.S., ALASKA, TEACHER-PUPIL RAPPORT SCALE

782 AUTH DENNIS, WAYNE; DENNIS, MARSENA G.
    TITL CRADLES AND CRADLING PRACTICES OF THE PUEBLO INDIANS.
    SOUR AMERICAN ANTHROPOLOGIST, 1940, V42, PP 107-115.
    YEAR 1940
    DESC MOTOR PROCESSES+, PUEBLO, CHILDREN-INFANTS AND
         PRESCHOOL+, TRADITIONAL CHILD REARING+, SOUTHWEST,
```

```
              RESERVATION
       IDEN   U.S.

783    AUTH   CHANCE, NORMAN A.; TRUDEAU, JOHN
       TITL   SOCIAL ORGANIZATION, ACCULTURATION, AND INTEGRATION
              AMONG THE ESKIMO AND THE CREE: A COMPARATIVE STUDY.
       SOUR   ANTHROPOLOGICA, 1963, V5, PP 47-56.
       YEAR   1963
       DESC   ESKIMO, WESTERN ARCTIC, CREE, EASTERN SUB-ARCTIC,
              CULTURAL ADAPTATION+, INTERTRIBAL COMPARISONS,
              LEADERSHIP, DISCRIMINATION+, OFF-RESERVATION
       IDEN   U.S., ALASKA, CANADA, ONTARIO

784    AUTH   ERIKSON, ERIK H.
       TITL   CHILDHOOD AND TRADITION IN TWO AMERICAN INDIAN TRIBES
              WITH SOME REFLECTION ON THE CONTEMPORARY AMERICAN
              SCENE.
       SOUR   IN C. KLUCKHOHN AND H.A. MURRAY (EDS.), PERSONALITY IN
              NATURE, SOCIETY AND CULTURE, PP 176-203.  NEW YORK:
              KNOPF, 1948.
       YEAR   1948
       DESC   TRADITIONAL CHILD REARING+, SIOUX, PLAINS, YUROK,
              CALIFORNIA AREA, EXTENDED FAMILY, FAMILY FUNCTIONING+,
              INTERTRIBAL COMPARISONS, SEXUAL RELATIONS, PERSONALITY
              TRAITS, PSYCHOANALYSIS
       IDEN   U.S.

785    AUTH   FORSLUND, MORRIS A.; MEYERS, RALPH E.
       TITL   DELINQUENCY AMONG WIND RIVER INDIAN RESERVATION YOUTH.
       SOUR   CRIMINOLOGY, MAY 1974, V12(1), PP 97-106.
       YEAR   1974
       DESC   SOCIALLY DEVIANT BEHAVIOR+, ADOLESCENTS+, CRIME,
              EPIDEMIOLOGICAL STUDY, RESERVATION, SEX DIFFERENCES
       IDEN   U.S., WYOMING, WIND RIVER RESERVATION

786    AUTH   ADAIR, JOHN; DEUSCHLE, KURT; MCDERMOTT, WALSH
       TITL   PATTERNS OF HEALTH AND DISEASE AMONG THE NAVAHOS.
       SOUR   ANNALS OF THE AMERICAN ACADEMY OF POLITICAL AND SOCIAL
              SCIENCE, 1957, V311,PP 80-94.
       YEAR   1957
       DESC   NAVAJO, SOUTHWEST, RESERVATION, NATIVE AMERICAN
              ETIOLOGY+, UNIVERSAL HARMONY, TRADITIONAL HEALERS+,
              MEDICAL PROGRAMS AND SERVICES+, DELIVERY OF SERVICES+,
              I.H.S., MEDICAL INSTITUTIONS
       IDEN   U.S., NAVAJO RESERVATION

787    AUTH   VOGT, EVON Z.
       TITL   THE ACCULTURATION OF AMERICAN INDIANS.
       SOUR   ANNALS OF THE AMERICAN ACADEMY OF POLITICAL AND SOCIAL
              SCIENCE, 1957, V311,PP 137-146.
       YEAR   1957
       DESC   CULTURAL ADAPTATION+, CULTURAL CONTINUITY+, ETHNIC
              IDENTITY, DISCRIMINATION+, CULTURAL REVIVAL
       IDEN   U.S., MEXICO
```

788 AUTH UNDERHILL, RUTH
     TITL RELIGION AMONG AMERICAN INDIANS.
     SOUR ANNALS OF THE AMERICAN ACADEMY OF POLITICAL AND SOCIAL
           SCIENCE, 1957, V311,PP 127-136.
     YEAR 1957
     DESC NATIVE AMERICAN RELIGIONS+, TABOO BREAKING, DREAMS AND
           VISION QUESTS, TRADITIONAL HEALERS
     IDEN U.S.

789 AUTH FERNBERGER, SAMUEL W.
     TITL OBSERVATIONS ON TAKING PEYOTE (ANHALONIUM LEWINII).
     SOUR AMERICAN JOURNAL OF PSYCHOLOGY, 1923, V34, PP 267-270.
     YEAR 1923
     DESC DRUG USE+, TRADITIONAL USE OF DRUGS AND ALCOHOL+
     IDEN U.S.

790 AUTH FELDMAN, CAROL F.; BOCK, R. DARRELL
     TITL COGNITIVE STUDIES AMONG RESIDENTS OF WAINWRIGHT
           VILLAGE, ALASKA.
     SOUR ARCTIC ANTHROPOLOGY, 1970, V7(1), PP 100-108.
     YEAR 1970
     DESC COGNITIVE PROCESSES+, PSYCHOLOGICAL TESTING+,
           OFF-RESERVATION, LANGUAGE HANDICAPS, BILINGUALISM+
     IDEN U.S., ALASKA, RAVEN PROGRESSIVE MATRICES, GUILFORD
           ZIMMERMAN SPATIAL VISUALIZATION TEST, ENGLISH
           VOCABULARY TEST, CONCEPT INDUCTION TEST

791 AUTH GRAVES, THEODORE D.
     TITL THE PERSONAL ADJUSTMENT OF NAVAJO INDIAN MIGRANTS TO
           DENVER, COLORADO.
     SOUR AMERICAN ANTHROPOLOGIST, 1970, V72, PP 35-54.
     YEAR 1970
     DESC RELOCATION+, URBAN AREAS, CORRECTIONAL INSTITUTIONS,
           ALCOHOL USE+, GROUP NORMS AND SANCTIONS, NAVAJO,
           SOUTHWEST, URBANIZATION+, ECONOMIC ISSUES, EMPLOYMENT,
           NATIVE AMERICAN VALUES
     IDEN U.S., COLORADO

792 AUTH PELLETIER, WILFRED
     TITL CHILDHOOD IN AN INDIAN VILLAGE.
     SOUR CHAPTER IN FOR EVERY NORTH AMERICAN INDIAN WHO BEGINS
           TO DISAPPEAR I ALSO BEGIN TO DISAPPEAR, PP 18-31.
           TORONTO, CANADA: NEEWIN PUB. CO., 1971.
     YEAR 1971
     DESC NONCOMPETITIVENESS, CHILDREN-SCHOOL AGE+, TRADITIONAL
           CHILD REARING+, NONINTERFERENCE, LEARNING+,
           LEADERSHIP+, NATIVE AMERICAN VALUES+
     IDEN CANADA

793 AUTH MURPHY, JANE M.; LEIGHTON, ALEXANDER H.
     TITL NATIVE CONCEPTIONS OF PSYCHIATRIC DISORDER.
     SOUR IN JANE M. MURPHY AND ALEXANDER H. LEIGHTON (EDS.),
           APPROACHES TO CROSS-CULTURAL PSYCHIATRY, PP 64-107.
           ITHACA, NEW YORK: CORNELL UNIVERSITY PRESS, 1965.
     YEAR 1965

DESC   NATIVE AMERICAN ETIOLOGY+, TRADITIONAL HEALERS,
       CULTURE-BASED PSYCHOTHERAPY, CULTURE-SPECIFIC
       SYNDROMES+, ESKIMO, CENTRAL AND EASTERN ARCTIC, MENTAL
       DISORDERS+, MENTAL RETARDATION, SOCIALLY DEVIANT
       BEHAVIOR, PSYCHOSES, NEUROSES, DEPRESSION,
       PSYCHOPHYSIOLOGICAL DISORDERS, CHARACTER DISORDERS,
       OFF-RESERVATION
IDEN   U.S.

794 AUTH   PARKER, SEYMOUR; SASAKI, TOM T.
     TITL   SOCIETY AND SENTIMENT IN TWO CONTRASTING SOCIALLY
            DISTURBED AREAS.
     SOUR   IN JANE M. MURPHY AND ALEXANDER H. LEIGHTON (EDS.),
            APPROACHES TO CROSS-CULTURAL PSYCHIATRY, PP 329-359.
            ITHACA, NEW YORK: CORNELL UNIVERSITY PRESS, 1965.
     YEAR   1965
     DESC   STRESS+, ANOMIE+, URBAN AREAS, POWERLESSNESS+, NAVAJO,
            SOUTHWEST
     IDEN   U.S.

795 AUTH   MURPHY, JANE M.; HUGHES, CHARLES C.
     TITL   THE USE OF PSYCHOPHYSIOLOGICAL SYMPTOMS AS INDICATORS
            OF DISORDER AMONG ESKIMOS.
     SOUR   IN JANE M. MURPHY AND ALEXANDER H. LEIGHTON (EDS.),
            APPROACHES TO CROSS-CULTURAL PSYCHIATRY, PP 108-160.
            ITHACA, NEW YORK: CORNELL UNIVERSITY PRESS, 1965.
     YEAR   1965
     DESC   ESKIMO, CENTRAL AND EASTERN ARCTIC,
            PSYCHOPHYSIOLOGICAL DISORDERS+, PSYCHOLOGICAL
            TESTING+, EPIDEMIOLOGICAL STUDY, OFF-RESERVATION,
            MENTAL DISORDERS+, SURVEY
     IDEN   CANADA, HEALTH OPINION SURVEY

796 AUTH   SPINDLER, LOUISE S.
     TITL   MENOMINI WOMEN AND CULTURE CHANGE.
     SOUR   AMERICAN ANTHROPOLOGICAL ASSOCIATION MEMOIRS NO. 91,
            FEB. 1962, V64(1,PART 2), PP 1-113.
     YEAR   1962
     DESC   FEMALES+, ADULTS+, SOCIAL ROLES+, PSYCHOLOGICAL
            TESTING, CULTURAL ADAPTATION+, MENOMINEE, NORTHEAST
            WOODLAND, RESERVATION, SOCIAL STATUS+, NATIVE AMERICAN
            VALUES+, PERSONALITY TRAITS+, STRESS, SOCIAL GROUPS
            AND PEER GROUPS
     IDEN   U.S., WISCONSIN

797 AUTH   CODERE, HELEN
     TITL   THE AMIABLE SIDE OF KWAKIUTL LIFE: THE POTLATCH AND
            THE PLAY POTLATCH.
     SOUR   AMERICAN ANTHROPOLOGIST, APR. 1956, V58(2), PP 334-351.
     YEAR   1956
     DESC   KWAKIUTL, NORTHWEST COAST, PERSONALITY TRAITS+, SOCIAL
            STATUS
     IDEN   CANADA, BRITISH COLUMBIA

798 AUTH   CODERE, HELEN

```
       TITL  KWAKIUTL SOCIETY: RANK WITHOUT CLASS.
       SOUR  AMERICAN ANTHROPOLOGIST, JUN. 1957, V59(3), PP 473-486.
       YEAR  1957
       DESC  KWAKIUTL, NORTHWEST COAST, SOCIAL STATUS+, SOCIAL
             GROUPS AND PEER GROUPS+, GROUP NORMS AND SANCTIONS
       IDEN  CANADA, BRITISH COLUMBIA

799    AUTH  ANDERSON, ROBERT
       TITL  THE NORTHERN CHEYENNE WAR MOTHERS.
       SOUR  ANTHROPOLOGICAL QUARTERLY, 1956, V29 (3), PP 82-90.
       YEAR  1956
       DESC  CHEYENNE-NORTHERN, PLAINS, RESERVATION, MILITARY
             SERVICE+, FEMALES, ADULTS, CULTURAL CONTINUITY+,
             NATIVE AMERICAN COPING BEHAVIORS+, ECONOMIC ISSUES,
             SOCIAL GROUPS AND PEER GROUPS
       IDEN  U.S., MONTANA, NORTHERN CHEYENNE RESERVATION

800    AUTH  FOULKS, EDWARD F.
       TITL  THE ARCTIC HYSTERIAS OF THE NORTH ALASKAN ESKIMO.
       SOUR  DISSERTATION ABSTRACTS INTERNATIONAL, 1973, V33, P
             2905B.
       YEAR  1973
       DESC  ARCTIC HYSTERIA+, ESKIMO, WESTERN ARCTIC, TRADITIONAL
             SOCIAL CONTROL, NUTRITIONAL FACTORS
       IDEN  U.S., ALASKA

801    AUTH  DICK, ROBERT MARCUS, II
       TITL  SCREENING IDENTIFICATION OF FIRST GRADE PROBLEMS IN AN
             AMERICAN INDIAN POPULATION.
       SOUR  DISSERTATION ABSTRACTS INTERNATIONAL, 1971, V2, P
             1209B.
       YEAR  1971
       DESC  LEARNING DISABILITIES AND PROBLEMS+, CHILDREN-SCHOOL
             AGE+, PSYCHOLOGICAL TESTING+, SOUTHEAST WOODLAND,
             CHILDREN-INFANTS AND PRESCHOOL+, ELEMENTARY SCHOOLS
       IDEN  U.S., NORTH CAROLINA, PERCEPTUAL MATURITY SCALE,
             BENDER GESTALT TEST, PEABODY PICTURE VOCABULARY TEST,
             LEE CLARK READING READINESS TEST, LORGE THORNDIKE
             INTELLIGENCE TEST, CALIFORNIA ACHIEVEMENT TEST

802    AUTH  CANADIAN PSYCHIATRIC ASSOCIATION
       TITL  STATEMENT BY THE CANADIAN PSYCHIATRIC ASSOCIATION'S
             SECTION ON NATIVE PEOPLES' MENTAL HEALTH.
       SOUR  WHITE CLOUD JOURNAL, SUM. 1978, V(2), PP 11-12.
       YEAR  1978
       DESC  NATIVE AMERICAN ADMINISTERED PROGRAMS+, NATIVE
             AMERICAN PERSONNEL+
       IDEN  CANADA

803    AUTH  CENTER FOR SOCIAL RESEARCH AND DEVELOPMENT. DENVER
             RESEARCH INSTITUTE. UNIVERSITY OF DENVER
       TITL  INDIAN CHILD WELFARE: A STATE-OF-THE -FIELD STUDY.
       SOUR  DENVER: AUTHOR, 1976.  (421P)
       YEAR  1976
       DESC  CHILDREN-SCHOOL AGE+, CHILDREN-INFANTS AND PRESCHOOL+,
```

              LEGAL ISSUES+, URBAN AREAS, RESERVATION, SOCIAL
              SERVICES+, SOCIAL SERVICE PROFESSIONALS, ADOPTION AND
              FOSTER CARE+, B.I.A., I.H.S., ADOLESCENTS+, DELIVERY
              OF SERVICES+, NATIVE AMERICAN ADMINISTERED PROGRAMS
       IDEN   U.S.

804   AUTH   STRAIGHT, WILLIAM M.
       TITL   SEMINOLE INDIAN MEDICINE.
       SOUR   JOURNAL OF THE FLORIDA MEDICAL ASSOCIATION, AUG. 1970,
              V57(8), PP 19-27.
       YEAR   1970
       DESC   SEMINOLE, SOUTHEAST WOODLAND, TRADITIONAL HEALERS+,
              TRAINING PROGRAMS, SOUL LOSS, NATIVE AMERICAN
              ETIOLOGY+
       IDEN   U.S., FLORIDA

805   AUTH   BLOOM, JOSEPH D.; RICHARDS, WILLIAM W.
       TITL   MENTAL HEALTH PROGRAM DEVELOPMENT IN RURAL
              ALASKA--CHANGING ROLES OF PUBLIC AND PRIVATE
              PSYCHIATRISTS.
       SOUR   ALASKA MEDICINE, MAY 1976, V18(3), PP 25-28.
       YEAR   1976
       DESC   MENTAL HEALTH PROGRAMS AND SERVICES+, OFF-RESERVATION,
              PROGRAM DEVELOPMENT+, DELIVERY OF SERVICES+, MENTAL
              HEALTH PROFESSIONALS+, ALASKA NATIVES
       IDEN   U.S., ALASKA

806   AUTH   INDIAN HEALTH SERVICE
       TITL   ALCOHOLISM: A HIGH PRIORITY HEALTH PROBLEM, A REPORT
              OF THE INDIAN HEALTH SERVICE TASK FORCE ON ALCOHOLISM.
       SOUR   (DHEW PUBLICATION NO. (HSM) 73-12002), DEC 1969,
              SEC.1. (21P)
       YEAR   1969
       DESC   ALCOHOL USE+,
       IDEN   U.S.

807   AUTH   INDIAN HEALTH SERVICE
       TITL   ALCOHOLISM: A HIGH PRIORITY HEALTH PROBLEM: A REPORT
              OF THE INDIAN HEALTH SERVICE TASK FORCE ON ALCOHOLISM.
       SOUR   (DHEW PUBLICATION NO. (HSM) 73-12002), FEB 1970, SEC
              2. (19P)
       YEAR   1970
       DESC   I.H.S.+, ALCOHOLISM TREATMENT+, ALCOHOL USE+, PROGRAM
              DEVELOPMENT+, COMMUNITY INVOLVEMENT
       IDEN   U.S.

808   AUTH   INDIAN HEALTH SERVICE
       TITL   ALCOHOLISM: A HIGH PRIORITY HEALTH PROBLEM: A REPORT
              OF THE INDIAN HEALTH SERVICE TASK FORCE ON ALCOHOLISM.
       SOUR   (DHEW PUBLICATION NO. (HSM) 73-12002), APR. 1970, SEC.
              3. (19P)
       YEAR   1970
       DESC   ALCOHOLISM TREATMENT+, CHEMOTHERAPY, PSYCHOTHERAPY AND
              COUNSELING

809 AUTH CENTER FOR SOCIAL RESEARCH AND DEVELOPMENT. DENVER
          RESEARCH INSTITUTE. UNIVERSITY OF DENVER
     TITL INDIAN CHILD WELFARE: A REVIEW OF THE LITERATURE.
     SOUR DENVER: AUTHOR, 1976.
     YEAR 1976
     DESC REVIEW OF LITERATURE, CHILDREN-INFANTS AND PRESCHOOL+,
          CHILDREN-SCHOOL AGE+, SOCIAL SERVICES+, DELIVERY OF
          SERVICES+, ADOPTION AND FOSTER CARE, SOCIAL SERVICE
          PROFESSIONALS, FEDERAL GOVERNMENT, NATIVE AMERICAN
          PERSONNEL, RESERVATION, URBAN AREAS, TRADITIONAL CHILD
          REARING, TRADITIONAL SOCIAL CONTROL, NATIVE AMERICAN
          ADMINISTERED PROGRAMS
     IDEN U.S.

810 AUTH TRIMBLE, JOSEPH E.; RYAN, ROBERT A.
     TITL AN AMERICAN INDIAN AND ALASKA NATIVE MENTAL HEALTH
          TRAINING SYMPOSIUM: A SUMMARY REPORT OF THE
          PROCEEDINGS.
     SOUR PORTLAND, OR.: WHITE CLOUD CENTER, 1978. (19P)
     YEAR 1978
     DESC TRAINING PROGRAMS+, NATIVE AMERICAN PERSONNEL+, MENTAL
          HEALTH PROFESSIONALS+, EDUCATION PROGRAMS AND
          SERVICES+, RESEARCHERS+, COLLEGES AND UNIVERSITIES
     IDEN U.S., OREGON

811 AUTH LURIE, NANCY O.
     TITL THE ENDURING INDIAN.
     SOUR NATURAL HISTORY, NOV. 1966, V75, PP 10-22.
     YEAR 1966
     DESC ETHNIC IDENTITY+, ECONOMIC ISSUES, CULTURAL
          ADAPTATION+, CULTURAL CONTINUITY+, NATIVE AMERICAN
          POLITICAL MOVEMENTS+, LEADERSHIP, FEDERAL GOVERNMENT
     IDEN U.S.

812 AUTH FITZGERALD, J.A.; LUDEMAN W.W.
     TITL THE INTELLIGENCE OF INDIAN CHILDREN.
     SOUR JOURNAL OF COMPARATIVE PSYCHOLOGY, 1926, V6, PP
          319-328.
     YEAR 1926
     DESC CHILDREN-SCHOOL AGE, ABILITIES+, PSYCHOLOGICAL
          TESTING+, SECONDARY SCHOOLS, ADOLESCENTS, ELEMENTARY
          SCHOOLS, FULL BLOOD-MIXED BLOOD COMPARISONS, SEX
          DIFFERENCES, CULTURE-FAIR TESTS+
     IDEN U.S., SOUTH DAKOTA, NATIONAL INTELLIGENCE TEST,
          NEBRASKA, OTIS GROUP INTELLIGENCE TEST

813 AUTH CHADWICK, BRUCE A.; STAUSS, JOSEPH H.; BAHR, HOWARD
          M.; HALVERSON, LOWELL K.
     TITL CONFRONTATION WITH THE LAW: THE CASE OF THE AMERICAN
          INDIANS IN SEATTLE.
     SOUR PHYLON, JAN. 1976, V37(2), PP 163-171.
     YEAR 1976
     DESC URBAN AREAS, CORRECTIONAL INSTITUTIONS+,
          DISCRIMINATION+, LEGAL ISSUES+, SOCIAL SERVICES+,
          CRIME, NATIVE-NON-NATIVE COMPARISONS, ANGLO AMERICANS,

```
                  DELIVERY OF SERVICES+
         IDEN     U.S., WASHINGTON

814  AUTH     LURIE, NANCY O.
     TITL     FORKED TONGUE IN CHEEK OR LIFE AMONG THE NOBLE
              CIVILAGES.
     SOUR     INDIAN HISTORIAN, SPR. 1974, V7, PP 28-40.
     YEAR     1974
     DESC     RESERVATION, ETHNIC IDENTITY+, POLITICS-NONTRIBAL+,
              ADMINISTRATIVE ISSUES+, CULTURAL CONTINUITY+, FEDERAL
              GOVERNMENT+
     IDEN     U.S.

815  AUTH     KUTTNER, ROBERT E.
     TITL     USE OF ACCENTUATED ENVIRONMENTAL INEQUALITIES IN
              RESEARCH ON RACIAL DIFFERENCES.
     SOUR     MANKIND QUARTERLY, 1968, V8, PP 147-160.
     YEAR     1968
     DESC     GENETIC FACTORS, ENVIRONMENTAL FACTORS,
              NATIVE-NON-NATIVE COMPARISONS, BLACK AMERICANS,
              ABILITIES+, PSYCHOLOGICAL TESTING+, ACHIEVEMENT,
              MOTIVATION, DISCRIMINATION
     IDEN     U.S.

816  AUTH     BOZOF, RICHARD P.
     TITL     SOME NAVAHO ATTITUDES TOWARD AVAILABLE MEDICAL CARE.
     SOUR     AMERICAN JOURNAL OF PUBLIC HEALTH, 1972, V62(12), PP
              1620-1624.
     YEAR     1972
     DESC     NAVAJO, SOUTHWEST, RESERVATION, I.H.S., MEDICAL
              PROGRAMS AND SERVICES+, DELIVERY OF SERVICES+, MEDICAL
              INSTITUTIONS+, ADULTS, TRADITIONAL HEALERS, OUTPATIENT
              CARE+, ATTITUDES+
     IDEN     U.S., NEW MEXICO, SHIPROCK P.H.S. HOSPITAL

817  AUTH     THOMPSON, WILLIAM M.; ACKERSTEIN, HAROLD
     TITL     PEPTIC ULCER DISEASE IN THE ALASKA NATIVES: A
              FOUR-YEAR RETROSPECTIVE STUDY.
     SOUR     ALASKA MEDICINE, MAY 1975, V17(3), PP 43-44.
     YEAR     1975
     DESC     PSYCHOPHYSIOLOGICAL DISORDERS+, ALASKA NATIVES,
              EPIDEMIOLOGICAL STUDY
     IDEN     U.S., ALASKA

818  AUTH     WINN, W.
     TITL     AMERICAN INDIAN ALCOHOLISM: ETIOLOGY AND IMPLICATIONS
              FOR EFFECTIVE TREATMENT.
     SOUR     ALASKA MEDICINE, MAY 1978, V20(3), PP 30-32.
     YEAR     1978
     DESC     ALCOHOL USE+, ALCOHOLISM TREATMENT+

819  AUTH     ATTNEAVE, CAROLYN L.
     TITL     THE WASTED STRENGTHS OF INDIAN FAMILIES.
     SOUR     IN STEVEN UNGER (ED.), THE DESTRUCTION OF AMERICAN
              INDIAN FAMILIES, PP 29-33.  NEW YORK: ASSOCIATION ON
```

AMERICAN INDIAN AFFAIRS, 1977.
YEAR   1977
DESC   ADOPTION AND FOSTER CARE+, FAMILY FUNCTIONING+, B.I.A.
       BOARDING SCHOOLS, ETHNIC IDENTITY+, CHILDREN-SCHOOL
       AGE, EXTENDED FAMILY, ADOLESCENTS
IDEN   U.S.

820 AUTH   COOLIDGE, DANE
     TITL   "KID CATCHING" ON THE NAVAJO RESERVATION: 1930.
     SOUR   IN STEVEN UNGER (ED.), THE DESTRUCTION OF AMERICAN
            INDIAN FAMILIES, PP 18-21. NEW YORK: ASSOCIATION ON
            AMERICAN INDIAN AFFAIRS, 1977.
     YEAR   1977
     DESC   NAVAJO, SOUTHWEST, RESERVATION, B.I.A. BOARDING
            SCHOOLS+, FEDERAL GOVERNMENT+, CHILDREN-SCHOOL AGE+
     IDEN   U.S., NAVAJO RESERVATION

821 AUTH   ABOUREZK, JAMES
     TITL   THE ROLE OF THE FEDERAL GOVERNMENT: A CONGRESSIONAL
            VIEW.
     SOUR   IN STEVEN UNGER (ED.), THE DESTRUCTION OF AMERICAN
            INDIAN FAMILIES, PP 12-13. NEW YORK: ASSOCIATION ON
            AMERICAN INDIAN AFFAIRS, 1977.
     YEAR   1977
     DESC   FEDERAL GOVERNMENT+, ADOPTION AND FOSTER CARE+, FAMILY
            FUNCTIONING
     IDEN   U.S.

822 AUTH   BYLER, WILLIAM
     TITL   THE DESTRUCTION OF AMERICAN INDIAN FAMILIES.
     SOUR   IN STEVEN UNGER (ED.), THE DESTRUCTION OF AMERICAN
            INDIAN FAMILIES, PP 1-11. NEW YORK: ASSOCIATION ON
            AMERICAN INDIAN AFFAIRS, 1977.
     YEAR   1977
     DESC   ADOPTION AND FOSTER CARE+, FAMILY FUNCTIONING+,
            CHILDREN-SCHOOL AGE+, TRADITIONAL CHILD REARING+,
            EXTENDED FAMILY+, SOCIAL SERVICE PROFESSIONALS, CHILD
            ABUSE AND NEGLECT
     IDEN   U.S.

823 AUTH   BASSO, KEITH H.
     TITL   WESTERN APACHE WITCHCRAFT.
     SOUR   ANTHROPOLOGICAL PAPERS OF THE UNIVERSITY OF ARIZONA,
            NO. 15. TUCSON: UNIVERSITY OF ARIZONA PRESS, 1969.
            (75P)
     YEAR   1969
     DESC   WITCHCRAFT+, APACHE, SOUTHWEST, AGGRESSIVENESS, AGED,
            TRADITIONAL SOCIAL CONTROL
     IDEN   U.S., ARIZONA

824 AUTH   SLOTKIN, J.S.; MCALLESTER, DAVID P.
     TITL   MENOMINI PEYOTISM.
     SOUR   TRANSACTIONS OF THE AMERICAN PHILOSOPHICAL SOCIETY,
            DEC. 1952, V4(4), PP 565-700.
     YEAR   1952

DESC MENOMINEE, NORTHEAST WOODLAND, DRUG USE+, TRADITIONAL
USE OF DRUGS AND ALCOHOL+, NATIVE AMERICAN RELIGIONS+,
RESERVATION, RESEARCHERS+
IDEN U.S., WISCONSIN, MENOMINEE RESERVATION

825 AUTH KENNEDY, DONALD A.
    TITL EXPLORATIONS IN THE CROSS-CULTURAL STUDY OF MENTAL
DISORDERS.
    SOUR DISSERTATION ABSTRACTS INTERNATIONAL, JUL. 1959, V10,
PP 23-24.
    YEAR 1959
    DESC MENTAL DISORDERS+, NAVAJO, SOUTHWEST, MENTAL HEALTH
PROFESSIONALS+, NATIVE AMERICAN ETIOLOGY+
    IDEN U.S., NAVAJO RESERVATION

826 AUTH FISHER, CAROL A.
    TITL A SURVEY OF VANDALISM AND ITS CULTURAL ANTECEDENTS ON
FOUR NEW YORK STATE INDIAN RESERVATIONS.
    SOUR DISSERTATION ABSTRACTS INTERNATIONAL, JAN. 1960, V20,
PP 2489.
    YEAR 1960
    DESC RESERVATION, NORTHEAST WOODLAND, ADOLESCENTS+,
SOCIALLY DEVIANT BEHAVIOR+, IROQUOIS, TRADITIONAL
SOCIAL CONTROL, ROLE MODELS
    IDEN U.S., NEW YORK, CATTARAUGUS RESERVATION, ST. REGIS
RESERVATION, TONAWANDA RESERVATION, ONONDAGA
RESERVATION

827 AUTH WOLCOTT, HARRY F.
    TITL A KWAKIUTL VILLAGE AND ITS SCHOOL: CULTURAL BARRIERS
TO CLASSROOM PERFORMANCE.
    SOUR DISSERTATION ABSTRACTS INTERNATIONAL, JAN. 1965, V25,
PP 3791-3792.
    YEAR 1965
    DESC KWAKIUTL, NORTHWEST COAST, CHILDREN-SCHOOL AGE+,
ADOLESCENTS+, EDUCATION PROFESSIONALS+, PSYCHOLOGICAL
TESTING, STRESS, COMMUNITY INVOLVEMENT, SOCIAL ROLES,
ELEMENTARY SCHOOLS+, SECONDARY SCHOOLS+, LEARNING
DISABILITIES AND PROBLEMS+
    IDEN CANADA, BRITISH COLUMBIA

828 AUTH SPANG, ALONZO T.
    TITL INDIANNESS, WORK PREPARATION, AND GEOGRAPHIC MOBILITY
OF RESERVATION AND URBAN INDIANS.
    SOUR DISSERTATION ABSTRACTS INTERNATIONAL, MAR. 1973, V33,
P 4855A.
    YEAR 1973
    DESC ETHNIC IDENTITY+, RESERVATION, URBAN AREAS,
RELOCATION, EMPLOYMENT+, ADULTS, MALES, URBANIZATION
    IDEN U.S.

829 AUTH MCFEE, MALCOLM
    TITL MODERN BLACKFEET: CONTRASTING PATTERNS OF DIFFERENTIAL
ACCULTURATION.
    SOUR DISSERTATION ABSTRACTS INTERNATIONAL, MAY 1963, V23,

```
             PP 4066-4067.
      YEAR   1963
      DESC   BLACKFEET, PLAINS, RESERVATION, ADULTS, MALES, ETHNIC
             IDENTITY+, CULTURAL CONTINUITY+, CULTURAL ADAPTATION+
      IDEN   U.S., MONTANA

830   AUTH   BRIGGS, JEAN L.
      TITL   KAPLUMA DAUGHTER: LIVING WITH ESKIMOS.
      SOUR   TRANSACTION, JUN. 1970, V7(8), PP 12-24.
      YEAR   1970
      DESC   ESKIMO, CENTRAL AND EASTERN ARCTIC, ADOPTION AND
             FOSTER CARE+, RESEARCHERS+, FEMALES+, ADULTS+, SOCIAL
             ROLES+, STRESS+, TRADITIONAL SOCIAL CONTROL+,
             EMOTIONAL RESTRAINT+
      IDEN   CANADA

831   AUTH   CRUIKSHANK, JULIE
      TITL   NATIVE WOMEN IN THE NORTH: AN EXPANDING ROLE.
      SOUR   NORTH/NORD, NOV.-DEC. 1971, V18(6), PP 1-7.
      YEAR   1971
      DESC   FEMALES+, ADULTS+, SOCIAL ROLES+, SOCIAL STATUS,
             STRESS+, FAMILY FUNCTIONING, CULTURAL ADAPTATION+,
             YUKON SUB-ARCTIC, TRADITIONAL CHILD REARING+
      IDEN   CANADA

832   AUTH   CHADWICK, BRUCE A.; BAHR, HOWARD M.; STAUSS, JOSEPH H.
      TITL   INDIAN EDUCATION IN THE CITY: CORRELATES OF ACADEMIC
             PERFORMANCE.
      SOUR   JOURNAL OF EDUCATIONAL RESEARCH, JAN.-FEB. 1977,
             V70(3), PP 135-141.
      YEAR   1977
      DESC   URBAN AREAS, SELF-CONCEPT, ACHIEVEMENT+, MOTIVATION,
             DISCRIMINATION, FAMILY FUNCTIONING, STRESS, SECONDARY
             SCHOOLS+, ADOLESCENTS+, SEX DIFFERENCES
      IDEN   U.S., WASHINGTON

833   AUTH   GIORDANO, JOSEPH; GIORDANO, GRACE
      TITL   ETHNICITY AND COMMUNITY MENTAL HEALTH.
      SOUR   COMMUNITY MENTAL HEALTH REVIEW, 1976, V1(3), COVER
             PAGE, 4-26.
      YEAR   1976
      DESC   MENTAL HEALTH PROGRAMS AND SERVICES+, DELIVERY OF
             SERVICES+, ETHNIC IDENTITY+, ASIAN AMERICANS, BLACK
             AMERICANS, LATINOS, TRADITIONAL HEALERS, MENTAL HEALTH
             PROFESSIONALS, REVIEW OF LITERATURE
      IDEN   U.S.

834   AUTH   RED BIRD, AILEEN; MELENDY, PATRICK
      TITL   INDIAN CHILD WELFARE IN OREGON.
      SOUR   IN STEVEN UNGER (ED.), THE DESTRUCTION OF AMERICAN
             INDIAN FAMILIES, PP 43-46.  NEW YORK: ASSOCIATION ON
             AMERICAN INDIAN AFFAIRS, 1977.
      YEAR   1977
      DESC   EXTENDED FAMILY+, FAMILY FUNCTIONING+, SOCIAL
             SERVICES+, URBAN AREAS, NORTHWEST COAST, ADOPTION AND
```

```
          FOSTER CARE+, PLATEAU, RESERVATION
     IDEN  U.S., OREGON, WARM SPRINGS RESERVATION

835  AUTH  SPINDLER, GEORGE D.
     TITL  PERSONALITY AND PEYOTISM IN MENOMINI INDIAN
           ACCULTURATION.
     SOUR  PSYCHIATRY, 1952, V15, PP 151-159.
     YEAR  1952
     DESC  PERSONALITY TRAITS+, DRUG USE+, TRADITIONAL USE OF
           DRUGS AND ALCOHOL+, MENOMINEE, NORTHEAST WOODLAND,
           CULTURAL ADAPTATION+, ETHNIC IDENTITY+, NATIVE
           AMERICAN RELIGIONS, DREAMS AND VISION QUESTS,
           PSYCHOLOGICAL TESTING
     IDEN  U.S., WISCONSIN, RORSCHACH TEST

836  AUTH  TOBIN, PATRICIA L.; CLIFFORD, WILLIAM B.; MUSTIAN, R.
           DAVID; DAVIS, A. CLARKE
     TITL  VALUE OF CHILDREN AND FERTILITY IN A TRI-RACIAL RURAL
           COUNTY.
     SOUR  JOURNAL OF COMPARATIVE FAMILY STUDIES, SPR. 1975,
           V6(1), PP 46-55.
     YEAR  1975
     DESC  FAMILY PLANNING+, NATIVE-NON-NATIVE COMPARISONS, ANGLO
           AMERICANS, BLACK AMERICANS, SOUTHEAST WOODLAND,
           DEMOGRAPHIC DATA, SEX DIFFERENCES, GROUP NORMS AND
           SANCTIONS+
     IDEN  U.S., NORTH CAROLINA

837  AUTH  WHITE HOUSE CONFERENCE ON AGING, 1971
     TITL  REPORT OF THE SPECIAL CONCERNS SESSION ON THE ELDERLY
           INDIAN.
     SOUR  WASHINGTON, D.C.: GOVERNMENT PRINTING OFFICE, 1971.
     YEAR  1971
     DESC  AGED+, LEGAL ISSUES, PHYSICAL HEALTH AND ILLNESS,
           SOCIAL SERVICES, NUTRITIONAL FACTORS,
           INSTITUTIONALIZATION
     IDEN  U.S.

838  AUTH  MCDONALD, ARTHUR
     TITL  AMERICAN INDIAN COMMUNITY RESOURCE WORKER TRAINING.
     SOUR  IN RALPH SIMON, SAM SILVERSTEIN, AND BEATRICE M.
           SHRIVER (EDS.), EXPLORATION IN MENTAL HEALTH TRAINING,
           PP 36-37. (DHEW PUBLICATION NO. (ADM) 74-109)
           ROCKVILLE, MD: NATIONAL INSTITUTE OF MENTAL HEALTH,
           1975.
     YEAR  1975
     DESC  TRAINING PROGRAMS+, CHEYENNE-NORTHERN, MENTAL HEALTH
           PARAPROFESSIONALS+, PLAINS, COLLEGES AND UNIVERSITIES,
           NATIVE AMERICAN PERSONNEL+, MENTAL HEALTH PROGRAMS AND
           SERVICES, RESERVATION
     IDEN  U.S., MONTANA

839  AUTH  RATTRAY, RICHARD L.
     TITL  COMPREHENSIVE TREATMENT PROGRAMS FOR INDIAN PROBLEM
           DRINKERS.
```

```
       SOUR  (DHEW GRANT NO. 12-P-55241/7-02 (RD-2975-6F)).  DES
             MOINES, IOWA: OFFICE OF THE GOVERNOR, 1971.  (89P)
       YEAR  1971
       DESC  ALCOHOLISM TREATMENT+, ALCOHOL USE+, GROUP NORMS AND
             SANCTIONS,  URBAN AREAS, INSTITUTIONALIZATION,
             CHEMOTHERAPY, OUTPATIENT CARE, PSYCHOTHERAPY AND
             COUNSELING+, MENTAL HEALTH PARAPROFESSIONALS+,
             EMPLOYMENT, FAMILY FUNCTIONING, SELF-CONCEPT, TRAINING
             PROGRAMS
       IDEN  U.S., IOWA

840    AUTH  BROWN, R. CHRIS; GURUNANJAPPA, BALE A.; HAWK, RODNEY
             J.; BITSUIE, DELPHINE
       TITL  THE EPIDEMIOLOGY OF ACCIDENTS AMONG THE NAVAJO
             INDIANS.
       SOUR  PUBLIC HEALTH REPORTS, OCT. 1970, V85(10), PP 881-888.
       YEAR  1970
       DESC  ACCIDENTS+, EPIDEMIOLOGICAL STUDY, NAVAJO, SOUTHWEST,
             RESERVATION, I.H.S., AGE COMPARISONS, SEX DIFFERENCES
       IDEN  U.S., NAVAJO RESERVATION

841    AUTH  FARRIS, CHARLES E.
       TITL  THE AMERICAN INDIAN: SOCIAL WORK EDUCATION"S NEGLECTED
             MINORITY.
       SOUR  JOURNAL OF EDUCATION FOR SOCIAL WORK, SPR. 1975,
             V11(2), PP 37-43.
       YEAR  1975
       DESC  SOCIAL SERVICE PROFESSIONALS+, NATIVE AMERICAN
             PERSONNEL+, COLLEGES AND UNIVERSITIES+, ETHNIC
             IDENTITY+, EDUCATION PROGRAMS AND SERVICES+, ROLE
             MODELS, EDUCATION PROFESSIONALS+, NATIVE AMERICAN
             ADMINISTERED PROGRAMS
       IDEN  U.S.

842    AUTH  DIZMANG, LARRY H.
       TITL  OBSERVATIONS ON SUICIDAL BEHAVIOR AMONG THE
             SHOSHONE-BANNOCK INDIANS.
       SOUR  PAPER PRESENTED AT THE FIRST ANNUAL NATIONAL
             CONFERENCE ON SUICIDOLOGY, CHICAGO, MARCH 1968, (12P).
       YEAR  1968
       DESC  SUICIDE+, SHOSHONE, BANNOCK, PLATEAU, RESERVATION,
             ADOLESCENTS+, ALCOHOL USE, FAMILY FUNCTIONING,
             SELF-CONCEPT, CORRECTIONAL INSTITUTIONS, MENTAL HEALTH
             PROGRAMS AND SERVICES, NATIVE AMERICAN PERSONNEL
       IDEN  U.S., IDAHO, FORT HALL RESERVATION

843    AUTH  JOHNSON, DAVIS G.
       TITL  CONFERENCE ON INCREASING REPRESENTATION IN MEDICAL
             SCHOOLS OF AFRO-AMERICANS, MEXICAN-AMERICANS, AND
             AMERICAN INDIANS.
       SOUR  JOURNAL OF MEDICAL EDUCATION, AUG. 1969, V44, PP
             710-711.
       YEAR  1969
       DESC  COLLEGES AND UNIVERSITIES+, BLACK AMERICANS, LATINOS,
             EDUCATION PROGRAMS AND SERVICES+, NATIVE-NON-NATIVE
```

COMPARISONS

844 AUTH JENSEN, GARY F.; STAUSS, JOSEPH H.; HARRIS, V. WILLIAM
    TITL CRIME, DELINQUENCY, AND THE AMERICAN INDIAN.
    SOUR HUMAN ORGANIZATION, AUT. 1977, V36(3), PP 252-257.
    YEAR 1977
    DESC CRIME, ADOLESCENTS+, SOCIALLY DEVIANT BEHAVIOR+,
         CORRECTIONAL INSTITUTIONS, NATIVE-NON-NATIVE
         COMPARISONS, BLACK AMERICANS, ANGLO AMERICANS, ASIAN
         AMERICANS, LATINOS, CRIME, ALCOHOL USE, DRUG USE,
         INTERTRIBAL COMPARISONS, PUEBLO-HOPI, NAVAJO, APACHE,
         SOUTHWEST
    IDEN U.S.

845 AUTH KUNITZ, STEPHEN J.
    TITL UNDERDEVELOPMENT AND SOCIAL SERVICES ON THE NAVAJO
         RESERVATION.
    SOUR HUMAN ORGANIZATION, WIN. 1977, V36(4), PP 398-404.
    YEAR 1977
    DESC ECONOMIC ISSUES+, NAVAJO, SOUTHWEST, RESERVATION,
         SOCIAL SERVICES+, EMPLOYMENT+,
    IDEN U.S., NAVAJO RESERVATION

846 AUTH MCDONALD, THOMAS
    TITL GROUP PSYCHOTHERAPY WITH NATIVE AMERICAN WOMEN.
    SOUR INTERNATIONAL JOURNAL OF GROUP PSYCHOTHERAPY, OCT.
         1975, V25(4), PP 410-420.
    YEAR 1975
    DESC ADULTS+, FEMALES+, PSYCHOTHERAPY AND COUNSELING+,
         RELOCATION+, URBAN AREAS, SOCIAL GROUPS AND PEER
         GROUPS+, TRADITIONAL HEALERS
    IDEN U.S., CALIFORNIA

847 AUTH PARSONS, ELSIE CLEWS
    TITL TEWA MOTHERS AND CHILDREN.
    SOUR MAN, OCT. 1924, V24, PP 148-151.
    YEAR 1924
    DESC ADULTS+, FEMALES+, PUEBLO-TEWA, SOUTHWEST,
         CHILDREN-INFANTS AND PRESCHOOL+, TRADITIONAL CHILD
         REARING+
    IDEN U.S., NEW MEXICO

848 AUTH PARSONS, ELSIE CLEWS
    TITL MOTHERS AND CHILDREN AT ZUNI, NEW MEXICO.
    SOUR MAN, NOV. 1919, V19, PP 168-173.
    YEAR 1919
    DESC PUEBLO-ZUNI, SOUTHWEST, FEMALES+, ADULTS+,
         CHILDREN-INFANTS AND PRESCHOOL+, TRADITIONAL CHILD
         REARING+
    IDEN U.S., NEW MEXICO

849 AUTH EWERS, JOHN C.
    TITL DEADLIER THAN THE MALE.
    SOUR AMERICAN HERITAGE, JUN. 1965, V16(4), PP 10-13.
    YEAR 1965

```
      DESC  FEMALES+, ADULTS+, SOCIAL ROLES+, GROUP NORMS AND
            SANCTIONS, AGGRESSIVENESS+, PLAINS, BLACKFEET, CROW

850   AUTH  HALLOWELL, A. IRVING
      TITL  SHABWAN: A DISSOCIAL INDIAN GIRL.
      SOUR  AMERICAN JOURNAL OF ORTHOPSYCHIATRY, APR. 1938, V8(2),
            PP 329-340.
      YEAR  1938
      DESC  CHIPPEWA, EASTERN SUB-ARCTIC, FEMALES+, ADOLESCENTS+,
            SOCIALLY DEVIANT BEHAVIOR+, MENTAL DISORDERS,
            CULTURE-BASED PSYCHOTHERAPY+
      IDEN  CANADA

851   AUTH  ALILKATUKTUK, JEELA
      TITL  CANADA: STRANGER IN MY OWN LAND.
      SOUR  MS., FEB. 1974, V2(8), PP 8-10.
      YEAR  1974
      DESC  ESKIMO, CENTRAL AND EASTERN ARCTIC, FEMALES+, ADULTS+,
            CULTURAL ADAPTATION+, CULTURAL CONTINUITY+,
            RESERVATION
      IDEN  CANADA, NORTHWEST TERRITORIES

852   AUTH  SANDNER, DONALD F.
      TITL  NAVAJO MEDICINE.
      SOUR  HUMAN NATURE, JUL. 1978, V1(7), PP 54-62.
      YEAR  1978
      DESC  NAVAJO, SOUTHWEST, TRADITIONAL HEALERS+, MEDICAL
            PROFESSIONALS, CULTURE-BASED PSYCHOTHERAPY+, UNIVERSAL
            HARMONY+, RESERVATION
      IDEN  U.S., NAVAJO RESERVATION

853   AUTH  GRINDSTAFF, CARL F.; GALLOWAY, F.; NIXON, WILDA;
            NIXON, JOANNE
      TITL  RACIAL AND CULTURAL IDENTIFICATION AMONG CANADIAN
            INDIAN CHILDREN.
      SOUR  PHYLON, DEC. 1973, V34(4), PP 368-377.
      YEAR  1973
      DESC  CHILDREN-SCHOOL AGE+, ETHNIC IDENTITY+,
            CHILDREN-INFANTS AND PRESCHOOL+, DISCRIMINATION+,
            PSYCHOLOGICAL TESTING+, STEREOTYPES+, SELF-CONCEPT+,
            RESERVATION, ELEMENTARY SCHOOLS+
      IDEN  CANADA, ONTARIO

854   AUTH  BAXTER, CAROL
      TITL  TRAINING AMERICAN INDIANS FOR URBAN MENTAL HEALTH
            SETTINGS.
      SOUR  IN RALPH SIMON, SAM SILVERSTEIN, AND BEATRICE M.
            SHRIVER (EDS.), EXPLORATION IN MENTAL HEALTH TRAINING,
            PP 33-34. (DHEW PUBLICATION NO. (ADM) 74-109)
            ROCKVILLE, MD: NATIONAL INSTITUTE OF MENTAL HEALTH,
            1975.
      YEAR  1975
      DESC  MENTAL HEALTH PROGRAMS AND SERVICES+, TRAINING
            PROGRAMS+, MENTAL HEALTH PARAPROFESSIONALS+, URBAN
            AREAS, PROGRAM EVALUATION
```

```
       IDEN   U.S., CALIFORNIA

855    AUTH   ERIKSON, ERIK H.
       TITL   HUNTERS ACROSS THE PRAIRIE.
       SOUR   CHAPTER IN CHILDHOOD AND SOCIETY, PP 114-165.  NEW
              YORK: W.W. NORTON + CO., 1963.
       YEAR   1963
       DESC   SIOUX-OGLALA, PLAINS, RESERVATION, TRADITIONAL CHILD
              REARING+, PASSIVE RESISTANCE, CHILDREN-INFANTS AND
              PRESCHOOL+, CHILDREN-SCHOOL AGE+, GENEROSITY, STRESS+,
              MALES+, FEMALES+, SOCIAL ROLES+, DREAMS AND VISION
              QUESTS, ADOLESCENTS+
       IDEN   U.S., SOUTH DAKOTA, PINE RIDGE RESERVATION

856    AUTH   ERIKSON, ERIK H.
       TITL   FISHERMAN ALONG A SALMON RIVER.
       SOUR   CHAPTER IN CHILDHOOD AND SOCIETY, PP 166-186.  NEW
              YORK: W.W. NORTON + CO., 1963.
       YEAR   1963
       DESC   YUROK, NORTHWEST COAST, TRADITIONAL HEALERS,
              CHILDREN-SCHOOL AGE+, TRADITIONAL CHILD REARING+,
              CHILDREN-INFANTS AND PRESCHOOL+, NEUROSES, EMOTIONAL
              RESTRAINT, ECONOMIC ISSUES
       IDEN   U.S., CALIFORNIA

857    AUTH   RYAN, CHARLES W.
       TITL   COUNSELING THE CULTURALLY ENCAPSULATED AMERICAN
              INDIAN.
       SOUR   VOCATIONAL GUIDANCE QUARTERLY, DEC. 1969, V18, PP
              123-126.
       YEAR   1969
       DESC   PSYCHOTHERAPY AND COUNSELING+, ADOLESCENTS, TRAINING
              PROGRAMS, EDUCATION PROGRAMS AND SERVICES, ETHNIC
              IDENTITY+, PROGRAM DEVELOPMENT+
       IDEN   U.S.

858    AUTH   BRANDON, WILLIAM
       TITL   AMERICAN INDIANS: THE ALIEN AMERICANS.
       SOUR   PROGRESSIVE, DEC. 1969, V33, PP 13-17.
       YEAR   1969
       DESC   POLITICS-NONTRIBAL+, ECONOMIC ISSUES+, LEGAL ISSUES+,
              RESERVATION, CULTURAL CONTINUITY+, DISCRIMINATION+
       IDEN   U.S.

859    AUTH   SCHOTTSTAEDT, MARY F.; BJORK, JOHN W.
       TITL   INHALANT ABUSE IN AN INDIAN BOARDING SCHOOL
       SOUR   AMERICAN JOURNAL OF PSYCHIATRY, NOV. 1977, V134(11),
              PP 1290-1293.
       YEAR   1977
       DESC   DRUG USE+, ELEMENTARY SCHOOLS+, CHILDREN-SCHOOL AGE+,
              B.I.A. BOARDING SCHOOLS+, PLAINS, PREVENTIVE MENTAL
              HEALTH PROGRAMS+
       IDEN   U.S., OKLAHOMA

860    AUTH   FARRIS, CHARLES E.; FARRIS, LORENE S.
```

```
        TITL   INDIAN CHILDREN: THE STRUGGLE FOR SURVIVAL.
        SOUR   SOCIAL WORK, SEP. 1976, V21, PP 386-389.
        YEAR   1976
        DESC   CHILDREN-INFANTS AND PRESCHOOL+, CHILDREN-SCHOOL AGE+,
               SOCIAL SERVICE PROFESSIONALS+, NATIVE AMERICAN
               PERSONNEL, ETHNIC IDENTITY, DELIVERY OF SERVICES+,
               ADOPTION AND FOSTER CARE
        IDEN   U.S.

861     AUTH   CINGOLANI, WILLIAM
        TITL   ACCULTURATING THE INDIAN: FEDERAL POLICIES, 1834-1973.
        SOUR   SOCIAL WORK, NOV. 1973, V18(6), PP 24-28.
        YEAR   1973
        DESC   FEDERAL GOVERNMENT+, B.I.A.,  STRESS, CULTURAL
               CONTINUITY, ADMINISTRATIVE ISSUES+
        IDEN   U.S.

862     AUTH   LEWIS, RONALD G.; HO, MAN KEUNG
        TITL   SOCIAL WORK WITH NATIVE AMERICANS.
        SOUR   SOCIAL WORK, SEP. 1975, V20, PP 379-382.
        YEAR   1975
        DESC   SOCIAL SERVICE PROFESSIONALS+, NATIVE AMERICAN
               VALUES+, TIME PERCEPTION, EMOTIONAL RESTRAINT,
               NONINTERFERENCE+, SOCIAL GROUPS AND PEER GROUPS,
               PSYCHOTHERAPY AND COUNSELING
        IDEN   U.S.

863     AUTH   VAN LEEUWEN, MARY STEWART
        TITL   A CROSS-CULTURAL EXAMINATION OF PSYCHOLOGICAL
               DIFFERENTIATION IN MALES AND FEMALES.
        SOUR   INTERNATIONAL JOURNAL OF PSYCHOLOGY, 1978, V13(2), PP
               87-122.
        YEAR   1978
        DESC   COGNITIVE PROCESSES+, SEX DIFFERENCES, PSYCHOLOGICAL
               TESTING, REVIEW OF LITERATURE, NATIVE-NON-NATIVE
               COMPARISONS, MALES+, FEMALES+, TRADITIONAL CHILD
               REARING+, ENVIRONMENTAL FACTORS+, SOCIAL ROLES+
        IDEN   EMBEDDED FIGURE TEST, ROD AND FRAME TEST, BODY
               ADJUSTMENT TEST, HUMAN FIGURE DRAWING TEST

864     AUTH   JILEK, WOLFGANG G.; ROY, CHUNILAL
        TITL   HOMICIDE COMMITTED BY CANADIAN INDIANS AND
               NON-INDIANS.
        SOUR   INTERNATIONAL JOURNAL OF OFFENDER THERAPY AND
               COMPARATIVE CRIMINOLOGY, V20(3), 1976.
        YEAR   1976
        DESC   CRIME+, ADULTS, ALCOHOL USE, CORRECTIONAL
               INSTITUTIONS+, EPIDEMIOLOGICAL STUDY,
               NATIVE-NON-NATIVE COMPARISONS, ANGLO AMERICANS
        IDEN   CANADA, BRITISH COLUMBIA

865     AUTH   PERKINS, ANNE E.
        TITL   PSYCHOSIS OF THE AMERICAN INDIANS ADMITTED TO GOWANDA
               STATE HOSPITAL.
        SOUR   PSYCHIATRIC QUARTERLY, 1927, V1, PP 335-343.
```

```
        YEAR  1927
        DESC  IROQUOIS-SENECA, NORTHEAST WOODLAND, MENTAL HEALTH
              INSTITUTIONS+, RESERVATION, PSYCHOSES, MENTAL
              DISORDERS, DEPRESSION+, INSTITUTIONALIZATION,  GRIEF
              REACTION
        IDEN  U.S., NEW YORK, ALLEGANNY RESERVATION, CATTARAUGUS
              RESERVATION

866  AUTH  SPEISER, ABRAHAM M.
     TITL  ANOTHER CULTURE, ANOTHER TIME.
     SOUR  JOURNAL OF AMERICAN GERIATRIC SOCIETY, DEC. 1974, V22,
           PP 551-552.
     YEAR  1974
     DESC  I.H.S., AGED+, NAVAJO, SOUTHWEST, PHYSICAL HEALTH AND
           ILLNESS+, MEDICAL PROFESSIONALS+, DELIVERY OF
           SERVICES+, RESERVATION
     IDEN  U.S., NAVAJO RESERVATION

867  AUTH  PFISTER, OSKAR
     TITL  INSTINCTIVE PSYCHOANALYSIS AMONG THE NAVAJOS.
     SOUR  JOURNAL OF NERVOUS AND MENTAL DISEASE, 1932, V76, PP
           234-254.
     YEAR  1932
     DESC  NAVAJO, SOUTHWEST, CULTURE-BASED PSYCHOTHERAPY+,
           RESERVATION, DEPRESSION, PSYCHOANALYSIS+, TRADITIONAL
           HEALERS+, NATIVE AMERICAN RELIGIONS
     IDEN  U.S., NAVAJO RESERVATION

868  AUTH  HUNTER, WALTER S.; SOMMERMIER, ELOISE
     TITL  THE RELATIONS OF DEGREE OF INDIAN BLOOD TO SCORE ON
           THE OTIS INTELLIGENCE TEST.
     SOUR  JOURNAL OF COMPARATIVE PSYCHOLOGY, 1922, V2, PP
           257-277.
     YEAR  1922
     DESC  PSYCHOLOGICAL TESTING+, ABILITIES+, B.I.A. BOARDING
           SCHOOLS, FULL BLOOD-MIXED BLOOD COMPARISONS,
           CHILDREN-SCHOOL AGE, ADOLESCENTS, NATIVE-NON-NATIVE
           COMPARISONS, AGE COMPARISONS, SEX DIFFERENCES, ANGLO
           AMERICANS
     IDEN  U.S., HASKELL INSTITUTE, OTIS GROUP INTELLIGENCE TEST,
           KANSAS

869  AUTH  NASH, PHILLEO
     TITL  THE PLACE OF RELIGIOUS REVIVALISM IN THE FORMATION OF
           THE INTERCULTURAL COMMUNITY ON KLAMATH RESERVATION.
     SOUR  IN FRIEDRICH RUSSELL EGGAN (ED.), SOCIAL ANTHROPOLOGY
           OF NORTH AMERICAN TRIBES, PP. 375-442.  CHICAGO:
           UNIVERSITY OF CHICAGO PRESS, 1955.
     YEAR  1955
     DESC  KLAMATH, PLATEAU, CULTURAL REVIVAL+, NATIVE AMERICAN
           RELIGIONS+, RESERVATION, MODOC, STRESS
     IDEN  U.S., KLAMATH RESERVATION, GHOST DANCE, OREGON,
           CALIFORNIA, PROPHET DANCE

870  AUTH  NATIONAL INDIAN CONFERENCE ON AGING
```

```
        TITL  NATIONAL INDIAN CONFERENCE ON AGING: SUMMARY REPORT.
        SOUR  CONFERENCE SPONSORED BY THE NATIONAL TRIBAL CHAIRMEN"S
              ASSOCIATION, PHOENIX, JUNE 1976.  (61P)
        YEAR  1976
        DESC  AGED+, ECONOMIC ISSUES, INSTITUTIONALIZATION, LEGAL
              ISSUES, PHYSICAL HEALTH AND ILLNESS, NUTRITIONAL
              FACTORS, SOCIAL SERVICES
        IDEN  U.S.

871     AUTH  ALLEN, VIRGINIA R.
        TITL  THE WHITE MAN"S ROAD: THE PHYSICAL AND PSYCHOLOGICAL
              IMPACT OF RELOCATION ON THE SOUTHERN PLAINS INDIANS.
        SOUR  JOURNAL OF THE HISTORY OF MEDICINE, APR. 1975, V30, PP
              148-163.
        YEAR  1975
        DESC  RELOCATION+, PLAINS, B.I.A., FEDERAL GOVERNMENT,
              STRESS+, RESERVATION, PHYSICAL HEALTH AND ILLNESS
        IDEN  U.S.

872     AUTH  POSTAL, SUSAN KOESSLER
        TITL  BODY-IMAGE AND IDENTITY: A COMPARISON OF KWAKIUTL AND
              HOPI.
        SOUR  AMERICAN ANTHROPOLOGIST, 1965, V67, PP 455-462.
        YEAR  1965
        DESC  KWAKIUTL, NORTHWEST COAST, PUEBLO-HOPI, SOUTHWEST,
              SELF-CONCEPT+, PERSONALITY TRAITS+, COGNITIVE
              PROCESSES+
        IDEN  U.S., NEW MEXICO, CANADA, BRITISH COLUMBIA

873     AUTH  WALLACE, BEN J.
        TITL  OKLAHOMA KICKAPOO CULTURE CHANGE.
        SOUR  PLAINS ANTHROPOLOGIST, 1969, V14, PP 107-112.
        YEAR  1969
        DESC  KICKAPOO, PRAIRIE, OFF-RESERVATION, CULTURAL
              ADAPTATION+, CULTURAL CONTINUITY+, NATIVE AMERICAN
              RELIGIONS+, ETHNIC IDENTITY+, POW-WOWS
        IDEN  U.S., OKLAHOMA

874     AUTH  MCCONE, R. CLYDE
        TITL  DEATH AND THE PERSISTENCE OF BASIC PERSONALITY
              STRUCTURE AMONG THE LAKOTA.
        SOUR  PLAINS ANTHROPOLOGIST, 1968, V13, PP 305-309.
        YEAR  1968
        DESC  SIOUX, PLAINS, DEATH AND DYING+, TIME PERCEPTION,
              NATIVE AMERICAN RELIGIONS+, POW-WOWS+, RESERVATION
        IDEN  U.S., SOUTH DAKOTA, CHEYENNE RIVER RESERVATION,
              ROSEBUD RESERVATION, PINE RIDGE RESERVATION

875     AUTH  PASCAROSA, PAUL; FUTTERMAN, SANFORD; HALSWEIG, MARK
        TITL  OBSERVATIONS OF ALCOHOLICS IN THE PEYOTE RITUAL: A
              PILOT STUDY.
        SOUR  ANNALS OF THE NEW YORK ACADEMY OF SCIENCES, 1976,
              V273, PP 518-524.
        YEAR  1976
        DESC  PLAINS, NATIVE AMERICAN RELIGIONS+, ALCOHOL USE, DRUG
```

```
                  USE+, TRADITIONAL USE OF DRUGS AND ALCOHOL+,
                  ALCOHOLISM TREATMENT+, CULTURE-BASED PSYCHOTHERAPY+
          IDEN    U.S., NATIVE AMERICAN CHURCH

876   AUTH    EDGERTON, ROBERT B.
      TITL    SOME DIMENSIONS OF DISILLUSIONMENT IN CULTURE CONTACT.
      SOUR    SOUTHWESTERN JOURNAL OF ANTHROPOLOGY, 1965, V21, PP
              231-243.
      YEAR    1965
      DESC    MENOMINEE, NORTHEAST WOODLAND, CULTURAL ADAPTATION+,
              SOCIAL STATUS+, STEREOTYPES+, SOCIAL ROLES+, STRESS+,
              RESEARCHERS
      IDEN    U.S., WISCONSIN

877   AUTH    BERRY, BREWTON
      TITL    THE MYTH OF THE VANISHING INDIAN.
      SOUR    PHYLON, 1960, V21, PP 51-57.
      YEAR    1960
      DESC    STEREOTYPES+, DEMOGRAPHIC DATA, CULTURAL ADAPTATION+,
              LUMBEE, SOUTHEAST WOODLAND
      IDEN    U.S.

878   AUTH    LEVINE, STUART
      TITL    OUR INDIAN MINORITY.
      SOUR    COLORADO QUARTERLY, 1968, V16, PP 297-320.
      YEAR    1968
      DESC    ETHNIC IDENTITY+, POW-WOWS, FEDERAL GOVERNMENT,
              B.I.A., TRIBAL POLITICAL ORGANIZATIONS+, NATIVE
              AMERICAN POLITICAL MOVEMENTS+, ECONOMIC ISSUES,
              CULTURAL CONTINUITY, CULTURAL ADAPTATION
      IDEN    U.S.

879   AUTH    MANBECK, JOHN B.
      TITL    AMERICAN INDIANS AND LAPPS: A COMPARATIVE STUDY.
      SOUR    AMERICAN SCANDINAVIAN REVIEW, 1971, V59, PP 365-373.
      YEAR    1971
      DESC    NATIVE-NON-NATIVE COMPARISONS, CULTURAL ADAPTATION+
      IDEN    U.S., EUROPE, LAPPS

880   AUTH    SPICER, EDWARD H.
      TITL    THE ISSUES IN INDIAN AFFAIRS.
      SOUR    ARIZONA QUARTERLY, 1965, V21, PP 293-307.
      YEAR    1965
      DESC    ETHNIC IDENTITY+, FEDERAL GOVERNMENT+, TRIBAL
              POLITICAL ORGANIZATIONS+, POWERLESSNESS+, B.I.A.+,
              RESERVATION, ADMINISTRATIVE ISSUES+, CULTURAL
              ADAPTATION+, CULTURAL CONTINUITY+
      IDEN    U.S.

881   AUTH    BERKHOFER, ROBERT F.
      TITL    PROTESTANTS, PAGANS, AND SEQUENCES AMONG THE NORTH
              AMERICAN INDIANS, 1760-1860.
      SOUR    ETHNOHISTORY, SUM. 1963, V10(3), PP 201-232.
      YEAR    1963
      DESC    RELIGIONS-NON-NATIVE+, NATIVE AMERICAN RELIGIONS,
```

RELIGIOUS-NON-NATIVE PERSONNEL+, STRESS+, TRIBAL
POLITICAL ORGANIZATIONS+
IDEN   U.S.

882 AUTH COOK, SHERBURNE F.
     TITL MIGRATION AND URBANIZATION OF THE INDIANS OF
           CALIFORNIA.
     SOUR HUMAN BIOLOGY, 1943, V15, PP 33-45.
     YEAR 1943
     DESC CALIFORNIA AREA, RELOCATION+, CULTURAL ADAPTATION+,
           DEMOGRAPHIC DATA, URBAN AREAS, OFF-RESERVATION, AGE
           COMPARISONS, SEX DIFFERENCES, FULL BLOOD-MIXED BLOOD
           COMPARISONS, GREAT BASIN, NORTHWEST COAST,
           URBANIZATION+
     IDEN U.S., CALIFORNIA

883 AUTH BARNOUW, VICTOR
     TITL A PSYCHOLOGICAL INTERPRETATION OF CHIPPEWA ORIGIN
           LEGEND.
     SOUR JOURNAL OF AMERICAN FOLKLORE, 1955, V68, PP 73-85,
           211-223, 341-355.
     YEAR 1955
     DESC CHIPPEWA, EASTERN SUB-ARCTIC, PERSONALITY TRAITS+,
           DREAMS AND VISION QUESTS+, PARANOIA, ANXIETY,
           AGGRESSIVENESS, PSYCHOANALYSIS
     IDEN U.S., WISCONSIN

884 AUTH SHEPARDSON, MARY
     TITL PROBLEMS OF THE NAVAJO TRIBAL COURTS IN TRANSITION.
     SOUR HUMAN ORGANIZATION, 1965, V24, PP 250-253.
     YEAR 1965
     DESC LEGAL ISSUES+, CORRECTIONAL INSTITUTIONS+, NAVAJO,
           SOUTHWEST, RESERVATION, FEDERAL GOVERNMENT, GROUP
           NORMS AND SANCTIONS+, TRADITIONAL SOCIAL 'CONTROL+,
           NATIVE AMERICAN ADMINISTERED PROGRAMS+, UNIVERSAL
           HARMONY, TRIBAL POLITICAL ORGANIZATIONS+, COMMUNITY
           INVOLVEMENT+
     IDEN U.S., NAVAJO RESERVATION, NAVAJO TRIBAL COURTS

885 AUTH MACNEISH, JUNE HELM
     TITL LEADERSHIP AMONG THE NORTHEASTERN ATHABASCANS.
     SOUR ANTHROPOLOGICA, 1956, V2, PP 131-163.
     YEAR 1956
     DESC LEADERSHIP+, ATHABASCAN, MACKENZIE SUB-ARCTIC, SLAVE,
           DOGRIB, HARE, CHIPEWYAN, YELLOWKNIFE, TRIBAL POLITICAL
           ORGANIZATIONS+, AGED, MALES, ADULTS, SOCIAL GROUPS AND
           PEER GROUPS+
     IDEN CANADA

886 AUTH BRAROE, NIELS W.
     TITL RECIPROCAL EXPLOITATION IN AN INDIAN-WHITE COMMUNITY.
     SOUR SOUTHWESTERN JOURNAL OF ANTHROPOLOGY, 1965, V21, PP
           166-178.
     YEAR 1965
     DESC SOCIAL ROLES+, SELF-CONCEPT+, RESERVATION,

```
                    DISCRIMINATION+, ANGLO AMERICANS, STEREOTYPES+,
                    NATIVE-NON-NATIVE COMPARISONS, CREE, PLAINS, ADULTS,
                    NATIVE AMERICAN COPING BEHAVIORS+
          IDEN      CANADA, SASKATCHEWAN

887    AUTH    ABERLE, DAVID F.
       TITL    SOME SOURCES OF FLEXIBILITY IN NAVAJO SOCIAL
               ORGANIZATION.
       SOUR    SOUTHWESTERN JOURNAL OF ANTHROPOLOGY, SPR. 1963,
               V19(1), PP 1-8.
       YEAR    1963
       DESC    CULTURAL ADAPTATION+, ENVIRONMENTAL FACTORS+, NAVAJO,
               SOUTHWEST, NATIVE AMERICAN COPING BEHAVIORS+,
               RESERVATION, RELOCATION
       IDEN    U.S., NAVAJO RESERVATION

888    AUTH    GARTH, THOMAS R.
       TITL    EMPHASIS ON INDUSTRIOUSNESS AMONG THE ATSUGEWI.
       SOUR    AMERICAN ANTHROPOLOGIST, 1945, V47, PP 554-566.
       YEAR    1945
       DESC    ATSUGEWI, CALIFORNIA AREA, LEADERSHIP+, SOCIAL
               STATUS+, NATIVE AMERICAN VALUES+, DREAMS AND VISION
               QUESTS+, MOTIVATION+
       IDEN    U.S., CALIFORNIA

889    AUTH    KOOLAGE, WILLIAM W.
       TITL    CONCEPTUAL NEGATIVISM IN CHIPEWYAN ETHNOLOGY.
       SOUR    ANTHROPOLOGICA, 1975, V17, PP 45-60
       YEAR    1975
       DESC    CHIPEWYAN, MACKENZIE SUB-ARCTIC, CULTURAL ADAPTATION+,
               RESEARCHERS+, STEREOTYPES+
       IDEN    CANADA

890    AUTH    CASE, CHARLES
       TITL    BLESSING WAY, THE CORE RITUAL OF NAVAJO CEREMONY.
       SOUR    PLATEAU, AUT. 1968, V41, PP 35-42.
       YEAR    1968
       DESC    NAVAJO, SOUTHWEST, NATIVE AMERICAN RELIGIONS+,
               TRADITIONAL HEALERS+, RESERVATION
       IDEN    U.S., NAVAJO RESERVATION

891    AUTH    BARNOUW, VICTOR
       TITL    THE PHANTASY WORLD OF A CHIPPEWA WOMAN.
       SOUR    PSYCHIATRY, 1949, V12, PP 67-76.
       YEAR    1949
       DESC    CHIPPEWA, EASTERN SUB-ARCTIC, FEMALES+, ADULTS+,
               PERSONALITY TRAITS+, TRADITIONAL HEALERS, DREAMS AND
               VISION QUESTS+, SCHIZOPHRENIA+
       IDEN    U.S., WISCONSIN

892    AUTH    EMERSON, GLORIA J.
       TITL    THE LAUGHING BOY SYNDROME.
       SOUR    SCHOOL REVIEW, NOV. 1970, V79, PP 94-98.
       YEAR    1970
       DESC    NAVAJO, SOUTHWEST, EDUCATION PROGRAMS AND SERVICES+,
```

```
              PROGRAM EVALUATION+, RESERVATION, RESEARCHERS+,
              ELEMENTARY SCHOOLS+, ADMINISTRATIVE ISSUES+,
              BICULTURALISM, NATIVE AMERICAN ADMINISTERED PROGRAMS+
      IDEN    U.S., ARIZONA, ROUGH ROCK DEMONSTRATION SCHOOL

893   AUTH    MUSKRAT, JOSEPH
      TITL    THE NEED FOR CULTURAL EMPATHY.
      SOUR    SCHOOL REVIEW, NOV. 1970, V79, PP 72-75.
      YEAR    1970
      DESC    EDUCATION PROGRAMS AND SERVICES+, EDUCATION
              PROFESSIONALS, BICULTURALISM+, NAVAJO, SOUTHWEST,
              NATIVE AMERICAN ADMINISTERED PROGRAMS+, ELEMENTARY
              SCHOOLS+, NATIVE AMERICAN PERSONNEL, COMMUNITY
              INVOLVEMENT, RESEARCHERS+, RESERVATION, ADMINISTRATIVE
              ISSUES
      IDEN    U.S., ARIZONA, ROUGH ROCK DEMONSTRATION SCHOOL

894   AUTH    COCKERHAM, WILLIAM C.
      TITL    PATTERNS OF ALCOHOL AND MULTIPLE DRUG USE AMONG RURAL
              WHITE AND AMERICAN INDIAN ADOLESCENTS.
      SOUR    INTERNATIONAL JOURNAL OF THE ADDICTIONS, 1977,
              V12(2-3), PP 271-285.
      YEAR    1977
      DESC    ALCOHOL USE+, DRUG USE+, ADOLESCENTS+,
              OFF-RESERVATION, NATIVE-NON-NATIVE COMPARISONS, ANGLO
              AMERICANS, RESERVATION, ARAPAHO-NORTHERN, SHOSHONE
      IDEN    U.S., WYOMING, WIND RIVER RESERVATION

895   AUTH    BLANCHARD, EVELYN
      TITL    CHILD WELFARE SERVICES TO INDIAN PEOPLES IN THE
              ALBUQUERQUE AREA.
      SOUR    IN STEVEN UNGER (ED.), THE DESTRUCTION OF AMERICAN
              INDIAN FAMILIES, PP 37-42.  NEW YORK: ASSOCIATION ON
              AMERICAN INDIAN AFFAIRS, 1977.
      YEAR    1977
      DESC    SOCIAL SERVICES+, CHILDREN-SCHOOL AGE+, ADOPTION AND
              FOSTER CARE+, SOCIAL SERVICE PROFESSIONALS+, NATIVE
              AMERICAN ADMINISTERED PROGRAMS+, NATIVE AMERICAN
              PERSONNEL+, DELIVERY OF SERVICES+
      IDEN    U.S.

896   AUTH    PLATZ, DONALD L.
      TITL    FANTASY PREDISPOSITION, PLAY PREFERENCE AND EARLY HOME
              EXPERIENCE OF WHITE AND NAVAJO KINDERGARTEN CHILDREN.
      SOUR    DISSERTATION ABSTRACTS INTERNATIONAL, JUL.-AUG. 1977,
              V38(1), P 105A.
      YEAR    1977
      DESC    NAVAJO, SOUTHWEST, CHILDREN-INFANTS AND PRESCHOOL+,
              NATIVE-NON-NATIVE COMPARISONS, ANGLO AMERICANS,
              PSYCHOLOGICAL TESTING+, LEARNING
      IDEN    U.S., ARIZONA, RORSCHACH TEST, PLAY PREFERENCE
              INVENTORY, CHILD SURVEY

897   AUTH    SHIPP, PATRICK E.
      TITL    A COMPARATIVE STUDY OF THIRD GRADE PERFORMANCE IN THE
```

EASTERN NAVAJO AGENCY B.I.A. SCHOOLS.
SOUR DISSERTATION ABSTRACTS INTERNATIONAL, JUN. 1977,
V37(12), PP 7462A-7463A.
YEAR 1977
DESC EDUCATION PROGRAMS AND SERVICES+, PROGRAM EVALUATION+,
NAVAJO, SOUTHWEST, ELEMENTARY SCHOOLS, B.I.A. BOARDING
SCHOOLS, CHILDREN-SCHOOL AGE+, EXPERIMENTAL STUDY,
PSYCHOLOGICAL TESTING+, ACHIEVEMENT+
IDEN U.S., NEW MEXICO, CALIFORNIA ACHIEVEMENT TEST

898 AUTH GOODLUCK, CHARLOTTE T.; ECKSTEIN, FLORENCE
TITL INDIAN ADOPTION PROGRAM: AN ETHNIC APPROACH TO CHILD
WELFARE.
SOUR PAPER PRESENTED AT THE 54TH ANNUAL MEETING OF THE
AMERICAN ORTHOPSYCHIATRIC ASSOCIATION, NEW YORK, APR.
1977. (15P)
YEAR 1977
DESC CHILDREN-INFANTS AND PRESCHOOL, CHILDREN-SCHOOL AGE,
ADOPTION AND FOSTER CARE+, EXTENDED FAMILY, SOCIAL
SERVICES+, FAMILY FUNCTIONING, ETHNIC IDENTITY+
IDEN U.S., ARIZONA, INDIAN ADOPTION PROGRAM

899 AUTH REED, WILLIAM H.
TITL A STUDY OF HIGH SCHOOL STUDENT"S ATTITUDE CORRELATES
WITH SCHOLASTIC PERFORMANCE, ETHNICITY, SEX, AND
PERSONALITY TYPE.
SOUR DISSERTATION ABSTRACTS INTERNATIONAL, JUN. 1977, V37,
P 7670A.
YEAR 1977
DESC ADOLESCENTS+, SECONDARY SCHOOLS+, NATIVE-NON-NATIVE
COMPARISONS, ANGLO AMERICANS, PSYCHOLOGICAL TESTING+,
B.I.A. BOARDING SCHOOLS, ACHIEVEMENT, ATTITUDES+
IDEN U.S., MYERS BRIGGS TYPE INDICATOR

900 AUTH GUSSOW, ZACHARY
TITL PIBLOKTOG (HYSTERIA) AMONG THE POLAR ESKIMO: AN
ETHNOPSYCHIATRIC STUDY.
SOUR PSYCHOANALYTIC STUDY OF SOCIETY, 1960, V1, PP 218-236.
YEAR 1960
DESC ESKIMO, CENTRAL AND EASTERN ARCTIC, ARCTIC HYSTERIA+,
ENVIRONMENTAL FACTORS, ANXIETY+, POWERLESSNESS+,
OFF-RESERVATION
IDEN CANADA

901 AUTH WALLIS, RUTH S.
TITL THE OVERT FEARS OF DAKOTA INDIAN CHILDREN.
SOUR CHILD DEVELOPMENT, 1954, V25(3), PP 185-192.
YEAR 1954
DESC TRADITIONAL CHILD REARING+, SIOUX, PLAINS, TRADITIONAL
SOCIAL CONTROL+, CHILDREN-INFANTS AND PRESCHOOL+,
CHILDREN-SCHOOL AGE+
IDEN U.S., CANADA, MANITOBA, MINNESOTA

902 AUTH ALLARD, IRENE
TITL NATIVE WOMEN AND SELF ESTEEM.

```
        SOUR   PAPER PRESENTED AT THE ANNUAL MEETING OF THE AMERICAN
               PSYCHIATRIC ASSOCIATION, TORONTO, MAY 1977.  (12P)
        YEAR   1977
        DESC   FEMALES+, ADULTS+, NATIVE AMERICAN COPING BEHAVIORS+,
               SELF-CONCEPT+, NATIVE AMERICAN VALUES+, UNIVERSAL
               HARMONY, STRESS, PSYCHOTHERAPY AND COUNSELING
        IDEN   CANADA

903     AUTH   MAY, PHILIP A.
        TITL   ARRESTS, ALCOHOL, AND ALCOHOL LEGALIZATION AMONG AN
               AMERICAN INDIAN TRIBE.
        SOUR   PLAINS ANTHROPOLOGIST, MAY 1975, V20, PP 129-134.
        YEAR   1975
        DESC   LEGAL ISSUES+, PLAINS, RESERVATION, CORRECTIONAL
               INSTITUTIONS+,  ALCOHOL USE
        IDEN   U.S.

904     AUTH   DENSMORE, FRANCES
        TITL   NATIVE SONGS OF TWO HYBRID CEREMONIES AMONG THE
               AMERICAN INDIANS.
        SOUR   AMERICAN ANTHROPOLOGIST, 1938, V43, PP 77-82.
        YEAR   1938
        DESC   NATIVE AMERICAN RELIGIONS+, CULTURAL ADAPTATION+,
               YAQUI, SOUTHWEST
        IDEN   U.S., NATIVE AMERICAN CHURCH, DEER DANCE

905     AUTH   CLIFTON, JAMES A.
        TITL   SOCIOCULTURAL DYNAMICS OF THE PRAIRIE POTAWATOMI DRUM
               CULT.
        SOUR   PLAINS ANTHROPOLOGIST, MAY 1969, V14(44), PP 85-93.
        YEAR   1969
        DESC   POTAWATOMI, PRAIRIE, NATIVE AMERICAN RELIGIONS+,
               CULTURAL REVIVAL+, ETHNIC IDENTITY
        IDEN   U.S., KANSAS, DRUM CULT, PRAIRIE POTAWATOMI DRUM CULT

906     AUTH   HOWARD, JAMES H.
        TITL   THE HENRY DAVIS DRUM RITE: AN UNUSUAL DRUM RELIGION
               VARIANT OF THE MINNESOTA OJIBWA.
        SOUR   PLAINS ANTHROPOLOGIST, MAY 1966, V11, PP 117-126.
        YEAR   1966
        DESC   NATIVE AMERICAN RELIGIONS+, CHIPPEWA, EASTERN
               SUB-ARCTIC, CULTURAL REVIVAL+, CULTURAL ADAPTATION+
        IDEN   U.S., MINNESOTA, HENRY DAVIS DRUM RITE

907     AUTH   BARKER, GEORGE C.
        TITL   SOME FUNCTIONS OF CATHOLIC PROCESSIONS IN PUEBLO AND
               YAQUI CULTURE CHANGE.
        SOUR   AMERICAN ANTHROPOLOGIST, JUN. 1958, V60, PP 449-455.
        YEAR   1958
        DESC   NATIVE AMERICAN RELIGIONS+, YAQUI, PUEBLO, SOUTHWEST,
               RELIGIONS-NON-NATIVE+, CULTURAL ADAPTATION+,
               INTERTRIBAL COMPARISONS
        IDEN   U.S., NEW MEXICO, ARIZONA, CATHOLIC CHURCH

908     AUTH   BERRY, JOHN W.; ANNIS, ROBERT C.
```

TITL ECOLOGY, CULTURE AND PSYCHOLOGICAL DIFFERENTIATION.
SOUR INTERNATIONAL JOURNAL OF PSYCHOLOGY, 1974, V9(3), PP
     173-193.
YEAR 1974
DESC ENVIRONMENTAL FACTORS+, SOCIAL STATUS+, PERSONALITY
     TRAITS+, TSIMSHIAN, CARRIER, CREE, NORTHWEST COAST,
     EASTERN SUB-ARCTIC, PLATEAU, PSYCHOLOGICAL TESTING+,
     COGNITIVE PROCESSES+, INTERTRIBAL COMPARISONS, SEX
     DIFFERENCES
IDEN CANADA, RAVEN PROGRESSIVE MATRICES, KOHS BLOCK DESIGN
     TEST

909 AUTH GOODWIN, GRENVILLE
    TITL WHITE MOUNTAIN APACHE RELIGION.
    SOUR AMERICAN ANTHROPOLOGIST, JAN.-MAR. 1938, V40, PP 24-37.
    YEAR 1938
    DESC APACHE-WHITE MOUNTAIN, SOUTHWEST, NATIVE AMERICAN
         RELIGIONS+, TRADITIONAL HEALERS, CULTURAL REVIVAL
    IDEN U.S., NEW MEXICO

910 AUTH OPLER, MORRIS E.
    TITL REACTION TO DEATH AMONG THE MESCALERO APACHE.
    SOUR SOUTHWESTERN JOURNAL OF ANTHROPOLOGY, WIN. 1946,
         V2(4), PP 454-467.
    YEAR 1946
    DESC APACHE-MESCALERO, SOUTHWEST, DEATH AND DYING+, GHOST
         SICKNESS+
    IDEN U.S., NEW MEXICO

911 AUTH WELLS, ROBERT N.; WHITE, MINERVA
    TITL OPERATION KANYENGEHAGA: AN AMERICAN INDIAN CROSS
         CULTURAL PROGRAM.
    SOUR AMERICAN INDIAN CULTURE AND RESEARCH JOURNAL, 1975,
         V1, PP 22-28.
    YEAR 1975
    DESC IROQUOIS-MOHAWK, NORTHEAST WOODLAND, RESERVATION,
         ELEMENTARY SCHOOLS+, CHILDREN-SCHOOL AGE+, EDUCATION
         PROGRAMS AND SERVICES+, COLLEGES AND UNIVERSITIES,
         COMMUNITY INVOLVEMENT+, PROGRAM DEVELOPMENT+
    IDEN U.S., CANADA, ST. REGIS RESERVATION

912 AUTH MALAN, VERNON D.; MCCONE, R. CLYDE
    TITL THE TIME CONCEPT, PERSPECTIVE, AND PREMISE IN THE
         SOCIO-CULTURAL ORDER OF THE DAKOTA INDIANS.
    SOUR PLAINS ANTHROPOLOGIST, MAY 1960, V5, PP 12-15.
    YEAR 1960
    DESC TIME PERCEPTION+, SIOUX, PLAINS, ANGLO AMERICANS,
         NATIVE-NON-NATIVE COMPARISONS, DEATH AND DYING
    IDEN U.S.

913 AUTH STUCKI, LARRY R.
    TITL ANTHROPOLOGISTS AND INDIANS: A NEW LOOK AT THE FOX
         PROJECT.
    SOUR PLAINS ANTHROPOLOGIST, AUG. 1967, V12, PP 300-317.
    YEAR 1967

```
      DESC  RESEARCHERS+, CULTURAL ADAPTATION, MESQUAKIE, PRAIRIE,
            PROGRAM EVALUATION+, ECONOMIC ISSUES, LEADERSHIP+,
            POW-WOWS, TRIBAL POLITICAL ORGANIZATIONS+, COMMUNITY
            INVOLVEMENT+
      IDEN  U.S., IOWA

914   AUTH  SUTTLES, WAYNE
      TITL  PRIVATE KNOWLEDGE, MORALITY, AND SOCIAL CLASSES AMONG
            THE COAST SALISH.
      SOUR  AMERICAN ANTHROPOLOGIST, JUN. 1958, V60, PP 497-507.
      YEAR  1958
      DESC  NORTHWEST COAST, COAST SALISH, SOCIAL STATUS+,
            TRADITIONAL SOCIAL CONTROL+, RESERVATION
      IDEN  U.S., WASHINGTON, LUMMI RESERVATION

915   AUTH  JERDONE, CLARE G.
      TITL  DAY CARE FOR INDIAN CHILDREN.
      SOUR  YOUNG CHILDREN, 1965, V20(3), PP 143-151.
      YEAR  1965
      DESC  CHILDREN-INFANTS AND PRESCHOOL+, DAY CARE+, B.I.A.,
            SOCIAL SERVICES+
      IDEN  U.S.

916   AUTH  BROWN, PAULA
      TITL  CHANGES IN OJIBWA SOCIAL CONTROL.
      SOUR  AMERICAN ANTHROPOLOGIST, JAN.-MAR. 1952, V54, PP 57-70.
      YEAR  1952
      DESC  CHIPPEWA, EASTERN SUB-ARCTIC, TRADITIONAL SOCIAL
            CONTROL+, RESERVATION, LEADERSHIP+, WITCHCRAFT, GROUP
            NORMS AND SANCTIONS, RESERVATION
      IDEN  U.S., MINNESOTA, RED LAKE RESERVATION

917   AUTH  HALPERN, KATHERINE SPENCER
      TITL  NAVAJO HEALTH AND WELFARE AIDES: A FIELD STUDY.
      SOUR  SOCIAL SERVICE REVIEW, 1971, V45(1), PP 37-52.
      YEAR  1971
      DESC  NAVAJO, SOUTHWEST, RESERVATION, MEDICAL PROGRAMS AND
            SERVICES+, SOCIAL SERVICES+, MEDICAL
            PARAPROFESSIONALS+, SOCIAL SERVICE PARAPROFESSIONALS+,
            NATIVE AMERICAN PERSONNEL+, B.I.A., I.H.S., STRESS, ,
            ADMINISTRATIVE ISSUES
      IDEN  U.S., NAVAJO RESERVATION

918   AUTH  SPINDLER, LOUISE S.; SPINDLER, GEORGE D.
      TITL  MALE AND FEMALE ADAPTATION IN CULTURE CHANGE.
      SOUR  AMERICAN ANTHROPOLOGIST, APR. 1958, V60, PP 217-233.
      YEAR  1958
      DESC  MALES+, FEMALES+, CULTURAL ADAPTATION+, MENOMINEE,
            NORTHEAST WOODLAND, SEX DIFFERENCES, ANXIETY,
            PSYCHOLOGICAL TESTING+, PERSONALITY TRAITS+, STRESS+,
            ADULTS
      IDEN  U.S., WISCONSIN, RORSCHACH TEST

919   AUTH  HONIGMANN, JOHN J.
      TITL  INTERCULTURAL RELATIONS AT GREAT WHALE RIVER.
```

SOUR AMERICAN ANTHROPOLOGIST, OCT.-DEC. 1952, V54, PP
510-522.
YEAR 1952
DESC ESKIMO, CENTRAL AND EASTERN ARCTIC, CREE, INTERTRIBAL
COMPARISONS, NATIVE-NON-NATIVE COMPARISONS, ANGLO
AMERICANS, COOPERATION+, LANGUAGE HANDICAPS, SOCIAL
GROUPS AND PEER GROUPS, ETHNIC IDENTITY+,
DISCRIMINATION, OFF-RESERVATION
IDEN CANADA

920 AUTH SCHUSKY, ERNEST L.
TITL CONTEMPORARY MIGRATION AND CULTURE CHANGE ON TWO
DAKOTA RESERVATIONS.
SOUR PLAINS ANTHROPOLOGIST, AUG. 1962, V7, PP 178-183.
YEAR 1962
DESC SIOUX, PLAINS, RESERVATION, RELOCATION+, CULTURAL
ADAPTATION+, ETHNIC IDENTITY, CULTURAL CONTINUITY+
IDEN U.S., SOUTH DAKOTA, PINE RIDGE RESERVATION, LOWER
BRULE RESERVATION

921 AUTH BRANT, CHARLES S.
TITL WHITE CONTACT AND CULTURAL DISINTEGRATION AMONG THE
KIOWA APACHE.
SOUR PLAINS ANTHROPOLOGIST, FEB. 1964, V9, PP 8-13.
YEAR 1964
DESC KIOWA APACHE, PLAINS, NATIVE AMERICAN RELIGIONS+,
CULTURAL REVIVAL+, RESERVATION
IDEN U.S., GHOST DANCE

922 AUTH KLUCKHOHN, CLYDE
TITL SOUTHWESTERN STUDIES OF CULTURE AND PERSONALITY.
SOUR AMERICAN ANTHROPOLOGIST, 1954, V56, PP 685-697.
YEAR 1954
DESC PERSONALITY TRAITS+, SOUTHWEST, REVIEW OF LITERATURE,
RESEARCHERS
IDEN U.S.

923 AUTH SPICER, EDWARD H.
TITL SPANISH-INDIAN ACCULTURATION IN THE SOUTHWEST.
SOUR AMERICAN ANTHROPOLOGIST, AUG. 1954, V56, PP 663-684.
YEAR 1954
DESC PUEBLO, SOUTHWEST, CULTURAL ADAPTATION+,
RELIGIONS-NON-NATIVE+, NATIVE AMERICAN RELIGIONS+,
YAQUI, MAYO, INTERTRIBAL COMPARISONS
IDEN U.S., MEXICO, CATHOLIC CHURCH

924 AUTH SANFORD, MARGARET
TITL PAN-INDIANISM, ACCULTURATION AND THE AMERICAN IDEAL.
SOUR PLAINS ANTHROPOLOGIST, AUG. 1971, V16, PP 222-227.
YEAR 1971
DESC POW-WOWS, CULTURAL REVIVAL+, ETHNIC IDENTITY+,
CULTURAL CONTINUITY+, DISCRIMINATION
IDEN U.S.

925 AUTH DEER, ADA E.

```
     TITL  THE EFFECTS OF TERMINATION ON THE MENOMINEE.
     SOUR  AMERICAN INDIAN CULTURE AND RESEARCH JOURNAL, WIN.
           1973, V4, PP 6-14.
     YEAR  1973
     DESC  MENOMINEE, NORTHEAST WOODLAND, RESERVATION, FEDERAL
           GOVERNMENT+, LEGAL ISSUES+, ECONOMIC ISSUES+, ETHNIC
           IDENTITY+
     IDEN  U.S., WISCONSIN, MENOMINEE RESERVATION

926  AUTH  MCALLESTER, DAVID P.
     TITL  WATER AS A DISCIPLINARY AGENT AMONG THE CROW AND
           BLACKFOOT.
     SOUR  AMERICAN ANTHROPOLOGIST, OCT.-DEC. 1941, V43, PP
           593-604.
     YEAR  1941
     DESC  BLACKFEET, CROW, PLAINS, TRADITIONAL CHILD REARING+,
           TRADITIONAL SOCIAL CONTROL+, ANXIETY+
     IDEN  U.S.

927  AUTH  BOGGS, STEPHEN T.
     TITL  CULTURE CHANGE AND THE PERSONALITY OF OJIBWA CHILDREN.
     SOUR  AMERICAN ANTHROPOLOGIST, FEB. 1953, V60, PP 47-58.
     YEAR  1953
     DESC  CHIPPEWA, EASTERN SUB-ARCTIC, PERSONALITY TRAITS+,
           TRADITIONAL CHILD REARING+, FAMILY FUNCTIONING+, CHILD
           ABUSE AND NEGLECT+, CHILDREN-INFANTS AND PRESCHOOL+,
           SELF-CONCEPT+, ADULTS+
     IDEN  U.S., WISCONSIN, CANADA, MANITOBA

928  AUTH  DEVEREUX, GEORGE
     TITL  MOHAVE BELIEFS CONCERNING TWINS.
     SOUR  AMERICAN ANTHROPOLOGIST, OCT.-DEC. 1941, V43, PP
           573-592.
     YEAR  1941
     DESC  MOHAVE, SOUTHWEST, CHILDREN-INFANTS AND PRESCHOOL+,
           TRADITIONAL CHILD REARING+
     IDEN  U.S.

929  AUTH  RICHARDSON, EDWIN H.
     TITL  COUNSELING ALCOHOLIC MINORITIES.
     SOUR  PAPER PRESENTED TO THE 6TH INTERNATIONAL CONGRESS OF
           GROUP PSYCHOTHERAPY, PHILADELPHIA, AUG. 1, 1977.
           (13P)
     YEAR  1977
     DESC  ALCOHOLISM TREATMENT+, PSYCHOTHERAPY AND COUNSELING+,
           NATIVE-NON-NATIVE COMPARISONS, LATINOS, ASIAN
           AMERICANS, BLACK AMERICANS, ANGLO AMERICANS, MENTAL
           HEALTH PROFESSIONALS+
     IDEN  U.S.

930  AUTH  COOK, SHERBURNE F.
     TITL  THE STABILITY OF INDIAN CUSTOM MARRIAGE.
     SOUR  INDIAN HISTORIAN, SUM. 1974, V7, PP 33-34.
     YEAR  1974
     DESC  CALIFORNIA AREA, MARITAL RELATIONSHIPS+, DEMOGRAPHIC
```

```
              DATA, LEGAL ISSUES
        IDEN  U.S., CALIFORNIA

931  AUTH  WINFREE, L. THOMAS; GRIFFITHS, C. TAYLOR
     TITL  AN EXAMINATION OF FACTORS RELATED TO THE PAROLE
           SURVIVAL OF AMERICAN INDIANS.
     SOUR  PLAINS ANTHROPOLOGIST, NOV. 1975, V20, PP 311-319.
     YEAR  1975
     DESC  CORRECTIONAL INSTITUTIONS+, ADULTS, CRIME,
           NATIVE-NON-NATIVE COMPARISONS,,LEGAL ISSUES+
     IDEN  U.S.

932  AUTH  MCCONE, R. CLYDE
     TITL  CULTURAL FACTORS IN CRIME AMONG THE DAKOTA INDIANS.
     SOUR  PLAINS ANTHROPOLOGIST, MAY 1966, V11, PP 144-151.
     YEAR  1966
     DESC  SIOUX, PLAINS, CRIME+, GROUP NORMS AND SANCTIONS+,
           TRADITIONAL SOCIAL CONTROL+, RESERVATION, URBAN AREAS
     IDEN  U.S., SOUTH DAKOTA, NORTH DAKOTA

933  AUTH  PARKER, ALAN
     TITL  DELINQUENTS AND TRIBAL COURTS IN MONTANA.
     SOUR  AMERICAN INDIAN CULTURE AND RESEARCH JOURNAL, AUT.
           1972, V3, PP 3-6.
     YEAR  1972
     DESC  RESERVATION,  LEGAL ISSUES, CHEYENNE-NORTHERN, PLAINS,
           ADOLESCENTS, SOCIALLY DEVIANT BEHAVIOR

934  AUTH  MACLACHLAN, BRUCE B.
     TITL  ON "INDIAN JUSTICE."
     SOUR  PLAINS ANTHROPOLOGIST, NOV. 1963, V8, PP 257-261.
     YEAR  1963
     DESC  APACHE-MESCALERO, SOUTHWEST, CRIME+, RESERVATION,
           TRADITIONAL SOCIAL CONTROL+
     IDEN  U.S., NEW MEXICO

935  AUTH  BARBER, CARROLL G.
     TITL  PEYOTE AND DEFINITION OF NARCOTIC.
     SOUR  AMERICAN ANTHROPOLOGIST, 1959, V61, PP 641-646.
     YEAR  1959
     DESC  DRUG USE+, TRADITIONAL USE OF DRUGS AND ALCOHOL+
     IDEN  U.S.

936  AUTH  VOGET, FRED W.
     TITL  A SHOSHONE INNOVATOR.
     SOUR  AMERICAN ANTHROPOLOGIST, 1950, V52, PP 53-63
     YEAR  1950
     DESC  NATIVE AMERICAN RELIGIONS+, CULTURAL REVIVAL+,
           LEADERSHIP, PERSONALITY TRAITS+, SHOSHONE, PLAINS
     IDEN  U.S., WYOMING, SUN DANCE RELIGION

937  AUTH  TRAGER, GEORGE L.
     TITL  A STATUS SYMBOL AND PERSONALITY AT TAOS PUEBLO.
     SOUR  SOUTHWESTERN JOURNAL OF ANTHROPOLOGY, 1948, V4, PP
           299-304.
```

```
        YEAR  1948
        DESC  PUEBLO-TAOS, SOUTHWEST, MALES+, ADULTS+, ETHNIC
              IDENTITY+, PERSONALITY TRAITS, STRESS+, CULTURAL
              ADAPTATION+, RESERVATION, SOCIAL STATUS+
        IDEN  U.S., NEW MEXICO

938     AUTH  DAVIS, THOMAS; PYATSKOWIT, ALFRED
        TITL  BICOGNITIVE EDUCATION: A NEW FUTURE OF THE INDIAN
              CHILD.
        SOUR  JOURNAL OF AMERICAN INDIAN EDUCATION, MAY 1976, V15,
              PP 14-20.
        YEAR  1976
        DESC  BICULTURALISM+, NATIVE AMERICAN VALUES+, SELF-CONCEPT,
              LEARNING, EDUCATION PROGRAMS AND SERVICES+, MENOMINEE,
              NORTHEAST WOODLAND, CHILDREN-SCHOOL AGE
        IDEN  U.S., WISCONSIN

939     AUTH  MARTIG, ROGER; DEBLASSIE, RICHARD
        TITL  SELF-CONCEPT COMPARISONS OF ANGLO AND INDIAN CHILDREN.
        SOUR  JOURNAL OF AMERICAN INDIAN EDUCATION, MAY 1973, V12,
              PP 9-16.
        YEAR  1973
        DESC  CHILDREN-SCHOOL AGE+, SELF-CONCEPT+, NATIVE-NON-NATIVE
              COMPARISONS, ANGLO AMERICANS, PSYCHOLOGICAL TESTING+,
              ELEMENTARY SCHOOLS, SEX DIFFERENCES
        IDEN  U.S., NEW MEXICO, PRIMARY SELF-CONCEPT SCALE

940     AUTH  BOUTWELL, RICHARD C.; LOW, WILLIAM C.; WILLIAMS,
              KRISTIN; PROFFIT, THOMAS
        TITL  RED APPLES.
        SOUR  JOURNAL OF AMERICAN INDIAN EDUCATION, JAN. 1973, V12,
              PP 11-14.
        YEAR  1973
        DESC  COLLEGES AND UNIVERSITIES+, ACHIEVEMENT+,
              DISCRIMINATION, ETHNIC IDENTITY+, ADOLESCENTS
        IDEN  U.S.

941     AUTH  SMITH, J.L.
        TITL  THE SACRED CALF PIPE BUNDLE: ITS EFFECT ON THE PRESENT
              TETON DAKOTA.
        SOUR  PLAINS ANTHROPOLOGIST, MAY 1970, V15, PP 87-93.
        YEAR  1970
        DESC  CULTURAL REVIVAL+, NATIVE AMERICAN RELIGIONS+,
              RELIGIONS-NON-NATIVE+, CULTURAL ADAPTATION+,
              SIOUX-OGLALA, PLAINS
        IDEN  U.S., SOUTH DAKOTA, SACRED PIPE, CATHOLIC CHURCH

942     AUTH  LIBERTY, MARGOT P.
        TITL  PRIEST AND SHAMAN ON THE PLAINS: A FALSE DICHOTOMY.
        SOUR  PLAINS ANTHROPOLOGIST, MAY 1970, V15(48), PP 73-79.
        YEAR  1970
        DESC  TRADITIONAL HEALERS+, CHEYENNE-NORTHERN, CROW, PLAINS,
              INTERTRIBAL COMPARISONS, NATIVE AMERICAN RELIGIONS+,
              DREAMS AND VISION QUESTS
        IDEN  U.S., SUN DANCE
```

943 AUTH STEINMETZ, PAUL
    TITL THE RELATIONSHIP BETWEEN PLAINS INDIAN RELIGION AND
          CHRISTIANITY: A PRIEST"S VIEWPOINT.
    SOUR PLAINS ANTHROPOLOGIST, MAY 1970, V15, PP 83-86.
    YEAR 1970
    DESC SIOUX-OGLALA, PLAINS, NATIVE AMERICAN RELIGIONS+,
          RELIGIONS-NON-NATIVE+, CULTURAL ADAPTATION+,
          RESERVATION
    IDEN U.S., SOUTH DAKOTA, CATHOLIC CHURCH, SACRED PIPE, PINE
          RIDGE RESERVATION

944 AUTH LEWIS, THOMAS H.
    TITL THE OGLALA (TETON DAKOTA) SUN DANCE: VISSICITUDES OF
          ITS STRUCTURES AND FUNCTIONS.
    SOUR PLAINS ANTHROPOLOGIST, FEB. 1972, V17, PP 44-49.
    YEAR 1972
    DESC SIOUX-OGLALA, PLAINS, NATIVE AMERICAN RELIGIONS+,
          CULTURAL ADAPTATION+, RESERVATION, ETHNIC IDENTITY
    IDEN U.S., SOUTH DAKOTA, PINE RIDGE RESERVATION, SUN DANCE

945 AUTH HURT, WESLEY R.
    TITL A YUWIPI CEREMONY AT PINE RIDGE.
    SOUR PLAINS ANTHROPOLOGIST, NOV. 1960, V5(10), PP 48-52.
    YEAR 1960
    DESC NATIVE AMERICAN RELIGIONS+, SIOUX-OGLALA, PLAINS,
          RESERVATION, TRADITIONAL HEALERS+, TRIBAL POLITICAL
          ORGANIZATIONS+
    IDEN U.S., SOUTH DAKOTA, YUWIPI CEREMONY, PINE RIDGE
          RESERVATION

946 AUTH KUNITZ, STEPHEN J.
    TITL NAVAJO AND HOPI FERTILITY, 1971-1972.
    SOUR HUMAN BIOLOGY, SEP. 1974, V46(3), PP 435-451.
    YEAR 1974
    DESC FAMILY PLANNING+, NAVAJO, PUEBLO-HOPI, SOUTHWEST,
          RESERVATION, INTERTRIBAL COMPARISONS, DEMOGRAPHIC
          DATA, CULTURAL ADAPTATION, AGE COMPARISONS, FEMALES,
          ADULTS
    IDEN U.S., NAVAJO RESERVATION, HOPI RESERVATION, NEW
          MEXICO, ARIZONA

947 AUTH DOZIER, EDWARD P.
    TITL SPANISH INFLUENCES ON RIO GRANDE PUEBLO RELIGION.
    SOUR AMERICAN ANTHROPOLOGIST, JUN. 1958, V60, PP 441-448.
    YEAR 1958
    DESC PUEBLO, SOUTHWEST, NATIVE AMERICAN RELIGIONS+,
          RELIGIONS-NON-NATIVE+, CULTURAL ADAPTATION+, CULTURAL
          CONTINUITY+
    IDEN U.S., CATHOLIC CHURCH

948 AUTH KLUCKHOHN, CLYDE
    TITL PARTICIPATION IN CEREMONIES IN A NAVAJO COMMUNITY.
    SOUR AMERICAN ANTHROPOLOGIST, JUL.-SEP. 1938, V40, PP
          359-369.
    YEAR 1938

```
       DESC   NAVAJO, SOUTHWEST, NATIVE AMERICAN RELIGIONS+,
              COMMUNITY INVOLVEMENT+, RESERVATION, ADULTS, ECONOMIC
              ISSUES+
       IDEN   U.S., NAVAJO RESERVATION

949    AUTH   STEWART, OMER C.
       TITL   ORIGIN OF THE PEYOTE RELIGION IN THE UNITED STATES.
       SOUR   PLAINS ANTHROPOLOGIST, AUG. 1974, V19, PP 211-223.
       YEAR   1974
       DESC   DRUG USE+, TRADITIONAL USE OF DRUGS AND ALCOHOL+,
              PRAIRIE, PLAINS, SOUTHWEST
       IDEN   U.S.

950    AUTH   WAGNER, ROLAND M.
       TITL   SOME PRAGMATIC ASPECTS OF NAVAJO PEYOTISM.
       SOUR   PLAINS ANTHROPOLOGIST, AUG. 1975, V20, PP 197-205.
       YEAR   1975
       DESC   NAVAJO, SOUTHWEST, NATIVE AMERICAN RELIGIONS+, DRUG
              USE+, TRADITIONAL USE OF DRUGS AND ALCOHOL+,
              RESERVATION, NATIVE AMERICAN COPING BEHAVIORS+
       IDEN   U.S., NAVAJO RESERVATION, NATIVE AMERICAN CHURCH

951    AUTH   OPLER, MORRIS E.
       TITL   A DESCRIPTION OF A TONKAWA PEYOTE MEETING HELD IN
              1902.
       SOUR   AMERICAN ANTHROPOLOGIST, 1939, V41, PP 433-439.
       YEAR   1939
       DESC   DRUG USE+, TRADITIONAL USE OF DRUGS AND ALCOHOL+,
              TONKAWA, SOUTHWEST
       IDEN   U.S.

952    AUTH   LIBERTY, MARGOT P.
       TITL   POPULATION TRENDS AMONG PRESENT-DAY OMAHA INDIANS.
       SOUR   PLAINS ANTHROPOLOGIST, AUG. 1975, V20, PP 225-230.
       YEAR   1975
       DESC   OMAHA, PRAIRIE, RESERVATION, URBAN AREAS, FAMILY
              PLANNING+, ADULTS+, FEMALES+, DEMOGRAPHIC DATA
       IDEN   U.S., NEBRASKA

953    AUTH   WEIST, KATHERINE M.
       TITL   GIVING AWAY: THE CEREMONIAL DISTRIBUTION OF GOODS
              AMONG THE NORTHERN CHEYENNE OF SOUTHEASTERN MONTANA.
       SOUR   PLAINS ANTHROPOLOGIST, MAY 1973, V18(60), PP 97-103.
       YEAR   1973
       DESC   CHEYENNE-NORTHERN, PLAINS, RESERVATION, GENEROSITY+,
              SOCIAL STATUS+, POW-WOWS+, MILITARY SERVICE, SOCIAL
              NETWORKS+
       IDEN   U.S., MONTANA

954    AUTH   FANSHEL, DAVID
       TITL   INDIAN ADOPTION RESEARCH PROJECT.
       SOUR   CHILD WELFARE, NOV. 1964, V43(9), PP 486-488.
       YEAR   2964
       DESC   ADOPTION AND FOSTER CARE+, CHILDREN-INFANTS AND
              PRESCHOOL, ADULTS, ANGLO AMERICANS, PROGRAM
```

```
                    EVALUATION+
          IDEN      U.S., INDIAN ADOPTION PROJECT

955   AUTH      HUGHES, CHARLES C.
      TITL      ANOMIE, THE AMMASSALIK, AND THE STANDARDIZATION OF
                ERROR.
      SOUR      SOUTHWESTERN JOURNAL OF ANTHROPOLOGY, WIN. 1958, V14,
                PP 352-377.
      YEAR      1958
      DESC      ESKIMO, CENTRAL AND EASTERN ARCTIC, COOPERATION+,
                SOCIAL NETWORKS+, ANOMIE
      IDEN      GREENLAND

956   AUTH      ABERLE, DAVID F.
      TITL      THE PROPHET DANCE AND REACTIONS TO WHITE CONTACT.
      SOUR      SOUTHWESTERN JOURNAL OF ANTHROPOLOGY, SPR. 1959, V15,
                PP 74-83.
      YEAR      1959
      DESC      NATIVE AMERICAN RELIGIONS+, CULTURAL REVIVAL+,
                NORTHWEST COAST, STRESS+
      IDEN      U.S., PROPHET DANCE

957   AUTH      BASSO, KEITH H.
      TITL      TO GIVE UP ON WORDS: SILENCE IN WESTERN APACHE
                CULTURE.
      SOUR      SOUTHWESTERN JOURNAL OF ANTHROPOLOGY, AUG. 1970,
                V26(3), PP 213-230.
      YEAR      1970
      DESC      APACHE, SOUTHWEST, RESERVATION, EMOTIONAL RESTRAINT+,
                GRIEF REACTION, NONINTERFERENCE+, GROUP NORMS AND
                SANCTIONS+
      IDEN      U.S., ARIZONA, FORT APACHE RESERVATION

958   AUTH      BENNET, J.W.
      TITL      THE INTERPRETATION OF PUEBLO CULTURE: A QUESTION OF
                VALUES.
      SOUR      SOUTHWESTERN JOURNAL OF ANTHROPOLOGY, WIN. 1946,
                V2(4), PP 361-374.
      YEAR      1946
      DESC      PUEBLO, SOUTHWEST, UNIVERSAL HARMONY+, TRADITIONAL
                SOCIAL CONTROL+, COOPERATION, EMOTIONAL RESTRAINT,
                RESEARCHERS+
      IDEN      U.S., NEW MEXICO

959   AUTH      EGGAN, DOROTHY
      TITL      INSTRUCTION AND AFFECT IN HOPI CULTURAL CONTINUITY.
      SOUR      SOUTHWESTERN JOURNAL OF ANTHROPOLOGY, WIN. 1956,
                V12(4), PP 347-370.
      YEAR      1956
      DESC      LEARNING+, TRADITIONAL SOCIAL CONTROL+, PUEBLO-HOPI,
                SOUTHWEST, TRADITIONAL CHILD REARING+, CULTURAL
                CONTINUITY, EXTENDED FAMILY, COOPERATION+, RESERVATION
      IDEN      U.S., NEW MEXICO

960   AUTH      OPLER, MORRIS E.; BITTLE, WILLIAM E.
```

TITL THE DEATH PRACTICES AND ESCHATOLOGY OF THE KIOWA
      APACHE.
SOUR SOUTHWESTERN JOURNAL OF ANTHROPOLOGY, WIN. 1961, V17,
      PP 383-394.
YEAR 1961
DESC DEATH AND DYING+, KIOWA APACHE, PLAINS, GRIEF
      REACTION, GHOST SICKNESS+, ANXIETY
IDEN U.S.

961 AUTH GOLDFRANK, ESTHER S.
     TITL THE IMPACT OF SITUATION AND PERSONALITY ON FOUR HOPI
           EMERGENCE MYTHS.
     SOUR SOUTHWESTERN JOURNAL OF ANTHROPOLOGY, AUT. 1948,
           V4(3), PP 241-262.
     YEAR 1948
     DESC PERSONALITY TRAITS+, PUEBLO-HOPI, SOUTHWEST,
           AGGRESSIVENESS+, UNIVERSAL HARMONY+, GROUP NORMS AND
           SANCTIONS
     IDEN U.S.

962 AUTH SWANSON, ROSEMARY A.; HENDERSON, RONALD W.
     TITL EFFECTS OF TELEVISED MODELING AND ACTIVE PARTICIPATION
           ON RULE-GOVERNED QUESTION PRODUCTION AMONG NATIVE
           AMERICAN PRESCHOOL CHILDREN.
     SOUR CONTEMPORARY EDUCATIONAL PSYCHOLOGY, OCT. 1977, V2(4),
           PP 345-352.
     YEAR 1977
     DESC CHILDREN-INFANTS AND PRESCHOOL+, PAPAGO, SOUTHWEST,
           LEARNING+, EDUCATION PROGRAMS AND SERVICES+,
           NONINTERFERENCE, EMOTIONAL RESTRAINT, TRADITIONAL
           CHILD REARING
     IDEN U.S., ARIZONA, PAPAGO RESERVATION, HEAD START

963 AUTH LEMERT, EDWIN M.
     TITL THE LIFE AND DEATH OF AN INDIAN STATE.
     SOUR HUMAN ORGANIZATION, AUT. 1954, V13, PP 23-27.
     YEAR 1954
     DESC COAST SALISH, NORTHWEST COAST, RELIGIONS-NON-NATIVE+,
           CULTURAL ADAPTATION+, TRADITIONAL SOCIAL CONTROL+
     IDEN CANADA, BRITISH COLUMBIA, CATHOLIC CHURCH

964 AUTH LEMERT, EDWIN M.
     TITL STUTTERING AMONG THE NORTH PACIFIC COASTAL INDIANS.
     SOUR SOUTHWESTERN JOURNAL OF ANTHROPOLOGY, WIN. 1952, V8,
           PP 429-441.
     YEAR 1952
     DESC COAST SALISH, NORTHWEST COAST, PSYCHOPHYSIOLOGICAL
           DISORDERS+, KWAKIUTL, NOOTKA, ANXIETY+,
           CHILDREN-SCHOOL AGE, ADULTS, GROUP NORMS AND
           SANCTIONS, ATTITUDES+, LANGUAGE HANDICAPS+, LANGUAGE
           HANDICAPS+
     IDEN CANADA, BRITISH COLUMBIA

965 AUTH HARDING, JAMES
     TITL CANADA"S INDIANS: A POWERLESS MINORITY.

```
        SOUR  IN JOHN HARP AND JOHN HOFLEY (EDS.), POVERTY IN
              CANADA, PP 239-252.  SCARBOROUGH: PRENTICE-HALL, 1971.
        YEAR  1971
        DESC  POWERLESSNESS+,  DISCRIMINATION+,  SOCIAL STATUS+,
              ECONOMIC ISSUES+
        IDEN  CANADA

966  AUTH  KUNITZ, STEPHEN J.
     TITL  FACTORS INFLUENCING RECENT NAVAJO AND HOPI POPULATION
           CHANGES.
     SOUR  HUMAN ORGANIZATION, SPR. 1974, V33(1), PP 7-16.
     YEAR  1974
     DESC  NAVAJO, PUEBLO-HOPI, SOUTHWEST, DEMOGRAPHIC DATA+,
           RESERVATION, RELOCATION, FAMILY PLANNING, INTERTRIBAL
           COMPARISONS
     IDEN  U.S., NAVAJO RESERVATION, HOPI RESERVATION

967  AUTH  BALIKCI, ASEN
     TITL  SUICIDAL BEHAVIOR AMONG THE NETSILIK ESKIMOS.
     SOUR  NORTH, 1961, V8(4), PP 12-19.
     YEAR  1961
     DESC  SUICIDE+, ESKIMO, CENTRAL AND EASTERN ARCTIC
     IDEN  CANADA

968  AUTH  BRIGGS, JEAN L.
     TITL  THE ISSUES OF AUTONOMY AND AGGRESSION IN THE
           THREE-YEAR-OLD: THE UTKU ESKIMO CASE.
     SOUR  SEMINARS IN PSYCHIATRY, NOV. 1972, V4(4), PP 317-329.
     YEAR  1972
     DESC  ESKIMO, CENTRAL AND EASTERN ARCTIC, CHILDREN-INFANTS
           AND PRESCHOOL+, AGGRESSIVENESS, TRADITIONAL CHILD
           REARING+, TRADITIONAL SOCIAL CONTROL, NONINTERFERENCE
     IDEN  CANADA

969  AUTH  BASEHEART, HARRY W.
     TITL  MESCALERO APACHE BAND ORGANIZATION AND LEADERSHIP.
     SOUR  SOUTHWESTERN JOURNAL OF ANTHROPOLOGY, SPR. 1970, V26,
           PP 87-106.
     YEAR  1970
     DESC  APACHE-MESCALERO, LEADERSHIP+, SOUTHWEST, TRIBAL
           POLITICAL ORGANIZATIONS+
     IDEN  U.S.

970  AUTH  KRAUS, ROBERT F.
     TITL  SUICIDAL BEHAVIOR IN ALASKAN NATIVES.
     SOUR  ALASKA MEDICINE, JAN. 1974, PP 2-6.
     YEAR  1974
     DESC  SUICIDE+, ALASKA NATIVES, EPIDEMIOLOGICAL STUDY,
           ADOLESCENTS, ADULTS, SEX DIFFERENCES, URBAN AREAS,
           OFF-RESERVATION, WESTERN ARCTIC, YUKON SUB-ARCTIC,
           NORTHWEST COAST
     IDEN  U.S., ALASKA

971  AUTH  ADAMS, G.W.; KANNER, LEO
     TITL  GENERAL PARALYSIS AMONG THE NORTH AMERICAN INDIAN.
```

```
       SOUR   AMERICAN JOURNAL OF PSYCHIATRY, 1926, V6, PP 125-133.
       YEAR   1926
       DESC   ORGANIC BRAIN SYNDROMES+, PLAINS, MENTAL HEALTH
              INSTITUTIONS+
       IDEN   U.S., SOUTH DAKOTA, ASYLUM FOR INSANE INDIANS

972    AUTH   BOYER, L. BRYCE; BOYER, RUTH M.; BRAWER, FLORENCE B.;
              KAWAI, HAYAO; KLOPFER, BRUNO
       TITL   APACHE AGE GROUPS.
       SOUR   JOURNAL OF PROJECTIVE TECHNIQUES, 1964, V28, PP
              397-402.
       YEAR   1964
       DESC   APACHE-MESCALERO, APACHE-CHIRICAHUA, SOUTHWEST,
              PSYCHOLOGICAL TESTING+, RESERVATION, PERSONALITY
              TRAITS+, AGE COMPARISONS, ADULTS, AGED, INTERTRIBAL
              COMPARISONS, ADOLESCENTS, PSYCHOANALYSIS
       IDEN   U.S., NEW MEXICO, MESCALERO RESERVATION, RORSCHACH
              TEST

973    AUTH   HOWARD, JAMES H.
       TITL   PAN-INDIAN CULTURE OF OKLAHOMA.
       SOUR   SCIENTIFIC MONTHLY, 1956, V81, PP 215-220.
       YEAR   1956
       DESC   OKLAHOMA INDIANS, OFF-RESERVATION, POW-WOWS+, ETHNIC
              IDENTITY+, CULTURAL ADAPTATION+
       IDEN   U.S., OKLAHOMA

974    TITL   INSANITY AMONG THE NORTH AMERICAN INDIANS.
       SOUR   IN H.M. HURD (ED.), THE INSTITUTIONAL CARE OF THE
              INSANE IN THE UNITED STATES AND CANADA, V1, PP
              381-385.  BALTIMORE: JOHNS HOPKINS UNIVERSITY PRESS,
              1916.
       YEAR   1916
       DESC   MENTAL DISORDERS+, EPIDEMIOLOGICAL STUDY
       IDEN   U.S., CANADA

975    AUTH   LOWRY, R.B.
       TITL   THE KLIPPEL-FEIL ANOMALAD AS PART OF THE FETAL ALCOHOL
              SYNDROME.
       SOUR   TERATOLOGY, AUG. 1977, V16(1), PP 53-56.
       YEAR   1977
       DESC   ALCOHOL USE+, CHILDREN-INFANTS AND PRESCHOOL+,
              PHYSICAL HEALTH AND ILLNESS+, FEMALES+, ADULTS+,
              CLINICAL STUDY
       IDEN   U.S.

976    AUTH   TOPPER, MARTIN D.
       TITL   NAVAJO CULTURE, SOCIAL PATHOLOGY, AND ALCOHOL ABUSE.
       SOUR   PAPER PRESENTED AT THE 32ND ANNUAL MEETING OF THE
              SOCIETY FOR APPLIED ANTHROPOLOGY, TUCSON, 1973. (22P)
       YEAR   1973
       DESC   NAVAJO, SOUTHWEST, RESERVATION, SOCIALLY DEVIANT
              BEHAVIOR+, ALCOHOL USE+, STRESS+, GROUP NORMS AND
              SANCTIONS, ALCOHOLISM TREATMENT
       IDEN   U.S., NAVAJO RESERVATION
```

977 AUTH GUILMET, GEORGE M.
     TITL THE NONVERBAL AMERICAN INDIAN CHILD IN THE URBAN
           CLASSROOM.
     SOUR DISSERTATION ABSTRACTS INTERNATIONAL, 1977, V37, PP
           6587A-6588A.
     YEAR 1977
     DESC CHILDREN-SCHOOL AGE, NAVAJO, SOUTHWEST, LEARNING+,
           NONINTERFERENCE, EMOTIONAL RESTRAINT+, TRADITIONAL
           CHILD REARING+, URBAN AREAS, ELEMENTARY SCHOOLS,
           NATIVE-NON-NATIVE COMPARISONS, ANGLO AMERICANS,
           CHILDREN-INFANTS AND PRESCHOOL+
     IDEN U.S., CALIFORNIA

978 AUTH CASSELL, RUSSELL N.; SANDERS, RICHARD A.
     TITL COMPARATIVE ANALYSIS OF SCORES FROM TWO LEADERSHIP
           TESTS FOR APACHE INDIAN AND ANGLO-AMERICAN YOUTH.
     SOUR JOURNAL OF EDUCATIONAL RESEARCH, SEP. 1961, V55(1), PP
           19-23.
     YEAR 1961
     DESC ADOLESCENTS+, LEADERSHIP+, APACHE, SOUTHWEST,
           NATIVE-NON-NATIVE COMPARISONS, ANGLO AMERICANS,
           PSYCHOLOGICAL TESTING+, SECONDARY SCHOOLS, RESERVATION
     IDEN U.S., ARIZONA, LEADERSHIP Q-SORT TEST, LEADERSHIP
           ABILITY EVALUATION

979 AUTH MIDDLETON, ALLEN H.
     TITL STRUCTURE-OF-INTELLECT IN AMERICAN INDIAN CHILDREN.
     SOUR DISSERTATION ABSTRACTS INTERNATIONAL, FEB. 1977, V37,
           PP 4156B-4157B.
     YEAR 1977
     DESC CHILDREN-INFANTS AND PRESCHOOL+, ABILITIES+, SOCIAL
           STATUS, SEX DIFFERENCES, URBAN AREAS, OFF-RESERVATION,
           NATIVE-NON-NATIVE COMPARISONS, ANGLO AMERICANS, BLACK
           AMERICANS
     IDEN U.S., GUILFORD STRUCTURE OF INTELLECT

980 AUTH HAYNES, TERRY L.
     TITL SOME FACTORS RELATED TO CONTRACEPTIVE BEHAVIOR AMONG
           WIND RIVER SHOSHONE AND ARAPAHOE FEMALES.
     SOUR HUMAN ORGANIZATION, SPR. 1977, V36(1), PP 72-76.
     YEAR 1977
     DESC SHOSHONE, ARAPAHO-NORTHERN, PLAINS, FAMILY PLANNING+,
           RESERVATION, FEMALES+, ADULTS+
     IDEN U.S., WIND RIVER RESERVATION, WYOMING

981 AUTH OPLER, MORRIS E.
     TITL THE LIPAN APACHE DEATH COMPLEX AND ITS EXTENSIONS.
     SOUR SOUTHWESTERN JOURNAL OF ANTHROPOLOGY, SPR. 1945,
           V1(1), PP 122-141.
     YEAR 1945
     DESC APACHE-LIPAN, SOUTHWEST, RESERVATION, DEATH AND
           DYING+, GHOST SICKNESS+, AGED
     IDEN U.S., NEW MEXICO, MESCALERO APACHE RESERVATION

982 AUTH LEE, DOROTHY

```
      TITL  NOTES ON THE CONCEPTION OF THE SELF AMONG THE WINTU
            INDIANS.
      SOUR  JOURNAL OF ABNORMAL PSYCHOLOGY, 1950, V45, PP 538-543.
      YEAR  1950
      DESC  WINTU, SELF-CONCEPT+, CALIFORNIA AREA
      IDEN  U.S., CALIFORNIA

983   AUTH  BURKE, BEVERLY A.
      TITL  THE EFFECT OF TEACHING COMMUNICATION SKILLS TO
            TEACHERS IN AN ELEMENTARY BUREAU OF INDIAN AFFAIRS
            SCHOOL.
      SOUR  DISSERTATION ABSTRACTS INTERNATIONAL, 1977, V37(12), P
            7627A.
      YEAR  1977
      DESC  B.I.A. BOARDING SCHOOLS+, ELEMENTARY SCHOOLS+,
            EDUCATION PROFESSIONALS+, TRAINING PROGRAMS+
      IDEN  U.S.

984   AUTH  BROWN, JANET W.; GREEN, RAYNA D.
      TITL  NATIVE AMERICANS IN SCIENCE.
      SOUR  THE EXCHANGE: A JOURNAL OF NATIVE AMERICAN
            PHILANTHROPIC NEWS, MAY 1976, V1(1), PP 15-17.
      YEAR  1976
      DESC  SCIENCE PROGRAMS+, EDUCATION PROGRAMS AND SERVICES+,
            ROLE MODELS
      IDEN  U.S., AMERICAN ASSOCIATION FOR THE ADVANCEMENT OF
            SCIENCE

985   AUTH  WALLACE, WILLIAM J.; TAYLOR, EDITH S.
      TITL  HUPA SORCERY.
      SOUR  SOUTHWESTERN JOURNAL OF ANTHROPOLOGY, SUM. 1950,
            V6(2), PP 188-196.
      YEAR  1950
      DESC  HOOPA, NORTHWEST COAST, WITCHCRAFT+, AGGRESSIVENESS
      IDEN  U.S., CALIFORNIA

986   AUTH  VALENCIA-WEBER, GLORIA
      TITL  TRAINING AMERICAN INDIANS IN PSYCHOLOGY.
      SOUR  PAPER PRESENTED AT A MEETING OF THE AMERICAN
            PSYCHOLOGICAL ASSOCIATION, SAN FRANCISCO, AUG. 1977.
            (28P)
      YEAR  1977
      DESC  COLLEGES AND UNIVERSITIES+, EDUCATION PROGRAMS AND
            SERVICES+, MENTAL HEALTH PROFESSIONALS+, NATIVE
            AMERICAN PERSONNEL+, ECONOMIC ISSUES, SOCIAL NETWORKS,
            ROLE MODELS
      IDEN  U.S., OKLAHOMA, OKLAHOMA STATE UNIVERSITY

987   AUTH  NORMAN, RALPH D.; MIDKIF, KATHERINE L.
      TITL  NAVAJO CHILDREN ON RAVEN PROGRESSIVE MATRICES AND
            GOODENOUGH DRAW-A-MAN TESTS.
      SOUR  SOUTHWESTERN JOURNAL OF ANTHROPOLOGY, SUM. 1955,
            V11(2), PP 129-136.
      YEAR  1955
      DESC  NAVAJO, SOUTHWEST, CHILDREN-SCHOOL AGE, PSYCHOLOGICAL
```

```
                  TESTING+, CULTURE-FAIR TESTS+, ABILITIES+, ELEMENTARY
                  SCHOOLS
          IDEN    U.S., NEW MEXICO, GOODENOUGH HARRIS DRAW A PERSON
                  TEST, RAVEN PROGRESSIVE MATRICES

988  AUTH    RAY, VERNE F.
     TITL    THE CONTRARY BEHAVIOR PATTERN IN AMERICAN INDIAN
             CEREMONIALISM.
     SOUR    SOUTHWESTERN JOURNAL OF ANTHROPOLOGY, SPR. 1945,
             V1(1), PP 75-113.
     YEAR    1945
     DESC    GROUP NORMS AND SANCTIONS+, PLAINS, SOCIALLY DEVIANT
             BEHAVIOR+, TRADITIONAL HEALERS
     IDEN    U.S.

989  AUTH    KLEINFELD, JUDITH S.
     TITL    EFFECTIVE TEACHERS OF ESKIMO AND INDIAN STUDENTS.
     SOUR    SCHOOL REVIEW, FEB. 1975, V83, PP 301-344.
     YEAR    1975
     DESC    ETHNIC IDENTITY, EDUCATION PROFESSIONALS+, PASSIVE
             RESISTANCE+, SECONDARY SCHOOLS+, DISCRIMINATION, URBAN
             AREAS, LEARNING+, ALASKA NATIVES, ADOLESCENTS
     IDEN    U.S., ALASKA

990  AUTH    LAZEWSKI, TONY
     TITL    AMERICAN INDIAN MIGRATION TO AND WITHIN CHICAGO,
             ILLINOIS.
     SOUR    DISSERTATION ABSTRACTS INTERNATIONAL, APR. 1977, V37,
             P 6751A.
     YEAR    1977
     DESC    RELOCATION+, URBAN AREAS, URBANIZATION+
     IDEN    U.S., ILLINOIS

991  AUTH    MARTIN, JAMES C.
     TITL    CHOICE OF DEFENSE MECHANISMS BY INDIAN AND WHITE
             ADOLESCENTS.
     SOUR    JOURNAL OF CLINICAL PSYCHOLOGY, OCT. 1977, V33, PP
             1027-1028.
     YEAR    1977
     DESC    ADOLESCENTS+, NATIVE-NON-NATIVE COMPARISONS, ANGLO
             AMERICANS, NATIVE AMERICAN COPING BEHAVIORS+,
             SECONDARY SCHOOLS, PSYCHOLOGICAL TESTING+, SEX
             DIFFERENCES, AGGRESSIVENESS+, PASSIVE RESISTANCE+
     IDEN    U.S., OKLAHOMA, DEFENSE MECHANISM INVENTORY

992  AUTH    RICHARDSON, EDWIN H.
     TITL    THE ROLE OF THE MEDICINE MAN AS A PART OF THE MODERN
             THERAPEUTIC TEAM IN PSYCHOTHERAPY FOR INDIANS.
     SOUR    PAPER PRESENTED TO THE 6TH INTERNATIONAL CONGRESS OF
             GROUP PSYCHOTHERAPY AND THE UNIVERSITY OF
             PENNSYLVANIA, PHILADELPHIA, AUG. 1977.  (24P)
     YEAR    1977
     DESC    TRADITIONAL HEALERS+, CULTURE-BASED PSYCHOTHERAPY+,
             MENTAL HEALTH PROFESSIONALS, NATIVE AMERICAN VALUES+,
             MEDICAL PROFESSIONALS, SIOUX, PLAINS
```

```
       IDEN  U.S.

993    AUTH  KRAUS, ROBERT F.
       TITL  A PSYCHOANALYTIC INTERPRETATION OF SHAMANISM.
       SOUR  PSYCHOANALYTIC REVIEW, 1972, V59(1), PP 19-32
       YEAR  1972
       DESC  TRADITIONAL HEALERS+, PERSONALITY TRAITS
       IDEN  NORTH AMERICA, ASIA

994    AUTH  ADAMS, DAVID
       TITL  SELF-DETERMINATION AND INDIAN EDUCATION.
       SOUR  JOURNAL OF AMERICAN INDIAN EDUCATION, JAN. 1974, V13,
             PP 21-27.
       YEAR  1974
       DESC  ELEMENTARY SCHOOLS+, NATIVE AMERICAN ADMINISTERED
             PROGRAMS+, EDUCATION PROGRAMS AND SERVICES+, ETHNIC
             IDENTITY+, BILINGUALISM, BICULTURALISM, NATIVE
             AMERICAN PERSONNEL+, EDUCATION PROFESSIONALS
       IDEN  U.S., ARIZONA, ROUGH ROCK DEMONSTRATION SCHOOL

995    AUTH  COLLIER, PETER
       TITL  THE RED MAN"S BURDEN.
       SOUR  RAMPARTS, FEB. 1970, V8, PP 26-38.
       YEAR  1970
       DESC  NATIVE AMERICAN POLITICAL MOVEMENTS+, B.I.A. BOARDING
             SCHOOLS+, DISCRIMINATION+, B.I.A.+, URBAN AREAS,
             RESERVATION, ECONOMIC ISSUES, POWERLESSNESS
       IDEN  U.S.

996    AUTH  SORKIN, ALAN L.
       TITL  SOME ASPECTS OF INDIAN MIGRATION.
       SOUR  SOCIAL FORCES, DEC. 1969, V48, PP 243-250.
       YEAR  1969
       DESC  RELOCATION+, RESERVATION, URBAN AREAS, ADULTS,
             TRAINING PROGRAMS+, EMPLOYMENT+
       IDEN  U.S.

997    AUTH  STEWART, KENNETH M.
       TITL  MOJAVE INDIAN SHAMANISM.
       SOUR  THE MASTERKEY, JAN.-MAR. 1970, V44, PP 19-27.
       YEAR  1970
       DESC  MOHAVE, SOUTHWEST, TRADITIONAL HEALERS+, DREAMS AND
             VISION QUESTS+, NATIVE AMERICAN ETIOLOGY+, WITCHCRAFT,
             GHOST SICKNESS, CULTURE-SPECIFIC SYNDROMES+
       IDEN  U.S.

998    AUTH  SHEPS, EFRAIM
       TITL  INDIAN YOUTH"S ATTITUDES TOWARD NON-INDIAN PATTERNS OF
             LIFE.
       SOUR  JOURNAL OF AMERICAN INDIAN EDUCATION, JAN. 1970, V9,
             PP 19-27.
       YEAR  1970
       DESC  PSYCHOLOGICAL TESTING+, ADOLESCENTS+, SECONDARY
             SCHOOLS, B.I.A. BOARDING SCHOOLS, NATIVE AMERICAN
             VALUES+, NATIVE-NON-NATIVE COMPARISONS, ANGLO
```

```
                 AMERICANS, INTERTRIBAL COMPARISONS, SEX DIFFERENCES,
                 ATTITUDES+
          IDEN   U.S.

999   AUTH   DAVIS, THOMAS; SANDERSON, FRED
      TITL   COMMUNITY COUNSELORS AND THE COUNSELING PROCESS.
      SOUR   JOURNAL OF AMERICAN INDIAN EDUCATION, OCT. 1974, V13,
             PP 26-29.
      YEAR   1974
      DESC   EDUCATION PROFESSIONALS, PSYCHOTHERAPY AND
             COUNSELING+, COMMUNITY INVOLVEMENT+, PREVENTIVE MENTAL
             HEALTH PROGRAMS, NATIVE AMERICAN PERSONNEL+,
             MENOMINEE, NORTHEAST WOODLAND, EDUCATION
             PARAPROFESSIONALS+, RESERVATION, SECONDARY
             SCHOOLS,DROPOUTS+
      IDEN   U.S., WISCONSIN MENOMINEE RESERVATION

1000  AUTH   KALRA, R.M.
      TITL   SCIENCE TAUGHT WITH A FOCUS ON VALUES.
      SOUR   JOURNAL OF AMERICAN INDIAN EDUCATION, JAN. 1975, V14,
             PP 21-25.
      YEAR   1975
      DESC   NATIVE AMERICAN VALUES, EDUCATION PROGRAMS AND
             SERVICES, SCIENCE PROGRAMS+
      IDEN   U.S.

1001  AUTH   STAUB, HENRY P.
      TITL   AMERICAN INDIAN MEDICINE AND CONTEMPORARY HEALTH
             PROBLEMS. III. AMERICAN INDIANS. NEW OPPORTUNITY  FOR
             HEALTH CARE.
      SOUR   NEW YORK STATE JOURNAL OF MEDICINE, JUN. 1978, V78
             (7), PP 1137-1141.
      YEAR   1978
      DESC   PHYSICAL HEALTH AND ILLNESS+, IROQUOIS-SENECA,
             NORTHEAST WOODLAND, MEDICAL PROGRAMS AND SERVICES+,
             PROGRAM DEVELOPMENT+, COMMUNITY INVOLVEMENT+, NATIVE
             AMERICAN PERSONNEL, MEDICAL PROFESSIONALS, MEDICAL
             PARAPROFESSIONALS, SURVEY
      IDEN   U.S., NEW YORK

1002  AUTH   JUDKINS, RUSSELL A.
      TITL   AMERICAN INDIAN MEDICINE AND CONTEMPORARY HEALTH
             PROBLEMS. IV. DIABETES AND PERCEPTION OF DIABETES
             AMONG SENECA INDIANS.
      SOUR   NEW YORK STATE JOURNAL OF MEDICINE, JUL. 1978, V78
             (8), PP 1320-1323.
      YEAR   1978
      DESC   PHYSICAL HEALTH AND ILLNESS+, IROQUOIS-SENECA,
             NORTHEAST WOODLAND, RESERVATION, NUTRITIONAL FACTORS,
             STRESS, PERSONALITY TRAITS+, NATIVE AMERICAN ETIOLOGY
      IDEN   U.S., NEW YORK, ALLEGANY RESERVATION

1003  AUTH   DINGES, NORMAN G.; TOLLEFSON, GWEN D.; PARKS, GEORGE
             A.; HOLLENBECK, ALBERT R.
      TITL   ANTICIPATED REWARD AND TIME ESTIMATION IN YOUNG NAVAJO
```

```
       CHILDREN.
SOUR   PERCEPTUAL AND MOTOR SKILLS, 1978, V47, PP 1011-1014.
YEAR   1978
DESC   TIME PERCEPTION+, MOTIVATION+, NAVAJO, SOUTHWEST,
       CHILDREN-SCHOOL AGE, B.I.A. BOARDING SCHOOLS,
       COGNITIVE PROCESSES+, SEX DIFFERENCES, RESERVATION,
       EXPERIMENTAL STUDY
IDEN   U.S., ARIZONA, NAVAJO RESERVATION

1004 AUTH   STRATTON, RAY; ZEINER, ARTHUR R.; PAREDES, ALFONSO
     TITL   TRIBAL AFFILIATION AND PREVALENCE OF ALCOHOL PROBLEMS.
     SOUR   JOURNAL OF STUDIES ON ALCOHOL, 1978, V39 (7), PP
            1166-1177.
     YEAR   1978
     DESC   INTERTRIBAL COMPARISONS, OKLAHOMA INDIANS, ALCOHOL
            USE+, PLAINS, SOUTHEAST WOODLAND, TRADITIONAL SOCIAL
            CONTROL+, DREAMS AND VISION QUESTS, CULTURAL
            ADAPTATION
     IDEN   U.S., OKLAHOMA

1005 AUTH   DEVEREUX, GEORGE
     TITL   THE MOHAVE NEONATE AND ITS CRADLE.
     SOUR   PRIMITIVE MAN, JAN.-APR. 1948, V21 (1-2), PP 1-18.
     YEAR   1948
     DESC   MOHAVE, SOUTHWEST, CHILDREN-INFANTS AND PRESCHOOL+,
            TRADITIONAL CHILD REARING+
     IDEN   U.S.

1006 AUTH   ISSACS, HOPE L.
     TITL   AMERICAN INDIAN MEDICINE AND CONTEMPORARY HEALTH
            PROBLEMS. I. TOWARD IMPROVED HEALTH CARE FOR NATIVE
            AMERICANS. COMPARATIVE PERSPECTIVE ON AMERICAN INDIAN
            MEDICINE CONCEPTS.
     SOUR   NEW YORK STATE JOURNAL OF MEDICINE, APR. 1978, V78
            (5), PP 824-829.
     YEAR   1978
     DESC   CHIPPEWA, NAVAJO, IROQUOIS, EASTERN SUB-ARCTIC,
            SOUTHWEST, NORTHEAST WOODLAND, INTERTRIBAL
            COMPARISONS, NATIVE AMERICAN ETIOLOGY+, UNIVERSAL
            HARMONY
     IDEN   U.S., CANADA

1007 AUTH   MARGETTS, EDWARD L.
     TITL   SYMPOSIUM--CANADA'S NATIVE PEOPLES:
            INTRODUCTION--METHODOLOGY AND TOPICS OF RESEARCH.
     SOUR   CANADIAN PSYCHIATRIC ASSOCIATION JOURNAL, AUG. 1974,
            V19 (4), PP 329-330.
     YEAR   1974
     DESC   RESEARCHERS+, MENTAL HEALTH PROGRAMS AND SERVICES+,
            CLINICAL STUDY, EPIDEMIOLOGICAL STUDY, TRADITIONAL
            HEALERS
     IDEN   CANADA

1008 AUTH   HERRICK, JAMES W.
     TITL   AMERICAN INDIAN MEDICINE AND CONTEMPORARY HEALTH
```

PROBLEMS. II. POWERFUL MEDICINAL PLANTS IN TRADITIONAL
IROQUOIS CULTURE.
SOUR NEW YORK STATE JOURNAL OF MEDICINE, MAY 1978, V78 (6),
PP 979-987.
YEAR 1978
DESC TRADITIONAL USE OF DRUGS AND ALCOHOL+, UNIVERSAL
HARMONY, NATIVE AMERICAN ETIOLOGY+, IROQUOIS-SENECA,
NORTHEAST WOODLAND, TABOO BREAKING, WITCHCRAFT
IDEN U.S.

1009 TITL GOLD AWARD: PROVIDING PSYCHIATRIC CARE AND
CONSULTATION IN REMOTE INDIAN VILLAGES--DEPARTMENT OF
PSYCHIATRY, UNIVERSITY OF TORONTO, TORONTO, ONTARIO.
SOUR HOSPITAL AND COMMUNITY PSYCHIATRY, OCT. 1978, V29
(10), PP 678-680.
YEAR 1978
DESC DELIVERY OF SERVICES+, MENTAL HEALTH PROGRAMS AND
SERVICES+, CONSULTATION+, MENTAL HEALTH
PROFESSIONALS+, CREE, CHIPPEWA, EASTERN SUB-ARCTIC,
RESERVATION
IDEN CANADA, ONTARIO, SIOUX LOOKOUT ZONE

1010 AUTH FRITZ, W.B.
TITL INDIAN PEOPLE AND COMMUNITY PSYCHIATRY IN
SASKATCHEWAN.
SOUR CANADIAN PSYCHIATRIC ASSOCIATION JOURNAL, FEB. 1978,
V23 (1), PP 1-7.
YEAR 1978
DESC DELIVERY OF SERVICES+, MENTAL HEALTH PROGRAMS AND
SERVICES+, NATIVE-NON-NATIVE COMPARISONS, OUTPATIENT
CARE+, RESERVATION, MENTAL HEALTH INSTITUTIONS+,
INSTITUTIONALIZATION+, ANGLO AMERICANS, MENTAL
DISORDERS, NEUROSES, PSYCHOSES, CHARACTER DISORDERS,
EPIDEMIOLOGICAL STUDY
IDEN CANADA, SASKATCHEWAN

1011 AUTH ISHISAKA, HIDEKI
TITL AMERICAN INDIANS AND FOSTER CARE: CULTURAL FACTORS AND
SEPARATION.
SOUR CHILD WELFARE, MAY 1978, V57 (5), PP 299-308.
YEAR 1978
DESC CHILDREN-SCHOOL AGE+, CHILDREN-INFANTS AND PRESCHOOL+,
ADOPTION AND FOSTER CARE+, FAMILY FUNCTIONING+, CHILD
ABUSE AND NEGLECT, SOCIAL SERVICES+, URBAN AREAS
IDEN U.S., INDIAN CHILD WELFARE ACT

1012 AUTH RESCHLY, DANIEL J.
TITL WISC-R FACTOR STRUCTURES AMONG ANGLOS, BLACKS,
CHICANOS, AND NATIVE-AMERICAN PAPAGOS.
SOUR JOURNAL OF CONSULTING AND CLINICAL PSYCHOLOGY, JUN.
1978, V46 (3), PP 417-422.
YEAR 1978
DESC CHILDREN-SCHOOL AGE+, ABILITIES+, NATIVE-NON-NATIVE
COMPARISONS, BLACK AMERICANS, ANGLO AMERICANS,
LATINOS, PAPAGO, SOUTHWEST, PSYCHOLOGICAL TESTING+,

```
              CULTURE-FAIR TESTS+, ELEMENTARY SCHOOLS
        IDEN  U.S., ARIZONA, WESCHLER INTELLIGENCE SCALE CHILDREN

1013  AUTH  FRITZ, W.B.
      TITL  PSYCHIATRIC DISORDERS AMONG NATIVES AND NON-NATIVES IN
            SASKATCHEWAN.
      SOUR  CANADIAN PSYCHIATRIC ASSOCIATION JOURNAL, OCT. 1976,
            V21 (6), PP 393-400.
      YEAR  1976
      DESC  EPIDEMIOLOGICAL STUDY, MENTAL DISORDERS+, MENTAL
            HEALTH INSTITUTIONS+, ADULTS, INSTITUTIONALIZATION+,
            SEX DIFFERENCES,PSYCHOSES, NEUROSES, CHARACTER
            DISORDERS, MENTAL RETARDATION, AGE COMPARISONS,
            NATIVE-NON-NATIVE COMPARISONS, ANGLO AMERICANS
      IDEN  CANADA, SASKATCHEWAN

1014  AUTH  ROHRER, JOHN H.
      TITL  THE INTELLIGENCE OF OSAGE INDIANS.
      SOUR  JOURNAL OF SOCIAL PSYCHOLOGY, 1942, V16, PP 99-105.
      YEAR  1942
      DESC  OSAGE, PRAIRIE, ABILITIES+, PSYCHOLOGICAL TESTING+,
            CULTURE-FAIR TESTS+, CHILDREN-SCHOOL AGE+,
            NATIVE-NON-NATIVE COMPARISONS, ANGLO AMERICANS
      IDEN  U.S., GOODENOUGH HARRIS DRAW A PERSON TEST, OTIS SELF
            ADMINISTERING TEST OF MENTAL ABILITY

1015  AUTH  CALLAN, JOHN P.; PATTERSON, CARROLL D.
      TITL  PATTERNS OF DRUG ABUSE AMONG MILITARY INDUCTEES.
      SOUR  AMERICAN JOURNAL OF PSYCHIATRY, MAR. 1973, V130 (3),
            PP 260-264.
      YEAR  1973
      DESC  DRUG USE+, MILITARY SERVICE+, NATIVE-NON-NATIVE
            COMPARISONS, ANGLO AMERICANS, BLACK AMERICANS, LATINOS
      IDEN  U.S.

1016  AUTH  MEDICINE, BEATRICE
      TITL  LEARNING TO BE AN ANTHROPOLOGIST AND REMAINING
            "NATIVE".
      SOUR  IN E.M. EDDY AND W.L. PARTRIDGE (EDS.), APPLIED
            ANTHROPOLOGY IN AMERICA, PP 182-196. NEW YORK:
            COLUMBIA UNIVERSITY PRESS, 1976.
      YEAR  1976
      DESC  RESEARCHERS+, ETHNIC IDENTITY+, SELF-CONCEPT+,
            FEMALES+, ROLE MODELS+, SOCIAL ROLES+, STRESS
      IDEN  U.S.

1017  AUTH  RITZENTHALER, ROBERT
      TITL  PRIMITIVE THERAPEUTIC PRACTICES AMONG THE WISCONSIN
            CHIPPEWA.
      SOUR  IN IAGO GALDSTON (ED.), MAN'S IMAGE IN MEDICINE AND
            ANTHROPOLOGY, PP 316-334. NEW YORK: INTERNATIONAL
            UNIVERSITIES PRESS, 1963.
      YEAR  1963
      DESC  CHIPPEWA, EASTERN SUB-ARCTIC ,TRADITIONAL HEALERS+,
            NATIVE AMERICAN ETIOLOGY+, TABOO BREAKING, SPIRIT
```

```
         INTRUSION
     IDEN U.S., WISCONSIN

1018 AUTH HALLOWELL, A. IRVING
     TITL OJIBWA WORLD VIEW AND DISEASE.
     SOUR IN IAGO GALDSTON (ED.), MAN'S IMAGE IN MEDICINE AND
          ANTHROPOLOGY, PP 258-315. NEW YORK: INTERNATIONAL
          UNIVERSITIES PRESS, 1963.
     YEAR 1963
     DESC CHIPPEWA, EASTERN SUB-ARCTIC, NATIVE AMERICAN
          ETIOLOGY+, TRADITIONAL SOCIAL CONTROL+, CONFESSION+,
          ANXIETY+, GROUP NORMS AND SANCTIONS+, TRADITIONAL
          HEALERS, CULTURE-BASED PSYCHOTHERAPY+, TABOO BREAKING,
          WINDIGO PSYCHOSIS, GENEROSITY, NONCOMPETITIVENESS,
          EMOTIONAL RESTRAINT, SEXUAL RELATIONS
     IDEN CANADA

1019 AUTH ROEHL, C. ALLEN
     TITL THE INDIGENOUS AMERICAN INDIAN MENTAL HEALTH WORKER:
          EVOLUTION OF A JOB AND A CONCEPT.
     SOUR IN A. BEIGEL AND A. LEVENSON (EDS.), THE COMMUNITY
          MENTAL HEALTH CENTER, PP 337-346. NEW YORK: BASIC
          BOOKS, 1972.
     YEAR 1972
     DESC MENTAL HEALTH PARAPROFESSIONALS+, NATIVE AMERICAN
          PERSONNEL+, MENTAL HEALTH INSTITUTIONS, RESERVATION,
          SOCIAL ROLES+, STRESS+, SIOUX, PLAINS
     IDEN U.S., SOUTH DAKOTA, PINE RIDGE RESERVATION

1020 AUTH OSTENDORF, DONALD; HAMMERSCHLAG, CARL A.
     TITL AN INDIAN-CONTROLLED MENTAL HEALTH PROGRAM.
     SOUR HOSPITAL AND COMMUNITY PSYCHIATRY, SEP. 1977, V28 (9),
          PP 682-685.
     YEAR 1977
     DESC NATIVE AMERICAN ADMINISTERED PROGRAMS+, MENTAL HEALTH
          PROGRAMS AND SERVICES+, RESERVATION, APACHE-WHITE
          MOUNTAIN, SOUTHWEST, MENTAL HEALTH INSTITUTIONS+,
          TRIBAL POLITICAL ORGANIZATIONS+, FEDERAL GOVERNMENT,
          ADMINISTRATIVE ISSUES+
     IDEN U.S., FORT APACHE RESERVATION, ARIZONA, APACHE TRIBAL
          GUIDANCE CENTER

1021 AUTH FOWLER, LORETTA
     TITL WIND RIVER RESERVATION POLITICAL PROCESS: AN ANALYSIS
          OF THE SYMBOLS OF CONSENSUS.
     SOUR AMERICAN ETHNOLOGIST, NOV. 1978, V5 (4), PP 748-769.
     YEAR 1978
     DESC ARAPAHO-NORTHERN, PLAINS, RESERVATION, TRIBAL
          POLITICAL ORGANIZATIONS+, LEADERSHIP+, GROUP NORMS AND
          SANCTIONS+, SOCIAL NETWORKS, AGED+, GENEROSITY
     IDEN U.S., WYOMING, WIND RIVER RESERVATION

1022 AUTH BACHTOLD, LOUISE M.; DE JACKSON, OLIVIA R.
     TITL THE HUPA INDIANS: A CULTURALLY-BASED PRESCHOOL.
     SOUR CHILDREN TODAY, NOV.-DEC. 1978, PP 22-23, 26
```

```
        YEAR  1978
        DESC  CHILDREN-INFANTS AND PRESCHOOL+, EDUCATION PROGRAMS
              AND SERVICES+, NATIVE AMERICAN VALUES+,DROPOUTS,
              ETHNIC IDENTITY, HOOPA, NORTHWEST COAST, RESERVATION,
              DAY CARE+
        IDEN  U.S., CALIFORNIA

1023    AUTH  KERRI, JAMES N.
        TITL  BRIEF COMMUNICATIONS: "PUSH" AND "PULL" FACTORS:
              REASONS FOR MIGRATION AS A FACTOR IN AMERINDIAN URBAN
              ADJUSTMENT.
        SOUR  HUMAN ORGANIZATION, SUM. 1976, V35 (2), PP 215-220.
        YEAR  1976
        DESC  RELOCATION+, URBAN AREAS, RESERVATION, URBANIZATION+
        IDEN  CANADA

1024    AUTH  ALEXANDER, FRANKLIN D.
        TITL  THE CHICKASAW INDIAN TRIBE AND SELF-DETERMINATION: A
              STUDY OF ORGANIZATION AND ORGANIZATIONAL CHANGE.
        SOUR  DISSERTATION ABSTRACTS INTERNATIONAL, 1978, V39 (6), P
              3685-A.
        YEAR  1978
        DESC  CHICKASAW, SOUTHEAST WOODLAND, TRIBAL POLITICAL
              ORGANIZATIONS+, ADMINISTRATIVE ISSUES+
        IDEN  U.S., OKLAHOMA

1025    AUTH  BRUCHMAN, ROBERT C.
        TITL  NATIVE AMERICAN REVITALIZED PROPHECY: A PROCESS OF
              ENCULTURATION.
        SOUR  DISSERTATION ABSTRACTS INTERNATIONAL, 1978, V39 (5), P
              3010-A.
        YEAR  1978
        DESC  CULTURAL REVIVAL+, CULTURAL ADAPTATION+, NATIVE
              AMERICAN RELIGIONS+
        IDEN  U.S., DELAWARE PROPHECY, GHOST DANCE

1026    AUTH  MILLER, NANCY B.
        TITL  UTILIZATION OF SERVICES FOR THE DEVELOPMENTALLY
              DISABLED BY AMERICAN INDIAN FAMILIES IN LOS ANGELES.
        SOUR  DISSERTATION ABSTRACTS INTERNATIONAL, 1978, V39 (5), P
              3016-A.
        YEAR  1978
        DESC  PHYSICAL HEALTH AND ILLNESS+, MENTAL RETARDATION+,
              URBAN AREAS, DELIVERY OF SERVICES+, SOCIAL SERVICES+
        IDEN  U.S., CALIFORNIA

1027    AUTH  BURCHELL, LINDA N.
        TITL  NATIVE AMERICAN HEALING IN PSYCHOTHERAPY.
        SOUR  DISSERTATION ABSTRACTS INTERNATIONAL, 1978, V39 (1), P
              354-B.
        YEAR  1978
        DESC  PSYCHOTHERAPY AND COUNSELING+, ALASKA NATIVES, MENTAL
              HEALTH PROGRAMS AND SERVICES+, BICULTURALISM+

1028    AUTH  ROWE, CHESTER A.
```

```
        TITL  THE ACADEMIC ACHIEVEMENT OF NAVAJO INDIAN STUDENTS: A
              STUDY OF SELECTED VARIABLES AND THEIR CORRELATIONS
              WITH THE ACADEMIC ACHIEVEMENT OF NAVAJO INDIAN
              STUDENTS WHO LIVE IN A RURAL RESERVATION SETTING.
        SOUR  DISSERTATION ABSTRACTS INTERNATIONAL,1979, 1978, V39
              (7), P 4107-A.
        YEAR  1978
        DESC  ACHIEVEMENT+, NAVAJO, SOUTHWEST, RESERVATION,
              SECONDARY SCHOOLS, ADOLESCENTS
        IDEN  U.S., NAVAJO RESERVATION

1029    AUTH  CHISHOLM, JAMES S.
        TITL  DEVELOPMENTAL ETHOLOGY OF THE NAVAJO.
        SOUR  DISSERTATION ABSTRACTS INTERNATIONAL, 1978, V39 (7), P
              4363-A.
        YEAR  1978
        DESC  NAVAJO, SOUTHWEST, CHILDREN-INFANTS AND PRESCHOOL+,
              TRADITIONAL CHILD REARING+, NATIVE-NON-NATIVE
              COMPARISONS, ANGLO AMERICANS, FEMALES, ADULTS, FAMILY
              FUNCTIONING
        IDEN  U.S.

1030    AUTH  LODER, RICHARD R.
        TITL  THE AMERICAN INDIAN BAR AS GATE KEEPER: AN EXPLORATORY
              STUDY IN SYRACUSE, NEW YORK.
        SOUR  DISSERTATION ABSTRACTS INTERNATIONAL, 1978, V39 (6), P
              3857-A.
        YEAR  1978
        DESC  IROQUOIS, NORTHEAST WOODLAND, ALCOHOL USE+, NATIVE
              AMERICAN COPING BEHAVIORS+
        IDEN  U.S., NEW YORK

1031    AUTH  MEDICINE, BEATRICE
        TITL  THE NATIVE AMERICAN WOMAN: A PERSPECTIVE.
        SOUR  AUSTIN, TEXAS: NATIONAL EDUCATIONAL LABORATORY
              PUBLISHERS, 1978.
        YEAR  1978
        DESC  FEMALES+, SOCIAL ROLES+, RESEARCHERS, STRESS, MARITAL
              RELATIONSHIPS, SEXUAL RELATIONS

1032    AUTH  JOHNSTON, THOMAS F.
        TITL  ALASKAN NATIVE SOCIAL ADJUSTMENT AND THE ROLE OF
              ESKIMO AND INDIAN MUSIC.
        SOUR  JOURNAL OF ETHNIC STUDIES, WIN. 1976, V3 (4), PP 21-36.
        YEAR  1976
        DESC  ALASKA NATIVES, CULTURAL ADAPTATION+, CULTURAL
              CONTINUITY+, COGNITIVE PROCESSES+
        IDEN  U.S., ALASKA

1033    AUTH  BASSO, ELLEN B.
        TITL  THE ENEMY OF EVERY TRIBE: "BUSHMAN" IMAGES IN NORTHERN
              ATHABASKAN NARRATIVES.
        SOUR  AMERICAN ETHNOLOGIST, NOV. 1978, V5 (4), PP 690-709.
        YEAR  1978
        DESC  ATHABASCAN, YUKON SUB-ARCTIC, MACKENZIE SUB-ARCTIC,
```

```
              TRADITIONAL SOCIAL CONTROL+
       IDEN   CANADA

1034   AUTH   WARNER, RICHARD
       TITL   THE RELATIONSHIP BETWEEN LANGUAGE AND DISEASE
              CONCEPTS.
       SOUR   INTERNATIONAL JOURNAL OF PSYCHIATRY IN MEDICINE,
              1976-77, V7 (1), PP 57-68.
       YEAR   1976-77
       DESC   NATIVE AMERICAN ETIOLOGY+, LANGUAGE HANDICAPS+,
              NATIVE-NON-NATIVE COMPARISONS, INTERTRIBAL COMPARISONS

1035   AUTH   KELLER, GORDON N.
       TITL   BICULTURAL SOCIAL WORK AND ANTHROPOLOGY.
       SOUR   SOCIAL CASEWORK, OCT. 1972, PP 455-456.
       YEAR   1972
       DESC   NAVAJO, SOUTHWEST, RESEARCHERS+, SOCIAL SERVICE
              PROFESSIONALS+, RESERVATION, ANOMIE, SOCIAL SERVICES+,
              ECONOMIC ISSUES, POWERLESSNESS
       IDEN   U.S., UTAH

1036   AUTH   TEICHER, MORTON I.
       TITL   ADOPTION PRACTICES AMONG THE ESKIMOS ON SOUTHAMPTON
              ISLAND.
       SOUR   CANADIAN WELFARE, JUN. 1953, V29 (2), PP 32-27.
       YEAR   1953
       DESC   ADOPTION AND FOSTER CARE+, CENTRAL AND EASTERN ARCTIC,
              ESKIMO, TRADITIONAL CHILD REARING
       IDEN   CANADA

1037   AUTH   DINGES, NORMAN G.; HOLLENBECK, ALBERT R.
       TITL   THE EFFECT OF INSTRUCTIONAL SET ON THE SELF-ESTEEM OF
              NAVAJO CHILDREN.
       SOUR   JOURNAL OF SOCIAL PSYCHOLOGY, FEB. 1978, V104, PP 9-13.
       YEAR   1978
       DESC   NAVAJO, SOUTHWEST, CHILDREN-SCHOOL AGE+,
              SELF-CONCEPT+, RESERVATION, PSYCHOLOGICAL TESTING+,
              B.I.A. BOARDING SCHOOLS, CULTURE-FAIR TESTS
       IDEN   U.S., NAVAJO RESERVATION, CHILDREN'S SELF-SOCIAL
              CONSTRUCTS TEST

1038   AUTH   ALBERT, ETHEL M.
       TITL   THE CLASSIFICATION OF VALUES: A METHOD AND
              ILLUSTRATION.
       SOUR   AMERICAN ANTHROPOLOGIST, APR. 1956, V58, PP 221-263.
       YEAR   1956
       DESC   NATIVE AMERICAN VALUES+, GROUP NORMS AND SANCTIONS+,
              NAVAJO, SOUTHWEST, UNIVERSAL HARMONY+, RESERVATION
       IDEN   U.S., NAVAJO RESERVATION

1039   AUTH   CUNDICK, BERT P.
       TITL   MEASURES OF INTELLIGENCE ON SOUTHWEST INDIAN STUDENTS.
       SOUR   JOURNAL OF SOCIAL PSYCHOLOGY, 1970, V81, PP 151-156.
       YEAR   1970
       DESC   SOUTHWEST, ABILITIES+, PSYCHOLOGICAL TESTING+,
```

```
              CHILDREN-SCHOOL AGE+, ELEMENTARY SCHOOLS,
              CHILDREN-INFANTS AND PRESCHOOL+, AGE COMPARISONS
       IDEN   U.S., WECHSLER INTELLIGENCE SCALE CHILDREN, PEABODY
              PICTURE VOCABULARY TESTS, GOODENOUGH HARRIS DRAW A
              PERSON TEST, WECHSLER PRESCHOOL AND PRIMARY SCALE OF
              INTELLIGENCE

1040   AUTH   SLOTKIN, J.S.
       TITL   RELIGIOUS DEFENSES: THE NATIVE AMERICAN CHURCH.
       SOUR   JOURNAL OF PSYCHEDELIC DRUGS, WIN. 1967, V1(2), PP
              77-95.
       YEAR   1967
       DESC   NATIVE AMERICAN RELIGIONS+, DRUG USE+, TRADITIONAL USE
              OF DRUGS AND ALCOHOL+, RELIGIONS-NON-NATIVE, CULTURAL
              ADAPTATION
       IDEN   U.S., NATIVE AMERICAN CHURCH

1041   TITL   PROCEEDINGS OF THE THIRD NATIONAL CONFERENCE ON INDIAN
              HEALTH.
       SOUR   NEW YORK: ASSOCIATION ON AMERICAN INDIAN AFFAIRS,
              1964. (43P)
       YEAR   1964
       DESC   MENTAL DISORDERS, PREVENTIVE MENTAL HEALTH PROGRAMS+,
              ALCOHOL USE, MENTAL HEALTH PROGRAMS AND SERVICES+,
              PROGRAM DEVELOPMENT+, DRUG USE, COMMUNITY INVOLVEMENT
       IDEN   U.S.

1042   AUTH   BAILEY, FLORA L.
       TITL   NAVAJO MOTOR HABITS.
       SOUR   AMERICAN ANTHROPOLOGIST, JAN.-MAR. 1942, V44, PP
              210-234.
       YEAR   1942
       DESC   NAVAJO, SOUTHWEST, MOTOR PROCESSES+, TRADITIONAL CHILD
              REARING ,RESERVATION
       IDEN   U.S., NAVAJO RESERVATION

1043   AUTH   WOOD, ROSEMARY; KEKAHBAH, JANICE; CORNELIUS, HELEN
       TITL   INDIAN MEDICINE AND NURSING.
       SOUR   PAPER PRESENTED AT THE FIRST NATIONAL AMERICAN INDIAN
              NURSES ASSOCIATION CONFERENCE, HASKELL INDIAN COLLEGE,
              1974. (8P)
       YEAR   1974
       DESC   NATIVE AMERICAN PERSONNEL+, MEDICAL PROFESSIONALS+,
              CULTURE-BASED PSYCHOTHERAPY+, TRADITIONAL HEALERS+
       IDEN   U.S.

1044   AUTH   BEE, ROBERT L.
       TITL   "SELF-HELP" AT FORT YUMA: A CRITIQUE.
       SOUR   HUMAN ORGANIZATION, FALL 1970, V29 (3), PP 155-161.
       YEAR   1970
       DESC   YUMA, SOUTHWEST, RESERVATION, COOPERATION+, ECONOMIC
              ISSUES, LEADERSHIP, GROUP NORMS AND SANCTIONS+,
              FEDERAL GOVERNMENT
       IDEN   U.S., CALIFORNIA, FORT YUMA RESERVATION
```

```
1045  AUTH  BRUNER, EDWARD M.; ROTTER, JULIAN B.
      TITL  A LEVEL-OF-ASPIRATION STUDY AMONG THE RAMAH NAVAJO.
      SOUR  JOURNAL OF PERSONALITY, 1953, V21, PP 375-385.
      YEAR  1953
      DESC  NAVAJO, SOUTHWEST, RESERVATION, MOTIVATION+, GROUP
            NORMS AND SANCTIONS+, ADULTS, SEX DIFFERENCES, PASSIVE
            RESISTANCE
      IDEN  U.S., NAVAJO RESERVATION, DART TEST, NEW MEXICO

1046  AUTH  ADAIR, JOHN
      TITL  THE INDIAN HEALTH WORKER IN THE CORNELL-NAVAJO
            PROJECT.
      SOUR  HUMAN ORGANIZATION, 1960, V19, PP 59-64.
      YEAR  1960
      DESC  NATIVE AMERICAN PERSONNEL+, MEDICAL
            PARAPROFESSIONALS+, BILINGUALISM, NAVAJO, SOUTHWEST,
            STRESS, BICULTURALISM+, TRAINING PROGRAMS+, SOCIAL
            ROLES+, PROGRAM EVALUATION, RESERVATION
      IDEN  U.S., NAVAJO RESERVATION

1047  AUTH  BUSHNELL, JOHN H.
      TITL  FROM AMERICAN INDIAN TO INDIAN AMERICAN: THE CHANGING
            IDENTITY OF THE HUPA.
      SOUR  AMERICAN ANTHROPOLOGIST, 1968, V70, PP 1108-1116.
      YEAR  1968
      DESC  HOOPA, NORTHWEST COAST, RESERVATION, CULTURAL
            ADAPTATION+, CULTURAL CONTINUITY+
      IDEN  U.S., CALIFORNIA, HOOPA VALLEY RESERVATION

1048  AUTH  PATTON, WALTER; EDINGTON, EVERETT D.
      TITL  FACTORS RELATED TO THE PERSISTENCE OF INDIAN STUDENTS
            AT COLLEGE LEVEL.
      SOUR  JOURNAL OF AMERICAN INDIAN EDUCATION, MAY 1973, V12,
            PP 19-23.
      YEAR  1973
      DESC  COLLEGES AND UNIVERSITIES+, SEX DIFFERENCES,
            MOTIVATION+, AGE COMPARISONS
      IDEN  U.S., NEW MEXICO

1049  AUTH  RAMEY, JOSEPH H.; SILEO, THOMAS W.; ZONGOLOWICZ, HELEN
      TITL  RESOURCE CENTERS FOR CHILDREN WITH LEARNING
            DISABILITIES.
      SOUR  JOURNAL OF AMERICAN INDIAN EDUCATION, MAY 1975, V14,
            PP 13-20.
      YEAR  1975
      DESC  NAVAJO, SOUTHWEST, RESERVATION, LEARNING DISABILITIES
            AND PROBLEMS+, MOTOR PROCESSES, COGNITIVE PROCESSES,
            LANGUAGE HANDICAPS, EDUCATION PROGRAMS AND SERVICES+,
            PSYCHOLOGICAL TESTING+, LEARNING+, B.I.A. BOARDING
            SCHOOLS
      IDEN  U.S., GREASEWOOD BOARDING SCHOOL, VALETT INVENTORY OF
            PSYCHOEDUCATIONAL LEARNING ABILITIES, NAVAJO
            RESERVATION

1050  AUTH  ARMSTRONG, ROBERT L. ; HOLMES, BARBARA
```

TITL   COUNSELING FOR SOCIALLY WITHDRAWN INDIAN GIRLS.
SOUR   JOURNAL OF AMERICAN INDIAN EDUCATION, JAN. 1971, V10,
       PP 4-7.
YEAR   1971
DESC   FEMALES+, ADOLESCENTS+, PSYCHOTHERAPY AND COUNSELING+,
       B.I.A. BOARDING SCHOOLS, PASSIVE RESISTANCE+, SOCIAL
       GROUPS AND PEER GROUPS+, SELF-CONCEPT
IDEN   U.S.

1051   AUTH   JILEK, WOLFGANG G.
       TITL   A QUEST FOR IDENTITY: THERAPEUTIC ASPECTS OF THE
              SALISH INDIAN GUARDIAN SPIRIT CEREMONIAL.
       SOUR   JOURNAL OF OPERATIONAL PSYCHIATRY, 1977, V8 (2), PP
              46-57.
       YEAR   1977
       DESC   COAST SALISH, NORTHWEST COAST, ANOMIE+, DEPRESSION+,
              CULTURE-BASED PSYCHOTHERAPY+, ETHNIC IDENTITY+,
              CULTURAL REVIVAL
       IDEN   U.S., WASHINGTON, CANADA, BRITISH COLUMBIA

1052   AUTH   HAYNER, NORMAN S.
       TITL   VARIABILITY IN THE CRIMINAL BEHAVIOR OF AMERICAN
              INDIANS.
       SOUR   AMERICAN JOURNAL OF SOCIOLOGY, 1942, V47, PP 602-613.
       YEAR   1942
       DESC   NORTHWEST COAST, PLAINS, CRIME+, ALCOHOL USE,
              INTERTRIBAL COMPARISONS, PLATEAU, COLVILLE, YAKIMA,
              KLAMATH, ECONOMIC ISSUES+
       IDEN   U.S.

1053   AUTH   COWEN, PHILIP A.
       TITL   TESTING INDIAN SCHOOL PUPILS IN THE STATE OF NEW YORK.
       SOUR   MENTAL HYGIENE, 1943, V27, PP 80-82.
       YEAR   1943
       DESC   PSYCHOLOGICAL TESTING+, ABILITIES+, CHILDREN-SCHOOL
              AGE+, ELEMENTARY SCHOOLS, RESERVATION, NORTHEAST
              WOODLAND
       IDEN   U.S., NEW YORK, KUHLMANN-ANDERSON TEST OF MENTAL
              ABILITY

1054   AUTH   GOLDFRANK, ESTHER S.
       TITL   IRRIGATION AGRICULTURE AND NAVAJO COMMUNITY
              LEADERSHIP: CASE MATERIAL ON ENVIRONMENT AND CULTURE.
       SOUR   AMERICAN ANTHROPOLOGIST, 1945, V47, PP 262-277.
       YEAR   1945
       DESC   NAVAJO, SOUTHWEST, RESERVATION, LEADERSHIP+,
              COOPERATION+, ENVIRONMENTAL FACTORS+, TRIBAL POLITICAL
              ORGANIZATIONS+
       IDEN   U.S , NAVAJO RESERVATION

1055   AUTH   KLUCKHOHN, CLYDE; MORGAN, WILLIAM
       TITL   SOME NOTES ON NAVAJO DREAMS.
       SOUR   IN GEORGE B. WILBUR AND WARNER MUENSTERBERGER (EDS.),
              PSYCHOANALYSIS AND CULTURE: ESSAYS IN HONOR OF GEZA
              ROHEIM, PP 120-131. NEW YORK: INTERNATIONAL

UNIVERSITIES PRESS, 1951.
YEAR 1951
DESC PSYCHOANALYSIS+, DREAMS AND VISION QUESTS+, FEMALES+,
FAMILY FUNCTIONING+, SEXUAL RELATIONS+, NAVAJO,
SOUTHWEST, RESERVATION
IDEN U.S., NAVAJO RESERVATION

1056 AUTH DENNIS, WAYNE
TITL ANIMISM AND RELATED TENDENCIES IN HOPI CHILDREN.
SOUR JOURNAL OF ABNORMAL AND SOCIAL PSYCHOLOGY, 1943, V38,
PP 21-36.
YEAR 1943
DESC PUEBLO-HOPI, SOUTHWEST, ADOLESCENTS+, PSYCHOLOGICAL
TESTING+, COGNITIVE PROCESSES+, NATIVE-NON-NATIVE
COMPARISONS, ANGLO AMERICANS, RESERVATION, SECONDARY
SCHOOLS, ABILITIES
IDEN U.S., PIAGETIAN TASKS, GOODENOUGH HARRIS DRAW A PERSON
TEST, HOPI RESERVATION

1057 AUTH WALLACE, WILLIAM J.
TITL HUPA CHILD-TRAINING: A STUDY IN PRIMITIVE EDUCATION.
SOUR EDUCATIONAL ADMINISTRATION AND SUPERVISION, 1947, V33,
PP 13-25.
YEAR 1947
DESC HOOPA, NORTHWEST COAST, TRADITIONAL CHILD REARING+,
CHILDREN-INFANTS AND PRESCHOOL+, CHILDREN-SCHOOL AGE+,
SEX DIFFERENCES, ADOLESCENTS+
IDEN U.S., CALIFORNIA

1058 AUTH CLIFTON, RODNEY A.
TITL THE SOCIAL ADJUSTMENT OF NATIVE STUDENTS IN A NORTHERN
CANADIAN HOSTEL.
SOUR CANADIAN REVIEW OF SOCIOLOGY AND ANTHROPOLOGY,1972,
V9(2), PP 163-166.
YEAR 1972
DESC MACKENZIE SUB-ARCTIC, BOARDING HOMES+, ESKIMO, METIS,
DROPOUTS, INTERTRIBAL COMPARISONS, CULTURAL
ADAPTATION+, ADOLESCENTS, SOCIALLY DEVIANT BEHAVIOR,
OFF-RESERVATION
IDEN CANADA, NORTHWEST TERRITORIES

1059 AUTH ARTHUR, GRACE
TITL AN EXPERIENCE IN TESTING INDIAN SCHOOL CHILDREN.
SOUR MENTAL HYGIENE, 1941, V25, PP 188-195.
YEAR 1941
DESC PSYCHOLOGICAL TESTING+, ADOLESCENTS+, ABILITIES+,
CHILDREN-SCHOOL AGE+
IDEN U.S., STANFORD BINET INTELLIGENCE SCALE

1060 AUTH PECORARO, JOSEPH
TITL THE EFFECT OF A SERIES OF SPECIAL LESSONS ON INDIAN
HISTORY AND CULTURE UPON THE ATTITUDE OF INDIAN AND
NON-INDIAN STUDENTS.
SOUR JOURNAL OF EDUCATION, FEB. 1973, V154(3), PP 70-78.
YEAR 1973

DESC   SELF—CONCEPT+, PSYCHOLOGICAL TESTING, CULTURAL
        CONTINUITY, ATTITUDES+ , ELEMENTARY SCHOOLS,
        EXPERIMENTAL STUDY, EDUCATION PROGRAMS AND SERVICES+,
        PASSAMAQUODDY, NORTHEAST WOODLAND, CHILDREN—SCHOOL
        AGE+
IDEN   U.S., MAINE, SEMANTIC DIFFERENTIAL, ATTITIDE SCALE

1061   AUTH   ALFRED, BRAXTON M.
       TITL   BLOOD PRESSURE CHANGES AMONG MALE NAVAJO MIGRANTS TO
               AN URBAN ENVIRONMENT.
       SOUR   CANADIAN REVIEW OF SOCIOLOGY AND ANTHROPOLOGY, AUG.
               1970, V7(3), PP 189-200.
       YEAR   1970
       DESC   PSYCHOPHYSIOLOGICAL DISORDERS+, STRESS+, NAVAJO,
               SOUTHWEST, MALES, ADULTS, RELOCATION, URBAN AREAS,
               RESERVATION
       IDEN   U.S.

1062   AUTH   GARTH, THOMAS R.
       TITL   MENTAL FATIGUE OF MIXED AND FULL BLOOD INDIANS.
       SOUR   JOURNAL OF APPLIED PSYCHOLOGY, 1922, V6, PP 331-341.
       YEAR   1922
       DESC   ABILITIES+, CHILDREN—SCHOOL AGE+, ADOLESCENTS+,
               PLAINS, SOUTHEAST WOODLAND, CHEYENNE, CREEK, CHEROKEE,
               CHOCTAW, NATIVE—NON—NATIVE COMPARISONS, ANGLO
               AMERICANS, FULL BLOOD—MIXED BLOOD COMPARISONS,
               MOTIVATION+
       IDEN   U.S.

1063   AUTH   GARTH, THOMAS R.
       TITL   A COMPARISON OF MENTAL ABILITIES OF MIXED AND FULL
               BLOOD INDIANS ON A BASIS OF EDUCATION.
       SOUR   PSYCHOLOGICAL REVIEW, 1972, V29(3), PP 221-236.
       YEAR   1922
       DESC   ABILITIES+, FULL BLOOD—MIXED BLOOD COMPARISONS,
               GENETIC FACTORS, ENVIRONMENTAL FACTORS,
               CHILDREN—SCHOOL AGE, ADOLESCENTS
       IDEN   U.S.

1064   AUTH   HAMMOND, D. CORYDON
       TITL   CROSS—CULTURAL REHABILITATION.
       SOUR   JOURNAL OF REHABILITATION, SEP.—OCT. 1971, V37(5), PP
               34-36, 44.
       YEAR   1971
       DESC   NATIVE AMERICAN VALUES+, PSYCHOTHERAPY AND
               COUNSELING+, MENTAL HEALTH PROFESSIONALS+
       IDEN   U.S.

1065   AUTH   WORTH, SOL; ADAIR, JOHN
       TITL   NAVAJO FILMMAKERS.
       SOUR   AMERICAN ANTHROPOLOGIST, 1970, V72, PP 9-34.
       YEAR   1970
       DESC   COGNITIVE PROCESSES+, NAVAJO, SOUTHWEST, RESERVATION,
               LEARNING, LANGUAGE HANDICAPS, NONINTERFERENCE
       IDEN   U.S., NAVAJO RESERVATION

1066 AUTH BAHR, HOWARD M.; CHADWICK, BRUCE A.
     TITL CONTEMPORARY PERSPECTIVES ON INDIAN AMERICANS: A
           REVIEW ESSAY.
     SOUR SOCIAL SCIENCE QUARTERLY, DEC. 1972, V53(3), PP
           606-618.
     YEAR 1972
     DESC URBAN AREAS, RESERVATION, CULTURAL ADAPTATION+,
           CULTURAL CONTINUITY+, CULTURAL REVIVAL+, REVIEW OF
           LITERATURE, RESEARCHERS+
     IDEN U.S.

1067 AUTH GUNSKY, FREDERIC R.
     TITL SCHOOL PROBLEMS OF INDIAN YOUTH.
     SOUR CALIFORNIA EDUCATION, 1966, V3(5), PP 20-22.
     YEAR 1966
     DESC SELF-CONCEPT+, CHILDREN-SCHOOL AGE+, ELEMENTARY
           SCHOOLS+, CALIFORNIA AREA
     IDEN U.S., CALIFORNIA STATE

1068 AUTH HENNINGER, DANIEL; ESPOSITO, NANCY
     TITL REGIMENTED NON-EDUCATION: INDIAN SCHOOLS.
     SOUR THE NEW REPUBLIC, FEB. 15, 1969, PP 18-21.
     YEAR 1969
     DESC B.I.A. BOARDING SCHOOLS+, SUICIDE, SOCIALLY DEVIANT
           BEHAVIOR, CHILDREN-SCHOOL AGE, ADOLESCENTS
     IDEN U.S.

1069 AUTH HANSEN, H.C.
     TITL SCHOLASTIC ACHIEVEMENT OF INDIAN PUPILS.
     SOUR JOURNAL OF GENETIC PSYCHOLOGY, 1937, V50, PP 361-369.
     YEAR 1937
     DESC ACHIEVEMENT+, CHILDREN-SCHOOL AGE+, ELEMENTARY
           SCHOOLS, NATIVE-NON-NATIVE COMPARISONS, ANGLO
           AMERICANS, FULL BLOOD-MIXED BLOOD COMPARISONS,
           PSYCHOLOGICAL TESTING, ABILITIES+
     IDEN U.S., OKLAHOMA, TRACY SHORT ANSWER TESTS

1070 AUTH HAUGHT, B.F.
     TITL MENTAL GROWTH OF THE SOUTHWESTERN INDIAN.
     SOUR JOURNAL OF APPLIED PSYCHOLOGY, 1934, V18, PP 137-142.
     YEAR 1934
     DESC ABILITIES+, PSYCHOLOGICAL TESTING+, SOUTHWEST,
           CHILDREN-SCHOOL AGE+, ADOLESCENTS+, B.I.A. BOARDING
           SCHOOLS, NATIVE-NON-NATIVE COMPARISONS, ANGLO
           AMERICANS
     IDEN U.S., PINTER CUNNINGHAM PRIMARY MENTAL TEST, NATIONAL
           INTELLIGENCE TEST, TERMAN GROUP TEST OF MENTAL ABILITY

1071 AUTH HANSEN, H.C.
     TITL RELATIONSHIP BETWEEN SEX AND SCHOOL ACHIEVEMENT OF ONE
           THOUSAND INDIAN CHILDREN.
     SOUR JOURNAL OF SOCIAL PSYCHOLOGY, 1939, V10, PP 399-406.
     YEAR 1939
     DESC ACHIEVEMENT+, ABILITIES+, SEX DIFFERENCES,
           PSYCHOLOGICAL TESTING+, CHILDREN-SCHOOL AGE+, OKLAHOMA

```
                    INDIANS, ELEMENTARY SCHOOLS, MALES, FEMALES,
                    NATIVE-NON-NATIVE COMPARISONS, ANGLO AMERICANS
          IDEN      U.S., OKLAHOMA, TRACY SHORT ANSWER TESTS

1072      AUTH      GAUDIA, GIL
          TITL      RACE, SOCIAL CLASS, AND AGE OF ACHIEVEMENT OF
                    CONSERVATION ON PIAGET'S TASKS.
          SOUR      DEVELOPMENTAL PSYCHOLOGY, 1972, V6(1), PP 158-165.
          YEAR      1972
          DESC      PSYCHOLOGICAL TESTING+, COGNITIVE PROCESSES+,
                    ABILITIES+, CHILDREN-SCHOOL AGE+, NATIVE-NON-NATIVE
                    COMPARISONS, ANGLO AMERICANS, BLACK AMERICANS,
                    IROQUOIS-SENECA, NORTHEAST WOODLAND, SOCIAL STATUS+,
                    ELEMENTARY SCHOOLS
          IDEN      U. S., NEW YORK, CONSERVATION CONCEPT DIAGNOSTIC KIT,
                    PEABODY PICTURE VOCABULARY, PIAGETIAN TASKS

1073      AUTH      LEWIS, RONALD G.
          TITL      "...BUT WE HAVE BEEN HELPING INDIANS FOR A LONG
                    TIME..."
          SOUR      IN GERALD C. ST. DENIS AND LOUISE DOSS (EDS.), HEALTH
                    CARE DELIVERY TO MEET THE CHANGING NEEDS OF THE
                    AMERICAN FAMILY; PROCEEDINGS OF THE 1977 MEDICAL
                    SOCIAL CONSULTANTS' ANNUAL MEETING, PP 51-58, 1977.
          YEAR      1977
          DESC      DELIVERY OF SERVICES+, FAMILY FUNCTIONING+, SOCIAL
                    SERVICES+, SOCIAL NETWORKS+, SOCIAL SERVICE
                    PROFESSIONALS+
          IDEN      U.S.

1074      AUTH      WALLACE, WILLIAM J.
          TITL      PERSONALITY VARIATION IN A PRIMITIVE SOCIETY.
          SOUR      JOURNAL OF PERSONALITY, 1947, V15, PP 321-328.
          YEAR      1947
          DESC      HOOPA, NORTHWEST COAST, PERSONALITY TRAITS+,
                    TRADITIONAL SOCIAL CONTROL+, GENEROSITY,
                    AGGRESSIVENESS
          IDEN      U.S., CALIFORNIA

1075      AUTH      BRUNER, EDWARD M.
          TITL      PRIMARY GROUP EXPERIENCE AND THE PROCESS OF
                    ACCULTURATION.
          SOUR      AMERICAN ANTHROPOLOGIST, 1956, V58, PP 605-623.
          YEAR      1956
          DESC      MANDAN, HIDATSA, PRAIRIE, GENEROSITY+, CULTURAL
                    ADAPTATION+, NATIVE AMERICAN VALUES, CULTURAL
                    CONTINUITY+, FAMILY FUNCTIONING, ROLE MODELS+,
                    EXTENDED FAMILY, GROUP NORMS AND SANCTIONS,
                    BICULTURALISM+, POW-WOWS
          IDEN      U.S.

1076      AUTH      GOLDFRANK, ESTHER S.
          TITL      HISTORIC CHANGE AND SOCIAL CHARACTER: A STUDY OF THE
                    TETON DAKOTA.
          SOUR      AMERICAN ANTHROPOLOGIST, 1943, V45, PP 67-83.
```

```
         YEAR  1943
         DESC  SIOUX, PLAINS, PERSONALITY TRAITS+, AGGRESSIVENESS+,
               GENEROSITY, COOPERATION+
         IDEN  U.S.

1077  AUTH  GARTH, THOMAS R.; BARNARD, MARY A.
      TITL  THE WILL-TEMPERAMENT OF INDIANS.
      SOUR  JOURNAL OF APPLIED PSYCHOLOGY, 1927, V9, PP 512-518.
      YEAR  1927
      DESC  NATIVE-NON-NATIVE COMPARISONS, ANGLO AMERICANS, BLACK
            AMERICANS, ADOLESCENTS, MOTIVATION+, PSYCHOLOGICAL
            TESTING+
      IDEN  U.S., WILL-TEMPERAMENT TEST

1078  AUTH  BROWN, JUDITH K.
      TITL  A CROSS-CULTURAL STUDY OF FEMALE INITIATION RITES.
      SOUR  AMERICAN ANTHROPOLOGIST, 1963, V65, PP 837-853.
      YEAR  1963
      DESC  FEMALES+, ADOLESCENTS+, SOCIAL ROLES+, INTERTRIBAL
            COMPARISONS, NATIVE-NON-NATIVE COMPARISONS

1079  AUTH  FOLK-WILLIAMS, JOHN A.
      TITL  ON BEING NON-INDIAN.
      SOUR  FOUNDATION NEWS, MAR.-APR. 1979, PP 15-20.
      YEAR  1979
      DESC  RESEARCHERS+, NATIVE AMERICAN VALUES+, TIME
            PERCEPTION, ADMINISTRATIVE ISSUES+

1080  AUTH  BAILEY, FLORA L.
      TITL  SUGGESTED TECHNIQUES FOR INDUCING NAVAHO WOMEN TO
            ACCEPT HOSPITALIZATION DURING CHILDBIRTH AND FOR
            IMPLEMENTING HEALTH EDUCATION.
      SOUR  AMERICAN JOURNAL OF PUBLIC HEALTH, OCT. 1948, V38, PP
            1418-1423.
      YEAR  1948
      DESC  NAVAJO, SOUTHWEST, RESERVATION, FEMALES+, ADULTS+,
            MEDICAL INSTITUTIONS+, INSTITUTIONALIZATION+,
            CHILDREN-INFANTS AND PRESCHOOL, PASSIVE RESISTANCE,
            TRADITIONAL HEALERS, MEDICAL PROFESSIONALS, ATTITUDES
      IDEN  U.S., NAVAJO RESERVATION

1081  AUTH  GEYNDT, WILLY DE
      TITL  HEALTH BEHAVIOR AND HEALTH NEEDS OF URBAN INDIANS IN
            MINNEAPOLIS.
      SOUR  HEALTH SERVICE REPORTS, APR. 1973, V88(4), PP 360-366.
      YEAR  1973
      DESC  URBAN AREAS, DEMOGRAPHIC DATA, SURVEY, MEDICAL
            PROGRAMS AND SERVICES+, DELIVERY OF SERVICES+ ,
            ATTITUDES
      IDEN  U.S., MINNESOTA

1082  AUTH  BARNETT, DON C.
      TITL  ATTITUDES OF ESKIMO SCHOOL CHILDREN.
      SOUR  INTEGRATED EDUCATION, JAN.-FEB. 1973, V11(1), PP 52-57.
      YEAR  1973
```

DESC   ATTITUDES+, ESKIMO, CENTRAL AND EASTERN ARCTIC,
        CHILDREN-SCHOOL AGE+, OFF-RESERVATION, URBAN AREAS,
        URBANIZATION+, ELEMENTARY SCHOOLS, EDUCATION
        PROFESSIONALS+
IDEN   CANADA

1083   AUTH   VOGET, FRED W.
        TITL   INDIVIDUAL MOTIVATION IN THE DIFFUSION OF THE WIND
                RIVER SHOSHONE SUNDANCE TO THE CROW INDIANS.
        SOUR   AMERICAN ANTHROPOLOGIST, 1948, V50, PP 634-646.
        YEAR   1948
        DESC   NATIVE AMERICAN RELIGIONS+, SHOSHONE, CROW, PLAINS,
                RESERVATION, MOTIVATION+, CULTURAL REVIVAL+, MALES,
                AGED, ADULTS, NATIVE AMERICAN VALUES
        IDEN   U.S., MONTANA, CROW RESERVATION, SUNDANCE RELIGION

1084   AUTH   ANDERSON, JAMES G.; SAFAR, DWIGHT
        TITL   THE INFLUENCE OF DIFFERENTIAL COMMUNITY PERCEPTIONS ON
                THE PROVISION OF EQUAL EDUCATIONAL OPPORTUNITIES.
        SOUR   SOCIOLOGY OF EDUCATION, SUM. 1967, V40(2), PP 219-230.
        YEAR   1967
        DESC   CHILDREN-SCHOOL AGE+, NATIVE-NON-NATIVE COMPARISONS,
                ANGLO AMERICANS, LATINOS, ABILITIES+, ATTITUDES+,
                SELF-CONCEPT+, STEREOTYPES, COMMUNITY INVOLVEMENT+,
                EDUCATION PROGRAMS AND SERVICES+, SOUTHWEST
        IDEN   U.S.

1085   AUTH   TEFFT, STANTON K.
        TITL   TASK EXPERIENCE AND INTERTRIBAL VALUE DIFFERENCES ON
                THE WIND RIVER RESERVATION.
        SOUR   SOCIAL FORCES, JUN. 1971, V49(4), PP 604-614.
        YEAR   1971
        DESC   SHOSHONE, PLAINS, RESERVATION, NATIVE AMERICAN
                VALUES+, ARAPAHO-NORTHERN, INTERTRIBAL COMPARISONS,
                SOCIAL GROUPS AND PEER GROUPS+, NATIVE-NON-NATIVE
                COMPARISONS, ANGLO AMERICANS, ACHIEVEMENT+,
                COOPERATION+, ADULTS
        IDEN   U.S., WYOMING, WIND RIVER RESERVATION

1086   AUTH   ARNEKLEV, BRUCE L.
        TITL   THE USE OF DEFENSIVENESS AS A COVARIATE OF SELF-REPORT
                IN THE ASSESSMENT OF SELF-CONCEPT AMONG NAVAJO
                ADOLESCENTS.
        SOUR   DISSERTATION ABSTRACTS INTERNATIONAL, 1972, V32(7), PP
                3772-A - 3773-A.
        YEAR   1972
        DESC   NAVAJO, SOUTHWEST, ADOLESCENTS+, SELF-CONCEPT+,
                PSYCHOLOGICAL TESTING+, B.I.A. BOARDING SCHOOLS
        IDEN   U.S., TENNESSEE SELF CONCEPT SCALE

1087   AUTH   GARTH, THOMAS R.
        TITL   THE INCIDENCE OF COLOR BLINDNESS AMONG RACES.
        SOUR   SCIENCE, MAR. 1933, V177, PP 333-334.
        YEAR   1933
        DESC   COGNITIVE PROCESSES+, NATIVE-NON-NATIVE COMPARISONS,

ANGLO AMERICANS, LATINOS, BLACK AMERICANS, SEX
DIFFERENCES
IDEN U.S., ISHIHARA COLOR BLINDNESS TEST

1088 AUTH GARTH, THOMAS R.
      TITL THE COLOR PREFERENCES OF FIVE HUNDRED AND FIFTY-NINE
            FULL-BLOOD INDIANS.
      SOUR JOURNAL OF EXPERIMENTAL PSYCHOLOGY, 1922, V5, PP
            392-418.
      YEAR 1922
      DESC COGNITIVE PROCESSES+, FULL BLOOD-MIXED BLOOD
            COMPARISONS, NATIVE-NON-NATIVE COMPARISONS, ANGLO
            AMERICANS, ADOLESCENTS, CHILDREN-SCHOOL AGE, AGE
            COMPARISONS
      IDEN U.S.

1089 AUTH GARTH, THOMAS R.
      TITL WHITE, INDIAN AND NEGRO WORK CURVES.
      SOUR JOURNAL OF APPLIED PSYCHOLOGY, 1921, V5, PP 14-25.
      YEAR 1921
      DESC NATIVE-NON-NATIVE COMPARISONS, ANGLO AMERICANS, BLACK
            AMERICANS, MOTIVATION+
      IDEN U.S.

1090 AUTH GARTH, THOMAS R.; SMITH, HALE W.; ABELL, WENDELL
      TITL A STUDY OF THE INTELLIGENCE AND ACHIEVEMENT OF
            FULL-BLOOD INDIANS.
      SOUR JOURNAL OF APPLIED PSYCHOLOGY, 1928, V12(5), PP
            511-516.
      YEAR 1928
      DESC ABILITIES+, ACHIEVEMENT+, PSYCHOLOGICAL TESTING+,
            CHILDREN-SCHOOL AGE, ADOLESCENTS, B.I.A. BOARDING
            SCHOOLS, AGE COMPARISONS, NATIVE-NON-NATIVE
            COMPARISONS, ANGLO AMERICANS
      IDEN U.S., OTIS CLASSIFICATION TEST

1091 AUTH GARTH, THOMAS R.; SMITH, OWEN D.
      TITL THE PERFORMANCE OF FULL-BLOOD INDIANS ON LANGUAGE AND
            NON-LANGUAGE INTELLIGENCE TESTS.
      SOUR JOURNAL OF ABNORMAL AND SOCIAL PSYCHOLOGY, 1937, V32,
            PP 376-381.
      YEAR 1937
      DESC B.I.A. BOARDING SCHOOLS, CHILDREN-SCHOOL AGE,
            ADOLESCENTS, ABILITIES+, PSYCHOLOGICAL TESTING+,
            LANGUAGE HANDICAPS+, AGE COMPARISONS, CULTURE-FAIR
            TESTS+, NATIVE-NON-NATIVE COMPARISONS, ANGLO AMERICANS
      IDEN U.S., PINTER NON-LANGUAGE MENTAL TEST, OTIS
            CLASSIFICATION TEST

1092 AUTH GARTH, THOMAS R.
      TITL THE INTELLIGENCE OF FULL BLOOD INDIANS.
      SOUR JOURNAL OF APPLIED PSYCHOLOGY, 1925, V9, PP 382-389.
      YEAR 1925
      DESC ABILITIES+, PSYCHOLOGICAL TESTING+, NATIVE-NON-NATIVE
            COMPARISONS, ANGLO AMERICANS, B.I.A. BOARDING SCHOOLS,

```
            SOCIAL STATUS, AGE COMPARISONS,
      IDEN  U.S., NATIONAL INTELLIGENCE TESTS

1093  AUTH  GARTH, THOMAS R.
      TITL  THE RESULTS OF SOME TESTS ON FULL AND MIXED BLOOD
            INDIANS.
      SOUR  JOURNAL OF APPLIED PSYCHOLOGY, 1921, V5, PP 359-372.
      YEAR  1921
      DESC  ABILITIES+, PSYCHOLOGICAL TESTING+, B.I.A. BOARDING
            SCHOOLS, CHILDREN-SCHOOL AGE, ADOLESCENTS, SEX
            DIFFERENCES, AGE COMPARISONS, FULL BLOOD-MIXED BLOOD
            COMPARISONS
      IDEN  U.S.

1094  AUTH  SCHLEGEL, ALICE
      TITL  THE ADOLESCENT SOCIALIZATION OF THE HOPI GIRL.
      SOUR  ETHNOLOGY, OCT. 1973, V12(4), PP 449-462.
      YEAR  1973
      DESC  PUEBLO-HOPI, SOUTHWEST, FEMALES+, ADOLESCENTS+, SOCIA
            ROLES+, SEXUAL RELATIONS, TRADITIONAL CHILD REARING+
      IDEN  U.S.

1095  AUTH  CARNEY, RICHARD E.; TROWBRIDGE, NORMA
      TITL  INTELLIGENCE TEST PERFORMANCE OF INDIAN CHILDREN AS A
            FUNCTION OF TYPE OF TEST AND AGE.
      SOUR  PERCEPTUAL AND MOTOR SKILLS, 1962, V14, PP 511-514.
      YEAR  1962
      DESC  MESQUAKIE, PRAIRIE, ABILITIES+, CHILDREN-SCHOOL AGE,
            PSYCHOLOGICAL TESTING+, AGE COMPARISONS, RESERVATION,
            COGNITIVE PROCESSES+, CULTURE-FAIR TESTS+
      IDEN  U.S., IOWA, TAMA RESERVATION, CALIFORNIA TEST OF
            MENTAL MATURITY, GOODENOUGH HARRIS DRAW A PERSON TEST

1096  AUTH  POSINSKY, S.H.
      TITL  NAVAJO INFANCY AND CHILDHOOD.
      SOUR  PSYCHIATRIC QUARTERLY, 1963, V37, PP 306-321.
      YEAR  1963
      DESC  NAVAJO, SOUTHWEST, CHILDREN-INFANTS AND PRESCHOOL+,
            PERSONALITY TRAITS+, TRADITIONAL CHILD REARING+,
            PSYCHOANALYSIS+, NONINTERFERENCE, ANXIETY,
            AGGRESSIVENESS, STRESS, WITCHCRAFT
      IDEN  U.S., NAVAJO RESERVATION

1097  AUTH  ROBERTS, ALAN H.; GREENE, JOEL E.
      TITL  CROSS-CULTURAL STUDY OF RELATIONSHIPS AMONG FOUR
            DIMENSIONS OF TIME PERSPECTIVE.
      SOUR  PERCEPTUAL AND MOTOR SKILLS, 1971, V33, PP 163-173.
      YEAR  1971
      DESC  TIME PERCEPTION+, NATIVE-NON-NATIVE COMPARISONS, ANGL
            AMERICANS, LATINOS, COGNITIVE PROCESSES+,
            CHILDREN-SCHOOL AGE, ADOLESCENTS, PSYCHOLOGICAL
            TESTING+, AGE COMPARISONS, STEREOTYPES, SOUTHWEST
      IDEN  U.S.

1098  AUTH  HALLOWELL, A. IRVING
```

```
      TITL  ACCULTURATION PROCESSES AND PERSONALITY CHANGES AS
            INDICATED BY THE RORSCHACH TECHNIQUE.
      SOUR  JOURNAL OF PROJECTIVE TECHNIQUES, 1942, V6, PP 42-50.
      YEAR  1942
      DESC  PERSONALITY TRAITS+, PSYCHOLOGICAL TESTING+, CULTURAL
            ADAPTATION+, CULTURAL CONTINUITY+, CHIPPEWA, EASTERN
            SUB-ARCTIC, ADULTS, SEX DIFFERENCES
      IDEN  CANADA, RORSCHACH TEST

1099  AUTH  U.S. CONGRESS. SENATE. COMMITTEE ON LABOR AND PUBLIC
            WELFARE. SUBCOMMITTEE ON INDIAN EDUCATION
      TITL  THE EDUCATION OF AMERICAN INDIANS: A COMPENDIUM OF
            FEDERAL BOARDING SCHOOL EVALUATIONS.
      SOUR  WASHINGTON,D.C.: GOVERNMENT PRINTING OFFICE, 1969.
      YEAR  1969
      DESC  B.I.A. BOARDING SCHOOLS+, ADOLESCENTS, CHILDREN-SCHOOL
            AGE, SOCIALLY DEVIANT BEHAVIOR, ADMINISTRATIVE
            ISSUES+, EDUCATION PROFESSIONALS+, EDUCATION
            PARAPROFESSIONALS+,  EDUCATION PROGRAMS AND SERVICES+,
            DROPOUTS, PROGRAM EVALUATION+
      IDEN  U.S., ALBUQUERQUE INDIAN SCHOOL, BUSBY BOARDING
            SCHOOL, CHILOCCO INDIAN SCHOOL, FLANDREAU INDIAN
            SCHOOL, PIERRE INDIAN SCHOOL, HASKELL INSTITUTE,
            INTERMOUNTAIN INDIAN SCHOOL, MAGDALENA DORMITORY,
            MOUNT EDGECUMBE BOARDING SCHOOL, WRANGELL INSTITUTE,
            OGLALA COMMUNITY SCHOOL, PHOENIX BOARDING SCHOOL,
            SENECA BOARDING SCHOOL, JAMES ACADEMY, EUFALA SCHOOL

1100  AUTH  LEVY, JERROLD E.
      TITL  THE OLDER AMERICAN INDIAN.
      SOUR  IN E. GRANT YOUMANS (ED.), OLDER RURAL AMERICANS, PP
            221-238. LEXINGTON: UNIVERSITY OF KENTUCKY PRESS,
            1967.
      YEAR  1967
      DESC  AGED+, DEATH AND DYING+, SOCIAL ROLES+, EXTENDED
            FAMILY+, FAMILY FUNCTIONING+
      IDEN  U.S.

1101  AUTH  GARTH, THOMAS R.
      TITL  A COMPARISON OF THE INTELLIGENCE OF MEXICAN AND MIXED
            AND FULL BLOOD INDIAN CHILDREN.
      SOUR  PSYCHOLOGICAL REVIEW, 1923, V30, PP 388-401.
      YEAR  1923
      DESC  CHILDREN-SCHOOL AGE, ABILITIES+, PSYCHOLOGICAL
            TESTING+, NATIVE-NON-NATIVE COMPARISONS, LATINOS,
            ADOLESCENTS, FULL BLOOD-MIXED BLOOD COMPARISONS,
            INTERTRIBAL COMPARISONS, SOCIAL STATUS
      IDEN  U.S., NATIONAL INTELLIGENCE TESTS

1102  AUTH  ZEINER, ARTHUR R.; PAREDES, ALFONSO; COWDEN, LAWRENCE
      TITL  PHYSIOLOGIC RESPONSES TO ETHANOL AMONG THE TARAHUMARA
            INDIANS.
      SOUR  ANNALS OF THE NEW YORK ACADEMY OF SCIENCES, 1976,
            V273, PP 154-158.
      YEAR  1976
```

```
           DESC  ALCOHOL USE+, GENETIC FACTORS, EXPERIMENTAL STUDY,
                 MALES, ADULTS, TARAHUMARA, NATIVE-NON-NATIVE
                 COMPARISONS, ANGLO AMERICANS
           IDEN  MEXICO

1103  AUTH  FEAGIN, JOE; ANDERSON, RANDALL
      TITL  INTERTRIBAL ATTITUDES AMONG NATIVE AMERICAN YOUTH.
      SOUR  SOCIAL SCIENCE QUARTERLY, 1973, V54(1), PP 117-131.
      YEAR  1973
      DESC  B.I.A. BOARDING SCHOOLS, SOUTHWEST, ATTITUDES+,
            PSYCHOLOGICAL TESTING+, BLACK AMERICANS,
            DISCRIMINATION+, ANGLO AMERICANS, INTERTRIBAL
            COMPARISONS, NATIVE-NON-NATIVE COMPARISONS,
            CHILDREN-SCHOOL AGE, ADOLESCENTS
      IDEN  U.S., CALIFORNIA

1104  AUTH  HODGE, WILLIAM H.
      TITL  NAVAHO PENTECOSTALISM.
      SOUR  ANTHROPOLOGICAL QUARTERLY, 1964, V37(3), PP 73-93.
      YEAR  1964
      DESC  NAVAJO, SOUTHWEST, RELIGIONS-NON-NATIVE+, URBAN AREAS
            TRADITIONAL HEALERS+, CULTURAL ADAPTATION
      IDEN  U.S., NEW MEXICO

1105  AUTH  ELLIS, FLORENCE H.
      TITL  PATTERNS OF AGGRESSION AND THE WAR CULT IN
            SOUTHWESTERN PUEBLOS.
      SOUR  SOUTHWESTERN JOURNAL OF ANTHROPOLOGY, 1951, V7(2), PP
            177-201.
      YEAR  1951
      DESC  PUEBLO, SOUTHWEST, AGGRESSIVENESS+,
            NONCOMPETITIVENESS+, TRADITIONAL SOCIAL CONTROL,
            COOPERATION, RESERVATION
      IDEN  U.S.

1106  AUTH  JACOBS, MELVILLE
      TITL  INDICATIONS OF MENTAL ILLNESS AMONG PRE-CONTACT
            INDIANS OF THE NORTHWEST STATES.
      SOUR  PACIFIC NORTHWEST QUARTERLY, APR. 1964, V55, PP 49-54
      YEAR  1964
      DESC  NORTHWEST COAST, PLATEAU, MENTAL DISORDERS+, NATIVE
            AMERICAN ETIOLOGY+, SOCIALLY DEVIANT BEHAVIOR+,
            ADOLESCENTS, ADULTS, SPIRIT INTRUSION,
            CULTURE-SPECIFIC SYNDROMES+
      IDEN  U.S.,WASHINGTON, OREGON

1107  AUTH  AGINSKY, BURT W.
      TITL  THE INTERACTION OF ETHNIC GROUPS: A CASE STUDY OF
            INDIANS AND WHITES.
      SOUR  AMERICAN SOCIOLOGICAL REVIEW, 1949, V14, PP 288-293.
      YEAR  1949
      DESC  POMO, CALIFORNIA AREA, CULTURAL ADAPTATION+,
            RESERVATION, URBAN AREAS, RELOCATION
      IDEN  U.S., CALIFORNIA
```

1108 AUTH AGINSKY, BURT W.
      TITL THE SOCIO-PSYCHOLOGICAL SIGNIFICANCE OF DEATH AMONG
            THE POMO INDIANS.
      SOUR AMERICAN IMAGO, JUN. 1940, V1(3), PP 1-11.
      YEAR 1940
      DESC DEATH AND DYING+, POMO, CALIFORNIA AREA, NATIVE
            AMERICAN ETIOLOGY+, TABOO BREAKING, ACCIDENTS,
            TRADITIONAL HEALERS+, CULTURE-BASED PSYCHOTHERAPY,
            GHOST SICKNESS, SOUL LOSS, WITCHCRAFT, ANXIETY
      IDEN U.S., CALIFORNIA

1109 AUTH KENNARD, E.A.
      TITL HOPI REACTIONS TO DEATH.
      SOUR AMERICAN ANTHROPOLOGIST, 1937, V39, PP 491-496.
      YEAR 1937
      DESC PUEBLO-HOPI, SOUTHWEST, DEATH AND DYING+, NATIVE
            AMERICAN ETIOLOGY+, RESERVATION
      IDEN U.S.

1110 AUTH DORAN, CHRISTOPHER M.
      TITL ATTITUDES OF 30 AMERICAN INDIAN WOMEN TOWARD BIRTH
            CONTROL.
      SOUR HEALTH SERVICE REPORTS, 1972, V87(7), PP 658-664.
      YEAR 1972
      DESC NAVAJO, SOUTHWEST, FEMALES+, ADULTS, FAMILY PLANNING+,
            ATTITUDES+, RESERVATION
      IDEN U.S., NAVAJO RESERVATION

1111 AUTH STUCKI, LARRY R.
      TITL THE CASE AGAINST POPULATION CONTROL: THE PROBABLE
            CREATION OF THE FIRST AMERICAN INDIAN STATE.
      SOUR HUMAN ORGANIZATION, WIN. 1971, V30(4), PP 393-399.
      YEAR 1971
      DESC FAMILY PLANNING+, ECONOMIC ISSUES, NAVAJO, SOUTHWEST,
            RESERVATION, POLITICS-NONTRIBAL+
      IDEN U.S., NAVAJO RESERVATION

1112 AUTH EULER, ROBERT C.; NAYLOR, HARRY L.
      TITL SOUTHERN UTE REHABILITATION PLANNING: A STUDY IN
            SELF-DETERMINATION.
      SOUR HUMAN ORGANIZATION, 1952, V11(4), PP 27-32.
      YEAR 1952
      DESC ECONOMIC ISSUES+, UTE, GREAT BASIN, RESERVATION,
            TRIBAL POLITICAL ORGANIZATIONS+, CONSULTATION+,
            PROGRAM DEVELOPMENT+, ADMINISTRATIVE ISSUES+, B.I.A.,
            LEADERSHIP+
      IDEN U.S., UTAH, COLORADO

1113 AUTH HILGER, M. INEZ
      TITL NOTES ON CHEYENNE CHILD LIFE.
      SOUR AMERICAN ANTHROPOLOGIST, 1944-46, V47, PP 60-69.
      YEAR 1944-1946
      DESC CHEYENNE-NORTHERN, PLAINS, TRADITIONAL CHILD REARING+,
            CHILDREN-INFANTS AND PRESCHOOL+, FEMALES, ADULTS,
            CHEYENNE-SOUTHERN

```
       IDEN  U.S.

1114   AUTH  ROWE,E.C.
       TITL  FIVE HUNDRED FORTY-SEVEN WHITE AND TWO HUNDRED
             SIXTY-EIGHT INDIAN CHILDREN TESTED BY THE BINET-SIMON
             TESTS.
       SOUR  PEDAGOGICAL SEMINARY, 1914, V21, PP 454-468.
       YEAR  1914
       DESC  CHILDREN-SCHOOL AGE+, PSYCHOLOGICAL TESTING+,
             ABILITIES+, B.I.A. BOARDING SCHOOLS, NATIVE-NON-NATIVE
             COMPARISONS, ANGLO AMERICANS
       IDEN  U.S., BINET-SIMON TESTS, MICHIGAN

1115   AUTH  BREWER, WILLIS R.; DU VAL, MERLIN K.; DAVIS, GLORIA M.
       TITL  INCREASING MINORITY RECRUITMENT TO THE HEALTH
             PROFESSIONS BY ENLARGING THE APPLICANT POOL.
       SOUR  NEW ENGLAND JOURNAL OF MEDICINE, JUL. 1979, V301(2),
             PP 74-76.
       YEAR  1979
       DESC  COLLEGES AND UNIVERSITIES+, SECONDARY SCHOOLS,
             DISCRIMINATION, LATINOS, ASIAN AMERICANS, EDUCATION
             PROGRAMS AND SERVICES+, BLACK AMERICANS, PREVENTIVE
             MENTAL HEALTH PROGRAMS,DROPOUTS+
       IDEN  U.S., ARIZONA

1116   AUTH  DYK, WALTER
       TITL  NOTES AND ILLUSTRATIONS OF NAVAHO SEX BEHAVIOR.
       SOUR  IN GEORGE B. WILBUR AND WARNER MUENSTERBERGER (EDS.),
             PSYCHOANALYSIS AND CULTURE: ESSAYS IN HONOR OF GEZA
             ROHEIM, PP 108-119. NEW YORK: INTERNATIONAL
             UNIVERSITIES PRESS, 1951.
       YEAR  1951
       DESC  NAVAJO, SOUTHWEST, SEXUAL RELATIONS+, ADULTS ,
             RESERVATION
       IDEN  U.S., NAVAJO RESERVATION

1117   AUTH  BAYNE, STEPHEN L.; BAYNE, JUDITH E.
       TITL  MOTIVATING NAVAHO CHILDREN.
       SOUR  JOURNAL OF AMERICAN INDIAN EDUCATION, JAN. 1969,
             V8(2), PP 1-9.
       YEAR  1969
       DESC  NAVAJO, SOUTHWEST, CHILDREN-SCHOOL AGE+, MOTIVATION+,
             ACHIEVEMENT+, ELEMENTARY SCHOOLS+, B.I.A. BOARDING
             SCHOOLS+, RESERVATION, TRADITIONAL SOCIAL CONTROL,
             ATTITUDES, TIME PERCEPTION, COMMUNITY INVOLVEMENT+,
             EDUCATION PROFESSIONALS+
       IDEN  U.S., NAVAJO RESERVATION

1118   AUTH  ZENTNER, HENRY
       TITL  PARENTAL BEHAVIOR AND STUDENT ATTITUDES TOWARD FURTHER
             TRAINING AMONG INDIAN AND NON-INDIAN STUDERTS IN
             OREGON AND ALBERTA.
       SOUR  ALBERTA JOURNAL OF EDUCATIONAL RESEARCH, MAR. 1963,
             V9(1), PP 22-30.
       YEAR  1963
```

<pre>
       DESC ATTITUDES+, COLLEGES AND UNIVERSITIES+, SECONDARY
             SCHOOLS, ADOLESCENTS, ADULTS, INTERTRIBAL COMPARISONS,
             NATIVE-NON-NATIVE COMPARISONS
       IDEN U.S., CANADA, OREGON, ALBERTA

1119   AUTH SNOW, ALBERT J.
       TITL ETHNO-SCIENCE IN AMERICAN INDIAN EDUCATION.
       SOUR SCIENCE TEACHER, OCT. 1972, V39(7), PP 30-33.
       YEAR 1972
       DESC SCIENCE PROGRAMS+, CULTURAL ADAPTATION+, EDUCATION
             PROGRAMS AND SERVICES+, CULTURAL CONTINUITY+, NAVAJO,
             SOUTHWEST, RESERVATION
       IDEN U.S., NAVAJO RESERVATION

1120   AUTH KLUCKHOHN, CLYDE
       TITL THE PHILOSOPHY OF THE NAVAHO INDIANS.
       SOUR IN F.S.C. NORTHROP (ED.), IDEOLOGICAL DIFFERENCES AND
             WORLD ORDER: STUDIES IN THE PHILOSOPHY AND SCIENCE OF
             THE WORLD CULTURES, PP 356-384. NEW HAVEN: YALE
             UNIVERSITY PRESS, 1949.
       YEAR 1949
       DESC NATIVE AMERICAN ETIOLOGY+, UNIVERSAL HARMONY+, TABOO
             BREAKING+, NAVAJO, SOUTHWEST, RESERVATION, TRADITIONAL
             SOCIAL CONTROL, SOCIALLY DEVIANT BEHAVIOR,
             COOPERATION, NATIVE AMERICAN VALUES, GROUP NORMS AND
             SANCTIONS+
       IDEN U.S., NAVAJO RESERVATION

1121   AUTH KUPFERER, HARRIET J.
       TITL CHEROKEE CHANGE: A DEPARTURE FROM LINEAL MODES OF
             ACCULTURATION.
       SOUR ANTHROPOLOGICA, 1963, V5(2), PP 187-198.
       YEAR 1963
       DESC CHEROKEE, SOUTHEAST WOODLAND, CULTURAL ADAPTATION+,
             NATIVE AMERICAN VALUES+, OFF-RESERVATION, COOPERATION,
             AGGRESSIVENESS, NONINTERFERENCE
       IDEN U.S., NORTH CAROLINA

1122   AUTH HOLLAND, R. FOUNT
       TITL SCHOOL IN CHEROKEE AND ENGLISH.
       SOUR ELEMENTARY SCHOOL JOURNAL, 1972, V72(8), 412-418.
       YEAR 1972
       DESC CHEROKEE, SOUTHEAST WOODLAND, EDUCATION PROGRAMS AND
             SERVICES+, BILINGUALISM+, SELF-CONCEPT, EDUCATION
             PARAPROFESSIONALS+, NATIVE AMERICAN PERSONNEL,
             CHILDREN-SCHOOL AGE, LANGUAGE HANDICAPS+
       IDEN U.S., OKLAHOMA

1123   AUTH WICKER, LESLIE C.
       TITL RACIAL AWARENESS AND RACIAL IDENTIFICATION AMONG
             AMERICAN INDIAN CHILDREN AS INFLUENCED BY
             NATIVE-AMERICAN POWER IDEOLOGY AND SELF-CONCEPT.
       SOUR DISSERTATION ABSTRACTS INTERNATIONAL, AUG. 1978,
             V39(2), P 1148-A.
       YEAR 1978
</pre>

```
          DESC  CHILDREN-SCHOOL AGE+, ETHNIC IDENTITY+, SELF-CONCEPT+
                AGE COMPARISONS
          IDEN  U.S.

1124  AUTH  RINER, REED D.
      TITL  ATTITUDES TOWARD FORMAL EDUCATION AMONG AMERICAN
            INDIAN PARENTS AND STUDENTS IN SIX COMMUNITIES.
      SOUR  DISSERTATION ABSTRACTS INTERNATIONAL, JAN. 1978,
            V38(7), P 4241-A.
      YEAR  1978
      DESC  ATTITUDES+, EDUCATION PROGRAMS AND SERVICES+, PLAINS,
            SOUTHWEST, COMMUNITY INVOLVEMENT+
      IDEN  U.S., MONTANA, SOUTH DAKOTA, ARIZONA

1125  AUTH  MURDOCK, MARGARET M.
      TITL  THE POLITICAL ATTITUDES OF NATIVE AMERICAN CHILDREN:
            THE ARAPAHOE AND SHOSHONE OF THE WIND RIVER
            RESERVATION IN WYOMING.
      SOUR  DISSERTATION ABSTRACTS INTERNATIONAL, SEP. 1978,
            V39(3), P 1809-A.
      YEAR  1978
      DESC  ATTITUDES+, CHILDREN-SCHOOL AGE+, ARAPAHO, SHOSHONE,
            PLAINS, RESERVATION, FEDERAL GOVERNMENT, TRIBAL
            POLITICAL ORGANIZATIONS+
      IDEN  U.S., WYOMING, WIND RIVER RESERVATION

1126  AUTH  BEUKE, VERNON L.
      TITL  THE RELATIONSHIP OF CULTURAL IDENTIFICATION TO
            PERSONAL ADJUSTMENT OF AMERICAN INDIAN CHILDREN IN
            SEGREGATED AND INTEGRATED SCHOOLS.
      SOUR  DISSERTATION ABSTRACTS INTERNATIONAL, JUN. 1978,
            V38(12), P 7203-A.
      YEAR  1978
      DESC  CHILDREN-SCHOOL AGE+, ELEMENTARY SCHOOLS, ETHNIC
            IDENTITY+, ATTITUDES+
      IDEN  U.S., ARIZONA

1127  AUTH  FOX, DENNIS R.
      TITL  PERCEPTIONS OF STUDENT RIGHTS AND RESPONSIBILITIES IN
            SECONDARY-LEVEL BUREAU OF INDIAN AFFAIRS BOARDING
            SCHOOLS.
      SOUR  DISSERTATION ABSTRACTS INTERNATIONAL, APR. 1978,
            V38(10), P 5819-A.
      YEAR  1978
      DESC  B.I.A. BOARDING SCHOOLS+, ADOLESCENTS, ATTITUDES+,
            ADULTS , SECONDARY SCHOOLS+
      IDEN  U.S.

1128  AUTH  YINGER, J. MILTON; SIMPSON, GEORGE E.
      TITL  THE INTEGRATION OF AMERICANS OF INDIAN DESCENT.
      SOUR  ANNALS OF THE AMERICAN ACADEMY OF POLITICAL AND SOCIA
            SCIENCE, MAR. 1978, V436, PP 137-151.
      YEAR  1978
      DESC  CULTURAL ADAPTATION+, ETHNIC IDENTITY+, CULTURAL
            CONTINUITY+, NATIVE AMERICAN VALUES
```

1129 AUTH MUNSELL, MARVIN R.
      TITL FUNCTIONS OF THE AGED AMONG SALT RIVER PIMA.
      SOUR IN DONALD O. COWGILL AND LOWELL D. HOLMES (EDS.),
            AGING AND MODERNIZATION, PP 127-132. NEW YORK:
            APPLETON-CENTURY-CROFTS, EDUCATIONAL DIVISION,
            MEREDITH CORPORATION, 1972.
      YEAR 1972
      DESC AGED+, PIMA, SOUTHWEST, RESERVATION, FAMILY
            FUNCTIONING+, SOCIAL STATUS+, EXTENDED FAMILY, SOCIAL
            ROLES+, SEX DIFFERENCES, FEMALES, MALES
      IDEN U.S., ARIZONA, SALT RIVER MARICOPA RESERVATION

1130 AUTH WAX, MURRAY L.; WAX, ROSALIE H.
      TITL RELIGION AMONG AMERICAN INDIANS.
      SOUR ANNALS OF THE AMERICAN ACADEMY OF POLITICAL AND SOCIAL
            SCIENCE, MAR. 1978, V436, PP 27-39.
      YEAR 1978
      DESC NATIVE AMERICAN RELIGIONS+, DREAMS AND VISION QUESTS,
            UNIVERSAL HARMONY, RELIGIONS-NON-NATIVE, CULTURAL
            REVIVAL, TRADITIONAL USE OF DRUGS AND ALCOHOL, DRUG
            USE
      IDEN U.S., GHOST DANCE, NATIVE AMERICAN CHURCH

1131 AUTH HAVIGHURST, ROBERT J.
      TITL INDIAN EDUCATION SINCE 1960.
      SOUR ANNALS OF THE AMERICAN ACADEMY OF POLITICAL AND SOCIAL
            SCIENCE, MAR. 1978, V436, PP 13-26.
      YEAR 1978
      DESC EDUCATION PROGRAMS AND SERVICES+, ACHIEVEMENT,
            ABILITIES, B.I.A. BOARDING SCHOOLS, COLLEGES AND
            UNIVERSITIES, BILINGUALISM, BICULTURALISM
      IDEN U.S.

1132 AUTH SPINDLER, GEORGE D.; SPINDLER, LOUISE S.
      TITL IDENTITY, MILITANCY, AND CULTURAL CONGRUENCE: THE
            MENOMINEE AND KAINAI.
      SOUR ANNALS OF THE AMERICAN ACADEMY OF POLITICAL AND SOCIAL
            SCIENCE, MAR. 1978, V436, PP 73-85.
      YEAR 1978
      DESC MENOMINEE, NORTHEAST WOODLAND, BLACKFEET-BLOOD,
            PLAINS, NATIVE AMERICAN VALUES+, INTERTRIBAL
            COMPARISONS, CULTURAL ADAPTATION+, STRESS, CULTURAL
            REVIVAL, NATIVE AMERICAN COPING BEHAVIORS+, ETHNIC
            IDENTITY+, NATIVE AMERICAN POLITICAL MOVEMENTS, NATIVE
            AMERICAN RELIGIONS, RESERVATION
      IDEN U.S., CANADA, WISCONSIN, ALBERTA

1133 AUTH TAX, SOL
      TITL THE IMPACT OF URBANIZATION ON AMERICAN INDIANS.
      SOUR ANNALS OF THE AMERICAN ACADEMY OF POLITICAL AND SOCIAL
            SCIENCE, MAR. 1978, V436, PP 121-136.
      YEAR 1978
      DESC URBANIZATION+, URBAN AREAS, DEMOGRAPHIC DATA, NATIVE
            AMERICAN VALUES, CULTURAL ADAPTATION
      IDEN U.S.

1134 AUTH STANLEY, SAM; THOMAS, ROBERT K.
      TITL CURRENT DEMOGRAPHIC AND SOCIAL TRENDS AMONG NORTH
            AMERICAN INDIANS.
      SOUR ANNALS OF THE ACADEMY OF POLITICAL AND SOCIAL SCIENCE,
            1978, V436, PP 111-120.
      YEAR 1978
      DESC DEMOGRAPHIC DATA, URBAN AREAS, RELOCATION+,
            URBANIZATION+, ETHNIC IDENTITY
      IDEN U.S.

1135 AUTH DIAL, ADOLPH L.
      TITL DEATH IN THE LIFE OF NATIVE AMERICANS.
      SOUR INDIAN HISTORIAN, SEP. 1978, V11(3), PP 32-37.
      YEAR 1978
      DESC DEATH AND DYING+, ATTITUDES+, INTERTRIBAL COMPARISONS,
            GRIEF REACTION
      IDEN U.S.

1136 AUTH RANDALL, ARCHIE; RANDALL, BETTE
      TITL CRIMINAL JUSTICE AND THE AMERICAN INDIAN.
      SOUR INDIAN HISTORIAN, SPR. 1978, V11(2), PP 42-48.
      YEAR 1978
      DESC CRIME+, LEGAL ISSUES+, CORRECTIONAL INSTITUTIONS+,
            NATIVE-NON-NATIVE COMPARISONS, BLACK AMERICANS, ANGLO
            AMERICANS, URBAN AREAS, STEREOTYPES+, CORRECTIONS
            PERSONNEL+, ALCOHOL USE
      IDEN U.S.,WASHINGTON

1137 AUTH SMITH, FREDERICK D.
      TITL A NETWORK ANALYSIS OF A BUREAU OF INDIAN AFFAIRS
            SCHOOL SYSTEM TO DETERMINE FACTORS IN JOB
            SATISFACTION.
      SOUR DISSERTATION ABSTRACTS INTERNATIONAL, JAN. 1978,
            V38(7), P 4085-A.
      YEAR 1978
      DESC EDUCATION PROFESSIONALS+, B.I.A. BOARDING SCHOOLS+,
            NAVAJO, SOUTHWEST, RESERVATION, ADMINISTRATIVE
            ISSUES+, SOCIAL NETWORKS+
      IDEN U.S., NAVAJO RESERVATION

1138 AUTH ROARK-CALNEK, SUE N.
      TITL INDIAN WAY IN OKLAHOMA: TRANSACTIONS IN HONOR AND
            LEGITIMACY.
      SOUR DISSERTATION ABSTRACTS INTERNATIONAL, MAR. 1978,
            V38(9), P 5569-A.
      YEAR 1978
      DESC ETHNIC IDENTITY+, DELAWARE, SOUTHEAST WOODLAND,
            OFF-RESERVATION, POW-WOWS+, SOCIAL NETWORKS+
      IDEN U.S., OKLAHOMA

1139 AUTH BRANDENBURG, CARLOS E.
      TITL VALIDATION OF THE SOCIAL READJUSTMENT RATING SCALE
            WITH MEXICAN-AMERICANS AND NATIVE AMERICANS.
      SOUR DISSERTATION ABSTRACTS INTERNATIONAL, 1979, V39(7), P
            4020-B.

```
     YEAR  1979
     DESC  STRESS+, PSYCHOLOGICAL TESTING+, PHYSICAL HEALTH AND
           ILLNESS+, NATIVE-NON-NATIVE COMPARISONS, LATINOS
     IDEN  U.S., SOCIAL READJUSTMENT RATING SCALE

1140 AUTH  RAMOS, ALBERT A.
     TITL  THE RELATIONSHIP OF SEX AND ETHNIC BACKGROUND TO
           JOB-RELATED STRESS OF RESEARCH AND DEVELOPMENT
           PROFESSIONALS.
     SOUR  DISSERTATION ABSTRACTS INTERNATIONAL, SEP.-OCT. 1975,
           V36, P 1862-A.
     YEAR  1975
     DESC  STRESS+, RESEARCHERS+, SOCIAL ROLES+, SEX DIFFERENCES,
           NATIVE-NON-NATIVE COMPARISONS, LATINOS, ANGLO
           AMERICANS, BLACK AMERICANS, PHYSICAL HEALTH AND
           ILLNESS, PSYCHOLOGICAL TESTING
     IDEN  U.S., JOB-RELATED TENSION INDEX

1141 AUTH  POPE, ALBERT W.
     TITL  AN EXPLORATION OF THE UNIVERSITY ENVIRONMENT AS
           PERCEIVED BY NATIVE AMERICAN FRESHMEN.
     SOUR  DISSERTATION ABSTRACTS INTERNATIONAL, JAN. 1978,
           V38(7), P 4007-A.
     YEAR  1978
     DESC  COLLEGES AND UNIVERSITIES+, ATTITUDES+,
           NATIVE-NON-NATIVE COMPARISONS, ANGLO AMERICANS,
           PSYCHOLOGICAL TESTING
     IDEN  U.S., UTAH, COLLEGE AND UNIVERSITY ENVIRONMENT SCALES

1142 AUTH  STAUSS, JOSEPH H.
     TITL  MODERNIZATION: THE URBAN INDIAN EXPERIENCE.
     SOUR  DISSERTATION ABSTRACTS INTERNATIONAL, JAN.-FEB. 1973,
           V33, P 3823-A.
     YEAR  1973
     DESC  URBANIZATION+, URBAN AREAS, PSYCHOLOGICAL TESTING+,
           ATTITUDES+
     IDEN  U.S.

1143 AUTH  BLANCHARD, JOSEPH D.
     TITL  BIOBEHAVIORAL CORRELATES OF PERCEPTUAL-COGNITIVE-MOTOR
           PERFORMANCE IN A SAMPLE OF SOUTHWEST INDIAN JUNIOR
           HIGH SCHOOL STUDENTS.
     SOUR  DISSERTATION ABSTRACTS INTERNATIONAL, MAR.-APR. 1974,
           V34, P 6641-A.
     YEAR  1974
     DESC  COGNITIVE PROCESSES+, PSYCHOLOGICAL TESTING+,
           ADOLESCENTS+, SECONDARY SCHOOLS, ABILITIES+,
           SOUTHWEST, B.I.A. BOARDING SCHOOLS, MOTOR PROCESSES+,
           LEARNING DISABILITIES AND PROBLEMS+
     IDEN  U.S., NEW MEXICO, WECHSLER INTELLIGENCE SCALE
           CHILDREN, WIDE RANGE ACHIEVEMENT TEST, ILLINOIS TEST
           OF PSYCHOLINGUISTIC ABILITY

1144 AUTH  VINCENT, LAURA L.
     TITL  THE PERFORMANCE OF NAVAJO AND APACHE INDIAN CHILDREN
```

ON THE BENDER GESTALT TEST USING THE KOPPITZ
DEVELOPMENTAL SCORING SYSTEM FOR VISUAL-MOTOR
PERCEPTION.
SOUR   DISSERTATION ABSTRACTS INTERNATIONAL, MAY-JUN. 1975,
V35, P 5628-B.
YEAR   1975
DESC   COGNITIVE PROCESSES+, CHILDREN-SCHOOL AGE+, NAVAJO,
APACHE, SOUTHWEST, PSYCHOLOGICAL TESTING+, ABILITIES+,
INTERTRIBAL COMPARISONS, SEX DIFFERENCES,
NATIVE-NON-NATIVE COMPARISONS, ANGLO AMERICANS
IDEN   U.S., BENDER GESTALT TEST

1145   AUTH   DEGHER, DOUGLAS W.
TITL   NATIVE AMERICANS IN THE JUSTICE SYSTEM: AN ANALYSIS OF
TWO RURAL WASHINGTON COUNTIES.
SOUR   DISSERTATION ABSTRACTS INTERNATIONAL, JUL.-AUG. 1975,
V36, P 1105-A.
YEAR   1975
DESC   LEGAL ISSUES+, CORRECTIONAL INSTITUTIONS+,
DISCRIMINATION+, SURVEY, CORRECTIONS PERSONNEL+
IDEN   U.S., WASHINGTON

1146   AUTH   HOOTON, RICHARD J.
TITL   RACE, SKIN COLOR, AND DRESS AS RELATED TO THE AMERICAN
INDIAN STEREOTYPE.
SOUR   DISSERTATION ABSTRACTS INTERNATIONAL, JAN.-FEB. 1973,
V33, P 3822-A.
YEAR   1973
DESC   STEREOTYPES+, MALES, ADULTS, DISCRIMINATION+
IDEN   U.S.

1147   AUTH   HALL, EDWIN L; SIMKUS, ALBERT A.
TITL   INEQUALITY IN THE TYPES OF SENTENCES RECEIVED BY
NATIVE AMERICANS AND WHITES.
SOUR   CRIMINOLOGY, AUG. 1975, V13(2), PP 199-222.
YEAR   1975
DESC   CRIME+, LEGAL ISSUES+, DISCRIMINATION+, CORRECTIONAL
INSTITUTIONS+, POWERLESSNESS, STEREOTYPES, ATTITUDES
IDEN   U.S.

1148   AUTH   MARTIN, JAMES C.
TITL   LOCUS OF CONTROL AND SELF-ESTEEM IN INDIAN AND WHITE
STUDENTS.
SOUR   JOURNAL OF AMERICAN INDIAN EDUCATION, OCT. 1978,
V18(1), PP 23-29.
YEAR   1978
DESC   SELF-CONCEPT+, PSYCHOLOGICAL TESTING+, CHILDREN-SCHOOL
AGE, ADOLESCENTS, NATIVE-NON-NATIVE COMPARISONS, ANGLO
AMERICANS, ELEMENTARY SCHOOLS, SECONDARY SCHOOLS, AGE
COMPARISONS, PERSONALITY TRAITS+, COGNITIVE PROCESSES+
IDEN   U.S., COOPERSMITH SELF-ESTEEM INVENTORY,
NOWICKI-STRICKLAND LOCUS OF CONTROL SCALE

1149   AUTH   MAIL, PATRICIA D.
TITL   HIPPOCRATES WAS A MEDICINE MAN: THE HEALTH CARE OF

NATIVE AMERICANS IN THE TWENTIETH CENTURY.
SOUR ANNALS OF THE AMERICAN ACADEMY OF POLITICAL AND SOCIAL
SCIENCES, MAR, V436, PP 40-47.
YEAR 1978
DESC PHYSICAL HEALTH AND ILLNESS+, I.H.S.+, MEDICAL
PROGRAMS AND SERVICES+, DELIVERY OF SERVICES+, ALCOHOL
USE, MEDICAL PARAPROFESSIONALS, NATIVE AMERICAN
PERSONNEL, RESERVATION
IDEN U.S.

1150 AUTH FORSLUND, MORRIS A.
TITL FUNCTIONS OF DRINKING FOR NATIVE AMERICAN AND WHITE
YOUTH.
SOUR JOURNAL OF YOUTH AND ADOLESCENCE, 1978, V7(3), PP
327-332.
YEAR 1978
DESC ALCOHOL USE+, ADOLESCENTS+, SURVEY, SECONDARY SCHOOLS,
SHOSHONE, ARAPAHO, PLAINS, SEX DIFFERENCES,
NATIVE-NON-NATIVE COMPARISONS, ANGLO AMERICANS ,
RESERVATION
IDEN U.S., WYOMING, WIND RIVER RESERVATION

1151 AUTH BORUNDA, PATRICK; SHORE, JAMES H.
TITL NEGLECTED MINORITY--URBAN INDIANS AND MENTAL HEALTH.
SOUR INTERNATIONAL JOURNAL OF SOCIAL PSYCHIATRY, AUT. 1978,
V24(3), PP 220-224.
YEAR 1978
DESC URBAN AREAS, SOCIAL SERVICES, MEDICAL PROGRAMS AND
SERVICES, DELIVERY OF SERVICES+, MENTAL HEALTH
PROGRAMS AND SERVICES, PROGRAM DEVELOPMENT+
IDEN U.S., OREGON

1152 AUTH MURDOCK, STEVE H.; SCHWARTZ, DONALD F.
TITL FAMILY STRUCTURE AND THE USE OF AGENCY SERVICES: AN
EXAMINATION OF PATTERNS AMONG ELDERLY NATIVE
AMERICANS.
SOUR GERONTOLOGIST, OCT. 1978, V18(5), PP 475-487.
YEAR 1978
DESC AGED+, EXTENDED FAMILY+, RESERVATION, PLAINS, SOCIAL
SERVICES+
IDEN U.S., SOUTH DAKOTA, NORTH DAKOTA

1153 AUTH ROGERS, C. JEAN; GALLION, TERESA E.
TITL CHARACTERISTICS OF ELDERLY PUEBLO INDIANS IN NEW
MEXICO.
SOUR GERONTOLOGIST, OCT 1978, V18(5), PP 482-487.
YEAR 1978
DESC AGED+, SOUTHWEST, RESERVATION, SURVEY, DEMOGRAPHIC
DATA, DELIVERY OF SERVICES+, SOCIAL SERVICES
IDEN U.S., NEW MEXICO

1154 AUTH SNIDER, JAMES G.; COLADARCI, ARTHUR P.
TITL INTELLIGENCE TEST PERFORMANCE OF INDIAN CHILDREN.
SOUR JOURNAL OF EDUCATIONAL RESEARCH, 1961, V7, PP 39-41.
YEAR 1961

```
          DESC  CULTURAL ADAPTATION+, ABILITIES+, PSYCHOLOGICAL
                TESTING+, NATIVE-NON-NATIVE COMPARISONS, ANGLO
                AMERICANS, NEZ PERCE, PLATEAU, ELEMENTARY SCHOOLS,
                SECONDARY SCHOOLS, CHILDREN-SCHOOL AGE, ADOLESCENTS,
                CULTURE-FAIR TESTS
          IDEN  U.S., IDAHO, PINTER GENERAL ABILITY TEST, PINTER
                ADVANCED TEST, CALIFORNIA TEST OF MENTAL MATURITY,
                AMERICAN COUNCIL ON EDUCATION PSYCHOLOGICAL
                EXAMINATION

1155  AUTH  FORSLUND, MORRIS A.; CRANSTON, VIRGINIA A.
      TITL  A SELF-REPORT COMPARISON OF INDIAN AND ANGLO
            DELINQUENCY IN WYOMING.
      SOUR  CRIMINOLOGY, AUG. 1975, V13(2), PP 193-197.
      YEAR  1975
      DESC  ADOLESCENTS+, SOCIALLY DEVIANT BEHAVIOR+, RESERVATION,
            NATIVE-NON-NATIVE COMPARISONS, ANGLO AMERICANS, SEX
            DIFFERENCES,   SOCIAL STATUS
      IDEN  U.S., WYOMING, WIND RIVER RESERVATION

1156  AUTH  MARETZKI, THOMAS W.
      TITL  ANTHROPOLOGY AND MENTAL HEALTH: REFLECTIONS ON
            INTERDISCIPLINARY GROWTH.
      SOUR  CULTURE, MEDICINE AND PSYCHIATRY, 1979, V3, PP 95-110.
      YEAR  1979
      DESC  REVIEW OF LITERATURE, RESEARCHERS+, MENTAL HEALTH
            PROFESSIONALS+, CULTURE-BASED PSYCHOTHERAPY+,
            TRADITIONAL HEALERS
      IDEN  U.S.

1157  AUTH  ADAMS, L. LA MAR; HIGLEY, H. BRUCE ; CAMPBELL, LELAND
            H.
      TITL  ACADEMIC SUCCESS OF AMERICAN INDIAN STUDENTS AT A
            LARGE PRIVATE UNIVERSITY.
      SOUR  COLLEGE AND UNIVERSITY, FALL 1977, V51(1), PP 100- 107.
      YEAR  1977
      DESC  COLLEGES AND UNIVERSITIES+, ACHIEVEMENT+, ADOPTION AND
            FOSTER CARE, RESERVATION, URBAN AREAS
      IDEN  U.S.

1158  AUTH  ROSS, BRUCE M.
      TITL  PREFERENCES FOR NONREPRESENTATIONAL DRAWINGS BY NAVAHO
            AND OTHER CHILDREN.
      SOUR  JOURNAL OF CROSS-CULTURAL PSYCHOLOGY, JUN. 1976,
            V7(2), PP 145-155.
      YEAR  1976
      DESC  NAVAJO, SOUTHWEST, CHILDREN-SCHOOL AGE+, COGNITIVE
            PROCESSES+, B.I.A. BOARDING SCHOOLS, PSYCHOLOGICAL
            TESTING+, CULTURE-FAIR TESTS+, NATIVE-NON-NATIVE
            COMPARISONS, ANGLO AMERICANS, SEX DIFFERENCES
      IDEN  U.S.

1159  AUTH  JILEK-AALL, LOUISE
      TITL  ALCOHOL AND THE INDIAN-WHITE RELATIONSHIP.
      SOUR  CONFINIA PSYCHIATRICA, 1978, V21(4), PP 195-233.
```

YEAR 1978
DESC COAST SALISH, NORTHWEST COAST, ALCOHOLISM TREATMENT+,
      SOCIAL GROUPS AND PEER GROUPS+, PSYCHOTHERAPY AND
      COUNSELING+, DISCRIMINATION+, GROUP NORMS AND
      SANCTIONS, MALES, FEMALES, AGGRESSIVENESS, ADULTS,
      NATIVE AMERICAN VALUES, ALCOHOL USE, CULTURAL REVIVAL,
      NATIVE AMERICAN RELIGIONS, RESERVATION
IDEN CANADA, BRITISH COLUMBIA, ALCOHOLICS ANONYMOUS

1160 AUTH STEPHENS, RICHARD C.; AGAR, MICHAEL H.
      TITL RED TAPE--WHITE TAPE: FEDERAL-INDIAN FUNDING
            RELATIONSHIPS.
      SOUR HUMAN ORGANIZATION, FALL 1979, V38(3), PP 283-293.
      YEAR 1979
      DESC DRUG TREATMENT, DRUG USE, FEDERAL GOVERNMENT+,
            RESEARCHERS+, PROGRAM DEVELOPMENT+, CONSULTATION+,
            ADMINISTRATIVE ISSUES+, TRIBAL POLITICAL
            ORGANIZATIONS+, RESERVATION, OFF-RESERVATION
      IDEN U.S., NATIONAL INSTITUTE ON DRUG ABUSE

1161 AUTH FERGUSON, FRANCES N.
      TITL STAKE THEORY AS AN EXPLANATORY DEVICE IN NAVAJO
            ALCOHOLISM TREATMENT RESPONSE.
      SOUR HUMAN ORGANIZATION, SPR. 1976, V35(1), PP 65-78.
      YEAR 1976
      DESC NAVAJO, SOUTHWEST, MALES, ADULTS, ALCOHOLISM
            TREATMENT+, GROUP NORMS AND SANCTIONS+, SOCIALLY
            DEVIANT BEHAVIOR, RESERVATION, BICULTURALISM, CULTURAL
            CONTINUITY, MOTIVATION, TRADITIONAL SOCIAL CONTROL,
            EXTENDED FAMILY
      IDEN U.S., NAVAJO RESERVATION

1162 AUTH TANNER, ADRIAN
      TITL BRINGING HOME ANIMALS: RELIGIOUS IDEOLOGY AND MODE OF
            PRODUCTION OF THE MISTASSINI CREE HUNTERS.
      SOUR DISSERTATION ABSTRACTS INTERNATIONAL, OCT. 1978,
            V39(4), P 2390-A.
      YEAR 1978
      DESC CREE, EASTERN SUB-ARCTIC, NATIVE AMERICAN RELIGIONS+,
            SOCIAL GROUPS AND PEER GROUPS+, ECONOMIC ISSUES,
            LEADERSHIP, ENVIRONMENTAL FACTORS
      IDEN CANADA, QUEBEC

1163 AUTH MERRILL, ORVILLE W.
      TITL GROUP PSYCHOTHERAPY WITH AMERICAN-INDIAN ADOLESCENTS:
            A STUDY OF REPORTED CHANGES.
      SOUR DISSERTATION ABSTRACTS INTERNATIONAL, SEP.-OCT. 1974,
            V35, P 1392-B.
      YEAR 1974
      DESC ADOLESCENTS+, SOCIAL GROUPS AND PEER GROUPS+,
            PSYCHOTHERAPY AND COUNSELING+
      IDEN U.S.

1164 AUTH CHICKADONZ, GRACE H.
      TITL MOTHERING AND ILLNESS IN YOUNG APACHE CHILDREN.

SOUR   DISSERTATION ABSTRACTS INTERNATIONAL, APR. 1975,
         V35(10), P 4955-B --4956-B.
YEAR   1975
DESC   RESERVATION, APACHE, SOUTHWEST, CHILDREN-INFANTS AND
         PRESCHOOL+, TRADITIONAL CHILD REARING+, FEMALES+,
         ADULTS+, PHYSICAL HEALTH AND ILLNESS+
IDEN   U.S., ARIZONA, APACHE RESERVATION

1165 AUTH   BEE, ROBERT L.
      TITL   TO GET SOMETHING FOR THE PEOPLE: THE PREDICAMENT OF
           THE AMERICAN INDIAN LEADER.
      SOUR   HUMAN ORGANIZATION, FALL 1979, V38(3), PP 239-247.
      YEAR   1979
      DESC   LEADERSHIP+, RESERVATION, SOCIAL NETWORKS+,
           POLITICS-NONTRIBAL, FEDERAL GOVERNMENT+, YUMA,
           SOUTHWEST, TRIBAL POLITICAL ORGANIZATIONS+
      IDEN   U.S., CALIFORNIA, WASHINGTON D.C.

1166 AUTH   COCKERHAM, WILLIAM C.; BLEVINS, AUDIE L.
      TITL   OPEN SCHOOL VS. TRADITIONAL SCHOOL:
           SELF-IDENTIFICATION AMONG NATIVE AMERICAN AND WHITE
           ADOLESCENTS.
      SOUR   SOCIOLOGY OF EDUCATION, APR. 1976, V49, PP 164-169.
      YEAR   1976
      DESC   SELF-CONCEPT+, ADOLESCENTS+, RESERVATION, ACHIEVEMENT,
           SECONDARY SCHOOLS+, LEARNING+, SHOSHONE, ARAPAHO,
           PSYCHOLOGICAL TESTING+, NATIVE-NON-NATIVE COMPARISONS,
           ANGLO AMERICANS, PLAINS
      IDEN   U.S., WYOMING, WIND RIVER RESERVATION, TWENTY
           STATEMENTS TEST

1167 AUTH   THORNTON, RUSSELL; MARSH-THORNTON, JOAN
      TITL   ON "OPEN SCHOOL VS. TRADITIONAL SCHOOL: SELF
           IDENTIFICATION AMONG NATIVE AMERICAN AND WHITE
           ADOLESCENTS.
      SOUR   SOCIOLOGY OF EDUCATION, JUL. 1976, V49(3), PP 247-248.
      YEAR   1976
      DESC   SELF-CONCEPT+, RESERVATION, ADOLESCENTS+, SHOSHONE,
           ARAPAHO, PLAINS, PSYCHOLOGICAL TESTING+, LEARNING,
           SECONDARY SCHOOLS, NATIVE-NON-NATIVE COMPARISONS,
           ANGLO AMERICANS
      IDEN   U.S., WYOMING, WIND RIVER RESERVATION, TWWENTY
           STATEMENTS TEST

1168 AUTH   GEORGE, DEBORAH M.; HOPPE, RONALD A.
      TITL   RACIAL IDENTIFICATION, PREFERENCE, AND SELF-CONCEPT:
           CANADIAN INDIAN AND WHITE SCHOOLCHILDREN.
      SOUR   JOURNAL OF CROSS-CULTURAL PSYCHOLOGY, MAR. 1979,
           V10(1), PP 85-99.
      YEAR   1979
      DESC   SELF-CONCEPT+, ETHNIC IDENTITY+, SEX DIFFERENCES,
           PSYCHOLOGICAL TESTING+, CHILDREN-SCHOOL AGE+,
           ELEMENTARY SCHOOLS, NATIVE-NON-NATIVE COMPARISONS,
           ANGLO AMERICANS, AGE COMPARISONS, ATTITUDES+
      IDEN   CANADA, BRITISH COLUMBIA, TWENTY STATEMENTS TEST

1169 AUTH BOWD, ALAN D.
     TITL FIELD-DEPENDENCE AND PERFORMANCE ON PIAGETIAN
          INVARIANCE TASKS: A CROSS-CULTURAL COMPARISON.
     SOUR JOURNAL OF GENETIC PSYCHOLOGY, 1977, V130, PP 157-158.
     YEAR 1977
     DESC COGNITIVE PROCESSES+, CHILDREN-SCHOOL AGE+,
          PSYCHOLOGICAL TESTING+, RESERVATION, NATIVE-NON-NATIVE
          COMPARISONS, ANGLO AMERICANS
     IDEN CANADA, MANITOBA, CHILDREN'S EMBEDDED FIGURES TEST,
          GOODENOUGH HARRIS DRAW A PERSON TEST, PIAGETIAN TASKS

1170 AUTH RED HORSE, JOHN G.; LEWIS, RONALD G.; FEIT, MARVIN;
          DECKER, JAMES
     TITL FAMILY BEHAVIOR OF URBAN AMERICAN INDIANS.
     SOUR SOCIAL CASEWORK, FEB. 1978, PP 67-72.
     YEAR 1978
     DESC FAMILY FUNCTIONING+, EXTENDED FAMILY+, SOCIAL
          NETWORKS+, SOCIAL SERVICE PROFESSIONALS, URBAN AREAS
     IDEN U.S.

1171 AUTH TAYLOR, L.J.; SKANES, G.R.
     TITL A CROSS-CULTURAL EXAMINATION OF SOME OF JENSEN'S
          HYPOTHESES.
     SOUR CANADIAN JOURNAL OF BEHAVIORAL SCIENCE, OCT. 1977,
          V9(4), PP 315-322.
     YEAR 1977
     DESC ABILITIES+, PSYCHOLOGICAL TESTING+, NATIVE-NON-NATIVE
          COMPARISONS, ANGLO AMERICANS, ESKIMO, CHILDREN-SCHOOL
          AGE+, SOCIAL STATUS+
     IDEN CANADA, RAVENS COLOURED PROGRESSIVE MATRICES, DIGIT
          SPAN TESTS

1172 AUTH WILLIAMS, LESLIE R.
     TITL MENDING THE HOOP: A STUDY OF ROLES, DESIRED
          RESPONSIBILITIES AND GOALS FOR PARENTS OF CHILDREN IN
          TRIBALLY SPONSORED HEAD START PROGRAMS.
     SOUR DISSERTATION ABSTRACTS INTERNATIONAL, SEP.-OCT. 1975,
          V36, P 1361-A.
     YEAR 1975
     DESC TRAINING PROGRAMS+, ADULTS, COMMUNITY INVOLVEMENT+,
          EDUCATION PROGRAMS AND SERVICES+, NATIVE AMERICAN
          ADMINISTERED PROGRAMS+
     IDEN U.S., HEAD START, LIFE COPING SKILLS TRAINING MODEL

1173 AUTH PIKE, WILLIAM A.
     TITL A STUDY OF SELF CONCEPT AS A FACTOR IN SOCIAL
          GROUPINGS OF THREE INDIAN SOCIAL GROUPS IN SIOUX CITY.
     SOUR DISSERTATION ABSTRACTS INTERNATIONAL, JAN.-FEB. 1976,
          V36, P5158-A.
     YEAR 1976
     DESC SELF-CONCEPT+, SIOUX, PLAINS, PSYCHOLOGICAL TESTING+,
          ADULTS
     IDEN U.S., TENNESSEE SELF CONCEPT SCALE, IOWA

1174 AUTH OETINGER, GEORGE

TITL   AN ATTITUDINAL STUDY OF AMERICAN INDIAN UPWARD BOUND
       STUDENTS WITH A PARTICULAR FOCUS ON TRADITIONAL AND
       NON-TRADITIONAL FAMILY BACKGROUND.
SOUR   DISSERTATION ABSTRACTS INTERNATIONAL, JAN.-FEB. 1974,
       V34, P 5339-A--5340-A.
YEAR   1974
DESC   FAMILY FUNCTIONING+, RESERVATION, OFF-RESERVATION,
       ACHIEVEMENT+, TRADITIONAL CHILD REARING+, ATTITUDES+,
       ADOLESCENTS+, SECONDARY SCHOOLS
IDEN   U.S., ARIZONA

1175   AUTH   MC AREAVEY, JAMES P.
       TITL   AN ANALYSIS OF SELECTED EDUCATIONALLY HANDICAPPED
              SOUTH DAKOTA SIOUX INDIAN CHILDREN'S RESPONSES TO THE
              WECHSLER INTELLIGENCE SCALE FOR CHILDREN AND WIDE
              RANGE ACHIEVEMENT TEST OF READING.
       SOUR   DISSERTATION ABSTRACTS INTERNATIONAL, JAN.-FEB. 1976,
              V36, P 5154-A.
       YEAR   1976
       DESC   ABILITIES+, PSYCHOLOGICAL TESTING+, CHILDREN-SCHOOL
              AGE+, SIOUX, PLAINS, LEARNING DISABILITIES AND
              PROBLEMS+
       IDEN   U.S., WECHSLER INTELLIGENCE SCALE CHILDREN, WIDE RANGE
              ACHIEVEMENT TEST OF READING

1176   AUTH   SNOW, ALBERT J.
       TITL   AMERICAN INDIAN ETHNO-SCIENCE: A STUDY OF ITS EFFECTS
              ON STUDENT ACHIEVEMENT.
       SOUR   DISSERTATION ABSTRACTS INTERNATIONAL, JUL.-AUG. 1975,
              V36, P 760-A.
       YEAR   1975
       DESC   SCIENCE PROGRAMS+, EDUCATION PROGRAMS AND SERVICES+,
              ACHIEVEMENT, NAVAJO, SOUTHWEST, ADOLESCENTS, SECONDARY
              SCHOOLS
       IDEN   U.S., NAVAJO RESERVATION

1177   AUTH   BOROVETZ, FRANK C.
       TITL   THE RELATIONSHIP BETWEEN SIXTH GRADE STUDENTS'
              PERCEPTIONS OF THEIR TEACHERS' FEELINGS TOWARD THEM
              AND READING ACHIEVEMENT.
       SOUR   DISSERTATION ABSTRACTS INTERNATIONAL, JUN. 1975, V35,
              P 7718-A.
       YEAR   1975
       DESC   CHILDREN-SCHOOL AGE+, ELEMENTARY SCHOOLS, ATTITUDES+,
              EDUCATION PROFESSIONALS+, ACHIEVEMENT+, READING
              PROGRAMS+
       IDEN   U.S., FEELING TONE QUESTIONNAIRE, METROPOLITAN
              ACHIEVEMENT TEST

1178   AUTH   BLAND, LAUREL L.
       TITL   VISUAL PERCEPTION AND RECALL OF SCHOOL-AGE NAVAJO,
              HOPI, JICARILLA APACHE, AND CAUCASION CHILDREN OF THE
              SOUTHWEST.
       SOUR   DISSERTATION ABSTRACTS INTERNATIONAL, SEP.-OCT. 1975,
              V36, P 1355-A.

```
      YEAR  1975
      DESC  CHILDREN-SCHOOL AGE+, LEARNING+, COGNITIVE PROCESSES+,
            NAVAJO, PUEBLO-HOPI, APACHE-JICARILLA, SOUTHWEST,
            RESERVATION, NATIVE-NON-NATIVE COMPARISONS, ANGLO
            AMERICANS, INTERTRIBAL COMPARISONS
      IDEN  U.S., VISUAL RECALL ABILITY INDICATORS

1179  AUTH  PORTER, MARGARET R.; VIEIRA, THEODORE A.; KAPLAN, GARY
            J. ; HEESCH, JACK R.; COLYAR, ARDELL B.
      TITL  DRUG USE IN ANCHORAGE, ALASKA.
      SOUR  JOURNAL OF THE AMERICAN MEDICAL ASSOCIATION, FEB.
            1973, V223 (6), PP 657-664.
      YEAR  1973
      DESC  ALASKA NATIVES, DRUG USE+, ELEMENTARY SCHOOLS,
            SECONDARY SCHOOLS, EPIDEMIOLOGICAL STUDY,
            CHILDREN-SCHOOL AGE, ADOLESCENTS, ALCOHOL USE, SEX
            DIFFERENCES
      IDEN  U.S., ALASKA

1180  AUTH  BLAIR, BOWEN
      TITL  AMERICAN INDIANS VS. AMERICAN MUSEUMS: A MATTER OF
            RELIGIOUS FREEDOM.
      SOUR  AMERICAN INDIAN JOURNAL, MAY 1979, V5(5), PP 13-21.
      YEAR  1979
      DESC  NATIVE AMERICAN RELIGIONS+, RESEARCHERS+, LEGAL
            ISSUES+
      IDEN  U.S.

1181  AUTH  GUILMET, GEORGE M.
      TITL  MATERNAL PERCEPTIONS OF URBAN NAVAJO AND CAUCASIAN
            CHILDREN'S CLASSROOM BEHAVIOR.
      SOUR  HUMAN ORGANIZATION, SPR. 1979, V38(1), PP 87-91.
      YEAR  1979
      DESC  CHILDREN-INFANTS AND PRESCHOOL+, NAVAJO, SOUTHWEST,
            FEMALES+, ADULTS+, AGGRESSIVENESS+, PASSIVE
            RESISTANCE, TRADITIONAL CHILD REARING, LEARNING, URBAN
            AREAS, NATIVE-NON-NATIVE COMPARISONS, ANGLO AMERICANS,
            EMOTIONAL RESTRAINT, NONINTERFERENCE
      IDEN  U.S., CALIFORNIA

1182  AUTH  LELAND, JOY
      TITL  ALCOHOL, ANTHROPOLOGISTS, AND NATIVE AMERICANS.
      SOUR  HUMAN ORGANIZATION, SPR. 1979, V38(1), PP 94-99.
      YEAR  1979
      DESC  RESEARCHERS+, ALCOHOLISM TREATMENT+, FEDERAL
            GOVERNMENT+, PROGRAM DEVELOPMENT+, I.H.S.,
            ADMINISTRATIVE ISSUES+,  PROGRAM EVALUATION
      IDEN  U.S.

1183  AUTH  BELTRANE, THOMAS; MCQUEEN, DAVID V.
      TITL  URBAN AND RURAL DRINKING PATTERNS: THE SPECIAL CASE OF
            THE LUMBEE.
      SOUR  INTERNATIONAL JOURNAL OF THE ADDICTIONS, 1979, V14(4),
            PP 533-548.
      YEAR  1979
```

```
         DESC  LUMBEE, SOUTHEAST WOODLAND, URBAN AREAS,
               OFF-RESERVATION, ALCOHOL USE+, MALES, ADULTS, SOCIAL
               STATUS+, PSYCHOLOGICAL TESTING, EMPLOYMENT,
               ACHIEVEMENT+, RELOCATION
         IDEN  U.S., MARYLAND, NORTH CAROLINA,
               QUANTITY-FREQUENCY-VARIABILITY, STATUS SATISFACTION
               INDEX

1184 AUTH  COCKERHAM, WILLIAM C.; FORSLUND, MORRIS A.; RABOIN,
           ROLLAND M.
     TITL  DRUG USE AMONG WHITE AND AMERICAN INDIAN HIGH SCHOOL
           YOUTH.
     SOUR  INTERNATIONAL JOURNAL OF THE ADDICTIONS, 1976, V11(2),
           PP 209-220.
     YEAR  1976
     DESC  RESERVATION, ADOLESCENTS+, SECONDARY SCHOOLS, DRUG
           USE+, PLAINS, SHOSHONE, ARAPAHO, NATIVE-NON-NATIVE
           COMPARISONS, ANGLO AMERICANS, ATTITUDES+
     IDEN  U.S., WYOMING, WIND RIVER RESERVATION

1185 AUTH  WESTERMEYER, JOSEPH
     TITL  SEX ROLES AT THE INDIAN-MAJORITY INTERFACE IN
           MINNESOTA.
     SOUR  INTERNATIONAL JOURNAL OF SOCIAL PSYCHIATRY, 1978,
           V24(3), PP 189-194.
     YEAR  1978
     DESC  SOCIAL ROLES+, MALES+, ADULTS+, DISCRIMINATION+,
           EMPLOYMENT+, STEREOTYPES+
     IDEN  U.S., MINNESOTA

1186 AUTH  WALKER, LILLY S.
     TITL  UNIVERSITY SUCCESS FOR CANADIAN INDIANS.
     SOUR  CANADIAN JOURNAL OF BEHAVIORAL SCIENCE, 1977, V9(2),
           PP 169-175.
     YEAR  1977
     DESC  COLLEGES AND UNIVERSITIES+, EDUCATION PROGRAMS AND
           SERVICES+, ACHIEVEMENT+, PSYCHOLOGICAL TESTING+,
           DROPOUTS, PROGRAM EVALUATION
     IDEN  CANADA, CORE EDUCATIONAL MODEL

1187 AUTH  SHANNON, LAEL
     TITL  DEVELOPMENT OF TIME PERSPECTIVE IN THREE CULTURAL
           GROUPS: A CULTURAL DIFFERENCE OR AN EXPECTANCY
           INTERPRETATION.
     SOUR  DEVELOPMENTAL PSYCHOLOGY, JAN. 1975, V11(1), PP
           114-115.
     YEAR  1975
     DESC  TIME PERCEPTION+, NATIVE AMERICAN COPING BEHAVIORS+,
           MALES, ADOLESCENTS, CHILDREN-SCHOOL AGE,
           NATIVE-NON-NATIVE COMPARISONS, LATINOS, ANGLO
           AMERICANS, PSYCHOLOGICAL TESTING+, AGE COMPARISONS
     IDEN  U.S., LINES TEST

1188 AUTH  RESCHLY, DANIEL J.; JIPSON, FREDERICK J.
     TITL  ETHNICITY, GEOGRAPHIC LOCALE, AGE, SEX, AND
```

URBAN-RURAL RESIDENCE AS VARIABLES IN THE PREVALENCE
OF MILD RETARDATION.
SOUR   AMERICAN JOURNAL OF MENTAL DEFICIENCY, SEP. 1976,
V81(2), PP 154-161.
YEAR   1976
DESC   MENTAL RETARDATION+, CHILDREN-SCHOOL AGE+, AGE
COMPARISONS, EPIDEMIOLOGICAL STUDY, PSYCHOLOGICAL
TESTING+, SEX DIFFERENCES, NATIVE-NON-NATIVE
COMPARISONS, URBAN AREAS, OFF-RESERVATION, ANGLO
AMERICANS, BLACK AMERICANS, LATINOS, PAPAGO,
SOUTHWEST, ABILITIES+
IDEN   U.S., WECHSLER INTELLIGENCE SCALE CHILDREN, ARIZONA

1189   AUTH   KRAUS, ROBERT F.; BUFFLER, PATRICIA A.
TITL   SOCIOCULTURAL STRESS AND THE AMERICAN NATIVE IN
ALASKA: AN ANALYSIS OF CHANGING PATTERNS OF
PSYCHIATRIC ILLNESS AND ALCOHOL ABUSE AMONG ALASKA
NATIVES.
SOUR   CULTURE, MEDICINE AND PSYCHIATRY, 1979, V3, PP 111-151.
YEAR   1979
DESC   EPIDEMIOLOGICAL STUDY, ALASKA NATIVES, MENTAL
DISORDERS+, ALCOHOL USE, STRESS+, MENTAL HEALTH
PROGRAMS AND SERVICES+, DELIVERY OF SERVICES+,
OFF-RESERVATION, I.H.S., INSTITUTIONALIZATION, MENTAL
HEALTH INSTITUTIONS, OUTPATIENT CARE, ACCIDENTS,
SUICIDE
IDEN   U.S., ALASKA

1190   AUTH   CROPLEY, A.J.; CARDEY, R.M.
TITL   CONTACT WITH THE DOMINANT CULTURE AND COGNITIVE
COMPETENCE IN CANADIAN INDIANS AND WHITES.
SOUR   CANADIAN JOURNAL OF BEHAVIORAL SCIENCE, 1975, V7(4),
PP 328-338.
YEAR   1975
DESC   COGNITIVE PROCESSES+, PSYCHOLOGICAL TESTING+,
NATIVE-NON-NATIVE COMPARISONS, ANGLO AMERICANS,
CULTURE-FAIR TESTS+, ABILITIES+, CHILDREN-SCHOOL AGE+,
RESERVATION, CREE, EASTERN SUB-ARCTIC, METIS
IDEN   CANADA, GOODENOUGH HARRIS DRAW A PERSON TEST, RAVEN
COLOURED PROGRESSIVE MATRICES, PINTER-CUNNINGHAM
PRIMARY TEST, OTIS QUICK-SCORING MENTAL ABILITY TEST,
SASKATCHEWAN

1191   AUTH   BOWD, ALAN D.
TITL   ITEM DIFFICULTY ON THE CHILDREN'S EMBEDDED FIGURES
TEST.
SOUR   PERCEPTUAL AND MOTOR SKILLS, 1976, V43, P 134.
YEAR   1976
DESC   PSYCHOLOGICAL TESTING+, COGNITIVE PROCESSES+,
CHILDREN-SCHOOL AGE+, RESERVATION, NATIVE-NON-NATIVE
COMPARISONS, ANGLO AMERICANS
IDEN   U.S., CHILDREN'S EMBEDDED-FIGURES TEST

1192   AUTH   SILVERN, STEVEN B.
TITL   AN INVESTIGATION OF THE EFFECTS OF SYMBOLIC PLAY ON

AURAL LANGUAGE COMPREHENSION IN FIVE-, SIX-, AND
SEVEN-YEAR-OLD NATIVE AMERICAN CHILDREN.
SOUR DISSERTATION ABSTRACTS INTERNATIONAL, APR. 1978,
V38(10),P 6000-A.
YEAR 1978
DESC ABILITIES+, CHILDREN-INFANTS AND PRESCHOOL+,
CHILDREN-SCHOOL AGE+, AGE COMPARISONS
IDEN U.S.

1193 AUTH ECHOHAWK, MARLENE; PARSONS, OSCAR A.
      TITL LEADERSHIP VS. BEHAVIORAL PROBLEMS AND BELIEF IN
            PERSONAL CONTROL AMONG AMERICAN INDIAN YOUTH.
      SOUR JOURNAL OF SOCIAL PSYCHOLOGY, 1977, V102, PP 47-54.
      YEAR 1977
      DESC ADOLESCENTS+, B.I.A. BOARDING SCHOOLS, LEADERSHIP+,
            PSYCHOLOGICAL TESTING+, SOCIALLY DEVIANT BEHAVIOR+,
            NATIVE AMERICAN VALUES, NATIVE-NON-NATIVE COMPARISONS,
            ANGLO AMERICANS, INTERTRIBAL COMPARISONS
      IDEN U.S., NOWICKI STRICKLAND LOCUS OF CONTROL SCALE,
            OKLAHOMA

1194 AUTH BROWN, JENNIFER
      TITL THE CURE AND FEEDING OF WINDIGOS: A CRITIQUE.
      SOUR AMERICAN ANTHROPOLOGIST, FEB. 1971, V73(1), PP 20-22.
      YEAR 1971
      DESC WINDIGO PSYCHOSIS+, NUTRITIONAL FACTORS, EASTERN
            SUB-ARCTIC
      IDEN U.S.

1195 AUTH RYAN, ROBERT A.
      TITL AN INVESTIGATION OF PERSONALITY TRAITS OF NATIVE
            AMERICAN COLLEGE STUDENTS AT THE UNIVERSITY OF SOUTH
            DAKOTA.
      SOUR DISSERTATION ABSTRACTS INTERNATIONAL, JUL. 1974,
            V35(1), P 198-A.
      YEAR 1974
      DESC COLLEGES AND UNIVERSITIES+, PERSONALITY TRAITS+, SEX
            DIFFERENCES, FULL BLOOD-MIXED BLOOD COMPARISONS,
            ADULTS, CULTURAL ADAPTATION+, NATIVE-NON-NATIVE
            COMPARISONS, ANGLO AMERICANS
      IDEN U.S., SOUTH DAKOTA, PERSONALITY RESEARCH FORM

1196 AUTH GRANZBERG, GARY
      TITL FURTHER EVIDENCE OF SITUATIONAL FACTORS IN DELAY OF
            GRATIFICATION.
      SOUR JOURNAL OF PSYCHOLOGY, 1977, V95, PP 7-8.
      YEAR 1977
      DESC CREE, EASTERN SUB-ARCTIC, EXPERIMENTAL STUDY,
            PSYCHOLOGICAL TESTING+, CHILDREN-SCHOOL AGE+,
            RESERVATION, SOCIAL GROUPS AND PEER GROUPS, GROUP
            NORMS AND SANCTIONS+
      IDEN U.S.

1197 AUTH BOYER, L. BRYCE; BOYER, RUTH M.
      TITL PROLONGED ADOLESCENCE AND EARLY IDENTIFICATION: A

```
         CROSS-CULTURAL STUDY.
  SOUR   PSYCHOANALYTIC STUDY OF SOCIETY, 1976, V7, PP 95-106.
  YEAR   1976
  DESC   PSYCHOANALYSIS+, ADOLESCENTS+, ADULTS+,
         APACHE-MESCALERO, RESERVATION, COGNITIVE PROCESSES+,
         AGED, EXTENDED FAMILY+, TRADITIONAL CHILD REARING+,
         CHILD ABUSE AND NEGLECT, CHILDREN-SCHOOL AGE,
         CHILDREN-INFANTS AND PRESCHOOL
  IDEN   U.S., MESCALERO RESERVATION, NEW MEXICO, RORSCHACH
         TEST

1198 AUTH   COOLEY, CARL R.
     TITL   AN APPLICATION OF SOCIAL LEARNING THEORY.
     SOUR   JOURNAL OF AMERICAN INDIAN EDUCATION, OCT. 1977,
            V17(1), PP 21-27.
     YEAR   1977
     DESC   LEARNING+, NATIVE AMERICAN VALUES+, CHILDREN-INFANTS
            AND PRESCHOOL+, MOTIVATION,COGNITIVE PROCESSES,
            BICULTURALISM, CHILDREN-SCHOOL AGE+
     IDEN   U.S.

1199 AUTH   SNOW, ALBERT J.
     TITL   ETHNO-SCIENCE AND THE GIFTED.
     SOUR   JOURNAL OF AMERICAN INDIAN EDUCATION, JAN. 1977,
            V16(2), PP 27-30.
     YEAR   1977
     DESC   SCIENCE PROGRAMS+, LEARNING+, NAVAJO, SOUTHWEST,
            ACHIEVEMENT+, COGNITIVE PROCESSES, EDUCATION PROGRAMS
            AND SERVICES+, RESERVATION
     IDEN   U.S., NAVAJO RESERVATION

1200 AUTH   ALBAS, DANIEL C.; MCCLUSKEY, KEN W.; ALBAS, CHERYL A.
     TITL   PERCEPTION OF THE EMOTIONAL CONTENT OF SPEECH: A
            COMPARISON OF TWO CANADIAN GROUPS.
     SOUR   JOURNAL OF CROSS-CULTURAL PSYCHOLOGY, DEC. 1976,
            V7(4), PP 481-489.
     YEAR   1976
     DESC   CREE, EASTERN SUB-ARCTIC, ANGLO AMERICANS,
            NATIVE-NON-NATIVE COMPARISONS, MALES, ADULTS, LANGUAGE
            HANDICAPS, EXPERIMENTAL STUDY
     IDEN   CANADA, MANITOBA

1201 AUTH   BUNGE, ROBERT P.
     TITL   THE AMERICAN INDIAN: A NATURAL PHILOSOPHER.
     SOUR   INTELLECT, JUN. 1978, V106, PP 493-498
     YEAR   1978
     DESC   UNIVERSAL HARMONY, NATIVE AMERICAN RELIGIONS+, NATIVE
            AMERICAN VALUES+, INTERTRIBAL COMPARISONS

1202 AUTH   GOLDSTEIN, GEORGE S.; OETTING, E.R.; EDWARDS, RUTH;
            GARCIA-MASON, VELMA
     TITL   DRUG USE AMONG NATIVE AMERICAN YOUNG ADULTS.
     SOUR   INTERNATIONAL JOURNAL OF THE ADDICTIONS, 1979, V14(6),
            PP 855-860.
     YEAR   1979
```

```
          DESC  ADULTS+, COLLEGES AND UNIVERSITIES+, DRUG USE+,
                ALCOHOL USE, URBAN AREAS
          IDEN  U.S.

1203  AUTH  WAGNER, ROLAND M.
      TITL  PATTERN AND PROCESS IN RITUAL SYNCRETISM: THE CASE OF
            PEYOTISM AMONG THE NAVAJO.
      SOUR  JOURNAL OF ANTHROPOLOGICAL RESEARCH, SUM. 1975,
            V31(2), PP 162-181.
      YEAR  1975
      DESC  TRADITIONAL USE OF DRUGS AND ALCOHOL+, RESERVATION,
            NAVAJO, SOUTHWEST, NATIVE AMERICAN RELIGIONS+,
            CULTURAL ADAPTATION+
      IDEN  U.S., NAVAJO RESERVATION

1204  AUTH  KRYWANIUK, L. W.
      TITL  FORTY CHILDREN.
      SOUR  MENTAL RETARDATION BULLETIN, 1972-73, V1(1), PP 17-20.
      YEAR  1972-73
      DESC  CHILDREN-SCHOOL AGE+, RESERVATION, ABILITIES+,
            PSYCHOLOGICAL TESTING+, COGNITIVE PROCESSES+,
            LEARNING+, LEARNING DISABILITIES AND PROBLEMS+
      IDEN  CANADA, ALBERTA, HOBBEMA RESERVATION, WECHSLER
            INTELLIGENCE SCALE CHILDREN, RAVEN'S PROGRESSIVE
            MATRICES, FIGURE COPYING TEST, MEMORY FOR DESIGNS,
            MAKING X'S, STROOP TEST, SERIAL LEARNING TEST,
            CROSS-MODAL TEST, SCHONELL'S GRADED WORD RECOGNITION
            TEST, VISUAL SHORT TERM MEMORY TEST

1205  AUTH  ALBAUGH, BERNARD J.; ALBAUGH, PATRICIA
      TITL  ALCOHOLISM AND SUBSTANCE SNIFFING AMONG THE CHEYENNE
            AND ARAPAHO INDIANS OF OKLAHOMA.
      SOUR  INTERNATIONAL JOURNAL OF THE ADDICTIONS,1979, V14(7),
            PP 1001-1007.
      YEAR  1979
      DESC  CHEYENNE, ARAPAHO, DRUG USE+, ALCOHOL USE+, PLAINS,
            PASSIVE RESISTANCE+, FAMILY FUNCTIONING+, CHARACTER
            DISORDERS, GROUP NORMS AND SANCTIONS, SOCIAL GROUPS
            AND PEER GROUPS
      IDEN  U.S., OKLAHOMA

1206  AUTH  WALLACE, ANTHONY F.C.
      TITL  HANDSOME LAKE AND THE GREAT REVIVAL IN THE WEST.
      SOUR  AMERICAN QUARTERLY, SUM. 1952, V4(2), PP 149-165.
      YEAR  1952
      DESC  NATIVE AMERICAN RELIGIONS+, NORTHEAST WOODLAND,
            RESERVATION, CONFESSION, IROQUOIS, DREAMS AND VISION
            QUESTS+, RELIGIONS-NON-NATIVE, STRESS+
      IDEN  U.S., NEW YORK, HANDSOME LAKE RELIGION, MORMON
            RELIGION

1207  AUTH  POPHAM, ROBERT E.
      TITL  PSYCHOCULTURAL BARRIERS TO SUCCESSFUL ALCOHOLISM
            THERAPY IN AN AMERICAN INDIAN PATIENT: THE RELEVANCE
            OF HALLOWELL'S ANALYSIS.
```

```
     SOUR  JOURNAL OF STUDIES ON ALCOHOL, 1979, V40(7), PP
           656-676.
     YEAR  1979
     DESC  ALGONKIN, EASTERN SUB-ARCTIC, FEMALES, ADULTS,
           ALCOHOLISM TREATMENT+, URBAN AREAS, EMOTIONAL
           RESTRAINT+, NONINTERFERENCE, NATIVE AMERICAN COPING
           BEHAVIORS, PSYCHOLOGICAL TESTING, PERSONALITY TRAITS+
     IDEN  CANADA, ONTARIO, RORSCHACH TEST

1208 AUTH  LELAND, JOY
     TITL  COMMENT ON "PSYCHOCULTURAL BARRIERS TO SUCCESSFUL
           ALCOHOLISM THERAPY IN AN AMERICAN INDIAN PATIENT."
     SOUR  JOURNAL OF STUDIES ON ALCOHOL, 1979, V40(7), PP
           737-742.
     YEAR  1979
     DESC  ALCOHOL USE, ALCOHOLISM TREATMENT+, EMOTIONAL
           RESTRAINT+
     IDEN  U.S.

1209 AUTH  RICHARDS, JOEL L.; FINGER, STANLEY
     TITL  MOTHER-CHILD HOLDING PATTERNS: A CROSS-CULTURAL
           PHOTOGRAPHIC SURVEY.
     SOUR  CHILD DEVELOPMENT, DEC. 1976, V46(4), PP 1001-1004.
     YEAR  1976
     DESC  ADULTS+, FEMALES+, CHILDREN-INFANTS AND PRESCHOOL,
           TRADITIONAL CHILD REARING+, MOTOR PROCESSES+,
           NATIVE-NON-NATIVE COMPARISONS, SURVEY
     IDEN  NORTH AMERICA, EUROPE, ASIA

1210 AUTH  ST. JOHN, JOAN; KRICHEV, ALAN; BAUMAN, EDWARD
     TITL  NORTHWESTERN ONTARIO INDIAN CHILDREN AND THE WISC.
     SOUR  PSYCHOLOGY IN THE SCHOOLS, OCT. 1976, V13(4), PP
           407-411.
     YEAR  1976
     DESC  CREE, CHIPPEWA, PSYCHOLOGICAL TESTING+, ABILITIES+,
           CHILDREN-SCHOOL AGE+, BOARDING HOMES, ADOLESCENTS,
           OFF-RESERVATION
     IDEN  CANADA, ONTARIO, WECHSLER INTELLIGENCE SCALE CHILDREN,
           WECHSLER ADULT INTELLIGENCE SCALE

1211 AUTH  BROCH, HARALD B.
     TITL  A NOTE ON BEDARCHE AMONG THE HARE INDIANS OF
           NORTHWESTERN CANADA.
     SOUR  WESTERN CANADIAN JOURNAL OF ANTHROPOLOGY, 1977, V7(3),
           PP 95-101.
     YEAR  1977
     DESC  HARE, MACKENZIE SUB-ARCTIC, SEXUAL RELATIONS+, GROUP
           NORMS AND SANCTIONS+, ADULTS, MALES, FEMALES, SOCIAL
           ROLES+, ATHABASCAN, OFF-RESERVATION
     IDEN  CANADA

1212 AUTH  ZINSER, OTTO; PERRY, JAMES S.; BAILEY, ROGER C.;
           LYDIATT, EDWARD W.
     TITL  RACIAL RECIPIENTS, VALUE OF DONATIONS, AND SHARING
           BEHAVIOR IN CHILDREN.
```

SOUR JOURNAL OF GENETIC PSYCHOLOGY, SEP. 1976, V129(1), PP
      29-35.
YEAR 1976
DESC CHILDREN-INFANTS AND PRESCHOOL+, CHILDREN-SCHOOL AGE+,
      ANGLO AMERICANS, DISCRIMINATION+, GENEROSITY+, AGE
      COMPARISONS, EXPERIMENTAL STUDY
IDEN U.S.

1213 AUTH ABOUD, FRANCES E.
      TITL INTEREST IN ETHNIC INFORMATION: A CROSS-CULTURAL
             DEVELOPMENTAL STUDY.
      SOUR CANADIAN JOURNAL OF BEHAVIORAL SCIENCE, APR. 1977,
             V9(2), PP 114-146.
      YEAR 1977
      DESC NATIVE-NON-NATIVE COMPARISONS, ANGLO AMERICANS, ETHNIC
             IDENTITY+, ASIAN AMERICANS, SELF-CONCEPT+,
             CHILDREN-SCHOOL AGE+, CHILDREN-INFANTS AND PRESCHOOL+,
             ATTITUDES+, DISCRIMINATION, SEX DIFFERENCES, AGE
             COMPARISONS, PSYCHOLOGICAL TESTING+, EXPERIMENTAL
             STUDY, URBAN AREAS
      IDEN CANADA, BRITISH COLUMBIA

1214 AUTH VAN DER KEILEN, MARGURITE
      TITL SOME EFFECTS OF A SPECIAL INDIAN CULTURE ORIENTED
             PROGRAM ON ATTITUDES OF WHITE AND INDIAN ELEMENTARY
             SCHOOL PUPILS.
      SOUR CANADIAN JOURNAL OF BEHAVIORAL SCIENCE, APR. 1977,
             V9(2), PP 161-168.
      YEAR 1977
      DESC CHIPPEWA, EASTERN SUB-ARCTIC, ACHIEVEMENT+,
             MOTIVATION+, EXPERIMENTAL STUDY, EDUCATION PROGRAMS
             AND SERVICES+, ATTITUDES+, ELEMENTARY SCHOOLS,
             DISCRIMINATION+, NATIVE-NON-NATIVE COMPARISONS, ANGLO
             AMERICANS, AGE COMPARISONS, OFF-RESERVATION,
             CHILDREN-SCHOOL AGE+, PSYCHOLOGICAL TESTING,
             ADOLESCENTS, SECONDARY SCHOOLS
      IDEN CANADA, ONTARIO

1215 AUTH ABOUD, FRANCES E.
      TITL ETHNIC ROLE TAKING: THE EFFECTS OF PREFERENCE AND
             SELF-IDENTIFICATION.
      SOUR INTERNATIONAL JOURNAL OF PSYCHOLOGY, 1977, V12(1), PP
             1-17.
      YEAR 1977
      DESC CHILDREN-SCHOOL AGE+, ETHNIC IDENTITY+,
             DISCRIMINATION+, ATTITUDES+, ANGLO AMERICANS, SOCIAL
             ROLES+, NATIVE-NON-NATIVE COMPARISONS, EXPERIMENTAL
             STUDY, PSYCHOLOGICAL TESTING+, ELEMENTARY SCHOOLS
      IDEN U.S.

1216 AUTH DAVIS, JAMES L.
      TITL AMERICAN INDIAN STUDENTS' PERCEPTIONS OF ACTUAL AND
             IDEAL DORMITORY AIDE PUPIL CONTROL BEHAVIOR, AND
             STUDENTS' ATTITIDES REGARDING THEIR DORMITORY AIDES.
      SOUR DISSERTATION ABSTRACTS INTERNATIONAL, JUN. 1979,

```
          V40(1), P 145-A.
YEAR      1979
DESC      ATTITUDES+, EDUCATION PARAPROFESSIONALS+, B.I.A.
          BOARDING SCHOOLS+, PSYCHOLOGICAL TESTING+,
          CHILDREN-SCHOOL AGE+, ADOLESCENTS+
IDEN      U.S., PUPIL CONTROL BEHAVIOR FORM, IDEAL PUPIL CONTROL
          BEHAVIOR
```

1217 AUTH HAYES, SUSANNA
     TITL THE COUNSELOR AIDE: HELPING SERVICES FOR NATIVE
AMERICAN STUDENTS.
     SOUR JOURNAL OF AMERICAN INDIAN EDUCATION, MAY 1979,
V18(3), PP 5-11.
     YEAR 1979
     DESC EDUCATION PARAPROFESSIONALS+, PSYCHOTHERAPY AND
COUNSELING+, TRAINING PROGRAMS+, MENTAL HEALTH
PARAPROFESSIONALS+, NATIVE AMERICAN PERSONNEL+, SOCIAL
ROLES+, ROLE MODELS
     IDEN U.S.

1218 AUTH BACHTOLD, LOUISE M.; ECKVALL, KARIN L.
     TITL CURRENT VALUE ORIENTATIONS OF AMERICAN INDIANS IN
NORTHERN CALIFORNIA: THE HUPA.
     SOUR JOURNAL OF CROSS-CULTURAL PSYCHOLOGY, SEP. 1978, V
9(3), PP 367-375.
     YEAR 1978
     DESC HOOPA, NORTHWEST COAST, NATIVE AMERICAN VALUES+,
CULTURAL CONTINUITY+, ETHNIC IDENTITY+, PSYCHOLOGICAL
TESTING+, ADULTS, AGED, TIME PERCEPTION+, RESERVATION,
RESEARCHERS+, ACHIEVEMENT+
     IDEN U.S., CALIFORNIA

1219 AUTH QUERY, JOY M.; QUERY, WILLIAM T.; SINGH, DEVENDRA
     TITL INDEPENDENCE TRAINING, NEED ACHIEVEMENT AND NEED
AFFILIATION: A COMPARISON BETWEEN WHITE AND INDIAN
CHILDREN.
     SOUR INTERNATIONAL JOURNAL OF PSYCHOLOGY, 1975, V10(4), PP
255-268.
     YEAR 1975
     DESC ACHIEVEMENT+, MOTIVATION+, NATIVE-NON-NATIVE
COMPARISONS, ANGLO AMERICANS, PLAINS, SEX DIFFERENCES,
B.I.A. BOARDING SCHOOLS, CHILDREN-SCHOOL AGE, SIOUX,
CHIPPEWA, ADOLESCENTS, ABILITIES, PSYCHOLOGICAL
TESTING+, EXPERIMENTAL STUDY
     IDEN U.S., WECHSLER INTELLIGENCE SCALE CHILDREN, PORTEUS
MAZES, FRENCH TEST OF INSIGHT

1220 AUTH THURBER, STEVEN
     TITL CHANGES IN NAVAJO RESPONSES TO THE DRAW-A-MAN TEST.
     SOUR JOURNAL OF SOCIAL PSYCHOLOGY, 1976, V99, PP 139-140.
     YEAR 1976
     DESC NAVAJO, SOUTHWEST, PSYCHOLOGICAL TESTING+, ABILITIES+,
CHILDREN-SCHOOL AGE+, SEX DIFFERENCES
     IDEN U.S., GOODENOUGH HARRIS DRAW A PERSON TEST

1221   AUTH   PRICE, THOMAS L.
         TITL   SIOUX CHILDREN'S KOPPITZ SCORES ON THE BENDER-GESTALT
              GIVEN BY WHITE OR NATIVE AMERICAN EXAMINERS.
         SOUR   PERCEPTUAL AND MOTOR SKILLS, 1976, V43, PP 1223-1226.
         YEAR   1976
         DESC   CHILDREN-SCHOOL AGE+, SIOUX, ABILITIES, PSYCHOLOGICAL
              TESTING+, NATIVE-NON-NATIVE COMPARISONS, ANGLO
              AMERICANS, RESERVATION, CHILDREN-INFANTS AND
              PRESCHOOL+ , AGE COMPARISONS
         IDEN   U.S., BENDER GESTALT TEST, NEBRASKA

1222   AUTH   SPIVEY, GEORGE H.
         TITL   THE HEALTH OF AMERICAN INDIAN CHILDREN IN
              MULTI-PROBLEM FAMILIES.
         SOUR   SOCIAL SCIENCE AND MEDICINE, MAR. 1977, V11(5), PP
              357-359.
         YEAR   1977
         DESC   FAMILY FUNCTIONING+, PHYSICAL HEALTH AND ILLNESS+,
              RESERVATION, SOUTHWEST, CHILDREN-INFANTS AND
              PRESCHOOL+, CHILDREN-SCHOOL AGE+, EPIDEMIOLOGICAL
              STUDY, MEDICAL PROGRAMS AND SERVICES
         IDEN   U.S.

1223   AUTH   LEFLEY, HARRIET P.
         TITL   SOCIAL AND FAMILIAL CORRELATES OF SELF-ESTEEM AMONG
              AMERICAN INDIAN CHILDREN.
         SOUR   CHILD DEVELOPMENT, 1974, V45, PP 829-833.
         YEAR   1974
         DESC   SELF-CONCEPT+, DISCRIMINATION, CULTURAL ADAPTATION,
              SEMINOLE, MICCOSUKEE, SOUTHEAST WOODLAND, RESERVATION,
              CHILDREN-SCHOOL AGE+, INTERTRIBAL COMPARISONS,
              NATIVE-NON-NATIVE COMPARISONS, ANGLO AMERICANS, SEX
              DIFFERENCES, AGE COMPARISONS, FAMILY FUNCTIONING+,
              CULTURAL CONTINUITY+, ADULTS+, FEMALES+
         IDEN   U.S., PIERS-HARRIS CHILDREN'S SELF CONCEPT SCALE, WORD
              RATING SCALES, FLORIDA

1224   AUTH   TERMANSEN, PAUL E.; RYAN, JOAN
         TITL   HEALTH AND DISEASE IN A BRITISH COLUMBIAN INDIAN
              COMMUNITY.
         SOUR   CANADIAN PSYCHIATRIC ASSOCIATION JOURNAL, 1970,
              V15(2), PP 121-127.
         YEAR   1970
         DESC   EPIDEMIOLOGICAL STUDY, PHYSICAL HEALTH AND ILLNESS+,
              DELIVERY OF SERVICES, DEMOGRAPHIC DATA, ACCIDENTS+,
              MENTAL DISORDERS+, NORTHWEST COAST, MACKENZIE
              SUB-ARCTIC, PLATEAU, ALCOHOL USE, ORGANIC BRAIN
              SYNDROMES, SCHIZOPHRENIA, PARANOIA, DEPRESSION,
              MENTAL RETARDATION
         IDEN   CANADA, BRITISH COLUMBIA

1225   AUTH   SHANNON, LAEL
         TITL   AGE CHANGE IN TIME PERCEPTION IN NATIVE AMERICANS,
              MEXICAN AMERICANS, AND ANGLO AMERICANS.
         SOUR   JOURNAL OF CROSS-CULTURAL PSYCHOLOGY, MAR. 1976,

```
                V7(1), PP 117-122.
        YEAR    1976
        DESC    TIME PERCEPTION+, COGNITIVE PROCESSES+,
                NATIVE-NON-NATIVE COMPARISONS, ANGLO AMERICANS,
                LATINOS, ACHIEVEMENT+, MOTIVATION+, ADOLESCENTS,
                MALES, URBAN AREAS, AGE COMPARISONS
        IDEN    U.S.

1226    AUTH    AUSTIN, GREGORY A.; JOHNSON, BRUCE D.; CARROLL,
                ELEANOR E.; LETTIERI, DAN J.
        TITL    DRUGS AND MINORITIES.
        SOUR    (DHEW PUBLICATION NO. (ADM) 78-507). WASHINGTON, D.C.:
                GOVERNMENT PRINTING OFFICE, 1978.
        YEAR    1978
        DESC    DRUG USE+, REVIEW OF LITERATURE, NATIVE-NON-NATIVE
                COMPARISONS, ASIAN AMERICANS, LATINOS, BLACK AMERICANS
        IDEN    U.S.

1227    AUTH    CENTER FOR MULTICULTURAL AWARENESS; NATIONAL INSTITUTE
                ON DRUG ABUSE
        SOUR    PROCEEDINGS OF THE FORUM ON SUBSTANCE ABUSE PREVENTION
                OF, BY, AND FOR, BICULTURAL WOMEN, WASHINGTON, D.C.,
                AUG. 23-25, 1979.
        YEAR    1979
        DESC    FEMALES+, ADULTS+, DRUG USE+, ALCOHOL USE+, PREVENTIVE
                MENTAL HEALTH PROGRAMS+, NATIVE AMERICAN COPING
                BEHAVIORS, NATIVE-NON-NATIVE COMPARISONS, ASIAN
                AMERICANS, BLACK AMERICANS, LATINOS
        IDEN    U.S.

1228    AUTH    STREIT, FRED; NICOLICH, MARK J.
        TITL    MYTHS VERSUS DATA ON AMERICAN INDIAN DRUG ABUSE.
        SOUR    JOURNAL OF DRUG EDUCATION, 1977, V7(2), PP 117-122.
        YEAR    1977
        DESC    ADOLESCENTS+, SURVEY, SECONDARY SCHOOLS, ALCOHOL USE+,
                DRUG USE+, FULL BLOOD-MIXED BLOOD COMPARISONS, FAMILY
                FUNCTIONING, ATTITUDES, CHILDREN-SCHOOL AGE,
                EPIDEMIOLOGICAL STUDY, ROLE MODELS+
        IDEN    U.S., MONTANA

1229    AUTH    BERGMAN, ROBERT L.
        TITL    A SECOND REPORT ON THE PROBLEMS OF BOARDING SCHOOLS.
        SOUR    PAPER PRESENTED TO THE SECOND MEETING OF THE COMMITTEE
                ON INDIAN HEALTH OF THE AMERICAN ACADEMY OF
                PEDIATRICS, SPRING, 1968.
        YEAR    1968
        DESC    B.I.A. BOARDING SCHOOLS+, CHILDREN-SCHOOL AGE+,
                ADOLESCENTS, EDUCATION PARAPROFESSIONALS+, ROLE
                MODELS+, NATIVE AMERICAN PERSONNEL+, MENTAL HEALTH
                PROGRAMS AND SERVICES+, CONSULTATION, MENTAL
                RETARDATION, RESERVATION, NAVAJO, SOUTHWEST
        IDEN    U.S., NAVAJO RESERVATION

1230    AUTH    BERGMAN, ROBERT L.
        TITL    BOARDING SCHOOLS AND PSYCHOLOGICAL PROBLEMS OF INDIAN
```

```
        CHILDREN.
  SOUR  PAPER PRESENTED AT THE FIRST MEETING OF THE COMMITTEE
        ON INDIAN HEALTH OF THE AMERICAN ACADEMY OF
        PEDIATRICS, FALL, 1967. (10P)
  YEAR  1967
  DESC  B.I.A. BOARDING SCHOOLS+, CHILDREN-SCHOOL AGE+,
        ADOLESCENTS+, BILINGUALISM, NAVAJO, SOUTHWEST,
        EDUCATION PARAPROFESSIONALS+, NATIVE AMERICAN
        PERSONNEL+, SOCIALLY DEVIANT BEHAVIOR, PASSIVE
        RESISTANCE, RESERVATION, LEARNING DISABILITIES AND
        PROBLEMS
  IDEN  U.S., NAVAJO RESERVATION

1231 AUTH  DEVEREUX, GEORGE
     TITL  THE PRIMAL SCENE AND JUVENILE HETEROSEXUALITY IN
           MOHAVE SOCIETY.
     SOUR  IN GEORGE B. WILBUR AND WARNER MUENSTERBERGER(EDS.),
           PSYCHOANALYSIS AND CULTURE: ESSAYS IN HONOR OF GEZA
           ROHEIM, PP 90-107. NEW YORK: INTERNATIONAL
           UNIVERSITIES PRESS, 1951.
     YEAR  1951
     DESC  SEXUAL RELATIONS+, CHILDREN-SCHOOL AGE+,
           PSYCHOANALYSIS, MOHAVE, SOUTHWEST, GROUP NORMS AND
           SANCTIONS+, RESERVATION
     IDEN  U.S.

1232 AUTH  EELS, WALTER C.
     TITL  MENTAL ABILITY OF THE NATIVE RACES OF ALASKA.
     SOUR  JOURNAL OF APPLIED PSYCHOLOGY, 1933, V17, PP 417-438.
     YEAR  1933
     DESC  ALASKA NATIVES,ABILITIES+, PSYCHOLOGICAL
           TESTING+,ESKIMO, ALEUT, INTERTRIBAL COMPARISONS, FULL
           BLOOD-MIXED BLOOD COMPARISONS, SEX DIFFERENCES,
           LANGUAGE HANDICAPS
     IDEN  U.S, STANFORD BINET INTELLIGENCE SCALE, GOODENOUGH
           HARRIS DRAW A PERSON TEST

1233 AUTH  BERGAN,K.W.
     TITL  THE SECONDARY SCHOOL AND THE ACCULTURATION OF INDIAN
           PEOPLE.
     SOUR  BULLETIN OF THE NATIONAL ASSOCIATION OF SECONDARY
           SCHOOL PRINCIPALS, OCT. 1959, V43(249), PP 115-118.
     YEAR  1959
     DESC  SECONDARY SCHOOLS+, CULTURAL ADAPTATION+, RESERVATION,
           BLACKFEET,FLATHEAD, CHEYENNE-NORTHERN, CROW, PLAINS,
           EDUCATION PROGRAMS AND SERVICES, RELOCATION+,
           ADOLESCENTS, PLATEAU
     IDEN  U.S., MONTANA, BLACKFEET RESERVATION, FLATHEAD
           RESERVATION, FORT BELKNAP RESERVATION, ROCKYBOY
           RESERVATION, NORTHERN CHEYENNE RESERVATION

1234 AUTH  DIPPIE, BRIAN W.
     TITL  POPCORN AND INDIANS: CUSTER ON THE SCREEN.
     SOUR  CULTURES, 1974, V2(1), PP 139-169.
     YEAR  1974
```

```
        DESC   STEREOTYPES+, DISCRIMINATION+, ROLE MODELS+
        IDEN   U.S.

1235    AUTH   FRANKLYN, G.J.
        TITL   ALIENATION AND ACHIEVEMENT AMONG INDIAN-METIS AND
               NON-INDIANS IN THE MACKENZIE DISTRICT OF THE NORTHWEST
               TERRITORIES.
        SOUR   ALBERTA JOURNAL OF EDUCATIONAL RESEARCH, JUN. 1974,
               V20(2), PP 157-169.
        YEAR   1974
        DESC   ACHIEVEMENT+, NATIVE AMERICAN VALUES+, SECONDARY
               SCHOOLS, ANOMIE+, POWERLESSNESS+, ATTITUDES+,
               MACKENZIE SUB-ARCTIC, STRESS, SEX DIFFERENCES,
               NATIVE-NON-NATIVE COMPARISONS, ANGLO AMERICANS,
               ADOLESCENTS
        IDEN   CANADA, ALBERTA, KOLESAR'S PUPIL ATTITUDE
               QUESTIONNAIRE, SCAT, ALBERTA DEVELOPMENTAL GRADE IX
               EXAMINATIONS

1236    AUTH   ARCHIBALD, CHARLES W.
        TITL   GROUP PSYCHOTHERAPY WITH AMERICAN INDIANS.
        SOUR   IN MAX ROSENBAUM (ED.), GROUP PSYCHOTHERAPY, PP 43-47.
               NEW YORK: GORDON AND BREACH SCIENCE PUBLISHERS, 1974.
        YEAR   1974
        DESC   SOCIAL GROUPS AND PEER GROUPS+, PSYCHOTHERAPY AND
               COUNSELING+, PASSIVE RESISTANCE, GROUP NORMS AND
               SANCTIONS, NONINTERFERENCE, RESERVATION
        IDEN   U.S.

1237    AUTH   GOLDFRANK, ESTHER S.
        TITL   "OLD MAN" AND THE FATHER IMAGE IN BLOOD (BLACKFOOT)
               SOCIETY.
        SOUR   IN GEORGE B. WILBUR AND WARNER MUENSTERBERGER (EDS).,
               PSYCHOANALYSIS AND CULTURE: ESSAYS IN HONOR OF GEZA
               ROHEIM, PP 132-141. NEW YORK: INTERNATIONAL
               UNIVERSITIES PRESS, 1951.
        YEAR   1951
        DESC   BLACKFEET-BLOOD, ATTITUDES+, MALES+, ADULTS+, SOCIAL
               ROLES+, TRADITIONAL CHILD REARING, FAMILY PLANNING,
               FAMILY FUNCTIONING+, SOCIAL STATUS+, PSYCHOANALYSIS
        IDEN   CANADA, ALBERTA

1238    AUTH   JILEK-AALL, LOUISE; JILEK, WOLFGANG G.; FLYNN, FRANK
        TITL   SEX ROLE, CULTURE AND PSYCHOTHERAPY: A COMPARATIVE
               STUDY OF THREE ETHNIC GROUPS IN WESTERN CANADA.
        SOUR   JOURNAL OF PSYCHOLOGICAL ANTHROPOLOGY, FALL 1978,
               V1(4), PP 473-488.
        YEAR   1978
        DESC   COAST SALISH, NORTHWEST COAST, SOCIAL ROLES+, SEX
               DIFFERENCES, MALES+, FEMALES+, NATIVE-NON-NATIVE
               COMPARISONS, RELIGIONS-NON-NATIVE+, MENTAL DISORDERS+,
               ADULTS, PARANOIA, ALCOHOL USE, PSYCHOPHYSIOLOGICAL
               DISORDERS, DEPRESSION, SCHIZOPHRENIA, ANXIETY,
               SUICIDE, SOCIALLY DEVIANT BEHAVIOR
        IDEN   CANADA, BRITISH COLUMBIA
```

1239 AUTH FREEMAN, DANIEL M.A.; FOULKS, EDWARD F.; FREEMAN.
            PATRICIA, A.
      TITL CHILD DEVELOPMENT AND ARCTIC HYSTERIA IN THE NORTH
            ALASKAN ESKIMO MALE.
      SOUR JOURNAL OF PSYCHOLOGICAL ANTHROPOLOGY, SPR. 1978,
            V1(2), PP 203-210.
      YEAR 1978
      DESC ARCTIC HYSTERIA+, MALES+, PERSONALITY TRAITS,
            TRADITIONAL CHILD REARING+, EMOTIONAL RESTRAINT,
            WESTERN ARCTIC, ESKIMO, AGGRESSIVENESS, TRADITIONAL
            SOCIAL CONTROL+, FAMILY FUNCTIONING+, ANXIETY+,
            CHILDREN-INFANTS AND PRESCHOOL
      IDEN U.S., ALASKA

1240 AUTH LOMBARDI, THOMAS P.
      TITL PSYCHOLINGUISTIC ABILITIES OF PAPAGO INDIAN SCHOOL
            CHILDREN.
      SOUR EXCEPTIONAL CHILDREN, MARCH 1970, PP 485-493.
      YEAR 1970
      DESC PAPAGO, SOUTHWEST, CHILDREN-SCHOOL AGE+, ABILITIES+,
            PSYCHOLOGICAL TESTING+, RESERVATION, LANGUAGE
            HANDICAPS+, ACHIEVEMENT, COGNITIVE PROCESSES,
            NATIVE-NON-NATIVE COMPARISONS, ANGLO AMERICANS,
            ELEMENTARY SCHOOLS
      IDEN U.S., ARIZONA, ILLINOIS TEST OF PSYCHOLINGUISTIC
            ABILITIES

1241 AUTH LEFLEY, HARRIET P.
      TITL ACCULTURATION, CHILD-REARING, AND SELF-ESTEEM IN TWO
            NORTH AMERICAN INDIAN TRIBES.
      SOUR ETHOS, 1976, V4(3), PP 385-401.
      YEAR 1976
      DESC MICCOSUKEE, SOUTHEAST WOODLAND, STRESS+, SEMINOLE,
            CULTURAL ADAPTATION+, SELF-CONCEPT+, CHILDREN-INFANTS
            AND PRESCHOOL+, TRADITIONAL CHILD REARING+,
            RESERVATION, CULTURAL CONTINUITY+, ADULTS+, FEMALES+,
            INTERTRIBAL COMPARISONS, PSYCHOLOGICAL TESTING+, SEX
            DIFFERENCES, FAMILY FUNCTIONING, EXTENDED FAMILY,
            SOCIALLY DEVIANT BEHAVIOR, ROLE MODELS
      IDEN U.S., FLORIDA, PIERS HARRIS CHILDREN'S SELF-CONCEPT
            SCALE, SARASON AND GANZER, WORD RATING SCALES, INDIAN
            STIMULUS SCALE, PARENT ATTITUDE RESEARCH INSTRUMENT

1242 AUTH JOHN, VERA P.
      TITL STYLES OF LEARNING--STYLES OF TEACHING: REFLECTIONS ON
            THE EDUCATION OF NAVAJO CHILDREN.
      SOUR IN COURTNEY B. CAZDEN, VERA P. JOHN, AND DELL HYMES
            (EDS.), FUNCTIONS OF LANGUAGE IN THE CLASSROOM, PP
            331-343. NEW YORK: TEACHERS COLLEGE PRESS, 1972.
      YEAR 1972
      DESC NAVAJO, SOUTHWEST, CHILDREN-SCHOOL AGE+, LANGUAGE
            HANDICAPS+, RESERVATION, ELEMENTARY SCHOOLS+,
            LEARNING+, BILINGUALISM+, BICULTURALISM+, COGNITIVE
            PROCESSES+
      IDEN U.S., NAVAJO RESERVATION, ROUGH ROCK DEMONSTRATION

SCHOOL

1243 AUTH DUMONT, ROBERT V.
     TITL LEARNING ENGLISH AND HOW TO BE SILENT: STUDIES IN
          SIOUX AND CHEROKEE CLASSROOMS.
     SOUR IN COURTNEY B. CAZDEN, VERA P. JOHN, DELL HYMES
          (EDS.), FUNCTIONS OF LANGUAGE IN THE CLASSROOM, PP
          344-369. NEW YORK: TEACHERS COLLEGE PRESS, 1972.
     YEAR 1972
     DESC PASSIVE RESISTANCE+, LEARNING+, ELEMENTARY SCHOOLS+,
          CHILDREN-SCHOOL AGE+, EDUCATION PROFESSIONALS+,
          OFF-RESERVATION, NONINTERFERENCE, COOPERATION+,
          LANGUAGE HANDICAPS+, CHEROKEE, SIOUX, PLAINS,
          SOUTHEAST WOODLAND
     IDEN U.S., SOUTH DAKOTA, OKLAHOMA

1244 AUTH PHILIPS, SUSAN U.
     TITL PARTICIPANT STRUCTURES AND COMMUNICATIVE COMPETENCE:
          WARM SPRINGS CHILDREN IN COMMUNITY AND CLASSROOM.
     SOUR IN COURTNEY B. CAZDEN, VERA P. JOHN, AND DELL HYMES
          (EDS.), FUNCTIONS OF LANGUAGE IN THE CLASSROOM, PP
          370-394. NEW YORK: TEACHERS COLLEGE PRESS, 1972.
     YEAR 1972
     DESC WARM SPRINGS, PLATEAU, CHILDREN-SCHOOL AGE+,
          RESERVATION, SOCIAL GROUPS AND PEER GROUPS+, EDUCATION
          PROFESSIONALS+, SOCIAL ROLES+, LEADERSHIP+,
          NONINTERFERENCE, NONCOMPETITIVENESS, LEARNING+,
          TRADITIONAL CHILD REARING, ELEMENTARY SCHOOLS+
     IDEN U.S., OREGON, WARM SPRINGS RESERVATION

1245 AUTH KLEINFELD, JUDITH S.; BLOOM, JOSEPH D.
     TITL BOARDING SCHOOLS: EFFECTS ON THE MENTAL HEALTH OF
          ESKIMO ADOLESCENTS.
     SOUR AMERICAN JOURNAL OF PSYCHIATRY, APR. 1977, V134(4), PP
          411-417.
     YEAR 1977
     DESC B.I.A. BOARDING SCHOOLS+, ADOLESCENTS+, ESKIMO,
          WESTERN ARCTIC, MENTAL DISORDERS+, SOCIALLY DEVIANT
          BEHAVIOR+, ENVIRONMENTAL FACTORS, BOARDING HOMES,
          STRESS+
     IDEN U.S., ALASKA, HEALTH OPINION SURVEY

1246 AUTH MILLER, MARV
     TITL SUICIDES ON A SOUTHWESTERN AMERICAN INDIAN
          RESERVATION.
     SOUR WHITE CLOUD JOURNAL, 1979, V1(3), PP 14-18.
     YEAR 1979
     DESC SUICIDE+, RESERVATION, SOUTHWEST, EPIDEMIOLOGICAL
          STUDY, ADOLESCENTS+, ADULTS, AGE COMPARISONS, MARITAL
          RELATIONSHIPS, MALES+, CORRECTIONAL INSTITUTIONS,
          EMPLOYMENT, PREVENTIVE MENTAL HEALTH PROGRAMS,
          DEMOGRAPHIC DATA
     IDEN U.S.

1247 AUTH MANSON, SPERO M.; PAMBRUN, AUDRA M.

```
          TITL   SOCIAL AND PSYCHOLOGICAL STATUS OF THE AMERICAN INDIAI
                 ELDERLY: PAST RESEARCH , CURRENT ADVOCACY, AND FUTURE
                 INQUIRY.
          SOUR   WHITE CLOUD JOURNAL, 1979, V1(3), PP 18-25.
          YEAR   1979
          DESC   AGED+, SURVEY, ATTITUDES+, RESERVATION, URBAN AREAS,
                 FAMILY FUNCTIONING, DELIVERY OF SERVICES,
                 SELF-CONCEPT, SOCIAL GROUPS AND PEER GROUPS, REVIEW OI
                 LITERATURE
          IDEN   U.S.

1248  AUTH   MCSHANE, DAMIAN
      TITL   A REVIEW OF SCORES OF AMERICAN INDIAN CHILDREN ON THE
             WECHSLER INTELLIGENCE SCALES.
      SOUR   WHITE CLOUD JOURNAL, 1980, V1(4), PP 3-10.
      YEAR   1980
      DESC   CHILDREN-SCHOOL AGE+, ABILITIES+, PSYCHOLOGICAL
             TESTING+, REVIEW OF LITERATURE, LANGUAGE HANDICAPS,
             ADOLESCENTS+, COGNITIVE PROCESSES+, LEARNING
      IDEN   U.S., WECHSLER INTELLIGENCE SCALE CHILDREN

1249  AUTH   JARANSON, JAMES M.; GREGORY, C. DELORES
      TITL   JOB SATISFACTION IN THE PORTLAND AREA INDIAN HEALTH
             SERVICE.
      SOUR   WHITE CLOUD JOURNAL, 1980, V1(4), PP 20-28.
      YEAR   1980
      DESC   I.H.S., EMPLOYMENT+, NATIVE AMERICAN PERSONNEL+,
             SURVEY, SEX DIFFERENCES, NATIVE-NON-NATIVE
             COMPARISONS, ANGLO AMERICANS
      IDEN   U.S., OREGON, MINNESOTA SATISFACTION QUESTIONNAIRE

1250  AUTH   LIBERMAN, DAVID; FRANK, JOEL
      TITL   INDIVIDUAL'S PERCEPTIONS OF STRESSFUL LIFE EVENTS: A
             COMPARISON OF NATIVE AMERICAN, RURAL, AND URBAN
             SAMPLES USING THE SOCIAL READJUSTMENT RATING SCALE.
      SOUR   WHITE CLOUD JOURNAL, 1980, V1(4), PP 15-19.
      YEAR   1980
      DESC   MICCOSUKEE, SOUTHEAST WOODLAND, STRESS+, ADULTS,
             RESERVATION, URBAN AREAS, NATIVE-NON-NATIVE
             COMPARISONS, ANGLO AMERICANS
      IDEN   U.S., FLORIDA, SOCIAL READJUSTMENT RATING SCALE

1251  AUTH   PENISTON, EUGENE; BURNS, THOMAS R.
      TITL   AN ALCOHOLIC DEPENDENCY BEHAVIOR INVENTORY FOR NATIVE
             AMERICANS.
      SOUR   WHITE CLOUD JOURNAL, 1980, V1(4), PP 11-15.
      YEAR   1980
      DESC   ALCOHOLISM TREATMENT+, PSYCHOLOGICAL TESTING+,
             CLINICAL STUDY, SEX DIFFERENCES
      IDEN   U.S., M.M.P.I., ALCOHOLIC DEPENDENCY BEHAVIOR
             INVENTORY

1252  AUTH   KELSO, DIANNE
      TITL   ANNOUNCING A BIBLIOGRAPHY ON AMERICAN INDIAN/ALASKAN
             NATIVE MENTAL HEALTH.
```

```
         SOUR  WHITE CLOUD JOURNAL, 1979, V1(3), PP 26-28.
         YEAR  1979
         DESC  REVIEW OF LITERATURE, RESEARCHERS+, CULTURE-SPECIFIC
               SYNDROMES, NATIVE AMERICAN COPING BEHAVIORS

   1253  AUTH  LIBERMAN, DAVID; KNIGGE, ROSE MARIE
         TITL  HEALTH CARE PROVIDER- CONSUMER COMMUNICATION IN THE
               MICCOSUKEE INDIAN COMMUNITY.
         SOUR  WHITE CLOUD JOURNAL, 1979, V1(3), PP 5-13.
         YEAR  1979
         DESC  MICCOSUKEE, SOUTHEAST WOODLAND, MEDICAL INSTITUTIONS,
               LANGUAGE HANDICAPS+, MEDICAL PROGRAMS AND SERVICES+,
               MEDICAL PROFESSIONALS+, CLINICAL STUDY, RESERVATION,
               ATTITUDES+, ADULTS, AGE COMPARISONS, NATIVE AMERICAN
               ETIOLOGY, TRADITIONAL HEALERS
         IDEN  U.S., FLORIDA

   1254  AUTH  HAVEN,GEORGE A.; IMOTICHEY, PAUL J.
         TITL  MENTAL HEALTH SERVICES FOR AMERICAN INDIANS: THE USET
               PROGRAM.
         SOUR  WHITE CLOUD JOURNAL, 1979, V1(3), PP 3-5.
         YEAR  1979
         DESC  MENTAL HEALTH PROGRAMS AND SERVICES+, NORTHEAST
               WOODLAND, SOUTHEAST WOODLAND, I.H.S., CONSULTATION,
               NATIVE AMERICAN ADMINISTERED PROGRAMS+
         IDEN  U.S., FLORIDA, MISSISSIPPI, LOUISIANA, NEW YORK, MAINE

   1255  AUTH  STRODBECK, FRED L.
         TITL  HUSBAND-WIFE INTERACTION OVER REVEALED DIFFERENCES.
         SOUR  AMERICAN SOCIOLOGICAL REVIEW, 1951, V16(4), PP 468-473.
         YEAR  1951
         DESC  MARITAL RELATIONSHIPS+, NAVAJO, SOUTHWEST, FAMILY
               FUNCTIONING+, SOCIAL ROLES+, FEMALES, MALES, ADULTS,
               NATIVE-NON-NATIVE COMPARISONS, ANGLO AMERICANS,
               RESERVATION
         IDEN  U.S., NAVAJO RESERVATION

   1256  AUTH  HEINRICH, ALBERT
         TITL  DIVORCE AS AN INTEGRATIVE SOCIAL FACTOR.
         SOUR  JOURNAL OF COMPARATIVE FAMILY STUDIES, 1972, V3(2), PP
               265-272.
         YEAR  1972
         DESC  MARITAL RELATIONSHIPS+, FAMILY FUNCTIONING+, EXTENDED
               FAMILY+, ESKIMO, WESTERN ARCTIC
         IDEN  U.S., ALASKA

   1257  AUTH  REICHARD, GLADYS A.
         TITL  THE FAMILY AND MARRIAGE.
         SOUR  IN IRWIN T. SANDERS (ED.), SOCIETIES AROUND THE WORLD,
               V1, PP 269-279. NEW YORK: DRYDEN PRESS, 1953.
         YEAR  1953
         DESC  NAVAJO, SOUTHWEST, EXTENDED FAMILY+, FAMILY
               FUNCTIONING+, RESERVATION, FEMALES+, SOCIAL ROLES,
               MARITAL RELATIONSHIPS, MALES+
         IDEN  U.S., NAVAJO RESERVATION
```

1258 AUTH BALLINGER, THOMAS O.
      TITL SOME NOTES ON DIRECTIONAL MOVEMENT IN THE DRAWINGS AND
            PAINTINGS OF PUEBLO AND NAVAJO CHILDREN.
      SOUR AMERICAN ANTHROPOLOGIST, 1964, V66, PP 880-883.
      YEAR 1964
      DESC PUEBLO, NAVAJO, SOUTHWEST, CHILDREN-SCHOOL AGE+,
            ADOLESCENTS+, PSYCHOLOGICAL TESTING+, COGNITIVE
            PROCESSES+, MOTOR PROCESSES, ABILITIES
      IDEN U.S., NEW MEXICO

1259 AUTH VOGT, EVON Z.
      TITL NAVAHO VETERANS: A STUDY OF CHANGING VALUES.
      SOUR PAPERS OF THE PEABODY MUSEUM OF AMERICAN ARCHEOLOGY
            AND ETHNOLOGY, 1951, V41(1, REPORTS OF THE RIMROCK
            PROJECT VALUES SERIES, NO. 1).
      YEAR 1951
      DESC NATIVE AMERICAN VALUES+, MILITARY SERVICE+, NAVAJO,
            SOUTHWEST, CULTURAL ADAPTATION+, CULTURAL CONTINUITY+,
            EXTENDED FAMILY, B.I.A. BOARDING SCHOOLS, RESERVATION,
            PERSONALITY TRAITS, STRESS+, NATIVE AMERICAN COPING
            BEHAVIORS, NATIVE AMERICAN RELIGIONS,
            RELIGIONS-NON-NATIVE, GHOST SICKNESS, WITCHCRAFT,
            UNIVERSAL HARMONY
      IDEN U.S., NAVAJO RESERVATION

1260 AUTH LANDAR, HERBERT J. ; ERVIN, SUSAN M.; HOROWITZ, ARNOLD
            E.
      TITL NAVAHO COLOR CATEGORIES.
      SOUR LANGUAGE, 1960, V36, PP 368-382.
      YEAR 1960
      DESC COGNITIVE PROCESSES+, NAVAJO, SOUTHWEST, LANGUAGE
            HANDICAPS, ADULTS, BILINGUALISM, NATIVE-NON-NATIVE
            COMPARISONS, ANGLO AMERICANS, RESERVATION
      IDEN U.S., NAVAJO RESERVATION

1261 AUTH LLOYD, DAVID O.
      TITL COMPARISON OF STANDARDIZED TEST RESULTS OF INDIAN AND
            NON-INDIAN IN AN INTEGRATED SCHOOL SYSTEM.
      SOUR JOURNAL OF AMERICAN INDIAN EDUCATION, 1961, V1(1), PP
            8-16.
      YEAR 1961
      DESC PIMA, MARICOPA, APACHE, ELEMENTARY SCHOOLS, SECONDARY
            SCHOOLS, CHILDREN-SCHOOL AGE+, ADOLESCENTS+,
            PSYCHOLOGICAL TESTING+, ABILITIES, ACHIEVEMENT+,
            CULTURAL ADAPTATION+
      IDEN U.S., ARIZONA, SALT RIVER RESERVATION, FORT MCDOWELL
            RESERVATION, CALIFORNIA TESTS OF MENTAL MATURITY,
            CALIFORNIA ACHIEVEMENT TESTS

1262 AUTH STAFFORD, KENNETH
      TITL PROBLEM SOLVING BY NAVAJO CHILDREN IN RELATION TO
            KNOWLEDGE OF ENGLISH.
      SOUR JOURNAL OF AMERICAN INDIAN EDUCATION, 1965, V4(2), PP
            23-25.
      YEAR 1965

DESC COGNITIVE PROCESSES+, NAVAJO, SOUTHWEST, ADOLESCENTS+,
ABILITIES+, EXPERIMENTAL STUDY, LANGUAGE HANDICAPS+,
BILINGUALISM+
IDEN U.S., ARIZONA

1263 AUTH SNIDER, JAMES G.
TITL ACHIEVEMENT TEST PERFORMANCE OF ACCULTURATED INDIAN
CHILDREN.
SOUR ALBERTA JOURNAL OF EDUCATIONAL RESEARCH, 1961, V7(1),
PP 39-41.
YEAR 1961
DESC NEZ PERCE, PLATEAU, PSYCHOLOGICAL TESTING+, SECONDARY
SCHOOLS, NATIVE-NON-NATIVE COMPARISONS, ANGLO
AMERICANS , ADOLESCENTS+, ACHIEVEMENT+, CULTURAL
ADAPTATION+
IDEN U.S., IDAHO, COOPERATIVE ENGLISH, ESSENTIAL H.S.
CONTENT BATTERY

1264 AUTH WESTERMEYER, JOSEPH
TITL ALCOHOLISM FROM THE CROSS CULTURAL PERSPECTIVE: A
REVIEW AND CRITIQUE OF CLINICAL STUDIES.
SOUR AMERICAN JOURNAL OF DRUG AND ALCOHOL ABUSE, 1974,
V1(1), PP 89-105.
YEAR 1974
DESC ALCOHOL USE+, CLINICAL STUDY, NATIVE-NON-NATIVE
COMPARISONS, ANGLO AMERICANS, REVIEW OF LITERATURE,
RESEARCHERS+
IDEN U.S.

1265 AUTH ROHNER, RONALD P.
TITL FACTORS INFLUENCING THE ACADEMIC PERFORMANCE OF
KWAKIUTL CHILDREN IN CANADA.
SOUR COMPARATIVE EDUCATION REVIEW, 1965, V9, PP 331-340.
YEAR 1965
DESC KWAKIUTL, NORTHWEST COAST, ABILITIES+, CHILDREN-SCHOOL
AGE+, ACHIEVEMENT+, ELEMENTARY SCHOOLS, PSYCHOLOGICAL
TESTING, LEARNING, FAMILY FUNCTIONING, DROPOUTS,
EDUCATION PROFESSIONALS, COMMUNITY INVOLVEMENT,
ADOLESCENTS, TRADITIONAL CHILD REARING
IDEN CANADA, BRITISH COLUMBIA, WECHSLER INTELLIGENCE SCALE
CHILDREN, CALIFORNIA TEST OF MENTAL MATURITY

1266 AUTH STEGGERDA, MORRIS
TITL FORM DISCRIMINATION TEST AS GIVEN TO NAVAJO, NEGRO AND
WHITE SCHOOL CHILDREN.
SOUR HUMAN BIOLOGY, 1941, V13, PP 237-246.
YEAR 1941
DESC CHILDREN-SCHOOL AGE+, PSYCHOLOGICAL TESTING+,
ABILITIES+, SEX DIFFERENCES, NATIVE-NON-NATIVE
COMPARISONS, ANGLO AMERICANS, NAVAJO, SOUTHWEST, BLACK
AMERICANS, AGE COMPARISONS
IDEN U.S., JAMAICA, FORM DISCRIMINATION TEST

1267 AUTH STEGGERDA, MORRIS; MACOMBER, EILEEN
TITL A REVISION OF THE MCADORY ART TEST APPLIED TO AMERICAN

INDIANS, DUTCH, WHITES AND COLLEGE GRADUATES.
SOUR JOURNAL OF COMPARATIVE PSYCHOLOGY, 1938, V26, PP
349-353.
YEAR 1938
DESC NAVAJO, SOUTHWEST, RESERVATION, ABILITIES+, COGNITIVE
PROCESSES+, PSYCHOLOGICAL TESTING+, NATIVE-NON-NATIVE
COMPARISONS, ANGLO AMERICANS, ADULTS
IDEN U.S., NAVAJO RESERVATION, MCADORY ART TEST

1268 AUTH STEGGERDA, MORRIS
TITL THE MCADORY ART TEST APPLIED TO NAVAHO INDIAN
CHILDREN.
SOUR JOURNAL OF COMPARATIVE PSYCHOLOGY, 1936, V22, PP
283-285.
YEAR 1936
DESC NAVAJO, SOUTHWEST, RESERVATION, SEX DIFFERENCES,
PSYCHOLOGICAL TESTING+, ABILITIES+, NATIVE-NON-NATIVE
COMPARISONS, ANGLO AMERICANS, COGNITIVE PROCESSES+,
CHILDREN-SCHOOL AGE+
IDEN U.S., NAVAJO RESERVATION, MCADORY ART TEST

1269 AUTH RUSSELL, R.W.
TITL THE SPONTANEOUS AND INSTRUCTED DRAWINGS OF ZUNI
CHILDREN.
SOUR JOURNAL OF COMPARATIVE PSYCHOLOGY, 1943, V35, PP 11-15
YEAR 1943
DESC CHILDREN-SCHOOL AGE+, ABILITIES+, PUEBLO-ZUNI,
SOUTHWEST, AGE COMPARISONS, SEX DIFFERENCES,
NATIVE-NON-NATIVE COMPARISONS, ANGLO AMERICANS,
CULTURE-FAIR TESTS+, PSYCHOLOGICAL TESTING+,
ELEMENTARY SCHOOLS
IDEN U.S., GOODENOUGH HARRIS DRAW A PERSON TEST, NEW MEXICO

1270 AUTH TURNER, G.H.; PENFOLD, D.J.
TITL THE SCHOLASTIC APTITUDE OF THE INDIAN CHILDREN OF THE
CARADOC RESERVE.
SOUR CANADIAN JOURNAL OF PSYCHOLOGY, 1952, V6(1), PP 31-44.
YEAR 1952
DESC ABILITIES+, PSYCHOLOGICAL TESTING+, RESERVATION,
CHIPPEWA, MUNSEE, EASTERN SUB-ARCTIC, NORTHEAST
WOODLAND, IROQUOIS-ONEIDA, ELEMENTARY SCHOOLS,
CHILDREN-SCHOOL AGE+, NATIVE-NON-NATIVE COMPARISONS,
ANGLO AMERICANS, ADOLESCENTS+, SECONDARY SCHOOLS, AGE
COMPARISONS, SELF-CONCEPT, LANGUAGE HANDICAPS
IDEN CANADA, ONTARIO, CARADOC RESERVE, WECHSLER
INTELLIGENCE SCALE CHILDREN, OTIS QUICK SCORING MENTAL
ABILITY TEST, HENMON-NELSON TEST OF MENTAL ABILITY,
PROGRESSIVE MATRICES

1271 AUTH TROIKE, RUDOLPH C.
TITL THE ORIGINS OF PLAINS MESCALISM.
SOUR AMERICAN ANTHROPOLOGIST, 1962, V64, PP 946-963.
YEAR 1962
DESC TRADITIONAL USE OF DRUGS AND ALCOHOL+, TRADITIONAL
HEALERS+, DREAMS AND VISION QUESTS+, NATIVE AMERICAN

```
          RELIGIONS+, PRAIRIE, CADDO, PONCA, WICHITA, IOWA,
          OMAHA, OTO, ARIKARA, TONKAWA
     IDEN U.S.

1272 AUTH TORREY, E. FULLER
     TITL INDIGENOUS PSYCHOTHERAPY: THEORIES AND TECHNIQUES.
     SOUR CURRENT PSYCHIATRIC THERAPIES, 1970, V10, PP 118-129.
     YEAR 1970
     DESC CULTURE-BASED PSYCHOTHERAPY+, GROUP NORMS AND
          SANCTIONS, TRADITIONAL HEALERS+, PERSONALITY TRAITS,
          PSYCHOTHERAPY AND COUNSELING+, CHEMOTHERAPY,
          CONFESSION, NATIVE-NON-NATIVE COMPARISONS,
          PSYCHOANALYSIS, DREAMS AND VISION QUESTS, BEHAVIOR
          MODIFICATION
     IDEN NORTH AMERICA, SOUTH AMERICA, EUROPE, AFRICA

1273 AUTH MAIL, PATRICIA D.; MCDONALD, DAVID R.
     TITL NATIVE AMERICANS AND ALCOHOL: A PRELIMINARY ANNOTATED
          BIBLIOGRAPHY.
     SOUR BEHAVIOR SCIENCE RESEARCH, 1977, V12(3), PP 169-196.
     YEAR 1977
     DESC ALCOHOL USE+, REVIEW OF LITERATURE, STRESS, GENETIC
          FACTORS

1274 AUTH JONES, KENNETH L.; SMITH, DAVID W.
     TITL THE FETAL ALCOHOL SYNDROME.
     SOUR TERATOLOGY, 1975, V12, PP 1-10.
     YEAR 1975
     DESC CHILDREN-INFANTS AND PRESCHOOL+, ALCOHOL USE+,
          FEMALES+, ADULTS, MENTAL RETARDATION, PHYSICAL HEALTH
          AND ILLNESS
     IDEN U.S.

1275 AUTH HAWLEY, FLORENCE
     TITL THE KERESAN HOLY ROLLERS: AN ADAPTATION TO AMERICAN
          INDIVIDUALISM.
     SOUR SOCIAL FORCES, 1948, V26(3), PP 272-280.
     YEAR 1948
     DESC STRESS+, CULTURAL ADAPTATION+, PUEBLO, SOUTHWEST,
          RELIGIONS-NON-NATIVE+, NATIVE AMERICAN VALUES+, NATIVE
          AMERICAN RELIGIONS+, GROUP NORMS AND SANCTIONS,
          DISCRIMINATION, RESERVATION, BLACK AMERICANS
     IDEN U.S.

1276 AUTH COOLEY, RICHARD C.; OSTENDORF, DONALD; BICKERTON,
          DOROTHY
     TITL OUTREACH SERVICES FOR ELDERLY NATIVE AMERICANS.
     SOUR SOCIAL WORK, MAR. 1979, V24, PP 151-153.
     YEAR 1979
     DESC AGED+, RESERVATION,MENTAL HEALTH PROGRAMS AND
          SERVICES+, SOUTHWEST, APACHE, DELIVERY OF SERVICES+,
          INSTITUTIONALIZATION+,MENTAL HEALTH PARAPROFESSIONALS,
          NATIVE AMERICAN PERSONNEL, COMMUNITY INVOLVEMENT+,
          URBAN AREAS
     IDEN U.S., ARIZONA, FORT APACHE RESERVATION
```

1277　AUTH　STARR, FRED M.
　　　　TITL　INDIANS AND THE CRIMINAL JUSTICE SYSTEM.
　　　　SOUR　CANADIAN JOURNAL OF CRIMINOLOGY, JUL. 1978, V20(3), PP
　　　　　　　317-323.
　　　　YEAR　1978
　　　　DESC　LEGAL ISSUES+, CORRECTIONS PERSONNEL+, ADMINISTRATIVE
　　　　　　　ISSUES+, COMMUNITY INVOLVEMENT+, NATIVE AMERICAN
　　　　　　　PERSONNEL+, CORRECTIONAL INSTITUTIONS+, PLAINS,
　　　　　　　PROGRAM DEVELOPMENT
　　　　IDEN　CANADA, SASKATCHEWAN

1278　AUTH　LANE, E.B.; DANIELS, H.W.; BLYAN, J.D.; ROGER R.
　　　　TITL　THE INCARCERATED NATIVE.
　　　　SOUR　CANADIAN JOURNAL OF CRIMINOLOGY, JUL. 1978, V20(3), PP
　　　　　　　308-316.
　　　　YEAR　1978
　　　　DESC　CORRECTIONAL INSTITUTIONS+, INSTITUTIONALIZATION+,
　　　　　　　SURVEY, SOCIAL GROUPS AND PEER GROUPS, ECONOMIC
　　　　　　　ISSUES, RESERVATION, URBAN AREAS, OFF-RESERVATION,
　　　　　　　COMMUNITY INVOLVEMENT
　　　　IDEN　CANADA

1279　AUTH　SUE, STANLEY; ALLEN, DAVID B.; CONAWAY, LINDA
　　　　TITL　THE RESPONSIVENESS AND EQUALITY OF MENTAL HEALTH CARE
　　　　　　　TO CHICANOS AND NATIVE AMERICANS.
　　　　SOUR　AMERICAN JOURNAL OF COMMUNITY PSYCHOLOGY, APR. 1978,
　　　　　　　V6(2), PP 137-147.
　　　　YEAR　1978
　　　　DESC　MENTAL HEALTH PROGRAMS AND SERVICES+, DELIVERY OF
　　　　　　　SERVICES+, LATINOS, DISCRIMINATION, PSYCHOTHERAPY AND
　　　　　　　COUNSELING+, NATIVE-NON-NATIVE COMPARISONS, ANGLO
　　　　　　　AMERICANS, BLACK AMERICANS, ASIAN AMERICANS, MENTAL
　　　　　　　HEALTH INSTITUTIONS, DROPOUTS
　　　　IDEN　U.S., WASHINGTON

1280　AUTH　HUNSBERGER, BRUCE
　　　　TITL　RACIAL AWARENESS AND PREFERENCE OF WHITE AND INDIAN
　　　　　　　CANADIAN CHILDREN.
　　　　SOUR　CANADIAN JOURNAL OF BEHAVIORAL SCIENCE, APR. 1978,
　　　　　　　V10(2), PP 176-180.
　　　　YEAR　1978
　　　　DESC　ATTITUDES+, DISCRIMINATION+, ELEMENTARY SCHOOLS,
　　　　　　　CHILDREN-INFANTS AND PRESCHOOL+, CHILDREN-SCHOOL AGE+,
　　　　　　　AGE COMPARISONS, NATIVE-NON-NATIVE COMPARISONS, ANGLO
　　　　　　　AMERICANS, SELF-CONCEPT+, PSYCHOLOGICAL TESTING+
　　　　IDEN　CANADA

1281　AUTH　ZELIGS, ROSE
　　　　TITL　CHILDREN'S CONCEPTS AND STEREOTYPES OF NORWEGIAN, JEW,
　　　　　　　SCOTCH, CANADIAN, SWEDISH, AND AMERICAN INDIAN.
　　　　SOUR　JOURNAL OF EDUCATIONAL RESEARCH, 1952, V45, PP 349-36(
　　　　YEAR　1952
　　　　DESC　STEREOTYPES+, DISCRIMINATION+, CHILDREN-SCHOOL AGE+,
　　　　　　　ANGLO AMERICANS, PSYCHOLOGICAL TESTING+, ATTITUDES+
　　　　IDEN　U.S., OHIO, ZELIG'S INTERGROUP ATTITUDES TEST

1282 AUTH WALLACE, ANTHONY F.C.
     TITL THE INSTITUTION OF CATHARTIC AND CONTROL STRATEGIES IN
           IROQUOIS RELIGIOUS PSYCHOTHERAPY.
     SOUR IN M.K. OPLER (ED.), CULTURE AND MENTAL HEALTH, PP
           63-96. NEW YORK: MACMILLAN CO., 1959.
     YEAR 1959
     DESC IROQUOIS, NORTHEAST WOODLAND, MENTAL DISORDERS+,
           DEPRESSION+, NATIVE AMERICAN ETIOLOGY+, CHARACTER
           DISORDERS, CULTURE-BASED PSYCHOTHERAPY+, DREAMS AND
           VISION QUESTS+, HYSTERIA, GRIEF REACTION, DEATH AND
           DYING, NATIVE AMERICAN RELIGIONS+, CONFESSION,
           PSYCHOTHERAPY AND COUNSELING+
     IDEN U.S.

1283 AUTH DAY, RICHARD; BOYER, L. BRYCE; DE VOS, GEORGE A.
     TITL TWO STYLES OF EGO DEVELOPMENT: A CROSS-CULTURAL,
           LONGITUDINAL COMPARISON OF APACHE AND ANGLO SCHOOL
           CHILDREN.
     SOUR ETHOS, 1975, V3(3), PP 345-380.
     YEAR 1975
     DESC APACHE-CHIRICAHUA, APACHE-MESCALERO, SOUTHWEST,
           RESERVATION, CHILDREN-SCHOOL AGE+, PSYCHOLOGICAL
           TESTING+, NATIVE-NON-NATIVE COMPARISONS, ANGLO
           AMERICANS, ADOLESCENTS+, ELEMENTARY SCHOOLS,
           LEARNING+, COGNITIVE PROCESSES, ABILITIES, NATIVE
           AMERICAN COPING BEHAVIORS+, PASSIVE RESISTANCE+,
           ETHNIC IDENTITY, PERSONALITY TRAITS, SECONDARY
           SCHOOLS, PSYCHOANALYSIS
     IDEN U.S., APACHE RESERVATION, RORSCHACH TEST

1284 AUTH SNYDER, PETER Z.
     TITL SOCIAL INTERACTION PATTERNS AND RELATIVE URBAN
           SUCCESS: THE DENVER NAVAJO.
     SOUR URBAN ANTHROPOLOGY, 1973, V2(1), PP 1-24.
     YEAR 1973
     DESC URBAN AREAS, NAVAJO, SOUTHWEST, URBANIZATION+, SOCIAL
           GROUPS AND PEER GROUPS, SOCIAL NETWORKS+, STRESS,
           EMPLOYMENT+, ECONOMIC ISSUES, ALCOHOL USE, NATIVE
           AMERICAN COPING BEHAVIORS, ADULTS
     IDEN U.S., COLORADO

1285 AUTH ABERLE, DAVID F.
     TITL THE PSYCHOSOCIAL ANALYSIS OF A HOPI LIFE-HISTORY.
     SOUR IN R. HUNT (ED.), PERSONALITY AND CULTURE, PP 79-138.
           NEW YORK: NATURAL HISTORY PRESS, 1967.
     YEAR 1967
     DESC PUEBLO-HOPI, SOUTHWEST, EXTENDED FAMILY, MARITAL
           RELATIONSHIPS+, NATIVE AMERICAN RELIGIONS, TRADITIONAL
           SOCIAL CONTROL+, WITCHCRAFT+, TRADITIONAL CHILD
           REARING+, SOCIAL STATUS, AGGRESSIVENESS
     IDEN U.S.

1286 AUTH HALLOWELL, A. IRVING
     TITL INTELLIGENCE OF NORTHEASTERN INDIANS.
     SOUR IN R. HUNT (ED.), PERSONALITY AND CULTURE, PP 49-55.

NEW YORK: NATURAL HISTORY PRESS, 1967.
YEAR 1967
DESC ABILITIES+, NORTHEAST WOODLAND, PSYCHOLOGICAL TESTING+
IDEN U.S., RORSCHACH TEST

1287 AUTH HONIGMANN, JOHN J.
      TITL WORLD VIEW AND SELF-VIEW OF THE KASKA INDIANS.
      SOUR IN R. HUNT (ED.), PERSONALITY AND CULTURE, PP 33-48.
            NEW YORK: NATURAL HISTORY PRESS, 1967.
      YEAR 1967
      DESC KASKA, YUKON SUB-ARCTIC, NATIVE AMERICAN COPING
            BEHAVIORS+, PERSONALITY TRAITS+, SELF-CONCEPT+,
            ANXIETY, TRADITIONAL CHILD REARING+, PSYCHOANALYSIS+
      IDEN U.S., ALASKA

1288 AUTH WALLACE, ANTHONY F.C.
      TITL NEW RELIGIONS AMONG THE DELAWARE INDIANS, 1600-1900.
      SOUR SOUTHWESTERN JOURNAL OF ANTHROPOLOGY, SPR. 1956,
            V12(1), PP 1-21.
      YEAR 1956
      DESC NATIVE AMERICAN RELIGIONS+, DELAWARE, SOUTHEAST
            WOODLAND, CULTURAL REVIVAL+, CULTURAL ADAPTATION+,
            RELIGIONS-NON-NATIVE+
      IDEN U.S.

1289 AUTH SCHLESIER, KARL H.
      TITL ACTION ANTHROPOLOGY AND THE SOUTHERN CHEYENNE.
      SOUR CURRENT ANTHROPOLOGY, SEP. 1974, V15(3), PP 277-283.
      YEAR 1974
      DESC CHEYENNE-SOUTHERN, PLAINS, RESEARCHERS+
      IDEN U.S., OKLAHOMA

1290 AUTH SHEPARDSON, MARY
      TITL VALUE THEORY IN THE PREDICTION OF POLITICAL BEHAVIOR:
            THE NAVAJO CASE.
      SOUR AMERICAN ANTHROPOLOGIST, 1962, V64, PP 742-750.
      YEAR 1962
      DESC NAVAJO, SOUTHWEST, NATIVE AMERICAN VALUES+, TRIBAL
            POLITICAL ORGANIZATIONS+, RESERVATION, CULTURAL
            CONTINUITY+, LEADERSHIP+, GROUP NORMS AND SANCTIONS,
            ECONOMIC ISSUES+, CULTURAL ADAPTATION+
      IDEN U.S., NAVAJO RESERVATION

1291 AUTH WAX, MURRAY L.
      TITL AMERICAN INDIAN EDUCATION AS A CULTURAL TRANSACTION.
      SOUR TEACHER'S COLLEGE RECORD, MAY 1963, V64, PP 693-704.
      YEAR 1963
      DESC CULTURAL CONTINUITY+, CULTURAL ADAPTATION+, PASSIVE
            RESISTANCE, ELEMENTARY SCHOOLS, SECONDARY SCHOOLS,
            B.I.A. BOARDING SCHOOLS, NATIVE AMERICAN VALUES,
            STRESS, ACHIEVEMENT, SELF-CONCEPT, EDUCATION PROGRAMS
            AND SERVICES+
      IDEN U.S.

1292 AUTH KRAUS, ROBERT F.; BUFFLER, PATRICIA A.

TITL INTERCULTURAL VARIATION IN MORTALITY DUE TO VIOLENCE.
SOUR IN EDWARD F. FOULKS, RONALD M. WINTROB, JOSEPH
     WESTERMEYER, AND ARMANDO R. FAVAZZA (EDS.), CURRENT
     PERSPECTIVES IN CULTURAL PSYCHIATRY, PP 81-91. NEW
     YORK: SPECTRUM PUBLICATIONS, 1977.
YEAR 1977
DESC ALASKA NATIVES, EPIDEMIOLOGICAL STUDY, WESTERN ARCTIC,
     DEATH AND DYING+, CRIME+, INTERTRIBAL COMPARISONS,
     SUICIDE, ACCIDENTS, ALCOHOL USE, NATIVE-NON-NATIVE
     COMPARISONS, ANGLO AMERICANS
IDEN U.S., ALASKA

1293 AUTH SHORE, JAMES H.
     TITL PSYCHIATRIC RESEARCH ISSUES WITH AMERICAN INDIANS.
     SOUR IN EDWARD F. FOULKS, RONALD M. WINTROB, JOSEPH
          WESTERMEYER, AND ARMANDO R. FAVAZZA (EDS.), CURRENT
          PERSPECTIVES IN CULTURAL PSYCHIATRY, PP 73-80. NEW
          YORK: SPECTRUM PUBLICATIONS, 1977.
     YEAR 1977
     DESC RESEARCHERS+, COMMUNITY INVOLVEMENT+, SUICIDE,
          ALCOHOLISM TREATMENT, B.I.A. BOARDING SCHOOLS, MENTAL
          HEALTH PROGRAMS AND SERVICES, PROGRAM EVALUATION+,
          ADOPTION AND FOSTER CARE
     IDEN U.S.

1294 AUTH SIEVERS, MAURICE L.; HENDRIKX, MARGARET E.
     TITL TWO WEIGHT-REDUCTION PROGRAMS AMONG SOUTHWESTERN
          INDIANS.
     SOUR HEALTH SERVICES REPORTS, JUN.-JUL. 1972, V87, PP
          530-536.
     YEAR 1972
     DESC PHYSICAL HEALTH AND ILLNESS+, EXPERIMENTAL STUDY,
          CLINICAL STUDY, MEDICAL INSTITUTIONS, SOUTHWEST
     IDEN U.S.

1295 AUTH WAHRHAFTIG, ALBERT L.; THOMAS, ROBERT K.
     TITL RENAISSANCE AND REPRESSION; THE OKLAHOMA CHEROKEE.
     SOUR TRANS-ACTION, FEB. 1969, PP 42-48.
     YEAR 1969
     DESC CHEROKEE, SOUTHEAST WOODLAND, CULTURAL ADAPTATION+,
          CULTURAL CONTINUITY+, SOCIAL STATUS+, DISCRIMINATION+,
          OFF-RESERVATION
     IDEN U.S., OKLAHOMA

1296 AUTH RHOADES, EVERETT R.; MARSHALL, MELODY; ATTNEAVE,
          CAROLYN L.; ECHOHAWK, MARLENE; BJORK, JOHN W.; BEISER,
          MORTON
     TITL IMPACT OF MENTAL DISORDERS UPON ELDERLY AMERICAN
          INDIANS AS RELFECTED IN VISITS TO AMBULATORY CARE
          FACILITIES.
     SOUR JOURNAL OF THE AMERICAN GERIATRICS SOCIETY, JAN. 1980,
          V28(1), PP 33-39.
     YEAR 1980
     DESC AGED+, I.H.S.+, MENTAL DISORDERS+, EPIDEMIOLOGICAL
          STUDY, AGE COMPARISONS, PSYCHOSES, NEUROSES, ORGANIC

```
                    BRAIN SYNDROMES, CHARACTER DISORDERS, MENTAL HEALTH
                    INSTITUTIONS+, ADULTS, ANXIETY, DELIVERY OF SERVICES,
                    SCHIZOPHRENIA
          IDEN      U.S., OREGON, NEW MEXICO

1297  AUTH  FARKAS, CAROL S.
      TITL  CAFFEINE INTAKE AND POTENTIAL EFFECT ON HEALTH OF A
            SEGMENT OF NORTHERN CANADIAN INDIGENOUS PEOPLE.
      SOUR  INTERNATIONAL JOURNAL OF THE ADDICTIONS, 1979, V14(1),
            PP 27-43.
      YEAR  1979
      DESC  CREE, EASTERN SUB-ARCTIC, DRUG USE
      IDEN  CANADA, QUEBEC

1298  AUTH  DINGES, NORMAN G.; TRIMBLE, JOSEPH E.; HOLLENBECK,
            ALBERT R.
      TITL  AMERICAN INDIAN ADOLESCENT SOCIALIZATION; A REVIEW OF
            THE LITERATURE.
      SOUR  JOURNAL OF ADOLESCENCE, 1979, V2, PP 259-296.
      YEAR  1979
      DESC  REVIEW OF LITERATURE, ADOLESCENTS+, RESEARCHERS

1299  AUTH  PRIMEAUX, MARTHA H.
      TITL  AMERICAN INDIAN HEALTH CARE PRACTICES: A
            CROSS-CULTURAL PERSPECTIVE.
      SOUR  NURSING CLINICS OF NORTH AMERICA, MAR. 1977, V12(1),
            PP 55-65.
      YEAR  1977
      DESC  DEMOGRAPHIC DATA, STEREOTYPES, TRADITIONAL HEALERS+,
            MEDICAL INSTITUTIONS+, EXTENDED FAMILY+, TABOO
            BREAKING, INSTITUTIONALIZATION+, CHILDREN-INFANTS AND
            PRESCHOOL, DELIVERY OF SERVICES+
      IDEN  U.S.

1300  AUTH  WESTERMEYER, JOSEPH
      TITL  ETHNIC IDENTITY PROBLEMS AMONG TEN INDIAN PSYCHIATRIC
            PATIENTS.
      SOUR  INTERNATIONAL JOURNAL OF PSYCHIATRY, AUT. 1979,
            V25(3), PP 188-197.
      YEAR  1979
      DESC  ETHNIC IDENTITY+, ADULTS+, URBAN AREAS, ADOLESCENTS+,
            SUICIDE, CLINICAL STUDY, MENTAL HEALTH INSTITUTIONS,
            DRUG USE, AGE COMPARISONS, SELF-CONCEPT+, DEPRESSION,
            ALCOHOL USE, SOCIAL STATUS+, ROLE MODELS+
      IDEN  U.S., MINNESOTA

1301  AUTH  JUUL, SANDRA
      TITL  PORTRAIT OF AN ESKIMO TRIBAL HEALTH DOCTOR.
      SOUR  ALASKA MEDICINE, NOV. 1979, V21(6), PP 66-71.
      YEAR  1979
      DESC  TRADITIONAL HEALERS+, WESTERN ARCTIC, ESKIMO, MEDICAL
            PROFESSIONALS, NATIVE AMERICAN PERSONNEL+, I.H.S.,
            MEDICAL PROGRAMS AND SERVICES+
      IDEN  U.S., ALASKA
```

1302 AUTH ROGERS, LINDA; TENHOUTEN, WARREN; KAPLAN, CHARLES D.;
            GARDINER, MARTIN
      TITL HEMISPHERIC SPECIALIZATION OF LANGUAGE: AN EEG STUDY
            OF BILINGUAL HOPI CHILDREN.
      SOUR INTERNATIONAL JOURNAL OF NEUROSCIENCE, 1977, V8, PP
            1-6.
      YEAR 1977
      DESC PUEBLO-HOPI, SOUTHWEST, BILINGUALISM+, CHILDREN-SCHOOL
            AGE+, COGNITIVE PROCESSES+, LANGUAGE HANDICAPS+,
            RESERVATION, ELEMENTARY SCHOOLS, PSYCHOLOGICAL
            TESTING+
      IDEN U.S.

1303 AUTH MEALEY, SHIRLEY A.; KANE, ROBERT L.
      TITL FACTORS THAT INFLUENCE NAVAJO PATIENTS TO KEEP
            APPOINTMENTS.
      SOUR NURSE PRACTITIONER, MAR.-APR. 1977, V2(4), PP 18-22.
      YEAR 1977
      DESC MEDICAL PROGRAMS AND SERVICES+, CLINICAL STUDY,
            ATTITUDES, NAVAJO, SOUTHWEST, RESERVATION, DELIVERY OF
            SERVICES+, AGE COMPARISONS
      IDEN U.S., NAVAJO RESERVATION

1304 AUTH TRIMBLE, JOSEPH E.; MEDICINE, BEATRICE
      TITL DEVELOPMENT OF THEORETICAL MODELS AND LEVELS OF
            INTERPRETATION IN MENTAL HEALTH.
      SOUR IN JOSEPH WESTERMEYER (ED.), ANTHROPOLOGY AND MENTAL
            HEALTH, PP 161-200. THE HAGUE: MOUTON PUBLISHING CO.,
            1976.
      YEAR 1976
      DESC RESEARCHERS+, PSYCHOANALYSIS+, PERSONALITY TRAITS+,
            REVIEW OF LITERATURE, DREAMS AND VISION QUESTS,
            PSYCHOLOGICAL TESTING, GROUP NORMS AND SANCTIONS,
            MENTAL DISORDERS
      IDEN U.S., RORSCHACH TEST, M.M.P.I.

1305 AUTH TRIMBLE, JOSEPH E.
      TITL THE SOJOURNER IN THE AMERICAN INDIAN COMMUNITY:
            METHODOLOGICAL ISSUES AND CONCERNS.
      SOUR JOURNAL OF SOCIAL ISSUES, 1977, V33(4), PP 159-174.
      YEAR 1977
      DESC RESEARCHERS+, COMMUNITY INVOLVEMENT+, NATIVE AMERICAN
            PERSONNEL+, OFF-RESERVATION, RESERVATION
      IDEN U.S.

1306 AUTH MCGEE, HAROLD F.
      TITL WINDIGO PSYCHOSIS.
      SOUR AMERICAN ANTHROPOLOGIST, 1972, V74, PP 244-246.
      YEAR 1972
      DESC NUTRITIONAL FACTORS+, WINDIGO PSYCHOSIS+, EASTERN
            SUB-ARCTIC, MICMAC
      IDEN CANADA

1307 AUTH OPLER, MARVIN K.
      TITL DREAM ANALYSIS IN UTE INDIAN THERAPY.

```
          SOUR   IN M.K. OPLER (ED.), CULTURE AND MENTAL HEALTH, PP
                 97-117 . NEW YORK: MACMILLAN CO., 1959.
          YEAR   1959
          DESC   UTE, GREAT BASIN, DREAMS AND VISION QUESTS+,
                 TRADITIONAL HEALERS+, STRESS+, CULTURAL CONTINUITY,
                 MENTAL DISORDERS, CULTURE-BASED PSYCHOTHERAPY+,
                 HYSTERIA, GHOST SICKNESS, NATIVE AMERICAN RELIGIONS,
                 WITCHCRAFT
          IDEN   U.S.

   1308   AUTH   MICHAEL, DONALD N.
          TITL   A CROSS-CULTURAL INVESTIGATION OF CLOSURE.
          SOUR   JOURNAL OF ABNORMAL AND SOCIAL PSYCHOLOGY, 1953,
                 V48(2), PP 225-230.
          YEAR   1953
          DESC   NAVAJO, SOUTHWEST, COGNITIVE PROCESSES+, PSYCHOLOGICAL
                 TESTING+, NATIVE-NON-NATIVE COMPARISONS, ANGLO
                 AMERICANS, EXPERIMENTAL STUDY, RESERVATION
          IDEN   U.S., NEW MEXICO, NAVAJO RESERVATION

   1309   AUTH   SPINDLER, LOUISE S.
          TITL   WITCHCRAFT IN MENOMONI ACCULTURATION.
          SOUR   AMERICAN ANTHROPOLOGIST, 1952, V54, PP 593-602.
          YEAR   1952
          DESC   WITCHCRAFT+, MENOMINEE, NORTHEAST WOODLAND, CULTURAL
                 ADAPTATION+, RESERVATION, ADULTS, PERSONALITY TRAITS+,
                 EMOTIONAL RESTRAINT, AGGRESSIVENESS, NATIVE AMERICAN
                 COPING BEHAVIORS+
          IDEN   U.S., WISCONSIN, MENOMONI RESERVATION

   1310   AUTH   GUE, LESLIE R.
          TITL   VALUE ORIENTATIONS IN AN INDIAN COMMUNITY.
          SOUR   ALBERTA JOURNAL OF EDUCATIONAL RESEARCH, MAR. 1971,
                 V17(1), PP 19-31.
          YEAR   1971
          DESC   NATIVE AMERICAN VALUES+, CREE, PLAINS, ADOLESCENTS,
                 METIS, STRESS, COOPERATION, FULL BLOOD-MIXED BLOOD
                 COMPARISONS, NATIVE-NON-NATIVE COMPARISONS, ANGLO
                 AMERICANS, SECONDARY SCHOOLS, EDUCATION PROGRAMS AND
                 SERVICES+
          IDEN   CANADA, ALBERTA

   1311   AUTH   MANSON, SPERO M.; MEDICINE, BEATRICE; FUNMAKER, WALTER
          TITL   TRAINING OF AMERICAN INDIANS AND ALASKA NATIVES IN
                 MENTAL HEALTH RELATED SCIENCES.
          SOUR   PRACTICING ANTHROPOLOGY, FEB.-MAR. 1980, V2(3), PP
                 4-5, 22-24.
          YEAR   1980
          DESC   TRAINING PROGRAMS+, MENTAL HEALTH PROFESSIONALS+,
                 NATIVE AMERICAN PERSONNEL+, EDUCATION PROGRAMS AND
                 SERVICES+, COLLEGES AND UNIVERSITIES+
          IDEN   U.S.

   1312   AUTH   STEVENSON, IAN
          TITL   THE BELIEF AND CASES RELATED TO REINCARNATION AMONG
```

```
          THE HAIDA.
SOUR   JOURNAL OF ANTHROPOLOGICAL RESEARCH, WIN. 1975,
          V31(4), PP 364-375.
YEAR   1975
DESC   NORTHWEST COAST, HAIDA, NATIVE AMERICAN RELIGIONS,
          DEATH AND DYING+, DREAMS AND VISION QUESTS+,
          OFF-RESERVATION
IDEN   CANADA, BRITISH COLUMBIA, U.S. , ALASKA
```

```
1313  AUTH   STORM, THOMAS; KNOX, ROBERT E.; STORM, CHRISTINE;
                 GUTMAN, GLORIA; MITCHELL, DIANA
        TITL   A DEVELOPMENTAL STUDY OF BALANCE THEORY IN FOUR
                 CULTURAL GROUPS.
        SOUR   CANADIAN JOURNAL OF BEHAVIOURAL SCIENCE, 1976, V8(1),
                 PP 9-22.
        YEAR   1976
        DESC   NATIVE-NON-NATIVE COMPARISONS, ANGLO AMERICANS,
                 OFF-RESERVATION, NORTHWEST COAST, CHILDREN-SCHOOL
                 AGE+, ELEMENTARY SCHOOLS, COGNITIVE
                 PROCESSES+,PSYCHOLOGICAL TESTING+, AGE COMPARISONS
        IDEN   CANADA, BRITISH CLOUMBIA, NEW ZEALAND
```

```
1314  AUTH   BUREAU OF INDIAN AFFAIRS
        TITL   AN INTERDISCIPLINARY APPROACH IN THE IDENTIFICATION OF
                 MENTALLY RETARDED INDIAN CHILDREN: PILOT STUDY.
        SOUR   WASHINGTON, D.C.: AUTHOR, 1965.
        YEAR   1965
        DESC   CHILDREN-SCHOOL AGE+, RESERVATION, NAVAJO, SOUTHWEST,
                 ABILITIES+, MENTAL RETARDATION+, PSYCHOLOGICAL
                 TESTING, PHYSICAL HEALTH AND ILLNESS, LEARNING
                 DISABILITIES AND PROBLEMS+, MOTOR PROCESSES, CLINICAL
                 STUDY, SOCIAL SERVICE PROFESSIONALS, EDUCATION
                 PROFESSIONALS, MEDICAL PROFESSIONALS, MENTAL HEALTH
                 PROFESSIONALS
        IDEN   NAVAJO RESERVATION, WECHSLER INTELLIGENCE SCALE
                 CHILDREN, PORTEUS MAZE TEST, BENDER GESTALT TEST,
                 GOODENOUGH HARRIS DRAW A PERSON TEST
```

```
1315  AUTH   BUREAU OF INDIAN AFFAIRS
        TITL   AN INTERDISCIPLINARY APPROACH IN THE IDENTIFICATION OF
                 MENTALLY RETARDED INDIAN CHILDREN: ADDENDUM.
        SOUR   WASHINGTON, D.C.: AUTHOR, 1966.
        YEAR   1966
        DESC   MENTAL RETARDATION+, LEARNING DISABILITIES AND
                 PROBLEMS+, CHILDREN-SCHOOL AGE+, NAVAJO, SOUTHWEST,
                 EDUCATION PROGRAMS AND SERVICES+, B.I.A. BOARDING
                 SCHOOLS, ADMINISTRATIVE ISSUES+, EDUCATION
                 PROFESSIONALS, PSYCHOLOGICAL TESTING+, LANGUAGE
                 HANDICAPS, CULTURE-FAIR TESTS
        IDEN   NAVAJO RESERVATION, BENDER GESTALT TEST, PORTEUS MAZE
                 TEST, GOODENOUGH HARRIS DRAW A PERSON TEST, THEMATIC
                 APPERCEPTION TEST
```

```
1316  AUTH   STONE, ELAINE J.; CROUCH, ALTHA
        TITL   CHILDREN'S PERCEPTION OF VULNERABILITY TO HEALTH
```

```
              PROBLEMS FROM A CROSS-CULTURAL PERSPECTIVE.
       SOUR   JOURNAL OF SCHOOL HEALTH, JUN. 1979, PP 347-350.
       YEAR   1979
       DESC   CHILDREN-SCHOOL AGE+, COGNITIVE PROCESSES+, ELEMENTARY
              SCHOOLS, SOUTHWEST, NAVAJO, ANGLO AMERICANS, LATINOS,
              PSYCHOLOGICAL TESTING+, PHYSICAL HEALTH AND ILLNESS+,
              ATTITUDES+, SEX DIFFERENCES, NATIVE-NON-NATIVE
              COMPARISONS, MEDICAL PROGRAMS AND SERVICES,
              MOTIVATION+
       IDEN   U.S., NOWICKI STRICKLAND INTERNAL EXTERNAL LOCUS OF
              CONTROL FOR CHILDREN, NEW MEXICO

1317   AUTH   HOWARD, JAMES H.
       TITL   THE PLAINS GOURD DANCE AS A REVITALIZATION MOVEMENT.
       SOUR   AMERICAN ETHNOLOGIST, MAY 1976, V3(2), PP 243-259.
       YEAR   1976
       DESC   CULTURAL REVIVAL+, PLAINS, PRAIRIE, COMANCHE, NATIVE
              AMERICAN RELIGIONS, SHOSHONE, KIOWA, CHEYENNE,
              ARAPAHO, OMAHA, POW-WOWS
       IDEN   U.S., GOURD DANCE

1318   AUTH   KUPFERER, HARRIET J.
       TITL   A CASE OF SANCTIONED DRINKING: THE RUPERT'S HOUSE
              CREE.
       SOUR   ANTHROPOLOGICAL QUARTERLY, OCT. 1979, V52(4), PP
              198-203.
       YEAR   1979
       DESC   ALCOHOL USE+, CREE, EASTERN SUB-ARCTIC,
              AGGRESSIVENESS, POWERLESSNESS, GROUP NORMS AND
              SANCTIONS+
       IDEN   CANADA

1319   AUTH   KEMNITZER, LUIS S.
       TITL   STRUCTURE, CONTENT, AND CULTURAL MEANING OF YUWIPI: A
              MODERN LAKOTA HEALING RITUAL.
       SOUR   AMERICAN ETHNOLOGIST, MAY 1976, V3(2), PP 260-280.
       YEAR   1976
       DESC   NATIVE AMERICAN RELIGIONS+, SIOUX-OGLALA, PLAINS,
              TRADITIONAL HEALERS+, RESERVATION, PHYSICAL HEALTH AND
              ILLNESS, MEDICAL PROFESSIONALS+, RELIGIONS-NON-NATIVE,
              GHOST SICKNESS, SPIRIT INTRUSION
       IDEN   U.S., SOUTH DAKOTA, PINE RIDGE RESERVATION

1320   AUTH   RYAN, ROBERT A; TRIMBLE, JOSEPH E.
       TITL   TOWARD AN UNDERSTANDING OF MENTAL HEALTH AND SUBSTANCE
              ABUSE ISSUES OF RURAL AND MIGRANT ETHNIC MINORITIES: A
              SEARCH FOR COMMON EXPERIENCES.
       SOUR   PAPER PREPARED FOR THE NATIONAL CONFERENCE ON MINORITY
              GROUP ALCOHOL, DRUG ABUSE, AND MENAL HEALTH ISSUES,
              DENVER, COLORADO, MAY 22-24, 1978. (28P)
       YEAR   1978
       DESC   OFF-RESERVATION, URBAN AREAS, URBANIZATION+,
              RELOCATION+, STRESS+, NATIVE-NON-NATIVE COMPARISONS,
              LATINOS, BLACK AMERICANS, ASIAN AMERICANS, MENTAL
              DISORDERS+, SOCIAL NETWORKS, CULTURAL ADAPTATION+,
```

```
              ETHNIC IDENTITY, ANOMIE, ENVIRONMENTAL FACTORS, DRUG
              USE+, ALCOHOL USE+, REVIEW OF LITERATURE
      IDEN    U.S.

1321  AUTH    BOWD, ALAN D.
      TITL    TEN YEARS AFTER THE HAWTHORNE REPORT; CHANGING
              PSYCHOLOGICAL IMPLICATIONS FOR THE EDUCATION OF
              CANADIAN NATIVE PEOPLES.
      SOUR    CANADIAN PSYCHOLOGICAL REVIEW, OCT. 1977, V18(4), PP
              332-345.
      YEAR    1977
      DESC    EDUCATION PROGRAMS AND SERVICES+, RESERVATION,
              DROPOUTS, CHILDREN-SCHOOL AGE+, ELEMENTARY SCHOOLS,
              LEARNING DISABILITIES AND PROBLEMS+, REVIEW OF
              LITERATURE, LANGUAGE HANDICAPS+, RESEARCHERS+,
              LEARNING+, COGNITIVE PROCESSES, COMMUNITY INVOLVEMENT+
      IDEN    CANADA

1322  AUTH    DELORIA, VINE
      TITL    OUR NEW RESEARCH SOCIETY: SOME WARNINGS FOR SOCIAL
              SCIENTISTS.
      SOUR    SOCIAL PROBLEMS, FEB. 1980, V27(3), PP 265-271.
      YEAR    1980
      DESC    RESEARCHERS+, FEDERAL GOVERNMENT+, ADMINISTRATIVE
              ISSUES+
      IDEN    U.S.

1323  AUTH    DEUSCHLE, KURT; ADAIR, JOHN
      TITL    AN INTERDISCIPLINARY APPROACH TO PUBLIC HEALTH ON THE
              NAVAJO INDIAN RESERVATION: MEDICAL AND ANTHROPOLOGICAL
              ASPECTS.
      SOUR    ANNALS OF THE NEW YORK ACADEMY OF SCIENCES, DEC. 1960,
              V84(17), PP 887-904.
      YEAR    1960
      DESC    NAVAJO, SOUTHWEST, RESERVATION, PHYSICAL HEALTH AND
              ILLNESS+, MEDICAL PROGRAMS AND SERVICES+, DELIVERY OF
              SERVICES+, LANGUAGE HANDICAPS, MEDICAL
              PARAPROFESSIONALS, COMMUNITY INVOLVEMENT, NATIVE
              AMERICAN VALUES+
      IDEN    U.S., NAVAJO RESERVATION

1324  AUTH    SWENSON, JAMES D.
      TITL    EROSION OF INDIAN MENTAL HEALTH IN THE CITIES.
      SOUR    MINNESOTA MEDICINE, JUN. 1976, V59(6), PP 395-397.
      YEAR    1976
      DESC    ETHNIC IDENTITY+, CULTURAL ADAPTATION+
      IDEN    U.S., MINNESOTA

1325  AUTH    SHORE, MILTON F.
      TITL    NIMH AND MINORITY PROGRAMS.
      SOUR    PROFESSIONAL PSYCHOLOGY, MAY 1976, V7(2), PP 249-250.
      YEAR    1976
      DESC    RESEARCHERS+, LATINOS, ASIAN AMERICANS, BLACK
              AMERICANS, MENTAL HEALTH PROGRAMS AND SERVICES+,
              FEDERAL GOVERNMENT+, CONSULTATION
```

```
        IDEN   U.S.

1326    AUTH   BEAUVAIS, FREDERICK
        TITL   COUNSELING PSYCHOLOGY IN A CROSS-CULTURAL SETTING.
        SOUR   COUNSELING PSYCHOLOGIST, 1977, V7(2), PP 80-82.
        YEAR   1977
        DESC   NAVAJO, SOUTHWEST, RESERVATION, PSYCHOTHERAPY AND
               COUNSELING+, COLLEGES AND UNIVERSITIES+, SCIENCE
               PROGRAMS, ACHIEVEMENT, LEARNING DISABILITIES AND
               PROBLEMS+, ADULTS
        IDEN   U.S., NAVAJO RESERVATION, NAVAJO COMMUNITY COLLEGE

1327    AUTH   PASCAROSA, PAUL; FUTTERMAN, SANFORD
        TITL   ETHNOPSYCHEDELIC THERAPY FOR ALCOHOLICS: OBSERVATIONS
               OF THE PEYOTE RITUAL OF THE NATIVE AMERICAN CHURCH.
        SOUR   JOURNAL OF PSYCHEDELIC DRUGS, JUL.-SEP. 1976, V8(3),
               PP 215-221.
        YEAR   1976
        DESC   TRADITIONAL USE OF DRUGS AND ALCOHOL+, NATIVE AMERICAN
               RELIGIONS+, DRUG USE+, ALCOHOLISM TREATMENT+,
               CULTURE-BASED PSYCHOTHERAPY+, TRADITIONAL HEALERS+,
               SOCIAL GROUPS AND PEER GROUPS, PSYCHOTHERAPY AND
               COUNSELING, SOCIAL NETWORKS, ANXIETY
        IDEN   U.S.

1328    AUTH   KICKINGBIRD, KIRKE
        TITL   IN OUR IMAGE..., AFTER OUR LIKENESS: THE DRIVE FOR THE
               ASSIMILATION OF INDIAN COURT SYSTEMS.
        SOUR   AMERICAN CRIMINAL LAW REVIEW, 1976, V13(4), PP 675-700.
        YEAR   1976
        DESC   CRIME+, TRADITIONAL SOCIAL CONTROL+, LEGAL ISSUES+,
               TRIBAL POLITICAL ORGANIZATIONS+, POLITICS-NONTRIBAL+
        IDEN   U.S.

1329    AUTH   DINGES, NORMAN G.; TRIMBLE, JOSEPH E.; MANSON, SPERO
               M.; PASQUALE, FRANK L.
        TITL   THE SOCIAL ECOLOGY OF COUNSELING AND PSYCHOTHERAPY
               WITH AMERICAN INDIANS AND ALASKAN NATIVES.
        SOUR   IN A.J. MARSELLA AND P. PEDERSEN(EDS.), CROSS-CULTURAL
               COUNSELING AND PSYCHOTHERAPY: FOUNDATIONS, EVALUATION,
               CULTURAL CONSIDERATIONS. ELMSFORD, N.Y.: PERGAMON
               PRESS, 1980.
        YEAR   1980
        DESC   MENTAL HEALTH PROFESSIONALS+, PSYCHOTHERAPY AND
               COUNSELING+, MENTAL HEALTH PROGRAMS AND SERVICES+,
               TRADITIONAL HEALERS+, PREVENTIVE MENTAL HEALTH
               PROGRAMS+, TRAINING PROGRAMS+, I.H.S., NATIVE AMERICAN
               PERSONNEL, MENTAL HEALTH PARAPROFESSIONALS, DELIVERY
               OF SERVICES+, PROGRAM EVALUATION+, RESEARCHERS
        IDEN   U.S.

1330    AUTH   ZINTZ, MILES V.
        TITL   PROBLEMS OF CLASSROOM ADJUSTMENT OF INDIAN CHILDREN IN
               PUBLIC ELEMENTARY SCHOOLS IN THE SOUTHWEST.
        SOUR   SCIENCE EDUCATION, APR. 1962, V46(3), PP 261-269.
```

```
      YEAR  1962
      DESC  NATIVE AMERICAN VALUES, ELEMENTARY SCHOOLS+,
            SOUTHWEST, LATINOS, ABILITIES, ACHIEVEMENT+, SECONDARY
            SCHOOLS+, LANGUAGE HANDICAPS+, BILINGUALISM+,
            CHILDREN-SCHOOL AGE+, ADOLESCENTS+
      IDEN  U.S., NEW MEXICO

1331  AUTH  BYLER, WILLIAM; DELORIA, SAM; GURWITT, ALAN
      TITL  AMERICAN INDIANS AND WELFARE.
      SOUR  CURRENT, JAN. 1974, V158, PP 30-37.
      YEAR  1974
      DESC  ADOPTION AND FOSTER CARE+, SOCIAL SERVICES+,
            ADMINISTRATIVE ISSUES, LEGAL ISSUES, POWERLESSNESS,
            FAMILY FUNCTIONING
      IDEN  U.S.

1332  AUTH  KLEINFELD, JUDITH S.
      TITL  POSITIVE STEREOTYPING; THE CULTURAL RELATIVIST IN THE
            CLASSROOM.
      SOUR  HUMAN ORGANIZATION, FALL 1975, V34(3), PP 269-274.
      YEAR  1975
      DESC  STEREOTYPES+, EDUCATION PROFESSIONALS+, SOCIALLY
            DEVIANT BEHAVIOR, DISCRIMINATION+, ALASKA NATIVES,
            CULTURAL CONTINUITY+, ELEMENTARY SCHOOLS, SECONDARY
            SCHOOLS, ADOLESCENTS, CHILDREN-SCHOOL AGE
      IDEN  U.S., ALASKA

1333  AUTH  WHITE, ROBERT A.
      TITL  VALUE THEMES OF THE NATIVE AMERICAN TRIBALISTIC
            MOVEMENT AMONG THE DAKOTA SIOUX.
      SOUR  CURRENT ANTHROPOLOGY, SEP. 1974, V15(3), PP 284-289.
      YEAR  1974
      DESC  SIOUX, PLAINS, CULTURAL REVIVAL+, NATIVE AMERICAN
            POLITICAL MOVEMENTS, CULTURAL CONTINUITY+, NATIVE
            AMERICAN ADMINISTERED PROGRAMS, URBAN AREAS,
            RESERVATION
      IDEN  U.S., SOUTH DAKOTA, PINE RIDGE RESERVATION

1334  AUTH  WITT, SHIRLEY
      TITL  PRESSURE POINTS IN GROWING UP INDIAN.
      SOUR  PERSPECTIVES, SPR. 1980, V12(1), PP 24-31.
      YEAR  1980
      DESC  EXTENDED FAMILY+, TRADITIONAL CHILD REARING+,
            NUTRITIONAL FACTORS, NONINTERFERENCE,
            NONCOMPETITIVENESS
      IDEN  U.S.

1335  AUTH  SPECTOR, RACHEL E.
      TITL  HEALTH AND ILLNESS IN THE NATIVE AMERICAN COMMUNITY.
      SOUR  IN RACHEL SPECTOR (ED.), CULTURAL DIVERSITY IN HEALTH
            AND ILLNESS, PP 275-292. NEW YORK:
            APPLETON-CENTURY-CROFTS, 1979.
      YEAR  1979
      DESC  PHYSICAL HEALTH AND ILLNESS+, TRADITIONAL HEALERS+,
            UNIVERSAL HARMONY, NATIVE AMERICAN ETIOLOGY+, MEDICAL
```

PROGRAMS AND SERVICES+, I.H.S., MEDICAL PROFESSIONALS, DELIVERY OF SERVICES+
IDEN   U.S.

1336   AUTH   HAGAN, JOHN
       TITL   CRIMINAL JUSTICE IN RURAL AND URBAN COMMUNITIES: A STUDY OF THE BUREAUCRATIZATION OF JUSTICE.
       SOUR   SOCIAL FORCES, MAR. 1977, V55(3), PP 597-612.
       YEAR   1977
       DESC   URBANIZATION+, ADMINISTRATIVE ISSUES+, LEGAL ISSUES+, CRIME+, ADULTS, SEX DIFFERENCES, DISCRIMINATION+, URBAN AREAS, OFF-RESERVATION
       IDEN   CANADA, ALBERTA

1337   AUTH   TAYLOR, L.J.; SKANES, G.R.
       TITL   COGNITIVE ABILITIES IN INUIT AND WHITE CHILDREN FROM SIMILAR ENVIRONMENTS.
       SOUR   CANADIAN JOURNAL OF BEHAVIOURAL SCIENCE, 1976, V8(1), PP 1-8.
       YEAR   1976
       DESC   ABILITIES+, ESKIMO, CENTRAL AND EASTERN ARCTIC, WESTERN ARCTIC, CHILDREN-SCHOOL AGE+, COGNITIVE PROCESSES+, LANGUAGE HANDICAPS+, NATIVE-NON-NATIVE COMPARISONS, ANGLO AMERICANS, PSYCHOLOGICAL TESTING+, SOCIAL STATUS, ENVIRONMENTAL FACTORS+, ELEMENTARY SCHOOLS
       IDEN   CANADA, WECHSLER INTELLIGENCE SCALE CHILDREN, SAFRAN CULTURE REDUCED INTELLIGENCE TEST, RAVENS MATRICES

1338   AUTH   NATIONAL AMERICAN INDIAN SAFETY COUNCIL
       TITL   DATA AND MATERIALS TO SUPPORT A COMMUNITY EDUCATION AND SAFETY PROGRAM TO REDUCE ACCIDENTS AMONG ELDERLY INDIANS.
       SOUR   AUTHOR, (INDIAN HEALTH SERVICE CONTRACT NO. 78-30-134). 1978.
       YEAR   1978
       DESC   ACCIDENTS+, DEMOGRAPHIC DATA, I.H.S., AGED+, ENVIRONMENTAL FACTORS, RESERVATION, PREVENTIVE MENTAL HEALTH PROGRAMS+
       IDEN   U.S.

1339   AUTH   LAZURE, DENIS
       TITL   INDIAN CHILDREN OF CANADA: EDUCATIONAL SERVICES AND MENTAL HEALTH.
       SOUR   CHILD PSYCHIATRY AND HUMAN DEVELOPMENT, FALL 1973, V4(1), PP 44-52.
       YEAR   1973
       DESC   DEMOGRAPHIC DATA, ELEMENTARY SCHOOLS, CHILDREN-SCHOOL AGE+, EDUCATION PROGRAMS AND SERVICES+
       IDEN   CANADA

1340   AUTH   ERVIN, ALEXANDER M.
       TITL   CONFLICTING STYLES OF LIFE IN A NORTHERN CANADIAN TOWN.
       SOUR   ARCTIC, 1969, V 22(2), PP 90-105.

```
       YEAR  1969
       DESC  URBANIZATION+, OFF-RESERVATION, CENTRAL AND EASTERN
             ARCTIC, ESKIMO, SOCIAL NETWORKS+, SOCIAL GROUPS AND
             PEER GROUPS+, LEADERSHIP, ECONOMIC ISSUES, ROLE
             MODELS, ADOLESCENTS, ADULTS, ANOMIE, ALCOHOL USE,
             STRESS, EMPLOYMENT, MACKENZIE SUB-ARCTIC, KUTCHIN
       IDEN  CANADA, NORTHWEST TERRITORIES

1341   AUTH  ABEL, THEODORA M.
       TITL  FREE DESIGNS OF LIMITED SCOPE AS A PERSONALITY INDEX.
       SOUR  CHARACTER AND PERSONALITY, 1938, V7, PP 50-62.
       YEAR  1938
       DESC  SCHIZOPHRENIA+, PSYCHOLOGICAL TESTING+, NAVAJO,
             SOUTHWEST, NATIVE-NON-NATIVE COMPARISONS, ANGLO
             AMERICANS, PERSONALITY TRAITS+, MENTAL RETARDATION,
             PARANOIA+
       IDEN  U.S., BALI

1342   AUTH  WEST, L.W.; MACARTHUR, RUSSELL
       TITL  AN EVALUATION OF SELECTED INTELLIGENCE TESTS FOR TWO
             SAMPLES OF METIS AND INDIAN CHILDREN.
       SOUR  ALBERTA JOURNAL OF EDUCATIONAL RESEARCH, 1964, V10(1),
             PP 17-27.
       YEAR  1964
       DESC  ABILITIES+, METIS, CULTURE-FAIR TESTS+, PSYCHOLOGICAL
             TESTING+, CHILDREN-SCHOOL AGE+, ELEMENTARY SCHOOLS
       IDEN  CANADA, NORTHWEST TERRITORIES, ALBERTA, PROGRESSIVE
             MATRICES, LORGE THORNDIKE NON-VERBAL INTELLIGENCE
             TEST, SAFRAN CULTURE REDUCED INTELLIGENCE TEST,
             CALIFORNIA TEST OF MENTAL MATURITY, DETROIT BEGINNING
             FIRST GRADE INTELLIGENCE TEST

1343   AUTH  BRODT, E. WILLIAM
       TITL  URBANIZATION AND HEALTH PLANNING: CHALLENGE AND
             OPPORTUNITY FOR THE AMERICAN INDIAN COMMUNITY.
       SOUR  AMERICAN JOURNAL OF PUBLIC HEALTH, AUG. 1973, V63(8),
             PP 694-701.
       YEAR  1973
       DESC  URBAN AREAS, RESERVATION, URBANIZATION+, ENVIRONMENTAL
             FACTORS, MEDICAL PROGRAMS AND SERVICES+, PROGRAM
             DEVELOPMENT+, COMMUNITY INVOLVEMENT+, SOUTHWEST
       IDEN  U.S.

1344   AUTH  WYMAN, LELAND C.; BAILEY, FLORA L.
       TITL  TWO EXAMPLES OF NAVAJO PHYSIOTHERAPY.
       SOUR  AMERICAN ANTHROPOLOGIST, 1944, V46, PP 329-337.
       YEAR  1944
       DESC  NAVAJO, SOUTHWEST, CULTURE-BASED PSYCHOTHERAPY+,
             NATIVE AMERICAN ETIOLOGY+, TRADITIONAL HEALERS+,
             RESERVATION
       IDEN  U.S., NAVAJO RESERVATION

1345   AUTH  SKEELS, DELL
       TITL  THE FUNCTION OF HUMOR IN THREE NEZ PERCE MYTHS.
       SOUR  AMERICAN IMAGO, 1954, V11, PP 249-261.
```

```
           YEAR  1954
           DESC  NEZ PERCE, PLATEAU, PSYCHOANALYSIS, NATIVE AMERICAN
                 COPING BEHAVIORS+
           IDEN  U.S.

    1346   AUTH  PRESTON, CAROLINE E.
           TITL  PSYCHOLOGICAL TESTING WITH NORTHWEST COAST ESKIMOS.
           SOUR  GENETIC PSYCHOLOGY MONOGRAPHS, 1964, V69, PP 323-419.
           YEAR  1964
           DESC  ESKIMO, WESTERN ARCTIC, PSYCHOLOGICAL TESTING+,
                 OFF-RESERVATION, ABILITIES, SEX DIFFERENCES,
                 ATTITUDES, ADULTS, MEDICAL INSTITUTIONS
           IDEN  U.S., ALASKA, RORSCHACH TEST, THEMATIC APPERCEPTION
                 TEST, GOODENOUGH HARRIS DRAW A PERSON TEST, WECHSLER
                 BELLEVUE INTELLIGENCE SCALE

    1347   AUTH  SAVAGE, CHARLES; LEIGHTON, ALEXANDER H.; LEIGHTON,
                 DOROTHEA C.
           TITL  THE PROBLEM OF CROSS-CULTURAL IDENTIFICATION OF
                 PSYCHIATRIC DISORDERS.
           SOUR  IN JANE MURPHY AND ALEXANDER LEIGHTON (EDS.),
                 APPROACHES TO CROSS-CULTURAL PSYCHIATRY, PP 21-63. NEW
                 YORK: CORNELL UNIVERSITY PRESS, 1965.
           YEAR  1965
           DESC  SOCIALLY DEVIANT BEHAVIOR+, MENTAL DISORDERS+, ORGANIC
                 BRAIN SYNDROMES, MENTAL RETARDATION, SCHIZOPHRENIA,
                 PARANOIA, DEPRESSION, PSYCHOPHYSIOLOGICAL DISORDERS,
                 NEUROSES, CHARACTER DISORDERS, NATIVE-NON-NATIVE
                 COMPARISONS, ESKIMO, WESTERN ARCTIC, NAVAJO, SOUTHWEST
           IDEN  U.S., BRAZIL, INDIA

    1348   AUTH  HILL, THOMAS W.
           TITL  LIFE STYLES AND DRINKING PATTERNS OF URBAN INDIANS.
           SOUR  JOURNAL OF DRUG ISSUES, SPR. 1980, V10(2), PP 257-269.
           YEAR  1980
           DESC  URBAN AREAS, ALCOHOL USE+, MALES, ADOLESCENTS, ADULTS,
                 FAMILY FUNCTIONING, GROUP NORMS AND SANCTIONS+
           IDEN  U.S., IOWA

    1349   AUTH  ZENTNER, HENRY
           TITL  CULTURAL ASSIMILATION BETWEEN INDIANS AND NON-INDIANS
                 IN SOUTHERN ALBERTA.
           SOUR  ALBERTA JOURNAL OF EDUCATIONAL RESEARCH, 1963, V9(2),
                 PP 79-86.
           YEAR  1963
           DESC  BLACKFEET-BLOOD, PLAINS, RESERVATION,
                 NATIVE-NON-NATIVE COMPARISONS, ANGLO AMERICANS,
                 CULTURAL ADAPTATION+, ATTITUDES, ADOLESCENTS+,
                 SECONDARY SCHOOLS, DISCRIMINATION+, SURVEY, SEX
                 DIFFERENCES, AGE COMPARISONS
           IDEN  CANADA, ALBERTA

    1350   AUTH  ZENTNER, HENRY
           TITL  VALUE CONGRUENCE AMONG INDIAN AND NON-INDIAN HIGH
                 SCHOOL STUDENTS IN SOUTHERN ALBERTA.
```

SOUR ALBERTA JOURNAL OF EDUCATIONAL RESEARCH, 1963, V9(3), PP 168-178.
YEAR 1963
DESC SECONDARY SCHOOLS, ADOLESCENTS+, NATIVE AMERICAN VALUES+, SURVEY, CULTURAL ADAPTATION+, SEX DIFFERENCES, AGE COMPARISONS, BLACKFEET-BLOOD, PLAINS, NATIVE-NON-NATIVE COMPARISONS, ANGLO AMERICANS, RESERVATION
IDEN CANADA, ALBERTA

1351 AUTH FRENCH, LAURENCE A.; HORNBUCKLE, JIM
TITL ALCOHOLISM AMONG NATIVE AMERICANS: AN ANALYSIS.
SOUR SOCIAL WORK, JUL. 1980, V25(4), PP 275-280.
YEAR 1980
DESC ALCOHOL USE+, ALCOHOLISM TREATMENT+, CRIME, FEDERAL GOVERNMENT, ETHNIC IDENTITY, STRESS, GROUP NORMS AND SANCTIONS, FULL BLOOD-MIXED BLOOD COMPARISONS, POLITICS-NONTRIBAL
IDEN U.S.

1352 AUTH FRENCH, LAURENCE A.; HORNBUCKLE, JIM
TITL INDIAN STRESS AND VIOLENCE: A PSYCHO-CULTURAL PERSPECTIVE.
SOUR JOURNAL OF ALCOHOL AND DRUG EDUCATION, FALL 1979, V25, PP 36-43.
YEAR 1979
DESC CHEROKEE, SOUTHEAST WOODLAND, CRIME, STRESS+, SUICIDE, PHYSICAL HEALTH AND ILLNESS, ALCOHOL USE+, RESERVATION, ETHNIC IDENTITY, PSYCHOTHERAPY AND COUNSELING+, SOCIAL GROUPS AND PEER GROUPS+, SELF-CONCEPT, SOCIAL NETWORKS+
IDEN U.S., QUALLA BOUNDARY, UNITED SOUTHEASTERN TRIBAL ORGANIZATION

1353 AUTH MULLER, JOHN P.
TITL MEETING THE NEEDS OF EXCEPTIONAL CHILDREN ON THE ROSEBUD RESERVATION.
SOUR EDUCATION AND TRAINING OF THE MENTALLY RETARDED, OCT. 1977, V12(3), PP 246-248.
YEAR 1977
DESC SIOUX, PLAINS, LEARNING DISABILITIES AND PROBLEMS+, CHILDREN-SCHOOL AGE+, RESERVATION, EDUCATION PROGRAMS AND SERVICES+, MENTAL RETARDATION, EDUCATION PARAPROFESSIONALS+, TRAINING PROGRAMS+
IDEN U.S., SINTE GLESKA COMMUNITY COLLEGE, ROSEBUD RESERVATION, SOUTH DAKOTA

1354 AUTH TAYLOR, L.J.; SKANES, G.R.
TITL LEVEL I AND LEVEL II INTELLIGENCE IN INUIT AND WHITE CHILDREN FROM SIMILAR ENVIRONMENTS.
SOUR JOURNAL OF CROSS-CULTURAL PSYCHOLOGY, JUN. 1976, V7(2), PP 157-168.
YEAR 1976
DESC ESKIMO, CENTRAL AND EASTERN ARCTIC, CHILDREN-SCHOOL AGE+, ABILITIES+, NATIVE-NON-NATIVE COMPARISONS, ANGLO

```
            AMERICANS, COGNITIVE PROCESSES+, ENVIRONMENTAL
            FACTORS+, CULTURE-FAIR TESTS+, PSYCHOLOGICAL TESTING+
     IDEN   CANADA, RAVENS PROGRESSIVE MATRICES, DIGIT SPAN TEST,
            NEWFOUNDLAND

1355 AUTH   FARRIS, JOHN J.; JONES, BEN M.
     TITL   ETHANOL METABOLISM AND MEMORY IMPAIRMENT IN INDIAN AND
            WHITE WOMEN SOCIAL DRINKERS.
     SOUR   JOURNAL OF STUDIES ON ALCOHOL, 1978, V39(11), PP
            1975-1979.
     YEAR   1978
     DESC   ALCOHOL USE+, FEMALES+, ADULTS, PSYCHOLOGICAL TESTING,
            NATIVE-NON-NATIVE COMPARISONS, ANGLO AMERICANS,
            GENETIC FACTORS
     IDEN   U.S., FREE-RECALL VERBAL MEMORY TEST

1356 AUTH   HYND, GEORGE, W.; KRAMER, RICK; QUACKENBUSH, RAY;
            CONNER, ROBERT; WEED, WENDY
     TITL   CLINICAL UTILITY OF THE WISC-R AND THE FRENCH
            PICTORIAL TEST OF INTELLIGENCE WITH NATIVE AMERICAN
            PRIMARY GRADE CHILDREN.
     SOUR   PERCEPTUAL AND MOTOR SKILLS, OCT. 1979, V4(2), PP
            480-482.
     YEAR   1979
     DESC   PSYCHOLOGICAL TESTING+, ABILITIES+, CHILDREN-SCHOOL
            AGE+, ELEMENTARY SCHOOLS, CULTURE-FAIR TESTS
     IDEN   U.S., WECHSLER INTELLIGENCE SCALE CHILDREN

1357 AUTH   WEIBEL, JOAN; WEISNER, THOMAS
     TITL   THE ETHNOGRAPHY OF CALIFORNIA URBAN AMERICAN INDIAN
            DRINKING PATTERNS IN DRINKING SETTINGS.
     SOUR   (REPORT FOR CALIFORNIA DEPARTMENT OF ALCOHOL AND DRUG
            PROGRAMS, CONTRACT NO. OA-0256-7, A-1). LOS ANGELES:
            ALCOHOL RESEARCH CENTER, UCLA, 1980.
     YEAR   1980
     DESC   INTERTRIBAL COMPARISONS, PLAINS, CALIFORNIA INDIANS,
            SOUTHWEST, CALIFORNIA AREA, OKLAHOMA INDIANS, ALCOHOL
            USE+, URBAN AREAS, ENVIRONMENTAL FACTORS+, SOCIAL
            STATUS, POW-WOWS, SIOUX, NAVAJO
     IDEN   U.S., CALIFORNIA

1358 AUTH   FISHER, A.D.
     TITL   THE DIALECTIC OF INDIAN LIFE IN CANADA.
     SOUR   CANADIAN REVIEW OF SOCIOLOGY AND ANTHROPOLOGY, 1976,
            V13(4), PP 458-464.
     YEAR   1976
     DESC   ADMINISTRATIVE ISSUES+, RESERVATION, SOCIAL STATUS+,
            LEADERSHIP+, POWERLESSNESS+, MACKENZIE SUB-ARCTIC,
            SOCIAL ROLES+, STEREOTYPES, CENTRAL AND EASTERN ARCTIC
     IDEN   CANADA

1359 AUTH   SLOBODIN, RICHARD
     TITL   KUTCHIN CONCEPTS OF REINCARNATION.
     SOUR   WESTERN CANADIAN JOURNAL OF ANTHROPOLOGY, 1970, V2, PP
            67-79.
```

```
     YEAR  1970
     DESC  KUTCHIN, YUKON SUB-ARCTIC, DEATH AND DYING+, DREAMS
           AND VISION QUESTS+
     IDEN  CANADA, NORTHWEST TERRITORIES

1360 AUTH  JILEK, WOLFGANG G.; JILEK-AALL, LOUISE; TODD, NORMAN;
           GALLOWAY, B.
     TITL  SYMBOLIC PROCESSES IN CONTEMPORARY SALISH INDIAN
           CEREMONIALS.
     SOUR  WESTERN CANADIAN JOURNAL OF ANTHROPOLOGY, 1978, V8, PP
           36-56.
     YEAR  1978
     DESC  COAST SALISH, NORTHWEST COAST, SPIRIT INTRUSION+,
           TRADITIONAL HEALERS+, CULTURE-BASED PSYCHOTHERAPY+,
           SOUL LOSS+, NATIVE AMERICAN RELIGIONS+
     IDEN  CANADA, BRITISH COLUMBIA

1361 AUTH  CLARK, ANNETTE M.
     TITL  KOYUKON ATHABASCAN CEREMONIALISM.
     SOUR  WESTERN CANADIAN JOURNAL OF ANTHROPOLOGY, 1970, V2(1),
           PP 80-88.
     YEAR  1970
     DESC  ATHABASCAN, YUKON SUB-ARCTIC, DEATH AND DYING+, GHOST
           SICKNESS+
     IDEN  U.S., ALASKA

1362 AUTH  HENDERSON, RONALD W.; SWANSON, ROSEMARY
     TITL  APPLICATION OF SOCIAL LEARNING PRINCIPLES IN A FIELD
           SETTING.
     SOUR  EXCEPTIONAL CHILDREN, SEP. 1974, V41(1), PP 53-55.
     YEAR  1974
     DESC  PAPAGO, SOUTHWEST, CHILDREN-SCHOOL AGE+, LEARNING
           DISABILITIES AND PROBLEMS+, NONINTERFERENCE+,
           ELEMENTARY SCHOOLS, LANGUAGE HANDICAPS+, MENTAL HEALTH
           PARAPROFESSIONALS, PSYCHOTHERAPY AND COUNSELING+,
           BEHAVIOR MODIFICATION+, EXPERIMENTAL STUDY, NATIVE
           AMERICAN PERSONNEL, EDUCATION PROGRAMS AND SERVICES+
     IDEN  U.S., ARIZONA

1363 AUTH  FARRIS, JOHN J.; JONES, BEN M.
     TITL  ETHANOL METABOLISM IN MALE AMERICAN INDIANS AND
           WHITES.
     SOUR  ALCOHOLISM: CLINICAL AND EXPERIMENTAL RESEARCH, JAN.
           1978, V2(1), PP 77-81.
     YEAR  1978
     DESC  MALES+, ADULTS+, ALCOHOL USE+, GENETIC FACTORS,
           NATIVE-NON-NATIVE COMPARISONS, ANGLO AMERICANS
     IDEN  U.S.
```

Indexes

Descriptor Index

314 Descriptor Index

(CONT.)
ADULTS
110, 111, 112, 113, 120, 125, 127, 134, 138, 140, 141, 145, 149,
155, 158, 161, 164, 174, 179, 182, 185, 190, 195, 200, 202, 203,
207, 208, 212, 216, 218, 223, 225, 228, 238, 240, 241, 245, 248,
251, 253, 261, 265, 296, 307, 325, 335, 350, 354, 356, 358, 362,
370, 376, 379, 381, 388, 389, 391, 395, 406, 407, 410, 411, 417,
428, 442, 454, 465, 466, 470, 504, 514, 518, 519, 528, 529, 536,
537, 546, 550, 556, 564, 569, 577, 578, 606, 619, 620, 641, 645,
647, 657, 669, 673, 677, 681, 686, 699, 706, 712, 714, 749, 774,
776, 796, 799, 816, 828, 829, 830, 831, 846, 847, 848, 849, 851,
864, 885, 886, 891, 902, 918, 927, 931, 937, 946, 948, 952, 954,
964, 970, 972, 975, 980, 996, 1013, 1029, 1045, 1061, 1080, 1083,
1085, 1098, 1102, 1106, 1110, 1113, 1116, 1118, 1127, 1146, 1159,
1161, 1164, 1172, 1173, 1181, 1183, 1185, 1195, 1197, 1200, 1202,
1207, 1209, 1211, 1218, 1223, 1227, 1237, 1238, 1241, 1246, 1250,
1253, 1255, 1260, 1267, 1274, 1284, 1296, 1300, 1309, 1326, 1336,
1340, 1346, 1348, 1355, 1363

AGE COMPARISONS
57, 97, 118, 120, 121, 138, 142, 202, 228, 277, 306, 314, 351, 381,
392, 394, 410, 426, 438, 452, 466, 523, 586, 590, 644, 647, 677,
681, 682, 697, 710, 776, 840, 868, 882, 946, 972, 1013, 1039, 1048,
1088, 1090, 1091, 1092, 1093, 1095, 1097, 1123, 1148, 1168, 1187,
1188, 1192, 1212, 1213, 1214, 1221, 1223, 1225, 1246, 1253, 1266,
1269, 1270, 1280, 1296, 1300, 1303, 1313, 1349, 1350

AGED
35, 46, 123, 138, 147, 193, 194, 228, 236, 346, 430, 434, 442, 454,
475, 492, 620, 636, 823, 837, 866, 870, 885, 972, 981, 1021, 1083,
1100, 1129, 1152, 1153, 1197, 1218, 1247, 1276, 1296, 1338

AGGRESSIVENESS
46, 70, 89, 91, 97, 104, 105, 106, 107, 112, 116, 143, 190, 195,
211, 218, 227, 228, 242, 243, 260, 300, 320, 322, 335, 344, 348,
349, 368, 370, 406, 454, 471, 504, 512, 547, 556, 580, 601, 666,
739, 742, 745, 756, 757, 763, 771, 823, 849, 883, 961, 968, 985,
991, 1074, 1076, 1096, 1105, 1121, 1159, 1181, 1239, 1285, 1309,
1318

ALASKA NATIVES
6, 49, 157, 163, 189, 279, 307, 400, 444, 490, 495, 692, 781, 805,
817, 970, 989, 1027, 1032, 1179, 1189, 1232, 1292, 1332

ALCOHOL USE
15, 25, 28, 33, 40, 42, 44, 45, 49, 51, 55, 56, 61, 77, 89, 98, 99,
100, 102, 103, 104, 105, 106, 107, 108, 109, 112, 113, 120, 126,
127, 134, 138, 146, 154, 155, 161, 164, 203, 217, 218, 223, 260,
262, 264, 270, 274, 279, 284, 285, 286, 289, 294, 307, 310, 320,
330, 333, 335, 337, 339, 344, 349, 355, 360, 361, 362, 364, 366,
367, 368, 369, 385, 410, 411, 414, 415, 416, 419, 422, 432, 448,
468, 471, 478, 491, 512, 518, 523, 528, 529, 546, 563, 564, 569,
570, 623, 637, 638, 669, 677, 715, 737, 753, 762, 791, 806, 807,
818, 839, 842, 844, 864, 875, 894, 903, 975, 976, 1004, 1030, 1041,
1052, 1102, 1136, 1149, 1150, 1159, 1179, 1183, 1189, 1202, 1205,

(CONT.)
ALCOHOL USE
     1208, 1224, 1227, 1228, 1238, 1264, 1273, 1274, 1284, 1292, 1300,
     1318, 1320, 1340, 1348, 1351, 1352, 1355, 1357, 1363

ALCOHOLISM TREATMENT
     15, 33, 40, 42, 55, 77, 99, 109, 134, 146, 155, 174, 279, 286, 289,
     307, 330, 353, 361, 362, 369, 405, 414, 422, 453, 470, 519, 528,
     564, 569, 671, 807, 808, 818, 839, 875, 929, 976, 1159, 1161, 1182,
     1207, 1208, 1251, 1293, 1327, 1351

ALEUT
     108, 375, 489, 637, 1232

ALGONKIN
     1207

ANGLO AMERICANS
     34, 53, 56, 67, 76, 85, 90, 94, 96, 97, 98, 106, 107, 111, 112, 115,
     117, 118, 127, 128, 129, 130, 137, 141, 155, 161, 163, 165, 166,
     170, 173, 176, 177, 178, 210, 217, 222, 254, 255, 264, 266, 270,
     272, 273, 281, 282, 284, 285, 286, 315, 333, 362, 363, 371, 374,
     381, 394, 396, 401, 403, 404, 415, 416, 423, 434, 438, 444, 446,
     468, 482, 500, 501, 502, 517, 519, 522, 529, 552, 564, 569, 582,
     601, 602, 607, 610, 611, 614, 619, 631, 637, 644, 677, 680, 681,
     683, 687, 694, 697, 698, 705, 708, 711, 716, 754, 761, 764, 813,
     836, 844, 864, 868, 886, 894, 896, 899, 912, 919, 929, 939, 954,
     977, 978, 979, 991, 998, 1010, 1012, 1013, 1014, 1015, 1029, 1056,
     1062, 1069, 1070, 1071, 1072, 1077, 1084, 1085, 1087, 1088, 1089,
     1090, 1091, 1092, 1097, 1102, 1103, 1114, 1136, 1140, 1141, 1144,
     1148, 1150, 1154, 1155, 1158, 1166, 1167, 1168, 1169, 1171, 1178,
     1181, 1184, 1187, 1188, 1190, 1191, 1193, 1195, 1200, 1212, 1213,
     1214, 1215, 1219, 1221, 1223, 1225, 1235, 1240, 1249, 1250, 1255,
     1260, 1263, 1264, 1266, 1267, 1268, 1269, 1270, 1279, 1280, 1281,
     1283, 1292, 1308, 1310, 1313, 1316, 1337, 1341, 1349, 1350, 1354,
     1355, 1363

ANOMIE
     13, 26, 55, 100, 124, 127, 191, 211, 247, 330, 416, 429, 473, 504,
     556, 657, 715, 794, 955, 1035, 1051, 1235, 1320, 1340

ANXIETY
     68, 99, 107, 108, 162, 252, 280, 322, 347, 359, 370, 402, 441, 463,
     464, 514, 540, 553, 571, 572, 579, 580, 598, 601, 619, 657, 658,
     683, 734, 737, 742, 757, 763, 883, 900, 918, 926, 960, 964, 1018,
     1096, 1108, 1238, 1239, 1287, 1296, 1327

APACHE
     78, 236, 697, 711, 823, 844, 957, 978, 1144, 1164, 1261, 1276

APACHE-CHIRICAHUA
     70, 346, 352, 393, 402, 492, 520, 672, 704, 739, 766, 972, 1283

APACHE-JICARILLA
     174, 346, 1178

APACHE-LIPAN
   346, 574, 981

APACHE-MESCALERO
   26, 70, 103, 122, 271, 336, 346, 352, 393, 402, 492, 520, 577, 656,
   704, 739, 749, 910, 934, 969, 972, 1197, 1283

APACHE-WHITE MOUNTAIN
   367, 909, 1020

ARAPAHO
   55, 330, 361, 1125, 1150, 1166, 1167, 1184, 1205, 1317

ARAPAHO-NORTHERN
   51, 247, 752, 894, 980, 1021, 1085

ARCTIC HYSTERIA
   110, 242, 245, 251, 334, 354, 395, 800, 900, 1239

ARIKARA
   1271

ASIAN AMERICANS
   97, 150, 166, 217, 264, 308, 416, 522, 529, 833, 844, 929, 1115,
   1213, 1226, 1227, 1279, 1320, 1325

ASSINIBOINE-STONEY
   85

ATHABASCAN
   91, 107, 117, 172, 181, 370, 498, 657, 885, 1033, 1211, 1361

ATSUGEWI
   888

ATTITUDES
   51, 53, 76, 119, 121, 414, 553, 569, 614, 622, 683, 688, 722, 816,
   899, 964, 998, 1060, 1080, 1081, 1082, 1084, 1103, 1110, 1117, 1118,
   1124, 1125, 1126, 1127, 1135, 1141, 1142, 1147, 1168, 1174, 1177,
   1184, 1213, 1214, 1215, 1216, 1228, 1235, 1237, 1247, 1253, 1280,
   1281, 1303, 1316, 1346, 1349

BANNOCK
   65, 133, 420, 842

BEHAVIOR MODIFICATION
   58, 75, 144, 199, 514, 1272, 1362

BELLA BELLA
   85

BICULTURALISM
   1, 11, 21, 74, 83, 139, 151, 209, 210, 230, 330, 365, 375, 390, 458,
   460, 495, 531, 690, 691, 692, 740, 747, 751, 892, 893, 938, 994,
   1027, 1046, 1075, 1131, 1161, 1198, 1242

(CONT.)
CHILDREN-SCHOOL AGE
    1012, 1014, 1037, 1039, 1053, 1057, 1059, 1060, 1062, 1063, 1067,
    1068, 1069, 1070, 1071, 1072, 1082, 1084, 1088, 1090, 1091, 1093,
    1095, 1097, 1099, 1101, 1103, 1114, 1117, 1122, 1123, 1125, 1126,
    1144, 1148, 1154, 1158, 1168, 1169, 1171, 1175, 1177, 1178, 1179,
    1187, 1188, 1190, 1191, 1192, 1196, 1197, 1198, 1204, 1210, 1212,
    1213, 1214, 1215, 1216, 1219, 1220, 1221, 1222, 1223, 1228, 1229,
    1230, 1231, 1240, 1242, 1243, 1244, 1248, 1258, 1261, 1265, 1266,
    1268, 1269, 1270, 1280, 1281, 1283, 1302, 1313, 1314, 1315, 1316,
    1321, 1330, 1332, 1337, 1339, 1342, 1353, 1354, 1356, 1362

CHIPEWYAN
    141, 885, 889

CHIPPEWA
    30, 36, 44, 56, 68, 112, 118, 121, 155, 162, 191, 195, 217, 226,
    227, 242, 255, 284, 285, 294, 312, 313, 321, 331, 334, 359, 371,
    377, 387, 410, 462, 463, 473, 474, 512, 519, 525, 550, 580, 659,
    680, 693, 713, 722, 734, 757, 770, 850, 883, 891, 906, 916, 927,
    1006, 1009, 1017, 1018, 1098, 1210, 1214, 1219, 1270

CHOCTAW
    202, 254, 502, 1062

CHUMASH
    665

CLINICAL STUDY
    8, 58, 75, 80, 88, 99, 109, 144, 158, 171, 190, 231, 248, 294, 301,
    311, 352, 355, 362, 369, 405, 413, 428, 464, 480, 491, 514, 528,
    679, 713, 777, 975, 1007, 1251, 1253, 1264, 1294, 1300, 1303, 1314

COAST SALISH
    13, 14, 15, 104, 168, 304, 353, 553, 582, 583, 676, 780, 914, 963,
    964, 1051, 1159, 1238, 1360

COCOPAH
    78

COGNITIVE PROCESSES
    153, 235, 281, 282, 298, 396, 423, 433, 442, 446, 486, 520, 635,
    680, 694, 697, 698, 701, 702, 705, 710, 759, 764, 772, 790, 863,
    872, 908, 1003, 1032, 1049, 1056, 1065, 1072, 1087, 1088, 1095,
    1097, 1143, 1144, 1148, 1158, 1169, 1178, 1190, 1191, 1197, 1198,
    1199, 1204, 1225, 1240, 1242, 1248, 1258, 1260, 1262, 1267, 1268,
    1283, 1302, 1308, 1313, 1316, 1321, 1337, 1354

COLLEGES AND UNIVERSITIES
    7, 21, 90, 111, 166, 177, 180, 488, 655, 689, 690, 810, 838, 841,
    843, 911, 940, 986, 1048, 1115, 1118, 1131, 1141, 1157, 1186, 1195,
    1202, 1311, 1326

COLVILLE
    77, 478, 1052

COMANCHE
61, 763, 1317

COMMUNITY INVOLVEMENT
60, 286, 765, 807, 827, 884, 893, 911, 913, 948, 999, 1001, 1041,
1084, 1117, 1124, 1172, 1265, 1276, 1277, 1278, 1293, 1305, 1321,
1323, 1343

CONFESSION
68, 72, 226, 313, 571, 700, 1018, 1206, 1272, 1282

CONSULTATION
132, 160, 275, 450, 490, 525, 534, 545, 1009, 1112, 1160, 1229,
1254, 1325

COOPERATION
8, 37, 39, 63, 83, 113, 124, 176, 215, 218, 227, 242, 243, 247, 348,
451, 497, 498, 505, 506, 557, 558, 559, 561, 676, 712, 718, 770,
771, 919, 955, 958, 959, 1044, 1054, 1076, 1085, 1105, 1120, 1121,
1243, 1310

CORRECTIONAL INSTITUTIONS
27, 93, 146, 202, 219, 335, 341, 344, 360, 362, 363, 366, 369, 414,
416, 419, 432, 461, 546, 564, 612, 791, 813, 842, 844, 864, 884,
903, 931, 1136, 1145, 1147, 1246, 1277, 1278

CORRECTIONS PERSONNEL
134, 229, 239, 414, 1136, 1145, 1277

CREE
60, 141, 149, 170, 317, 334, 377, 439, 452, 474, 486, 525, 529, 580,
657, 664, 670, 680, 694, 713, 714, 723, 758, 783, 886, 908, 919,
1009, 1162, 1190, 1196, 1200, 1210, 1297, 1310, 1318

CREEK
1062

CRIME
98, 100, 146, 288, 300, 306, 335, 341, 344, 351, 360, 363, 367, 381,
410, 416, 420, 597, 669, 672, 712, 785, 813, 844, 864, 931, 932,
934, 1052, 1136, 1147, 1292, 1328, 1336, 1351, 1352

CROW
534, 545, 849, 926, 942, 1083, 1233

CULTURAL ADAPTATION
1, 17, 21, 23, 30, 39, 53, 58, 59, 63, 79, 94, 95, 127, 139, 140,
149, 153, 164, 177, 182, 191, 201, 202, 203, 207, 209, 210, 215,
222, 225, 230, 238, 254, 259, 280, 290, 293, 295, 308, 317, 331,
350, 357, 358, 359, 364, 365, 374, 375, 379, 382, 383, 384, 390,
404, 439, 443, 455, 456, 458, 463, 482, 485, 487, 489, 492, 500,
501, 502, 515, 520, 565, 638, 648, 652, 653, 658, 664, 670, 675,
686, 717, 722, 726, 743, 747, 750, 751, 752, 755, 783, 787, 796,
811, 829, 831, 835, 851, 873, 876, 877, 878, 879, 880, 882, 887,
889, 904, 906, 907, 913, 918, 920, 923, 937, 941, 943, 944, 946,

(CONT.)
DELIVERY OF SERVICES
    248, 275, 279, 354, 418, 437, 475, 508, 522, 525, 531, 534, 543,
    545, 576, 610, 611, 612, 614, 615, 616, 617, 618, 634, 640, 650,
    679, 724, 730, 769, 786, 803, 805, 809, 813, 816, 833, 860, 866,
    895, 1009, 1010, 1026, 1073, 1081, 1149, 1151, 1153, 1189, 1224,
    1247, 1276, 1279, 1296, 1299, 1303, 1323, 1329, 1335

DEMOGRAPHIC DATA
    31, 36, 49, 53, 121, 123, 126, 139, 140, 161, 182, 183, 184, 193,
    194, 196, 197, 205, 206, 207, 232, 240, 256, 261, 265, 288, 294,
    314, 367, 377, 382, 410, 420, 421, 426, 430, 431, 466, 586, 590,
    591, 592, 595, 596, 597, 602, 603, 605, 608, 612, 634, 659, 836,
    877, 882, 930, 946, 952, 966, 1081, 1133, 1134, 1153, 1224, 1246,
    1299, 1338, 1339

DEPRESSION
    13, 24, 28, 49, 117, 158, 162, 216, 321, 325, 395, 492, 560, 641,
    695, 776, 793, 865, 867, 1051, 1224, 1238, 1282, 1300, 1347

DIEGUENO
    668

DISCRIMINATION
    7, 48, 53, 73, 79, 92, 98, 119, 124, 128, 186, 196, 207, 208, 214,
    229, 239, 240, 247, 254, 258, 268, 291, 305, 315, 341, 344, 359,
    360, 382, 401, 412, 414, 463, 469, 500, 505, 506, 522, 533, 607,
    622, 640, 649, 652, 699, 706, 709, 729, 783, 787, 813, 815, 832,
    853, 858, 886, 919, 924, 940, 965, 989, 995, 1103, 1115, 1145, 1146,
    1147, 1159, 1185, 1212, 1213, 1214, 1215, 1223, 1234, 1275, 1279,
    1280, 1281, 1295, 1332, 1336, 1349

DOGRIB
    885

DREAMS AND VISION QUESTS
    69, 135, 158, 175, 226, 227, 228, 231, 246, 260, 302, 309, 312, 321,
    445, 457, 484, 491, 496, 512, 548, 566, 571, 575, 580, 599, 630,
    660, 663, 668, 722, 731, 734, 741, 745, 770, 780, 788, 835, 855,
    883, 888, 891, 942, 997, 1004, 1055, 1130, 1206, 1271, 1272, 1282,
    1304, 1307, 1312, 1359

DROPOUTS
    60, 76, 129, 130, 145, 173, 212, 258, 265, 447, 589, 606, 631, 690,
    693, 765, 999, 1022, 1058, 1099, 1115, 1186, 1265, 1279, 1321

DRUG TREATMENT
    715, 1160

DRUG USE
    24, 55, 78, 101, 102, 166, 185, 224, 287, 415, 441, 445, 479, 484,
    491, 513, 524, 540, 571, 574, 575, 585, 599, 600, 629, 644, 665,
    669, 715, 726, 727, 741, 753, 768, 789, 824, 835, 844, 859, 875,
    894, 935, 949, 950, 951, 1015, 1040, 1041, 1130, 1160, 1179, 1184,
    1202, 1205, 1226, 1227, 1228, 1297, 1300, 1320, 1327

EASTERN SUB-ARCTIC
    30, 36, 44, 56, 68, 89, 112, 118, 121, 149, 155, 162, 191, 195, 217,
    226, 227, 242, 255, 264, 284, 285, 294, 312, 313, 317, 321, 322,
    331, 334, 347, 359, 371, 387, 410, 429, 452, 462, 463, 464, 473,
    474, 486, 512, 519, 525, 529, 550, 580, 652, 664, 670, 680, 693,
    694, 713, 714, 722, 723, 734, 757, 758, 770, 783, 850, 883, 891,
    906, 908, 916, 927, 1006, 1009, 1017, 1018, 1098, 1162, 1190, 1194,
    1196, 1200, 1207, 1214, 1270, 1297, 1306, 1318

ECONOMIC ISSUES
    24, 42, 61, 73, 80, 83, 89, 93, 100, 113, 114, 121, 123, 127, 142,
    149, 179, 194, 210, 214, 223, 237, 238, 258, 280, 344, 366, 388,
    396, 397, 417, 420, 426, 430, 432, 463, 466, 485, 505, 506, 518,
    543, 557, 558, 590, 591, 592, 593, 608, 610, 624, 659, 685, 707,
    729, 761, 770, 771, 791, 799, 811, 845, 856, 858, 870, 878, 913,
    925, 948, 965, 986, 995, 1035, 1044, 1052, 1111, 1112, 1162, 1278,
    1284, 1290, 1340

EDUCATION PARAPROFESSIONALS
    9, 378, 999, 1099, 1122, 1216, 1217, 1229, 1230, 1353

EDUCATION PROFESSIONALS
    43, 48, 60, 67, 82, 234, 239, 323, 469, 693, 720, 721, 740, 827,
    841, 893, 983, 989, 994, 999, 1082, 1099, 1117, 1137, 1177, 1243,
    1244, 1265, 1314, 1315, 1332

EDUCATION PROGRAMS AND SERVICES
    9, 48, 60, 66, 76, 83, 84, 94, 119, 128, 129, 130, 144, 145, 151,
    167, 169, 199, 248, 276, 288, 293, 308, 323, 327, 427, 460, 469,
    488, 495, 507, 521, 562, 581, 594, 606, 690, 691, 692, 693, 708,
    720, 721, 736, 740, 810, 841, 843, 857, 892, 893, 897, 911, 938,
    962, 984, 986, 994, 1000, 1022, 1049, 1060, 1084, 1099, 1115, 1119,
    1122, 1124, 1131, 1172, 1176, 1186, 1199, 1214, 1233, 1291, 1310,
    1311, 1315, 1321, 1339, 1353, 1362

ELEMENTARY SCHOOLS
    60, 67, 75, 81, 84, 94, 96, 115, 119, 144, 176, 198, 235, 258, 271,
    392, 423, 427, 473, 526, 568, 582, 590, 591, 596, 603, 612, 622,
    651, 680, 682, 683, 684, 685, 687, 688, 691, 692, 693, 696, 705,
    711, 720, 721, 736, 740, 746, 757, 801, 812, 827, 853, 859, 892,
    893, 897, 911, 939, 977, 983, 987, 994, 1012, 1039, 1053, 1060,
    1067, 1069, 1071, 1072, 1082, 1117, 1126, 1148, 1154, 1168, 1177,
    1179, 1214, 1215, 1240, 1242, 1243, 1244, 1261, 1265, 1269, 1270,
    1280, 1283, 1291, 1302, 1313, 1316, 1321, 1330, 1332, 1337, 1339,
    1342, 1356, 1362

EMOTIONAL RESTRAINT
    158, 172, 181, 190, 195, 243, 312, 322, 347, 348, 471, 486, 512,
    552, 556, 645, 718, 734, 739, 742, 752, 757, 763, 830, 856, 862,
    957, 958, 962, 977, 1018, 1181, 1207, 1208, 1239, 1309

EMPLOYMENT
    36, 61, 93, 106, 149, 159, 196, 207, 208, 212, 214, 237, 240, 254,
    255, 259, 280, 288, 366, 388, 430, 460, 502, 506, 526, 536, 557,
    577, 586, 590, 591, 592, 593, 603, 612, 664, 670, 686, 714, 774,

(CONT.)

FAMILY FUNCTIONING
834, 839, 842, 898, 927, 1011, 1029, 1055, 1073, 1075, 1100, 1129, 1170, 1174, 1205, 1222, 1223, 1228, 1237, 1239, 1241, 1247, 1255, 1256, 1257, 1265, 1331, 1348

FAMILY PLANNING
265, 417, 606, 738, 774, 836, 946, 952, 966, 980, 1110, 1111, 1237

FEDERAL GOVERNMENT
18, 132, 215, 233, 269, 280, 290, 397, 412, 443, 472, 506, 610, 611, 613, 659, 691, 729, 809, 811, 814, 820, 821, 861, 871, 878, 880, 884, 925, 1020, 1044, 1125, 1160, 1165, 1182, 1322, 1325, 1351

FEMALES
71, 87, 92, 105, 110, 124, 135, 138, 141, 158, 179, 188, 223, 231, 241, 242, 245, 248, 249, 265, 278, 305, 311, 350, 379, 389, 391, 406, 407, 417, 434, 442, 454, 504, 509, 514, 526, 533, 536, 537, 577, 578, 606, 620, 638, 647, 706, 749, 770, 774, 775, 796, 799, 830, 831, 846, 847, 848, 849, 850, 851, 855, 863, 891, 902, 918, 946, 952, 975, 980, 1016, 1029, 1031, 1050, 1055, 1071, 1078, 1080, 1094, 1110, 1113, 1129, 1159, 1164, 1181, 1207, 1209, 1211, 1223, 1227, 1238, 1241, 1255, 1257, 1274, 1355

FLATHEAD
210, 1233

FULL BLOOD-MIXED BLOOD COMPARISONS
518, 586, 590, 596, 597, 599, 602, 603, 607, 610, 612, 614, 619, 623, 631, 649, 812, 868, 882, 1062, 1063, 1069, 1088, 1093, 1101, 1195, 1228, 1232, 1310, 1351

GENEROSITY
30, 82, 89, 105, 113, 135, 148, 180, 225, 247, 259, 277, 345, 380, 398, 451, 467, 518, 561, 593, 620, 667, 703, 730, 747, 855, 953, 1018, 1021, 1074, 1075, 1076, 1212

GENETIC FACTORS
217, 235, 264, 270, 284, 333, 355, 516, 529, 710, 815, 1063, 1102, 1273, 1355, 1363

GHOST SICKNESS
23, 69, 70, 158, 190, 311, 346, 352, 393, 413, 496, 745, 910, 960, 981, 997, 1108, 1259, 1307, 1319, 1361

GOSIUTE
727

GREAT BASIN
22, 115, 154, 314, 432, 506, 641, 663, 727, 745, 882, 1112, 1307

GRIEF REACTION
28, 158, 190, 329, 346, 393, 492, 542, 639, 695, 865, 957, 960, 1135, 1282

GROUP NORMS AND SANCTIONS
  35, 40, 44, 51, 54, 99, 103, 104, 105, 106, 107, 124, 135, 188, 223,
  226, 241, 320, 334, 352, 360, 375, 383, 389, 405, 406, 407, 408,
  419, 424, 454, 458, 459, 470, 471, 481, 503, 523, 546, 623, 632,
  704, 712, 715, 717, 730, 745, 791, 798, 836, 839, 849, 884, 916,
  932, 957, 961, 964, 976, 988, 1018, 1021, 1038, 1044, 1045, 1075,
  1120, 1159, 1161, 1196, 1205, 1211, 1231, 1236, 1272, 1275, 1290,
  1304, 1318, 1348, 1351

HAIDA
  538, 1312

HALIWA
  256, 315

HARE
  243, 767, 885, 1211

HAVASUPAI
  78

HIDATSA
  1075

HOOPA
  645, 985, 1022, 1047, 1057, 1074, 1218

HUALAPAI
  78

HYSTERIA
  122, 236, 245, 309, 311, 325, 339, 395, 704, 713, 723, 1282, 1307

INSTITUTIONALIZATION
  80, 123, 147, 171, 186, 193, 202, 288, 294, 341, 366, 369, 378, 414,
  416, 418, 419, 432, 440, 461, 465, 572, 598, 650, 724, 837, 839,
  865, 870, 1010, 1013, 1080, 1189, 1276, 1278, 1299

INTERTRIBAL COMPARISONS
  22, 27, 28, 30, 41, 61, 66, 78, 82, 85, 87, 102, 126, 133, 137, 149,
  197, 202, 217, 242, 247, 255, 264, 331, 371, 415, 439, 455, 520,
  538, 544, 644, 682, 737, 763, 783, 784, 844, 907, 908, 919, 923,
  942, 946, 966, 972, 998, 1004, 1006, 1034, 1052, 1058, 1078, 1085,
  1101, 1103, 1118, 1132, 1135, 1144, 1178, 1193, 1201, 1223, 1232,
  1241, 1292, 1357

IOWA
  1271

IROQUOIS
  175, 198, 349, 456, 457, 826, 1006, 1030, 1206, 1282

IROQUOIS-MOHAWK
  911

MILITARY SERVICE
   383, 645, 699, 760, 799, 953, 1015, 1259

MODOC
   869

MOHAVE
   78, 105, 246, 277, 278, 406, 408, 425, 496, 537, 542, 551, 578, 660,
   731, 735, 738, 928, 997, 1005, 1231

MOTIVATION
   11, 128, 129, 165, 177, 214, 233, 248, 473, 589, 622, 651, 761, 815,
   832, 888, 1003, 1045, 1048, 1062, 1077, 1083, 1089, 1117, 1161,
   1198, 1214, 1219, 1225, 1316

MOTOR PROCESSES
   273, 423, 782, 1042, 1049, 1143, 1209, 1258, 1314

MUNSEE
   83, 1270

NANTICOKE
   500

NATIVE AMERICAN ADMINISTERED PROGRAMS
   3, 15, 19, 33, 40, 65, 77, 84, 88, 174, 186, 192, 361, 427, 495,
   511, 527, 562, 610, 613, 691, 692, 693, 707, 728, 729, 740, 802,
   803, 809, 841, 884, 892, 893, 895, 994, 1020, 1172, 1254, 1333

NATIVE AMERICAN COPING BEHAVIORS
   42, 44, 68, 69, 72, 91, 216, 218, 226, 243, 313, 335, 366, 385, 459,
   462, 486, 497, 506, 518, 525, 552, 571, 593, 619, 623, 696, 700,
   709, 712, 722, 737, 739, 744, 752, 762, 781, 799, 886, 887, 902,
   950, 991, 1030, 1132, 1187, 1207, 1227, 1252, 1259, 1283, 1284,
   1287, 1309, 1345

NATIVE AMERICAN ETIOLOGY
   4, 12, 17, 29, 42, 62, 68, 69, 71, 156, 175, 189, 226, 227, 250,
   252, 301, 309, 313, 395, 413, 417, 425, 475, 483, 487, 508, 532,
   538, 547, 548, 550, 554, 573, 616, 658, 745, 786, 793, 804, 825,
   997, 1002, 1006, 1008, 1017, 1018, 1034, 1106, 1108, 1109, 1120,
   1253, 1282, 1335, 1344

NATIVE AMERICAN PERSONNEL
   1, 3, 5, 6, 7, 45, 48, 67, 73, 74, 75, 84, 92, 109, 111, 157, 160,
   219, 269, 280, 378, 400, 431, 435, 465, 527, 531, 535, 572, 618,
   655, 671, 691, 692, 693, 740, 765, 802, 809, 810, 838, 841, 842,
   860, 893, 895, 917, 986, 994, 999, 1001, 1019, 1043, 1046, 1122,
   1149, 1217, 1229, 1230, 1249, 1276, 1277, 1301, 1305, 1311, 1329,
   1362

NATIVE AMERICAN POLITICAL MOVEMENTS
   3, 21, 145, 197, 268, 291, 317, 327, 364, 503, 649, 811, 878, 995,
   1132, 1333

NATIVE AMERICAN RELIGIONS
4, 17, 29, 34, 40, 55, 101, 156, 167, 175, 185, 190, 209, 224, 225,
230, 242, 250, 267, 298, 302, 304, 330, 373, 376, 383, 436, 456,
457, 461, 484, 510, 513, 515, 540, 547, 548, 575, 585, 604, 609,
626, 627, 628, 629, 630, 632, 633, 676, 722, 727, 732, 733, 743,
744, 750, 766, 768, 780, 788, 824, 835, 867, 869, 873, 874, 875,
881, 890, 904, 905, 906, 907, 909, 921, 923, 936, 941, 942, 943,
944, 945, 947, 948, 950, 956, 1025, 1040, 1083, 1130, 1132, 1159,
1162, 1180, 1201, 1203, 1206, 1259, 1271, 1275, 1282, 1285, 1288,
1307, 1312, 1317, 1319, 1327, 1360

NATIVE AMERICAN VALUES
30, 53, 86, 94, 150, 159, 221, 222, 225, 234, 237, 247, 261, 298,
398, 458, 476, 486, 495, 497, 504, 517, 518, 558, 561, 593, 609,
613, 615, 617, 620, 648, 667, 686, 696, 703, 711, 730, 747, 751,
791, 792, 796, 862, 888, 902, 938, 992, 998, 1000, 1022, 1038, 1064,
1075, 1079, 1083, 1085, 1120, 1121, 1128, 1132, 1133, 1159, 1193,
1198, 1201, 1218, 1235, 1259, 1275, 1290, 1291, 1310, 1323, 1330,
1350

NATIVE-NON-NATIVE COMPARISONS
34, 53, 56, 67, 76, 81, 85, 90, 94, 96, 97, 98, 102, 106, 107, 111,
112, 115, 117, 118, 127, 128, 129, 130, 137, 141, 142, 150, 155,
161, 163, 165, 166, 170, 173, 176, 177, 178, 183, 199, 210, 217,
222, 247, 254, 264, 270, 272, 273, 281, 282, 284, 285, 286, 294,
295, 308, 333, 341, 354, 355, 362, 363, 371, 374, 381, 390, 394,
396, 401, 403, 409, 410, 415, 416, 423, 434, 438, 444, 445, 446,
468, 477, 482, 501, 502, 516, 517, 519, 522, 529, 544, 552, 564,
569, 582, 586, 601, 602, 607, 610, 611, 614, 619, 631, 637, 644,
651, 677, 680, 681, 683, 685, 687, 694, 697, 698, 705, 708, 710,
711, 716, 717, 737, 754, 761, 764, 813, 815, 836, 843, 844, 863,
864, 868, 879, 886, 894, 896, 899, 912, 919, 929, 931, 939, 977,
978, 979, 991, 998, 1010, 1012, 1013, 1014, 1015, 1029, 1034, 1056,
1062, 1069, 1070, 1071, 1072, 1077, 1078, 1084, 1085, 1087, 1088,
1089, 1090, 1091, 1092, 1097, 1101, 1102, 1103, 1114, 1118, 1136,
1139, 1140, 1141, 1144, 1148, 1150, 1154, 1155, 1158, 1166, 1167,
1168, 1169, 1171, 1178, 1181, 1184, 1187, 1188, 1190, 1191, 1193,
1195, 1200, 1209, 1213, 1214, 1215, 1219, 1221, 1223, 1225, 1226,
1227, 1235, 1238, 1240, 1249, 1250, 1255, 1260, 1263, 1264, 1266,
1267, 1268, 1269, 1270, 1272, 1279, 1280, 1283, 1292, 1308, 1310,
1313, 1316, 1320, 1337, 1341, 1347, 1349, 1350, 1354, 1355, 1363

NAVAJO
1, 4, 5, 9, 11, 16, 17, 24, 26, 29, 37, 38, 39, 41, 43, 45, 46, 58,
61, 62, 69, 74, 81, 84, 93, 97, 99, 100, 101, 126, 137, 139, 151,
161, 167, 171, 179, 190, 197, 202, 204, 205, 207, 214, 220, 221,
228, 237, 241, 248, 250, 252, 253, 255, 261, 265, 276, 282, 283,
311, 339, 342, 343, 350, 365, 366, 369, 373, 379, 381, 383, 388,
403, 404, 405, 409, 414, 417, 423, 427, 440, 442, 453, 459, 465,
470, 475, 494, 505, 508, 509, 523, 526, 530, 531, 535, 536, 546,
555, 566, 567, 637, 638, 650, 697, 700, 711, 719, 721, 722, 728,
730, 736, 740, 741, 744, 759, 786, 791, 794, 816, 820, 825, 840,
844, 845, 852, 866, 867, 884, 887, 890, 892, 893, 896, 897, 917,
946, 948, 950, 966, 976, 977, 987, 1003, 1006, 1028, 1029, 1035,
1037, 1038, 1042, 1045, 1046, 1049, 1054, 1055, 1061, 1065, 1080,

(CONT.)
PERSONALITY TRAITS
1074, 1076, 1096, 1098, 1148, 1195, 1207, 1239, 1259, 1272, 1283, 1287, 1304, 1309, 1341

PHYSICAL HEALTH AND ILLNESS
31, 87, 92, 123, 126, 161, 193, 251, 252, 262, 270, 284, 285, 367, 428, 430, 443, 448, 474, 531, 532, 538, 543, 591, 603, 614, 647, 658, 837, 866, 870, 871, 975, 1001, 1002, 1026, 1139, 1140, 1149, 1164, 1222, 1224, 1274, 1294, 1314, 1316, 1319, 1323, 1335, 1352

PIMA
78, 217, 688, 697, 1129, 1261

PLAINS
11, 22, 25, 26, 30, 41, 43, 51, 55, 59, 60, 61, 63, 79, 80, 85, 86, 94, 102, 106, 112, 114, 133, 135, 137, 138, 141, 145, 148, 170, 176, 183, 184, 188, 202, 222, 223, 231, 234, 240, 244, 247, 255, 260, 261, 267, 302, 318, 329, 330, 331, 356, 361, 371, 377, 398, 399, 407, 436, 447, 454, 462, 477, 481, 493, 515, 517, 518, 534, 545, 554, 560, 565, 585, 586, 587, 588, 589, 590, 591, 592, 593, 594, 595, 596, 597, 598, 599, 600, 601, 602, 603, 604, 605, 606, 607, 608, 609, 610, 611, 612, 613, 614, 615, 616, 617, 618, 619, 620, 621, 622, 623, 624, 625, 626, 627, 628, 629, 630, 631, 632, 633, 634, 635, 637, 646, 654, 666, 677, 684, 695, 722, 743, 747, 752, 755, 760, 761, 763, 768, 784, 799, 829, 838, 849, 855, 859, 871, 874, 875, 886, 901, 903, 912, 920, 921, 926, 932, 933, 936, 941, 942, 943, 944, 945, 949, 953, 960, 971, 980, 988, 992, 1004, 1019, 1021, 1052, 1062, 1076, 1083, 1085, 1113, 1124, 1125, 1132, 1150, 1152, 1166, 1167, 1173, 1175, 1184, 1205, 1219, 1233, 1243, 1277, 1289, 1310, 1317, 1319, 1333, 1349, 1350, 1353, 1357

PLATEAU
22, 65, 77, 88, 133, 210, 219, 238, 257, 304, 309, 384, 413, 420, 449, 478, 488, 548, 549, 725, 750, 754, 834, 842, 869, 908, 1052, 1106, 1154, 1224, 1233, 1244, 1263, 1345

POLITICS-NONTRIBAL
269, 472, 506, 624, 814, 858, 1111, 1165, 1328, 1351

POMO
1107, 1108

PONCA
1271

POTAWATOMI
224, 357, 471, 512, 707, 905

POWERLESSNESS
48, 186, 497, 504, 512, 572, 607, 608, 610, 611, 613, 619, 659, 722, 728, 752, 774, 794, 880, 900, 965, 995, 1035, 1147, 1235, 1318, 1331, 1358

PSYCHOSES
  12, 120, 162, 205, 218, 301, 793, 865, 1010, 1013, 1296, 226

PSYCHOTHERAPY AND COUNSELING
  8, 12, 14, 17, 32, 40, 54, 58, 74, 75, 82, 109, 111, 144, 152, 168,
  171, 190, 199, 229, 231, 263, 271, 311, 352, 353, 373, 405, 413,
  435, 451, 464, 491, 499, 507, 514, 561, 572, 639, 660, 679, 713,
  723, 777, 808, 839, 846, 857, 862, 902, 929, 999, 1027, 1050, 1064,
  1159, 1163, 1217, 1236, 1272, 1279, 1282, 1326, 1327, 1329, 1352,
  1362

PUEBLO
  40, 211, 409, 479, 711, 782, 907, 923, 947, 958, 1105, 1258, 1275

PUEBLO-COCHITI
  71

PUEBLO-HOPI
  11, 26, 38, 41, 43, 64, 78, 100, 116, 126, 137, 143, 158, 272, 273,
  455, 505, 637, 697, 718, 722, 732, 742, 844, 872, 946, 959, 961,
  966, 1056, 1094, 1109, 1178, 1285, 1302

PUEBLO-SAN FELIPE
  26

PUEBLO-SANTO DOMINGO
  26

PUEBLO-TAOS
  937

PUEBLO-TEWA
  455, 847

PUEBLO-ZIA
  11, 41, 137

PUEBLO-ZUNI
  11, 30, 41, 43, 52, 134, 137, 281, 332, 383, 403, 404, 453, 673,
  718, 848, 1269

QUINAULT
  142

READING PROGRAMS
  199, 220, 688, 736, 746, 1177

RELIGIONS-NON-NATIVE
  40, 50, 304, 339, 368, 376, 379, 412, 456, 457, 515, 549, 585, 591,
  603, 612, 625, 627, 630, 678, 703, 732, 743, 750, 881, 907, 923,
  941, 943, 947, 963, 1040, 1104, 1130, 1206, 1238, 1259, 1275, 1288,
  1319

RELIGIOUS-NON-NATIVE PERSONNEL
239, 339, 349, 636, 678, 723, 881

RELOCATION
36, 39, 61, 86, 93, 110, 150, 196, 197, 202, 207, 212, 214, 234,
237, 238, 240, 243, 254, 255, 344, 364, 365, 366, 380, 388, 398,
442, 466, 490, 505, 507, 532, 709, 714, 755, 759, 791, 828, 846,
871, 882, 887, 920, 966, 990, 996, 1023, 1061, 1107, 1134, 1183,
1233, 1320

RESEARCHERS
167, 244, 283, 286, 292, 500, 527, 541, 558, 565, 653, 741, 751,
810, 824, 830, 876, 889, 892, 893, 913, 922, 958, 1007, 1016, 1031,
1035, 1066, 1079, 1140, 1156, 1160, 1180, 1182, 1218, 1252, 1264,
1289, 1293, 1298, 1304, 1305, 1321, 1322, 1325, 1329

RESERVATION
1, 2, 4, 5, 9, 11, 13, 14, 15, 16, 17, 23, 24, 25, 26, 27, 37, 38,
39, 41, 43, 45, 46, 51, 52, 57, 58, 59, 60, 61, 62, 63, 65, 66, 69,
70, 71, 74, 75, 77, 78, 81, 83, 84, 85, 88, 94, 97, 99, 100, 101,
103, 105, 106, 115, 116, 118, 120, 121, 123, 126, 133, 135, 137,
140, 141, 143, 144, 145, 147, 148, 158, 160, 161, 174, 179, 182,
184, 191, 193, 195, 203, 205, 210, 218, 219, 224, 225, 226, 227,
228, 232, 233, 244, 247, 248, 253, 258, 259, 260, 263, 265, 272,
273, 275, 280, 281, 282, 283, 300, 311, 314, 317, 331, 336, 339,
342, 343, 350, 351, 352, 357, 359, 360, 361, 365, 367, 377, 379,
381, 384, 389, 397, 402, 407, 411, 412, 413, 417, 420, 423, 428,
430, 431, 436, 447, 452, 455, 456, 463, 465, 466, 472, 473, 475,
477, 479, 481, 486, 492, 493, 494, 499, 502, 503, 504, 505, 506,
508, 512, 515, 517, 518, 520, 523, 526, 531, 534, 535, 536, 545,
546, 548, 550, 554, 555, 558, 560, 565, 574, 576, 577, 581, 583,
585, 586, 587, 588, 589, 590, 591, 592, 593, 594, 595, 596, 597,
598, 599, 600, 601, 602, 603, 604, 605, 606, 607, 608, 609, 610,
611, 612, 613, 614, 615, 616, 617, 618, 619, 620, 621, 622, 623,
624, 625, 626, 627, 628, 629, 630, 631, 632, 633, 634, 635, 638,
641, 645, 652, 659, 666, 672, 676, 677, 684, 688, 695, 704, 715,
721, 722, 728, 730, 731, 732, 733, 736, 739, 740, 742, 743, 744,
747, 752, 754, 755, 757, 759, 765, 769, 770, 778, 779, 782, 785,
786, 796, 799, 803, 809, 814, 816, 820, 824, 826, 828, 829, 834,
838, 840, 842, 845, 851, 852, 853, 855, 858, 865, 866, 867, 869,
871, 874, 880, 884, 886, 887, 890, 892, 893, 894, 903, 911, 914,
916, 917, 920, 921, 925, 932, 933, 934, 937, 943, 944, 945, 946,
948, 950, 952, 953, 957, 959, 966, 972, 976, 978, 980, 981, 995,
996, 999, 1002, 1003, 1009, 1010, 1019, 1020, 1021, 1022, 1023,
1028, 1035, 1037, 1038, 1042, 1044, 1045, 1046, 1047, 1049, 1053,
1054, 1055, 1056, 1061, 1065, 1066, 1080, 1083, 1085, 1095, 1105,
1107, 1109, 1110, 1111, 1112, 1116, 1117, 1119, 1120, 1125, 1129,
1132, 1137, 1149, 1150, 1152, 1153, 1155, 1157, 1159, 1160, 1161,
1164, 1165, 1166, 1167, 1169, 1174, 1178, 1184, 1190, 1191, 1196,
1197, 1199, 1203, 1204, 1206, 1218, 1221, 1222, 1223, 1229, 1230,
1231, 1233, 1236, 1240, 1241, 1242, 1244, 1246, 1247, 1250, 1253,
1255, 1257, 1259, 1260, 1267, 1268, 1270, 1275, 1276, 1278, 1283,
1290, 1302, 1303, 1305, 1308, 1309, 1314, 1319, 1321, 1323, 1326,
1333, 1338, 1343, 1344, 1349, 1350, 1352, 1353, 1358

SHOSHONE
51, 65, 133, 247, 314, 420, 515, 743, 842, 894, 936, 980, 1083,
1085, 1125, 1150, 1166, 1167, 1184, 1317

SIOUX
11, 25, 30, 41, 43, 86, 102, 106, 112, 135, 137, 138, 188, 197, 202,
223, 234, 240, 244, 255, 260, 261, 302, 331, 356, 371, 398, 436,
447, 462, 495, 554, 565, 585, 637, 646, 677, 695, 784, 874, 901,
912, 920, 932, 992, 1019, 1076, 1173, 1175, 1219, 1221, 1243, 1333,
1353, 1357

SIOUX-OGLALA
26, 59, 145, 477, 481, 517, 518, 560, 586, 587, 588, 589, 590, 591,
592, 593, 594, 595, 596, 597, 598, 599, 600, 601, 602, 603, 604,
605, 606, 607, 608, 609, 610, 611, 612, 613, 614, 615, 616, 617,
618, 619, 620, 621, 622, 623, 624, 625, 626, 627, 628, 629, 630,
631, 632, 633, 634, 635, 684, 722, 755, 855, 941, 943, 944, 945,
1319

SKAGIT
756

SLAVE
885

SOCIAL GROUPS AND PEER GROUPS
40, 54, 89, 99, 101, 102, 103, 104, 106, 107, 109, 115, 152, 191,
203, 213, 223, 229, 230, 243, 263, 271, 344, 375, 405, 411, 435,
447, 470, 471, 499, 503, 523, 546, 599, 623, 637, 638, 747, 796,
798, 799, 846, 862, 885, 919, 1050, 1085, 1159, 1162, 1163, 1196,
1205, 1236, 1244, 1247, 1278, 1284, 1327, 1340, 1352

SOCIAL NETWORKS
8, 37, 83, 197, 240, 255, 261, 296, 331, 342, 376, 497, 503, 505,
511, 518, 557, 675, 676, 726, 751, 953, 955, 986, 1021, 1073, 1137,
1138, 1165, 1170, 1284, 1320, 1327, 1340, 1352

SOCIAL ROLES
87, 92, 110, 124, 138, 179, 200, 241, 242, 277, 305, 350, 352, 378,
379, 442, 454, 481, 503, 531, 577, 620, 653, 704, 707, 714, 739,
747, 749, 770, 775, 796, 827, 830, 831, 849, 855, 863, 876, 886,
1016, 1019, 1031, 1046, 1078, 1094, 1100, 1129, 1140, 1185, 1211,
1215, 1217, 1237, 1238, 1244, 1255, 1257, 1358

SOCIAL SERVICE PARAPROFESSIONALS
488, 671, 917

SOCIAL SERVICE PROFESSIONALS
10, 213, 229, 336, 400, 465, 533, 572, 655, 803, 809, 822, 841, 860,
862, 895, 1035, 1073, 1170, 1314

SOCIAL SERVICES
20, 88, 123, 131, 147, 187, 188, 192, 194, 206, 213, 233, 249, 258,
288, 297, 343, 400, 507, 511, 643, 707, 803, 809, 813, 834, 837,
845, 870, 895, 898, 915, 917, 1011, 1026, 1035, 1073, 1151, 1152,

Author Index

ABELL, WENDELL
1090

ABEL, THEODORA M.
409, 1341

ABERLE, DAVID F.
887, 956, 1285

ABLON, JOAN
150, 255, 380, 398

ABOUD, FRANCES E.
1213, 1215

ABOUREZK, JAMES
821

ACKERKNECHT, ERWIN H.
424

ACKERMAN, LILLIAN A.
257

ACKERMAN, ROBERT E.
251

ACKERSTEIN, HAROLD
817

ADAIR, JOHN
1, 383, 786, 1046, 1065, 1323

ADAMS, DAVID
994

ADAMS, G.W.
971

ADAMS, L. LA MAR
1157

AGAR, MICHAEL H.
1160

AGINSKY, BURT W.
1107, 1108

ALASKA NATIVE HEALTH BOARD
279, 307, 310

ALBAS, CHERYL A.
1200

ANASTASI, ANNE
392

ANDERSON, FORREST N.
568

ANDERSON, JAMES G.
1084

ANDERSON, PHILIP O.
55

ANDERSON, RANDALL
1103

ANDERSON, ROBERT
148, 799

ANDRE, JAMES M.
332

ANDROES, SHARON T.
488

ANNIS, ROBERT C.
694, 908

ARCHIBALD, CHARLES W.
1236

ARMSTRONG, HARVEY
713

ARMSTRONG, ROBERT L.
1050

ARNEKLEV, BRUCE L.
1086

ARSDALE, MINOR V.
237

ARTHUR, GRACE
552, 1059

ASSOCIATION OF AMERICAN INDIAN PHYSICIANS
193

ASTROV, MARGOT
759

ATCHESON, J.D.
354

ATTNEAVE, CAROLYN L.
2, 8, 345, 640, 679, 819, 1296

AUSTIN, GREGORY A.
1226

BACHTOLD, LOUISE M.
1022, 1218

BAHR, HOWARD M.
53, 212, 813, 832, 1066

BAILEY, FLORA L.
1042, 1080, 1344

BAILEY, ROGER C.
1212

BAIZERMAN, MICHAEL
534

BAKER, JAMES L.
335

BALES, ROBERT
737

BALIKCI, ASEN
547, 556, 967

BALLINGER, THOMAS O.
1258

BARBER, CARROLL G.
935

BARCLAY, W.S.
426, 438

BARGER, KENNETH
149

BARKER, GEORGE C.
907

BARNARD, MARY A.
1077

BARNETT, DON C.
1082

BARNOUW, VICTOR
331, 883, 891

BELTRANE, THOMAS
1183

BENEDICT, ROBERT
430

BENNET, J.W.
958

BENNION, LYNN
333

BERGAN,K.W.
1233

BERGER, A.
60

BERGMAN, ROBERT L.
5, 62, 101, 340, 373, 1229, 1230

BERG, DAVID.
48

BERG, GREG
765

BERKHOFER, ROBERT F.
881

BERLIN, IRVING N.
266

BERNARD, JESSIE
326

BERREMAN, GERALD D.
108, 375, 489

BERRY, BREWTON
877

BERRY, JOHN W.
153, 710, 908

BEUKE, VERNON L.
1126

BICKERTON, DOROTHY
1276

BIENVENUE, RITA M.
341

BIGART, ROBERT J.
210, 259

BITSUIE, DELPHINE
840

BITTKER, THOMAS E.
78, 154

BITTLE, WILLIAM E.
760, 960

BJORK, JOHN W.
234, 399, 859, 1296

BLACK HORSE, FRANCIS D.
461

BLAIR, BOWEN
1180

BLANCHARD, EVELYN
211, 297, 895

BLANCHARD, JOSEPH D.
211, 378, 1143

BLANCHARD, KENDALL
379

BLAND, LAUREL L.
1178

BLEVINS, AUDIE L.
1166

BLOOM, JOSEPH D.
6, 110, 805, 1245

BLYAN, J.D.
1278

BOAG, THOMAS A.
334

BOCK, PHILIP K.
389

BOCK, R. DARRELL
790

BOGGS, STEPHEN T.
927

BRANT, CHARLES S.
768, 921

BRAROE, NIELS W.
886

BRATRUDE, AMON P.
478

BRAWER, FLORENCE B.
236, 492, 972

BREKKE, BEVERLY
52

BRETT, BRIAN
437

BREWER, WILLIS R.
1115

BRICKNER, PHILIP W.
441

BRIGGS, JEAN L.
830, 968

BRILL, A.A.
245

BRINKER, PAUL A.
61

BROCH, HARALD B.
1211

BRODT, E. WILLIAM
1343

BRODY, HUGH
344

BROD, THOMAS M.
337

BROMBERG, WALTER
433, 540

BROWDER, J. ALBERT
530

BROWNLEE, ALETA
233

BURTON, R. FISHER
280

BUSHNELL, JOHN H.
645, 1047

BUTLER, G.C.
539

BUTT, DORCAS S.
706

BUXBAUM, ROBERT C.
7

BYLER, WILLIAM
822, 1331

BYNUM, JACK
338

CALLAN, JOHN P.
1015

CAMERON, ANN
651

CAMPBELL, LELAND H.
1157

CANADIAN PSYCHIATRIC ASSOCIATION
802

CARDELL, GEORGE W.
271

CARDEY, R.M.
1190

CARLIN, WALTER
261

CARLSON, ERIC J.
32

CARNEY, RICHARD E.
1095

CARPENTER, EDMUND S.
457, 573

CARROLL, ELEANOR E.
1226

FITZGERALD, J.A.
812

FLANNERY, REGINA
749

FLINT, GARRY
528

FLYNN, FRANK
1238

FOLEY, JOHN P.
392

FOLK-WILLIAMS, JOHN A.
1079

FORSLUND, MORRIS A.
785, 1150, 1155, 1184

FOSTER, DOROTHY A.
647

FOULKS, EDWARD F.
49, 800, 1239

FOWLER, LORETTA
1021

FOX, DENNIS R.
1127

FOX, J. ROBIN.
71

FRANKLYN, G.J.
1235

FRANK, JOEL
1250

FREDERICK, CALVIN
146

FREDERIKSEN, SVEND
510

FREEMAN, DANIEL M.A.
318, 1239

FREEMAN. PATRICIA, A.
1239

GALVEZ, EUGENE
  263

GARBARENO, MERWYN S.
  364

GARCIA-MASON, VELMA
  1202

GARCIA, ANTHONY
  261

GARDINER, MARTIN
  1302

GARDNER, RICHARD E.
  376

GARDNER, RUTH
  688

GARFIELD, SOL L.
  222

GARTH, THOMAS R.
  888, 1062, 1063, 1077, 1087, 1088, 1089, 1090, 1091, 1092, 1093,
  1101

GAUDIA, GIL
  1072

GEORGE, DEBORAH M.
  1168

GEYNDT, WILLY DE
  1081

GHUCHU, STANLEY
  332

GIBBINS, ROBERT J.
  217

GILBERT, J.A.L.
  355

GILLIAM, OLIVIA L.
  476

GILLIN, JOHN
  359

GIORDANO, GRACE
  833

GUTMAN, GLORIA
   1313

HACKENBERG, ROBERT A.
   140, 232, 466

HAGAN, JOHN
   1336

HALLOWELL, A. IRVING
   68, 226, 227, 312, 313, 322, 374, 550, 850, 1018, 1098, 1286

HALL, EDWIN L
   1147

HALPERN, KATHERINE SPENCER
   917

HALSWEIG, MARK
   875

HALVERSON, LOWELL K.
   813

HAMAMSY, LAILA S.
   179

HAMER, JOHN H.
   471, 512

HAMMERSCHLAG, CARL A.
   48, 435, 499, 1020

HAMMES, LAUREL M.
   444

HAMMOND, BLODWEN
   139

HAMMOND, D. CORYDON
   1064

HAMPSON, JOHN L.
   120

HANDELMAN, DON
   653, 663

HANNON, THOMAS A.
   81

HANSEN, H.C.
   1069, 1071

HEATH, DWIGHT B.
523

HEESCH, JACK R.
1179

HEIDENREICH, C. ADRIAN
753

HEINRICH, ALBERT
1256

HELLON, C.P.
480

HELPER, MALCOLM M.
222

HENDERSON, NORMAN B.
453

HENDERSON, RONALD W.
962, 1362

HENDRIE, HUGH C.
80

HENDRIKX, MARGARET E.
1294

HENNINGER, DANIEL
1068

HERMAN, FREDERICK
680

HERREID, CLYDE F.
163

HERREID, JANET, R.
163

HERRICK, JAMES W.
1008

HIGLEY, H. BRUCE
1157

HILGER, M. INEZ
1113

HILKEVITCH, RHEA R.
137

HILL, CHARLES A.
306

HILL, THOMAS W.
320, 1348

HILL, W.W.
241

HIPPLER, ARTHUR E.
91, 181, 189, 370

HIPPLE, J.L.
221

HIRABAYASHI, JAMES
751

HODGE, WILLIAM H.
365, 1104

HOFFMANN, HELMUT
56, 294, 519

HOFFMAN, VIRGINIA
740

HOLDEN, DAVID E.W.
714

HOLE, L.W.
426

HOLLAND, R. FOUNT
1122

HOLLENBECK, ALBERT R.
282, 1003, 1037, 1298

HOLMES, BARBARA
1050

HOLSINGER, DAVID N.
118

HONIGMANN, IRMA
107, 164

HONIGMANN, JOHN J.
107, 164, 657, 919, 1287

HOOD, WILLIAM R.
270

ISSACS, HOPE L.
  1006

JACKSON, DOUGLAS N.
  56

JACOBS, MELVILLE
  1106

JALES, WILLIAM M.
  183

JAMES, BERNARD J.
  429, 463

JAMIESON, ELMER
  198

JARANSON, JAMES M.
  1249

JENKINS, ALMA
  131

JENNESS, DIAMOND
  309

JENSEN, GARY F.
  844

JERDONE, CLARE G.
  915

JETMALANI, N.B.
  221

JEWELL, DONALD P.
  171

JILEK-AALL, LOUISE
  15, 168, 353, 482, 583, 1159, 1238, 1360

JILEK, WOLFGANG G.
  12, 13, 14, 95, 353, 864, 1051, 1238, 1360

JIMSON, LEONARD B.
  343

JIPSON, FREDERICK J.
  1188

JOHNSON, BRUCE D.
  1226

LIBERMAN, DAVID
1250, 1253

LIBERTY, MARGOT P.
942, 952

LIEBOW, ELLIOT
664

LINTON, RALPH
34

LISMER, MARJORIE
493

LITTMAN, GERARD
42

LI, TING-KAI
333

LLOYD, DAVID O.
1261

LOCASSO, RICHARD M.
173

LOCKLEAR, HERBERT H.
467

LODER, RICHARD R.
1030

LOEB, EDWIN M.
672

LOMBARDI, THOMAS P.
1240

LONG, ROGER
323

LOPEZ, BARRY
298

LORINCZ, ALBERT B.
102, 223

LOWERY, MARY J.
564, 569

LOWRY, R.B.
975

MANSON, SPERO M.
   1247, 1311, 1329

MARETZKI, THOMAS W.
   1156

MARGETTS, EDWARD L.
   584, 1007

MARQUIS, JAMES R.
   428

MARRIOTT, ALICE
   296

MARSHALL, MELODY
   1296

MARSH-THORNTON, JOAN
   1167

MARTIG, ROGER
   939

MARTIN, DAVID S.
   119

MARTIN, HARRY W.
   183, 202, 490

MARTIN, JAMES C.
   991, 1148

MASHBURN, WILLIAM
   441

MASON-BROWNE, N.L.
   667

MASON, EVELYN P.
   128, 129, 130, 165, 173, 708

MATCHETT, WILLIAM F.
   158

MAYBEE, CHRIS
   261

MAYNARD, EILEEN
   244, 589, 595, 607, 623, 634

MAYNARD, JAMES E.
   444

PAREDES, ALFONSO
1004, 1102

PARKER, ALAN
933

PARKER, ARTHUR C.
412

PARKER, SEYMOUR
242, 348, 580, 794

PARKIN, MICHAEL
117

PARKS, GEORGE A.
1003

PARSONS, ELSIE CLEWS
847, 848

PARSONS, OSCAR A.
1193

PASCAROSA, PAUL
875, 1327

PASQUALE, FRANK L.
1329

PATTERSON, CARROLL D.
1015

PATTERSON, PAUL
713

PATTISON, E. MANSELL
120, 160, 413

PATTON, WALTER
1048

PECK, RAYMOND LESTER
687

PECORARO, JOSEPH
1060

PELLETIER, WILFRED
792

PELNER, LOUIS
484

RABOIN, ROLLAND M.
 1184

RACHLIN, CAROL
 296

RAE-GRANT, QUENTIN
 525

RAMEY, JOSEPH H.
 1049

RAMOS, ALBERT A.
 1140

RAMSTAD, VIVIAN V.
 754

RANDALL, ARCHIE
 1136

RANDALL, BETTE
 1136

RANKIN, JAMES G.
 217

RANKIN, L.S.
 125

RATTRAY, RICHARD L.
 839

RAY, VERNE F.
 988

REASONS, CHARLES
 416

REBOUSSIN, ROLAND
 177

RED BIRD, AILEEN
 834

RED HORSE, JOHN G.
 1170

REED, T. EDWARD
 217, 264, 285

REED, WILLIAM H.
 899

SCHOENFELD, LAWRENCE S.
24, 190, 204, 205

SCHOTTSTAEDT, MARY F.
859

SCHUBERT, JOSEF
170

SCHULTES, RICHARD E.
575

SCHUSKY, ERNEST L.
920

SCHWARTZ, DONALD F.
1152

SCHWARTZ, DORIS R.
475

SELLERS, MARY
36

SHANNON, LAEL
1187, 1225

SHAUGHNESSY, TIM
316

SHEPARDSON, MARY
139, 884, 1290

SHEPS, EFRAIM
998

SHERWIN, DUANE
563

SHIMKIN, D.B.
515

SHIPP, PATRICK E.
897

SHORE, JAMES H.
27, 28, 77, 87, 88, 120, 160, 174, 219, 449, 642, 1151, 1293

SHORE, MILTON F.
1325

SHUTT, DONALD L.
81

STULL, DONALD D.
   182

ST. JOHN, JOAN
   1210

SUE, STANLEY
   111, 522, 1279

SUTKER, SARA SMITH
   183

SUTTLES, WAYNE
   304, 676, 914

SWANSON, DAVID M.
   478

SWANSON, ROSEMARY A.
   962, 1362

SWENSON, DAVID D.
   41

SWENSON, JAMES D.
   1324

SYDIAHA, D.
   761

TABACHNICK, NORMAN
   777

TADLOCK, L.D.
   221

TAMERIN, JOHN S.
   564, 569

TANNER, ADRIAN
   1162

TAX, SOL
   1133

TAYLOR, BENJAMIN J.
   61

TAYLOR, EDITH S.
   985

WATSON, JANE
    65

WAX, MURRAY L.
    1130, 1291

WAX, ROSALIE H.
    299, 447, 1130

WEED, WENDY
    1356

WEIBEL, JOAN
    1357

WEISNER, THOMAS
    1357

WEIST, KATHERINE M.
    184, 953

WELLMANN, KLAUS F.
    665

WELLS, ROBERT N.
    911

WEPPNER, ROBERT S.
    207

WERNER, RUTH E.
    721

WESTERMEYER, JOSEPH
    33, 44, 132, 155, 186, 206, 262, 289, 410, 450, 462, 1185, 1264,
    1300

WEST, L.W.
    1342

WHITE HOUSE CONFERENCE ON AGING, 1971
    837

WHITE, LYNN C.
    238

WHITE, MINERVA
    911

WHITE, ROBERT A.
    1333

WHITING, BEATRICE B.
    745

WINTROB, RONALD M.
    317

WITHYCOMBE, JERALDINE S.
    115

WITT, SHIRLEY
    774, 1334

WOLCOTT, HARRY F.
    827

WOLFF, PETER H.
    529

WOLMAN, CAROL
    405

WOODWARD, RICHARD G.
    145

WOOD, ROSEMARY
    92, 1043

WORTH, SOL
    1065

WYMAN, LELAND C.
    253, 567, 1344

YAZZIE, MYRA
    74

YINGER, J. MILTON
    201, 1128

YOUNGMAN, GERALDINE
    82

YOUNG, BILOINE W.
    728

YOUNG, PHILIP
    391

ZEINER, ARTHUR R.
    1004, 1102

ZELIGS, ROSE
    1281

ZENTNER, HENRY
    372, 1118, 1349, 1350

About the Compilers

DIANNE R. KELSO is Information Analyst at the White Cloud Center for American/Indian Alaska Native Mental Health Research and Development at the University of Oregon's Health Services Center in Portland.

CAROLYN L. ATTNEAVE is a member of the Delaware Cherokee tribes of Oklahoma and Professor of Psychology and Psychiatry and Behavioral Sciences at the University of Washington, Seattle.